LATIN AMERICA

An Economic and Social Geography

ENGLAND: BUTTERWORTH & CO. (PUBLISHERS) LTD.
                    LONDON: 88 Kingsway, W.C.2

AUSTRALIA: BUTTERWORTH & CO. (AUSTRALIA) LTD.
                    SYDNEY: 20 Loftus Street
                    MELBOURNE: 473 Bourke Street
                    BRISBANE: 240 Queen Street

CANADA: BUTTERWORTH & CO. (CANADA) LTD.
                    TORONTO: 1367 Danforth Avenue, 6

NEW ZEALAND: BUTTERWORTH & CO. (NEW ZEALAND) LTD.
                    WELLINGTON: 49/51 Ballance Street
                    AUCKLAND: 35 High Street

SOUTH AFRICA: BUTTERWORTH & CO. (SOUTH AFRICA) LTD.
                    DURBAN: 33/35 Beach Grove

U.S.A.:   BUTTERWORTH INC.
                    WASHINGTON, D.C. 20014: 7300 Pearl Street

LATIN AMERICA

AN ECONOMIC AND
SOCIAL GEOGRAPHY

J. P. COLE, M.A., Ph.D.

Lecturer in Geography at
Nottingham University

LONDON
BUTTERWORTHS
1965

Suggested U.D.C. Number 911·3 : 33 (8 : 6)

Printed in the United Kingdom by R. J. Acford Ltd., Chichester, Sussex.

To

my Wife

Quotations

Excellency,

I am urgently advised by cablegram this morning of my government's extreme desire that its Sister Republic Uruguay, shall appoint three Representatives, to the International Commission of Engineers, meeting at my country's capital, in October next, 'to study the possible routes, determine their true length, estimate their respective cost, and compare their reciprocal advantages', for a Railroad to unite the systems of South and North America.

In support of my government's earnest wishes in this particular, I trust you will forgive the suggestion, that, vast as may appear the undertaking of connecting the three Americas, by a Continuous Railway, for impartial service, to all their different Nations, its successful accomplishment need not be despaired of, since apart from multiplying many times their material wealth, such a trunk line, with the branches it must attract, will serve to bind with bands of steel, all to harmony with one another, and each to internal tranquility; the whole that is needed to assure them ultimate destinies of the greatest happiness and prosperity.

To His Excellency Blas Vidal
   Minister of Foreign Relations, Uruguay

From Geo. Money, Legation of the United States,
   Montevideo, August 15th 1890

Part of a letter in *Despatches from U.S. Ministers to Paraguay and Uruguay, 1855–1906*, The National Archives of the United States, 1934.

The conference of the Inter-American Economic and Social Council of the Organization of American States began at Punta del Este, Uruguay, on 5th August. In a message to the conference, President Kennedy stated that the U.S.A. would allocate more than U.S. $ 1,000 m. to Latin America in the first year of the Alliance for Progress programme. The U.S.A. could and should provide sufficient resources to achieve a breakthrough to self-sustaining economic growth. But the U.S.A. would do this only after the Latin American governments had mobilized their internal resources for planned development. The message stressed that social reform was an essential condition for economic growth and political peace, and called for land and tax reform and greater emphasis in government spending on education, health and housing.

Fortnightly Review of the
BANK OF LONDON & SOUTH AMERICA LIMITED
12th August 1961

CONTENTS

CONTENTS

CONTENTS

CONTENTS

PREFACE

The purpose of this book is to give an account of the economic and social geography of Latin America in the early 1960s. The author feels that it is unreasonable to expect to cover every aspect of the geography of the region in one volume; the justification for an incomplete approach is that a great deal of material on the economic and social aspects is missing from the various books currently available on the geography of Latin America. Again, several books already deal with Latin America regionally, usually devoting most of their space to a country by country description. *Latin America* by P. E. James is widely considered to be one of the best geography books written in English on a large region. Although sovereign states have undoubtedly been significant units of political and economic organization, the creation of the Latin American Free Trade Association (LAFTA) has made it desirable also to have a systematic account of different topics such as roads, oil refining and urban growth for the region as a whole. There is a case too for bringing the picture of the human geography of Latin America up to date by using material from the numerous censuses of 1960–61 and from statistical yearbooks of the larger countries, as well as from United Nations publications, bank reports and similar sources, often neglected in geography books on the region. But it is extremely difficult to assemble such material and it is hoped that the reader will forgive the incomplete coverage of many areas and the failure to mention either in the text or in the final bibliography all recent important works on the geography of the region; for some areas, of course, there is very little information anyway. A brief account of the physical geography and of the political and economic history are included for the reader who has little or no knowledge about Latin America, but further publications are recommended on these aspects at appropriate places in the text for anyone wishing to cover them more fully. It was hoped to include a chapter with large scale maps of rural and urban settlements, farms, mines and so on, but lack of space prevented the inclusion of this feature; the reader is recommended to refer to R. Platt, *Latin America, Countrysides and United Regions*, 1942, New York.

It is superfluous here to open a discussion on methodology concerning the arrangement of material in regional geography books and to attempt to justify the somewhat unorthodox arrangement of topics and regions in this book. In the view of the author, however, there is no special reason to follow the traditional sequence of topics in studying a region. Let us say, for simplicity, that the following 10 main topics should be covered in a complete regional description and that they are expected in this order: 1 Geology, and/or structure, 2 Relief, 3 Climate, 4 Soils, 5 Vegetation, 6 Agriculture, 7 Mining, 8 Manufacturing, 9 Population, 10 Communications. It seems not only arrogant but even absurdly inflexible to say that this is the only possible sequence, when the 10 topics listed can in reality be arranged in more than 3 million different ways. The same, of course, applies to the arrangement of the regional studies in the second half of the book.

Turning to more practical questions, each map is placed in the text as near as possible to the point at which it is most relevant. An attempt has been made to indicate on at least one map the location of almost every place mentioned in the text. Except for places commonly referred to in English by an English equivalent (e.g. Guatemala City for Ciudad de Guatemala), the Spanish or Portuguese word has been used and necessary diacritical marks (stresses, etc.) indicated. The metric system has been used throughout the book except in a few special cases, but no equivalents are included in the text; they appear on pages xiii and xiv. Numerous works published in Latin America in Spanish or Portuguese have been consulted, and although many readers may not be familiar with these languages and would certainly find some difficulty in obtaining the publications, it has been considered desirable to refer to a considerable number.

The illustrations have been drawn by the author's father, Philip Cole. His help is greatly appreciated. They are based on photographs taken by the author or collected from other sources. Much information has been collected from the Fortnightly Review of the Bank of London and South America. The Petroleum Information Bureau has also kindly sent much up-to-date material. The maps were drawn by Mr. A. Bailey and Miss G. Scholtz at Nottingham University and their work and help is much valued. The author would also like to thank in particular a number of Latin Americans who, unlike so many of their fellows in that part of the world, have regularly sent material: Senhor Marcelo Stern in Rio de Janeiro, Dr. Eduardo Neira Alva in Caracas, Dr. Jorge Vivó Escoto and Señora María Teresa Mac-Gregor in Mexico City and Dr. Ricardo Podestá in Buenos Aires. He is greatly indebted to Dr. C. W. J. Granger of Nottingham University for help in applying certain simple statistical techniques in this book and to Dr. J. A. S. Grenville of the History Department, Nottingham University, for providing the quotation from 1890 at the beginning of the book. Dr. Grenville is working on the subject of politics and strategy in American Diplomacy. He is also greatly indebted to Dr. C. A. M. King of the Department of Geography, Nottingham University, for advice on some aspects of the physical background, to Dr. S. R. Eyre of the Department of Geography, Leeds University, for advice on the vegetation of the region, and to Mr. J. C. Crossley of the Department of Geography, Leicester University, with whom he has had many fruitful discussions on the subject of Latin America. The author himself takes responsibility for all the shortcomings in the book, consoling himself with the old Spanish proverb: 'En el reino de los ciegos, el tuerto es rey'. Finally, he wishes to thank his wife, Isabel, for her patience and help, and apologizes to the reader if her own country, Peru, and her home town, Lima, have been given somewhat greater prominence in this book than they really merit.

ACKNOWLEDGEMENTS

The author wishes to thank the following for permissions to reproduce figures and sketches.
Coast Outline of Latin America

The Oxford University Press for permission to use the outline of the coast, based on a map in the Oxford Atlas for figures on pages 13, 14, 15, 18, 106, 118, 122, 131, 132, 176, 179, 409, 414, 424 and 438.

Figure 3.6

Edward Arnold for permission to reproduce data from maps 5, 6 and 7 of *Vegetation and Soils* by S. R. Eyre.

Figure on Page 24.

The Standard Oil Company of New Jersey for permission to reproduce as a sketch the photograph of a Mestizo from Central Colombia.

Figure 3.1

Oliver and Boyd for permission to reproduce this figure from *The Morphology of the Earth,* 1962 by L. C. King.

Figures on pages 109 and 151

The Venezuela Information Services for permission to reproduce as sketches, photographs from *Venezuela Up-to-Date* 1962 and 1961.

Figures on pages 24 and 142

Tiroler Graphic for permission to reproduce as sketches, photographs on pages 157 and 142 from *Cordillera Blanca (Peru)* by Hans Kinzl and Erwin Schneider

Figures on pages 24 and 151

Companhia Editora Nacional for permission to reproduce as sketches, figures from pages 97, 173 and 126 of *Geografia do Brasil* by Aroldo de Azevedo.

Figure on page 186

New York Times for permission to reproduce as a sketch the photograph of an 'Outstanding Realization in Argentina, I.A.F.A. under Peugeot licence', from a Special Supplement on Argentina.

Figure on page 261

Ministry of Commerce and Industry—Department of Tourism, Venezuela for permission to reproduce as a sketch the photograph of Area Metropolitana Centre Simón Bolívar from *Venezuela* p. 25.

Figures on pages 24, 67

Imprimerie Aulard, Paris for permission to reproduce as sketches photographs from *Brazil* on pages 212, 63 and 181.

Figures on page 66

L'Ambassade du Mexique à Paris for permission to reproduce as a sketch a photograph from *Nouvelles* de Mexique No. 15, 1958.

Figure 8.10c

M. C. Megee for permission to base this figure on one in *Monterrey.*

PLACE NAMES AND TERMS

The following place names have been used consistently throughout for certain areas:

Central America   Guatemala, El Salvador, Honduras, Nicaragua, Costa Rica, Panama

Hispaniola   Haiti and Dominican Republic

the Islands   All the islands in the Caribbean and Gulf of Mexico between the U.S.A. and South America

Latin America   Everywhere in the Americas south of the U.S.A.

North America   The U.S.A. and Canada

South America   Latin America excluding Mexico, Central America and the Islands

The following terms should be noted:

Oil = petroleum

Combined gross domestic product = the total gross domestic product of all countries in Latin America (or other relevant area)

Major civil division = political-administrative unit at highest level in hierarchy within a Sovereign State (e.g. departments of Colombia, states of Brazil)

Pre-Columbian refers to Latin American history (or pre-history) before the arrival of the Europeans around 1500. Spelling with u from Columbus, not to be confused with Colombia the country.

NOTE ON THE PRONUNCIATION OF PLACE NAMES

A number of diacritical marks are used in both Spanish and Portuguese but are usually omitted from capital letters. Some indicate the syllable on which the stress falls in words in which this does not follow recognized rules. Others affect the pronunciation of certain letters. In Spanish (´) as in Mérida and in Portuguese (´) as in Anápolis and (^) as in Rondônia indicate the syllable with the stress. In Spanish (ñ) as in Viña del Mar is pronounced like ni in onion and (¨) which is rare (as in Camagüey) means that the u is pronounced and does not merely harden the g for the following e or i (as in Miguel); in Portuguese (~) is found on certain vowels (as in São Paulo), indicating a nasal sound. In this book such diacritical marks have been put on all but the most commonly used place names (not, for example, on México, Perú, Bogotá).

There is considerable possibility for confusion over the following fairly similar names:

Pará,   state in northern Brazil
Paraguaná, Peninsula in northwest Venezuela
Paraíba,   state in northeast Brazil, river behind Rio
Paraná,   state and river in Brazil, town and river in Argentina
Paranaguá, town in Paraná state Brazil
Paranaíba, tributary of R. Paraná
Parnaíba,   river in northeast Brazil (Ceará state)

NUMERACY

A large amount of quantitative data are presented in this book both in the text and in tables. The reader should be careful to distinguish between absolute figures and figures *per caput* (per inhabitant). This material is of little use unless it means something to the reader. In order therefore to provide a very approximate guide to the magnitude of quantities involved, the following may be used for comparison.

1. Population
10,000   a small town
100,000   a town about the size of York in England
1 m.   roughly the population of a British county, and of major civil divisions in larger Latin American countries
10 m.   roughly the population of Belgium, of Peru
100 m.   somewhat less than half of the total population of Latin America

2. Area

In square kilometres	In hectares	
1	100	a large arable farm
1,000	100,000	a small British county
100,000	10 m.	roughly the area of Cuba
1 m.		roughly the area of Bolivia
10 m.		roughly half the area of Latin America

3. Cost in United States dollars (U.S. $)
100,000   the cost of drilling an oil well
1 m.   sufficient to build a few kilometres of road
10 m.   the cost of building a small oil refinery
100 m.   the investment needed to open a large copper mine, or roughly the value of exports of Guatemala in one year
1,000 m.   the cost of constructing a giant hydroelectric power station
10,000 m.   the gross domestic product of Mexico in one year or roughly the value of all Latin American exports in one year
100,000 m.   one fifth of the gross domestic product of the U.S.A. in one year

GENERAL INFORMATION

ABBREVIATIONS

GDP   gross domestic product
GNP   gross national product
m.   million, millions
km   kilometre, kilometres

Since the following works have been referred to frequently in the book their titles have for convenience been abbreviated:

AEB 1961		*Anuario Estatístico do Brasil, 1961*
BOLSA		*Bank of London and South America*
	(FR)	*Fortnightly Review*
	(QR)	*Quarterly Review*
FAO		*Food and Agriculture Organization of the United Nations*
	PY	*Production Yearbook*
	SFA	*The State of Food and Agriculture 1963*
	TY	*Trade Yearbook*
UN		*United Nations Organization*
	DY	*Demographic Yearbook*
	PIG	*Patterns of Industrial Production 1938–1958*
	SBLA	*Statistical Bulletin for Latin America*, Vol. 1, No. 1
	SY	*Statistical Yearbook*

CONVERSIONS

(Metric to British units)

Distance

1 centimetre = 0·39 inch
1 metre   = 3·28 feet
1 kilometre = 0·62 mile

Area

1 hectare = 10,000 square metres = 2·47 acres
1 square kilometre = 100 hectares = 0·386 square miles

Weight

All weights are in metric tons
1,000 kilogrammes = 1 metric ton = 0·98 long tons

GENERAL INFORMATION

Climatic data

Precipitation, millimetres to inches (nearest half inch)

2,500	98½	800	31½
2,000	79	600	23½
1,500	59	500	19½
1,400	55	400	16
1,300	51	200	8
1,200	47	150	6
1,100	43½	100	4
1,000	39½	50	2

Temperature, degrees Centigrade to degrees Farenheit

Quick reference

$0°C = 32°F$
$10°C = 50°F$
$20°C = 68°F$
$30°C = 86°F$

Conversion to nearest degree F

0:32	1:34	7:45	13:55	19:66	25:77
	2:36	8:46	14:57	20:68	26:79
	3:37	9:48	15:59	21:70	27:81
	4:39	10:50	16:61	22:72	28:82
	5:41	11:52	17:63	23:73	29:84
	6:43	12:54	18:64	24:75	30:86

CHAPTER 1

INTRODUCTION

1.1. GENERAL FEATURES

Latin America is widely though not universally accepted to be everywhere
in the Americas south of the U.S.A.; that is its meaning in this book. The
remainder (U.S.A. and Canada) is referred to as North America. One
argument against using the term Latin, which refers to people speaking a
Romance Language (derived from Latin) and implies perhaps, also,
adherence to the Roman Catholic religion, is that Latin America has some
non-Latin population (e.g. English speaking Jamaicans) and has received
many immigrants (e.g. slaves from Africa, more recently, Germans,
Japanese) from countries in which Romance languages are not spoken,
while conversely in North America there are people of Latin origin (French
Canadians, Italian immigrants, Puerto Rican immigrants). Another
objection to the twofold division of the Americas into North (or Anglo-) and
Latin is that it separates Mexico from southwest U.S.A. when the two are
related structurally and closely associated economically.*

Latin America covers an area of 20,541,000 km², approximately 14 per
cent of the world's land surface. In 1961 it had approximately 217,000,000
inhabitants, about 7 per cent of the total population of the world. It may
be noted for comparison (see also Chapter 20.2) that Latin America covers
roughly the same area and has roughly as many people as each of the following: North America, the U.S.S.R., and Africa south of the Sahara. It lies
mainly within the tropics, but extends to about 55°S, while even within the
tropics much of the population lives at an altitude high enough to give
appreciably cooler conditions than in adjoining lowlands. The inclusion of
Mexico and Central America does not make Latin America very compact as
a land mass, a feature that casts some doubt on the wisdom of forming at this
stage the Latin American Free Trade Association,† which came into being
at the beginning of 1962.

Although so large, and so long from end to end, Latin America has
certain features that at least give it cultural unity. Most important, perhaps,
is its location in a particular part of the world relatively remote from outside
influences. Mexico, Brazil and Chile may be very different from each other,
but they are more like one another than any is like an African or Asian
country. Spanish or Portuguese (in Brazil) is the official language of 95 per
cent of the total population. In theory the Roman Catholic religion is
virtually universal; in practice it is not adhered to everywhere in a pure
form but at all events it is the only religion organized throughout the region.

* Wreford Watson[1] stresses the intermediate position and role of Mexico in the Americas:
'it is the bridge between these two great New World regions'

† This Association referred to in the book as LAFTA from now on, is discussed in
Section 20.2.

In reality, apparent cultural uniformity has been superimposed upon very different Indian and negro traditions, preserved particularly in rural areas, in many parts of Latin America. Since the Second World War, thanks to some extent probably to frequent and reasonably cheap international air services, professional people have been travelling more and more between countries and meeting at conferences. Out of this has grown a new consciousness of the similarities between remote parts of the region and of the desirability of collaborating in order to resist being overrun economically by the U.S.A. The precarious dependence on one or a small number of agricultural or mineral products for export has also been a feature shared by every country, and has strengthened this desire to pool resources to achieve greater industrialization and less economic dependence on the leading industrial countries of the world. The areas least in step with this movement are the Islands of the Caribbean and the small mainland countries of Central America.

The unity of Latin America has been stressed, but much of this book will be devoted to showing the great diversity in both physical and human conditions in the region. In such a large area, virtually every kind of climate is to be expected and almost all types of vegation are encountered, and crops grown. The 22 independent countries vary enormously in size and in levels of economic development. Within the larger countries themselves, great contrasts occur between the population of modern, highly sophisticated cities, and forest Indians practising the simplest economic activities possible to maintain an existence at all. The present population has come from many different parts of the world and in many parts of Latin America mixed physiological characteristics are evident. Indeed, Latin America is full of variety* and surprises, many too trivial to record in a geography book. Who, for example, would expect, turning a corner in the centre of Buenos Aires, to be confronted with a large Harrods shop, or emerging from a hotel in Bogota, almost to walk into a red pillar box exactly like an English one?

1.2. THE POSITION OF LATIN AMERICA

In *Figure 1.1* the hemisphere centred on Quito, Ecuador shows those parts of the world nearest to Latin America. Mexico and the Islands lie close to the U.S.A., and Northeast Brazil fairly close to Africa and Europe, but most of Latin America is separated from other continents by great stretches of ocean. Relative to other populated land areas of the world it is remote; the author has definitely sensed this in a number of places without consciously looking for it. The feeling is most marked in the lack of urgency and even concern over world shattering crises such as Suez (1956) and Berlin (1961), but events in Cuba have suddenly drawn Latin America into direct contact with other parts of the world for the first time.

The direction and nature of the various influences and currents of settlers that have reached Latin America in the last few hundred years will be outlined in Chapter 4, and here only the most outstanding implication of the

---

* A glance at a list of selected place names in Appendix 1.1 will show clearly one aspect of the variety.

position of Latin American today, its proximity to the U.S.A., will be discussed. *Figure 1.2* shows the position of Latin America in relation to Europe (Lisbon) and the U.S.A. (Miami and places along the United States—Mexico boundary). In (a) and (b) distances are correct from Lisbon and Miami respectively.* Nowhere in Latin America is less than

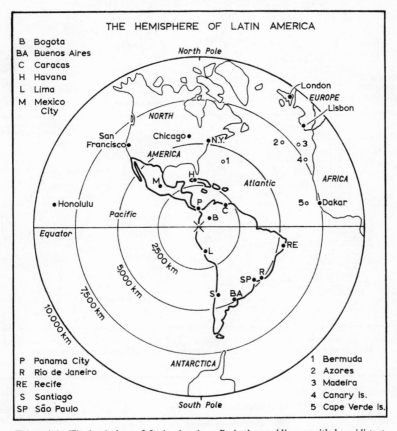

Figure 1.1. *The hemisphere of Latin America. Projection: oblique zenithal equidistant, centred on the coast of Ecuador at the Equator*

about 3,500 miles from Europe, whereas more than half of it lies at less than this distance from the U.S.A. In (c), Miami in map (b) is placed on Lisbon in map (a) and Latin America seen from Miami is rotated to show the relative distances from the two places to different parts of the region. In (d), Latin America is divided according to comparative distance from the U.S.A. and Europe. Only the extreme tip of Northeast Brazil is closer to Europe than to the U.S.A., but much of South America is less than twice as far from Europe as from the U.S.A. In contrast, Mexico, Central America and most of the Caribbean are at least four times as far from Europe as from

* Special maps were constructed for this purpose.

3

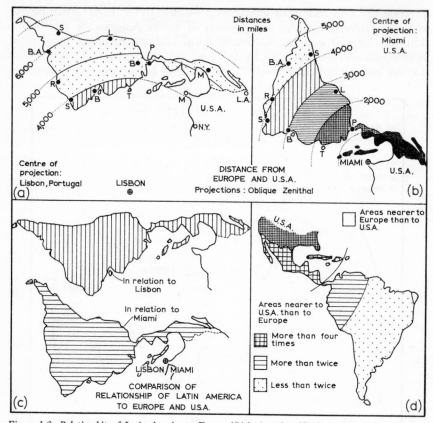

Figure 1.2. Relationship of Latin America to Europe (Lisbon) and to North America (Miami). Distances are correct from Lisbon in map (a), from Miami in map (b)

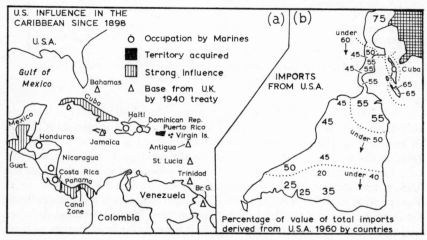

Figure 1.3. (a) U.S. influence in the Caribbean since 1898: (b) Latin American imports from the U.S.A. in 1960

the U.S.A. Does U.S. influence diminish and presumably West European influence increase with distance away from the U.S.A?

From a study of some of the ways in which the U.S.A. may be said to influence Latin America the following conclusions may be drawn*: firstly, physical intervention (the landing of marines and so on) has occurred only in some of the Islands and some Central American countries (see *Figure 1.3*), while the U.S.A. invaded Mexico in the middle of the nineteenth century. Secondly, the dependence of Latin American countries on the U.S.A. for their imports diminishes fairly regularly as distance increases. Thirdly, on the other hand there is only a slight correlation between distance from the U.S.A. and *per caput* value of U.S. investments per country, and none between distance and U.S. aid *per caput*.

Strategically and politically the U.S.A. has thus clearly been much more concerned during the present century about the countries closest to it in Latin America than about most of South America; the amount of trade also appears to be related to proximity, but the fact that the more remote Atlantic facing countries produce goods needed more in Europe than in the U.S.A. should not be overlooked. In contrast, investment and aid appear to be distributed without diminishing with distance, and varying with local conditions, needs and priorities.

1.3. PROBLEMS OF LATIN AMERICA

Latin America has slightly more people than North America yet the combined gross domestic product† of its member countries amounts to about 12 per cent of that of North America. Even allowing that exchange rates prevent precise comparison and exaggerate the gap, and that some production is not recorded in Latin America because it is of a subsistence nature, living standards must be at least several times as high in North America as in Latin America. Yet in the eighteenth century the value of exports of Haiti alone exceeded that of the British colonies that were to become the nucleus of the U.S.A. Some features that have delayed economic development and social improvement in Latin America may be suggested here.

The far-flung nature of the region, the difficulty of communication by land between different parts, and the generally unfavourable deployment of population and resources in relation to one another should be noted. Further, some resources present in North America, including large coal reserves and a very large and continuous area of good farm land, are lacking in Latin America. Since independence early in the nineteenth century the region has been divided into almost 20 political units, each concerned more with its own problems, and several in recent decades deliberately pursuing a policy leading towards self-sufficiency in manufacturing. There has therefore never been a single large market and rarely the opportunity to build large establishments in those branches of industry that benefit from economies of a large scale. Until very recently, nationalism has prevented any move towards continental cohesion. In addition, many moves towards

* See Appendix 1.2 for the figures on which these conclusions are based.
† See Section 1.4 for note of explanation about this and associated terms.

achieving superior material conditions have been stifled by a social structure inherited from the colonial period, by attitudes indifferent to or even hostile to the growth of manufacturing and the changes this would bring, and by lack of financial and other institutions necessary in a manufacturing economy. Matters are further complicated, in the short run anyway, by a very high rate of natural increase of population (see *Figure 1.4*).* Ultimately

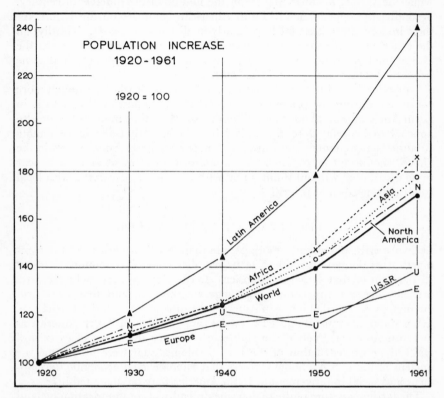

Figure 1.4. Population increase in major regions of the world, 1920–1961. Note: North America and Asia coincide during 1940–50. See Appendix 3 for absolute figures and for source

this will create larger markets and provide settlers to open up new areas, but in the early stages of industrial growth it means that a large proportion of the population is under employable age and that the economy must expand at about 3 per cent per year merely to keep pace with population growth, and to expand at more than twice this rate to achieve even modest material progress. Although pressure of population on resources is felt acutely locally in Latin America, in most regions there is plenty of slack to take up, and Latin America as a whole has a population/resource balance far superior to that of India or China.

Returning to the question of differences in gross domestic product and therefore in living standards in the Americas, it should be appreciated that

* See Appendix 3 for relevant figures.

although the gap is enormous between North and Latin America, the latter is not one of the poorest of the major regions of the world. Below are 1958 figures[2]:

Region	Total gross domestic product in thousand million U.S. dollars	Per caput gross domestic product in U.S. dollars
North America	437	2,300
Latin America	59	300
West Europe	246	810
Asia (excl. U.S.S.R. and China)	99	106
Africa	29	121

Though impossible to calculate exactly, the Soviet figure was between two and three times as great as that of Latin America both in total and in *per caput* terms.

Figure 1.5 illustrates the great difference between North and Latin America. The two states of New York and New Jersey alone have a combined income greater than that of the *whole* of Latin America. The *increase*

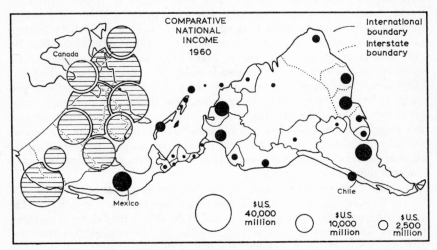

Figure 1.5. Comparative national income of North American and Latin American countries [3,4,5] in 1960. Data for the U.S.A. and Brazil have been presented for groups of states, not for the countries as a whole

in income in the U.S.A. between 1956 and 1960 was alone greater than the *total* for Latin America in 1960. The reader may feel that all this is remote from reality. At all events it cannot be ignored in a study of the economic and social geography of Latin America since it is the most complete way of comparing the material development and achievement of different areas. Latin America does not of course lag behind North America to the same extent in everything. North America produces no coffee, so no comparison is possible here. On the other hand, recently the U.S.A. was spending *fifty* times more on higher education than Latin America. The following figures give some idea of the contrasts in production or expenditure. North America (or U.S.A. only) = 100. The figures are mostly for 1960 or near that year[4].

Mining production	19	Value of exports	31
Light manufacturing	11	Gross domestic product	13·5
Heavy manufacturing	5	Motor vehicles in circulation	5
Engineering	3	Higher education (U.S.A. only)	2

1.4. UNEQUAL LEVELS OF DEVELOPMENT AMONG LATIN AMERICAN COUNTRIES*

Just as the *per caput* gross national or domestic product of North America and Latin America differs greatly, so it differs between Latin American countries themselves. There are obvious difficulties in using indices of *per caput* gross national product to assess levels of development of countries, and figures are very imprecise. But, to quote Gill[6]: 'The truth is that the differences are *so* enormous that even the most defective measuring sticks could not fail to detect them.' Within Latin America itself, differences are great, both between individual countries and from region to region within the larger ones. Since these great contrasts will appear and be discussed on many occasions in the book it is necessary to present their main features briefly at this stage. In a very broad sense they summarize and reflect the ability of given groups of people to make use, materially speaking, of the resources with which their home area is endowed; of course by trading with other areas, resources from elsewhere may also be used, but these presumably have to be paid for. In explaining the differences that exist at any given time, at least the following considerations must be taken into account: the population/resource balance of each area being studied, the actual spatial arrangement, favourable or otherwise, of people and resources, the current level of technology, organization and education, and attitudes towards material development.[7]

Table 1.1 shows the *per caput* income assessed in slightly different ways† for the 22 sovereign states of Latin America, together with Puerto Rico. The great difference between Venezuela and Haiti shows that the two extremes are very far apart in income levels, about as far, for example, as Italy and Ethiopia. No indication is given, of course, of the way in which this income is distributed among the population. In most Latin American countries the spread is very uneven, but this does not affect the basic implications of the figures in the table, which may be considered by the reader.

In Table 1.2 the 15 countries of Latin America having more than 2·5 m. inhabitants in 1961 (and together containing 92 per cent of the total popu-

* See also Ginsberg, N.[56] especially the final section by B. Berry.

† The total value of production of goods and services in a country (or in a major civil division) may be assessed in several different ways. Gross national product (GNP) (e.g. in the U.K. in 1962, £24,905 m.) may be modified to gross domestic product (GDP) (£24,580 m.) by subtracting net property income from abroad, or to national income (£22,630 m.) by subtracting capital consumption. GDP may further be modified to GDP at market prices by adding taxes on expenditure, less subsidies.

lation of the region) are ranked according to various criteria. Some, such as *per caput* consumption of sources of energy, would be expected to produce roughly the same order as *per caput* national income. Others, such as size of country, would not necessarily do so. Even in the limited amount of

TABLE 1.1

U.S. Dollars Per Caput

	I 1958 GDP	II 1961 GNI	III 1962 GNP	IV 1960 GDP	Ranking of fifteen largest			
					I	II	III	I-III
Venezuela	715	896	1044	1120	1	1	1	1
Puerto Rico	581	606	n.a.	n.a.				
Trinidad	529	717	n.a.	n.a.				
Argentina	476	394	391	505	2	2	4	2
Uruguay	450	306	302	n.a.	3	5	5	5
Cuba	379	361	420	n.a.	4	4	2	4
Jamaica	357	353	n.a.	n.a.				
Chile	352	362	399	370	5	3	3	3
Panama	352	313	434	503				
Costa Rica	348	344	356	350				
Colombia	301	222	215	325	6	7	9	7
LATIN AMERICA	300			325				
Mexico	255	275	309	310	7	6	6	6
Brazil	252	160	99	240	8	10	14	11
Nicaragua	220	202	220	n.a.				
Dominican Rep.	213	220	231	230	9	7	7	8
El Salvador	208	152	220	270	10	11	8	9
Honduras	192	164	210	215				
Ecuador	180	175	187	180	11	9	11	10
Guatemala	164	136	174	190	12	13	12	13
Peru	150	144	195	230	13	12	10	12
Paraguay	126	130	124	105				
Bolivia	96	114	147	100	14	14	13	14
Haiti	86	58	48	n.a.	15	15	15	15

n.a. = not available
Other countries of the world (1958) for comparison with column I

U.S.A.	2324	Portugal	212
Canada	1767	Ghana	158
U.K.	1084	Egypt	116
Italy	493	Sudan	82
South Africa	385	Burma	47
Spain	324	Ethiopia	40
Japan	285		

I *Per caput* gross domestic product in 1958 in U.S. dollars[8]. Allowances were made in the calculation for special exchange rates in Brazil, Argentina and Chile.
II *Per caput* gross national income in 1961 in U.S. dollars[9,10].
III *Per caput* gross national product at the end of 1962 in U.S. dollars[11]. Converted to U.S. dollars at official exchange rate, which is unrealistic at least in the following cases: Cuba, Chile, Brazil.
IV *Per caput* gross domestic product in 'real' terms in 1960 in U.S. dollars[12].

material presented here, there is considerable scope for testing for correlations. The following relationships, using Spearman Rank Correlation Coefficient, $r = 1 - \dfrac{6\Sigma d^2}{n^3 - n}$ (For further notes on this test, see Section 11.6) may be noted:

1. Size of total population and *per caput* gross domestic product: a correlation of $+0\cdot415$ suggests slight advantage only in having a large total population.
2. Size of population and amount of value of exports *per caput*: a correlation of $0\cdot0$, no relationship at all.
3. *Per caput* gross domestic product and *per caput* value of foreign trade: a correlation of $+0\cdot74$, a fairly strong relationship.

9

TABLE 1.2

Indices of Degree of Economic and Social Development:
Per Caput Data Ranked

	Population[13]	Area[13]	Density[13]	GDP (1958)[8]	Energy[14]	Cement[14]	Newspapers[14]	Physicians[14]	Telephones[14]	Private cars[14]	Exports[15]	% Urban[16]	% Literate[17]
Brazil	1	1	13	8	9	8	10	7	8	8	13	9	9
Mexico	2	3	6	7	3	7	6	5	7	5	12	6	6
Argentina	3	2	14	2	2	2	2	1	1	3	4	2	1
Colombia	4	5	9	6	7	5	8	8	6	9	9	8	5
Peru	5	4	11	13	8	9	7	6	9	6	8	7	10
Chile	6	8	10	5	4	4	3	4	5	10	3	3	3
Venezuela	7	7	12	1	1	1	5	3	4	1	1	5	8
Cuba	8	11	4	4	5	6	4	2	3	2	2	4	4
Ecuador	9	9	7	11	11	10	9	10	10	14	10	12	7
Guatemala	10	12	5	12	10	11	14	13	13	11	11	14	14
Haiti	11	14	1	15	15	14	15	15	15	15	15	15	15
Bolivia	12	6	15	14	13	15	12	11	14	12	14	11	13
Dominican r.	13	13	3	9	12	13	13	14	11	13	5	13	11
Uruguay	14	10	8	3	6	3	1	9	2	4	7	1	2
El Salvador	15	15	2	10	14	12	11	12	12	7	6	10	12

REFERENCES

[1] Wreford Watson, J. *North America, its Countries and Regions*, p. 818, 1963, London; Longmans

[2] *UN Yearbook of National Account Statistics 1962*, 1963, New York; United Nations

[3] *UNSY*, 1961

[4] *UNSY*, 1962

[5a] *Statistical Abstract of the United States*, 1962 and 1963.

[5b] Ginsberg, N. *Atlas of Economic Development*, 1961. Chicago.

[6] Gill, R. T. *Economic Development: Past and Present*, p. 81, 1963, New Jersey; Englewood Cliffs.

[7] Keller, F. L. 'Institutional Barriers to Economic Development—Some Examples from Bolivia', *Economic Geography* 31 (1955) 351–363

[8] *UN Yearbook of National Account Statistics 1962*, 1963, New York; United Nations

[9] *UNSY, 1962*. Table 162, 'Estimates of National Income' and Table 167, 'Exchange Rates'

[10] *Pick's World Currency Report, July 1962*

[11] *Pick's World Currency Yearbook, 1963*. 1963, N.Y. Pick's Publishing Corporation;

[12] *The Panama Canal Review*, Vol. 14, No. 2, Sept. 1963 quoting U.N. Economic Commission for Latin America

[13] *UNSY, 1962*, Table 1

[14] *UNSY, 1962*, appropriate tables, mostly 1961 data

[15] *Pick's Currency Year Book 1963*, p. 29, 1963, New York; '*per caput* of exports, 1962'

[16] Cole, J. P. *Notes on the Towns of Latin America*, 1962, Nottingham Univ.

[17] El Correo, *UNESCO*, June 1961, p. 33

CHAPTER 2

POPULATION

2.1. GENERAL FEATURES

Some time during 1962 the population of Latin America passed 220 m. Almost every country in the region had a census of population in the early 1960s and this figure is therefore reasonably accurate.[1] Unfortunately, censuses have not been held simultaneously throughout the region in the past and some countries have not held them regularly at all (e.g. Uruguay none between 1908 and 1963). What is more, as time has passed the censuses have tended to be more complete and fewer people have missed enumeration. As a result, the intercensal rates of growth appear to be somewhat greater than they probably were. Thus in Brazil, for example,[2] the 1950 census figure was 51,976,000, the 1960 figure 70,799,000, whereas projections based on an assumed annual increase from 1950 to 1959 gave only 64,216,000 for 1959. An increase of 6m. between 1959 and 1960 is inconceivable. The discrepancy probably arose both through underestimating the annual

TABLE 2.1

	Population in millions			Increase 1935–61 1935 = 100	Pop'n[6] in millions 1961	% Annual[6] increase 1953–60	Population[7] in thousands 1963
	Early[3] 1880s	Circa[4] 1910	1935[5]				
Mexico	9,6	15,1	18,1	200	36,1	3·1	39,855
Guatemala	1,2	2,0	2,0	195	3,9	3·0	4,096
El Salvador	0,6	1,2	1,5	180	2,7	2·5	2,684
Honduras	0,3	0,6	1,0	190	1,9	2·5	2,161
Nicaragua	0,3	0,6	0,7	215	1,5	3·4	1,638
Costa Rica	0,2	0,4	0,6	200	1,2	4·1	1,358
Panama*		0,4	0,6	185	1,1	2·7	1,145
Venezuela	2,1	2,7	3,3	230	7,6	4·3	8,136
Colombia	3,0	5,4	8,2	175	14,4	2·2	16,821
Ecuador	1,1	1,5	2,2	205	4,5	3·2	4,726
Peru	2,8	4,5	6,3	165	10,4	2·7	10,931
Bolivia	1,1	2,3	2,5	140	3,5	1·4	3,951
Cuba	1,5	2,2	4,2	165	6,9	2·1	7,224
Haiti	0,9	2,0	2,5	170	4,2	1·2	4,432
Dominican R.	0,3	0,7	1,5	205	3,1	3·5	3,350
Puerto Rico	0,8	1,1	1,7	140	2,4	1·1	2,460 ('62)
Jamaica	0,6	0,8	1,1	145	1,6	1·2	1,641 ('62)
Trinidad	0,2	0,3	0,4	225	0,9	3·2	894 ('62)
Brazil	12,0	22,0	37,2	195	73,1	3·4	76,744
Paraguay	0,3	0,7	1,0	180	1,8	2·4	1,906
Uruguay	0,5	1,2	2,0	145	2,9	1·6	2,586
Argentina	2,8	7,2	13,0	160	21,1	1·2	22,117
Chile	2,4	3,4	4,7	165	7,8	1·8	8,176
Latin America†	45	79	118,2	185	217,4		224,000

* Part of Colombia in 1880s.
† As some small areas are not listed, the total does not in some cases agree precisely with the sum of figures listed. In the right-hand column it is for 20 countries only.

11

rate of growth and through the 1950 census being less complete than the 1960 census, understating the actual population total perhaps by several million.

In spite of this drawback it is worth while studying population figures in Latin America for past decades (see Table 2.1). Roughly between the early 1930s and the early 1960s, in just over a generation, the population of Latin America has doubled. Currently it appears to be increasing each year at about 3 per cent or by 6–7 m. Recent projections have suggested that by 2000 A.D. it will have around 600 m. people or 10 per cent of the total population of the world; in 1900 it had about 5 per cent. Population growth and regional changes will be discussed more fully in Chapter 19.2*.

As will be seen in Table 2.1, countries vary greatly in population. Brazil has almost exactly one third of the total, Mexico, Argentina and Colombia together have almost another third. The remaining third is shared among 18 independent countries and a number of dependent units.

One feature of a rapidly growing population is the large proportion of children. This is accompanied by a lower proportion of employable population to total population than in countries with a more stable population. The following are recent figures for selected countries:

Percentage of total population under 15 years of age[8]			
Costa Rica	46	Paraguay	40
Venezuela	45	Chile	39
Mexico	44	Argentina	31
Peru	44	U.S.A.	31
Puerto Rico	43	England and Wales	24

2.2. DISTRIBUTION AND DENSITY OF POPULATION

Figure 2.1 shows the distribution of population in Latin America in 1960. Each dot represents approximately 1 per cent of the total population in that year and is placed at the centroid of 2,100,000 persons.† The purpose is not to give a visual impression of the distribution, as has often been done for the region by using a much larger number of dots, but to make it possible quickly to calculate roughly how many people or what percentage of the total population is in any given area.

Figure 2.1 suggests that although no single limited part of the region has a large proportion of the total population (as occurs in North America, the U.S.S.R., China), population is nevertheless concentrated in several clusters, while large areas appear to be virtually uninhabited.

In *Figure 2.1* the two inset maps have been included as a basis for comparison with the actual distribution. The even distribution of dots is

* The high rate of increase in population almost everywhere and the growing practice of seeking abortions, virtually the only method of family limitation available to most (though illegal) appears to be causing a sudden interest in family planning, and there has been very little opposition from the Roman Catholic Church to the opening of clinics in some places[9].

† The location of each dot has been chosen by considering the data for population in major civil divisions. Where precisely each dot has been placed depends of course on personal judgement, but the general distribution would not be fundamentally altered if the map were redrawn, since each dot is tied to its quota of the total population.

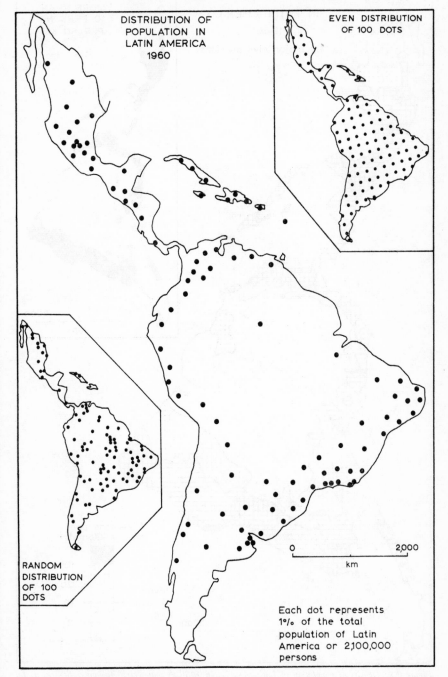

Figure 2.1. Distribution of population in Latin America in 1960. Sources: for countries and various national censuses for major civil division data UNSY[10]

Outline of coast based on a map in the Oxford Atlas published by the Oxford University Press

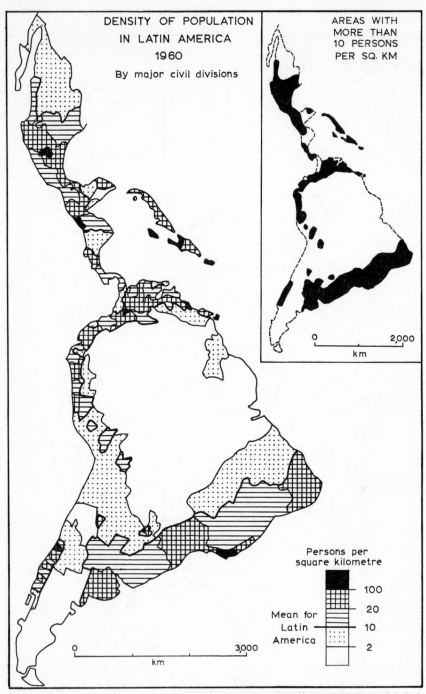

Figure 2.2. Density of population in Latin America in 1960 by major civil divisions. Sources as for Figure 2.1. Inset map: areas in Latin America with more than 10 persons/km²

Outline of coast based on a map in the Oxford Atlas published by the
Oxford University Press

self-explanatory.* In the view of the author this kind of distribution could be used as a basis for assessing the degree of concentration that actually exists, there being a possible range between the dispersed even distribution, and a completely concentrated distribution in which all hundred dots fall

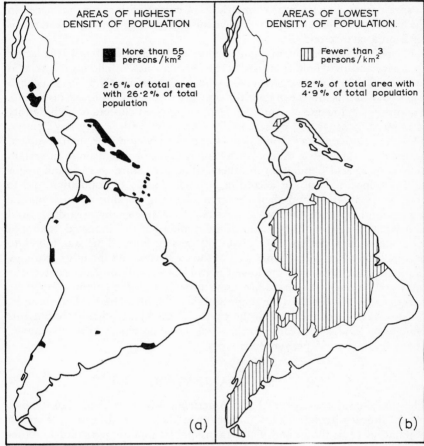

Figure 2.3. Latin America (a) Areas of highest density of population (b) Areas of lowest density of population

Outline of coast based on a map in the Oxford Atlas published by the
Oxford University Press

on one spot. The random distribution shows the kind of arrangement that can be expected if the hundred dots are spread over the area by chance. This map was constructed by placing a grid with very small squares over the area of Latin America. There turned out to be 739 squares, each of which

* The even distribution was produced by using a grid made of squares each proportional in area to 1 per cent of the total area of Latin America. A dot was placed in the centre of each whole square and in each square through which the coast line passed if the square contained over half land. A somewhat greater degree of dispersal would have been obtained by placing each dot at the centre of a hexagon proportional in area to 1 per cent of the area of Latin America. See reference 11 for the use of a hexagonal grid.

15

was numbered. From a list of random numbers the first hundred numbers listed between 1 and 739 were recorded on their appropriate squares. A different set of numbers is of course picked each time the exercise is done, but the same general picture emerges: some surprisingly marked clusters involving several dots, and empty areas that could easily lead the geographer to speculation, but no gaps comparable in extent with some that occur in the actual distribution. The arrangement of population in Latin America is far from a chance one.

Figure 2.2 shows density of population by major civil divisions in the larger countries and by whole countries in the smaller ones.* The scale is related to the mean for Latin America as a whole (approximately 10 persons/km²) and above and below mean densities only are distinguished in the inset map. The impression is one of a number of varying sized clusters of high density of population separated by sea, or by land areas with a very low density. The clusters themselves tend to be long and narrow rather than compact.

Figure 2.3 shows in a different way the extent of concentration in certain areas and lack of population in others. The procedure was to rank major civil divisions of countries according to their density of population and to add the population and then the area of each, working down from the highest and up from the lowest density. In map (a) this was done until somewhat more than 25 per cent of the population was included, taking in all units with a density over about 60 persons/km². This was found to occupy little more than 2·5 per cent of the total area. At the other extreme, the half of the area with the lowest density has less than 5 per cent of the total population. The maps are unfortunately to some extent affected by irregularities and freaks in the shape and size of political units. For example, Buenos Aires is not included in the part with the highest density because its population has been spread over the whole large province of the same name, giving fewer than 55 persons/km².

2.3. URBANIZATION

The study of urbanization in Latin America is full of problems. In the first place, almost all of the 22 countries have their own definition of urban population.† In the second place, many predominantly agricultural settlements are urban in layout and amenities though rural in function. In several Latin American countries (e.g. Mexico, Argentina) urban population is defined as that living in centres over a certain size (varying from 1,000 to 2,500 in different countries); in some others (e.g. Colombia) it is population living in the administrative centre of political units (major and minor civil divisions), regardless of the size of centre. Several countries have a different basis altogether, or no clearcut definition at all. In spite of these drawbacks, an attempt has been made to assess the urban population of each country, considering it to consist of the inhabitants of places with more than about

---

* The largest countries must obviously be divided into major civil divisions but if the smallest are as well (e.g. Dominican Republic, El Salvador) excessive detail is achieved in these areas. A compromise was made to break up Mexico and all the South American countries except Uruguay.

† See[12] for the definition of urban in most Latin American countries.

2,500 people. Latin America as a whole in the early 1960s has between 40 per cent and 45 per cent of its population urban on this basis, a figure much higher than those for Africa south of the Sahara, India or China, and not far below the figures for Japan and the U.S.S.R. There are great differences within the region, however, and each country must be considered individually. The range is between over 60 per cent urban in Argentina, Chile and Uruguay, and less than 30 per cent in Haiti, the Dominican Republic and parts of Central America. Venezuela and Cuba are also highly urbanized but Brazil is somewhat below the mean for Latin America*.

A narrower but more precise assessment of urban population can be achieved by considering only the population in towns of a much larger size than 2,500. This is done for many countries for towns of over 20,000 and 100,000 in the *United Nations Demographic Yearbook*[14], but figures are for different years. The figures below show the proportion of total population living in towns with over 50,000 inhabitants in 1960–61 in six major regions of Latin America:

Mexico	28	Islands	19
Central America	15	Brazil	24
Andean countries	30	South	47

Mean for Latin America 28·5

The main map in *Figure 2.4* shows the distribution of towns with more than about 50,000 inhabitants in 1960; these are mapped in greater detail and are named in later chapters†. Neighbouring towns have been considered as one, and where possible, outer suburbs of the larger towns have been included to give a figure for the population of greater urban areas‡. As would be expected, *Figure 2.4* suggests that most of the towns are in areas that in *Figure 2.2* have a density of population above the mean for Latin America.

One feature that emerges from the study of town sizes in Latin America is a relationship between size of town and frequency. This has been studied particularly in towns in the U.S.A., but applies in Latin America both to all towns over 50,000 and to towns of Brazil over 10,000. Briefly, the number of towns of different classes of size (number of inhabitants) increases as size diminishes in a predictable way and in a way similar to that found in towns in the U.S.A. and the U.S.S.R.§

* After writing this section, the following figures became available:
Urban population, expressed as a percentage of total population, in the early 1960s in countries for which data were available[18]

Chile	66·5	Panama	41·5	Ecuador	35·3
Venezuela	62·5	Nicaragua	41·1	Costa Rica	34·5
Mexico	50·7	El Salvador	38·5	Honduras	30·7
Peru	47·1	Paraguay	35·4	Dominican	
Brazil	45·1			Republic	30·5

† See *Figures 10.1, 11.2, 12.1, 13.1, 16.4, 17.3.*
‡ More recent or accurate data has become available for some towns since the map was drawn, and is included in appropriate tables in the regional chapters.
§ See 'On a class of skew distribution functions[15]. This feature of town sizes has been investigated by G. K. Zipf and is also discussed by A. Lösch[16].

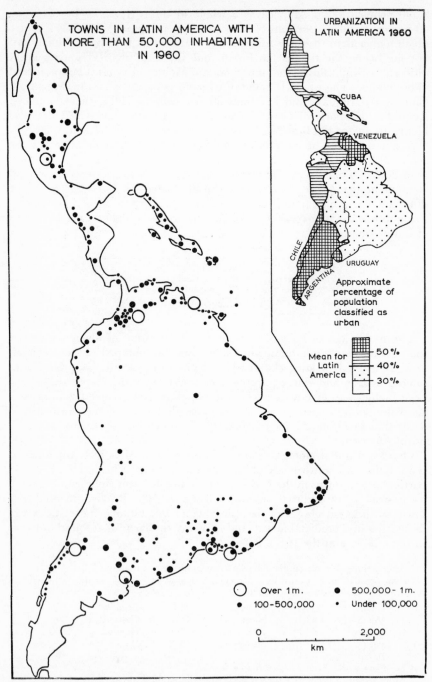

Figure 2.4. *Towns in Latin America with more than 50,000 inhabitants in 1960. Inset map: Urbanization in Latin America in 1960*

Outline of coast based on a map in the Oxford Atlas published by the Oxford University Press

18

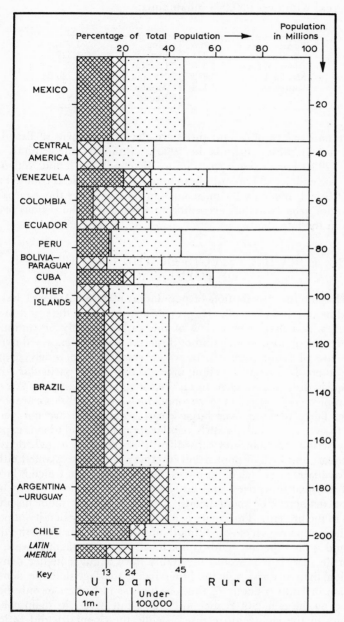

Figure 2.5. Urbanization in Latin America by countries according to size of urban centre. The urban percentage is for the late 1950s in most areas

There are 227 towns with over 50,000 inhabitants and they have a total population of nearly 62 m. Almost 30 m. of these people live in the 11 towns (greater area) with over 950,000 inhabitants:

Buenos Aires	6,763	Lima	1,978
Mexico City	4,871	Bogota	1,329
Rio de Janeiro	4,370	Caracas	1,265
São Paulo	3,872	Havana	1,220
Santiago	2,114	Montevideo	1,173
		Recife	974

Eight are national capitals and three are the largest towns of Brazil (Rio replaced as capital by Brasilia in 1960). Similarly, the capitals of 25 countries (22 sovereign states plus Puerto Rico and British and Netherlands Guianas) have almost 30 m. out of the total of 62 m. if Rio is counted as the capital of Brazil, but only 25 m. if not. *Figure 2.5* shows the approximate proportion of urban dwellers according to town size in the regions of Latin America in the late 1950s.

2.4. FURTHER ASPECTS OF THE DISTRIBUTION OF POPULATION

In this chapter the distribution of population of Latin America has been described in very broad terms. Its present distribution is the result of many influences, which may in the view of the author, largely be summarized under three categories. Some kind of dispersal would be expected over any area the size of Latin America, in which resources are widely scattered. Whether there is any justification in expecting some particular kind of fairly regular distribution, even in an area such as the pampa of Argentina or the tropical rain forest of Amazonia, in which conditions are by any reckoning fairly uniform over large areas, geographers are not yet in a position to say. If, initially, a fairly regular spread of population is expected, then any serious irregularities subsequently resulting in a high density in certain areas, and lack of population in others, may be explained either in terms of availability or lack of resources, the distribution of which is largely a result of physical influences, and lastly by human decisions (individual or collective, deliberate or spontaneous) made at different moments in time right up to the present. Thus there can be a much greater density of population in the pampa region of Argentina than in Patagonia because the quality of the land is far superior. This is not to say that if Patagonia were much more fertile than it is it would inevitably have a much higher density of population than it does. On the other hand, the fact that the density of population in Haiti is about $2\frac{1}{2}$ times as high as in Cuba can only be fully explained by the policy of France to develop intensively its main colony in the tropics in the eighteenth century (while the Spaniards did little with Cuba throughout the colonial period), for physical conditions in Cuba are on the whole far more favourable than those in Haiti. In practice, in explaining the particular features of distribution of population in any part of Latin America (or the world) it is necessary to take into account both physical influences and past human decisions (often referred to as historical factors). A further feature not to be overlooked in studying the distribution of population in the Latin American region is the shift from a predominantly agricultural economy to a non-agricultural one. Non-agricultural activities tend to benefit from concentration, and urbanization implies a gradual change from a fairly dispersed to a highly concentrated form of settlement. Some aspects of the relationship of population to physical features are tentatively suggested in Chapter 3 while in Chapter 4 the influence of political and economic activities on the distribution of population in the last four centuries will be discussed.

Two further points may in conclusion briefly be introduced here. In the first place, the relationship of the distribution of population to distance from the coast in South America is by no means as straightforward as is often made out. If only a coastal belt say 50–100 km deep is examined, then nothing useful can be concluded, for it contains in roughly equal proportions areas with a density of population above and below the mean for South America (see *Figure 2.6b*). If on the other hand the whole of South America is considered then something more conclusive may be asserted. *Figure 2.6a* illustrates a method that has been adopted here to relate distribution of population to distance from the interior of South America. The centre of the area of each major civil division is plotted and the divisions are then listed in descending order of distance to their centres from the nearest point on the coast. Thus the state of Amazonas (Brazil) is the most interior major civil division, Mato Grosso state next, and so on. The areas of these have been added until one quarter of the area of South America (the area with dots in *Figure 2.6a*) was reached; the population of these divisions was then added together. The same procedure was applied to the next most 'interior' quarter of the area. The following are the results:

	Area (per cent)	Population	% of South American total
Most interior	25	5,440,000	3·9
Next	25	13,350,000	9·6
Remaining	50	121,060,000	86·5
Total	100	139,850,000	100

Ideally, of course, the exercise should be carried out on a map with the population represented by a considerable number of dots, and the irregularities of major civil divisions should not affect the calculations of distance from the coast. Moreover, the area could usefully be divided into say ten parts rather than three. Even so, the lack of population in the interior part emerges very convincingly in spite of lack of population in many coastal areas.

Given the new interest in economic union resulting from the formation of the Latin American Free Trade Association, the actual dispersal of population over the region also deserves attention. The dispersed nature of the population of Latin America can be appreciated by a comparison with North America (U.S.A. and Canada), which is roughly similar in area and has only

21

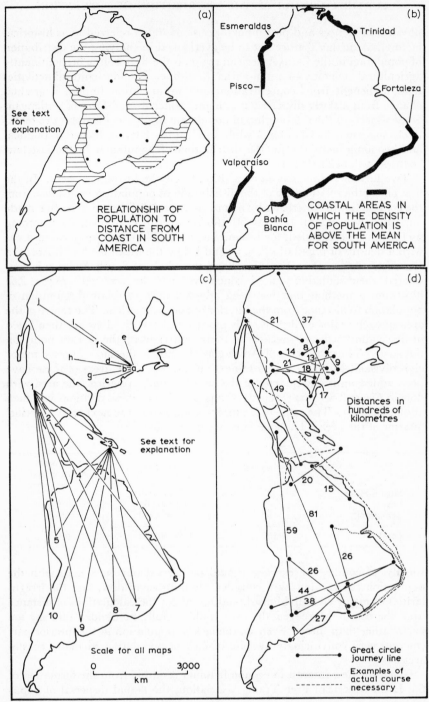

Figure 2.6. (a) (b) Relationship of population to distance from coast in South America. (c) (d) Comparative distances in Latin America and North America. See text for further explanation. In (c) only selected lines are drawn to illustrate the method

slightly fewer people. Economic union in Latin America implies that more journeys will be made between different parts of the region, in the way that long hauls of goods are already made across the North American continent. To compare the two regions, two methods have been used (see *Figure 2.6*). Firstly, the population of each region has been represented by 10 dots (letters a–j in North America, numbers 1–10 in Latin America) each equivalent to and located at the centroid of 10 per cent of the total population. In each region, the straight line journeys from each dot to all others have been measured. The procedure has been employed later in the book for journeys in Peru and is explained there more fully (see Section 6.7). Altogether, not counting a 'journey' of no distance from each dot to itself, there are 90 journeys (45 pairs) in each region. The total distance of these journeys is approximately 142,800 km in North America, a mean distance of 1,590 km, while in Latin America it is 370,400 km, a mean distance of 4,120 km, or more than $2\frac{1}{2}$ times the North American average. Even allowing for errors in the placing of the dots and in the measurement of distances, a fundamental difference emerges between the two regions. The broad implications are that in Latin America *either* greater effort is needed to achieve the same amount of interregional movement between different places *or* with the same amount of effort, less interregional movement can be achieved.

The problem has been approached, again, from another angle. From lists of towns with over 100,000 inhabitants in each region, ten pairs of towns

From	To	km
1 Roanoake	Seattle	3,700
2 Lorain	Corpus Christi	2,100
3 San Antonio	Atlanta	1,400
4 York	Fort Wayne	900
5 Milwaukee	Springfield	800
6 Omaha	San Bernadino	2,100
7 Corpus Christi	Asheville	1,800
8 Nashville	Lubbock	1,400
9 Tampa	Grand Rapids	1,700
10 Macon	Rockford	1,300
TOTAL		17,200
MEAN		1,720

From	To	km Great circle	Actual	Detour extra	Actual as % of great circle
1 Fortaleza (Brazil)	San Juan (Arg.)	4,400	6,000	1,600	136
2 Fortaleza (Brazil)	Paraná (Arg.)	3,800	5,400	1,600	142
3 Ponce (Puerto Rico)	Cali (Colombia)	2,000	2,500	500	125
4 Mar del Plata (Arg.)	Brasilia	2,700	3,200	500	118
5 La Paz (Bolivia)	Juiz de Fora (Brazil)	2,600	2,900	300	111
6 León (Mexico)	Rio de Janeiro	8,100	10,600	2,500	131
7 Georgetown	Maracaibo (Venez.)	1,500	1,900	400	127
8 Cartagena (Col.)	Mexicali (Mex.)	4,900	5,400	500	110
9 Manaus (Brazil)	Belo Horizonte (Br.)	2,600	5,400	2,800	208
10 Santa Fé (Arg.)	Tegucigalpa (Hond.)	5,900	6,700	800	114
TOTAL		38,500	50,000	11,500	*130*
MEAN		3,850	5,000	1,150	

COCAMOS INDIAN, ACRE
TERRITORY, BRAZIL

INDIAN, CENTRAL ANDES, PERU

MESTIZO (INDIAN AND EUROPEAN),
CENTRAL COLOMBIA

MULATO (AFRICAN AND EUROPEAN),
BRAZIL

LATIN AMERICA

CABOCLO (INDIAN AND EUROPEAN),
NORTHEAST BRAZIL

AFRICAN, BAHIA STATE,
NORTHEAST BRAZIL

INSET:
EUROPEAN, LIMA
SOCIALITE, A
MISS UNIVERSE
OF LATE 1950's

MESTIZO FAMILY, CIUDAD DE DIOS SHANTY TOWN, LIMA, 1955

more than 500 km apart have been randomly selected*. The direct distance (great circle) between each pair of towns was then measured. The journeys are shown in *Figure 2.6d*. The tables on p. 23 show the towns considered and the distances involved (note that Canadian towns were listed but none came up in the sample).

Again, Latin America comes out with an average journey more than twice as great as North America. In fact, the figures of 1,720 km for North America and 3,850 km for Latin America flatter Latin America for two main reasons. Firstly, three short journeys (under 500 km) were rejected in the North American sample and secondly, while in North America all the journeys could in reality be made by road and/or rail without appreciably exceeding the direct distance recorded, several of the Latin American journeys would in practice be impossible except by air, without making very substantial detours. Thus, for example, the direct distance from Manaus to Belo Horizonte (both in Brazil) is about 2,600 km but in reality it is about 5,400 km down the Amazon, along the coast, and in again by road or rail. If the essential detours (still without taking into account local detours) are added to the Latin American journeys, their mean is nearly *three* times as great as the North American mean.

The reader may not feel convinced at this stage that the greater distances in Latin America, revealed quantitatively in a very approximate way, have any implications for the future of the Latin American Free Trade Association. The question will be reconsidered in Chapter 20.2.

REFERENCES

[1] *UNSY*, 1963, Tables 2 and 3
[2] *Anuario Estatístico do Brazil*, 1961, IBGE, p. 20
[3] Various, including *Statesman's Yearbooks*
[4] Mainly *Statesman's Yearbook*, 1913
[5] *UNDY*, 1960, Table 4
[6] *UNSY*, 1962, Table 1
[7] *UNSBLA*, Vol. 1, Table 3, except for Puerto Rico, Jamaica, Trinidad
[8] *UNSBLA*, Vol. 1, No. 1, Table 4
[9] Maisel, A. Q. 'Latin America Turns to Family Planning', *Readers Digest*, May 1964
[10] *UNSY*, 1962
[11] Hägerstrand, T. 'The Propagation of Innovation Waves, *Lund Studies in Geography*, 1952; Gleerup, Lund. Sweden
[12] *UNDY*, 1955, Table 7
[13] *UNSBLA*, Vol. 1. No. 1. Table 5
[14] *U.N.Demographic Yearbook*, 1960, Table 8
[15] *Biometrika*, 42 (1956) p. 425
[16] Lösch, A, *The Economics of Location* (in translation) 1954, New Haven

* The randomness of the sample has to some extent been deliberately interfered with for convenience by rejecting pairs of towns less than 500 km apart. Three of these were drawn and rejected in North America, none in Latin America.

CHAPTER 3

PHYSICAL BACKGROUND AND RESOURCES

3.1. STRUCTURE AND RELIEF

South America and North America are two separate structural entities. The isthmus of Panama is an archlike incursion thrust from the Pacific between the two, standing on part of a submarine plateau belonging to neither continent. The Caribbean Sea to the east of Panama separates the east-west aligned islands, which continue the structure of western North America, Mexico and Central America south as far as Honduras on its northern side from the northern Andes, which splay out north and north-east in Colombia and Venezuela, only to disappear against its southern side. Indeed even the eastern extremity of the Andes of Venezuela disappears beyond Trinidad without apparently being associated with the arc of small islands at the eastern end of the Caribbean.

Structurally, South America consists of three main elements, the stable eastern shields, the high western fold mountains (*cordilleras*) and a great intervening trough largely filled by Tertiary or Quaternary sediments from the western ranges. Though the ancient crystalline massifs of the Guiana and Brazilian highlands are separated by later sedimentary rocks, they are in reality only the exposed parts of one great structural unit, the South American basement complex, which extends from the Orinoco, south as far as the pampa of Argentina (Sierra de Tandil). This basement disappears west beneath the sedimentaries of the mid-continental depression but probably widely underlies the mountains and basins, and even reappears in certain areas within the western zone of fold mountains (northern Colombia, Peru, south central Chile). *Figure 3.1a* does not show the subaerial deposits that cover much of the area indicated as exposed shield; see *Figure 16.2* (geology of Brazil) for greater detail.

The Brazilian Shield has for various reasons been studied much more thoroughly than the Guiana Shield, but the two areas appear to have certain features in common. There is another ancient massif in the extreme south of South America, Patagonia, largely covered by marine sediments dating from the Mesozoic or Tertiary when it was transgressed by the sea, but this massif is thought to be related to a similar feature in Antarctica and not to the original framework of South America.

The Brazilian Shield has not been invaded by the sea since the Palaeozoic, but during periods of deposition much of the original surface has received continental post-Palaeozoic deposits, especially in the later Cretaceous. The landforms of the Brazilian plateau are the result firstly of successive stages of denudation by pediplanation (scarp retreat and pedimentation) followed by deposition from Carboniferous times, and secondly of relatively recent polycyclic stream incision.

* See King[1] for most of the material in this section.

Though greatly modified by subsequent stream erosion, several stages of pediplanation remain in the landscape, often terminated by abrupt erosional scarps. For example, many present day flat interfluves are relics of the very widespread early Tertiary Sul-Americana pediplanation; in places these interfluves are extensive, but elsewhere they may be very narrow. Older planations stand above the Sul-Americana, and more recent ones below its level. These surfaces have been warped by later movements.

There is much evidence in the Brazilian plateau, including the presence of Cretaceous continental sands preserved on high watersheds (interfluves), which should have disappeared under a Davisian cycle of erosion, to offer evidence for pediplanation during the earlier evolution of the landscape. Much of Brazil to this day bears traces of these successive cycles of pediplanation and deposition, but subsequent stream erosion has excavated broad valleys in the interior and many gorges, where the land is highest, especially along the south-eastern coastal margin of the massif.

Most of the present relief was formed as a result of Plio-Pleistocene and recent upwarping. In the Guiana highlands older denudational landscapes now stand high, as they do in the Brazilian highlands, but the existing basins of the Amazon and Paraná regions were further filled. In the east of Brazil a number of rift valleys associated with upwarping were formed, including the upper and middle São Francisco and the Paraíba trough behind Rio. Nick points of about 100–150 m on the tributaries of the Amazon are the result of Quaternary rejuvenations. Waterfalls on many other rivers in Brazil mark various substages in relatively recent movements caused by arching. The remarkable scarp formed by the seaward face of the Serra do Mar between Rio and São Paulo is not due to faulting but to erosion (see *Figure 3.13*).

The Andes are characterized by their great length, for they form a continuous range or series of ranges more than 9,000 km in length between eastern Venezuela and southern Chile. The comparative recency of the modern Andes is no less striking than their great length; the area occupied by the present Andes was until early-Pleistocene no more than the relics of previous ranges reduced by erosion to a mature land (the Puna surface) with scattered hill residuals (only 300–450 m). The present ranges were uplifted as much as several thousand metres in places as a result of violent uparching; widespread block-faulting also took place, not necessarily in harmony with earlier structural axes.

Although there are relics of earlier ranges, especially along the coastal region of south Peru and Chile, the evolution of the present Andes began in the late Mesozoic. Their evolution through the Tertiary is considered to be the final stage in the development of a late Mesozoic igneous island arc, with a trough on the east separating it from the already existing massifs of Gondwanaland, already discussed. Indeed, since the late Mesozoic the western outline of the South American continent has hardly changed. The present Andes evolved as a result of four main tectonic stages. In the late Cretaceous there was uplifting in the western part of the present region of the Andes (see *Figure 3.1*), roughly the course of the present Western Cordillera, involving Mesozoic formations. This movement actually occurred later in Venezuela, at the end of the Cretaceous, when the Laramide earth movement of North America and Mexico also took place. There was large scale faulting in Venezuela. Since the Mesozoic there has been no marine transgression of the Andes, but thick fluviatile and lacustrine deposits occur.

A second major movement took place in the early Oligocene. Tertiary elements were affected (see *Figure 3.1a*) and the eastern part of the present Andes was formed, with great folding and much volcanic activity. A third movement took place in the Miocene, accompanied by igneous activity. Thereafter, as already explained, the whole region was reduced by erosion and finally uplifted a fourth time. Tectonic activity has not yet ceased in the region, as volcanic activity and frequent earthquakes suggest.

Throughout the evolution of the Andes there has been little lateral movement, but there has tended to be some thrust eastwards towards the Gondwana shield in the east. There are few overthrust masses, and inliers of older rocks are limited in extent (Santa Marta, Sierras Pampeanas). Most striking has been the great amount of vertical movement.

As a result of these varied and complex developments it is possible to find several distinct elements in the Andean region today, though the complete sequence (from west to east) does not of course occur throughout. Off the Pacific coast is a trench, the Peru–Chile deep; the continental shelf is narrow. On the mainland, close to the coast, or in the form of islands in southern Chile, are relics of ranges folded before the late Mesozoic. Then follow the Western Cordillera with its older marine sedimentaries and extensive areas of volcanic rocks with lavas over 2,000 m thick in parts of Peru, and the Eastern Cordillera, with newer sedimentaries and only limited volcanic activity. Finally there are eastern front ranges, the depression filled with Tertiary and Quaternary deposits, and the Gondwana shield itself.

Turning to the relief of the modern Andes (see *Figure 3.2* and appropriate regional chapters), it is necessary to divide the region into a number of fairly distinct parts. In Venezuela and Colombia there are several distinct ranges separated by basins caused by block faulting (Magdalena and Cauca valleys). From Ecuador south to northern Argentina the Andes widen and are characterized by Western and Eastern Cordillera with intervening plateaux from around 3,000 m in altitude in Ecuador to 4,000–4,500 m in altitude in southern Peru and Bolivia. The third distinct section of the Andes is the narrower, and generally lower, single main range, south of Aconcagua (Lat. 33°S) in central Chile. Finally, south of about 38°S the Andes are rather a series of parallel discontinuous ranges. The detailed relief features of these various parts of the Andes will be described under individual countries. The most striking feature of drainage, which is basically antecedent, is the proximity of the continental divide to the Pacific coast. It follows closely the crest of the Western Cordillera much of the way, leaving short rivers with precipitous courses usually flowing directly to the Pacific on the west, but great depressions, in places structural, along the eastern flanks, which are followed for many hundreds of kilometres by the upper courses of rivers flowing to the Atlantic. The Puna block remains largely an area of internal drainage, however, with its remarkably smooth surface only beginning to be dissected along the sides. Rapids, and great

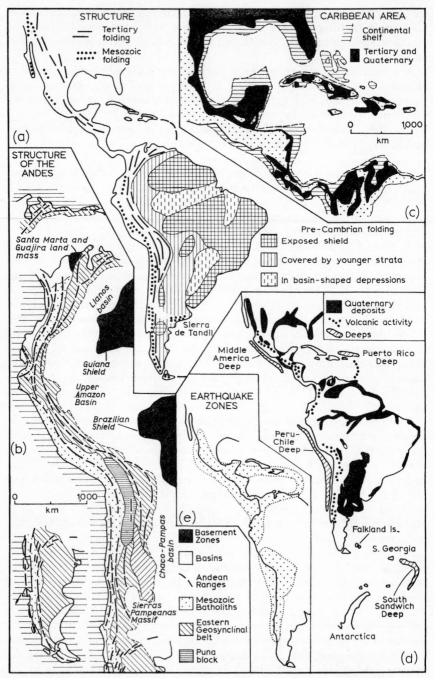

Figure 3.1. Structure and associated features of Latin America. (a) Main structural features, based on Umbgrove[2]. (b) Structural features of the Andes according to King[1]. (c) Features of the Caribbean area, King[1]. (d) Quaternary deposits, volcanic activity and ocean deeps. (e) Earthquake zones

(From L. C. King[1] by courtesy of Oliver and Boyd)

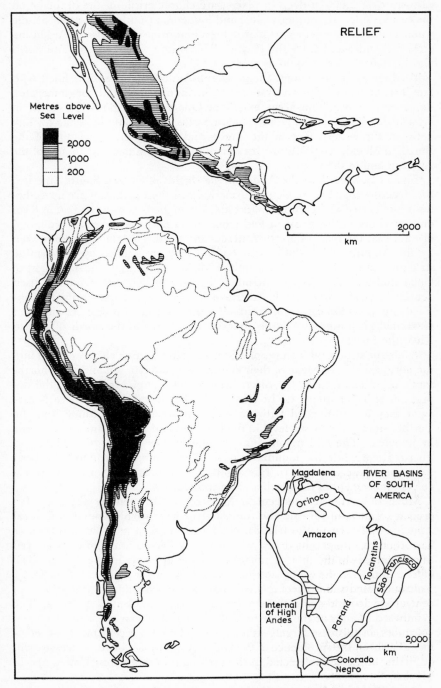

Figure 3.2. Main relief features of Latin America. See regional chapters for more detailed maps of most areas. Inset map: Main river basins of South America

canyons over 2,000 m deep in places, are characteristic of the drainage on the eastern side. In southern Chile and Patagonia (south of about 38°S), the watershed follows a very irregular course, and some rivers rise in Argentina cross the Andes and enter the Pacific. This region was glaciated, and fiords and limited glaciers remain as evidence today.

To the east of the Andes, the great sub-Andean depression is filled with late Tertiary and Quaternary deposits, including torrential conglomerates, sands and muds. The great extent of Quaternary deposits is shown in *Figure 3.1d*. There are in fact two main basins, joined only by a narrow link between the eastern foot of the Andes and the western extremity of the Brazilian Shield. Deposits are very thick in places, as near the mouth of the Amazon and in the Chaco.

Smaller in area than the Andes or the shields of eastern South America, the structures of Mexico, Central America and the Caribbean are nevertheless more varied and complex. In total, the higher parts of the region form one extremity of the girdle of fold mountains that form the circumvallation of Laurasia, the mass of North America and northern Asia, a girdle broken by the Atlantic*. To the east and north they are flanked by more stable structures of the lowlands of the gulf of Mexico, including Yucatán, most of Cuba and Florida. These surround the Gulf of Mexico, which is itself actually a part of the North American land mass that has gradually subsided but is tectonically quiescent. To the west of southern Mexico and Guatemala is the great Middle America deep, and to the north of Puerto Rico, the Puerto Rico deep.

While the structural features of western North America clearly extend into the northern part of Mexico, their continuity is interrupted and their north-south trend changed at the Sierra Madre del Sur of Mexico and the depression of Tehuantepec†. In Guatemala, Honduras and northern Nicaragua they are prolonged with an east-west trend and continue into the Caribbean only below sea level in the Rosalind and Pedro Bank, to reappear in Jamaica. The fold mountains continue further east in Hispaniola and Puerto Rico, while the mountains of southeast Cuba appear to have been split from those of northern Hispaniola by the Bartlett Trough, by transcurrent movement of the northern side westwards.

Much of northern and central Mexico was affected by the Nevadan orogeny of the late Jurassic and traces of its effects are also found in Central America and even in the Islands, but a succession of tectonic disturbances has occurred into recent times, with complex folding and faulting, as well as substantial uplift, though not of the same order as in the Andes. The older folding is in the west (Mesozoic) and the younger in the east (Tertiary). Volcanic activity has accompanied these movements and is widespread in central Mexico and again close to the Pacific coast in Central America. The Windward Islands at the extreme end of the Caribbean are a third area of volcanoes, in this case largely submerged. The most recent major development has been the subsidence of the Gulf of California; disturbances are still occurring and can be detected in this area both in south-west U.S.A. and in Mexico.

* L. C. King, *op. cit., Figure 177*, p. 453.
† See *Figure 11.1* for greater detail.

The present day relief of northern Mexico is dominated by the high plateau of the Sierra Madre Occidental; on its flanks, particularly to the west are relief features similar to those known as basin and range in southwestern U.S.A. To the east is the intermont plateau, terminating in the east in the Sierra Madre Oriental. The whole of Mexico and Central America is characterized by high land overlooking the Pacific, a watershed well on the Pacific side of the isthmus, and short rivers in the west; part of north central Mexico has interior drainage, however, and south of the Rio Grande there are no rivers to compare in scale with those of South America.

3.2. CLIMATE

Many geographical studies by Latin American authors of large areas such as countries contain maps with climatic regions, often based on the classification of Koppen[3]. In the view of the author such apparently tidy climatic compartments give a misleading picture of climatic conditions, inviting one to the view that there is a considerable degree of uniformity within each region and an abrupt change at the edges. This is of course the drawback of most regions in geography delimited by more than one criterion. Throughout this book, therefore, climatic maps show single features such as precipitation or temperature. The maps in this section only show the main features in the region as a whole, while more detailed maps of parts of Latin America appear later in the text. This and the following sections on soils and vegetation are merely introductory and are considered to be the most useful way of providing material on the physical background in the limited space available.

Latin America extends over a great range of latitude, from roughly 30°N to 50°S. Firstly, as mean annual temperature diminishes with increasing latitude, so the seasonal range tends to increase, at least to about 40°S. Secondly, long, relatively narrow but high mountain regions act as barriers, separating the lowest 3,000–6,000 m of atmosphere on either side over distances of thousands of kilometres. Since about half of the air above any given locality at sea level is within the first 5,000 m or so, the implications of such a barrier as the Andes can be appreciated. Mountain regions also of course contain their own varying climatic conditions. Thirdly, oceanic currents appear to affect profoundly at least the climates of coastal regions. The Gulf of Mexico-Caribbean area is virtually sealed off from the penetration of currents from colder latitudes and its surface waters are very warm. In contrast, cold currents converge from north and south along the Pacific coasts of the Americas towards the Panama area and are associated with dry coastal regions. The ocean on the eastern side of South America is, however, warmer than the western side at comparable latitudes.

Before giving an account of the broad features of temperature and precipitation it should be stressed that very great differences occur over very short distances, admittedly usually on account of differences of altitude or of the presence of intervening relief features. *Figure 3.3c* shows for example differences in mean annual precipitation in Haiti and *Figure 3.4d* differences in mean temperature in northern Colombia.

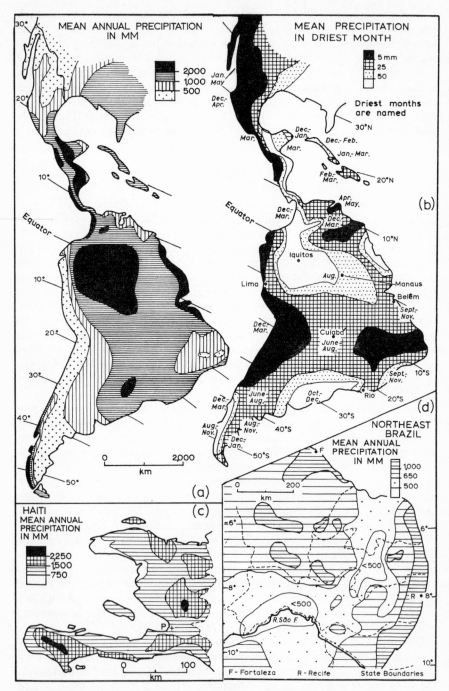

Figure 3.3. Features of precipitation in Latin America. (a) Mean annual precipitation. (b) Precipitation in driest month. (c) Annual precipitation in Haiti. (d) Annual precipitation in Northeast Brazil (based on map in Revista Brasileira de Geografia, Ano XXIV No. 4, p. 511)

CLIMATE

When dealing with climatic data in Latin America the occurrence of
the southern hemisphere summer season in December-February should be
borne in mind. Unfortunately, the terms summer (*verano*) and winter
(*invierno*) are in some areas used to refer to the dry and rainy seasons, which
do not necessarily coincide with warm and cool periods respectively.

The following table summarizes roughly the temperatures that may be
expected at different latitudes in lowland areas of the interior and eastern
side of Latin America.

Latitude	District	Winter	Summer	Range
30°N	North Mexico	(Jan.) 10°C	(July) 25–30°C	15–20°C
Equator	Amazonia	27°C	27°C	negligible
30°S	Chaco	(July) 10–12°C	25–30°C	15–20°C
50°C	South Patagonia	(July) 1–2°C	12–15°C	about 12°C

For what it is worth, the mean annual sea-level temperature in South
America exceeds about 20°C in lowland areas almost everywhere within
30 degrees of the Equator, but there are considerable regional differences
within this generally hot area. In Brazil, for example, the mean annual temperature exceeds 26°C around Manaus and Fortaleza, but is only 16°C at
a few hundred metres above sea level in Santa Catarina in the south (see
Figure 16.1d). The highest summer temperatures occur away from the
Equator itself. Hot areas such as the shores of the Gulf of California and
parts of the Chaco of Argentina have mean temperatures of over 30°C in the
hottest month.

Within about 30 degrees on each side of the equator, mean annual temperatures are considerably lower along most of the Pacific coastlands of
Latin America than on the eastern side at the same latitude. Compare for
example the mean annual temperature of less than 20°C in Lima (12°S)
with around 25°C at the same latitude in Northeast Brazil. Western
Colombia and the southern part of Central America are however as warm as
would be expected for their latitude. Great differences also occur as a result
of variations in altitude and more, perhaps, than in any other part of the
world, it is possible in Latin America to find the extremes of permanent snow
and tropical rain forest close to one another as in the Sierra Nevada de
Santa Marta in north Colombia where they are only 50 km apart. Some
effects of great altitude on human activities are discussed in Section 3.8.

Almost all of Latin America except the highest parts, limited in actual
areal extent, and the bleak, windswept extreme south, has high enough
temperatures for some kind of agriculture to be practised. Nevertheless, the
length of growing season and the cumulative temperatures set limits to
different crops at different latitudes and a map summarizing the occurrence
of frost is suggestive if only approximately of the limit of tropical agriculture.
Figure 3.4c shows that except in the very highest parts, almost all of tropical
South America is frost free, but whereas in the U.S.A. the period in which
frosts may be expected to occur grows in duration rapidly north from the
Gulf of Mexico, there is a large area in South America in similar latitudes in
which frosts may be expected to occur, though only in certain years.

35

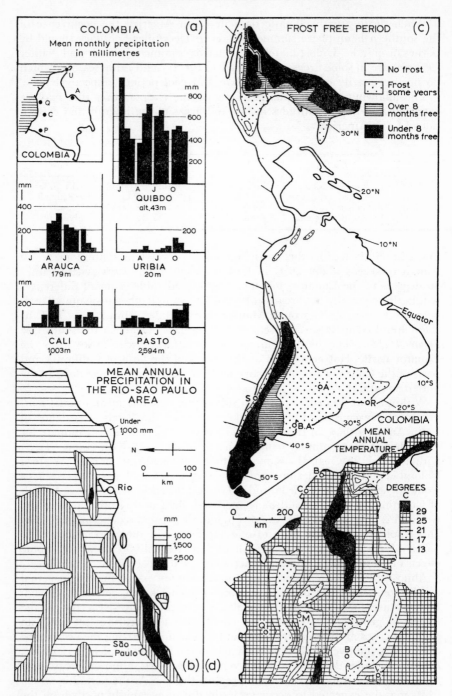

Figure 3.4. Features of precipitation and temperature in Latin America. (a) Precipitation in five selected stations in Colombia[4]. (b) Precipitation in part of Southeast Brazil. (c) Approximate duration of frost free period in Latin America. (d) Mean annual temperature in Colombia[4].

There are enormous differences in mean annual precipitation between different parts of Latin America. Places in northern Chile with virtually no rainfall at all contrast with part of the Pacific coast of Colombia receiving 6,000–7,000 mm/year. With exceptions and reservations it may be said that precipitation rather than temperature determines the broad differences in vegetation type and agricultural possibilities on a regional level, though temperature does this of course on a continental scale. An appreciation of the quantity, occurrence by seasons and reliability of precipitation in Latin America is therefore essential to an understanding of the human background but unfortunately data are inadequate for many areas. *Figure 3.3a* shows the main features of distribution of mean annual precipitation and *Figure 3.3b* gives an idea of the intensity and period of the dry season by showing the mean amount falling in the driest month*.

Although the effectiveness of a given amount of rain varies greatly from region to region in Latin America through differences in evaporation, surface conditions, nature of occurrence and so on, a mean annual rainfall in excess of about 1,000 mm is usually associated with a forest or savanna vegetation, or where this has been cleared for agriculture, allows cultivation to be practised without the need for irrigation. In contrast, in areas with less than 500 mm/year, xerophytic types of vegetation prevail and irrigation is needed to supplement rainfall for crop farming to succeed.

Marked differences in mean annual precipitation occur over short distances in many parts of Latin America but are not of course revealed on the general map; compare the detail on the inset map of Haiti with its generalized shading indicating 1,000–2,000 mm on the main map. In reality in Haiti a number of east-west highland areas receive 2–3 times as much rain as the deep intervening lowlands, while the distribution is complicated by the fact that north-facing sides of the highland areas receive more rain than south-facing sides. Such marked contrasts as these have been recorded in many parts of Latin America, including the Islands and the Andes. For example, over 2,000 mm are recorded on one mountain side in the eastern Andes of Peru, but about 350 mm in a valley floor only 20 km away and 1,000 m below. The transition here from tropical montane forest to cactus scrub is most impressive. Such abrupt contrasts have been noted for example along the coast in Ecuador. But *Figure 3.3d* also shows very marked contrasts in precipitation in northeast Brazil over short distances in an area in which relief features are not pronounced and heights of more than a few hundred metres are rare. *Figure 3.4a* shows precipitation data for five stations (heights indicated in metres) in Colombia covering tropical rain forest (Quibdó), savanna (Arauca), dry (Uribia) and mountain, conditions.

Marked seasonal differences in precipitation are found almost throughout Latin America, even in the areas of heaviest rain (over about 2,000 mm), which have no actual dry period. *Figure 3.3b* does not attempt to represent the length of the dry season but gives an idea of the amount of rain falling in the driest month in different parts of Latin America, thus representing only the peak of the dry season. A comparison with the left-hand map suggests a

* For more detailed precipitation maps, see *Figures 11.1a* (Mexico), *12.2b* (Venezuela), *14.2b* (Peru), *16.1c* (Brazil), *17.1c* (Southern Area).

fairly close correlation between high total precipitation and some rain even in the driest month. A rainfall regime with rain all the year is characteristic of Southern Brazil and Argentina, the tropical areas of western Amazonia, and the Caribbean lowlands of Central America. In contrast, large areas (in black) receive a negligible amount of rain (under 5 mm) in the driest month and may have several dry months, yet still receive a substantial total for the whole year; for example, parts of northeast Brazil, south Venezuela, and the Pacific coasts of southern Mexico and Central America.

Within a few degrees either side of the equator there tend to be two periods of maximum precipitation around December and June and two periods with less, around March and October. These differences are more accentuated towards the eastern end of Amazonia. To the south of the equatorial zone, a pronounced wet season in the southern hemisphere summer and autumn (January on) is characteristic, especially south of about 15°S, but there are many regional variations of this pattern, and in the west the Andes and the Pacific coastlands may have quite different regimes. The eastward facing coastlands of Brazil between Recife and Rio have more rain in winter (May, June) than in the summer. To the north of the equatorial belt the late summer maximum is in general more marked than to the south, with a very distinct wet season during June–August or somewhat later in some places and a relatively dry winter and spring. Almost throughout Latin America the period of heaviest rain coincides with the hot season and arrives therefore when most useful for agriculture but when susceptible to greatest evaporation; central Chile and northwest Mexico are exceptions.

The above data are based on means for periods of years and in a given year both the annual total and its occurrence in the year may deviate greatly. The following figures[6] show the actual amount of rain that fell each month in two Brazilian towns in 1959 and 1960 in millimetres:

	J	F	M	A	M	J	J	A	S	O	N	D	Total
Fortaleza 1959	127	198	456	209	317	84	4	24	12	5	7	5	1,448
Fortaleza 1960	16	10	428	281	95	71	4	6	4	28	2	34	980
Manaus 1959	356	370	321	183	47	23	2	49	10	315	187	228	2,091
Manaus 1960	357	320	229	410	119	174	68	59	80	226	240	299	2,580

Precipitation in the interior of northeast Brazil is notoriously unreliable, but many other areas for which data are limited, and which have attracted less attention because they have fewer people, are as adversely affected by droughts as northeast Brazil, and appear to suffer from great year to year variations. For example, desert localities of Peru and northern Chile may receive no appreciable rain for many years and then have all their 'quota' in a few heavy downpours. To bring home the devastating impact of weather in the Latin American environment from time to time, the following selected disasters in the single year of 1963 may be considered. During the winter months of 1963 (May–October) there were serious droughts over much of southern Brazil, Paraguay and northern Argentina. Throughout, crop yields were greatly reduced and there were water shortages and power cuts in Rio and São Paulo. The dry conditions allowed the spreading of fires, and in Paraná state some 30,000 people were rendered homeless. Exceptionally severe frosts afflicted the same general region, and some 650 million coffee trees were destroyed in north Paraná state, Brazil. On the other side of South America probably completely independent occurrences in 1963 were frosts destroying up to half of the vine harvest in parts of Central Chile, storms and heavy rain doing damage further south, floods in south coastal Peru affecting several towns, droughts affecting rice crops in north Peru and heavy rains also in the Peruvian Andes. The Caribbean area was swept by Hurricane Flora, which seriously damaged crops, including bananas, in many islands, and caused the loss of several thousand lives, and the destruction of tens of thousands of homes, mostly in Haiti. For example, most of the cocoa crop in Tobago was destroyed, and most of the bananas in several of the smaller British islands.

3.3. SOILS*

Several major soil types are present in Latin America. Their general characteristics are known but there has not been a great deal of study in detail of soils in different parts of the region. Some Latin American authors (e.g. in Mexico, Colombia) seem too ready to use terms applied to soil types of cool latitudes in classifying their own. This section is concerned merely with summarizing the outstanding features and assessing the fertility of the major soil types. The nature and fertility of the soils are related to the material from which they are derived, the climatic and vegetation conditions under which they have developed and, over wide areas, the influence of man. In their turn they affect vegetation and the productivity of land for agricultural purposes. In many areas, present day soils have been partly formed under different climatic conditions of past periods, while some (a-zonal soils) are formed not from underlying rock but from material transported from elsewhere.

Almost half of the area of Latin America consists of a very broad group of soils associated with humid lowland and upland areas of the tropics: latosols (laterific soils) and red-yellow podzolic soils. These soils vary according to the length of dry season, if any, but are found either in areas of tropical forest or of savanna. They are strongly weathered and leached and in spite of the luxuriant vegetation cover they often carry, may be poor in plant nutrients. They have only a limited nutrient carrying capacity and are not necessarily improved by the indiscriminate application of fertilizers. If cleared and cultivated they often lose fertility quickly and once interfered with may not readily acquire the same kind of vegetation cover that they had previously. Within this very generalized soil zone are considerable areas with special conditions; in Brazil for example, large areas of alluvial soils, especially in Amazonia, which if properly drained and protected from flooding could be very productive agriculturally, and, in the south, a large area with volcanic soils.

A particularly distinct set of soils occurs in Argentina and has counterparts in mid-U.S.A. and the blackearth belt of the U.S.S.R., the chernozems

---

* Much of the information in this section is based on material in FAO[7].

(blackearths) and reddish chestnut soils (see *Figure 3.5*). These are deep, fertile soils formed under grassland conditions. Towards the drier western fringes, however, they become poorer in humus (chestnut brown and reddish brown) and under present climatic conditions, characterized by a low rainfall and strong winds, are easily eroded (see *Figure 3.5b*). Black and

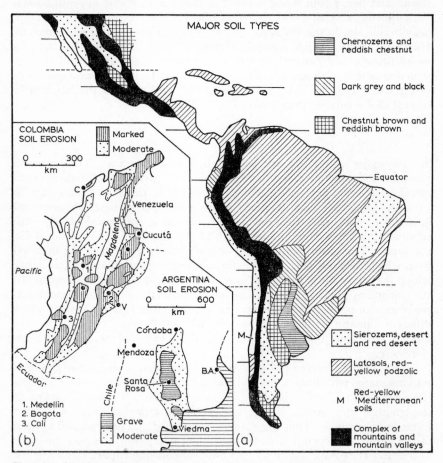

Figure 3.5. (a) *Major soil types in Latin America* (*based on Soil Map of the World in The State of Food and Agriculture 1963, p. 150*[7]), (b) *Soil erosion in Colombia*[4] *and in Argentina*

chestnut soils have been recorded elsewhere in Latin America at considerable altitudes, as in central Mexico and in Colombia, but they are limited in extent and probably of quite a different nature.

In the driest parts of Latin America, whether on the dry margin of the chestnut and reddish brown soils as in West and South Argentina, or along the desert coast of Peru and Chile, or in the dry northeast of Brazil, soils are often thin, and poor in organic matter, especially if sandy, but they may be rich in certain mineral nutrients. There is little scope for cultivation without irrigation, but once water is available and suitable fertilizers are added, very high yields may be obtained, as in the irrigated lands of Peru and Mexico.

Other soils tentatively shown on *Figure 3.5* are a very varied set of dark grey and black soils associated with the sub-tropical fringes of the tropical forest and savannas in South America, the soils of 'Mediterranean' Chile, and the soils of the highland areas. Steep slopes and great differences in climatic conditions over short distances give very varied conditions in the mountain regions, ranging from bare surfaces almost devoid of soil to prairie soils, alluvial soils and in southern Bolivia, saline soils.

Soil erosion is serious in many parts of Latin America. Indeed, almost every existing combination of soil and climate in the region is potentially destructible unless carefully cultivated, but the situation is most serious in the highland areas where alarmingly steep slopes may be cultivated, and on the semi-arid zone between the pampas and desert areas of Argentina.

3.4. VEGETATION

Of the four aspects of the physical environment most frequently referred to as the background of the activities of man in any large region, relief, climate, soils and vegetation, the last, perhaps, comes closest to summarizing the agricultural possibilities of a region. Vegetation regions are no more easy to define with precision than climatic or soil regions, since any given vegetation type is an arbitrarily chosen mass of tree, shrub and herbaceous species. Innumerable combinations are possible and completely different classifications of vegetation types could be devised for any large area by two different authorities. Nevertheless, reasonably distinct types of vegetation do often persist over large areas. Those occurring in Latin America have been grouped into four main classes, each of which is mapped separately in *Figure 3.6**. To supplement the relatively simple picture conveyed by these four maps, the vegetation of certain smaller parts of Latin America is shown in more detail separately†.

The types of vegetation combined are as follows:
(1) Humid forest:
    (*a*) Tropical (*i*) Rain
                (*ii*) Semi-evergreen and deciduous
    (*b*) Evergreen mixed forest, deciduous beech forest
(2) Dry: thorn forest, cactus scrub with or without desert grass, mid-latitude semi-desert scrub (Patagonia), sclerophyllous scrub (Chile and Mexico), desert (Peru, Chile)
(3) Mountain: Alpine, tropical montane forest, often with conifers.
(4) Savanna, grassland including pampa: broadleaved tree savanna (campos in Brazil, llanos in Venezuela), pampas and other temperate grasslands.

In addition to the physical influences that have shaped the various combinations of plant species making up the natural vegetation, the influence of man, in removing the original vegetation by cutting or burning it, in cultivating it and abandoning it, or using it for grazing, is considered to have

* This fourfold division of main vegetation types is based on maps by S. R. Eyre[8].
† See *Figures 3.7, 3.8, 16.1e*.

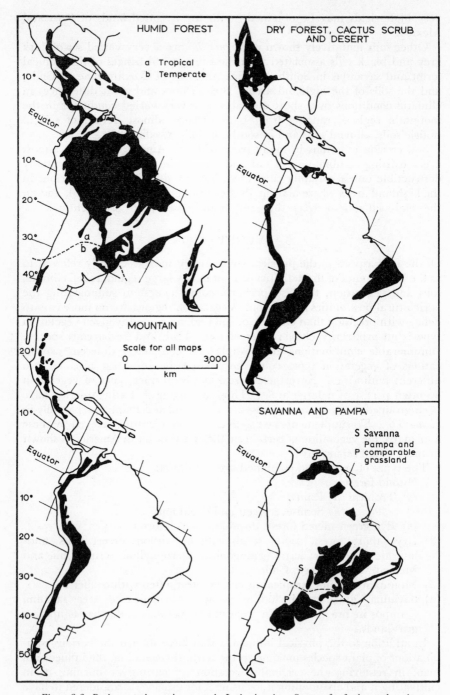

Figure 3.6. Basic vegetation environments in Latin America. See text for further explanation

(From S. R. Eyre[8] by courtesy of Edward Arnold)

been very profound over very large areas, even where there is only a low density of population. The population of Latin America was not, however, large before the sixteenth century except in certain limited areas, but even so, several thousand years of gradual modification could have had a considerable cumulative influence, and great activity in clearing vegetation in the last few centuries must be added. Even so, the natural vegetation would seem to have been interfered with by man less in Latin America than in Africa; for one thing, there was little grazing until the arrival of Old World livestock in the sixteenth century.

The widespread tropical rain forest is the densest and most continuous mass of vegetation in Latin America. On its drier margins it gives way to semi-evergreen and deciduous forest, or where the transition to dry conditions is abrupt, is replaced by thorn forest with dwarf trees. Where it reaches the margins of highland areas it merges into tropical montane forest, which eventually thins out around two or three thousand metres altitude, depending on local conditions. A further reduction in precipitation, or in the length of the rainy season, is frequently associated with savanna in the tropics, grassland and scrub further from the equator. The opposite extreme, desert conditions, is reached in Latin America over a large area only in the coastal region of Peru and northern Chile.

Since the tropical rain forest covers such a large part of Latin America its main features deserve attention. This forest has been called equatorial forest, but in certain parts of the tropical world it is found at a great distance from the equator. Such vegetation is permitted by high temperatures and heavy rainfall interrupted by only very short dry periods. It has at least several thousand different plant species, including in Amazonia some 2,500 species of large tree alone, but shrubs are few. The trees are evergreen and are constantly shedding their leaves and growing new ones. The leaves of the taller trees are leathery and dark green and are able to continue functioning under the strong heat of the sun. Often three distinct levels of forest can be detected. The forest itself generally exceeds 30 m in height and the uppermost layer is formed by the umbrella-shaped crowns of the tallest species; these alone intercept much of the light, but often two other layers of smaller trees, with their foliage around 20 and 15 m, grow below. Trees usually have straight trunks with few branches, and the ground beneath the forest is much clearer than is popularly imagined. It does of course contain the saplings waiting their opportunity to replace the existing trees as they die. Lianes are frequently found, trailing from tree to tree, and adding to the mass of foliage high above ground level; many species of epiphytes grow on the trees themselves. The nutrient cycle in the forest soil is very rich and very rapid but depends almost entirely upon the products of decayed vegetation from the forest. Well-known species of tall tree are the india-rubber tree (*Hevea braziliensis*), and the brazil nut (*Bertholletia excelsa*); shorter trees are the cacao (*Theombroma cacao*), and banana (*Musa species*) trees. The tropical montane forest has many of the features of the tropical rain forest but is found mainly between about 1,500 and 3,000 m. The largest area of tropical rain forest in Latin America is in Amazonia and extends several degrees north and south of the Equator with only small interruptions. Smaller areas of this forest are found along the coast of Brazil between 10° and 25°S, in western Colombia, along the Caribbean coast of Central America and in the Islands, where, however, very little of the original forest remains.

Mainly within the tropics but in areas with a more limited and more seasonal rainfall (about 750 to 1,250 mm), the tropical semi-evergreen and deciduous forest displaces the tropical rain forest. The largest area of this forest is in middle Brazil, and long galleries of the forest extend south into the savanna lands. In temperate South America there are two more limited zones of lowland and upland forest. These mostly contain both deciduous and evergreen species and are found in areas with more than about 1,000 mm of rain. The uplands of South Brazil still have large areas of forest with one very characteristic species of pine, the *Araucaria angustifolia* (Paraná pine), one of the most important commercial trees in Latin America. The other area of forest extends from south central Chile, along the flanks of the Andes to the southern tip of the continent, and also includes valuable coniferous species. The Patagonian side of the Andes has mainly deciduous forest (southern 'beech').

Between the humid forest environments and the decidedly dry environments, large areas of savanna and grassland characterize the central part of South America and much of Argentina. The savanna vegetation has been considered to be associated with a particular climate, but its origin is now in question and in Brazil, at least, it occurs in areas with very different rainfall regimes. It consists of plant communities in which grasses and sedges cover most of the ground but trees also occur, sometimes wide apart, sometimes close together. It is thought that fires may have had much to do with the development of savanna vegetation, but certain types of soil may also encourage this coexistence of grass and tree species. The savanna belt of Latin America is less continuous than that in West Africa, where the great east-west belt appears to be a transition between the dense humid forest to the south and the desert to the north. Savanna vegetation is rare in Mexico, Central America and the Islands, and in South America occurs mainly in the llanos of the Orinoco Valley and in south central Brazil.

In South Brazil, Uruguay and east central Argentina a large area receiving from about 400 to 1,000 mm of rain per year had a grassland vegetation before most was cleared for cultivation or was intensively grazed in the last 100 years. The grassland was tall prairie with feather-grass and melic growing in closely spaced tussocks. Small areas of tree vegetation were also to be found, and it is thought that possibly these are relics of an earlier forest cover, at least in those parts receiving more than about 750 mm of rain per year. On its northern margins the temperate grassland terminates against the forests of southern Brazil, but in the west, with increasing aridity, the grass is shorter and is replaced by xerophytic shrubs.

The grassland area in Argentina is generally referred to as the *pampa*, but according to usage in the countries concerned, the grasslands of Rio Grande do Sul (Brazil), Uruguay and the Mesopotamian region of Argentina (between the Paraná and Uruguay rivers) is termed provincia Uruguayensis, with *vegetación de pradera* (meadow).

Most of the dry environment of Latin America consists of varying combinations of scanty grass, dwarf tree species, shrubs and succulent plants

44

adapted to long periods of drought. A large area of dry steppe and semi-desert extends from southern Bolivia, through western Argentina, over almost 40 degrees of latitude, and consists of thorn forest in the north and lower growing scrub in the south. This area is of little use agriculturally except where irrigated. The interior of Northeast Brazil also consists mainly of thorn forest, with occasional taller trees (e.g. bottle trees and xerophytic palms). Most of the area receives considerable total precipitation but this occurs with great irregularity, which explains the dominance of drought-resisting species, though underlying rock conditions may also contribute. A smaller area with drier species occurs in parts of northern Venezuela and Colombia, and unexpected dry patches occur also in the Islands and Yucatán. Most of northern and western Mexico consists either of thorn forest where precipitation is sufficient, or towards the north, semi-desert with cactus scrub; savanna vegetation is not widely found. Central Chile and small areas in the extreme northwest of Mexico have a 'mediterranean' type of vegetation, with distinct species but many characteristics in common, as a result of dry summer conditions.

In coastal Peru, northern Chile and parts of the central Andes are found the most arid conditions in the whole of Latin America. With a very limited precipitation, large areas are virtually without vegetation, and bare rock surfaces and sand dunes are frequent. Desert conditions are only relieved where rivers cross the arid zone from the Andes to the Pacific, where the water table is close to the surface or where ephemeral plants appear in places along the coast exposed to light drizzle (*garúa*) from sea mists.

The mountain environments are characterized by sharp changes in vegetation with altitude. In general, an increase in altitude above about 3,000 m is accompanied by diminished precipitation and by a thinning out of forest in areas humid enough for this to occur below this altitude. Four distinct highland environments may be distinguished in Latin America (see *Figure 3.6*; that of southeast Brazil is not shown on the map). Firstly, the Andes north of 30 degrees south are continuous, high and, in places, very wide. In the adjoining lowlands completely different types of vegetation are found, ranging from desert in Peru and Chile on the Pacific side to tropical rain forest on the eastern side. On the western side cactus scrub extends high along the western Cordillera, while on the eastern side tropical montane forest may extend to beyond 2,500 m. Above about 3,000 m, however, the characteristic Alpine grassland type of vegetation, with local names (e.g. *páramo* in the north, *puna* in the south) according to precipitation and type of grass, occur almost throughout the region, thinning out and disappearing around 4,500 m into bare rock and small patches of permanent snow. In southern Bolivia and northern Argentina desert-like conditions occur.

The second mountain region consists of the Andes south of about 30 degrees south. The range here is narrower, and for the most part lower, and less continuous. There is a more scanty grassland cover, while the lower flanks are largely covered by temperate forest. The third high mountain region extends discontinuously from northern Mexico far into Central America. The higher ranges in Mexico are distinguished by their relatively dense forest vegetation, containing many conifers, while in southern Mexico and Central America coniferous species appear in the higher parts of the tropical montane

45

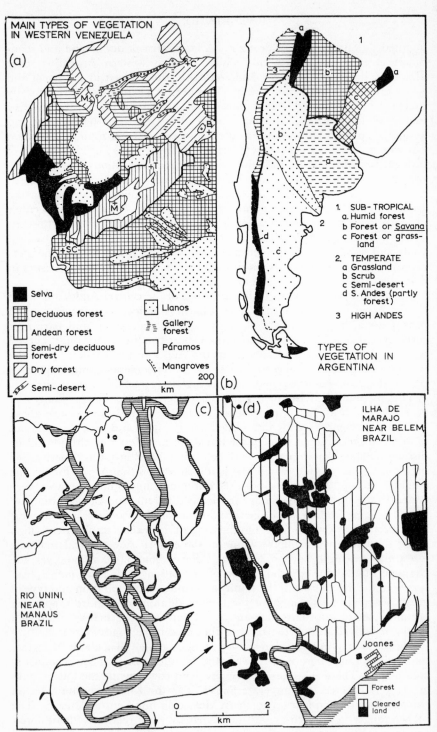

Figure 3.7. Examples of vegetation and land use. (a) Vegetation in Western Venezuela (based on Atlas de Venezuela, map No. 12). (b) Vegetation in Argentina (based on A. C. Rampa[15], p. 192). (c) (d) Small areas in Amazonia of Brazil, (c) above Manaus, (d) near the mouth of the Amazon

46

VEGETATION

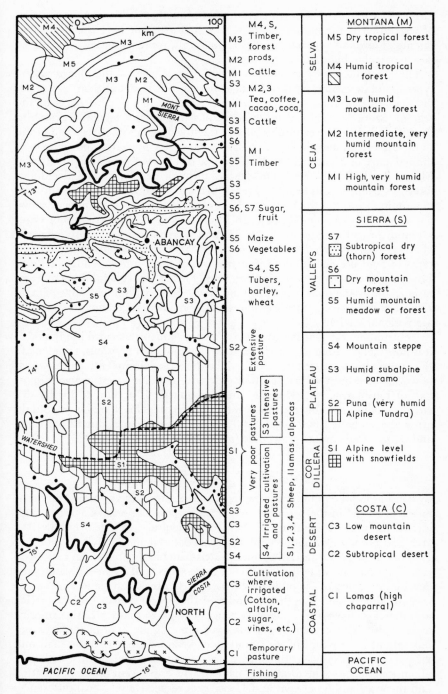

Figure 3.8. The coastal desert (costa), high Andes (sierra) and tropical rain forest (selva) of Southern Peru[9]. The black dots are the principal nucleated settlements. Different types of shading are used to help to distinguish different types of vegetation

47

forest. The fourth area in which altitude indirectly modifies the distribution of vegetation is the high parts of southern Brazil, but here a complicated mixing of lowland vegetation types is the result, rather than the appearance of a particular highland vegetation.

These comments on vegetation give a rough idea of the characteristic types found in various parts of Latin America, but in detail there are many different interpretations of vegetation conditions in different parts of the region. More detailed vegetation maps of selected areas have therefore also been included to give examples both of the diversity in some areas and of the Latin American terminology. *Figure 3.7a* shows how it is possible in a limited part of Venezuela to pass over a distance of some 200 km in the Maracaibo lowlands from semi-desert, through dry forest and deciduous forest, to tropical rain forest. Over a further 200 km one can pass through mountain forest into the high grassland of the Andes, over permanent snow, and down into savanna (*llanos*). In *Figure 3.7b* are the main types of vegetation in Argentina, and in *Figures 3.7c* and *d*, on a larger scale, forested areas of Amazonia. *Figure 3.8* illustrates the great variety of environments and types of land use encountered in a traverse of the southern Andes of Peru. Brazil also has a great variety of interesting terms for regional types of vegetation; the main ones are shown in *Figure 16.1*, with their approximate English equivalents. Other references will be made to vegetation in appropriate regional sections.

Returning to the four main vegetation environments mapped in *Figure 3.6*, it is possible, by using as a basis the area of major civil divisions, to calculate the approximate extent of each. The forest environment, from which however have been subtracted both dry and montane forest, covers almost half of Latin America. Roughly another quarter is accounted for by dry environments, including the dry forest. The remainder is shared by mountain areas above about 1,000 m (about 8 per cent), savanna (about 12 per cent) and pampa and similar grasslands (about 6 per cent).

3.5. VEGETATION AND POPULATION

By considering the number of people in each of the main vegetation environments discussed in the previous section*, it is possible to have a very rough idea of the present usefulness of these for agriculture. Table 3.1 shows the area and population, both calculated from data for major civil divisions, of 17 areas (*Figure 3.9a*) in Latin America according to the four main categories (see *Figure 3.6*) showing the location of these areas, and *Figure 3.9b* shows the densities recorded in the table for each of the 17 areas. Lowland forest areas contain almost half of both the land and the population in Latin America and therefore have a mean density roughly equal to that for Latin America as a whole. The dry environments have some 25 per cent of the area but only about 20 per cent of the population, savanna areas 12·5 per cent and 2·5 per cent respectively. In contrast, the mountain environments, with only about 8 per cent of the total area, have nearly 20 per cent of the population and the grassland 6 per cent and 11 per cent respectively. Local differences

* For comparison, major environments proposed by Platt[10] are illustrated in *Figure 3.10*.

within these main vegetation regions are, of course, so great that the mean density represents a very wide range of densities in different areas. Further, very large towns such as Mexico City and Buenos Aires undoubtedly owe their size partly to the fact that their influence extends beyond the vegetation regions in which they are located and the study could be continued to eliminate them from the calculation. In spite of these drawbacks however it seems useful to show the broad relationship between population and vegetation.

TABLE 3.1

	Area (thousand km²)	Pop'n (millions)	Persons per km²	% of total area	% of total pop'n
I MOUNTAIN	1,690	38·8	23	8·2	18·6
(a) Mexico—Guatemala	150	13·9	93		6·7
(b) Venezuela—Colombia —Ecuador	430	16·1	37		7·7
(c) Peru—Bolivia— N. Argentina	1,110	8·8	8		4·2
II DRY	5,226	41·4	8	25·3	19·7
(a) Mexico	1,560	17·5	11		8·4
(b) Venezuela—Colombia	220	2·8	13		1·3
(c) Peru—N. Chile	566	9·9	17		4·7
(d) Northeast Brazil	500	6·5	13		3·1
(e) Bolivia—Paraguay— Argentina	2,380	4·7	2		2·2
III FOREST	9,843	100·2	10	48·0	48·0
(a) Mexico—C. America	800	15·1	19		7·2
(b) Islands	230	19·6	85		9·4
(c) Venezuela—Colombia —Ecuador	264	3·7	14		1·8
(d) 'Amazonia'	6,641	9·2	1·4		4·4
(e) Brazil—Paraguay	1,558	50·3	33		24·1
(f) S. Chile	350	2·3	7		1·1
IV SAVANNA	2,573	5·2	2	12·5	2·5
(a) Venezuela—Colombia	395	1·3	3·3		0·6
(b) Brazil	2,178	3·9	1·8		1·9
V GRASSLAND INCLUDING PAMPA	1,243	23·1	19	6·0	11·2
LATIN AMERICA	20,575	208·7	10	100	100

Occurrence of large towns: Ia Mexico City (5 m.)
Ib Caracas (1½ m.), Bogota (1¼ m.)
IIc Lima (2 m.), Santiago (2 m.)
IIIb Havana (1¼ m.)
IIIe Rio (4½ m.), São Paulo (4½ m.)
V Buenos Aires (7 m.), Montevideo (1 m.)

The lowland forest environment supports very high densities of population in the Islands (IIIb) where, of course, much of it has been cleared, yet is virtually uninhabited in the interior of Amazonia (IIId). Southeast Brazil and Paraguay (IIIe) contain roughly one quarter of the total population of Latin America. The great differences in density in the forest environment appear to be due partly to differences in soil conditions but

49

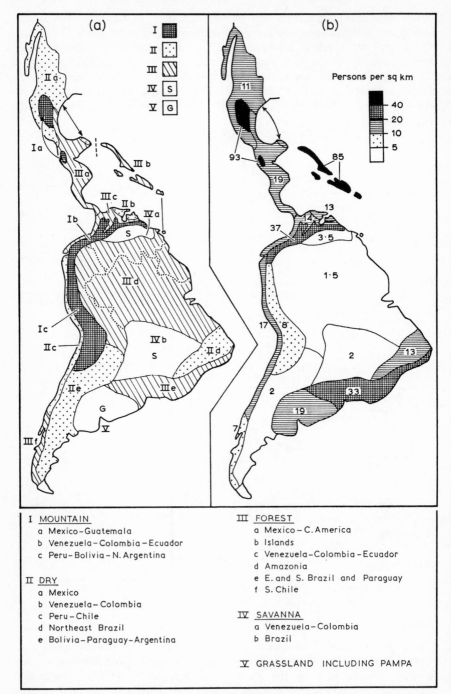

Figure 3.9. Physical environments in Latin America based largely on vegetation types (see Figure 3.6). (b) Density of population calculated on the basis of major civil division figures, for regions in (a). See also Figure 3.10a and Table 3.1

50

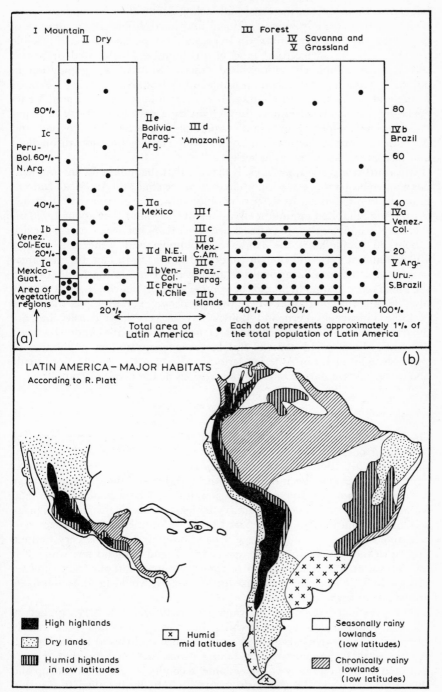

Figure 3.10. (a) Comparative density of population on major physical environments (see Figure 3.9).
(b) For comparison with Figure 3.9, major habitats of Latin America according to Platt[10]. Shading is
used to distinguish different types of habitat

51

largely to distance from the coast and lack of penetration by modern settlement. In the dry environment regional and local differences in density of population are even more marked. In coastal Peru for example, it is possible to step from the agricultural land of an intensively cultivated oasis into surrounding, completely uninhabited desert. Most of the population in dry environments is dependent on water supply from elsewhere, or is related to mineral production. In contrast, the savanna lands of Brazil and Venezuela are characterized almost throughout by a very low density of population. The temperate grassland region of South Brazil, Uruguay and Argentina, however, supports a considerable rural population throughout and has several large towns as well.

Most surprising of all, perhaps, is the fact that the mountain environment has a much larger share of population than of area in Latin America. Indeed, in pre-Columbian times its share of population was far greater than it is now. Within the inhabited mountain environments (say land over about 1,000 m) there are striking regional contrasts (see *Figure 3.9b*) between Central Mexico (about 90 people/km²) the Andes of Colombia and Venezuela (almost 40/km²) and of Peru and Bolivia (under 10). This is, in fact, because areas with good conditions for agriculture are less numerous in the Andes than in the much more limited highlands of Central Mexico, but can support equally high densities of population where they do occur. For example, the shores of Lake Titicaca in Peru and Bolivia have a very high density but are separated from other concentrations of population in the Andes by great distances. In a world context this large concentration of population at great altitudes in Latin America seriously affects any generalizations made about the adverse nature of mountain regions as the home of man.

3.6. WATER SUPPLY

Once taken for granted except in arid areas, water is now beginning to be counted as one of the basic resources or assets of a region, and to be considered on a national rather than a local level. Although spectacular irrigation works have been built in Latin America and there are a few large hydroelectric power stations in the region, little has been done to assess total water resources and much still has to be learned about the sheer quantity available, about rainfall regimes, and so on. Movement of water over considerable distances to supply large urban consuming areas is very limited. Owing to the complexity of the availabity of, and demand for, water it is difficult to produce a useful map of water resources, but the map showing precipitation (*Figure 3.3*) gives an idea of where it would be expected to be abundant and where deficient.

The principal 'consumer' of water is agriculture. Most is supplied of course by rain, but in recent decades the irrigated area has been greatly extended. The water background to agriculture is discussed in Section 7.2. Hydroelectricity is generated by falling water, the amount that can be expected depending firstly on the volume, secondly on the vertical drop and thirdly of course on the generating capacity actually installed to use this. A reasonably regular flow of water is desirable and a water-course with an irregular regime requires a reservoir constructed above the site of the power station. Other users of water are mining, industrial and domestic consumers. Finally, inland navigation on rivers uses water even if it does not consume it, and inland fisheries should not be overlooked.

To some extent the various users of the water resources compete. If used to generate electricity, falling water may reach too low a level to be available for irrigation where needed, while agricultural and urban consumers may also at times compete. Reservoirs can usefully regulate water supply for power and for other users and even improve navigation, but are liable to silt up in time and if they greatly increase the water surface, evaporation can actually reduce supplies, while in some places loss is caused by seepage of water through the underlying rock*. Sometimes, on the other hand, several functions may usefully be fulfilled by the construction of a single works. Thus the Tres Marias in Minas Gerais, Brazil (see *Figure 16.3*) will not only generate hydroelectricity, but will help navigation on the São Francisco River, prevent floods further downstream, regulate the supply of water to the Paulo Alfonso station much further downstream and allow some irrigation.

The work of regulating and using to the full the water resources of Latin America has only just seriously started. In theory, none of the water in rivers flowing across arid areas need ever reach the sea, a situation that may soon exist in western North America. Thus almost all the rivers rising in the mountains of northern Mexico and in the Andes could be exploited to improve water supply in agriculture, even if only to supplement existing precipitation. Northeast Brazil is less fortunate, but the São Francisco can contribute to parts of this dry area. The greatest hydroelectric potential also occurs in the mountain regions, but suitable sites are often remotely placed and the need for great preparatory work such as road building has discouraged efforts so far. Both the Guiana and Brazilian shield areas offer many excellent sites, and the Paraná basin, with a number of rapids, has a very large potential.

In spite of apparently abundant water resources in most parts of Latin America, water supply is inadequate in most settlements. Large cities such as Mexico, Monterrey, Rio and Lima have already exhausted resources in their immediate vicinity and are having to look further afield. Lima, for example, is now receiving water piped through a long tunnel under the main Andean watershed from the headwaters of rivers flowing to the Amazon. Many mining and smelting centres in dry areas, being large consumers, have also had water problems. Eventually considerable quantities of sea water may be distilled in coastal areas for human consumption and possibly even for irrigation. This is not an economic proposition at present but is done as a last resort, as in the Netherlands Antilles, which have two large oil refineries requiring far more water than the small islands can provide.

3.7. DISTRIBUTION OF ECONOMIC MINERALS

This section merely attempts to find some order in what at first sight appears to be a haphazard distribution of different economic mineral deposits in

* These problems have already been encountered for example in Southwest U.S.A. and in the southern part of European U.S.S.R.

Latin America. Their extraction is considered in Section 8.2. Most of the region has not been seriously explored yet for minerals and if important new deposits are still being found in such thoroughly studied areas as the U.S.A. (e.g. iron ore in Missouri) and Western Europe (e.g. oil and gas in the Netherlands, Italy), certainly the inventory of minerals in Latin America will grow in time. Even so there is good reason not to expect certain minerals in

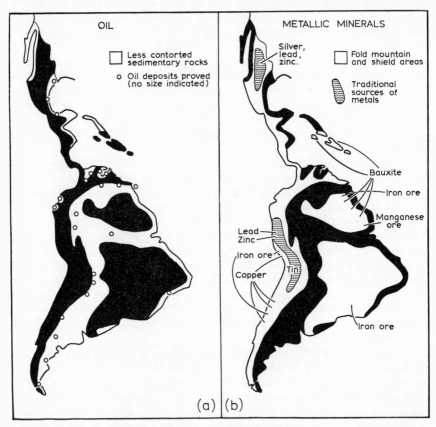

Figure 3.11. Areas of occurrence of (a) oil and (b) metallic minerals in Latin America

areas with certain types of structure and geology. If coal is ignored, since proved reserves are very small and prospects of finding large reserves are poor, then the main commercial minerals known and exploited in the region may be divided into three groups.

Firstly, there is a much greater probability of finding oil and natural gas in commercial quantities in areas of sedimentary rocks that are not greatly contorted than elsewhere. Their age does not matter, but an arrangement in appropriate layers of porous beds to hold the hydrocarbons, and impervious beds above to trap them there, is essential in some form. Traces of oil are found very widely in greatly different geological circumstances but useful quantities may only be expected in the areas left white in *Figure 3.11a*, though

54

even here there need not *necessarily* be any at all, either because it has never formed, or because it has not been retained. Most of the more important discoveries of oil are recorded on the map, which is of course greatly simplified, but prospecting is also under way in many districts not indicated.

Secondly, most metallic minerals known and mined in Latin America occur in precisely the opposite kinds of conditions from those favouring the

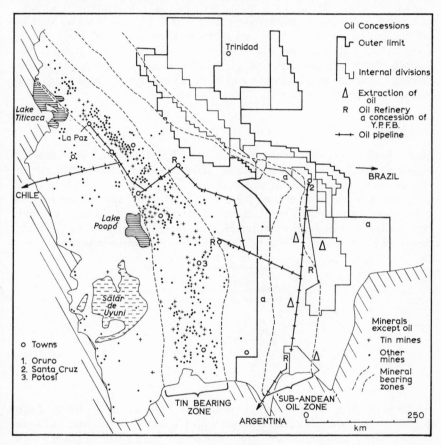

Figure 3.12. Mining in Bolivia. The map brings out the spatial distinction between metal bearing[11] and oil bearing areas.

occurrence of oil and gas, namely the fold mountains and shield areas. The actual metal bearing deposits within these areas occupy of course only a tiny part of the total area. Useful metallic ores could lie beneath the sedimentary basins, but their exploration would be very costly. Although iron is contained in commercial quantities in a large number of forms, almost all the high grade iron ore extracted in Latin America is found in the shield areas and fold mountains, and at present little low grade iron ore is extracted at all. Silver, gold, copper, lead, zinc and tin are particularly associated with the fold mountains, while precious stones also come either from here or the Brazilian Shield.

Thirdly, a number of minerals, including those containing iron and aluminium, as well as non-metallic minerals used in the chemicals industry and in the production of building materials, are found in both areas shown in *Figure 3.11*. The nitrate of Chile and the guano of Peru are associated with a particularly dry climate rather than with geological conditions.

The mutually exclusive character of oil and several metallic minerals is a feature of other parts of the world as well as Latin America (e.g. U.S.A., U.S.S.R.), and comes out strikingly in *Figure 3.12*, which shows that in Bolivia, petroleum concessions, and mines producing tin and other metals, occur in two quite separate belts. One considerable drawback of this is that there is rarely any possibility of achieving a saving in investment by the sharing of roads, urban services and so on by enterprises producing these two distinct kinds of mineral.

3.8. ALTITUDE

Since about 20 per cent of the population of Latin America lives above a height at which the effects of altitude make conditions different in one or several ways from those in adjoining lowlands, and since high altitude populations occur in several major countries, it seems appropriate here to draw attention to some general aspects of the influence of altitude. Pressure decreases with altitude in a predictable way, though small local variations in time and place occur. The following data seem widely accepted:

Altitude in metres	Expected pressure in millimetres
Sea level	760
1,000	674
2,000	596
3,000	526
4,000	462
5,000	405

At about 5,600 m the atmospheric pressure is half that at sea level. Temperature also diminishes with altitude with reasonable regularity, but since temperatures, unlike pressure, vary enormously from place to place at sea level and in the same place over time, the temperature at a given altitude can only be predicted, and even then only roughly, if sea level temperature is known at that place. The following figures show diminution of temperature in Venezuela in an area with a mean annual temperature of 27°C at sea level; the mean figures at given altitudes are[12]:

Altitude in metres	Temperature in 0°C
Sea level	27°
1,000	21
2,000	15
3,000	9
4,000	2·5

Precipitation and relative humidity are much less precisely related to changes in altitude, but perhaps above 2,500–3,000 m the rareness of the atmosphere begins to affect its moisture retaining capacity and precipitation appears to diminish, having apparently reached a maximum at least in the northern Andes in a zone around 1,000 to 2,000 m.

A difference in altitude of about 1,000 m brings appreciable changes in temperature (e.g. between Santos and São Paulo, La Guaira and Caracas). At 2,000 m, climate and vegetation are very different and agricultural patterns distinct. At about 3,000 m, low pressure, which is roughly ⅔ sea level pressure, begins to have profound effects on the physiology of new-comers from lowland areas, though some people are already affected below this altitude and others little affected at greater heights. Almost inevitably, great variations in altitude are also accompanied by widespread steep slopes, and movement is therefore seriously affected. Thus human activities are affected in many ways by appreciable changes in altitude, there being a series of influences originating in differences in temperature affecting particularly crop farming, differences in pressure affecting animal and human physiology and even the performance of steam and internal combustion engines, and widespread steep slopes affecting cultivation, facilitating soil erosion, and through steep gradients raising transport costs and necessitating detours to avoid physical obstacles.

Much of the population of Mexico and the northern Andean countries lives between 2,000 and 3,000 m, but only in Peru and Bolivia do large numbers live between 3,000 and 4,000 m. There are few settlements anywhere above 4,000 m, but roads and railways pass above this in places and many small mining settlements are above 4,000 m, including one town of considerable size (see *Figure 8.6*), Cerro de Pasco, Peru, at over 4,200 m.

Agriculture is affected by altitude in various ways, but most profound is the influence of decreasing temperatures. Very broadly the main crops grown in Latin America can occur either below 2,000 m or above this or throughout. The following are figures for Colombia[13]:

Low altitude		High altitude	
Sugar cane	below 1,750	Wheat	1,900–3,200
Cotton	750–1,750	Potatoes	2,100–3,500
Bananas	below 1,900	Beans (*haba*)	2,150–3,500
Coffee (best)	1,100–2,000		
	Large range		
	Maize	below 3,200	

Appropriate fodder grasses are grown at different altitudes.

Lack of oxygen affects animal life above a certain altitude. This problem is serious only in Peru and Bolivia, with their large populations above 3,000 m. The immediate effect of a visit to a high altitude may be *soroche*—various unpleasant symptoms affecting digestion in particular; these are usually overcome after a short time. A move in the reverse direction may also cause discomfort. More disturbing are the long term effects of infertility on settlers from lowland areas moving into high altitudes and of respiratory

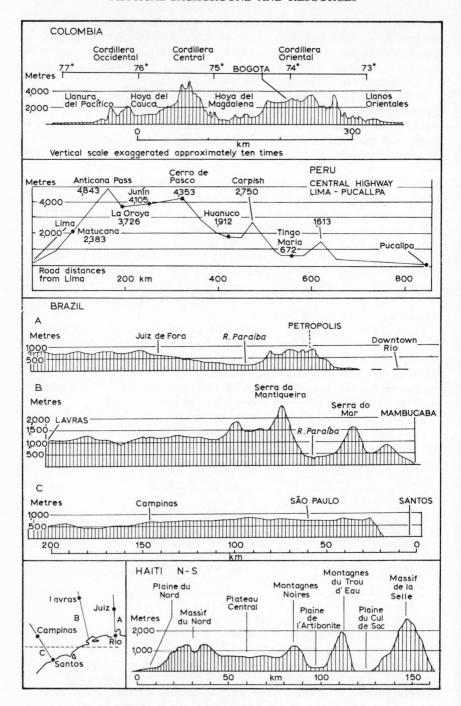

Figure 3.13. Selected relief profiles in Latin America

troubles for those moving down into lowland areas. When the Spaniards overcame the Inca Empire they soon encountered the problem of infertility, for they could not raise European livestock where they first proposed to put their capital (Jauja at 3,410 m). But they had eventually to settle in the high Andes to supervise mining activities and long remained either infertile or unable to keep babies alive after birth.

Carlos Monge[14] quotes early Spanish chroniclers and also describes modern experience and experiments concerning infertility among living things newly introduced to high altitudes. Many a farmer has invested in high grade livestock for breeding purposes, only to be disappointed, but the general experience is that adaptation comes in time. In Potosí it was 53 years before the first child was born of Spanish parents, though with mixed Indian and Spanish parents success was achieved sooner. Monge quotes Antonio de la Calancha (1639)[14] on the difficulty of bringing up European babies.

'In Potosí all children born of Spanish parents died either at birth or within a fortnight thereafter, because the great cold and freezing air would kill them; the mothers used to leave in order to give birth in the neighbouring valleys and until their child was more than a year old the mothers would exile themselves from this city. Francisco Flores, who is now Secretary to the Royal High Court of Lima, did not succeed in raising a single child of the several that he had for they either died as soon as born or froze when brought up from the hot valleys. He was a devotee of Saint Nicholas and decided to dedicate his first child to his protection, trusting that the Saint would preserve the child even without taking it away from Potosí, he promised to name him after the Saint, who subsequently gave him a son. His relatives and friends, before the child was born, thought him foolhardy for wanting it to be born in Potosí but he would repeat that with confidence in Saint Nicholas he surely would raise it there. It was born on Christmas Eve in the year 1598, he gave it the name of Nicholas and raised it there.'

Perhaps more serious for the economic development of the countries with large highland populations than difficulties of plant and animal adaptation is the costs added to transportation. In an economy in which single communities or small groups of these are largely self-sufficient, transportation is less important than in one in which most products are sold off farms and large quantities of modern manufactured goods are consumed. Road and rail routes between two places are often forced to make detours to avoid excessive gradients, the gradient being more serious for railways than for roads, while even air transport has drawbacks, for take-off is difficult in a rare atmosphere and sites are often dangerous. Detours may be local in nature to negotiate or avoid steep slopes (e.g. hairpin bends), or regional in nature, to avoid major obstacles. But even if gradients are minimized, they cannot be eliminated, and they remain a burden on an upward journey and a hazard on a downhill journey, while curves are also a danger. The implications of these are well illustrated in an extreme case, the railway in Peru from Lima to Cerro de Pasco, which is actually in two parts belonging to separate companies. The direct distance from Lima to Cerro is 185 km, the general course the railway takes to follow the Rimac valley to the summit of the Cordillera is

240 km and the actual rail distance, added by curves and zig zags is 350 km, almost twice the direct distance. In addition, extra fuel is needed to climb, speed is much slower than on a level railway, only one track is possible and time is further lost at passing places. Finally, the load safely pulled by a locomotive is less than normal (e.g. 5–6 passenger coaches). A journey that would take 2–3 h in a flat area takes 10, with staff thus engaged longer for the same amount of work. Altogether, transport costs are *several times greater*. This matter is discussed again in Section 6.7, and some selected profiles are shown in *Figure 3.13*.

REFERENCES

[1] King, L. C. *The Morphology of the Earth.* 1962, Edinburgh. Oliver and Boyd
[2] Umbgrove, J. H. F. *The Pulse of the Earth,* 1947, The Hague; Nijhoff, Plate 5
[3] As in *Atlas do Brazil, IBGE,* 1960 Rio de Janeiro and in Tamayo, J. L. *Geografía Moderna de México.* 1960, Mexico, pp. 117–24
[4] *Atlas de Economía Colombiàna*
[5] Preston, D. 'Man-Land Relationships in Coastal Ecuador'. *Paper in IBG Annual Conf.* Jan. 1964
[6] *IBGE Anuario Estatístico do Brasil,* 1959, 1960
[7] FAO, 'The State of Food and Agriculture, 1963'. Rome 1963
[8] Eyre, S. R. *Vegetation and Soils. A World Picture.* 1963, London; Edward Arnold
[9] *Plan para el desarrollo der sur del Perú,* 1959
[10] Platt, R. S. 'Major Habitats' p. 487, *Latin America: Countrysides and United Regions.* 1942, New York; McGraw-Hill
[11] Ahlfeld, F. Banco Minero de Bolivia, Mapa de los yacimientos minerales de Bolivia. 1953
[12] Santos Rudulfo Cortés, 'Geografía Altitudinal de Venezuela', *Rev. Venezuela de Geografía.* pp. 45–87, June 1961
[13] Atlas de Colombia, Vol. 1. (Banco de la República) Cartograma, No. 6, 1959
[14] Monge, Carlos, *Acclimatization in the Andes,* p. 36, 1948, Baltimore; Johns Hopkins Press (in English)
[15] Rampa, A. C. *Geografía física de la República Argentina,* 1961, Buenos Aires

CHAPTER 4

HISTORY

4.1. PEOPLING

Opinions differ about how and when early man entered the Americas, but the most widely held view is that the first humans entered from East Asia at least ten thousand years ago, probably on several occasions, and certainly in small groups. Finds thought to be at least 10,000 years old have been discovered in the U.S.A. Since no Old World plants or domesticated animals were used or known in pre-Columbian* America it seems that the people who entered the continent were simple hunters and gatherers. Current views on race and on the importance of different physical characteristics of human beings are so uncertain at the moment that evidence of this kind is of little help in solving the problem; certain features such as hair and shape of face are reminiscent of East Asian features, but blood groups are quite different, gene M predominating in the indigenous population and A locally in northwest North America, when these are both uncommon in East Asia.

Early man in America was mainly a hunter and gatherer with a modest range of techniques. For example there were very few metal tools, the wheel was not used for transport, and there were no proper written languages, although the Mayas did develop sophisticated calendars and simple writing. New World plants were, however, cultivated several thousand years ago, while three thousand years ago, more complex communities were practising irrigation in parts of what are now Mexico and Peru, and there were sizable urban centres here and also in forested areas of Central America, but livestock made little contribution to the economy except in the Andes. When the Europeans explored the Americas in the sixteenth century they encountered some very densely populated districts but mainly vast virtually uninhabited areas. There are of course no records of population numbers in pre-Columbian America but attempts have been made to assess the number on the basis of the economy of the time and the natural conditions. For the area that became Spanish America, a Spanish source[1] puts the figure at $11\frac{1}{4}$ million in 1492. With Brazil this makes about 13 million altogether. Such a figure seems low considering that it gives a mean density of about 0·5 persons/km² for all Latin America, which definitely included several densely peopled areas. At all events much of the total was in the highlands of Mexico, the forest lowlands of Southern Mexico and northern Central America ($4\frac{1}{2}$ m.), in the northern Andes and in coastal Peru ($3\frac{1}{2}$ m.), about 8–9 million altogether.

During the three centuries following the discovery of Latin America two main streams of settlers entered the area and gradually mixed with the indigenous Amerind (American Indian) population: Spaniards and

* Before Columbus.

61

Portuguese* from Iberia and Africans mainly from the western part of tropical Africa. From Spain immigrants came initially mainly from the area of Castilian domination but later from other parts: Basques and Aragonese, for example. The impact on the Amerind population was devastating in some areas, very slight in others. In the Caribbean islands the Amerinds were reduced to about 10 per cent of their original numbers after a few decades, partly by Old World diseases. The highland Amerinds of Mexico and the Andes resisted better but were eventually reduced by about 20–30 per cent. The Amerinds of Amazonia and Patagonia and in much of North America were not directly affected until the nineteenth century.

During the colonial period, the early sixteenth to the early nineteenth century, Iberian and African settlers reached different parts of Latin America in varying numbers. The total number of Europeans arriving was at most several hundred thousand. The Spaniards for various reasons (see later sections) gravitated towards existing concentrations of Indians. The Africans on the other hand were deliberately brought to areas from which the Indians had disappeared or to areas where they had not been. Other Europeans (including Dutch, English and French) settled alongside the African slaves.

In Spanish America even by 1570 only just over 1 per cent of the population was white, and about the same proportion negro, while by 1650 over 80 per cent was still Indian and much of the rest mixed. Rapid mixing of Amerinds and Europeans took place in the early decades due to the lack of European women; this was permitted by the Church, and marriage was encouraged. The result was the emergence of the *mestizo* element. Europeans and Africans also mixed, but marriage with slaves was not usually accepted. The result was the mulatto element. When Amerinds and Africans mixed the result was called *zambo*, a type generally considered to be unsatisfactory. By about 1800 all six types were recognized and innumerable local combinations as well. In a total population of about 20·5 million around 1800 the various ingredients were represented as follows:

	Spanish areas	Brazil
Whites	3·3 m.	0·8
Mestizos	5·3 m.	
Indians	7·5 m.	0·3
Negroes	0·8 m.	1·9
Mixed (mainly mulatto)		0·6

Changes took place in the pattern of migration after independence around 1820. Africans were still brought in, especially to Brazil, until near the end of the nineteenth century, but in diminishing numbers. From about the middle of the century, thanks to the steamship, increasing numbers of Europeans came, both Iberians and others. Many Spaniards went to their remaining colonies, Cuba and Puerto Rico, or to southern South America;

* Referred to collectively as Iberians.

the Portuguese went mainly to Brazil. Italians, Germans and other Europeans went mainly to extra-tropical South America. Chinese, Japanese and Asian Indians settled in small numbers in many parts. In southern South America, in Cuba, Costa Rica and more recently in Venezuela the balance was changed, and the European element greatly strengthened. *Figure 4.1a* indicates the direction of migrations, excluding the Iberian colonization up to the nineteenth century. This was so widespread that it covered almost the whole area shaded.

To this day virtually 'pure' Europeans may be found in many parts, including most of Argentina; 'pure' negroes still remain in Northeast Brazil and Haiti; while Indians abound in many areas, including of course Amazonia. Most Latin Americans however must by now have some proportion of more than one element and it is therefore difficult to classify them according to race. This is nevertheless done in most national censuses but largely on the basis of skin colour and/or cultural characteristics; a further difficulty is that even if people could be classified into races by say skin colour, this is not done in practice, for often the decision is left to the individual to say what he considers himself to be*. Given that white is the most desirable skin colour, people tend to classify themselves as whites when they are brown, and mulatto or mestizo when they are virtually pure African or Indian; the result presumably is to make the European element seem larger than it is.

In Latin American countries the division of 'races' into such a rigid official twofold division as white and non-white, as in the U.S.A., is not found. Rather there are many rungs on a ladder leading up from darkest to lightest skin or most Indian or negro to most European. If social problems have not been so acute as in the U.S.A., Latin America, both past and present, cannot be fully understood unless it is appreciated that deep underlying prejudices exist over race. Naturally they are least of a problem in areas populated mainly by one particular race. To quote Harris[2]: 'In Minas Velhas (a small town in Bahia, Brazil), the superiority of the white man over the Negro is considered to be a scientific fact as well as the inconvertible lesson of daily experience.' Suitably adapted to local racial conditions, this might be applied in many parts of Latin America, in spite of the professed admiration the Mexicans and Chileans have for their pure Indian minorities, the southern Brazilians for their negro brothers, and so on.

Hutchinson[3] points out clearly the differing attitudes to race in Bahia state Brazil and in the U.S.A.:

'In the United States an absolute "line" is drawn between white and Negro. A person who is not white is a Negro, whatever his percentage of Negro heritage may be. In Vila Recôncavo, this "line" is recognized rather than drawn. A distinction between Negro and white is always kept in mind when classifying an individual. Everyone knows who is "pure" white and who is not. Classification by colour is one of the most important

---

* The author met a South African, half Indian (Hindu) half English, of brown skin colour, who was visiting Brazil with a view to emigrating there. It was made clear to him in Brazil that only whites were acceptable, but it was also suggested to him that there would be no difficulties if he *called himself* white.

63

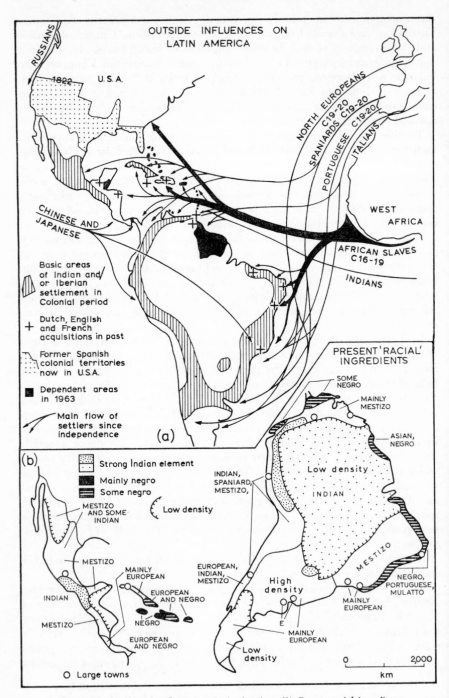

Figure 4.1. (*a*) *Outside influences on Latin America.* (*b*) *Present racial ingredients*

aspects of local culture, and one of the most difficult aspects for the outsider to grasp. Recôncavo Bahians feel that one may instantly recognize the difference between a "pure" white and a mixed white-Indian, white-Negro, or Negro-Indian, but they do not let it go at that. They classify or describe minutely each person; they classify according to skin colour, hair form, and facial features. Their classifications of physical types are used in everyday conversation. Just as it would be said in the United States that someone is short and fat, the people of Vila Recôncavo will describe a person's colour and hair form. . . .'

In Mexico, as in Northeast Brazil, complicated mixtures of European and non-European are recognized and terms are given. Galindo Villa[4] in a geography of Mexico, after pointing out that the white is superior intellectually, describes the mestizo: 'He is intelligent, patriotic, just as much as the white and more than the Indian; he disdains his forebear the Indian, however, and also dislikes the Spaniard.' The author then lists some of the variations, which have special terms down to several generations of mixing, and intriguing connotations such as 'salta atrás' (jump back) and 'torna atrás' (turn back) indicating a move, favourable or otherwise, towards a particular 'pure' race, or 'tente en el aire' (stay in the air) for a union of mestizo with mestizo, mulatto with mulatto, when two of the same intermediate colour join to produce offspring not going towards a particular pure race.

The proportion of the different racial ingredients in Latin American countries has been nicely mapped by Robinson[5] and in other publications. In reality, as will have become clear, it is misleading to imply clearcut divisions, for while pure African, Indian and Negro are reasonably straightforward concepts in a cultural sense, mulatto, mestizo and zambo have no universal definition. Moreover, each country has its own definitions of different racial types for its census, and comparison is difficult. The present distribution is therefore summarized as concisely as possible as follows and is very tentatively mapped in *Figure 4.1b*.

1. Indian: (a) Thinly peopled interior of South America (Amazonia)
   (b) Densely peopled rural areas of Southern Mexico and Central America, the Andean countries, parts of Chile, Paraguay.

2. Mestizo: Towns throughout 1(a) and 1(b), many rural areas also.

3. European: (a) Rural in the three southern states of Brazil, in Uruguay, most of Argentina, Cuba, Costa Rica.
   (b) Urban almost throughout Latin America

4. Mulatto: (a) European strong: parts of Cuba, Puerto Rico, Dominican republic, Northeast Brazil, Rio—São Paulo area.
   (b) European weak: Jamaica, parts of Northeast Brazil.

5. Negro: Relics in Northeast Brazil, interior Haiti, smaller West Indian islands.

6. Asian: Considerable element in Trinidad, Guianas, São Paulo state.

ZAPOTEC TEMPLE, MONTEALBAN, OAXACA STATE, MEXICO

MACHU PICCHU CITY RUINS, SOUTHERN PERU

P. COLE

LEFT:
GOLD MASK
FROM ZAPOTEC
TOMB, MONTEALBAN,
OAXACA STATE,
MEXICO

RIGHT:
MOCHICA *HUACO*
(ORNAMENTAL
WATER JAR),
COASTAL PERU

66

ABOVE LEFT:
INCA WALLS WITH COLONIAL
STRUCTURE ABOVE. CUSCO, PERU

ABOVE RIGHT:
THE PROPHET JOËL
BY ALEIJADINHO, LATE
18TH CENTURY, AT
CONGONHAS DO CAMPO,
MINAS GERAIS, BRAZIL

COLONIAL CHURCH, JOÃO PESSÔA, PARAÍBA, NORTHEAST BRAZIL

The official combined percentage of 'whites' and mestizos is shown for each of the main countries.

Argentina	99	Venezuela	55
Canada	98·4	El Salvador	49
Uruguay	98	Guatemala	46
Costa Rica	90	Mexico	40
U.S.A.	89·5	Bolivia	31
Cuba	80	Peru	27
Brazil	75	Ecuador	26
Chile	61	Haiti	2·5
Dominican Republic	58		

4.2.* POLITICAL HISTORY

In most of Pre-Columbian America clearly defined political units did not exist, though of course communities operated within recognized areas. Even in Mexico and Central America, large areas did not fall under one government, though there were loose associations of quite large groups. For example, Aztec control from Tenochtitlán at the end of the fifteenth century diminished sharply with distance, and was sporadic over peoples on the fringes. Only the Inca Empire was organized as a large political unit with constant communication between all the parts and the centre, cohesion being achieved by a remarkable system of roads, and a system of messengers working in relays. This delicately balanced system, spreading some 4,500 km along the Pacific side of South America, like other Indian units of organization, very quickly collapsed before the Spaniards, though the roads continued in use.

In 1493–94, a year after Columbus first reached America, the Pope made an agreement (the Treaty of Tordesillas) with Spain and Portugal, dividing the world, in effect the tropics, into two spheres of influence. The dividing line on one side of the world was to be a meridian 370 leagues west of the Cape Verde Isles. This line passes very close to Belém near the mouth of the Amazon, south near Goiania and Curitiba to Araranguá (*see Figure 16.2*). Subsequently, Portuguese influence extended west of the Tordesillas line into the interior of South America.

Soon after the arrival of Columbus, the Spaniards began the conquest of their part of the Americas. From 1493, just a year after the defeat of the last Moors in Spain, the whole area, initially believed to be part of Asia, and called the Indies (las Indias), was considered to be under the crown of Spain, and Spain (Las Españas) and America (Reynos de las Indias) became known as the Monarquía Universal Española. Conquest was largely carried out in the initial decades on a private basis by ambitious and enterprising individuals with small groups of followers, the *conquistadores*, who with remarkably small numbers of soldiers, overcame populations of millions. From 1493 to about 1520 most of the activity was in the Caribbean, Santo Domingo serving as the first base. When the Aztecs were overcome

*See references [6–8] for the principal works for the material in this and the following section.

after a bitter struggle around 1520 and the Inca Empire in 1533, Mexico (New Spain) and Peru became the main centres for further conquest. *Figure 4.2b* shows the area controlled by Spain in about 1550, and *Figure 4.2c* the further, more gradual expansion to about 1800. Two very large areas, Amazonia and southern South America, were not absorbed at all either by Spain or Portugal during the colonial period. During this period there were many mission areas on the fringes of the settled area (see *Figure 4.2d*), and these in a way represented the frontier of settlement.

The Portuguese annexation of Brazil was a more gradual and less spectacular process. Portugal had interests in the tropics in other continents, while the main difficulty in the Americas was not to establish control of coastal Brazil, the Indians here being relatively few, but later to keep out the Dutch and French. Until the 1540s Portugal left control of Brazil to a number of Captains General (see *Figure 4.2b*), each of whom held a stretch of coast and the land to the west of this; the Captaincies were hereditary. The system was then changed, and the whole of Brazil was thereafter administered from Portugal except during 1580–1640, when Spain and Portugal were united. During the period of union the Tordesillas line was no longer necessary and the Portuguese crossed it both west from São Paulo and along the Amazon (see *Figure 16.2*). By 1750 they had penetrated, though in small numbers, to within a short distance of the Andes, and by the Treaty of Madrid in 1750, Spain recognized their control of much of Amazonia. In spite of being divided initially, and of being split for a time, when the north, Maranhão, was administered separately, Brazil maintained its cohesion throughout the colonial period and in 1823 remained intact when it became independent. One reason seems to be that all the important centres were in close contact with one another along the coast between São Vicente and Fortaleza; the capital merely shifted from Salvador to Rio as the southern part gained in economic influence.

If the Portuguese Empire survived as modern Brazil, the Spanish area had broken into 16 independent countries by 1850 and 18 by just after 1900. How the Spanish American countries reached their present form can only be appreciated by following the main administrative developments in the colonial period. Not long after the arrival of the *conquistadores*, the administrators moved in; those conquerors who had not been killed, either by the Indians or by each other, soon lost the grandiose titles and vast lands they had acquired. Administrative centres, *Audiencias*, were set up by Spain in several places. In 1543, two viceroyalties were created, with their administrative centres in Mexico and Lima. From then until the eighteenth century almost all of Spanish America fell within one or other of these units though at certain periods Venezuela and various islands came directly under Spain. The viceroy in Mexico controlled Mexico, Central America (except Panama), various Caribbean islands and the Philippines. The viceroy in Lima ruled over Spanish South America. As the Spaniards moved into and organized other areas, further decentralization was desirable, and new Audiencias were formed within the two viceroyalties (see dates *Figure 4.3a*), and by 1700 there were some 10 Audiencias. Contact between the two viceroyalties was discouraged by Spain for various reasons and apart from limited trade and the movement of administrators there was

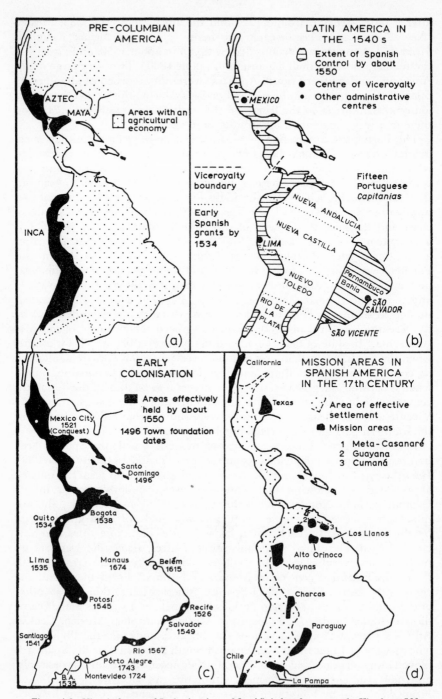

Figure 4.2. Historical maps of Latin America. Map (d) is based on a map by Vives[6], p. 568

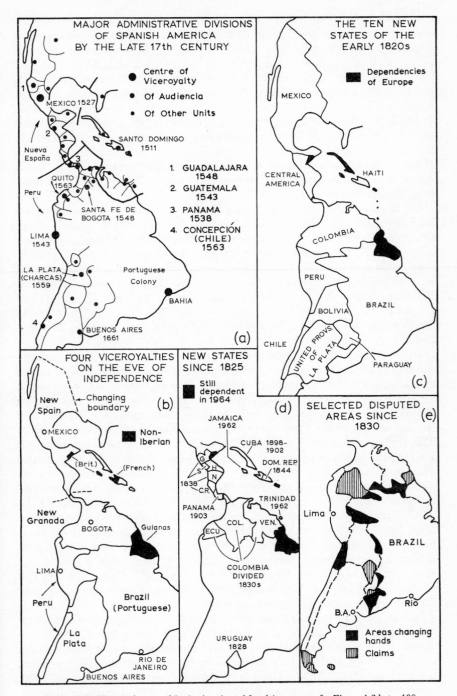

Figure 4.3. Historical maps of Latin America. Map (a) source as for Figure 4.2d, p. 480.

even little contact between most of the Audiencias. In the eighteenth century further decentralization took place, as two new viceroyalties were created: New Granada (1717–24 and from 1740) in Bogota and La Plata (1776) in Buenos Aires. In addition, in the 1770s, Cuba, Venezuela and Chile were given more direct links with Spain as captaincies-general. But virtually all major political decisions concerning the Spanish colonies were made in Madrid, and transferred to the Americas through the Casa de Indias in Seville. Local decisions were of course made in the Americas and local affairs run by the colonies themselves. It is not surprising, therefore, that between the conquerors of the early sixteenth century and the liberators of the early nineteenth there were few outstanding personalities in Latin American colonial history and no constant struggle between political units as in Europe at the time.

On the eve of independence, around 1800, Latin America was divided basically into four Spanish Viceroyalties, Mexico (New Spain), Peru, Colombia (New Granada) and Argentina (La Plata), and one Portuguese colony, Brazil. These are the five largest units at the present day, both in population and in area. In addition, several other modern republics could be distinguished as Audiencias or Captaincies: Chile, Venezuela, Bolivia, Ecuador, Cuba, Santo Domingo, Guatemala. England, Holland and France also had colonies in Latin America by 1800. Each had a colony in the Guianas, while France held Haiti and England held Jamaica, Trinidad and smaller islands.

Independence came rapidly to almost all the colonies once the movement started. The main cause was the resentment by the white settlers in the colonies against the rigid control of Iberia. The movement was encouraged by the American War of Independence. Spain's weak state during the Napoleonic wars was the opportunity to declare and fight for independence; the inspiration came from the *criollo* population, the European element. The Indian and negro masses were possibly pro-criollo in some areas but mainly indifferent or actually hostile *both* to the criollos *and* the Spaniards. The complicated and fascinating struggle for independence cannot be outlined here. By the early 1820s the struggle was over. Eight separate independent states emerged from the Spanish colonies (see *Figure 4.3c*), making ten altogether with Haiti and Brazil. Haiti achieved independence from France a little earlier, after a bitter struggle during which those French who did not leave were eliminated. Brazil, on the other hand, achieved an admirable compromise, detaching itself from Portugal but retaining as its ruler the son of the King of Portugal. The Court had fled to Brazil during the Napoleonic Wars. Cuba, Puerto Rico and the Philippines remained as Spanish colonies.

In the decades following the main struggle for independence, Central America broke into five separate parts, Colombia into three; Uruguay was recognized by Brazil and Argentina; and the Dominican republic became separated from Haiti. This brought the total number of independent countries to 18 by 1850. Cuba and Panama were added around 1900, when the U.S.A. also acquired Puerto Rico and the Philippines from Spain. The final stage in the retreat of the colonial powers has been taking place since the Second World War, with the granting of Commonwealth status to Puerto Rico, independence for Jamaica and Trinidad, disputes over British Honduras, the Panama Canal Zone, and probable independence for the Guianas.

After independence, the nature of Latin American political history changed completely. Here for the first time was a large number of new sovereign states outside Europe, many already conscious of their existence as entities in the eighteenth century. Admittedly they have taken a long time to settle down and in doing so there have been several serious conflicts and many boundary disputes (see *Figure 4.3e*), but the considerable age and experience of Latin American countries should not be overlooked. Most were running their own affairs reasonably successfully several decades before the Europeans even entered Africa.

4.3. ECONOMIC HISTORY

The inhabitants of pre-Columbian America could be divided into hunters and gatherers on the one hand and cultivators on the other. The cultivators were of two main kinds, shifting and sedentary. Shifting cultivation was found mainly in the tropical forest areas, sedentary cultivation in temperate forests (Southeast U.S.A.), drier areas and mountain areas. Irrigation was practised in parts of Mexico, coastal Peru and Chile, and the Andes. A fairly high density of population was reached both in a few areas of shifting cultivation (the Maya areas of southern Mexico and Central America) and in some areas of sedentary cultivation, especially in mountain basins and valleys (Aztecs, Incas, Chibchas). Towns of considerable size could be supported in all these areas.

As already stressed, the range of crops and livestock used in these basically agricultural economies was limited and the technology was far behind that of contemporary Europe, China or even much of Africa. According to their physical conditions, agricultural communities depended heavily on one particular basic food: maize in Mexico, Central America, the Islands, parts of South America; roots, especially manioc, in Amazonia; and potatoes and other tubers in the Andes. Beans, cacao, groundnuts, tomatoes and many tropical fruits were also available, while cotton was used as a fibre, *maguey* in Mexico as a beverage, tobacco for smoking, and the coca leaf in the Andes as a special luxury for the privileged, later to be greatly abused in the colonial period. The only important domesticated animals were the dog which was widespread, the turkey in Mexico, and the llama and alpaca in the Andes. The llama was easily tamed and widely used for carrying goods, for its wool, its dung and on occasions its meat. Animals were not used for draught purposes, either for ploughing or transport, the wheel not being in use; outside the Andean region all goods were conveyed by humans, and this greatly limited the distance over which most goods could be carried. The waterways were hardly used for transport in the civilized areas, and coastal navigation was very limited.

One great weakness of the Amerinds was their failure to develop metal tools, though bronze was made and silver and gold ornaments widely produced. Without metal tools stone could only be shaped by harder stone and wood could only be worked with difficulty. The Andes of Peru and

73

Bolivia were almost treeless anyway. The arms that were in use when the Europeans came were quite inadequate against the crossbow, musket, and armour of the Spaniards, while the horse gave the Spaniards great mobility and the trained hunting dog was also used against the Indians during the decades of the conquest.

Perhaps the main reason why both the Spaniards and the Portuguese acquired an empire was to obtain sources of raw materials, many of them not available in Europe. Other motives should not be overlooked: the prestige of having new lands, the missionary zeal and the desire to convert pagans to Christianity, and an outlet for surplus population from Iberia. Throughout the colonial period the Spaniards were concerned mainly with metals, whereas until the eighteenth century the Portuguese, like the English, French and Dutch throughout, concentrated on agricultural products, mainly sugar. Although Spain and Portugal were intent on getting everything possible out of the region, they made many changes that in the long run transformed and benefited the economic life of the Americas. Old World crops and livestock were introduced, particularly those used in Europe itself. Horses and asses for transport, the wheel, iron implements, firearms, all these spread through the region in the early decades of the sixteenth century. A further minor contribution was to spread New World crops that had been confined to certain limited parts of Latin America into new areas; for example, the potato from the Andes to Mexico. Even to this day, however, Indian populations of remoter areas cling tenaciously to their pre-Columbian plants and techniques.

As already shown, the Indian population was soon affected by the impact of the relatively few Europeans. In some areas the Indians were wiped out by fighting and diseases; they moved out of other areas away from the advancing Europeans; in places they resisted. The quechua speaking descendants of the Inca Empire held out until after 1570, while the Araucanian Indians in Chile were not tamed until the nineteenth century. Even now the Amazon Indians take their toll of explorers and missionaries and even interfere with road construction and the exploration for minerals[*]. In most areas, however, the Indian population formed the foundation for European exploitation of the resources. Their way of life was undermined and often they were reduced to apathy. Land tenure was changed in favour of European settlers and although the Indians were never considered to be slaves they virtually belonged to Spanish landowners under the system of encomiendas in the sixteenth century or were organized in large numbers to work in the mines of Mexico and the Andes. At one stage some 80,000 Indians were employed in the Potosí area of Bolivia alone. They provided the labour force for agriculture and the mines and also practised crafts. Strictly speaking the organization of land tenure and agriculture was not feudal, but the results were not unlike those in later Medieval Europe. By 1600, however, the position of the Indian had improved somewhat except in the mining areas, and most Indians were not tied to large estates;

* In May, 1964, for example, Mayoruna Indians in the Amazon region of Peru ambushed and attempted to wipe out a party of 42 men forming a road exploration expedition. The wounded had to be rescued by a U.S. Air Force helicopter brought specially from Panama and which landed in a clearing made by the besieged men[9].

many owned land as before. In some areas, especially away from the main area of Spanish penetration, missionaries organized the Indians in ideal communities, although throughout, the Indians have rarely been really reliable converts to Christianity. In Brazil the Indian population in the areas settled during the colonial period was small and was soon reduced or absorbed by the European and negro elements; but one reason for Portuguese penetration far into the interior was to search for more Indians to bring back as labourers.

For reasons of security and administrative convenience the Europeans first settled mainly in nucleated settlements, and many of the present towns of Latin America were founded in the sixteenth century. The Spaniards paid great attention to the position, siting and layout of their future urban centres and the foundation was a formal affair. In addition to the administrative and commercial centres there were special settlements in mining areas (*campamentos mineros*), forts (*presidios*) and missionary villages (*reducciones*). Often dispersed Indian rural dwellers were gathered into planned villages.

Where the Indians were few in numbers and commercial agriculture therefore difficult to organize on a large scale, African slaves were brought in. Slavery was authorized in Spanish America shortly after the discovery of the continent; both Spain and Portugal were already accustomed to slavery in their contacts with North Africa. Ironically, one pretext for bringing in African slaves was to save the American Indians themselves from this form of exploitation. Initially most African slaves reached Northeast Brazil; later they were fed into the Caribbean area and North America in large numbers, especially to the English and French possessions, but also to Spanish Cuba and Puerto Rico. Smaller numbers were taken to or spread to the coastlands of Venezuela, Colombia, Ecuador and Peru, while others spread south from Northeast Brazil to Rio and beyond. The negro element in Mexico and Central America is very small.

Brutally detached from their precarious homeland of Africa the slaves were transported to the Americas in incredibly bad conditions. The slave trade was a commercial enterprise permitted by European countries, both Catholic and Protestant. Once the survivors who reached the Americas had been sold and were settled, they were in general reasonably well cared for materially, since they were very costly pieces of equipment; they were of course the property of their owners; they usually received no education at all. They worked either in agriculture, labouring in the sugar and other plantations, or were domestic servants, while some were freed and others escaped. In time mixing with Europeans produced mulattoes.

By about 1600 there had emerged a very interesting spatial distribution of economic activities in the Americas and this remained with modifications until the early nineteenth century. The distribution of certain activities can only be fully appreciated by reference to distance from West Europe. *Figure 4.4a* shows the Americas with distances correct from Lisbon. The parts closest to Europe are Northeast Brazil, the coast of Amazonia, the Guianas, the Caribbean islands and eastern North America, all about 6,000 km away. The following types of economy may be distinguished:

(*a*) Almost all the sugar and other tropical crops grown in plantations for export to Europe were produced along the 6,000 km line. The main

75

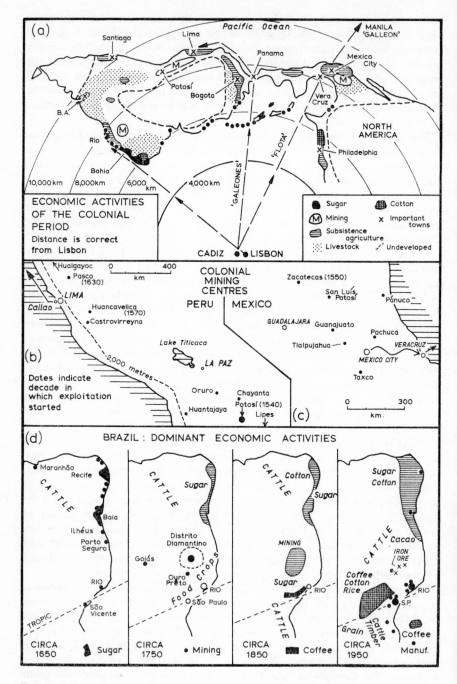

Figure 4.4. Economic history. (a) Major economic activities of the colonial period. (b) (c) Colonial mining areas in Peru and Mexico. (d) Dominant economic activities in Brazil at different periods

exception was the coast of Brazil to the south of this. Sugar was grown in smaller quantities elsewhere, but largely for local consumption. In view of the great inconvenience and cost of moving it far by land it had to be produced near the Atlantic coasts. Even moving it across Panama from the Pacific coastlands would have been unthinkable. As it was, given the small size of vessels and the difficulty of navigation, bringing large quantities of sugar in the seventeenth century, even from the coastal belt of Northeast Brazil, was a remarkable achievement, perhaps the first time in history that such a bulky commodity was taken so far across an ocean. Certainly European organized agriculture in the tropics was first applied on a large scale by the Portuguese in Brazil. In the eighteenth century, this area was eclipsed by the Caribbean Islands, and Haiti became the world's leading producer of sugar, but this area is just as close as Northeast Brazil is to Europe.

(b) In contrast to the plantations of tropical crops in the forested coastal lowlands of Atlantic-facing Latin America, the mining areas of Mexico, Peru and Minas Gerais in Brazil were not, of course, determined by distance from Europe but by the occurrence of accessible deposits of gold, silver and later precious stones. Once the silver had been refined it could be transported relatively easily, but its great value was obviously an embarrassment and its movement had to be heavily protected in the sixteenth and seventeenth centuries when piracy was widely practised and other European powers took a heavy toll of Spanish shipping.

(c) Scattered about the Americas were many areas of relatively dense agricultural settlement not producing crops for export to Europe. These included not only such temperate areas as New England in North America, Chile and La Plata in southern South America, but also the interior of Mexico and Central America, and the Andean countries; here the mining areas were fed by a surplus from the nearer agricultural areas, but there was virtually no export of agricultural products from these remoter areas to Europe.

(d) In lands that were neither humid and densely forested nor excessively dry, the raising of livestock, especially cattle, developed in the colonial period. These areas were relatively thinly populated; the cattle were either loosely organized in large estates (estancias) or left to roam wild. Extremely tough types of cattle evolved; their main contribution to the economy of other areas was hides, which were also exported in some quantity to Europe, but were mainly used in the colonies for a large number of purposes such as saddlery, storing water and carrying liquids, making clothing in mining activities and so on. The most extensive areas of cattle raising were in the northern part of Mexico, the northern part of Argentina, the lands behind the coast of Brazil, the llanos of Venezuela, and alone among the islands, Cuba.

(e) In the remotest parts of all from Europe either in terms of sheer distance or because of difficulty in penetration, vast areas remained in the hands of hostile Indian tribes until the nineteenth century: most of North America, of Argentina south of Buenos Aires, and of the interior of South America. Military expeditions, traders and missionaries did at times penetrate these areas but permanent settlements were few and conditions insecure, particularly in North America where the Indians adapted themselves to European

77

horsemanship and acquired firearms. In the nineteenth century these Indians were virtually eliminated from the extra tropical parts of the Americas but to this day they remain in Amazonia, little interfered with except along the main rivers.

The impact of the products of the Americas made itself felt in Europe soon after the conquest began. Silver and gold from the Aztec and Inca areas in particular were sent to Europe. Mines were taken over and new techniques introduced from Europe to raise production. Already in the 1540s regular production was organized by the Spaniards in certain areas in Mexico and Peru (see *Figure 4.4b,c*). By the eighteenth century production here was declining, but in Colombia and in Minas Gerais other mines were developed. These minerals were produced almost entirely for export. Plantation agriculture was slower to develop, and shipping in the sixteenth century was not capable of carrying much back to Europe. By the eighteenth century tropical agricultural products had become more important than minerals and even Spanish America, hitherto organized to produce metals, was diversifying its exports. Hides were a third item of export. In the plantation areas food crops were of course grown, but the slaves were discouraged from consuming sugar. During the colonial period therefore, the areas in the Americas geared to producing for export were: the Andes of southern Peru and Bolivia, central Mexico, Minas Gerais and Colombia (minerals), Northeast Brazil and all the islands except Cuba, and Southeastern North America (tropical and sub-tropical crops). Other areas only made a limited contribution, but in some, considerable concentrations of population grew up on regional economies.

Some implications of the economic development of Latin America for the modern period may now be noted. In the first place, it was the policy of European colonial powers and of Spain in particular to discourage manufacturing in colonial areas. Manufactured goods made in Spain or elsewhere in Europe and sent through Seville or Cadiz were sold at very high prices in the colonies. Competition from Asian manufactured goods such as silk was prevented and only one galleon a year was allowed between Manila in the Philippines and Acapulco (Mexico). Even so industries did develop in the colonies. Food processing was often essential before crops could be exported, and large quite highly capitalized sugar factories were built wherever sugar was grown commercially. Minerals were also processed, and in the later sixteenth century a complex process involving salt and mercury (deposits of which were discovered in Huancavelica, Peru, in 1563) was used in the Andean mines to refine silver. Mining equipment had to be maintained and iron, which was often short in the colonies, was worked in a limited way. Metal working developed particularly in Minas Gerais, Brazil, and there has been a continuous if modest tradition here. All the ships for use in the Pacific by the Armada del Sur were built on that side of the continent (in Guayaquil particularly), while Havana (La Habana) served the Atlantic side. Cloth was widely manufactured, though the highest quality textiles came from Europe.

A second feature was the tendency to work an area intensively for a particular product and then abandon it. Brazilian historians have traced periods in which one product and one area in their country have been exploited far more than any other (see *Figure 4.4d* and Chapter 16.4). Thirdly, throughout the colonial period Latin America was very closely tied to Iberia. Trade between colonies was not encouraged, and Mexico and South America had virtually no contact, for Spain organized its trade along rigid lines. Convoys sailing out from Seville (or more often Cadiz in the eighteenth century) one year and back the next went initially together (1543–1564) but later separately to Veracruz (the Flota) and to Portobello (the Galleons)*. Here the products of the colonies were assembled. This was convenient in view of the insecurity of the Atlantic crossing but it was hardly tolerable for many places on the periphery of the Empire, especially Buenos Aires, which could have reached Europe much more easily by other routes. Admittedly the system was eased in the eighteenth century and France was allowed to trade in the Spanish colonies, but the trading pattern changed little. After 1820 Latin America was still closely tied to Europe, but now to West Europe in general rather than to Iberia alone.

During the period 1815–25 Latin America was completely transformed politically, but economic changes were more gradual and social changes slower still. In the first place, other European countries were able to trade directly with the new countries. Soon Britain, France, Belgium and later Germany, Italy and other European countries, with manufactured goods to export, needing raw materials and food at home, and having capital to invest, replaced Spain and Portugal as the main trading partners. In the second place, rapid improvements in transportation (railways, speed and size of vessels, refrigeration and so on) made it possible to bring new areas of Latin America within easy reach of ports and to move more bulky commodities to Europe. Thirdly, it became possible for non-Iberian settlers to emigrate to Latin America; this they did mainly to the extra-tropical southern part. Though the same pattern of trade continued, the exports of Latin America changed. From about 1800, sugar beet was grown more and more widely in Europe and in the nineteenth century cane sugar declined in relative importance, while coffee, cacao, cotton and later bananas were exported from tropical areas, and cereals and livestock products were exported from Argentina and Uruguay, the organization of livestock farming having been greatly improved with the introduction of barbed wire fencing. Silver, gold and precious stones were still exported, but other minerals eclipsed these: guano and nitrates, non-ferrous metals, in the nineteenth century, oil and iron ore in the twentieth.

Each Latin American country came to depend heavily on one or a small number of goods for export to buy manufactured goods and any other items lacking. Many of the mines and the rail and shipping services were financed by European countries, or more recently also by the U.S.A. Before the First World War manufacturing in Latin America was limited in scale and was confined to certain areas: Monterrey in Mexico had the first modern iron and steel works, Puebla in Mexico, Medellín in Colombia and Juiz de Fora in Brazil had early cotton mills, while the larger capitals had

---

* Vives[1], p. 557, shows the career of one particular ship early in the seventeenth century. It sailed out from Seville via the Canary Islands to the Leeward Islands and then to Cartagena and Portobello; the return was via La Habana and the Azores to Seville.

some light industry. The First World War encouraged countries to manufacture goods not easily obtained during this period and since then most countries have tried to move towards self-sufficiency at least in simpler manufactured goods, often heavily protecting their young industries against outside competition. Industry is now widespread in Latin America but there are few really large and efficient establishments apart from those connected with extractive industries producing minerals for export. That industrialization was both vital to countries and inevitable was perhaps widely realized already in the 1930s, and these lines published in 1945 show that by then it was taken for granted by one authority: 'Under the economic and technological circumstances of the modern world, the number of nations which can develop manufacturing industries to advantage has increased considerably. At the same time, it must be recognized that the tempo and character of industrialization must be adapted to the special circumstances in each country. It is therefore necessary to guard against hasty generalizations about Latin America as a whole, for they tend to obscure the profound differences which exist between the various countries. It is also necessary to avoid conclusions based upon easy analogy with conditions of the United States and Europe'[10].

REFERENCES

[1] Vives, J. V. *Historia Social y Económica de España y América*, Vol. III, p. 391. 1957, Barcelona; Editorial Teide

[2] Harris, M. *Race and Class in Rural Brazil* Ed. C. Wagley, 'Race and Society' p. 51, 2nd. edn, 1963, Paris; UNESCO

[3] Hutchinson, H. W. *Village and Plantation Life in Northeastern Brazil*, p. 117, 1957, Seattle; The American Ethnological Soc.

[4] Galindo Y. Villa, J. *Geografía de México* (Colección Labor), pp: 85–90, 1950, Barcelona; Editorial Labor

[5] Robinson, H. *Latin America*, p. 39, 1961, London; McDonald and Evans

[6] *Historia Social y Económica de España y América* (especially) Vol. III pp. 387–578 Imperio, Aristocracia, Absolutismo, Ed. by J. Vincens Vives (Editorial Teide). 1957, Barcelona

[7] Herring, H. *A History of Latin America*. 1961, New York; McLelland and Stewart

[8] Bailey, H. M. and Nasatir, A. P. *Latin America*, 1960, London; Constable.

[9] *Peruvian Times*, 15 May 1964.

[10] Wythe, G. *Industry in Latin America*, p. 355, 1945, New York; Columbia U.P.

CHAPTER 5

PRESENT INSTITUTIONS AND ECONOMIC DEVELOPMENT

5.1. PRESENT POLITICAL GEOGRAPHY

There are now 22 independent states in Latin America and a number of colonial territories (see *Figure 5.1a,b*). These vary greatly in size. The smallest units of all are the Islands, but the long narrow isthmus of Central America is divided into six* small countries, while Uruguay, Paraguay and even Ecuador and Bolivia, the latter much larger than its population of 4 million suggests, have rather the appearance of buffer states surviving between more powerful neighbours. Even the apparently sizable Guianas are no more than coastal footholds with virtually empty forest behind. The size of the remaining states gives a misleading idea of their importance. Only Brazil, Argentina and Mexico each have a total gross domestic product roughly equal to that of Belgium or the Netherlands; Venezuela, Colombia, Chile and Cuba just about compare with the single state of Connecticut in the U.S.A.

Differences in actual area are enormous. Brazil is almost 400 times larger than the republic of El Salvador and 1,670 times larger than Trinidad. Brazil is divided into 24 states, several of which are larger than most other Latin American countries. The states are divided into *municipios*, and the largest of these, Altamira (see *Figure 5.2c*) in the state of Pará, in Amazonia, covers 279,000 km² and could comfortably hold El Salvador, with its 14 departments and 760 municipios; El Salvador is *two* levels higher in the hierarchy of administrative units.

Most Latin American countries have a unitary government, but some including Brazil, Mexico, Argentina and Venezuela term themselves federal. In reality federalism is strong only in Brazil, where the state governors are particularly influential figures; even here, however, state rights are not so strong as in the U.S.A. In all the larger countries, however, regional consciousness is strong, whatever the type of government. In Argentina for example, this has been expressed by frequent struggles between the capital and the interior provinces. In Brazil as recently as 1961 Rio Grande do Sul suddenly talked of secession when attempts were made in Rio and Brasilia to prevent the vice-president Goulart, one of its citizens, from taking office when President Quadros resigned. Other instances of regionalism and regional isolation will appear in regional chapters.

Some of the most ambitious claims to sovereignty over the ocean have been made by the countries of western South America. Ecuador, Peru and Chile all claim the right to prevent other countries from fishing within a 200 miles limit of their coasts. In fact, permission has in practice rarely been refused.

* Strictly speaking, Panama is not considered to be part of Central America, culturally at least.

81

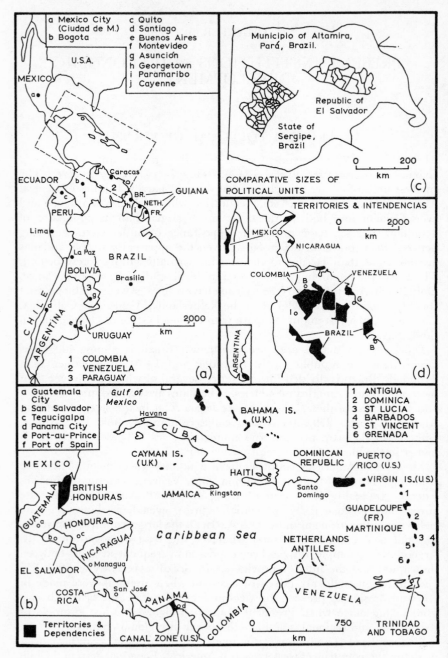

Figure 5.1. Present sovereign States and dependent areas of Latin America

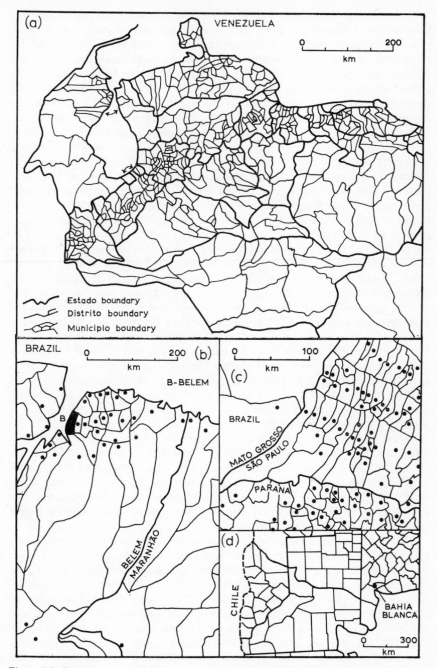

Figure 5.2. Examples of sizes and shapes of major and minor civil divisions. Civil divisions: (a) *Venezuela,* (b) *Brazil, near the mouth of the Amazon,* (c) *Brazil, western São Paulo state,* (d) *provinces and departments of south-central Argentina*

The major civil divisions of all the larger countries are mapped in appropriate regional chapters. They have many features of considerable geographical interest, but only a few points can be noted here. In most of the large and medium sized countries and even in some small ones there are marked differences in density of population between different areas. In almost all these countries there is a marked tendency for the major civil divisions to be small where density is high, large where it is low. Only in Argentina and Peru is this not so. In smaller countries such as Cuba, El Salvador and Haiti which have a high density throughout and only a small number of units anyway, such a generalization cannot be made.

Certain small (in area) units have been given major civil division level status round large cities: the federal districts of Mexico, Buenos Aires and formerly Rio de Janeiro (now called Guanbara state), and special small areas round Montevideo, Callao and Barranquilla. At the other extreme there are many very sparsely peopled areas designated as *territorios* (also *intendencias* in Colombia). These are usually on the periphery of sovereign states (see *Figure 5.1d*) and do not have the complete administrative functions of major civil divisions, being partially controlled by the central government. Some groups of small islands belonging to the larger countries are also run as territories. Many territories are in some way aided by the central government, and this is true also of normal civil divisions in pioneer areas in some countries. For example, the four Brazilian territories receive special subsidies from the capital, parts of the Peruvian selva are exempt from certain taxes, provinces in the extreme north and south of Chile have customs concessions, and in Argentina the province of Rio Negro receives special concessions, a feature being extended to other provinces as well.

The minor civil divisions of Latin American countries also have many features of geographical interest. As with major civil divisions there is a tendency for them to be small where the density of population is high; they are hardly ever small in sparsely peopled areas. *Figure 5.2a* shows administrative divisions on three levels in northwest Venezuela. They are smallest in the Andean region where, of course, the presence of many small isolated valleys would encourage this, but here also the density of population is high. They increase convincingly in size towards the southeast and are even larger still in southern Venezuela. This kind of arrangement is found in most Latin American countries.

The shape of minor civil divisions is also of interest, and some features are illustrated in *Figure 5.2b, c* and *d*. Long narrow municipios stretch back from the coast near the mouth of the Amazon. Away from the coastal area there are no settlements large enough to form administrative centres for further municipios. In *Figure 5.2c* ridge top settlements are distributed in lines in the western part of São Paulo state and their municipios stretch into the intervening valleys. Note here also the much larger size of units in the state of Mato Grosso and the smaller ones pressing against the northern boundary of Paraná state. In most parts of Latin America minor civil divisions are irregular in shape, rather than geometrical, but in much of Argentina (*Figure 5.2d*) and in parts of northern Mexico squares, rectangles and other angular shapes occur in areas laid out for settlement in the nineteenth century.

5.2. ECONOMIC AND SOCIAL FEATURES*

A great deal of thinking has been done in or on behalf of Latin America since the mid-1950s, especially by economists, on how to transform the region as quickly as possible into a predominantly non-agricultural economy with a reasonably high standard of living. This is not a new idea but it has taken a more concrete form with the growth of such international bodies as the United Nations, with growing apprehension in Latin America about the economic future as the postwar export boom, prolonged perhaps by the Korean War (1950–53), came to an end, and growing apprehension in the U.S.A. about the political future of the region. Only some of the main aspects can be considered here, but in the view of the author, the profound changes taking place in the human geography of Latin America cannot be fully appreciated without some knowledge of the economic and social background.

Perhaps the most fundamental division of the economic life of a country is the threefold one into agriculture, mining and manufacturing, and services. The relative importance of these three activities varies greatly among Latin American countries. The importance of each branch can be expressed broadly either according to the contribution it makes to the gross domestic product, or to the proportion it has of total employment. Usually there is a large discrepancy between the two sets of figures because persons engaged in mining and manufacturing and to a lesser extent services have a greater productivity than those in agriculture†. Since employment figures in the three main branches of the economy are unsatisfactory for many Latin American countries, industrial origin of the gross domestic product has been used. Figures are for 1959, 1960 or 1961[4,5]. Percentages are of total gross domestic product:

	A	M	S		A	M	S
Honduras	44	16	40	British Guiana	25	35	40
Paraguay	38	16	46	Peru	25	32	43
Ecuador	37	20	43	Panama	24	18	58
Costa Rica	37	15	48	Argentina	20	29	51
El Salvador	36	12	52	Chile	14	29	57
Colombia	34	26	40	Trinidad	13	52	35
Guatemala	32	25	43	Puerto Rico	12	32	56
Brazil	27	25	48	Venezuela	6	51	43

A—Agriculture. M—Mining, manufacturing, construction, electricity. S—other activities.

* Of numerous non-geographical publications on this subject, the three following may be mentioned:

(a) *The Latin American Common Market*[1].

(b) *Social Aspects of Economic Development in Latin America, I*[2], a very important document with a great deal of material of geographical interest.

(c) *Towards a Dynamic Development Policy for Latin America*[3]. Many of the economic and social problems facing Latin America are dealt with in a forthright way in this publication. The report includes a discussion of structural reforms needed to obtain capital for future economic growth, considers weaknesses of employment structure such as the excessive proportion of population in service activities, now 30 per cent for the region as a whole, gives examples of the unequal distribution of purchasing power among social classes, and deals with problems of trade.

† This is not so in the U.K. where agriculture is highly mechanized and accounts for both 4 per cent of the labour force and 4 per cent of gross domestic product.

ABOVE :
WEEDING MAIZE WITH OXEN,
SOUTHERN MEXICO

RIGHT :
SLOW TURNOVER IN A SMALL
MARKET, SOUTHERN MEXICO

PART OF ACESITA, FERRO-ALLOY PLANT AND TOWN,
MINAS GERAIS, BRAZIL

PEUGEOT MOTOR VEHICLE
PLANT, BUENOS AIRES,
ARGENTINA

AND EFFICIENCY IN LATIN AMERICA

ABOVE:
SMALL OVERSTAFFED
METAL WORKSHOP,
LA PAZ, BOLIVIA

LEFT:
REMOVAL OF
OVERBURDEN IN
1957, TOCQUEPALA
COPPER DEPOSITS,
SOUTHERN PERU

BELOW:
GIANT MEAT
REFRIGERATION
PLANT, BUENOS
AIRES, ARGENTINA

FRIGORIFICO LA PAMPA

In the region as a whole the relative importance of agriculture has been declining slowly but steadily in most countries, but at differing rates. The share of agriculture is expressed as a percentage of total gross domestic product in selected years in countries for which data are readily available[4,5]:

	Costa Rica	Venezuela	Colombia	Peru	Puerto Rico	Brazil	Argentina	Chile
1950 (48)	46	8	38	38	26 (48)	28 (48)	16	18
1953	44	8	38	33	19	29	22	17
1958	39	6	38	24	13	26	19	14
1959 (60 or 61)	37 (61)	6	34 (60)	25	12 (61)	27	20 (61)	14 (60)

A characteristic of the employment structure in most Latin American countries is the low proportion of the total population actually economically active, although figures quoted below probably exclude many people who are employed in agriculture on a part time basis only. One reason for this was suggested earlier: the high proportion of the population under 15. Of course many children under this age are in reality employed but would not normally be recorded. For what they are worth the figures are listed below (mainly for the 1950s):

Employed population as a percentage of total population[6]:

Haiti	56	Chile	37
Bolivia	50	Uruguay	36
U.K.	45	El Salvador, Guatemala, Panama	35
Jamaica	43	Trinidad, Venezuela, Costa Rica,	
Peru	42	Cuba	34
U.S.A.	41	Brazil, Colombia, Paraguay	33
Argentina	41	Mexico	32
Dominican Rep.	39	Nicaragua	31
Ecuador	38	Puerto Rico	26

The large proportion of children is not the only explanation of the low proportion in most countries, for almost everywhere unemployment is considerable. This is presumably due partly to the sheer inefficiency of many Latin American economies, but is due also to the transformation of the employment structure and the inability of new non-agricultural activities to absorb all the untrained rural dwellers who have moved to urban areas. Figures are not readily available for most countries but the following[7] give an idea of the situation. In Venezuela in 1963 there were 363,000 unemployed, compared with 2,330,000 in employment, a proportion of 13·5 per cent, and 70,000 were being added each year. In the same year Uruguay had 150,000 unemployed out of a labour force of about 1 million. In Chile as a whole and in Santiago and Concepción in particular the figure in 1961–62 was around 5 per cent. But is was 8–9 per cent in both Bogota and Buenos Aires in 1963.

The rapid increase in population in Latin America since the Second World War has only partly been matched by a satisfactory rate of economic growth. This has been irregular in most countries and too slow in several.

In many countries, *per caput* gross national product (at constant prices to overcome distortion by inflation) has risen, but this has not been so in Argentina and Chile, which, it should be recalled, have slower rates of population growth than most. The figures below[8] show the unevenness of growth among major countries:

	Mex.	Guat.	Venez.	Col.	Ecu.	Braz.	Arg.	Chile	Italy	Japan
1948	86					78	112		61	
1953	85	85	81	93	94	87	96	99	79	78
1958 (= 100)	100	100	100	100	100	100	100	100	100	100
1960	103	105	102	108	104	106	100	97	114	133

Index numbers of *per capita* product at constant prices.

No large or medium countries have recorded anything like the recent growth rates of Japan, the U.S.S.R. or Italy. On the other hand, impressive progress has been made in the region as a whole in raising electricity and steel output, and both mining and manufacturing output have grown, whereas agricultural production has failed to keep pace with population increase. Thus between 1938 and 1961, during which period population grew by 70 per cent, the volume of industrial production increased more than three times in Latin America[9], but it did so also in North America. During the 1950s there was almost a twofold increase, but this was unevenly spread among the countries with Brazil, Mexico, Venezuela and Puerto Rico among the most rapidly expanding, Chile and Argentina stagnating. Between 1938 and 1960 the increases in industrial production were as follows:

1960 (1938 = 100)

Brazil	545	Chile	265
Mexico	320	Argentina	170

Venezuela, for which 1938 figures are not readily available, recorded a fivefold increase merely between 1948 and 1961. Table 5.1 again shows how uneven rates of increase have been in both mining and manufacturing, this time between 1953 and 1960.

TABLE 5.1

Increase of Production in Mining and Manufacturing between 1953 and 1960 was as follows (1953 = 100).

Mining		Manufacturing	
Argentina	217	Venezuela	209
Brazil	201	Brazil	198
Venezuela	192	Mexico	178
Latin America	*160*	*Latin America*	*164*
Peru (1959)	157	Peru	135
Chile	126	Chile	119
Mexico	116	Argentina	112

Nor has the rate of increase in Latin America as a whole been uniform in the main branches:

1961 (1938 = 100)	
Mining and manufacturing	350
Textiles	250
Food	275
Base metals	335
Chemicals	540
Engineering	615

The relative increase has obviously been greater in those branches that hardly existed in the 1930s.

There are some striking resemblances between Latin America since the late 1950s and the U.S.S.R. in the years following the initiation of its 1st Five Year Plan in 1928. As in the U.S.S.R. then, there is currently in Latin America great emphasis on the need to expand steel production and engineering, perhaps an excessive emphasis on hydroelectric power, which needs enormous capital investment before 'cheap' power is available, a rapid increase in the consumption of energy (with the emphasis on oil and natural gas, not on coal as in interwar U.S.S.R.), a rapid increase in inter-regional movement of goods (road in Latin America, rail in the U.S.S.R.) and a move to overhaul agriculture completely. Capital is obtained differently, of course, while there is no complete single plan for the whole region or indeed for individual countries. On the other hand, the economic policy of the 20 independent states has led to a considerable degree of regional self-sufficiency, not unlike that aimed at in the 15 or so economic planning regions of the U.S.S.R. in the 1930s (see *Figure 20.1*), a policy now being abandoned in favour of greater regional specialization (a feature of North America of course during much of its history).

These comparisons are only mentioned to suggest that some lessons might be learned in Latin America from experience in other parts of the world. Certainly it has been appreciated in Latin American countries that dependence on agriculture must be decreased if rapid economic growth is to be achieved, and several countries have already gone so far along the path towards industrialization that they have passed the point of no return. Among the large countries, the contribution of manufacturing to total gross domestic product exceeds that of agriculture in Argentina and is about equal in Brazil and Mexico; in the medium countries, Venezuela in particular and also Chile are much more dependent on mining and manufacturing than on agriculture, and Peru, Colombia and Cuba are nearly at that stage. One cannot therefore consider Latin America as still a predominantly agricultural region. It is to be hoped that agriculture will not be neglected or exploited to obtain capital and manpower for industry as it so often has in the modern history of the more advanced countries (especially Western Europe and the U.S.S.R.) and has already in Argentina and Venezuela.

The kind of expansion needed in Latin America during 1960–1975 was outlined in *The Latin American Common Market*[1], p. 18. Between 1960 and

1975 the population of the region may be expected to grow by about 75 m.; the active population should increase by 38 m. but only 5 m. of this could be employed in agriculture and 33 m. new jobs would have to be found in other branches of the economy. By 1975 agriculture would only account for about 36 per cent of the employed population. The following increases would be desirable:

All agricultural production	120 per cent
Food production	130 per cent
Textiles	100 per cent
Basic chemicals	4 times
Trade	10 times
Steel	12 times
Capital goods	25 times

To prepare the ground for achieving anything near this ambitious increase in production, Latin America must overcome two basic problems at once: firstly, it must obtain sufficient capital without crippling itself in the future by interest rates and, secondly, it must alter institutions such as tax structure, financial organization and land tenure to enable the new capital to be invested as quickly and soundly as possible. A longer term problem is to contain the population explosion. The remainder of this section and the following section will consider the current sources of capital, the growing role of the State in the economy of Latin American economies, and education and land tenure questions.

In the post-war period capital has been derived from four main sources: from the private investor and from the State within countries, and, from private investors and State funds in foreign countries. These may of course combine to provide capital for large enterprises. The proportion of foreign investment to total investment is not so great as might be imagined. In broad terms it is estimated that about 30 per cent of economic activity in Latin America is government controlled and 70 per cent privately owned; of the latter, 90 per cent is in turn estimated to be owned domestically, only 10 per cent by foreigners[10].

The private investor in modern Latin America has generally been reluctant to invest in mining and manufacturing activities and has preferred a modest but steady income from agricultural land or has indulged in furious speculation in land in growing urban areas*. In fact, many industrial enterprises have been financed entirely by Latin Americans, but few of these are large. The textile industries of Puebla and Orizaba, Medellín and Juiz de Fora are examples. In recent decades the industrial boom in São Paulo has to a considerable extent been due to the accumulation of private capital from the coffee plantations of its hinterland. In recent years a tendency has been noted for Latin Americal capitalists to invest within the region but *outside* their own countries.

* That the classes with money that could be invested have not been pulling their weight is made clear in *Towards a Dynamic Development Policy for Latin America*[11], and the remedy (p. 11): 'Hence there is no way out but for the State deliberately to reduce the consumption of the higher income groups. . . .'

The public sector has not on the whole been strongly developed in Latin American countries until recently. In *per caput* terms, budgets are mostly very modest and much of the money is devoted to defence, education and so on. As long ago as the sixteenth century, however, the State (Spain then) did have control of some activities, such as the mercury mines of Huancavelica in Peru. Recently the public sector has become much stronger and is now responsible roughly for 30 per cent of all investment. For example, the development plans of both Venezuela and Brazil allow for one third of the capital to come from public funds. Further features of the public sector will be discussed below.

Private capital from outside has played a very large role in helping Latin America to break away from its colonial economy and limited range of products*. For at least a century it has been considerable, with British and French entering at first, and later German, Japanese and particularly U.S. capital (Britain and France both having other large commitments in the tropics). By the First World War, about 20 per cent of British investment abroad was in Latin America. During 1914–30, U.S. investment there increased four times, and by 1930 Latin America had about 30 per cent of all U.S. foreign investment.

During and after the depression, in which many Latin American countries suffered severely, the attitude to foreign investment changed, and less came to the region for a time, while the State took over many enterprises: for example Mexico nationalized its oil industry in the late 1930s, Argentina its railways after the Second World War, and Cuba its sugar plantations around 1960. Compensation varied greatly. Since the depression, therefore, the fortunes of the private foreign investor have fluctuated, but little European capital entered most countries between 1930 and 1955. Since 1955 the situation has improved and capital is now being welcomed by most countries.

Initially, foreign capital was invested in transport and urban utilities, then in mining enterprises, more recently in plantation agriculture, then in manufacturing and retail enterprises. At present, most is being placed in mining and manufacturing. The distribution of U.S. investment in Latin America is revealing[13]. Large items (in millions of U.S. $) in 1960 and 1961 were:

	Oil		Mining and smelting			Manufacturing		
	1960	1961		1960	1961		1960	1961
Venezuela	1995	2371	Chile	517	503	Mexico	391	414
Colombia	233	229	Peru	251	242	Brazil	515	543
			Mexico	130	130	Argentina	213	283
						Venezuela	180	196

In 1958 total direct foreign investment in Latin America was about U.S. $ 13,000 m. of which nearly 70 per cent was from the U.S.A. In 1961 the U.S. total was U.S. $ 8,166 m. of which 37 per cent was in Venezuela.

* See 'Foreign Investment in Latin America'[10], p. 113; also *Foreign Private Investments in the Latin American Free-Trade Area*[12].

Recently capital has reached Latin America from still different sources in grants (gifts) or credits (loans usually at a very favourable rate of interest) from foreign governments and in sums of money lent by international banks (financed privately or with both private and public funds). The U.S. government has in recent years given considerable aid to Latin America, while West Europe, Japan, the U.S.S.R. and China are all involved to varying degrees in financing projects. A development of particular importance was the establishment of the Alliance for Progress, proposed in Punta del Este, Uruguay, in August 1961.

To quote the late President Kennedy:

> 'From this meeting will emerge a vigorous and imaginative new development effort to bring economic progress and increasing social justice to the Americas.'

It was proposed that countries should work out their needs* for the next 10 years and also their immediate problems, and that $ U.S. 2,000 m. per year should be assured to Latin America for the 1960s from various overseas capital exporting countries, from both public and private sources, to add to the $8,000 m. per year expected from internal sources. Appendix 5.1 contains notes on the main bodies concerned with providing capital and on other bodies concerned in the economic development of Latin America.

The interest and involvement of the State in domestic economic affairs has grown rapidly in Latin America in the last three decades. This is to be expected in view of the concern to foster private industry by protecting it. To ensure sound industrial growth the State has itself had to invest in such branches of heavy industry as electricity and iron and steel, which often required more capital than could be provided from local private sources. Further, it is obviously desirable for the State, rather than private investors, to use financial aid actually given in the form of grants by outside countries. So far, the public sector in Latin American countries has made most progress in the oil industry, the iron and steel industry†, and electricity. It has little to do with agricultural production but is often responsible for irrigation works and for providing advisory and other facilities in rural areas, and for carrying out road construction, while most of the main line railways are also State run. Some undertakings are actually run by autonomous public authorities. In other words, in most of the large and medium countries the State runs a far larger proportion of the national economy than it does in the U.S.A. In addition, in some countries there are state bodies to study and stimulate the expansion of industry, notably CORFO in Chile and a more recent equivalent in Venezuela‡, as well as development banks in some countries.

Since many of the largest State concerns in Latin America are connected with oil, and State control of oil is perhaps the most controversial question in the region, this will briefly be discussed to illustrate the public sector in

---

* For a very useful note on many of these, see[14].

† Largely state owned in Chile, Colombia, Peru and Venezuela, partly so in Argentina, Mexico and Brazil.

‡ Venezuelan Development Corporation (CVF) an autonomous institution established in 1947. It now owns few shares in companies but still has a hand in sugar refining, shipping and air services.

the region[15]. There are three main types of arrangement. Firstly, in Mexico since 1938 and in Cuba since 1960 the industry has been entirely state owned, while in Argentina, Brazil and Chile, oil (and gas) *production* is entirely or largely state owned*. Foreign control is not admitted, but foreign companies may be invited to help in exploration or exploitation. Secondly, in Colombia and Peru most production is in the hands of foreign companies but there are state owned enterprises, ECOPETROL and EPF, while in Bolivia the complete State monopoly established in 1937 was changed in 1956 to admit foreign companies, but since 1962 no new concessions have been granted. Thirdly, in Venezuela the industry is almost completely in the hands of foreign companies, though the position of the government is now by no means unfavourable financially, and in Ecuador it is completely private.

With taxes on exploration, exploitation, transportation, profits and so on, Venezuela was receiving roughly half of the profits of the foreign companies in the mid-1950s. By 1962 it was obtaining 67 per cent of profits on an inflexible royalty plus a flexible tax†. In these circumstances policy is naturally to avoid sudden nationalization and to obtain control gradually of at least part of the industry. The 1943 Hydrocarbons Act was a move to make the oil companies expand refining in Venezuela. In 1960 the Venezuelan Government company became a producer of oil, but its wells only accounted in 1962 for 1/10,000 of all production. This company has interests in pipelines, in a refinery, and in its own areas of exploration, and is likely to expand greatly soon, for policy is to discourage foreign companies from developing new areas. Almost two thirds of the Venezuelan oil production in 1962 was accounted for by two companies[16] alone:

	%
Creole (Standard Oil)	39
Royal Dutch-Shell	26
Menegrande	13
Venezuelan Sun	5
Mobil	4

In recent years altogether about 15 companies have been operating in the country.

The position in Venezuela is better now than it was around 1960, when production was stagnating after the post-Suez boom, and political conditions

* The following are the titles and initials:

Mexico	PEMEX	Petróleos Mexicanos
Brazil	PETROBRÁS	
Argentina	YPF	Yacimientos Petrolíferos Fiscales
Cuba	CPI	Cuban Petroleum Institute
Chile	ENAP	Empresa Nacional de Petróleo
Peru	EPF	Empresa Petrolera Fiscal
Bolivia	YPBF	Yacimientos Petrolíferos Fiscales Bolivianos
Colombia	ECOPETROL	Empresa Colombiana de Petróleos
Venezuela	CORVEPET	Corporación Venezolana de Petróleo

† Venezuela is a prominent member of OPEC, the Organization of Petroleum Exporting Countries, to which several Middle East countries also belong. There are no other Latin American members.

were very unstable. This is not so in Argentina, where contracts with foreign companies made in 1958 under one government have been renounced in 1963 by its successor, nor in Brazil, where PETROBRAS is planning to take over all foreign owned refineries and distribution facilities. Peru, too, is negotiating with the International Petroleum Company and may nationalize the industry completely.

A problem of a more geographical nature is the question of where in Latin America to invest new capital most usefully and where to direct new financial and technical assistance. Immediately after the Second World War the policy throughout less-developed areas tended to be to provide an infrastructure on which economic growth could take place. Remote areas were opened up with costly roads, schools were built widely, local amenities such as water improved, small scale industries encouraged and so on, and capital was spread thinly over large areas. Policy now appears to be changing. Most areas must for the time being largely be neglected, and only a few areas—poles of development—are to receive a large amount of capital. A steel works, oil refinery or petrochemicals plant, is considered useful because it attracts other activities and later spreads benefits outwards*. Certainly in the Latin American context the wisdom of pushing too rapidly into pioneer areas must be questioned when there is plenty of slack to be taken up without stretching communications, in areas in which population is relatively dense. Examples of this in practice are the investment of large sums in the new industrial complex in eastern Venezuela, and the policy in Brazil now to pave well the trunk roads of the country rather than to try to improve slightly all roads, whatever the volume of traffic they carry. Even on an international level funds now seem to be moving to certain countries in which they can find immediate use, and it may be hoped that in their turn these countries will later help more backward ones.

In addition to the numerous problems of an economic nature outlined in this section so far, Latin America is faced with basic cultural and social problems. On the cultural side it must be appreciated that educational facilities lag far behind those in the more advanced industrial countries. Probably only about half the children have a complete primary education, while secondary and higher education are largely confined to higher social classes. In some areas, over 90 per cent of the population is illiterate (remote parts of Guatemala, Haiti). Nor does literacy necessarily mean an ability to cope with literature given out to guide farmers towards improving their techniques. Illiterates, too, are denied the vote in many countries (e.g. Brazil, Peru). Furthermore, most higher educational institutions are biased heavily towards Law and Arts subjects. Technological education is directed towards training architects, doctors and engineers, many of the latter finding employment in foreign companies; it is rarely devoted to research and the advancement of industrial techniques. The fact that the U.S.A., with a somewhat smaller total population, spends about fifty times as much on higher education as Latin America, illustrates the backwardness of this part of the world.

* This has been practised in Italy since the late 1950s after the virtual failure of widespread investments in the South to achieve rapid economic growth.

5.3. LAND TENURE AND AGRARIAN REFORM*

There is no complete work on this very complex aspect of Latin America, yet problems connected with land tenure in the region are invariably assumed to have a great bearing on economic and social questions. The question of agrarian reform is therefore dealt with at this stage to give as complete a picture as possible and to avoid repeating the subject for each country. Land tenure and agrarian reform have several aspects. Among these are: type of ownership and size of holding, which are to some extent related, the agrarian reform legislation, if any, in a particular country, and the availability or otherwise in a country or other land that might be used for settlement following agrarian reform. In Latin America certain countries are virtually full agriculturally speaking, particularly El Salvador, Uruguay, Haiti and the smaller islands, but most have extensive unsettled areas. The type of land tenure in a region will usually, to some extent, be related to the type of agriculture practised, which may be related ultimately to physical conditions, and to some extent to the origin of the settlers in the area and the kind of system they have evolved there or have brought from elsewhere.

There is general agreement that in many parts of Latin America the system of land tenure is not satisfactory except perhaps for the limited number of people who own large holdings. The very uneven shareout of land characteristic of much of Latin America is harmful both socially and economically, socially because it leaves the mass of the agricultural population discontented, economically because large properties are usually farmed only in part, and often inefficiently, while still providing a satisfactory income for their owners. Unfortunately, experience has frequently shown that where large estates have been broken up, the land is no better farmed by a large number of individual peasant owners. If they have not already fundamentally changed their land tenure conditions, as has been done for example in Mexico and Bolivia, most countries in Latin America now have agrarian reform programmes, and agrarian reform is seriously regarded as one way of increasing agricultural production, in this case, by ensuring greater interest on the part of agricultural workers in the land they cultivate. Other ways of increasing production are of course to improve productivity by using fertilizers and so on, and to open up new areas.

Ownership of land is still regarded as the most desirable form of wealth among the elite of most Latin American countries. The acquisition of land was one of the main motives in the conquest and it is difficult to change this idea when land means not only wealth and prestige but also entry into the aristocracy. What is more, unless there is legislation to prevent it there seems to be a gradual tendency for land to concentrate in fewer and fewer hands. This has been noticed particularly in Mexico between 1850 and 1910 and more recently in Brazil in the 1950s. Such a tendency is not confined to Latin America, for it has been occurring in the U.S.A. and was a

---

* A very useful concise study of the subject, which contains many further references, is by Crossley[17]. For the study of agrarian problems in an individual Latin American country, see Ford[18].

feature of the U.S.S.R. in the 1920s, under the New Economic Policy, before collectivization, but after the large estates had been broken up and shared out among the peasantry.

Agrarian reform is a costly undertaking with serious political implications. It embitters the aristocracy more than anything else and has on many occasions been frustrated, as in Guatemala in the early 1950s, when much of the land that had been distributed was returned to its former owners. One reason for the Brazilian Revolution in 1964 appears to have been over compensation for lands that were to be expropriated. It is ironical that part of the U.S. aid to Latin America is to be used for this very purpose in some countries. Even, however, if large estates are broken up successfully, a new problem is created, that of ensuring that the new small farmers use the land more efficiently than it was previously used; this may involve the construction of roads, the establishment of training centres and the organization of loans. Even if this is successful it is by no means certain that the greater production will contribute to the economic development of the country as a whole; it may result in the appearance of a more prosperous peasantry with a higher standard of living, depriving the country even of the limited amount of capital for investment in industry that might have been expected from the large owners under previous conditions.

Turning first to the question of ownership, in any agrarian society there are more people using the land than owning any land. In Latin America this is particularly true of a type of land tenure based on the individualistic society of the Spanish; it is least true in a system still based on the collective organization of land ownership originating in many of the pre-Columbian Indian societies. Agricultural land may be worked under several different systems of ownership and labour. Firstly, there is the owner of a piece of land, who may possess a large farm with workers (or slaves in the past) in his employment, a medium sized farm worked by a family, perhaps with two or three labourers, or a very small farm hardly sufficient to satisfy the needs of the family owning and working it. Secondly, there are various arrangements whereby farmers pay in some form or other to use a particular piece of land owned by someone else; the tenant farmer pays a rent in money, the sharecropper pays by giving an agreed part of his crop to the owner of the land he works, while a labour/tenant works on the land of an owner for the right to use a small piece of land himself. Thirdly, there are landless labourers who in the past have been slaves in some areas, who have been tied to some particular estate or, now, are free to work where they wish, though in fact it may not be easy for them to move from the land of one owner to that of another. Other types of land tenure exist in Latin America, including a collective system in much of Mexico, collective and state farms in Cuba, and simple communities of savages in the Amazon with no legal organization at all; under this heading might come squatters occupying land that has no definite owner, as in Haiti and also in Paraguay and Venezuela. There are many variations on these types as, for example, under the heading of large owners of land, which may be not merely single families but the Church, a foreign company (for example bananas in Central America, beef in Argentina), or the State, as in pioneer areas and now in some circumstances in Cuba.

Turning now to the size and type of holding, Latin America is characterized by very large units (*latifundio*) and very small ones (*minifundio*), the latter worked by owner-occupiers, tenants or sharecroppers, often only a few hectares in area and in some cases fragmented due to splitting among heirs in the past. Medium sized farms, the characteristic family farm of North America and Australia, are relatively rare in Latin America. The following table gives a rough idea of the proportion of total area in farms in different parts of Latin America, distributed in different categories of size. The figures are very approximate.

	Percentage of area in farms		
	Under 100 hectares	*100–500 hectares*	*Over 500 hectares*
Mexico and Central America	9	9	82
Islands	44	25	31
South America	13	22	65
Latin America	13	19	68

A recent investigation showed that in South America more than half of the land in farms was actually in units of more than 1,000 hectares in extent. With regard to the figures in the table, it will be appreciated that they do not show the percentage of farm units of different sizes but the percentage of land in each size group. Not all the land in a property is necessarily cultivated and usually the larger ones have a smaller percentage of their total area cultivated than the smaller ones. Moreover, smaller units tend to be cultivated more intensively than large ones. For these reasons the farms with less than 100 hectares make a much larger contribution to total production in Latin America than their 13 per cent of the total area in farms would suggest. The desirable or optimum size for a farm varies greatly according to the fertility of the land and to the type of farming practised. Some of the very large cattle-raising estates in remoter parts of Latin America are not necessarily unduly large for the functions they fulfil.

Several distinct systems of land tenure are found in Latin America, and it is useful to mention these, as long as it is appreciated that there is a great deal of overlapping. Firstly, the Amazon Indians and those of certain forested areas elsewhere still practise a simple shifting cultivation, operating as a community with little concern over precise legal details of ownership. Secondly, the Spaniards introduced the *hacienda* system into many parts of the region conquered by them, including Mexico and Central America, and much of South America. Large properties including the Indians living on them were distributed among the Spaniards and the land was used mainly for the growing of food crops or the raising of livestock, but very little was ever exported to Europe. This semi-feudal system reached its peak around 1700 in Spanish America when it accounted for a large part of all agricultural land, though in places Indian communities remained without being absorbed in this system. In a sense the system of land tenure in Argentina, Uruguay and the extreme south of Brazil is a modern version of the hacienda system, but the units of land tenure are generally called estancias, are more efficiently used, and are often worked by tenants or sharecroppers under more satisfactory systems of tenure. Isacovich[19] quotes instances of three families each owning more than 200,000 hectares of land and twelve each owning more than 100,000 hectares in the most fertile part of Argentina, the province of Buenos Aires. This was in 1929, but the situation has not changed appreciably.

The third system of land tenure, the plantation, though used by the Spaniards, has been more characteristic of the Portuguese and of other European powers in sub-tropical and tropical America. The older plantations using slave labour were most developed in Northeast Brazil, the Caribbean area, and the southeast of North America, and concentrated on sugar, coffee, cacao and cotton during the colonial period; food crops were also grown on the plantations or on small pieces of land nearby. In the nineteenth century when the availability of slaves became more limited, indentured labour from Asian countries was brought in, while European farmers, particularly Italians, moved into Brazil to work on the expanding coffee plantations. The status of the worker on plantations has now changed and in some cases wages are reasonably high, as in the modern banana plantations of Central America, but the status of the workers is still low and insecure. Fourthly, the 'family' farm, the model for which is the 160 acre unit of the United States, or the much smaller peasant owned farm in France and other parts of Europe, is not widespread in Latin America, a fact that has frequently been lamented. It occurs in areas where North and Central European settlers (particularly Germans), in some cases Spanish settlers, and occasionally local settlers, have moved into new areas, clearing the land, often forest, for themselves. This type of land tenure occurs in southern parts of Brazil, in Argentina, south Central Chile, Costa Rica and Colombia.

The basic problem of agrarian reform is to expropriate and split up part, if not all, of the large holdings, without upsetting production and particularly without interfering with the production of crops for export. Very little reform of this kind was introduced in Latin America before the twentieth century. From about 1910 on there has been a gradual transformation of land tenure in Mexico, with much of the newly allocated land being placed in collectives (*ejidos*). In the interwar period conditions for tenants in Argentina and Uruguay were greatly improved by rural tenancy legislation, giving security to tenants by means of contracts lasting for a minimum of several years, and eventually in some cases in Argentina enabling the tenant actually to purchase the land. There have also been reforms in the Dominican Republic since the early 1930s and about 100,000 people have been resettled there, while following the 1952 Revolution in Bolivia, the agrarian reform law of 1953 was introduced to restore land in private hands to Indian communities.

But until the late 1950s or early 1960s little had been done in most of the other countries. Since the late 1950s much has been done to pave the way for agrarian reform, with Cuba going its own way since 1959–60, moving towards state ownership of farms, and with various other countries introducing programmes. These include Colombia (1961), Chile (1963 Agrarian

Reform Law), Peru, which in 1964 was planning with United States aid (U.S. $ 43 m.) to resettle about 100,000 peasant farmers, Paraguay, El Salvador, Honduras and Costa Rica. Uruguay has introduced legislation to reform the terms of ownership and tenancy, establishing a maximum size for estates owned by one person (600–2,500 hectares according to locality), and is excluding limited companies. By 1963, however, virtually nothing had been done in Brazil, where the most suitable form of compensation was being considered, and in 1964 this question was still being debated by the new government, but it was proposed to use heavy progressive taxation on unexploited land. It was being proposed by Goulart to ensure that most agricultural families should own land by raising the number of units of ownership from about 3 m. to some 10–12 m. In Brazil at present there are about 3,350,000 rural properties owned by only about a quarter of all farm families, but of this large number, only about 33,000 or 1 per cent of the total occupy 47 per cent of the total area in farms. The largest farms, those over about 1,000 hectares, usually have only 1–4 per cent in use for farming. Venezuela made a somewhat earlier start and, being a more prosperous country and having other sources of wealth, has found compensation less difficult. But between 1948 and 1958 only 5,000 families were resettled on 93,000 hectares of land, compared with 61,000 during 1959–1962 on 1,700,000. By 1963 it was planned to bring the total to 100,000 and eventually to double this, thus enabling the majority of farming families to own their land.

REFERENCES

[1] *The Latin American Common Market*, 1959. Prepared by the Secretariat of ECLA, United Nations
[2] *Social Aspects of Economic Development in Latin America, I. Technology and Society*, 1963, UNESCO
[3] *Towards an Dynamic Development Policy for Latin America*, 1963, New York; United Nations
[4] *UNSY* 1962, Table 164
[5] *UNSBLA*, Vol. 1, No. 1
[6] *UNDY*, 1960, Table 12
[7] *BOLSA (FR)*, 9 March 1963, 4 May 1963, 15 June 1963, 29 June 1963, 10 Aug. 1963, 16 Nov. 1963
[8] *UNSY*, 1962, Table 163
[9] *UNSY*, 1962, Table 10
[10] *BOLSA (QR)*, July 1963, 'Foreign Investment in Latin America', p. 132
[11] *Towards a Dynamic Development Policy*, 1963, United Nations
[12] *Foreign Private Investments in the Latin American Free-Trade Area*, 1961, New York; United Nations
[13] *U.S. Statistical Abstract 1962 and 1963*, p. 856
[14] *BOLSA (QR)*, July 1964, pp. 109–118. *Latin American Development Plans*
[15] *Petroleum Press Service*, Feb. 1963, 'State Interest in Oil', pp. 61–65
[16] *Venezuela Up-to-Date*, Fall 1962, Vol. XI, No. 1
[17] Crossley, J. C. 'Agrarian Reform in Latin America', *The Yearbook of World Affairs*, Vol. 17, 1963
[18] Ford, T. R. *Man and Land in Peru*, 1955, Gainsville
[19] Isacovich, M. *Argentina económica y social*, p. 37, 1961, Buenos Aires

CHAPTER 6

TRANSPORT

6.1. GENERAL

Virtually every form of transport used in the world is still of importance in some part of Latin America, but certain forms are of course far more widespread than others. Table 6.1 sets out the various forms roughly in their order of introduction into Latin America and suggests the kinds of distance likely to be covered by different forms at the present day. The meaning of local and interregional varies according to size of country and other conditions. Interregional in Brazil may be 1–2,000 km, whereas this distance would be international in say Central America. Intercontinental refers to distances of at least several thousand kilometres between Latin America and other parts of the world.

Given the great variety of forms of transport in use in an area the size of Latin America, the many kinds of goods carried and the great contrasts in distance, it is only possible to obtain a very general idea of comparative

TABLE 6.1

	Local	Inter-regional	Inter-national	Inter-continental	Where used
1 Human transport	X				Rugged areas, especially Haiti, the Andes
2 Pack animal	X				Mountain areas
3 Canoe, raft	X				Amazonia, other remote lowland areas with suitable rivers
4 Wheeled cart	X				Plantations, agricultural areas in general
5 Internal steam navigation	X	X	X		Large South American rivers, some lakes
6 Railway	X	X	(X)	(X)†	Most areas with above mean density of population for Latin America
7 Coastal navigation		X	X		South American countries, especially Chile, Brazil, Argentina, Peru; also Mexico
8 Oceanic navigation		(X)	X	X	Latin America to North America, Europe
9 Motor vehicles	X	X	(X)	(X)†	Most settled areas are being reached
10 Pipelines	X	X			Venezuela, Mexico, other oil producers
11 Electricity transmission	X	(X)			Long distance limited. Brazil
12 Air: passengers	X	X	X	X	Widespread except in very rugged and/or high areas
13 Air: freight		X	(X)	(X)	Limited except for inaccessible localities. Often subsidized

(X) Not much used.
† Mexico—U.S.A.

transport costs for goods by different forms of transport. It is widely accepted that for most purposes sea transport is the cheapest form, while railways are cheaper than road except for very short hauls, and that the transport of goods by air is exorbitant and can only be used in exceptional circumstances, as can the simpler forms depending on human or animal energy. But for various reasons the scheme does not clearly apply in Latin America. In the first place, there is little competition between land and sea transport except over short distances (coastal services), so the question of comparative efficiency rarely arises. Moreover, sea transport is not cheap for short journeys, nor when vessels are small or services infrequent. Secondly, for various reasons railways in Latin America have usually been very in-efficient, while road transport is rapidly improving.

Though this does not necessarily apply widely, our general picture of relative transport costs resembles in principle, if not in detail, the average charges for oil transport in the U.S.A[1].

Cost per ton mile, road = 100 units			
Road	100	Pipeline	6 to 7
Rail	27	Water	1·3

Precise charges depend on size of ship, capacity of pipeline and so on, but in the U.S.S.R. in 1961 completely different costs were recorded for general cargoes.

Cost per ton kilometre, road = 100 units			
Road	100	Inland waterway	5·4
Rail	5·5	Sea	3·8

The obvious efficiency of the Soviet railway system emerges, even if freight rates are to some extent fixed unrealistically to suit planning and accounting needs*. Unfortunately there is no such overall picture for Latin America, but certainly the situation is different from that in either the U.S.A. or the U.S.S.R. Railways are still apparently cheaper than roads for lengthy hauls of bulky goods, particularly in Mexico, Brazil and Argentina, but where a railway would carry little traffic, a road is in reality more desirable. Where serious competition has taken place between roads and railways linking the same areas, as for example in Venezuela, or in central Peru, the road has quickly taken traffic previously handled by the railway. Similarly, since coastal shipping services are usually run with small and slow vessels, these cannot always face competition from roads parallel to the coast (Brazil, Peru).

Air transport is usually at least two or three times as costly as land trans-port for passengers, but so much time is saved that it is widely used even for short journeys (e.g. Rio—São Paulo). For the movement of goods, costs are many times greater by air than by land or sea, though they are diminishing relatively, at least on long distance journeys, as the size and capacity of

* Kopeks per 10/ton/km in 1961, rail 3,1, sea 2,1, river 3,0, road 55,7; port facilities are not considered for sea or river[2].

aircraft increases*. Often in Latin America, however, air transport is the only form available. For example, many building materials were flown to Brasilia in the earlier stages of its construction; meat is flown to Caracas from remote estancias in the llanos of Venezuela; and in 1961 the author saw aircraft bring into a place in the Peruvian selva not served by road, rail or river: cement, bottled beer and the parts of a complete lorry; coffee and coca leaves were flown out from the same general area.

Only a rough idea may be given of the relative importance of the major forms of transport†. For goods, almost all the total carried between Latin America and other regions goes by sea, as does most trade between countries within the region itself. In northern Mexico, much of Brazil, Argentina and Chile, railways still carry much of the traffic. In most other areas roads now account for a greater volume.

Latin America does not have an integrated transportation system like that in North America, a system that covers virtually all the U.S.A. as well as the southern part of Canada and the northern part of Mexico. In North America it is possible within reason to go by rail, road or air between any two places without the actual distance travelled appreciably exceeding the direct distance except, of course, from areas like Florida projecting seawards. In addition, there are extensive complex systems of pipelines and electricity transmission lines. In contrast, in Latin America there are many separate road and rail systems of varying extent and shape, while pipelines and electricity transmission are mainly local in scope (these two forms are not dealt with in this chapter but where they occur regionally). Shipping services make up for the deficiency to a small extent, but usually need long detours, whether or not they use the Panama Canal; for example, Buenos Aires to Valparaiso, Veracruz to Manzanillo. Services are not usually regular.

Only the combined international and internal air network forms a reasonably integrated and complete system in Latin America as a whole, and since the Second World War it has become possible to fly between any two major centres without undue delay or appreciable detours, though changes often have to be made. As yet it is not possible to do this by using only rail and road services, though it is now feasible to go by road, nearly all paved, from the U.S.A. at least to Costa Rica and from north Peru via Chile to Northeast Brazil.

In reality there are three major transport systems in Latin America: Mexico (one end of the North American system; quality and efficiency decline south of Mexico City); southern Brazil; and Argentina. Secondary systems in terms of extent and quantity of goods carried exist in Chile, Venezuela, Colombia, Peru, Cuba and Uruguay, and are being formed in central America and Northeast Brazil. Several smaller systems exist elsewhere: other Caribbean islands, Ecuador, Bolivia, Paraguay. Some of these are linked with each other, but there is very little traffic between them.

* For example, a ton of machinery can now be flown by Pan American Airways across the Atlantic from London to New York for U.S. $ 500—nearly 5,000 km—some 10 cents per ton/km. Such items as chemicals, electrical appliances and shoes are now regularly handled.

† Contrast the share of goods accounted for by different forms in the U.S.S.R. in 1961; railways 78·4%, sea 8·0%, river 5·3%, pipeline 3·0%, road 5·3%, air 0·04% of all ton kilometres[3]. The total volume involved was of course many times greater than the total for Latin America.

Much of the goods traffic in Latin America falls into one of the following classes: movement of goods between rural areas and urban centres; movement of goods between ports and inland localities, and movement of goods between ports and other countries, most of it between Latin America on the one hand and North America or Europe on the other. The following tendencies may be noted in the early 1960s: rail transport is stagnating, with existing lines being closed in some areas (Venezuela, Argentina) but a few new lines being constructed elsewhere (Brazil, Colombia); the road network is growing rapidly and the number of motor vehicles in circulation is likely to increase greatly with their manufacture in the region; pipelines and electricity transmission (especially Brazil) are just beginning to play a role in long distance movement; air transport is increasing very impressively; and there are moves to improve or introduce regular shipping services between various LAFTA countries (see Section 20.2).

6.2. INLAND WATERWAYS

Although the main form of transport over vast areas in the interior of South America, the rivers of the continent carry only a very limited traffic. There are two systems of international significance, the Amazon basin (concerning six countries) and the Paraná-Uruguay basin (concerning five countries), each with several thousand kilometres of navigable waterway, and three more limited national systems, the Magdalena in Colombia, the Orinoco in Venezuela, and the São Francisco in Brazil. Elsewhere in Latin America, rivers are mostly short or unsuitable for navigation or both. Many estuaries and lower reaches carry traffic 50–100 km inland (e.g. Ecuador, Guianas) but are thereafter useless.

As elsewhere in the world, navigation on inland waterways is faced with many drawbacks. Firstly, rivers do not necessarily flow in the most useful directions; that they drain Amazonia to a virtually undeveloped coastal region and not to a point near say Rio has no doubt discouraged penetration via the system. The Paraná system runs parallel to the Atlantic coast for too long, at least to be an ideal outlet for Paraguay and the interior of Brazil. The Orinoco in Venezuela is only now beginning to serve as a possible line of penetration into the interior of the country. The Magdalena on the other hand has been a blessing to the interior concentration of population in Colombia. A second drawback of the rivers is related to their regime. Most originate in or flow through areas with marked seasonal differences in rainfall, and the Amazon and its tributaries are afflicted by great floods causing differences in level of up to 10 m in Iquitos and 15 m in Manaus. In the Paraná, Orinoco and Magdalena basins navigation is curtailed during dry seasons and sometimes throughout dry years. Thirdly, the structure of South America is such that many of the rivers, including particularly the right bank tributaries of the Amazon and the left bank tributaries of the Paraná flow off the Brazilian Shield over a number of difficult rapids. In some instances the obstructions have been by-passed by roads or railways, but transhipment causes delays and raises costs.

The Amazon system carries a wide range of products, but invariably in vary small quantities. Ocean going vessels can comfortably reach Manaus

(10,000 tons) and Iquitos (4,000) and small sea going vessels can penetrate further still. Products are assembled at certain convenient points along the Amazon itself, and there are regular though not frequent services to North America and Europe as well as to southeast Brazil and even round to the Pacific coast of Peru. Belem is the focus for the lower part of the basin. The Paraná basin likewise has regular navigation, but seagoing vessels do not penetrate easily beyond Rosario. At present only the lower part of the Orinoco, to its confluence with the Caroní, is used to any great extent; this stretch has been specially dredged to accommodate iron ore carriers. The Magdalena was formerly Colombia's main link with the outside world, but the growth of Buenaventura on the Pacific, the development of air services and the opening of a parallel railway in 1961 have greatly reduced its role.

The prospect of increased traffic on the inland waterways of Latin America seems limited; new roads and railways to the coast are reorientating the traffic from the upper part of the Paraná; the same could happen with the Amazon as new roads extend from Brasilia into interior Brazil, and possibly even the apparently promising Orinoco may not be needed as more north-south roads link the llanos with the Caribbean coast of Venezuela. There is a scheme to provide a navigable waterway through from the the Amazon to the Paraná basin but it would link regions that at present have similar products.

6.3. SEA TRANSPORT

Very broadly there are three sets of shipping service affecting Latin America; they are largely organized independently, but are to some extent competitive. Firstly, several countries have their own shipping services linking different ports on their coastline. Chile, for example has services to its southern provinces in particular; the Brazilian ports are linked by regular services. Secondly, there are services between Latin American countries. Venezuela, for example, exports oil to several countries; Cape Horn is rounded by many vessels linking the Atlantic and Pacific ports of southern South America. A weekly service was started in 1963 between the Plate estuary ports and Salvador (Northeast Brazil). Part of the function of these international services is also, where possible, to carry goods between ports in the same country. Thirdly, there are regular services between sets of Latin American ports and single ports or sets of ports in other regions of the world. For example three liners of the Royal Mail Lines link London, a French port, a Spanish port and Lisbon with Rio, Santos, Montevideo and Buenos Aires. The six principal directions served by such intercontinental lines are:

Atlantic South America	
Pacific South America	Western Europe
Caribbean coasts	Eastern North America

There are only limited services to the Pacific side of Mexico and Central America, and little trade between Pacific North America and anywhere in Latin America. Japanese services go round both sides of the world to reach Latin America, while a service has just been started between Australia and South America, and Cuba has frequent services to eastern Europe. The

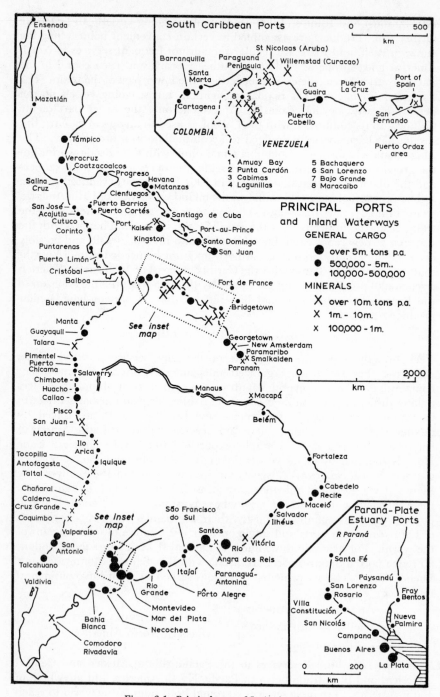

Figure 6.1. Principal ports of Latin America[6].

intercontinental services along the coasts of Latin America are also used to link ports within Latin American countries (e.g. goods from Valparaiso to Arica, from Santos to Recife) and in different countries (e.g. Valparaiso to Buenaventura, Buenos Aires to Rio), but Latin American shipping is usually required to do this where possible.

Several Latin American countries have merchant shipping fleets, but if the contributions of Panama and Honduras (3,851,000 tons and 113,000 tons) are excluded, these flags being used for convenience by various non-Latin American countries, then the total strength is modest, given the size of Latin America and its obvious need for good shipping services. The following are the gross registered tons (in thousands) of merchant shipping fleets[4].

	1955	1963		1955	1963
Argentina	1,043	1,308	Mexico	172	250
Brazil	893	1,227	Peru	98	117
Venezuela	216	319	Colombia	n.a.	114
Chile	230	286	Uruguay	66	n.a.

The combined shipping of all Latin American countries is only one sixth that of the U.K. and many of the vessels are small and antiquated.

Even *Figure 6.1*, which shows only the principal ones, suggests that Latin America has a large number of ports. These are strung irregularly along the coasts and vary greatly in size, facilities and functions. Very broadly there are two main types, those handling exclusively minerals and those dealing with general cargoes (usually including some minerals) and passengers. The outstanding importance of minerals in the total bulk of goods handled in Latin American ports can be judged by the fact that of some 225 m. tons of goods exported from Latin American ports in 1961[5] (excluding the exports of the Netherlands Antilles, which are merely refined Venezuelan oil already recorded as having been exported by Venezuela), 160 m. tons were oil, its products, and iron ore from Venezuela alone, and about 40 m. more were minerals of various kinds from the remaining countries including iron ore, bauxite, manganese ore and refined non-ferrous metals—nearly 90 per cent of the total. The total weight of goods entering Latin American ports (excluding the Netherlands Antilles and Trinidad) was under 40 m. tons; much of this was also oil (especially to Brazil). Altogether, then, only about 25 m. tons of goods other than minerals enter and leave Latin American ports each year. Total goods loaded and unloaded in 1962 were[7], in millions of tons:

	Mainly minerals loaded			Mainly goods other than minerals loaded	
	Loaded	Unloaded		Loaded	Unloaded
Venezuela	171,2	2,3	Argentina	11,7	7,3
Brazil	12,4	16,8	Central		
Trinidad	9,5	9,7	America	1,6	2,2
Chile	9,2	2,7	Ecuador	1,1	0,5
Jamaica	9,0	1,6			
Peru	8,6	2,1	U.S.A.	122,2	201,9
Colombia	5,5	1,5			

TRANSPORTATION PROBLEMS

LEFT:
PORTERS CARRY-
ING HEAVY
EQUIPMENT,
ANDES OF PERU

BELOW:
IMPRESSION
OF DIFFICULT
CONDITIONS
IN THE ANDES
OF PERU

TRANSPORT
WITH OXEN
IN SAN
SALVADOR,
EL SALVADOR

TOTORA REED
FISHING BOATS,
LAKE TITICACA,
BOLIVIA

IN LATIN AMERICA

RIGHT:
ASSEMBLING A LORRY
FLOWN IN BY AIR,
TARAPOTO, PERU

MIDDLE:
DIFFICULT MOUNTAIN
ROAD NEAR SAN MATEO,
CENTRAL ANDES OF PERU

BELOW:
SHIPS TOWED BY 'MULES'
PASSING IN MIRAFLORES
LOCKS, PANAMA CANAL

In *Figure 6.1* two types of port are distinguished, those handling almost exclusively minerals (e.g. Port Kaiser in Jamaica, Cruz Grande in Chile) and those handling mainly or entirely other goods (e.g. Veracruz in Mexico, Belem in Brazil). Some, like La Plata (Argentina) and Santos (Brazil) handle large quantities of oil as well as other cargoes. The ports of Western Venezuela account for nearly half of the total tonnage of cargo loaded in all Latin American ports. The inset map shows the formidable array on the Gulf of Maracaibo and the Paraguaná Peninsula. Puerto la Cruz handles much of the oil exported from Eastern Venezuela. There are several smaller oil ports elsewhere in Latin America including Comodoro Rivadavia in Argentina and Talara in Peru. The handling of oil requires a minimum of effort, the main concern being to construct jetties to convey pipelines to places where large tankers can moor in reasonably sheltered, deep waters. Iron ore and bauxite are also handled in millions of tons per year in several ports. The Puerto Ordaz area on the lower Orinoco serves the iron ore fields of Eastern Venezuela, Vitória, which is to be greatly enlarged, those of Minas Gerais in Brazil, and San Juan in Peru, the new iron ore deposits of Marcona, while the ports of Jamaica, British Guiana and Surinam handle most of the bauxite.

In contrast to the specialized mineral ports, the general ports are often large towns themselves and by the nature of their functions usually serve extensive hinterlands. The value per ton of the goods they handle generally exceeds many times that of the minerals in the specialized ports. They usually have to cater for many different sizes and types of vessel and often need complicated facilities for loading and storing goods. Only Santos, Rio de Janeiro and Buenos Aires with La Plata (50 km away) each handle more than about 5 m. tons of goods per year, a quantity exceeded several times in all the major ports of North America and Western Europe. Many of the exports of Mexico reach its chief trading partner, the U.S.A., by road or rail, and the leading port of the country, Veracruz, is not therefore among the busiest in Latin America for general cargoes; with Havana, Guayaquil, Callao, Valparaiso, Montevideo and certain ports of Brazil and Argentina, it is of medium size.

Some of the smaller ports are losing traffic to the large and medium ones. Ilhéus in Brazil, for example, is largely by-passed now by foreign shipping; the same fate faces some Peruvian and Chilean ports. Imports, in particular, are encouraged to enter countries by one or a few ports only, in order to centralize customs control. Certain small ports owe their existence almost exclusively to the exportation of one particular agricultural product; for example, several ports in Central America handle mainly bananas, some in Cuba only sugar, some in Argentina cereals or livestock products.

The areas served by Latin American ports deserve greater study than they have received. In view of the widespread lack of integration of land communications there is less overlapping of hinterlands than might be expected from the number of ports. Along many stretches of coast including the Pacific side of South America and most of Northeast Brazil, most places have only one obvious outlet on the coast. In Colombia, Bolivia and the Atlantic side of southern South America there is greater scope for competition between different ports.

The Panama Canal* (see *Figure 6.2*) has a special place in Latin American shipping connections. The history, present status and features of the Canal will be dealt with in Chapter 10.5 under Panama, and only the international aspect of it, the shipping using it, will be covered here. All but the largest

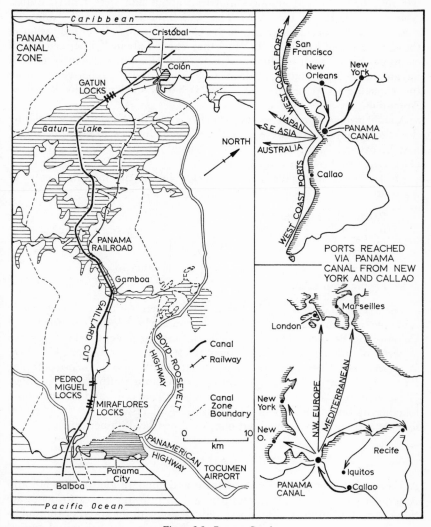

Figure 6.2. Panama Canal

vessels (depending on critical dimensions) can pass through the Canal. In the fiscal year 1963 (July 1962–June 1963), a total of 11,017 vessels of over 300 net tons passed through in both directions, an appreciable increase on the average number for 1951–55: 7,062. There are no noticeable seasonal differences. In 1963 a total of approximately 62,250,000 tons of cargo (36 m. average 1951–55) were carried through the Canal, about 33 m. from the

* Principal sources of information used for this section[8,9].

Atlantic to the Pacific, 29 m. from Pacific to Atlantic. The tolls collected in 1963 totalled about U.S. $ 56 m., roughly U.S. $ 5,000 per vessel, at first sight a large sum, but in fact little enough to have to pay for the days or even weeks saved. Of the number of vessels using the Canal (but the average size may have differed among countries), about half were United States, Norwegian, U.K. or German. The vessels of several Latin American countries make considerable use of the Canal, but there is no indication of the destination of journeys. In 1963 they carried about 2·5 per cent of all cargo passing through (excluding Panama and Honduras, which accounted for another 3·5 per cent). Chilean, Colombian and Peruvian vessels were the chief users. At present the Canal is hardly used at all by Brazil or Argentina.

A wide range of cargoes passes through. From the Pacific to the Atlantic side the heaviest items were ores (7 m. tons), lumber (4 m)., oil, sugar, metals, canned foods, bananas and fish meal. In the other direction, oil (11 m. tons) and coal were the heaviest.

Most services using the Panama Canal linked the following pairs of regions:

Pacific North America	
Pacific Mexico, Central America	Eastern North America
Far East	
Australasia	Western Europe
Pacific South America	

The least used direction is the Far East to Western Europe. Other possible routes not accounted for in the above diagram are both local (e.g. Caribbean Colombia to Pacific Colombia) or long distance (e.g. Venezuela to Japan). In terms of number of vessels, the two busiest routes were Eastern U.S.A. to Western South America (21 per cent of total) and Eastern U.S.A. to the Far East (19 per cent). Routes from Europe to Western South America (about 12 per cent), to Western North America (about 9 per cent) and to Australasia together accounted for about 24 per cent of all vessels. U.S. intercoastal services accounted for only about one vessel per day (3·5 per cent).

6.4. RAILWAYS*

As the steamship began to transform trade and immigration patterns of Latin American countries about a century ago, so railways began to penetrate the continent from the coastal ports, though not with the speed or thoroughness that they did in North America, for there was neither internal capital to finance railways nor industry capable of producing the rails or rolling stock. By about 1930, however, most of the present lines had been completed. The figures for Argentina† give an idea of the pattern of development, though railways came somewhat later to most other areas. The period of greatest growth was from about 1885 to 1915 and very little has been added since 1940. The figures are quoted in Chapter 17.7.

* See *Figure 6.3* for general features of the railways and detailed examples.
†See page 392.

The present length of route in Latin America is about one third as great as that in North America, but the tons/km handled are far less. The figures for the U.S.A. and Canada in 1961 were 822,000 m. and 96,000 m. respectively, compared with only 48,000 m. for all Latin America, which was therefore only about half of the total for Canada alone. It had risen to this from 38,500 m. in 1948, almost all of the increase having come in Mexico and Brazil.

The total distance of route in Latin America was about 146,000 km in the late 1950s. This contrasts with 418,000 km in North America (U.S.A. 348,000, Canada 70,000). It was distributed among countries as follows:

Argentina	45,000	31 per cent	5 Andean countries	11,000
Brazil	38,000	26 per cent	Central America	5,600
Mexico	18,400	13 per cent	Uruguay, Paraguay	4,200
Chile	10,600		Other islands, etc.	3,700
Cuba	9,600			

The total tons/km handled were distributed in 1960 as follows:

Argentina	15,100	31 per cent
Mexico	14,000	29 per cent
Brazil	12,700	26 per cent

These three countries have only about 60 per cent of the total population of Latin America but their railways handle over 85 per cent of the goods traffic, while Chile, Uruguay and Cuba account for most of the rest.

The main reason for the small amount of goods handled by Latin American railways is the fact that most bulky goods moved between regions are for export and are produced close to the coast, so there are few long hauls of these. The longest are of minerals in southeast Brazil and of farm products in Argentina. In spite of the poor standard of many lines and the fact that they are nearly all single track, it is rarely excessive traffic for capacity that keeps down the quantity of goods carried, usually lack of traffic.

The ownership of the Latin American railways varies among countries. Many of the more important systems are almost entirely State owned (Argentina, Colombia, Venezuela, Uruguay, Cuba) or largely State owned (Mexico), but in other countries they are privately operated either by national companies (many in Brazil) or by foreign companies (Peru, Central America). In addition there are many small systems operated by mining companies (e.g. in Chile the 191 km of the Ferrocarril Mineral de Chuquicamata) or on plantations (e.g. in Honduras on banana plantations).

If Latin America ever aspired to have an integrated railway system, one virtually insuperable obstacle would be the difficulty of deciding on one gauge. In fact the question seems unlikely to arise in the way it has in Australia. Many countries have two or more gauges and altogether half a dozen different gauges are to be found. Mexico has nearly all standard gauge (4ft. 8½in., 1·435 m) but central America has mainly narrow gauge (3ft. gauge, 0·914 m). In South America, Colombia, Ecuador and Bolivia have narrow gauge, but Peru, between them, mainly standard. Chile and Argentina have various gauges, with some broad gauge (5ft. 6in., 1·676 m) in Argentina. Uruguay again has standard, but neighbouring Brazil has

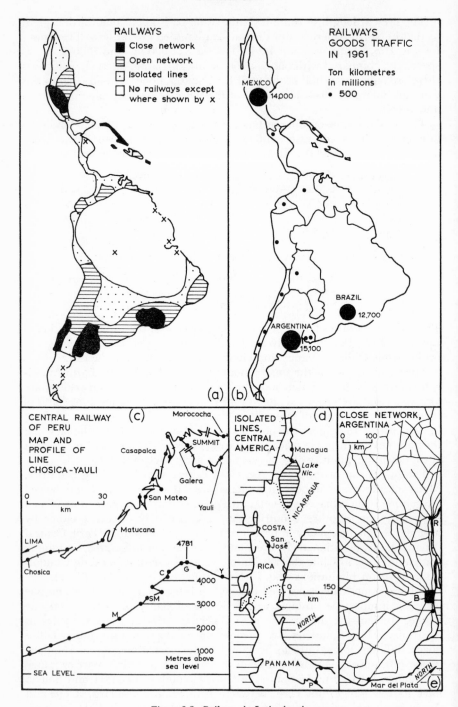

Figure 6.3. Railways in Latin America

mainly 1 m. A narrow gauge is convenient in rugged areas as it can negotiate curves and gradients more easily than standard gauge but its carrying capacity is limited. Ironically, too, Peru and Mexico, with some of the most difficult conditions, have standard gauge. So far, only about 2 per cent of all the railways are electrified. Most are in Brazil, on routes heavily used for mineral traffic, but an important stretch in Central Chile is also electrified. More progress has been made in replacing steam traction by diesel (Mexico, Peru, Brazil, Argentina).

Altogether, the position of the railways in Latin America is unsatisfactory. Almost all lines are single track; this may be adequate for the traffic they need to carry, but it makes train services very slow and discourages passengers. In 1961, the author made a journey by train in South Mexico from Arriaga to Tapachula, a distance of 160 km, in over 10 h. There was no other means of transport. But the journey by rail from La Paz to Buenos Aires takes four days and nights, compared with a few hours by air, and here the choice is obvious. Roads easily compete with railways in terms of both speed and fares almost everywhere in Latin America over shorter distances, while air is preferred to rail over greater distances, though it costs more. Many railways therefore depend largely on freight.

It must be stressed that a railway map of Latin America is very misleading. The representation of a railway on the map is no indication that one actually exists any longer or that if it does exist, more than a few trains actually run on it, or that if there is a railway between two places there is necessarily a service between them. Competition from other forms of traffic, bad management and lack of capital, poor equipment and inadequate facilities for maintenance, lack of an engineering industry, together with generally difficult physical conditions, make future prospects for many lines look unpromising. Perhaps half of the railways could be closed in the near future without causing more than slight inconvenience. In fact the volume of traffic is declining in Chile and Argentina, while nine out of fifteen railways in Venezuela have now closed down and Argentina is considering closing down some 2,000 km. On the other hand, the efficiency of certain Mexican lines is being improved with new rails and locomotives, while Colombia, Brazil and Mexico have built important new lines in the last decade. Most remarkable of all, Venezuela plans to rehabilitate and greatly extend its system.

After these many cautionary comments about the railways of Latin America the reader should see them in their true perspective. Maps of the complete railway network give an idea of large integrated systems whereas in reality there are many quite separate small systems with different gauges and under different owners; the idea of integration and cohesion is largely fictitious.

6.5. ROAD TRANSPORT

Outside the larger Latin American cities road transport has spread much more slowly than in North America or Western Europe, and even many relatively densely peopled parts of Latin America have not yet felt the impact of motor vehicles. The lack of suitable roads and the absence of a motor vehicle industry until the late 1950s were obvious reasons for lack of progress and most private passenger cars are still used mainly in and close to urban centres, while the railways presumably largely satisfied the needs of agriculture and mining until after the Second World War. Since then, however, the improvement of existing roads and the construction of new roads has proceeded very rapidly, while the number of vehicles in circulation has increased greatly. Total figures for Latin America as a whole are not easy to obtain but the case of several countries shows what has happened. Between 1948 and 1961 the number of commercial vehicles in Argentina and Chile roughly doubled, the number in Mexico increased about three times and in Central America, Colombia, Ecuador and Peru nearly four times. Every Latin American country has a road building programme of some sort and Brazil has one of the most ambitious in the world. The figures for commercial vehicles in 1960[10] give perhaps the best idea of likely degrees of impact of motor transport on different parts of Latin America if the number of vehicles per 1,000 inhabitants is calculated:

	Total commercial vehicles	Per thousand inhabitants		Total commercial vehicles	Per thousand inhabitants
Argentina	389,000	19·5	Colombia	83,000	6
Venezuela	101,000	13·5	Peru	64,000	6
Mexico	320,000	11·5	Brazil	400,000	5·5
Chile	69,000	9	Guatemala		3
			Haiti		about 1

But the total number of commercial vehicles in Latin America, 1,710,000, contrasts with Canada's 1,117,000 for less than one tenth the population, and, of course, 12,572,000 in the U.S.A. (1961). Passenger cars are even less evenly distributed among Latin American countries, with 36 per 1,000 people in Venezuela and 24/in Argentina contrasting with about 3 in Ecuador and Paraguay and less than 2 in Haiti. In general, the areas most affected by motor transport in Latin America so far are the areas tributary to large urban centres in a regional level, and countries with a relatively high *per caput* gross domestic product on a national level. Certain countries (especially Brazil and Argentina) now manufacture motor vehicles in large quantities and this may tell in their favour in the future.

The length of roads in use in many Latin American countries is at first sight impressive. In most, however, only a very small percentage is actually paved, the remainder having surfaces of varying quality, ranging from quite adequate hard surfaces to nothing more than rough ground used by motor vehicles only in dry periods. In the long run it is desirable to have as many roads as possible with a paved surface since as well as saving wear on vehicles, it needs much less maintenance, even though the initial cost is greater.

Most of the paved surface is to be found in towns and along the major interregional highways. The limited length of paved road in the early 1960s in Venezuela, 13,000 km and Brazil (federal road), 11,000 km, gives an idea of the inadequacy so far of major systems. Four lane motorways are very limited in length: for example between São Paulo and Santos, Caracas and La Guaira. The only direct road between São Paulo and Rio was being given two carriageways in 1961. A considerable proportion of all roads in Latin America are indeed not wide enough for two vehicles to pass conveniently. For example, in the Andes of Peru, where there are many such roads, traffic is arranged to go in different directions on alternate days. Road constructors in Latin America face many problems. Heavy downpours are frequent in most parts; forest has to be cleared in many areas; steep gradients have to be negotiated and high passes overcome in Mexico, Central America and the Andean countries; blown sand delays traffic in some regions, landslides in others.

Although goods are carried great distances by road in parts of Latin America there is so far no question of taking them over trans-continental distances as is occasionally done in the U.S.A. Buses cover over 1,000 km on some journeys (e.g. Laredo-Mexico City, Montevideo to Pôrto Alegre*, Rio to places in Northeast Brazil) but these are exceptional. Only occasionally do long distance lorry hauls exceed several hundred kilometres. For example, timber is carried from Santa Catarina to São Paulo; agricultural products are carried great distances to Mexico City and Lima.

Although the road network in Latin America is more complete now than the rail network, and there is no problem of difference in gauge, there are still several breaks in continuity (see *Figure 6.4*) and it is impossible to pass between certain road systems. Once the Pan-American Highway is completed, all the principal road systems will be linked, although few people are likely to follow the system from end to end.

Apart from the Islands, Guianas and other isolated road systems there are now three main systems, Mexico-Central America, Venezuela-Colombia-Ecuador, and Peru-Chile-Argentina-Brazil, with two major gaps to be filled: Panama-Colombia (see *Figure 6.4c*) and Ecuador-Peru. The former is incomplete on account of difficult terrain and the limited prospects of traffic anyway, the latter on account of friction between the two countries. Grandiose in scope and admirable in purpose, the Pan-American Highway system is in reality quite useless as a means of linking the Americas except for wealthy tourists who have at least several weeks to motor round the continent. If the distance from New York to San Francisco by road is about 5,000 km, the distance from Mexicali (in Northwest Mexico) to Concepción (in Chile) is 9,000 km by great circle and if, and when, the Pan-American Highway is completed the two places would be over 14,000 km apart, distributed as follows:

Mexicali	to Mexico City	2,400 km
Mexico City	to Panama City	3,800 km
Panama City	to South Ecuador	
	(incomplete)	about 2,500 km
Peru		2,800 km
North Chile	to Concepción	2,700 km

14,200 km

An imaginary lorry carrying petroleum products from one end of Latin America to the other would need to consume the equivalent of much of its

* The journey of about 1,000 km could be completed in 20 h in 1961.

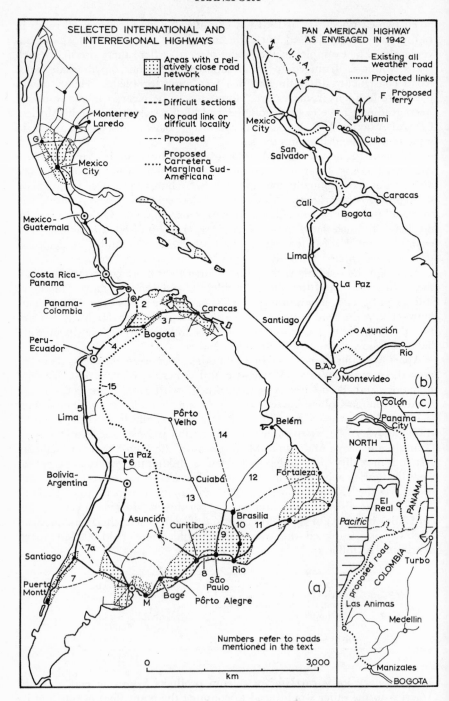

Figure 6.4. Roads in Latin America. (a) Selected main roads. (b) Pan-American Highway as envisaged in 1942. (c) Pan-American highway link as projected between Panama and Colombia

118

load before it reached its destination; it would probably fall off a precipice or break an axle long before it got there anyway. The usefulness of the Pan-American Highway concept has been firstly to stimulate individual countries to provide good stretches of road within their boundaries, and secondly to encourage neighbouring countries to link their road systems, which has happened particularly in Central America.

This section is concluded with notes on some recent major road developments in Latin America. Numbers refer to *Figure 6.4a*. It is now possible to go by road from the U.S.A. to Panama through Mexico City and along the recently completed highway through Central America (1). The total distance from Laredo to Panama City is approximately 5,000 km, and only 16 per cent is still unpaved. A gap of several hundred kilometres (2) still separates Panama City from Medellín and Manizales in Colombia; a route is being surveyed (*Figure 6.4c*). Venezuela has a good system of roads (see *Figure 6.5a*) and this is linked (3) to the Colombian system which has some good stretches (Cucutá-Bogota-Cali) but lacks a good link with the Caribbean ports. It is possible to go by road between Colombia and Ecuador (4) but conditions are very difficult near the boundary. Peru (5) has an excellent highway, almost entirely paved from end to end, along its coast, and the Chilean counterpart, which runs in the central valley much of the way has now been paved from Arica to Puerto Montt. The most spectacular road in Bolivia is the Cochabamba-Santa Cruz highway (6) completed in 1954 to link the Andean region with the eastern lowlands. At present there is only one inadequate road between Argentina and Chile (Mendoza-Santiago), but other roads are proposed (7), and one, 500 km in length, from San Juan to Coquimbo over the Aguas Negras Pass has apparently been completed.

In the last few years quite astounding progress has been made in road construction in Brazil. In the early 1960s the construction of a road from Brasilia to Belém made it possible (though unlikely) for vehicles to go from the mouth of the Amazon to the boundary of Uruguay (near Bagé)—hence the BBB—Belém-Brasilia-Bagé link. The new road from Belo Horizonte to Brasilia (10) was built at the rate of nearly one kilometre per day and that from Brasilia to Belém (12) was at least laid out if not completed at the incredible rate of about 5 km per day, construction extending from several bases along the course, some reached only by air. More ambitious still is the improvement and extension of a road northwest from Brasilia to Pôrto Velho (13) planned eventually to join the Central Highway of Peru and link Lima with Brasilia. In the meantime, roads have been built or improved between Curitiba and São Paulo (8) (1961), São Paulo and Brasilia (9) and Rio and Salvador (11) (1963).

Two further projects deserve mention. There has been talk of building a road between Brasilia and Bogota via Manaus (14); even the direct distance is enormous (3,750 km) and the road would have to make some detours; it would presumably serve as two new outlets for the interior of Amazonia rather than to carry traffic across. The Amazon border road (15) running along the foot of the Andes from Bolivia through Peru and Ecuador to Colombia is already being surveyed; the total length would be about 6,000 km. It is difficult to imagine at the moment what purpose this road

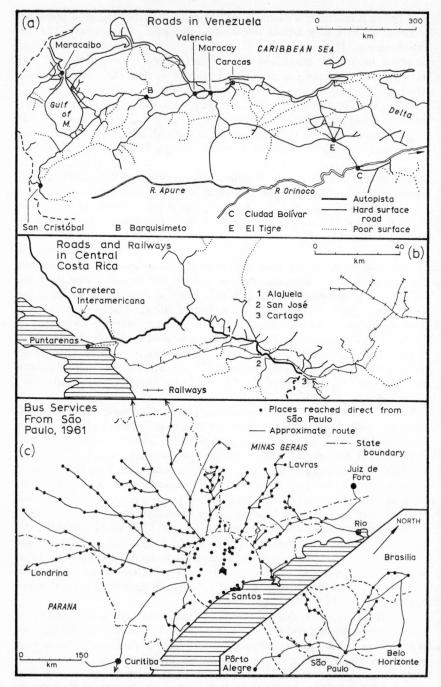

Figure 6.5. Roads and bus services. (a) Roads in northern Venezuela. (b) Roads and railways in central Costa Rica. (c) Bus Services direct from São Paulo in 1961 (not exhaustive)

would serve since it would only link a number of almost empty areas with similar products anyway.

6.6. AIR TRANSPORT

Air transport began to be used widely in Latin America soon after it was used in North America and there was not such a great time lag as in the spread of motor transport. One reason has been that in the interwar period many non-Latin American countries ran services to Latin America, another that air transport was a blessing to many Latin American governments faced with the difficulty of reaching and controlling remote provinces. In Peru in the nineteenth century for example it was more easy and safer to travel from Iquitos down the Amazon and then by sea to Europe than to travel across the forest and over the Andes to the capital, Lima, a journey taking as much as several weeks. Now there is a frequent air service to Lima taking 2 h. This is not to say that air transport has contributed more than slightly to economic integration of countries, for air transport costs are very high by any reckoning. Even in Brazil, ton/kilometres carried by air amount to only 1 per cent of those carried by rail. The proportion is much smaller in Argentina and Mexico, but is somewhat higher in Colombia. As already stressed, however, air transport offers the advantages of speed and flexibility, since within reason aircraft can fly between any two airfields in a direct line. Unfortunately for Latin America all its aircraft have to be imported and aviation fuel is a further costly item for most countries; not surprisingly, air lines are almost all subsidized by governments.

As with shipping services there are various scales of operation of air services. On a local level, small aircraft move from place to place in thinly peopled areas where there are no other forms of transport, using rudimentary landing strips or landing on rivers, and carrying passengers, mail and valuable goods. On a regional level, there are both frequent intercity links and services between the national capital or other major regional centres and distant peripheral areas. In Colombia for example there are 'air taxi' services between Bogota, Medellín and Cali, while between Rio, São Paulo and Brasilia there are step on services on each of the three 'air bridges'; according to *Time* (Aug. 30, 1963) the frequency of flights per week in 1963 was Rio-São Paulo 505, Rio-Brasilia 99, São Paulo-Brasilia 81. Chile and Argentina also depend on air transport to keep in touch with their distant southern provinces. On a smaller scale, Honduras is particularly air conscious, and before the opening of the Cochabamba–Santa Cruz highway, Bolivia was as well. The relative importance of air transport to different countries might be assessed in various ways. Using figures[11] for cargo ton/kilometres and total population in 1962 the following figures have been derived showing cargo ton/kilometres handled by scheduled air services *per inhabitant*, in selected countries, in 1962:

U.S.A.	7,9	Honduras	2,7	Bolivia	1,1
Venezuela	3,9	Chile	1,6	Mexico	1,0
Colombia	3,1	Brazil	1,5	Argentina	0,4

At present each country tends to have its own distinct system of internal air services, for while there are frequent services between Latin American

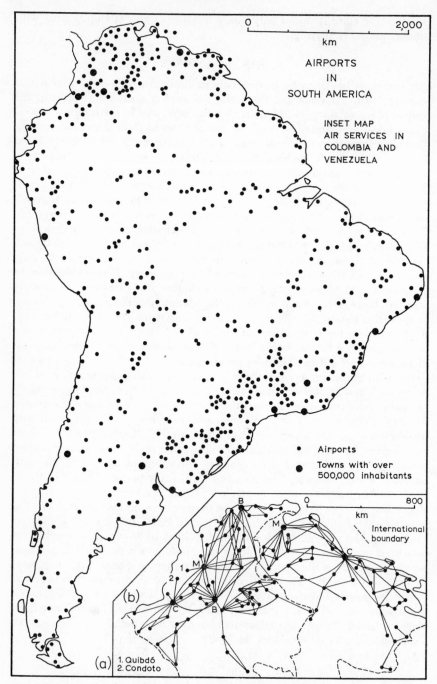

Figure 6.6. (a) *Airports in South America*[12] *showing only the main airports.* (b) *Airports and scheduled air services in Colombia and Venezuela*

Outline of coast based on a map in the Oxford Atlas published by the Oxford University Press

capitals there are often none between places in neighbouring countries at no great distance apart on either side of international boundaries (this is illustrated in *Figure 6.6b*). There are also frequent services between Latin American cities and those in North America and Europe. Routes from the east and west sides of North America converge on Panama, Caracas or Trinidad and then diverge to different parts of South America. With long range jets there is a tendency for more routes to fly across Amazonia instead of following the coasts as they did in the past, and New York has the advantage of non-stop flights to many Latin American capitals including Buenos Aires, the longest non-stop service in the world.

Whereas it was possible for passengers to travel reasonably fast over North America by rail several decades before air transport became widespread, Latin American countries were much more isolated from one another on account of their incomplete rail systems, the slowness and inadequacy of shipping links and the greater distances apart. The impact of air transport has therefore brought a revolution in inter-Latin American relations.

There are now at least several hundred airfields in Latin America with frequent scheduled air services (see *Figures 6.6, 6.7*) and thousands of landing places, including for example landing strips on large farms in the llanos of Venezuela, airfields operated by large oil companies for their own internal use, and landing places specially provided to bring in equipment for development projects in remote areas. There appears to be an inverse relationship between the frequency of airfields and of population in some parts of Latin

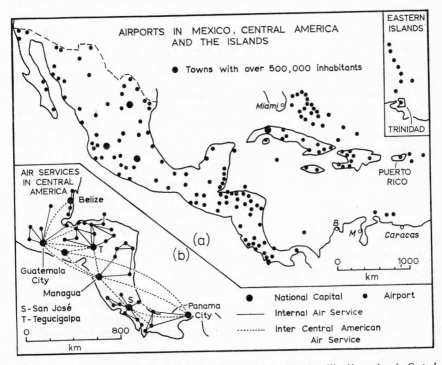

Figure 6.7. (a) Airports in Mexico, Central America and the Islands. (b) Air services in Central America

123

America though of course the largest and busiest airports are almost all associated with a large urban centre. In *Figure 6.6* it is easy to see the fringe of settlement in Brazil, the Amazon and its tributaries, and areas of development in Colombia, Peru and Bolivia. The Caribbean islands, particularly the Bahamas, also depend heavily on air transport. In contrast, there is a marked lack of airfields in the vicinity of many larger towns (São Paulo, Buenos Aires, Montevideo, Santiago, Lima) since these areas are close enough to the main centres to be able to reach quickly and use their frequent air services. Though not so obvious from the map, air transport is of limited scope in very high areas of settlement. This appears to be less a result of rugged conditions than of rarified atmosphere making take off hazardous. La Paz airport at about 4,100 m above sea level has a runway twice as long as normal for piston aircraft and the runway opened in 1964 for large jet aircraft is 4 km in length.

As already noted, it is inevitable that air services should be concentrated in certain directions and should focus on certain centres, rather than attempt to serve an area indiscriminately. In Latin America there has been a marked tendency for each country to organize its internal air routes with the capital as the focus* and also for there to be breaks along national boundaries. Even in a few years Brasilia has emerged as a great focus of air routes. The result is that it is usually much more easy to travel towards or away from the capital than to make journeys along routes at right angles to the radial lines. Thus in Colombia, for example, a journey from Condoto to Quibdó (see *Figure 6.6b*), only about 70 km apart, means flying into Cali, then to Medellin and finally back to Condoto, a distance of almost 700 km.

6.7. ACTUAL AND DIRECT DISTANCE, A CASE STUDY AND SOME EXAMPLES

A brief study of journeys by road between the main concentrations of population in Peru, represented for convenience by 10 urban centres, shows considerable differences between direct distance and the actual road distance on different journeys The 10 places and the roads linking them are shown in *Figure 6.8*. The road and the direct distance have each been measured and are recorded in Table 6.2a and b respectively. The excess of road distance over direct distance has been calculated for each journey in Table 6.2c, and is expressed as $\dfrac{\text{road distance}}{\text{direct distance}} \times 100$. Table 6.2d summarizes the results. The index ranges from 116 between Trujillo and Lima to 275 between Ayacucho and Arequipa.

Very broadly there are three sets of reasons why road distance can be expected to exceed direct distance. Firstly, minor or local deviations from the straight line may be made in order to negotiate steep slopes with hairpin bends (e.g. Ayacucho-Cusco, 236), or to serve places not far from the straight line. Secondly, regional detours may be required by the presence of a physical obstacle, such as the sea†, which obviously cannot be crossed, or

* See e.g. *Figure 9.3b* for Peru and also *Figure 6.6b*.
† As, for example, in England and Wales from places in Southwest Wales to places in Devon and Cornwall.

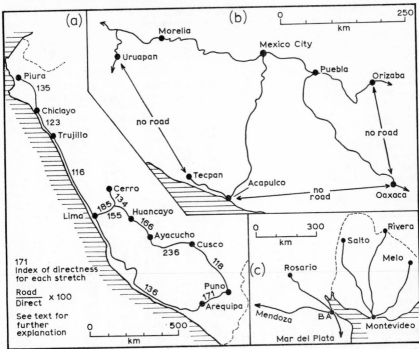

Figure 6.8. Routes and distances in (a) Peru, (b) Mexico, and (c) Argentina—Uruguay. (See text for further explanation)

a mountain area which is too costly to cross (e.g. Trujillo-Cerro, 211). Thirdly, a reasonably direct road may simply not exist between two places even of considerable importance owing to the incompleteness of the road system. These of course may combine (e.g. Ayacucho-Arequipa).

TABLE 6.2*

(a)	*Piura*	*Chiclayo*	*Trujillo*	*Lima*	*Cerro*	*Huancayo*	*Ayacucho*	*Cusco*	*Puno*	*Arequipa*	*Total*
Piura	0	270	480	1,050	1,365	1,360	1,625	2,210	2,365	2,080	12,805
Chiclayo	270	0	210	780	1,090	1,085	1,355	1,940	2,095	1,805	10,630
Trujillo	480	210	0	570	885	880	1,145	1,730	1,885	1,595	9,380
Lima	1,050	780	570	0	315	310	575	1,165	1,315	1,030	7,110
Cerro	1,365	1,090	885	315	0	255	520	1,110	1,500	1,340	8,380
Huancayo	1,360	1,085	880	310	255	0	265	855	1,245	1,180	7,435
Ayacucho	1,625	1,355	1,145	575	520	265	590	0	390	675	10,665
Cusco	2,210	1,940	1,730	1,165	1,110	855	590	0	390	290	12,065
Puno	2,365	2,095	1,885	1,315	1,500	1,245	980	390	0	290	12,065
Arequipa	2,080	1,805	1,595	1,030	1,340	1,180	1,265	675	290	0	11,260
Total	12,805	10,630	9,380	7,110	8,380	7,435	8,320	10,665	12,065	11,260	98,050

* Road distances have been obtained from tables in appropriate ESSO touring maps.

125

TABLE 6.2 (cont.)

(b)	Piura	Chiclayo	Trujillo	Lima	Cerro	Huancayo	Ayacucho	Cusco	Puno	Arequipa	Total
Piura	0	200	370	860	780	970	1,130	1,330	1,670	1,580	8,890
Chiclayo	200	0	170	660	590	780	940	1,140	1,460	1,400	7,340
Trujillo	370	170	0	490	420	610	770	970	1,290	1,220	6,310
Lima	860	660	490	0	170	200	330	570	860	760	4,900
Cerro	780	590	420	170	0	190	350	560	880	820	4,760
Huancayo	970	780	610	200	190	0	160	380	690	620	4,600
Ayacucho	1,130	940	770	330	350	160	0	250	540	460	4,930
Cusco	1,330	1,140	970	570	560	380	250	0	330	320	5,870
Puno	1,670	1,460	1,290	860	880	690	540	330	0	170	7,890
Arequipa	1,580	1,400	1,220	760	820	620	460	320	170	0	7,350
Total	8,890	7,340	6,310	4,900	4,760	4,600	4,930	5,870	7,890	7,350	62,840

(c)	Piura	Chiclayo	Trujillo	Lima	Cerro	Huancayo	Ayacucho	Cusco	Puno	Arequipa	Average
Piura	0	135	130	122	175	140	144	166	142	132	144
Chiclayo	135	0	123	118	185	139	144	170	143	139	145
Trujillo	130	123	0	116	211	144	148	178	146	130	149
Lima	122	118	116	0	185	155	174	204	153	136	145
Cerro	175	185	211	185	0	134	149	198	170	163	175
Huancayo	140	139	144	155	134	0	166	225	180	191	162
Ayacucho	144	144	149	174	149	166	0	236	182	275	167
Cusco	166	170	178	204	198	225	236	0	118	211	182
Puno	142	143	146	153	170	180	182	118	0	171	153
Arequipa	132	129	131	136	163	191	275	211	171	0	153
Average	144	145	149	145	176	162	167	182	153	153	156

(d)	Total road	Total direct	$\frac{Road}{direct} \times 100$	Total road Lima = 100	Mean road*
Lima	7,110	4,900	145	100	711
Huancayo	7,345	4,600	162	103	734
Ayacucho	8,320	4,930	167	117	832
Cerro	8,380	4,760	175	118	838
Trujillo	9,380	6,310	149	132	938
Chiclayo	10,630	7,340	145	150	1,063
Cusco	10,665	5,870	182	150	1,067
Arequipa	11,260	7,350	153	158	1,126
Puno	12,065	7,890	153	170	1,207
Piura	12,805	8,890	144	180	1,280

* Assuming 10 journeys, one of no distance to the place of origin itself.

Selected road journeys in Mexico

(e)	Road	Direct	Excess by road Direct = 100
Acapulco–Mexico	426	290	145
Acapulco–Morelia	736	340	216
Acapulco–Oaxaca	973	330	295
Acapulco–Uruapan	923	350	264
Tecpan–Uruapan	1,023	280	366
Oaxaca–Mexico	547	360	152
Oaxaca–Orizaba	595	200	298

TABLE 6.2 (*cont.*)

Selected road journeys in Southern South America

	Road	Direct	Excess by road Direct = 100
Rio –São Paulo	432	350	123
Rio–Belo Horizonte	532	335	159
Curitiba–Porto Alegre	686	540	127
Montevideo–Salto	498	425	115
Montevideo–Rivera	520	450	116
Montevideo–Melo	382	335	114
Buenos Aires–Rosario	324	270	120
Buenos Aires–Mar del Plata	410	375	109
Buenos Aires–Mendoza	1,115	960	116
Santiago–Concepción	525	430	122

The study also reveals the advantage of a central position. The sum of the journeys to all places from Lima is little more than half the sum of the journeys to all places from Puno or from Piura, at the extremities of the country. This means that an industrial establishment located in Lima would be able to distribute its goods over the national market with about half the total transport costs incurred by one in Puno or Piura, assuming that each was sending its goods uniformly over the whole national market. In this case, in fact, Lima represents a concentration of population about three times as large as any of the others, and if the exercise outlined so far in this section were further refined, it would have to be weighted. This would in practice mean that Lima would have to add two extra journeys to itself (of no distance) to its total, while Piura and Puno would each have to add two extra journeys to Lima. Even from such a simple study as this, a number of other interesting ideas emerge such as the implications of the inevitable advantage of being central unless there is a great concentration at *one* periphery, the possibility of using the procedure to detect where the next road could most usefully be added to the system, and so on[13].

In Table 6.2e, some other examples, which are self-explanatory, show that Peru is not the only part of Latin America with such discrepancies. On the other hand, indices are much more favourable in the lowland areas of Uruguay and Argentina. Nor does the problem only concern roads; if anything, water and rail routes are more liable to be diverted from direct courses than roads. On the other hand, theoretically at least, air routes can be direct.

REFERENCES

[1] *Petroleum Information Bureau*, 1954
[2] *Narodnoye khozyaystvo SSSR v 1961 godu*, pp. 75 and 509, 1962, Moscow
[3] *Narodnoye khozyaystvo SSSR v 1961 godu*, pp. 473–5 and 509, 1962, Moscow
[4] *UNSY*, 1963, Table 147
[5] *UNSY*, 1962, Table 143
[6] *Ports of the World*, 1962, 16th edn. Edited by D. Maxwell
[7] *UNSY*, 1963, Table 149
[8] *The Panama Canal Review*, Vol. 14, No. 2, Sept. 1963
[9] Fox, D. *Tijdschr. econ. Geogr.* 'Prospects for the Panama Canal' April, 1964
[10] *UNSY*, 1962, Table 140
[11] *UNSY*, 1963, Table 150
[12] *ABC World Airways Guide*, 1961
[13] Kansky, K. J. *Structure of Transportation Networks*, Chicago. 1963

CHAPTER 7

AGRICULTURE

7.1. GENERAL

In the late 1950s agriculture employed some 32 m. people in Latin America, nearly half of the total employed population of the region, but was only accounting for about one quarter of combined gross domestic product; the remaining activities therefore accounted for three quarters, while only accounting for half of the employed population. Figures for around 1950[1] showed that very approximately employment in agriculture was shared out as follows: Mexico 6 m., Central America 2 m., Andean countries 6 m., the Islands and Guianas $3\frac{1}{2}$ m., Brazil 10 m., Southern South America 3 m., a total of $30\frac{1}{2}$ m. In contrast, the figure for the U.S.A. in 1950 was 7,331,000; this has subsequently diminished, in spite of a rise in production.

The importance of agriculture to the economy varies greatly from country to country as is shown by the following figures, comparing employment in agriculture and contribution of this branch to gross domestic product.

TABLE 7.1[1,2]

	Agriculture as % of total employment (1950s)	Percentage contribution of agric. to GDP, 1960 or nearest year		Agriculture as % of total employment (1950s)	Percentage contribution of agric. to GDP, 1960 or nearest year
Haiti	83	(65)	Ecuador	53	37
Bolivia	72	(45)	Peru	(50)	25
Guatemala	68	32	Panama	50	24
Nicaragua	68	(45)	Jamaica	49	13
Honduras	66	44	Br. Guiana	46	25
El Salvador	63	36	Cuba	42	(30)
Brazil	58	27	Venezuela	41	6
Mexico	58	(25)	Chile	30	14
Dominican Rep.	56	(40)	Argentina	25	20
Costa Rica	55	37	Trinidad	25	13
Colombia	54	34	Puerto Rico	24	12
Paraguay	54	38	U.S.A.	12	4
			U.K.	4	4

( ) derived from other sources or estimated.

The contribution of agriculture to total gross domestic product varied from about two-thirds in Haiti to about 20 per cent in Argentina and only 6 per cent in Venezuela. Comparable figures for many African countries are near the level of Haiti, while the figures for the U.S.A. and U.K. are only around 4 per cent.

In view of the inefficient nature of employment in agriculture it is not surprising that throughout Latin America there is a discrepancy between the percentage of employed population engaged in agriculture and the percentage of the contribution made by agriculture to total gross domestic product (see Table 7.1). Which is the truer index of the importance of agriculture to any given country is debatable. Inefficiency of agricultural labour is almost a world-wide feature, but the figures suggest that agriculture is much more efficiently run in Argentina than, for example, in Venezuela and Jamaica, whose economies depend heavily on the extraction of minerals, an activity employing a small but very productive labour force.

One reason for the backwardness of agriculture in Latin America has been the failure to modernize it in the way that mining, manufacturing, and many service activities have been modernized. Figures show[3] that in most Latin American countries agriculture only receives a small share of total public investment, much less even than the share of its contribution to gross domestic product. Under these circumstances modernization and the expansion of production are likely to take place more slowly than in other branches of the economy, as has happened in the U.S.S.R. from about 1930 on.

The output of agricultural workers in Latin American countries is much lower than in the most advanced countries. The estimated output per adult male engaged in agriculture during 1956–60[4], after appropriate conversions and adjustments, shows that in relation to the productivity of Italian agricultural workers (Italy = 100) figures for selected Latin American countries were as follows: Argentina 91, Panama 54, Colombia 45, Venezuela 32, and Guatemala 21. At the other extreme the figures for the following countries were: U.S.A. 286, U.K. 231, Canada 199 and France 132. This inefficiency can be expressed in more concrete terms by showing, for example, how many days work is required (per worker) on average to produce 100 kilograms of maize in different countries[5]: U.S.A. 2, Argentina 5, Chile 30, Mexico 33, Colombia 47.

Turning to the use of land in Latin America, it is at first sight surprising to find that only about 5 per cent of the total area is used for the cultivation of field and tree crops, while another 17·5 per cent is classified as grazing, but this is mostly of very poor quality. Some 47·5 per cent of the total area is forest covered, though not all of this is of more than limited commercial use, and some 30 per cent is considered to be of no commercial use at all. In comparison approximately 10 per cent of both North America and the U.S.S.R. is used for the cultivation of field and tree crops. Table 7.2 shows that the proportion of arable land to total land varies greatly from region to region, with up to half of the land cultivated in some of the smaller Islands, compared with a mere 2 per cent in Brazil and even less than this in Peru and Bolivia. In almost every country the arable land is very unevenly spread over the total area, while in some countries, large areas of apparently suitable land remain untouched.

7.2. PHYSICAL CONDITIONS AFFECTING AGRICULTURE

In Chapter 3 the main physical features of Latin America were described in very general terms and conditions affecting agriculture were only briefly indicated. This section is intended to discuss physical features only in so

TABLE 7.2[6]†

	Total	Arable	Pasture	Forest	Non-agricultural
		Thousands of km² and percentages of total area of country (in italics)			
Mexico (1950)	1,969	199 *10·1*	752 *38*	388 *20*	630 *32*
Venezuela (1956)	912	25 *3*	178 *19*	190 *21*	492 *54*
Colombia (1960)	1,138	51 *4·5*	146 *13*	694 *61*	247 *21·5*
Peru (1961)	1,285	20 *1·5*	120 *9·5*	700 *54·5*	446 *34·5*
Bolivia (1950)	1,099	7 *0·6*	113 *10*	470 *43*	484 *44*
Brazil (1957)	8,514	191 *2*	1,076 *13*	5,179 *61*	1,724 *20*
Argentina (1957)	2,778	300 *11*	1,132 *41*	994 *36*	353 *13*
Chile (1956)	742	55* *7·5*	5 *1*	164 *22*	442 *57*
Latin America	20,540	1,070 *5*	3,790 *18·5*	9,750 *47·5*	5,930 *29*
North America	21,510	2,270 *10·5*	2,780 *13*	7,560 *35*	8,900 *41·5*

* Includes meadow.
† Discrepancies are due to rounding.

far as they may be expected to affect agriculture. By describing these features it is not implied that they are the only or even the main factors determining what is grown in different parts of Latin America. Commodity price fluctuations may also have a profound effect, as recently with coffee and sugar, while local traditions and prejudices still count as well.

Unlike the land masses in the northern hemisphere very little of Latin America has a growing season that is too short to permit cultivation of some sort. Only in the extreme south of the continent and in the highest parts of the mountain regions is arable farming impossible on account of low temperatures. On the other hand the growing season is not long enough for many crops to be cultivated in the southern part of South America, even at low altitudes, and the same is true within the tropics throughout the higher mountain regions. Further, frosts occur well within the tropics in certain places and exclude certain tropical crops or make their cultivation hazardous. This has been the case with coffee in Southeast Brazil. High temperatures also of course exclude the cultivation of most temperate crops within the lowlands of tropical Latin America.

Precipitation exerts a much wider influence on agriculture than features of temperature. In two large areas of Latin America agriculture is virtually impossible without irrigation (see *Figure 7.1*): much of the northern half of Mexico, and a belt of country extending along coastal Peru and northern Chile and crossing the Andes into western and southern Argentina. A third area, part of Northeast Brazil, also has a low rainfall, which is notoriously unreliable, while many smaller areas such as the northern part of the Maracaibo Lowlands in Venezuela and deep valleys in the Andes are dry. It could further be argued that excessive precipitation is one reason for the

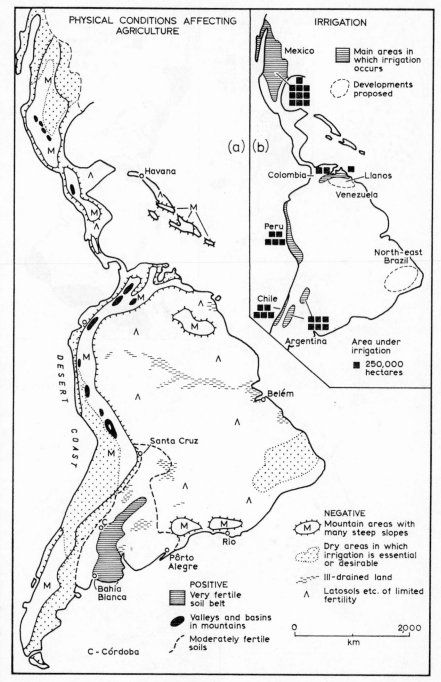

Figure 7.1. (a) Physical conditions affecting agriculture. Note: This map contains information already presented in Chapter 3. It is only suggestive and is to some extent controversial. (b) Irrigation

Outline of coast based on a map in the Oxford Atlas published by the Oxford University Press

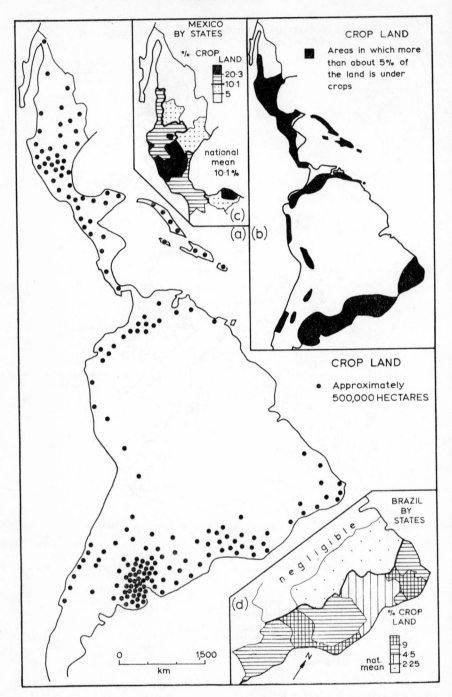

Figure 7.2. Distribution of crop-land in (a)(b) *Latin America,* (c) *in Mexico and* (d) *in Brazil*

Outline of coast based on a map in the Oxford Atlas published by the Oxford University Press

failure to extend cultivation in many of the forest areas of tropical Latin America.

Relief features, or rather slope, also make cultivation impossible, difficult or undesirable in many areas. These include much of Mexico, Central America and the Andean countries as well as all the Islands except Cuba, and considerable areas in Southeast Brazil. Steep slopes are frequently cultivated in Latin America but this may cause soil erosion and farming can never be fully mechanized. Lack of slope may also hinder cultivation, for large areas in the interior of South America in both the Amazon and Paraná basins are almost flat and at the present ill-drained. These areas include wide flood plains with potentially fertile land on which, however, cultivation is impossible without regulation of the rivers themselves.

Soils, which are of course largely a product of the other features of the physical environment, are on the whole of poor quality for agriculture in Latin America. In the mountain areas, good soils occur only over limited areas, notably on the floors of basins and valleys. In dry areas they are often thin and infertile. In the tropical forest they support a luxuriant vegetation yet are poor in plant nutrients. Once the vegetation cover is removed they may degenerate completely, or at best can be cultivated only for a few years and then have to be left perhaps some decades to recover.

For these reasons only a very small part of Latin America is suitable for cultivation without some negative feature to make conditions difficult. On the positive side the belt of chernozem and associated soils in Argentina is very fertile. The western fringe of this belt, however, suffers from low and somewhat unreliable precipitation. More widely in this same area, soils of moderate fertility are found in southern Brazil, in the interior of Argentina and in parts of Paraguay and Bolivia. Outside this general area (see *Figure 7.1*) the occurrence of good conditions for agriculture is the exception rather than the rule. This is not to say that the various oases, fertile flood plains, valley floors, volcanic soils and so on do not, in total, form an appreciable area.

One way in which the cultivated area has been greatly extended has been by the introduction of irrigation, and the possibilities of further expansion in this direction are great, though not without costly works of construction. At present about one third of the irrigated land in Latin America is in Mexico and another third in Chile and Peru. The following figures show the area of land under irrigation in thousands of hectares in 1957[7].

Mexico	2,504	Peru	1,212	Brazil	141
Argentina	1,500	Colombia	505	Dominican Rep.	135
Chile	1,363	Venezuela	246	Bolivia	64

In some areas there could be no cultivation without irrigation (e.g. coastal Peru, northern Chile) whereas in others (e.g. parts of Mexico, Venezuela) irrigation supplements a considerable but unreliable rainfall. Irrigation is almost entirely by gravity distribution, using water from rivers flowing from high mountain areas with a considerable rainfall across adjoining dry lowland areas. Irrigation is vital to the agricultural economy of several Latin American countries. In Peru 60 per cent of the arable land is irrigated, in Chile 40 per cent, in Venezuela nearly 20 per cent and in Mexico and Colombia about 10 per cent.

7.3. CROPS AND LIVESTOCK

Virtually every crop and every type of livestock can be found somewhere in Latin America but a surprisingly large number of crops, some of which would seem to be suited to the Latin American environment, at present

TABLE 7.3

E = export surplus B = own needs satisfied D = deficit O = little or none grown	Mexico	C. America	Venezuela— Col.—Ecuador	Peru—Bolivia	Islands	Brazil—Paraguay	Argentina—Uruguay	Chile
New World origin								
Maize	B	B	B	B	B	B	E	B
Cassava	O	O	B	O	O	B	O	O
Potatoes	O	O	B	B	O	O	B	B
Cacao	B	B	E	B	B	E	D	D
Tobacco	B	B	B	B	B	B	B	B
Sisal	E	O	O	O	E	O	O	O
Groundnut	B	O	O	O	B	B	B	O
Complex origin								
Cotton	E	E	B	E	B	E	B	D
Old World origin								
Sugar cane	E	B	B	E	E	E	E	D
Coffee	B	E	E	B	B	E	D	D
Wheat	B	B	D	D	D	D	E	B
Bananas	B	E	B	B	E	B	D	D
Rice	B	B	B	B	B	B	E	B
Livestock (all Old World)								
Cattle	B	B	B	B	B	B	E	B
Pigs	B	B	B	B	B	B	B	B
Sheep (wool)	B	B	D	E	D	D	E	E
Meat	B	B	B	B	D	B	E	B

More limited (*a*) New World: other tubers (Andes), other roots (forests), coconut palm (coasts), rubber tree in plantation, coca (Peru, Bolivia), yerba maté (South Brazil and Paraguay), sunflower (Argentina)

(*b*) Old World: linseed, oats, barley, rye (Argentina), millet and sorghum (Brazil), the vine (Chile, Argentina), olive trees, canary seed (Argentina), tea (Peru, Argentina), citrus fruits (Brazil), apples (Argentina)

Plants recently acquiring importance: oil palm (Colombia, Venezuela), pyrethrum, jute, soy beans (Brazil).

play only a very small part in the farming economy. This may to some extent be due to the failure of some Old World crops to be adopted in the New World. For this reason the main crops grown in Latin America are divided in Table 7.3 into those of New World origin and those of Old World origin. The oil palm, so widely grown in West Africa, has only very recently been introduced into comparable parts of Latin America. On the other hand, cane sugar and coffee have had a more distinguished history in recent centuries in Latin America than in the Old World where they originated. Some New World plants, including the rubber tree (*Hevea brasiliensis*) in plantations, have not been a success in their own environment. Similarly, of course, some New World crops such as the potato were an immediate success when introduced to parts of the Old World, whereas some others, such as maize, are not so widely grown as might have been expected (witness the 'discovery' of maize in the U.S.S.R. around 1955). The llama and alpaca are unknown in the Old World outside zoological gardens, yet might have proved useful in high parts of Asia.

In spite of intrusions of high land into the tropical parts of Latin America, complicating the distribution of tropical and non-tropical plants, the region may be divided into two main areas. The temperate south, including South Brazil, Uruguay, most of Argentina and Chile, together with land above about 2,000 m in Mexico and the Andean countries, is characterized by crops such as wheat and potatoes, and by sheep-raising, as well as by less important crops such as oats, barley, rye, vines and apples, excluded from the tropical lowlands of Latin America by unsuitable physical conditions. In contrast, cassava, sugar cane, cacao and bananas are confined to the tropical lowland areas. Some plants, notably maize, tobacco, cotton and rice, are not confined to one or other of the two main regions, but are grown almost everywhere except in the highest mountain regions and the extreme south of the continent, while cattle, pigs and poultry are also widely distributed. Certain plants (see examples in *Figure 7.3d*) are for reasons of suitability of physical conditions, or of local taste, confined to very limited parts of Latin America: for example, the vine, yerba maté, agaves and coca.

Some impression of the relative importance of different crops and types of livestock to the Latin American region may be judged from the contribution this region makes to total world production of each (see especially[8] Tables 10 A–B and others). Some of the figures are for Latin America's share of production in the non-Communist world only. It has 10 per cent of the population of this, and 7 per cent of total world population.

Coffee	77	Maize	11	Rice	3·5	Horses	36
Bananas	66	Oilseeds	8	Barley	2	Cattle	21
Cacao	27	Millet and		Oats	2	Pigs	14·5
Sugar	26	sorghum	5	Potatoes	2	Sheep	13
Cotton	20	Wheat	4	Rye	1·5	Goats	11
Pulses	11·5						

Latin America is clearly the major producer of coffee and bananas and also has a large surplus of cacao, sugar and cotton. It is roughly self-supporting in oilseeds, and in various basic food crops of regional rather than continental distribution such as bananas, cassava and potatoes. Maize hardly enters the foreign trade of any country except Argentina, being a basic food crop in most. Wheat is poorly represented in Latin America, but since bread made from this cereal is widely consumed in the region, most countries import some, the chief supplier now being the U.S.A., while only Argentina has a large surplus for export. In total, cereal farming is one of the less satisfactory branches of agriculture in Latin America and the region only accounts for 5 per cent of the world's total.

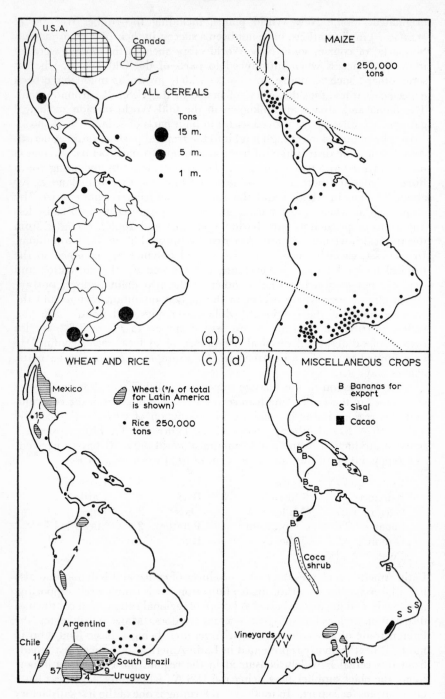

Figure 7.3. Cereals and miscellaneous crops in Latin America

Turning to livestock, Latin America, more than any other region, depends for traction purposes and transportation in difficult regions on horses, asses and particularly mules. In this respect it is at an intermediate level between the more highly mechanized countries of the world such as the U.S.A. and U.S.S.R. in which these animals are rapidly being reduced in numbers, and countries such as China and Japan, in which there is too little fodder, cultivated or natural, to keep many animals at all anyway. Latin America also has a large share of the world's cattle, but for the most part they are of poor quality, and make little contribution to the economy of the countries to which they belong, considering their numbers. Another major weakness of Latin American agriculture is the lack of development of dairying, except in a few areas. Even so, thanks to the large numbers of livestock including pigs and poultry, protein is generally more widely available than in African or Asian countries. The total *per caput* consumption of calories, too, is somewhat higher, but varies considerably from country to country[9].

Calories/day 1961/2			
U.S.A.	3,100	Paraguay	2,500
Argentina	2,930	Venezuela	2,490
Uruguay	2,900	Honduras	2,200
Brazil	2,710	Colombia	2,200
Mexico	2,550	Ecuador	2,110
Chile	2,530	Peru	2,030

7.4. FARMING ECONOMY AND MARKETING

Quite apart from the complicated regional differences in land tenure discussed in Chapter 5.3, agriculture in Latin America is characterized by virtually every major kind of farming economy. In forest lowlands of Amazonia and in a few small areas elsewhere, rural communities depend more on hunting, fishing and the gathering of wild plant products than on cultivation at all. Usually, however, a few crops are grown in these areas: cassava, maize, bananas, other root crops and fruits, all of which can be counted on to yield some food even when they receive little serious attention. Although goods from outside do penetrate these areas, most settlements are sufficiently isolated and independent still to be considered as having subsistence economies. In this way, several million people live virtually beyond the economic life of the countries they inhabit, for the perishable goods they could produce cannot be moved quickly by the inadequate river vessels and rafts in use. Even air routes so far still mainly serve towns and villages along rivers, or new areas of colonization (see *Figure 6.6*).

On the next level of rural economy, perhaps half of the agricultural population of Latin America practises an economy near subsistence but not entirely so[10]. Communities grow nearly all the food they consume and provide most of their own clothing and building materials, but achieve a surplus that can hardly be spared, to exchange for products from other regions. Usually the exchange is between rural areas on the one hand and, regional centres supplying services as well as manufactured and other goods from further afield on the other. Local and regional markets and fairs held at regular intervals are characteristic. Total turnover is small but the range of commodities can be very large. This kind of economy might be called subsistence on a regional level, or in small countries on a national level, intermediate between virtually complete subsistence already described and a proper market economy, characterized by the sale of most of production off the farms, and involving the world economy. A regional subsistence economy is to be found in southern Mexico and much of Central America, in the Andean area, some Islands, and the interior of Northeast Brazil.

The third kind of rural economy is also widespread in Latin America, commercial agriculture based on a market economy. In this kind of economy, a large part of the farm production, whatever the size of unit of land tenure, is sold off the farm, the typical procedure in North America and Western Europe. Commercial farming is practised widely in Argentina and Uruguay, much of Brazil, and northern Mexico, and elsewhere in Latin America in areas that are either close to the coast or have particularly favourable physical conditions. The special crops are grown either for consumption in large urban centres in the same country or for export. Though not necessarily associated with large holdings, many products grown commercially, especially sugar, are in fact grown in plantations. Bananas, cotton and coffee are often grown in plantations but are also grown for sale off the farm in moderate sized or even family sized holdings (e.g. coffee in Colombia, cotton in Haiti, bananas in Ecuador). Many commercial farming enterprises are or have been foreign owned and managed and have considerable capital investment. Commercial farms usually supply most of their own needs of food, whether by consuming part of their own commercial products (e.g. meat in Argentina) or by devoting some space to food crops, as on the sugar plantations of Northeast Brazil, where slaves were discouraged from acquiring a taste for sugar and lived mainly on manioc and maize. In some areas, plantations are accompanied by separate small farms catering for their needs. It goes without saying that the greater the proportion of produce sold off a farm, the more prosperous the farm will tend to be, though this does not necessarily mean that the people who work the land enjoy a higher standard of living, for the greater efficiency of farms in a commercial economy may lead only to the prosperity of a few large owners, whether individuals or companies.

The more agriculture in Latin America moves away from a subsistence level, the more it becomes essential to have efficient facilities for marketing: good means of transport, places for storage, and a satisfactory financial system; at present many farmers have to obtain loans before they harvest the crops they plan to sell to exist at all. Railways first began to break down subsistence agriculture in areas away from the old plantations, but these did not penetrate far in many areas. Now roads are carrying on the process, rapidly in some countries (e.g. Mexico, Venezuela, Southern Brazil), more gradually in poor and difficult areas (Central America, the Andes, Haiti). At present, however, very long hauls of perishable as well as other farm products have to be made because so much of the demand for farm surplus products is concentrated in a limited number of large and rapidly growing urban areas. Roads are often badly surfaced, journeys too long, the bodywork of lorries not properly constructed to carry perishable products, and costs very high. In some areas animal or even human transport still prevails. Nor are warehouse facilities often adequate. The impression is that at present the desire to sell products off the farm and to enter a commercial economy is greater than the ability to provide good marketing facilities and is therefore often frustrated. Again, both wholesale and retail trades are inefficient, and food products often badly prepared or overripe when eventually they reach the consumer.

7.5. BASIC FOOD CROPS

Lack of space prevents a full discussion of the climatic, soil and other physical conditions required by the various plants cultivated in Latin America; these have so often been dealt with in general texts on economic geography that it seems better here to discuss the areas in which different crops are actually grown. Table 7.4 shows the volume of different basic food crops grown in different Latin American countries or groups of countries. Bananas of course are grown in certain areas mainly for export, while maize and wheat are exported by Argentina. Otherwise the crops dealt with in this section are mainly consumed within the producing countries, often locally.

The root of the cassava plant (manioc) was the principal food in most areas of tropical forest lowland in South America in pre-Columbian times, but is virtually unknown in Mexico, Central America, the Islands or the South. In volume it is by far the largest crop grown in Brazil, but after processing it is greatly reduced. *Mandioca* is grown throughout the country, not least in Rio Grande do Sul. 1960 figures for Brazil for manioc, maize and wheat make an interesting comparison[11]

	Manioc	Maize	Wheat
Area (hectares)	1,342,000	6,681,000	1,141,000
Volume (tons)	17,613,000	8,672,000	713,000
Value ('000 cruz.)	23,700,000	49,075,000	11,721,000
Value per hectare ('000 cruz.)	18	7	11

The failure of manioc to attract attention in the New World outside its original area of cultivation is paralleled by the potato or rather by the various tubers, including many varieties of potato itself, grown in pre-Columbian America in the higher inhabited parts of the Andes. Just as manioc has been successful in Africa, the potato is widely grown in the Old World and also in southern South America, yet has made little impact on agriculture in Mexico and Guatemala, precisely where it might have been useful. As in the Andean countries, farmers prefer maize to the potato where the former will ripen, and most of the highland areas of Mexico and Guatemala are just low enough to allow this. Thus there are two main areas of potato cultivation in Latin America, the high Andes, especially of southern Peru and Bolivia, and the temperate South. Together, however, these only grow a mere 2 per cent of the world's potatoes.

AGRICULTURE

Sweet potatoes, yams and many similar plants are grown in Latin America, but largely for local consumption. Only in the Islands and parts of the tropical forest lowlands, are they of basic importance to the farming economy. Pulses* are also widely grown in Latin America but with the exception of dry (haricot) beans are less important relatively than in many parts of Asia. Again they are grown mainly for consumption on farms or for sale within regional markets.

TABLE 7.4

Basic food crops in millions of tons[12]

	Cassava	Potatoes	Sweet potatoes and yams	Dry beans	Bananas	Maize	Wheat	Rice
Mexico		0,3	0,1	0,6	0,3	5,6	1,4	0,4
C. America				0,1	2,0	1,2		0,2
Venezuela	0,5	0,1	0,1	0,1	1,0	0,4		0,1
Colombia	0,8	0,6			0,5	0,8	0,1	0,4
Ecuador	0,2	0,3			2,1	0,2	0,1	0,2
Peru	0,4	1,2	0,1			0,4	0,2	0,3
Bolivia	0,1	0,6				0,2		
Cuba	0,2	0,1	0,2			0,2		0,4
Other Islands and Guianas	0,2		0,4		1,3	0,2		0,2
Brazil and Paraguay	19,3	1,1	1,4	1,8	5,5	9,2	0,6	5,3
Argentina and Uruguay	0,2	1,2	0,4			5,4	5,5	0,2
Chile		0,7		0,1		0,2	1,1	0,1
Latin America	21,9	6,3	3,0	3,0	12,6	24,0	8,9	8,2
Latin America as % of the world total	29	2	3	31	66	11	4	3

In contrast to other fruits, bananas can provide a large volume of carbohydrate food and as such can be the basic food consumed at least in rural communities. They are, however, an unsatisfactory food as the sole item of diet, while their perishability makes them difficult to handle in a commercial economy. Moreover, while they are easy to plant and tend throughout the forested lowland areas of tropical Latin America and are therefore a great standby in more primitive communities, they are susceptible to disease, especially when grown in plantations, and are also easily damaged by wind if occupying large plantations without the protection of forest trees. There is a sharp distinction between the standard of cultivation of bananas grown for local consumption and those, grown mainly in Central America, Ecuador, certain Islands, and Brazil, destined for export. Control of diseases, assurance of presentable bunches of fruit, and efficient marketing facilities are essential for the latter. In practice there is considerable wastage between farm and port, and part of the crop intended for export may be lost or consumed locally. The conversion of overripe bananas to flour is a possible way of reducing the waste. Though they tend to be grown for export in large plantations, bananas may be grown commercially on medium and small farms, as particularly in Ecuador.

* Dry (haricot) beans, dry peas, dry broad beans, chickpeas and lentils[13].

Of the cereals cultivated in Latin America, the only cultivated New World cereal, maize, is the most important by far (see Table 7.4). Even so, Latin America was only able in 1961–62 to produce about one quarter as much as North America (23 m. and 94 m. tons respectively). In contrast to the potato, maize was known and cultivated almost throughout those parts of pre-Columbian America in which arable farming was practised, and today it is still represented throughout the region. It is however clearly favoured in certain areas rather than others, particularly central Mexico and Guatemala, southern Brazil, and the more humid parts of the Argentine pampa. Everywhere except Argentina it is grown more as a crop for human consumption than as animal fodder. Being the traditional food crop of so many areas it is understandably still grown where physical conditions are unsatisfactory. This, together with lack of attention to the quality of seed and failure to apply fertilizers, makes yields very low in most of the region:

Yield in 100 kg/hectare, *1961–62*[16]

North America	39	Canada	46	Brazil	13
Europe	20	U.S.A.	39	Colombia	11
Latin America	12	Chile	20	Mexico	9
Africa	10	Argentina	19	Guatemala	8

Yields are still particularly disappointing in Mexico, where the yields of wheat, cotton and other crops have been increased greatly in the 1950s. In fact, in Latin America as a whole, there has been little improvement since the war. Contrast 1,060 kg/hectare in 1948/49–1952/53 and around 1,200 kg/hectare in the early 1960s in Latin America with an increase in North America from 2,490 to 3,900 in the same period, a clear case of the advanced economy drawing ahead while the underdeveloped one stagnates. With a *diminution* in the area under maize cultivation in North America from about 30 m. to about 24 m. hectares, an *increase* in production of 18 m. tons was achieved!

In spite of the relatively unfavourable conditions of maize cultivation, the area under maize in Latin America has been extended in the 1950s from about 14 m. hectares to over 20 m. and output has risen in all the major producing countries except Colombia over this period, steadily in most, but unevenly in Argentina, as the following figures show[15]

	Thousands of tons			
	Mexico	*Argentina*	*Brazil*	*Colombia*
Average 1948–52	3,090	2,509	5,916	733
53	3,720	4,450	6,789	890
54	4,480	2,546	6,690	850
55	4,490	3,870	6,999	770
56	4,382	2,698	7,763	790
57	4,500	4,806	7,370	746
58	5,277	4,932	7,787	851
59	5,563	4,108	8,672	701
60	5,200	4,850	8,999	864
61	5,561	5,220	9,000	737
62	6,015	4,360	n.a.	762

Clearly Latin American agriculture would benefit greatly from a drive to improve standards of maize cultivation, for even if this cereal is not ideal as a basic item of diet it could form the basis for necessary improvements in livestock farming, as it is doing in the U.S.S.R. (production around 1950 6 m. tons p.a., 1961/62 24 m. tons).

Although an Old World plant, wheat was considered so desirable as an item of diet by the Spaniards that its cultivation was introduced in the Americas as widely as possible. Unlike maize, of course, it is precluded from the tropical lowlands of Latin America, but was grown in colonial times in the higher parts of Mexico, Central America and the Andes and in Central Chile and later in southern Brazil and Argentina. The amount grown in the Andes is very limited and almost all the wheat produced in Latin America is in fact grown outside the tropics. In contrast to maize yields, wheat yields in Latin America are hardly below those in North America and compare with those in Australia; they are however well below West European wheat yields. In spite of having wheat yields roughly equal to those for the world as a whole and maize yields only about half as high, there has not been an increase in the postwar period either in the area under wheat or in the amount produced. The area has remained at $7\frac{1}{2}$–8 m. hectares and production 8–9 m. tons/year. Compare the following figures[16] for wheat production in thousands of tons:

	Average 1948/49–1952/53	1961/62
Argentina	5,175	5,100
Uruguay	469	375
Chile	942	1,063
Brazil	498	545
Mexico	534	1,373

Only Mexico has made progress in improving wheat cultivation in the 1950s, increasing yields from 880 kg/hectare around 1950 to 1,680 in 1961/62. Yields in Brazil are depressingly low (530 kg/hectare in 1961/62) and poor also in Uruguay, which recently has had to import some.

The third major cereal cultivated in Latin America, rice (understand where necessary paddy), is also an Old World crop, but rice has come to Latin America much more recently than wheat, its adoption being largely connected with the arrival of settlers from Asia in the modern period, but it seems likely to overtake wheat very shortly. Both the area under rice cultivation, and rice production, have roughly doubled in the postwar period. Brazil is the leading rice growing country and in 1960 the four states of Minas Gerais (940,000 tons), São Paulo (920), Rio Grande do Sul (890) and Goiás (720) accounted for over 70 per cent of Brazilian production. The Northeast is too dry and grows little rice except in the state of Maranhão. Rice is grown elsewhere in Latin America, but even so the region only accounts for 3 per cent of the world total. It is essentially a crop of the lowland areas with humid tropical or sub-tropical conditions, but is becoming the main cereal in several areas, including coastal Peru and Ecuador, and Cuba, as well as parts of Brazil. Yields are somewhat lower in Latin America than in the world as a whole.

Other cereals are also grown in Latin America but are more localized in distribution and make a more modest contribution to the total economy of the region. The other cereals are grown mainly in Argentina, but appear also in Mexico and the Andes, as well as in southern Brazil. The following table[17] summarizes cereal cultivation in 1960/61

	Area (thousand hectares)	Production (thousand tons)	Production of Argentina	% Share of Argentina
Maize	20,280	23,990	5,220	22
Wheat	7,820	8,910	5,100	57
Rice	4,480	8,240	182	2
Millet and sorghum	1,450	2,320	1,857	80
Barley	1,540	1,580	800	51
Oats	900	970	700	72
Rye	740	540	510	94
Total	37,210	46,550	14,369	31

Clearly cereal cultivation in Latin America is very weakly developed compared with other parts of the world if the contribution of Argentina is excluded. The extension of both maize and rice cultivation and improvement in their yields seems to be the key to future progress. The general shortage of arable land outside Argentina has already been stressed and seems to be behind the failure to produce more cereals. Cereals have by nature a low value of production per unit of area, though maize and rice are more valuable than the others.

7.6. INDUSTRIAL AND OTHER CROPS

In addition to the basic food crops discussed in the previous section, a very large number of plants are grown for export or for more specialized uses within home markets. Many, however, only occupy a small area and are confined to certain parts of the region. The distribution of the main crops is summarized in Table 7.5 and illustrated in *Figure 7.4.*

TABLE 7.5[12]

	Millions of tons			Thousands of tons			
	Sugar (raw)	Groundnuts	Cottonseed	Coffee	Cacao	Tobacco	Cotton lint
Mexico	1,6	0,1	0,8	141	14	74	436
C. America	0,3		0,2	316	12	9	148
Venezuela	0,2			48	12	10	8
Colombia	0,4		0,2	468	17	28	77
Ecuador	0,1			48	44	1	4
Peru	0,8		0,2	45	5	2	134
Bolivia	0,5				2	1	
Cuba	4,8			48	2	47	
Other islands and Guianas	3,5	0,1		93	46	16	
Brazil and Parag.	3,6	0,6	1,2	2,085	168	179	606
Arg. and Uruguay	0,7	0,4	0,2			41	110
Chile	0,1 (beet)					7	
Latin America	16,0	1,2	2,8	3,293	1,180	450	1,540
LAM % of World	n.a.	8·5	13·5	77	27	12	14

143

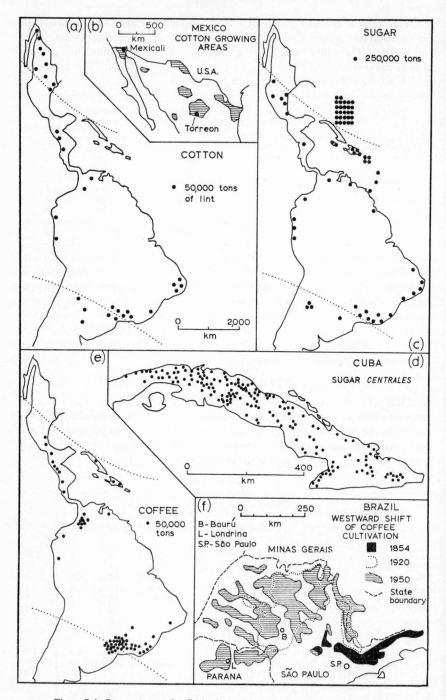

Figure 7.4. Cotton, sugar and coffee in Latin America.   Source for maps(d)[18](f)[19]

If the cultivation of sugar in the New World suffered a setback in the nineteenth century as a result of the expansion of beet sugar cultivation in Europe it has recovered with the growth of a nearby market, that of the U.S.A. This country produces both beet and cane sugar itself, but the proximity of the Caribbean area to U.S. markets and the lower production costs here have enabled Cuba and Puerto Rico in particular to build up a large sugar trade under special tariff arrangements in the present century. Like maize, cotton and tobacco, cane sugar is grown in almost every Latin American country, only Chile resorting to beet sugar. Moreover, it is usually grown for regional if not international markets rather than for consumption on farms. It is cultivated mainly in humid, tropical, lowland areas, especially the Caribbean Islands and mainland coasts and Northeast Brazil, but under irrigation in Peru and Argentina. Though cultivable annually in areas affected by frost (e.g. Louisiana, U.S.A.), it is more usefully cultivated in frost free areas and therefore is virtually absent in sub-tropical South America.

The cultivation of cane sugar has caused many economic and social problems in Latin America. It requires a large labour force per unit of area and was one of the main types of cultivation using slave labour. It also requires considerable capital, and can most economically be grown as a near monoculture with land under cane as near as possible to the processing factories (*centrales*), since the cane has to be processed within a very short time of cutting. The crop exhausts the land easily; although only a small part of the cane that is cut actually becomes sugar, the rest is not necessarily returned to the soil and may even be used as a raw material for industry; a large application of fertilizer is therefore desirable. Although labour is needed in large quantities this may be only seasonally; hitherto agricultural labour has been idle and in some circumstances unpaid for much of the year. Given the high degree of capitalization needed to make production efficient and the great interest of the U.S.A. in Latin American sugar it is not surprising that much of the cane is grown in foreign plantations, mainly U.S. owned. This is another reason for discontent, especially as the expansion of these has resulted in their encroachment on food producing lands. The situation was of course most explosive in Cuba, and is unsatisfactory in several other areas. In Brazil and Mexico on the other hand there is little foreign influence.

Of the sugar produced in Latin America, about half enters world trade, but whereas most of the Islands sell nearly all their output, the mainland countries have little surplus for export with the exception of Peru, British Guiana and Brazil. The progress of the Cuban sugar industry since 1958 will be dealt with under Cuba (Chapter 15.4). The figures in Table 7.6 show the distribution of raw sugar production in 1961/62 in greater detail than in Table 7.5[20] and also exports in 1961[21] in thousands of tons.

Within the larger countries sugar cane cultivation is limited to certain parts of the national area. In Argentina it is cultivated in the extreme northwest (Tucumán), in Peru in the northern coastal lowlands, in Mexico mainly along the Gulf coast, and in Colombia in the Cauca valley. Brazil has two main areas, the traditional northeast coast, and the newer inland areas of the southeast. Table 7.7 shows how raw sugar production has risen appreciably in the postwar period especially in mainland countries.

TABLE 7.6

	Islands			Mainland	
	Production	Exports		Production	Exports
Cuba	4,815	6,420	Brazil	3,615	783
Dominican Rep.	950	745	Mexico	1,548	570
Puerto Rico	915	890	Peru	810	545
Jamaica	441	386	Argentina	694	197
Trinidad	204	220	Colombia	400	46
Other British Is.	230	190	Br. Guiana	331	318
French	255	235	Central America	324	X
Haiti	58	X	Venezuela	258	X

X negligible.

TABLE 7.7[22,23]

	Cuba	Dominican Republic	Puerto Rico	Mexico	Peru	Brazil	Argentina
1948	6,055	421	1,005	666	498	1,750	565
1953	5,159	552	1,072	868	602	2,002	764
1954	4,890	658	1,092	894	612	2,118	845
1955	4,528	637	1,057	961	652	2,073	635
1956	4,740	780	1,045	823	690	2,268	800
1957	5,672	836	898	1,164	677	2,714	722
1958	5,784	838	856	1,210	681	3,004	1,114
1959	5,964	809	979	1,448	705	3,108	979
1960	5,862	1,112	933	1,518	807	3,319	859
1961	6,767	873	1,001	1,488	799	3,354	701
1962	4,815	902	913	1,531	765	3,238	799

The decline of Cuban production since 1961 and its economic isolation have indeed stimulated production in other Latin American countries. This may partly be the reason for the ambitious project in Colombia to achieve an exportable surplus of sugar of 3,200,000 tons by 1970 with mechanized cultivation of some 450,000 hectares in the Cauca valley[24].

Oilseeds* are cultivated in Latin America mainly for home consumption and are the principal source of cooking fat in many areas, being especially important in view of the lack of animal fat and of a proper dairying industry. Although the groundnut is a New World crop it is not grown as widely as might be expected. Latin America does however now produce more than the U.S.A., which it overtook in the late 1950s, and production has risen from 370,000 tons per year around 1950 to over 1 m. in 1961/62, the greatest expansion being in Brazil and Argentina. Cottonseed production in Latin America has also risen impressively since the Second World War (1,570,000 tons around 1950, 2,800,000 in 1961/62) with only Argentinian production stagnating:

	Cottonseed production	
	1948/49–1952/53 average	1961/62 average
Brazil	749	1,152
Mexico	384	766
Peru	121	221
Central America	33	171
Colombia	19	153

* Soybeans, groundnuts, cottonseed, linseed, rapeseed, sesame, and sunflower seed[25].

Linseed is less important than most other oils in the world as a whole, but Argentina is the leading producer, and Latin America accounts for nearly 33 per cent of the world's total, 990,000 tons out of 3 m. in 1961/62, with Argentina and Uruguay accounting for 920,000. Yields in these countries fluctuate greatly from year to year. As yet soybeans make only a small contribution to agriculture in Latin America and the region only accounts for about 1 per cent of the world total but production in Brazil has increased greatly in the 1950s (80,000 tons per year around 1950 to 280,000 in 1961/62) and the plant is being recommended in southern Brazil to farmers who are reducing their coffee plantations. Another moderately important source of oil, the sunflower, is confined largely to Argentina and Uruguay, which together (1961/62) account for 13·5 per cent of the world total, or 920,000 tons.

Other sources of oil, notably palm kernels, olives, rapeseed, sesame seed and copra are very limited in distribution and volume of production. Mexico is the chief producer (1961/62) of sesame seed (140,000 tons) and copra (180,000) and Brazil of palm kernels (120,000).

A very large number of tropical fruits* are grown in Latin America for local consumption but usually little care is taken over their cultivation. This is not so with bananas, already mentioned, and also pineapples, which are grown both for home consumption and for export. Latin America accounts for 23 per cent of the world total of pineapples, producing 640,000 tons in 1961/62 (Brazil 270,000 and Mexico 200,000).

Many sub-tropical and temperate fruits are grown widely in southern South America, but few are grown for export except to neighbouring Latin American countries. For example, Chile and Ecuador exchange apples and bananas. Apples and pears are cultivated mainly in Argentina, Chile and southern Brazil, but plums and cherries are hardly known. The vine is cultivated in this same region, with Argentina accounting for about two thirds of both the table grapes and wine grapes. Citrus fruits are grown throughout Latin America but in spite of a strong position in foreign trade some time ago not even Brazil now exports many oranges.

More than any other major crop in Latin America, coffee is cultivated for export, though much is also consumed at home. But in 1961/62, out of 3,290,000 tons of coffee produced in Latin America, about 1,800,000 tons were exported. While coffee prefers certain physical conditions within the tropical environment and high grades appear to prefer sloping ground at certain altitudes, there is enough space in the region to grow far more if there were a demand. The country by country distribution of coffee production in tropical Latin America can therefore no longer be explained by physical conditions but rather by the export quota allowed under international coffee agreements; of course there is no restriction on production for home consumption. Within countries, on the other hand, coffee cultivation occurs in clearly defined and highly localized areas.

The following figures show the quotas allowed to the main producing countries of the world. The total export quota for October 1963—September 1964 inclusive was 45,7 m. bags of 60 kg.

* e.g. mango, pawpaw, chirimoyo, avocado pear, all of which are too inconvenient to export in bulk.

TABLE 7.8

Latin America				Other areas	
Brazil	17,8	Peru	0,6	Former French Africa	4,3
Colombia	6,0	Ecuador	0,5	Uganda-Kenya	2,4
Mexico	1,5	Dominican R.	0,5	Portuguese Africa	2,2
El Salvador	1,4	Haiti	0,5	Ethiopia	1,0
Guatemala	1,3	Venezuela	0,5	Congo (Leopoldville)	0,9
Costa Rica	0,9			Indonesia	1,2

Thus Brazil was allowed roughly 39 per cent of total exports, Colombia 13 per cent and Central America 8 per cent, 60 per cent between them. These areas have been producing appreciably more than could be absorbed by combined home and export markets, in spite of the expansion of world coffee consumption since the war. Table 7.9 shows coffee production by countries or groups of countries in 1961/62. The distribution of production within countries will be dealt with in regional sections (see *Figures 10.2* and *13.1*). Here the changing position of coffee in the Latin American economy must be stressed. In Central America and Colombia the high quality of the coffee produced would seem to ensure that drastic changes are not necessary, but in both regions dependence on coffee as a major item of export is being diminished as cotton lint and cottonseed cultivation expands in Central America and sugar cultivation is encouraged in Colombia. In Brazil, on the other hand, it was planned in 1962[26] to destroy 2,000 m. out of Brazil's 4,300 m. coffee trees*. Between mid-1962 and mid-1963 450 m. were destroyed, freeing over 500,000 hectares, which were replanted to pasture (40 per cent), maize (25 per cent), rice, beans, cotton and other crops. The frosts of 1963 continued the devastation and in that year 70–80 per cent of the coffee trees in north Paraná were destroyed (650 m.); coffee production in Paraná state dropped from 18 m. to 3 m. bags. As a result, Brazilian stocks of coffee, stored at great expense, will have diminished between 1962 and 1965 from some 25 m. bags to almost nothing. The contribution of Brazil to the total coffee exports of the world has also diminished as follows:

$$
\left. \begin{array}{ll} 1959 & 41 \cdot 6 \\ 1960 & 39 \cdot 5 \\ 1961 & 38 \cdot 4 \\ 1962 & 35 \cdot 0 \end{array} \right\} \text{per cent}
$$

and in spite of its quota of 39 per cent for 1963/64 Brazil seems likely to supply appreciably less than this. Brazilian dependence on coffee is thus being reduced almost in a suicidal way, and such a swift end to the pre-dominance of coffee in its economy could not have been foreseen a few years ago, but figures of increased output in Table 7.9 suggest that expansion was excessive in the 1950s.

Latest figures confirm the decline of Brazilian coffee. In 1963, 19,7 m. bags were exported (value U.S. $ 748 m.), in 1964 only 14,9 m. bags (value U.S. $ 757 m.).

* Under the Grupo Executivo de Racionalisaçao da Cafeicultura.

TABLE 7.9[27]

	Coffee production in thousands of metric tons					
	Brazil	Colombia	Mexico	El Salvador	Guatemala	Costa Rica
1948–52	1,077	359	70	75	58	23
1953	1,111	403	85	60	61	23
1954	1,037	377	93	77	65	35
1955	1,370	335	88	73	69	24
1956	979	365	97	91	74	34
1957	1,409	468	122	84	81	46
1958	1,696	462	97	93	84	51
1959	2,629	480	98	98	96	54
1960	1,797	462	124	94	99	70
1961	2,085	468	123	123	104	66
1962	1,560	462	127	97	105	69

Coffee exports in 1961[28] in thousands of metric tons were as follows

Brazil	1,018	El Salvador	87	Peru	34
Colombia	339	Guatemala	79	Venezuela	25
Mexico	89	Costa Rica	52	Ecuador	23
		Haiti, Nicaragua, Dominican Republic each about 20			

Up to a point the production of cocoa beans has a history like that of coffee, this time with diseases rather than climatic disasters affecting fortunes. But in contrast to coffee, the cultivation of cacao has been dominated for some decades by Africa, and it is here, not in Latin America, that spectacular advances have been made since the Second World War. The leading producing countries in 1961/62[29] were (thousands of tons):

Africa		Latin America	
Ghana	415	Brazil	156
Nigeria	202	Ecuador	44
Ivory Coast	81	Dominican	
Cameroun	70	Republic	33

Compare the increase from 500,000 tons to 825,000 tons in Africa between 1950 and the early 1960s with 255,000 to 310,000 in Latin America. Many other countries in Latin America not listed above produce cocoa beans, but mainly for home consumption. In Ecuador bananas have superseded cacao as the leading export crop, while in Brazil inadequate marketing facilities in Ilhéus are hampering the industry.

Of other non-alcoholic beverages, Latin America produces very little tea, while yerba maté is grown only in one main area and is consumed mainly there, notably southern Brazil and Paraguay. Alcoholic beverages are manufactured from various plants. Sugar cane is the base of a great many, and is widely cultivated in small quantities, to be made into rum and other drinks; maize, too, is widely used. In Mexico the agave (maguey) is the origin of a particularly strong beverage, pulque. The coca shrub, cultivated on the eastern slopes of the Andes of Peru and Bolivia is a more sinister

TYPICAL HOUSE
OF THE TROPICAL
RAIN FOREST,
IQUITOS, PERU

ADOBE AND
THATCH HOUSE,
COMMON IN
SUB-HUMID
AREAS

OLD AND NEW
HOUSES WITH
ADOBE WALLS,
NEAR LAKE
TITICACA,
BOLIVIA

HOUSING IN
A COTTON
PLANTATION,
ARID ZONE
OF PERU

P. COLE

150

OLD AND NEW
RURAL
DWELLINGS,
VENEZUELA

TIMBER HOUSE,
PINE FOREST
AREA, SOUTH-
ERN BRAZIL

COFFEE
PLANTATION
OWNER'S
HOUSE,
SAÕ PAULO
STATE, BRAZIL

plant, its leaves being chewed as a stimulant in the high areas of the Andes and the drug cocaine is derived from them.

Although a New World plant, tobacco, does not have a prominent role in Latin American foreign trade. It is grown virtually in every part of Latin America, though in limited quantities in some areas, such as the Andes, where its consumption appears to be very limited. In many countries the tobacco industry is a state monopoly, and policy is to achieve near self-sufficiency. Brazil, Cuba and the Dominican Republic are the only major exporters but their combined exports (1961/62), about 90,000 tons, were only about equal to those of the Rhodesias and Nyasaland; Cuba specializes in the preparation of high grade products.

Cotton is cultivated for its lint (fibre) widely in Latin America, even in some places outside the tropics. More than most crops in the region it is found in drier areas, the inadequate rainfall being supplemented by irrigation. Indeed, the highest grades of cotton are grown in desert areas,

Cotton production in thousands of tons						
	Brazil	Mexico	C. America	Argentina	Peru	Colombia
1948–52	395	220	18	118	76	10
1955	428	491	76	122	109	23
1960	536	437	96	124	130	67
1961	606	447	154	118	134	78
1962	n.a.	512	191	132	152	81

and very little is now grown in the humid lowlands of the tropics, virtually none coming from the Islands. Cotton has been grown in Latin America both for export and to supply home industry, cotton spinning and weaving being one of the earliest and most convenient branches of modern industry to establish. Peru has for some decades produced high grade cotton, and Mexican cotton, grown under only somewhat less arid conditions, is of similarly high quality. The rise of cotton growing in northern Mexico may be regarded as part of the shift in cotton cultivation from the humid south-east of the U.S.A. to drier southwestern states, especially California. In Brazil there are two separate main areas, the dry interior of the Northeast and the more humid lands of the south. Cultivation is increasing particularly in Colombia and Central America[30].

Unlike sugar which is mostly plantation grown, cotton can be cultivated on small farms if harvested by hand, and the whole procedure is more casual than the sugar industry and less liable to over-production than coffee. Even so, the manufacture of cotton textiles is not likely to increase fast in the world as a whole and unless Latin America can concentrate on high grade varieties, dependence on cotton cannot be considered a sound alternative to dependence on sugar or coffee.

While cotton is by far the most widely grown textile fibre in Latin America, the region accounts for an even greater share, nearly half, of the world production of certain hard fibres*, Agave species. Sisal is the main

* Listed[31] are sisal (Agave sisalana); henequen (Agave fourcroydes); cantala (Agave cantala); lecheguilla (Agave lecheguilla); Mexican henequen (Agave lurida); letona (Agave letona).

variety produced and is grown in Northeast Brazil (170,000 tons), Mexico (156,000 tons)[32], Haiti (23,000) and Venezuela, while henequen is grown in Cuba.

The cultivation of jute in Latin America is very limited, and only Brazil has made serious attempts to cultivate this plant (48,000 tons in 1961/62 was less than 2 per cent of the world's total). Attempts to grow in plantations the rubber tree (Hevea brasiliensis), a native of Amazonia, have not yet passed the experimental stage, but small quantities of wild rubber are gathered, Latin America accounting for 1 per cent of the world's natural rubber. Flax and hemp are grown only in negligible quantities.

A great many other plants of economic importance grow wild or are cultivated in Latin America, but few are of more than local importance at present. In Brazil a number of trees yield products of some interest. The Brazil nut, gathered from wild trees (Bertholletia excelsa) is rich in oil and protein and would seem to offer an excellent source of food if grown in plantations, but the unwieldy size of the tree would make this difficult. The carnauba, babaçu, and other Brazilian species are discussed in Chapter 16.5.

7.7. LIVESTOCK FARMING

With only 7 per cent of the total population of the world, Latin America has at first sight a surprisingly high proportion of all kinds of livestock (see Table 7.10), not least horses, mules and asses. But the figures are flattering, for outside Argentina and Uruguay the productivity of animals is generally very low. The large number of horses, mules, asses and draught cattle merely underlines the lack of mechanization in farming and the lack of motor vehicles and presence of difficult conditions and great distances in transportation. Large herds of poor quality cattle roam the intermediate lands in South America between the continuous forest of Amazonia and the more densely peopled coastal regions. They belong most characteristically to the savanna lands. On a smaller scale, the same situation occurs in the Islands, in Mexico and in Central America. These animals are kept for their hides and meat rather than for dairy products. Little attempt has been made until recently either to improve pastures for them or to breed good herds, but more enterprising farmers have made improvements and zebu (Brahman) cattle have been widely introduced in places. Even so, it is often impossible to move products from these remote ranches except by air. Although the number of dairy cows is not known or distinguished in most Latin American countries many attempts have been made to improve dairying, especially in the vicinity of larger towns or in areas that have particularly favourable pastures (e.g. around Mexico City, in the lowlands of Maracaibo).

The most advanced cattle raising area is however the pampa of Argentina, together with Uruguay and southern Brazil. Here the emphasis is still on meat production rather than on dairying, and essentially meat production for export, though a growing proportion is being consumed at home. Since the land is reasonably if not very fertile, no serious attempt has been made to improve pastures in the way that has been done in Australia and New Zealand since the war. Beef and veal production has remained around two

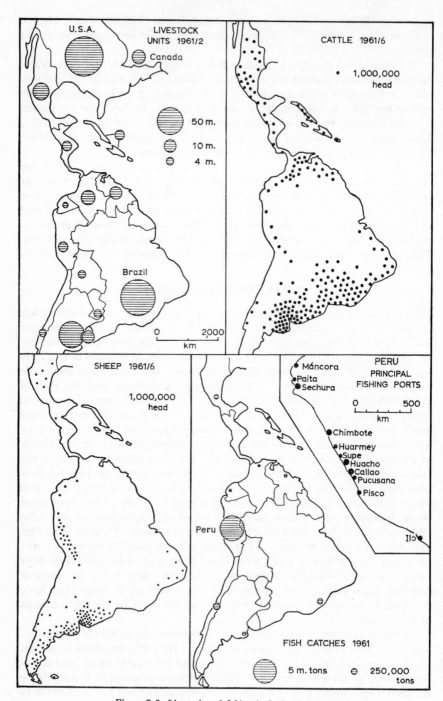

Figure 7.5. Livestock and fishing in Latin America

LIVESTOCK FARMING

TABLE 7.10

Livestock Totals and Fish Catch
Yearly Average 1961/62

	Cattle	Pigs	Sheep	Goats	Wool thousand quintals	Fish catch thousand tons
			Millions			
Mexico	21,1	9,4	5,7	10,7	36	191
C. America	6,4	1,8	1,2	0,1	negl.	negl.
Venezuela	9,2	2,4	negl.	0,9	negl.	85
Colombia	15,4	1,5	1,1	0,2	8	48
Ecuador	1,5	1,1	1,7	0,1	negl.	60
Peru	3,8	1,6	16,0	3,8	50	5,243
Bolivia	2,4	0,6	7,2	1,2	22	negl.
Cuba	5,0	1,4	0,2	0,2	negl.	31
Other islands and Guianas	2,7	3,0	negl.	2,3	negl.	negl.
Brazil and Paraguay	78,7	48,5	18,2	12,0	155	257
Argentina and Uruguay*	51,9	3,7	71,0	4,5	1,555†	100
Chile	3,0	1,0	6,3	1,3	111	430
Latin America	196,9	76,3	128,0	38,7	1,950	
Latin America as % of World	21	14	13	11	13	

* Includes Falkland Islands (0,6).
† Argentina 1,037, Uruguay 503, Falkland Islands 15.

million tons per year in Argentina and one quarter million in Uruguay since 1950 whereas it has risen in a spectacular fashion even in such countries as West Germany, the U.K. and Italy. Altogether Latin America produced 5,510,000 tons of beef and veal, 19 per cent of the world total in 1961/62, but nearly half came from Argentina and Uruguay. The production of hides and skins is difficult to assess and compare, but Latin America is a major exporting region of these.

Pigs and poultry are raised throughout Latin America but records of their numbers must be very approximate. They are not usually raised on modern lines in special farms but are rather an essential but neglected feature on farms of all kinds. Considering the number of pigs kept, the estimated amount of pork produced seems disappointing. The 55 m. pigs in the U.S.A. produced over 5 m. tons of pigmeat, the 75 m. in Latin America a little over 1 m. tons. Such an inferior position in Latin America is not only the result of less favourable physical conditions but also of greatly inferior farming practices.

Sheep raising is run on more efficient lines than most other branches of livestock farming. Wool is not in great demand in tropical Latin America except in the highlands of Mexico and the Andes; these areas have considerable flocks. However, the main sheep pastures are on the drier fringes of the

	Sheep in millions	Wool produced in thousands of quintals	Quintals per 1,000 sheep
Australia	152,7	4,395	28,7
New Zealand	48,5	1,900	39,2
Argentina	49,0	1,037	21,2
Uruguay	21,2	503	23,8

Argentinian pampa, in Uruguay, and still further south in Patagonia, Tierra del Fuego and the Falkland Islands (see Table 7.10). Flocks depend largely on little improved natural pastures, and the preoccupation with improvement (new fodder grasses, trace elements, elimination of pests) found in Australia and New Zealand is again not to be found. Comparative sheep and wool figures[33] (1961/62) show that in spite of its generally more favourable environment, Argentina lags behind Australia. Nor (1961/62) do Argentina and Uruguay compare with Australia and New Zealand in the production of mutton and lamb (about 250,000 tons compared with nearly 1 m.). Goats are also raised in considerable numbers in certain parts of Latin America. They replace sheep in tropical lowland areas and are particularly numerous in dry areas such as Northeast Brazil and parts of Peru and Mexico, but in view of the damage they do to vegetation, their position is under review in several countries.

7.8. YIELDS, FERTILIZERS AND MECHANIZATION

As already stressed, Latin America is extremely diverse, both physically and in levels of economic development, and for this reason it is unrealistic to take yields in the region as a whole as more than a very rough guide to efficiency of agriculture. Nor is it fair to infer too much from a comparison of yields in Latin America with those in other large regions of the world, since none combines tropical and temperate farming in the same proportions. With these reservations in mind, the following comparisons[8] are shown merely to underline the general proximity of Latin America to world levels and the great disparity in yields (in 100 kg/hectare) of key cereal crops between Latin America and the most advanced farming regions.

	World	Europe	North America	Latin America	Africa
Wheat	11·7	18·7	13·3	11·4	4·6
Maize	20·8	20·4	39·0	11·8	9·9
Rice	20·3	48·2	38·4	18·4	11·8
Cotton	3·1	3·4	4·9	2·9	0·9

The following summary table[12] seems the best way of showing differences in yields among different Latin American countries. Differences also occur of course within countries, from one part to another. Latin America as a whole has far to go to achieve yields as high as those in the most advanced farming economies: the wheat yields of Europe, the rice yields of Japan, the maize yields of North America. The potato lags farthest behind: compare the yield of 25,000 kg/hectare in Ireland with 3,400 in Bolivia. Again, cotton lint and cotton seed yields, though high in Mexico, Central America and Peru, are low in most of South America and the Islands. Without satisfactory figures it is not possible to assess yields of livestock industries, but it seems safe to assume that they are far lower than in Western Europe or North America, though there are local and even regional exceptions to this, and the meat industry of Argentina and Uruguay has not lost its high reputation in spite of lack of progress since the 1930s.

TABLE 7.11[12]

100 kg/hectare

	Wheat	Rice	Maize	Potatoes	Cotton (lint)
Latin America	11	18	12	58	2·9
Mexico	17	26	9	62	5·5
Guatemala	7	14	8	32	10·8*
Venezuela	†	14	11	79	1·7
Colombia	9	17	11	48	4·8
Ecuador	10	17	7	92	1·7
Peru	10	44	15	53	5·5
Cuba	†	19	11	140	†
Haiti	†	10	8	†	1·0
Brazil	5	18	13	55	1·9
Uruguay	9	35	6	†	†
Argentina	12	34	19	82	2·0
Chile	13	28	20	75	†
U.S.A.	16	38	39	220	4·9
U.S.S.R.	11	†	19	95	6·5
Canada	8	†	46	162	†
Japan	†	47	27	177	†

* El Salvador.
† Little or none grown.

Altogether, however, there is great scope for increasing yields in existing farming areas in Latin America.

The application of fertilizers in agriculture has been limited in scale and local in area until recently. Some Chilean nitrate and in recent decades virtually all Peruvian guano have been used locally, but otherwise Latin America has depended heavily on imported fertilizers, at least until the late 1950s. The manufacture of fertilizers will be dealt with in Chapter 8.5. Table 7.12[34] summarizes the impressive increase in consumption in Latin America since around 1950:

TABLE 7.12

Fertilizers	1948/49– 1952/53	1959/60	1960/61	1961/62	% of World	U.S.A. 1961/62
Production	Thousands of tons					Thousands of tons
Nitrogenous	300	280	260	320	3	2,940
Phosphate	70	130	130	160	1·5	2,840
Potash	10	20	10	20	negl.	2,480
Consumption						
Nitrogenous	140	350	440	470	4·5	2,900
Phosphate	140	230	270	310	3	2,400
Potash	80	170	240	240	3	2,010

The U.S.A. however is still far ahead both in production and in consumption.

Since different soils and other physical conditions require different kinds of fertilizer it is not realistic to assess total fertilizer consumed per unit of arable land, but the following figures for selected countries[35] show clearly

TABLE 7.13
Average Consumption in Tons
per 1,000 Hectares of Arable Land

	1961/62		
	N	P_2O_5	K_2O
Latin America	4·1	2·6	2·3
Mexico	6·8	2·1	0·4
Peru	21·6	11·2	3·0
Cuba	13·2	9·9	11·3
Dominican Rep.	6·6	1·7	4·5
Brazil	3·4	4·0	5·6
Chile	4·5	5·4	2·9
U.S.A.	14·8	12·9	10·6
Netherlands	215·2	107·9	133·0
Japan	124·0	80·9	98·9
Australia	0·8	19·2	1·1

great differences in Latin American countries and the low level of consumption compared with that in certain other parts of the world.

The consumption of fertilizers has increased in almost every Latin American country since the war but application has been uneven over the farmland of each country. In Mexico, for example, most is used in the northern part of the country, in Peru, most along the coast and very little in the Andes. The main consumers of fertilizer are in fact still those listed, and Argentina and Uruguay in particular are still relying on the fertility of their soils and use only negligible quantities. A further move towards greater farming efficiency has been made in Latin America by importing agricultural tractors and other machines. The number of tractors used in agriculture has risen from about 146,000 in 1949–52 to 386,000 in 1961. But per 1,000 inhabitants, North America still has nearly fifteen times as many (5,246,000), and per unit area of arable land, about seven times. The U.K. *alone* had 427,000 in use in 1960, and Australia and New Zealand 350,000.

Holding up the more rapid introduction of mechanization in farming have been the sheer cost of importing machinery and the lack of suitable conditions in many areas. Now that tractors are being manufactured in several Latin American countries the position should however improve, and abundant fuel is an asset of many countries. The total number of agricultural tractors in the main countries in 1960 or 1961 was as follows[36]

Mexico	39,000	Brazil	66,000
Venezuela	10,000	Uruguay	23,000
Colombia	11,000	Argentina	111,000

Figures for Cuba and Peru are not readily available but each has about 10,000. Much of the work on the land in Latin America is still done by draught animals. These consume fodder that might otherwise feed animals producing meat, milk and so on. In some areas arable land is still worked by hand; this is so not only in the primitive forest communities but also in the poorer parts of the Andes. Of other kinds of machinery, combine harvesters are only used widely in Argentina, Uruguay and southern Brazil.

7.9. FISHING AND FORESTRY

Until the late 1950s, none of the seas around Latin America were counted among the world's leading fishing regions. Since then, the Pacific coast of South America between about 20 degrees south and the equator has come to produce almost as much fish as the whole of Western Europe. The fortunes of fishing in Latin America revolve almost entirely round the rise of Peru and more recently Chile to places among the leading producing countries. The following are key figures[37] for selected years.

Catch in millions of tons	1938	1953	1957	1958	1959	1960	1961	1962
World	20,50	25,24	30,91	32,24	35,74	38,02	41,16	44,5
Latin America	0,24	0,73	1,33	1,84	3,19	4,68	6,52	8,0
% caught in Latin America	1·2	2·9	4·3	5·7	8·9	12·3	15·8	18·0

Of the total of 8 m. tons in Latin America, 6,8 m. was caught by Peru,* which came within a few thousand tons of the Japanese total. Chile accounted for about half of the remainder (640,000 in 1962). It is something of an anti-climax to find that nearly all the fish caught by Peru, Chile and Ecuador are anchovies, which are almost all converted into fishmeal fertilizer. Attempts are however being made to process them into forms suitable for livestock and even human consumption. The rapid expansion of fishing along the Peruvian and north Chilean coasts has had considerable economic repercussions. Existing ports have been enlarged, old ports revived, and numerous fishmeal factories erected. There is an element of insecurity in the boom both on account of the sudden appearance in world markets of large quantities of fertilizer and of the occasional disappearance of the shoals of fish. In 1963, for example, fishing was almost at a standstill for several weeks at one stage.

Elsewhere in Latin America, rich fishing grounds do not appear to exist, and the industry is unrewarding, and characterized by very low productivity of fishermen. But in some regions, particularly Northeast Brazil, fish are an important source of protein, while many riverside communities in the interior of Latin America depend on fishing as a main source of protein. Whaling is also practised by Latin American countries on a modest scale. Fish catches were as follows[38] (thousands of tons), regardless of nature or quality of catch:

	1961	1962		1961	1962
Peru	5,243	6,830	Argentina	94	94
Chile	430	639	Venezuela	83	n.a.
Brazil	282	n.a.	Ecuador	60	52
Mexico	225	219	Colombia	48	52

Although nearly half of the total area of Latin America is classed as forest, for various reasons forestry has not progressed far in most parts of the region and many countries actually import some of their requirements.

* In 1963 the catch was 6,6 m. tons of which 6,4 m. were anchovies, from which 1,2 m. tons of fishmeal were produced.

Very broadly the forests may be divided initially into a large area of tropical forest, mainly lowland but reaching to about 2,000 m in places, and a smaller area of temperate forest, found both outside the tropics and at high altitudes within the tropics. Much of the land classed as forest is in areas such as Northeast Brazil, where conditions are too dry for the growth of commercially useful stands. In addition, the tropical rain forest is characterized by the occurrence of a very large number of species in any given small area, with useful species scattered among more numerous useless ones and therefore costly to exploit. Many useful species do in fact occur in such areas as Amazonia, some hardwood, others soft, but the limited quantity that can be assembled in any one place and the cost of moving products to markets have so far limited exploitation of timber here. The Caribbean coastlands of Central America have been more exploited. Most of the timber produced commercially rather than for local consumption comes from the pine forests of the uplands of South Brazil, from southern Chile and from the high ranges of Mexico. The high Andes from Colombia to northern Argentina did not have a continuous forest cover and the region was notoriously deficient until the planting of Eucalyptus species in the nineteenth century. Many other parts of Latin America, especially southern Brazil, Uruguay and parts of Argentina have also greatly benefited from the introduction of this remarkable Australian tree.

The area under forest bears little relationship to the actual state of the industry in Latin America, but clearly the potential is great since of the larger countries, only Mexico and Chile are less than one third forest covered, while Brazil and Colombia are nearly two thirds covered. Actual production of timber is very modest indeed in most countries, as 1961 or near figures suggest[39]:

Estimated production in million cubic metres of roundwood			
U.S.A.	293	Peru	5
Brazil	106	Mexico	5
Colombia	13	Honduras	3
Chile	7	Costa Rica	2

Actual lumber (sawn timber) in thousands of cubic metres was in 1961 or 1962[40]:

	Coniferous (mainly temperate)	Broadleaved (mainly tropical)
Mexico	843	36
Central America	760	320
Venezuela—Ecuador— Peru	—	810
Guianas	—	130
Brazil	2,800	2,900
Argentina	29	565
Chile	455	576

Hitherto the production of woodpulp and newsprint in Latin American countries has been on a very limited scale and imports have been considerable. The two largest producers, Brazil and Chile combined, only produce about 270,000 tons, compared with over 5m. tons in Canada and over 1m. in Sweden, but an effort is being made in Chile to produce large quantities for export.

7.10. THE PROCESSING OF AGRICULTURAL PRODUCTS

The various aspects of handling, processing and manufacturing agricultural forest and fish products probably employ more persons in Latin America than any other single branch of industry. Figures for the early 1950s are available for most countries[41], and a rough idea of the relative importance of this branch in the industrial sector of the economy of each country may be gained by expressing employment in food, drink and tobacco as a percentage of total employment in industry

	Total number in thousands	% of all employment in mfg.		Total number in thousands	% of all employment in mfg.
Dominican Rep.	53	86	Honduras	6	30
Nicaragua	13	64	Colombia	59	30
Venezuela	78	57	Uruguay	50	29
Costa Rica	10	56	Mexico	167	26
El Salvador	29	56	Ecuador	8	25
Puerto Rico	29	41	Brazil	270	22
Peru	44	38	Chile	37	20
Paraguay	11	32	Argentina	280	20

The relative importance of food, drink and tobacco varies greatly from country to country, although to some extent this may be the result of differences in classification in industrial censuses. It also depends on the relative importance in different countries of products requiring a great deal of preparation, such as sugar. Moreover, many additional persons engaged in agriculture, but not necessarily even registered as being in employment at all, process agricultural products in some way. In spite of these drawbacks the table shows convincingly enough that the more highly industrialized countries (see Chapter 8) depend less on this branch than Central America or the Islands. The position has changed in Venezuela since 1953 with the rapid growth of other branches of manufacturing.

Like agriculture itself, the processing of products of the land and of fish is carried on in establishments of greatly varying size. At one extreme, most rural areas in tropical Latin America prepare manioc or maize or other basic food crops for consumption. Women in the Andes will spend an enormous amount of time, for example, separating different colours of maize grain to no purpose at all. At the other extreme, thousands of cattle a day may enter the largest slaughter houses in Buenos Aires, and vast *frigoríficos* store enormous numbers of carcasses. Much processing, such as the reduction of sugar cane or the drying and sorting of coffee beans, are carried on in moderate sized establishments. Very broadly the processing of agricultural products is carried out either in the immediate vicinity of their cultivation, especially if items are bulky, or, if it is more convenient to assemble products from over a wide area to process on a large scale ready for export, in ports. Unfortunately, it is not possible to obtain figures for the number of persons engaged in different branches of food, drink and tobacco in different areas, and it is therefore superfluous to attempt to map quantitatively the distribution of these industries.

7.11. FOREIGN TRADE IN AGRICULTURAL PRODUCTS

The proportion of agricultural, fish and forest products to total value of export trade varies greatly from country to country, and since the range is from 97 per cent in Argentina to less than 2 per cent in Venezuela the figures are worth recording[42]

Paraguay	almost 100	El Salvador	92	Peru	46
Guatemala	almost 100	Dominican Rep.	87	Jamaica	43
Argentina	97	Brazil	86	Surinam	16
Costa Rica	96	Honduras	86	Trinidad	13
Ecuador	94	Barbados	84	Chile	7
Panama	93	Nicaragua	83	Venezuela	1·4
Uruguay	92	Colombia	81	Bolivia	negligible
		Mexico	60		

It goes without saying that mineral products account for most of the remaining value of exports, though Brazil, Chile and Mexico in particular are beginning to export manufactured goods. Most Latin American countries also *import* some agricultural products; much, in fact, is inter-Latin American trade. The following are the percentages of imports made up of agricultural products in selected Latin American countries:

Jamaica	24	Brazil	14
Venezuela	19	Ecuador	13
Central America	10–20	Colombia	12
		Argentina	10

There seem several reasons why countries that apparently have enough land to be self-supporting agriculturally need to import food. In the first place, tropical areas need temperate products and vice versa; Argentinian wheat goes to Brazil, for example, Brazilian coffee to Argentina. Secondly, some areas still specialize to such a great extent in certain export crops, as often happened in the colonial period, that other parts of the same country do not have sufficient surplus to cover the deficit in food crops. Thirdly, areas that might be used to achieve a surplus to provide deficient areas in the same country are often too inconveniently placed to do so.

Latin America makes a major contribution to world trade in several agricultural commodities. These are listed in the order they occupied in 1962 as a share of total world trade[43]

	World total	Latin America	%
	Millions of tons		
Bananas	3,9	3,0	77
Coffee	2,8	1,9	68
Sugar	15,8	9,3	59
Cotton (lint)	2,74	0,85	31
Meat	1,94	0,52	17
Wool	1,44	0,24	17
Maize	17,5	2,6	15
Cocoa beans	1,03	0,15	14·5
Wheat and wheat flour	36,6	2,75	7·5

Coffee and sugar exports have already been dealt with in a previous section, and the dominant position of Brazil, Colombia and Central America in coffee exports and of Cuba and the other Islands in sugar exports was noted. Other agricultural exports may be briefly summarized as follows (exports in 1961 in thousands of tons).

Cotton lint: Mexico 305, Brazil 206, Peru 109, Central America 87
Bananas: Ecuador 985, Honduras 426, Panama 271, French Caribbean
                260, Brazil 246, Costa Rica 230, Colombia 206, Guatemala
                164, Dominican Republic 163, Jamaica 160
Apples: Argentina 150
Wheat: Argentina 1,066 (1960, 2,486)
Maize: Argentina 1,730 (1960, 2,570)
Cocoa beans: Brazil 104, Ecuador 32.

Imports of wheat or wheat flour, which rose from about 1,4 m. tons per year around 1950 to 3 m. in 1961 were distributed as follows (thousands of tons):

Brazil	1,881	Colombia	127
Peru	416	Chile	80
Venezuela	345	Guatemala	54
Cuba	192		

Much of the wheat imported in recent years has come from the U.S.A. under special agreements, and in 1961, Latin America took 4·2 per cent of world wheat imports.

7.12. SUMMARY AND FUTURE PROSPECTS

The general impression of agriculture in Latin America is that crop-farming is not well balanced, while livestock farming is generally inefficient and wasteful. These generalizations apply much less to Argentina and Uruguay than to other countries. With regard to crop farming, there still seems to be a hangover from colonial times and the nineteenth century when Latin America had to export either minerals or agricultural products to obtain all its needs of manufactured goods. Often the best land is devoted to the cultivation of coffee, sugar, bananas or whatever other crop a particular region finds itself well suited to produce, while food crops occupy less fertile land and have less thorough and regular attention. This is one explanation for the weak development of cereals except in Argentina and Uruguay, which grow them for export. With regard to livestock, large herds are kept but, again with the exception of Argentina and Uruguay, there has been little attempt to improve meat or milk yields by breeding and by improving the supply of fodder crops. This may, to some extent, also be a relic of the colonial period, when large numbers of cattle were kept mainly for their hides.

In general, then, Latin America is much less efficiently farmed in terms of output per farm worker than North America or Australia, and much less efficiently farmed in terms of output per unit of land than Western Europe, Japan or even much of China and India. Had the region been settled for several thousand years as heavily as southern Asia or eastern Asia and had it been subjected to Old World technology over this period, it could well now be supporting three or four times as many people as it is at the standard of living it has. More than any other region in the world except Africa there seems to be an enormous amount of slack to take up, whether by achieving more satisfactory land tenure systems, obtaining much higher yields in existing areas of cultivation or by extending agriculture into new areas.

While agricultural production has increased appreciably in Latin America during the present century, progress has been very erratic, with many setbacks due to both physical and social influences, and many periods of stagnation. For some decades now it has hardly kept pace with the increase in population, and in the region as a whole the *per caput* food production is indeed somewhat lower than it was in the 1930s. Between the early 1950s and the early 1960s there was an increase of about 30 per cent in the total volume of farm production, but this was matched by a similar population increase. There are, however, surprising differences in the rate of increase between individual countries, and if the region as a whole could achieve the progress made in some, then prospects would be very good. During the decade 1952–1961 food production in Mexico increased by nearly 85 per cent, in Brazil by nearly 50 per cent and in Venezuela by 40 per cent, whereas in Argentina the increase was only 6 per cent, in Chile 4 per cent, and in Cuba 2 per cent, and there was a decline in Uruguay. The Central American and Andean countries mainly stood between these two extremes.

There is a growing desire throughout Latin America to modernize agriculture and to increase production to a level more commensurate with needs and potential. This is more difficult in some respects than industrialization because many existing land tenure systems in Latin America cannot easily be adapted to rapid improvements yet are difficult to change, while physical setbacks are impossible to predict and difficult to allow for. Very broadly, an increase in total agricultural production can be achieved either by increasing yields in existing areas or by bringing new lands into use. An increase in the productivity of farm workers, on the other hand, depends largely on more mechanization, though changes in land tenure could help. In fact it is not so urgent at present to squeeze more people out of rural areas into non-agricultural activities in already overcrowded towns as to achieve a greater total volume of production: an increase of 3 per cent per year to keep up with population increase, plus several per cent more to improve diet and increase exports.

Increased yields in existing farming areas may be achieved by the greater use of fertilizers, pesticides and so on, the introduction of superior varieties of plant and breeds of livestock and even the introduction of completely new crops to areas in which they are better suited than are the traditional crops; it has been suggested, for example, that fodder crops could largely replace maize in the higher areas of Central Mexico. Similarly, rice could be grown in low lying areas of pasture. Irrigation schemes are, of course, also making a major contribution to improvements but these more often involve the use of new areas, formerly waste or poor pasture. Mechanization itself can also help to increase yields, particularly by allowing deeper ploughing, more effective weeding and so on.

164

Since only about 5 per cent of the total area of Latin America is under field and tree crops it would seem that there must also be scope for developing completely new areas. Only the smaller Islands, and El Salvador in Central America are completely without new farm land. On the other hand, not much is known about physical conditions in many areas, and given the generally poor quality of soils in the tropics, governments might well have reason to be apprehensive about embarking on large-scale colonization schemes in new areas, especially since some of these have been unsuccessful in the past. What is more, promising new areas usually lie at considerable distances from existing clusters of population and can usually only be reached by the building of new roads or railways (e.g. Bolivia, Peru, Venezuela). Even if such projects are successful and they produce a surplus, much of this would have to be carried to existing markets for a long period before the new areas themselves could be expected to become major clusters of population.

In the view of the author, in most cases more benefit could at present be derived from improving yields in existing areas than from stretching communications, scattering population thinly over wide areas, and chancing unknown conditions to open up new parts of countries. This will of course have to come in the end. Individual new development projects will be discussed in appropriate regional sections later. Here a few new developments may be noted to illustrate the kinds of change that are taking place. The replacement of one crop or set of crops by another is occurring on a more massive scale than has happened since the great development of farming in southern South America following the inflow of new immigrants in the nineteenth century. The rationalization of coffee growing in Brazil is one example, the plan to extend sugar cultivation in Colombia another. In Cuba immediately after the Revolution it was at first considered desirable to change much of the land under sugar to pasture or basic food crops; this seems largely to have been abandoned. Turning to water supply and irrigation, great progress is being made in Mexico, Venezuela, Peru, Chile and Northeast Brazil. Finally, new areas are being colonized in the interior of Brazil, in Bolivia, Peru and Venezuela.

REFERENCES

[1] *FAOPY, 1962*, Table 5A
[2] *UNSY, 1962*, Table 164
[3] *FAOSFA, 1963*, p. 63
[4] *FAOSFA, 1963*, p. 117
[5] *FAOSPA, 1963*, p. 113
[6] *FAOPY, 1962*, Table 1
[7] *FAOPY, 1962*, Table 2
[8] *FAOPY, 1962*, Table 10 A–B
[9] *FAOPY, 1962*, Table 45
[10] e.g. Aschmann, H. *Indian Pastoralists of the Guajira Peninsula* A.A.A.G. Dec. 1960, pp. 408–18
[11] *Anuario Estatístico do Brasil, 1961*, IBGE, pp. 81–82
[12] *FAOPY, 1962*, appropriate tables
[13] *FAOPY, 1962*, pp. 85–92
[14] *FAOPY, 1962*, Table 16
[15] *UNSY, 1962*, Table 17; *UNSY*, 1963, Table 22
[16] *FAOPY, 1962*, Table 11

[17] *FAOPY, 1962,* Table 19 A–B
[18] Jiménez, A. N. *Geografía de Cuba,* Havana, 1960
[19] França, A. *A marcha do café e as frentes pioneiras,* p. 16, 1960; Rio de Janiero
[20] *FAOPY, 1962,* Table 22
[21] *FAOPY, 1962,* Table 41
[22] *UNSY, 1962,* Table 75
[23] *UNSY, 1963,* Table 81
[24] *BOLSA (FR) July 13,* p. 620, 1963
[25] *FAOPY, 1962*
[26] *Peruvian Times,* 3 August 1962, *BOLSA (FR)* 13 July 1963 and 24 August 1963.
[27] *UNSY, 1962,* Table 28; 1963, Table 33
[28] *FAOTY, 1962,* Table 42
[29] *FAOPY, 1962,* Table 58A
[30] *UNSY, 1962,* Table 31, and 1963, Table 36
[31] *FAOPY, 1962,* p. 144
[32] Fox, D. J. 'Henequen in Yucatán', in *Transactions and Papers of I.B.G.* 29 (1961) pp. 215–229
[33] *FAOPY, 1962,* Tables 73 and 93
[34] *FAOPY, 1962,* Tables 98–100
[35] *FAOSFA, 1963,* pp. 226–7
[36] *FAOPY, 1962,* Table 101
[37] *FAOSFA, 1963,* p. 25
[38] *UNSY, 1963,* Table 42
[39] *UNSY, 1963,* Table 40
[40] *UNSY, 1963,* Table 98
[41] *UNPIG 1938–1958,* Part 2, 'Statistics and Explanatory Notes for Individual Countries'
[42] *FAOTY, 1962,* Table 1; South American Handbook, 1964
[43] *FAOSFA, 1963,* pp. 184–194

CHAPTER 8

MINING AND MANUFACTURING

8.1. GENERAL

In Chapter 4 the outlines of mining and manufacturing development were briefly traced through the colonial period into the nineteenth century. This section now considers developments in the modern period. In the latter part of the nineteenth century mining and the processing of certain agricultural products was advanced in parts of Latin America, but in general there were few industrial establishments run on modern lines. As Latin America became independent from Iberia, trade with other European countries grew rapidly and the region became an important market for the growing industries of Western Europe. Mines, railways and port facilities were developed with European capital, but this was not generally forthcoming for manufacturing, while throughout the century little was invested in industry from either private or public Latin American sources. By the First World War there were some modern textile mills, most of them manufacturing cotton, but little else. The two world wars were a stimulus to manufacturing development, the second more than the first, because in the second the traditional European suppliers of manufactured goods to Latin America were even more committed to their respective war efforts. During both of these wars attention was turned to import substitution to compensate for shortages of goods no longer available; since exports continued, the foreign exchange accumulated could be used to import equipment, particularly from the U.S.A. In an industrial country import substitution might be, for example, the manufacture of synthetic rubber to save importing natural rubber; in Latin America the question was to convert indigenous raw materials into consumer goods. Most of these consumer industries could not have survived without protection and it has now become widely accepted that, within reason, economic nationalism is beneficial* and not to be deplored by the leading industrial countries since it is more advantageous for the underdeveloped countries to produce at home, at least, certain industrial goods, even if prices are higher than they would be for the same goods imported, than to have no industry at all. To be effective, of course, such a situation presupposes improvements in technology and in productivity per worker in agriculture and a shift of working population to industrial centres.

* That it has been carried too far on some occasions is indicated in[1] p. 71. 'However, these tariffs have been carried to such a pitch that they are undoubtedly—on an average—the highest in the world. It is not uncommon to find tariff duties of over 500 per cent.
As is well known, the proliferation of industries of every kind in a closed market has deprived the Latin American countries of the advantages of specialization and economies of scale, and owing to the protection afforded by excessive tariff duties and restrictions, a healthy form of internal competition has failed to develop, to the detriment of efficient production'.

Following the manufacturing of textiles, the manufacture of iron and steel and of cement grew up on a limited scale in certain countries in the inter-war period. In the post-war period the manufacture of engineering products and chemicals has expanded impressively in some of the larger countries. Early centres of modern manufacturing were Monterrey and Mexico City in Mexico, Medellín in Colombia, Santiago in Chile, Buenos Aires, São Paulo and Rio. In the inter-war period modern industries spread to smaller countries and new industries appeared, especially in national capitals such as Havana, Lima and Montevideo. In the post-war period yet other areas have started to develop modern manufacturing, notably Venezuela, which is quickly becoming one of the most advanced, Central America, which is beginning to benefit from its economic union, Northeast Brazil, which is now receiving funds from Southeast Brazil, and certain Islands, especially Puerto Rico, Trinidad and Jamaica.

Crossley[2] proposes a division of manufacturing industries into four broad categories, 'basic and advanced consumer goods and basic and advanced capital goods'. These represent varying degrees of sophistication and complexity, from simple branches such as the preparation of food and soap and the manufacturing of textiles and footwear at one extreme, to the manufacture of heavy electrical equipment, petrochemicals and loco-motives at the other. Several of the smaller countries still only make basic consumer goods, but the numbers producing advanced consumer goods, such as pharmaceuticals and motor vehicles, is increasing. The medium and large countries all aspire now to producing basic capital goods such as cement and steel, but only Brazil, Mexico and Argentina have reached the final stage, and these only to a limited extent so far, making heavy machinery and complex chemicals.

There are no precise figures for the total value or volume of mining and manufacturing production in Latin America, and the basis for assessing these activities varies from country to country. Latin America is however far behind the more advanced industrial countries, as comparative figures for *per caput* consumption of steel indicate. Compare in 1961 488 kg consumed per inhabitant each year in the U.S.A. and 314 in the U.S.S.R. with approximately 50 in Latin America; but the figures for mainland China and India respectively were 25 and 12. The U.S.A. was already consuming 50 kg of pig iron per inhabitant in the 1870s and the U.S.S.R. in the early 1930s. The contrast is revealed again by figures for the total number of persons employed in manufacturing per thousand inhabitants in 1953: North America 115, West Europe 112, Latin America 35; but for East and South East Asia the figure was only 24, and Africa was certainly lower still. Very roughly, manufacturing accounted in the early 1960s for 20 per cent of the combined gross domestic product of Latin American countries but only for 10 per cent of the total employment. Mining accounts roughly for about another 5 per cent, but employs only a mere 1 per cent.

Table 8.1 shows the relative importance of mining and manufacturing in the more important Latin American countries, expressed as the per-centage contribution these make to total gross domestic product. On the whole, the larger countries depend more on manufacturing than the smaller ones, but this is not so in mining. Manufacturing is least developed in

TABLE 8.1[3]

Percentage of Total Gross Domestic Product Contributed by Mining and Manufacturing (1950 Percentage in Brackets Where Available).

Mining		Manufacturing			
Trinidad	33	Brazil	25† (22)	Ecuador	15 (16)
Venezuela	31	Mexico	23 (22)	Paraguay	15† (15)
Bolivia	20*	Chile	23 (14)	Br. Guiana	13 (15)
Surinam	15*	Argentina	22 (24)	Trinidad	13
Peru	12	Puerto Rico	21 (15)	Jamaica	13
Jamaica	9	Peru	17 (15)	Costa Rica	12
Br. Guiana	8	Colombia	16 (17)	Venezuela	12 (9)
Chile	5				

* Estimated.
† Includes mining and construction.

Central America, in most of the Islands apart from Cuba, and in Bolivia, Ecuador and Paraguay, areas that have already been shown in Chapter 1.4 to have a low *per caput* gross domestic product. At the other extreme, in 1958 Argentina, Brazil, Venezuela and Mexico each accounted for 18–19 per cent of all industrial production, including mining, while in that year, Brazil (23 per cent) Argentina (21 per cent) and Mexico (21 per cent) had 65 per cent of the manufacturing in the region.

TABLE 8.2[4]

Employment in Manufacturing in the Mid-1950s in Thousands

Brazil	(1953)	1,421*	Uruguay	(1956)	171
Argentina	(1954)	1,422	Venezuela	(1953)	138
Mexico	(1950)	632	Peru	(1954)	117
Colombia	(1953)	199	Puerto Rico	(1954)	70
Chile	(1953)	187	Dominican Rep.	(1954)	62

* Only in establishments employing over 4 persons. Part II, Data for individual countries.

The total number of persons employed in manufacturing in the early 1960s was 6–7 m., out of a total employed population of about 70 m. Table 8.2 shows more reliable figures for the mid-1950s. In relation to its total population, Argentina is by far the most highly industrialized country, but for a time in the early 1960s employment and production were declining. In the last decade mining and manufacturing production has risen more rapidly than employment in most areas, as the productivity of workers has increased.

The relative importance of major branches of manufacturing differed appreciably in 1953 in Latin America from that in North America and West Europe

TABLE 8.3[5]

Percentage Contributed

	All manufacturing	Food	Textiles	Clothing	Base metals	Metal manufacturing and engineering
North America	100	11	7	9	7·4	35·5
West Europe	100	12	12	11	5·5	31
Latin America	100	29	16	9	3·3	13·1

TABLE 8.4[6]

Contribution of Different Countries to Different Branches of Industry.
The Latin American Total for Each Item = 100 in 1958

	Mining and mfg.	Mining	Heavy mfg.	Light mfg.	Metals and engineering
Brazil	19·3	1·8	25·5	23·6	30·6
Mexico	18·7	10·7	25·6	20·6	21·7
Argentina	18·1	3·7	21·8	21·6	29·0
Venezuela	16·2	56·7	5·1	6·3	4·0
Colombia	5·1	4·6	3·5	5·2	3·3
Chile	4·9	5·5	5·6	4·7	3·2
Peru	3·0	6·3	1·5	2·3	0·9
Islands	8·5	6·6	7·9	9·0	2·8
LAFTA	67	30·4	82·4	70·9	88·5

While food and textile industries were relatively more important in Latin America, metal manufacturing and engineering were far less developed.

To some extent the size of a country determines the branches of manufacturing that can successfully be developed there (see Table 8.4). This is not so with industries such as cotton textile manufacturing in which economies of large-scale are negligible once a plant is above a moderate minimum size. At the other extreme the modern aircraft industry needs a very large plant and a large home or export market to be competitive. Thus even the smallest and least developed Latin American countries manufacture textiles, but in the early 1960s only four made motor vehicles, Brazil, Mexico, Argentina and Venezuela; aircraft were not, of course, manufactured at all although the manufacture of light aircraft was being considered in Brazil. The iron and steel industry, which benefits from economies of large scale, but can still function in small establishments, exists on a large scale (by Latin American standards) precisely in the seven largest countries (see *Figure 8.7*). Until recently, oil refineries also seem to some extent to have been related to size of country, occurring either in oil-producing countries, regardless of

TABLE 8.5[7]

Per caput Consumption of Energy in Kilograms of Coal
Equivalent in 1961 and 1962

	Large and medium countries		1961	1962	Smaller countries		1961	1962
	Venezuela		2,764	2,917				
	Argentina		1,178	1,194	Puerto Rico		1,448	1,700
	Mexico		959	916				
	Chile		874	970	Uruguay		718	767
Mean for Latin America in 1961, 680	Cuba		866	920				
	Colombia		549	576	Jamaica		602	607
	Peru		354	390	Ecuador		184	166
	Brazil		345	367	Guatemala		174	162
					Dominican R.		148	141
					Bolivia		145	156
					Paraguay		91	93
					Haiti		36	34

their size, of processing imported oil in the larger countries. Recently, however, it has become a matter of national policy and of prestige to have a refinery, whatever its size; by 1965, for example, five of the six Central American countries will have one.

It is less obvious why the *per caput* consumption of energy (see Table 8.5) also tends to be much higher in the larger countries. It is related either to large size or to special local circumstances (as in Puerto Rico, Trinidad, certain smaller islands, the Panama Canal zone and so on). Again, the poorer Islands, Central America and the three poorest South American countries come low. The low position of Brazil is due partly to the presence of the Northeast, partly to the unfair conversion factor for hydroelectric power (now used in United Nations publications), the main source of home-produced energy in Brazil.

8.2. MINING

The areas in which minerals of various kinds might be expected to occur in Latin America were briefly mentioned in Chapter 3.7 and the history of mining was outlined in Chapter 4.3. In this section the present production of minerals in the region is summarized and important new deposits are noted. The minerals will then be reconsidered in the following sections in the groups of industry to which they are related (power, chemicals, iron and steel).

Only a small part of Latin America has been explored thoroughly for minerals and large areas remain as yet unknown, while often there has been an element of luck in the discovery and exploitation of particular deposits. The manganese ore in Amapá, Brazil, for example was found initially during a search for gold. In the extreme north of Peru oil has been exploited for many decades, but large deposits of phosphates near the oilfields were only revealed in the late 1950s.

In very broad terms one would expect the countries with the largest area to have the most minerals, but it may also be lack of interest in the particular areas concerned that explains the virtual lack of mining in the six Central American countries, and in Cuba, Hispaniola, Ecuador, Paraguay and Uruguay. These are not included in Table 8.6, which shows the contribution made by individual countries to the total Latin American production of 12 major economic minerals. In each case the total equals 100, but the absolute amount produced is expressed also in weight and is compared with that produced in North America. From the table it is easy to distinguish (vertically) both the range and relative importance of different minerals produced in each country and (horizontally) the countries contributing to the production of each individual mineral.

Since most of the minerals produced in Latin America are exported, it is understandable that most of the output comes from places near the coast. The coastal areas are not necessarily more abundant in economic minerals, but in the first place tend to have been more thoroughly explored and, secondly, are preferred by mining companies even if comparable deposits are known to exist inland. Thus in Peru appreciable oil and gas deposits have been discovered on the interior side of the Andes but little is produced

TABLE 8.6

	Mexico	Venezuela	Colombia	Peru	Bolivia	Chile	Argentina	Brazil	Guianas	Jamaica	Trinidad	Others	Latin America	Latin America absolute*	North America absolute*
a Coal	13		33	2		20	4	27				1	100	8	386
b Oil	7·5	76	3·5	1	1	1	6	2			3		100	206	384
c Gas	46	22	3			12	11	2			4		100	22,1	398,7
d Sulphur	100												100	1,2	8,3
e Phosphates				15				85					100	1,1	18,9
f Bauxite									44	50		6	100	13,2	1,5
g Iron ore	3	38	1	13		18		26				>1	100	24,2	49,2
h Manganese ore	11					2		70	13			3	100	0,5	negl.
i Copper	6			25		68						1	100	0,8	1,5
j Lead	38			30	3		6	22				1	100	0,5	0,4
k Zinc	55			36			6					3	100	0,5	0,8
l Tin	2				90		2	6					100	21	negl.

* In millions of tons except tin (thousands) and gas (thousands of millions of cubic metres)

here, whereas costly but fruitless exploration has continued in the coastal and offshore areas.

Table 8.6 shows that in spite of the strong association of mining with several Latin American countries and the fact that these depend heavily on minerals for their exports, of the 12 minerals listed, Latin America appreciably exceeds North America only in the production of three, bauxite, manganese ore and tin, while lead is mined in roughly equal quantities. In 1958[9], Latin America only accounted for 8·4 per cent of the production of minerals in the non-communist world, compared with 44·7 per cent produced in North America, 25·4 per cent in West Europe, and 6·9 per cent in Asia. Its contribution to total world production of the more important minerals was as follows:

Bauxite	53 per cent	Manganese ore	11 per cent
Lead	25	Iron ore	10
Copper	21	Sulphur, phosphates,	
Oil	18·5	natural gas,	
Zinc	18	all under	5
		Coal	0·6

A study of the value of mining production in 1958[10] shows the striking dominance of Venezuela. Figures show the percentage contributed by each country to the value of the Latin American total:

Venezuela	56·7 per cent	Argentina		3·7 per cent
Mexico	10·7	Bolivia	about	2·1
Peru	6·3	Brazil		1·8
Chile	5·5	Islands		6·8
Colombia	4·6	Guianas	about	1·0
		Rest		<1

Oil and gas account for about three quarters of the value of all minerals produced in Latin America. The small proportion contributed by Brazil is

172

unlikely to alter much for some time to come and should be noted by those who talk with such enthusiasm about mining there.

Many new deposits of minerals with importance for the future if not the present have been found in the last decade. They occur particularly in certain areas: Venezuela, the Guianas and the extreme northeast of Brazil, where new deposits of oil, iron ore, bauxite and manganese ore have been found; the interior side of the Andes in Peru (oil, natural gas, manganese ore), the Manaus area in Brazil (oil, manganese ore), Argentina (iron ore, oil).

Most minerals are now produced in Latin America from highly capitalized establishments run on efficient modern lines although prospecting and small scale mining is still carried on in places, for example in Chile and in the interior of Brazil. Generally, therefore, large numbers of workers are not involved, although those who are employed are better paid and usually much better housed than their compatriots in agricultural activities. Since most of the minerals are produced by foreign companies and are exported, the main benefits derived by the host countries are the wages of their nationals employed in mining, the services such as roads, schools and hospitals provided by the companies, and the revenues (royalties) derived from the companies from taxes on their concessions, output, profits and so on. The oil industry in Venezuela, which accounts for over half of the value of mining production in Latin America, employs only about 40,000 persons, less than 2 per cent of the total employed population of Venezuela, yet the value of oil production is several times greater than that of farm production and in terms of value of output the productivity of a worker in the oil industry is nearly *one hundred times greater* than that of a worker in agriculture.

In order to make mining play a greater part in their economic life, Latin American countries have taken steps, some drastic, some gradual, to reduce dependence on foreign capital. One way has been to take over the production of certain minerals, particularly oil. Bolivia and Mexico did this before the Second World War, while several countries, including Argentina and Brazil, also now control production, and some (Venezuela itself, Peru) have a small share in total production and refining; Chilean companies now account for much of the iron ore output. Other ways of participating more in mining have been to compel foreign companies to employ national workers in technical and administrative as well as manual work, to make them do as much refining as possible before exporting, and to sell to host countries at a cheap rate that part of the mining output that can be consumed at home (e.g. oil, iron ore, in Peru, iron ore in Venezuela).

Although mining directly employs only a limited labour force it has managed to attract large numbers of people to mining areas. Some, of course, are in employment that serves mine workers, but others are never satisfactorily absorbed. One preoccupation of all Latin American countries that depend heavily on mining is the danger of exhaustion of reserves in a particular area, or their closure for political reasons. This would seriously affect government revenues and would also leave many sizable communities with no economic basis. In fact, few centres in Latin America that exist solely for mining have more than 50,000 people, but there are now several larger than this in Venezuela.

8.3. ENERGY

In 1961 Latin America produced roughly twice as much energy as it consumed (in terms of coal equivalent). The main reason is that the South Caribbean countries, Venezuela, Trinidad and Colombia, which produce over 75 per cent of the total, export about 87 per cent of the oil they produce. The other countries mostly have a deficit, though some are approaching a balance.

The rise to prominence of Latin America as an energy producing region has been due to the great expansion of oil production in the last four decades. The impact of this might have been less profound if the region had been able to develop a coal industry earlier. As it was, most of the requirements of coal were imported by sea from other continents (e.g. even coal from Australia to the mines of the Andes) while wood has been used widely in some areas (e.g. eucalypts are grown in Brazil for fuel). Coal production increased gradually in a few areas but even now the whole continent only produces about $\frac{1}{20}$ as much coal as the U.K., and only half as much as Australia. The discovery and exploitation of oil in Latin America was a gradual process until the 1920s, and several of the larger countries came on the scene even later. Although the region has many promising areas, lack of capital and experience has hindered exploration by countries themselves, but few have opened the door to foreign companies without some misgivings. The approximate year in which commercial oil production began in the main oil producing countries was as follows:

Peru (Zorritos) about	1870	Venezuela (E. region)	1913
Mexico (near Támpico)	1901	Venezuela (W. region)	1917
Argentina (Comodoro		Colombia	1926
Rivadavia)	1907	Brazil	1941
Trinidad	1909	Chile	1945

The production of hydroelectric energy except in very small quantities has been even more recent. Again, lack of appropriate branches of engineering have necessitated the importation of virtually all equipment. Many power stations have been constructed by foreign mining companies to serve their mines and smelters.

The *per caput* consumption of energy in different Latin American countries was discussed in the first section of this chapter. The following are figures (in kilograms per inhabitant of coal equivalent in 1961) for major countries:

U.S.A.	8,042	Mainland China	528
U.K.	4,925	India	150
U.S.S.R.	2,921	Indonesia	140
Latin America	680	Nigeria	50

The more advanced Latin American countries are far ahead of almost all Asian and African countries (except Japan, South Africa) but far behind the most advanced industrial countries. Latin America differs from the industrial countries in cooler latitudes in that little fuel is consumed for domestic heating, and it would seem that the region has a different emphasis than the more advanced countries, with an appreciable share (perhaps 20 per cent) used in the mining and processing of minerals, and a large share (perhaps 30 per cent) in transport. Table 8.7 illustrates the difference between production and consumption in 1961:

TABLE 8.7

Energy Production and Consumption in Latin America,
in Millions of Tons of Coal Equivalent 1961

	Production	Consumption	Surplus or deficit	Main types of energy consumed
Venezuela	210	21	+189	oil and gas
Mexico	35	35	0	oil, gas, coal, hydroelec.
Argentina	19	25	− 6	oil, gas
Colombia	13	8	+ 5	oil, coal
Brazil*	11	25	− 14	hydroelec., oil, coal
Trinidad	10	2	+ 8	oil
Chile	5	7	− 2	coal, oil
Peru	4	4	0	oil
Others	about 1	21	− 20	
		148 (cf. U.K. 261)		

* Hydroelectricity is underrated in this conversion and affects Brazil especially.

About 3 per cent of the energy production of Latin America and 6 per cent of its consumption is accounted for by home produced coal. Colombia is the only country with appreciable reserves, but these have not been easy to exploit and it seems unlikely that any large reserves will be found in the continent. Production in thousands of tons in 1961 and 1962 was[12]:

	1961	1962		1961	1962
Colombia	2,650	3,000	Mexico	1,060	1,110
Brazil	2,390	2,450	Argentina	240	210
Chile	1,530	1,640	Peru	167	163

Only the economies of Chile and Colombia depend heavily on coal as a source of energy. The existence and proposed expansion of the iron and steel industry has perhaps been the main reason for prolonging the life of many mines in Latin America and even stimulating the expansion of output by the four leading producers, but mines are small, productivity per worker low and conditions difficult. Where coal cannot be replaced by other sources of energy it can be brought by sea from the U.S.A. to most parts of Latin America at a lower price than home produced coal.

Oil and more recently natural gas now account for most of the energy consumed in Latin America. Ten countries produce oil on some scale but only three have an appreciable surplus.

Surplus	Rough balance	Deficit
Venezuela	Mexico	Brazil
Trinidad	Peru	Argentina
Colombia	Ecuador	
	Bolivia	

Peru and Bolivia could become exporters if the output from their main reserves could be easily moved to the coast. The remaining areas (Central

175

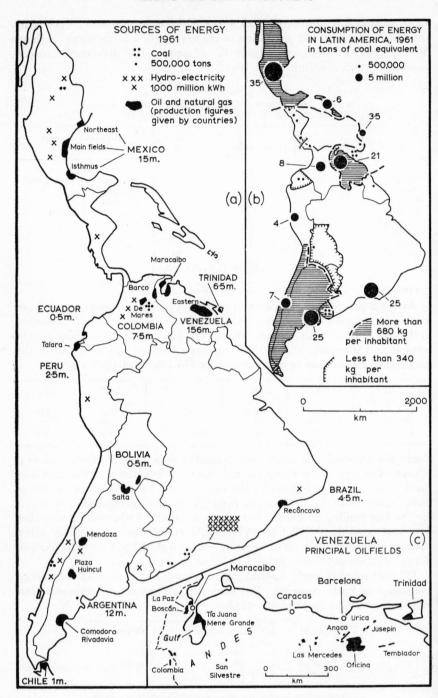

Figure 8.1. Sources and consumption of energy in Latin America in 1961

Outline of coast based on a map in the Oxford Atlas published by the
Oxford University Press

America, the Islands) import, mainly from Venezuela, as do Brazil and Argentina, but in the early 1960s Argentina was well on the way to becoming self-sufficient. Production in millions of tons in 1961 and 1963 was as follows:

	1961	1963		1961	1963
Venezuela	155,9	169,7	Brazil	4,5	5,0
Mexico	15,3	16,5	Peru	2,6	3,0
Argentina	12,1	13,8	Chile	1,2	1,8
Colombia	7,3	8,3	Ecuador	0,4	0,3
Trinidad	6,5	7,0	Bolivia	0,4	0,4

The production of natural gas was as follows in 1961 and 1962 in thousands of millions of cubic metres[14].

	1961	1962		1961	1962
Mexico	10,2	10,5	Trinidad	0,8	0,9
Venezuela	4,8	5,2	Brazil	0,5	0,5
Chile	2,5	3,7	Colombia	0,4	0,4
Argentina	2,4	3,0			

This source of energy is only beginning to make a major contribution to energy consumption in Latin America.

Progress to present oil production totals has been uneven over the region*. Mexican production stagnated for nearly two decades between nationalization (1938) and the late 1950s, while Venezuelan output increased five times in this period. Disappointing progress was made until 1958 in both Argentina and Brazil, while in Colombia and Trinidad progress has been steady but not spectacular since the war.

Figure 8.1 shows the main areas of oil production in Latin America, but many minor producing areas have been omitted. Roughly half of all the oil produced in Latin America comes from one area, the Gulf of Maracaibo in western Venezuela, and another quarter from eastern Venezuela, about 100 m. and 50 m. tons per year respectively. The main fields around Támpico are next (about 12 m.), while Trinidad, Colombia, Comodoro Rivadavia and the Recôncavo fields (Agua Grande, Candeias) each account for several million tons.

The northeast coastal strip of the Gulf of Maracaibo and the offshore wells produce mainly heavy oil; newer fields west of the Gulf produce lighter types; a new area, developed since 1957, is the centre of the lake. The wells in the lake are on platforms linked by complicated systems of pipelines and electricity transmission lines, mainly on the lake bed. In eastern Venezuela, fields are more scattered, but the Oficina area is the major producer. Both areas are reasonably near the coast. Trinidad may be considered an extension of the eastern Venezuelan area.

In the 1920s Mexico had some of the most productive oil wells in the world, around Támpico. This area has continued to produce most of

* See Appendix A5.2 for growth of oil production in recent decades.

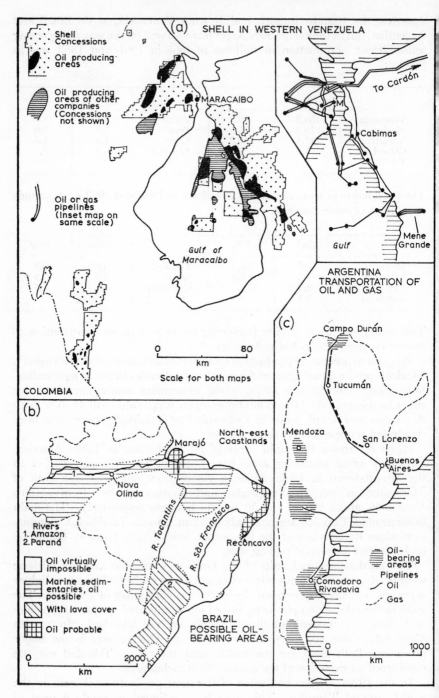

Figure 8.2. Oil in (a) Venezuela, (b) Brazil and (c) Argentina

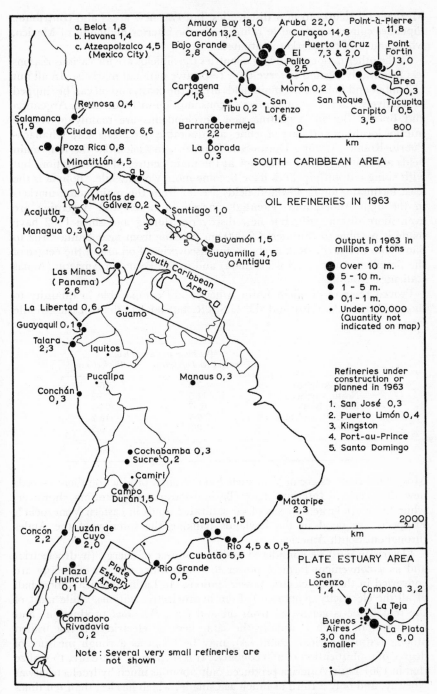

Figure 8.3. Oil refineries in Latin America, 1963[17]

Outline of coast based on a map in the Oxford Atlas published by the
Oxford University Press

Mexico's oil thanks to new discoveries, but two new areas also contribute. Pipelines convey crude oil to refineries in the interior highlands of Mexico, where much of the market is situated.

In the other major producing countries the oilfields are for various reasons less favourably located to serve their respective national markets. In all but Colombia and Bolivia, the main fields are on the coast, and oil can be shipped to relatively distant home centres of consumption in Peru, Chile, Argentina and Brazil. But in Argentina new developments are mainly in remote interior localities and long pipelines are desirable (see *Figure 8.2*; Challaco-Puerto Rosales, Campo Durán-San Lorenzo), in Colombia the four main fields are neither on the coast nor at the main centres of consumption, but with rising output, pipelines have become more worth while. Bolivia is the least fortunate, for its lowland fields are far from the main home markets in the high Andes, and potential markets in Brazil and Argentina are even more distant still, but new discoveries during and since 1962 have made it possible to consider a 2,000 km pipeline from near Santa Cruz to São Paulo in Brazil. Relatively recent discoveries of oil are in the centre of the Brazilian Amazon (Nova Olinda) and in the Peruvian Amazon (Aguas Calientes, Maquia).

Proved reserves of oil in Latin America are comparable in quantity to those in North America and the U.S.S.R. but far less than in the Middle East:

	Percentages of world total	
	Reserves (end of 1962)	*Production*
Latin America	7·8	16·9
North America	11·5	35·7
Middle East	62·7	24·7
U.S.S.R. and bloc	9·7	16·2
Other	8·3	6·5
	100	100

Most of the reserves are in Venezuela but currently production there exceeds new discoveries. Interior areas (Barinas-Paré) are promising, however, while there are large deposits of tar saturated sands in eastern Venezuela*. Prospects are good in the lowlands flanking the interior of the Andes throughout South America.

Electricity must be considered both as a source of energy (hydroelectric) and as a convenient form of power to which other sources of energy are converted in thermal electric power stations. In Latin America almost half of all the electricity generated is from hydroelectric stations, while most of the remainder is generated from oil and gas. *Per caput* production (and consumption, which is usually the same because electricity is not traded among Latin American countries), may be taken as a rough measure of degree of sophistication of an economy. It is surprising, therefore, to realize that in 1961 Latin America produced only about as much hydroelectricity as Norway, and only a third as much as Canada, which has less than ten times

* The Orinoco Tar Belt Area is estimated to have heavy crude reserves of about 28,000 m. tons. New techniques may soon make it commercially feasible to exploit these.

as many people. Its total output of electricity from all sources was only half that of the U.K. It is even more revealing to note that in 1948 output was less than one third what it was in 1961. In contrast to most other branches of production in Latin America, electricity output has risen steadily in all the major countries. This is because each plant is being planned and constructed over a considerable period, and increasing capacity rides smoothly over other irregularities in the economy that appear as year to year fluctuations. It seems likely that a further threefold increase may be expected in a comparable period.

TABLE 8.8[15]

	Total	1961	
		Hydro	% Hydro
Brazil	23,8	18,5	78
Mexico	11,7	5,0	43
Argentina	11,6	1,0	9
Chile	4,8	3,1	65
Colombia	3,8	2,6	68
Venezuela	3,4	0,1	3
Peru	2,4	1,4	58
Puerto Rico	2,4	0,3	12
All Latin America	72,6	34,1	

The relative importance of thermal electricity and hydroelectricity in the main producing countries can be seen in Table 8.8 (thousand million kWh generated). There are very ambitious electrification plans for several Latin American countries. Brazil plans to have several of the largest hydroelectricity power stations in the world, and others are being constructed or projected elsewhere. But thermal stations are also under construction in many areas, as for example in Buenos Aires.

8.4. OIL REFINING

In the late 1930s the oil refining capacity of Latin America was only about one sixth what it was in 1963. It was distributed as follows in 1937[16]:

Netherlands Antilles	20 m.	Venezuela	1 m.
Mexico	4½ m.	Peru	¾ m.
Argentina	2½ m.	Colombia	¼ m.
Trinidad	2 m.		

A little: Cuba, Bolivia, Ecuador, Uruguay.
Brazil only began refining in 1939.

Now, as in 1937, about two thirds of the total capacity is in the Caribbean area, but relatively the importance of the Netherlands Antilles has declined, while that of Venezuela has grown. Table 8.9 shows the distribution of refining capacity by regions in 1963.

About one third is still refined in the Islands, most in the Netherlands Antilles, where the two main Venezuelan producing companies each have a very large refinery, and in Trinidad. Venezuela and Colombia together have another 30 per cent of the total. About 50 per cent of the total refining capacity is owned by U.S. companies, 21 per cent by Netherlands and U.K. companies, the rest mainly by Latin American nationalized enterprises.

TABLE 8.9[17]

Regional Distribution of Refining Capacity, 1963,
in Thousands of Metric Tons

		Percentage of Latin American total			Percentage of Latin American total
Mexico	18,750	10·3	Ecuador	775	0·4
Central America	3,755	2·1	Peru	2,735	1·5
Cuba	4,235	2·3	Bolivia	640	0·3
Puerto Rico	6,000	3·3	Chile	2,235	1·2
Trinidad	15,050	8·2	Argentina	18,455	10·1
Neth. Antilles	36,750	20·1	Uruguay	2,250	1·2
Venezuela	51,640	28·3	Brazil	15,035	8·2
Colombia	4,275	2·3	TOTAL	182,625	100

In 1963 there were approximately 90 oil refineries in Latin America, varying greatly in size. Sixty eight had a capacity of over about 100,000 tons per year. The twelve refineries shown in Table 8.10 are the largest in Latin America and were accounting for about 65 per cent of all the oil processed in the early 1960s. Other refineries are shown in *Figure 8.3*.

The six largest refineries are based on the oil of Venezuela and Trinidad, especially western Venezuela, and produce primarily for shipment outside

TABLE 8.10

Location	Country	Ownership	Output 1963
Aruba	Neth. Antilles	Lago	22,000
Amuay Bay	Venezuela	Creole	18,000
Curaçao	Neth. Antilles	Shell	14,750
Cardón	Venezuela	Shell	13,150
Point-à-Pierre	Trinidad	Texaco	11,750
Puerto la Cruz	Venezuela	Gulf/Texas	7,250
Mexico City	Mexico	Pemex	6,650
La Plata	Argentina	Y.P.F.	6,000
Cubatão	Brazil	Petrobras	5,500
Rio	Brazil	Petrobras	4,500
Atzeapolzalco	Mexico	Pemex	4,500
Minatitlán	Mexico	Pemex	4,500
			118,300

the region. Aruba and Curaçao are served by tankers from the Maracaibo area, while the Venezuelan refineries receive oil by pipeline. Other refineries in or near oilfields are in Mexico, Colombia, Peru, southern Argentina, and Northeast Brazil. In the 1950s there was a growing tendency for large concentrations of population to have one or more refineries either based on home produced oil (Mexico City) or on home and imported (Buenos Aires area) or largely on imported (Cubatão, near São Paulo).

CHEMICALS

Oil refineries have understandably come to be considered as major sources of energy for industrial and other development in many parts of Latin America and almost every country now has one, or plans to have one, while many secondary concentrations of population aspire to having them, including several states in Brazil, where, however, a minimum size is fixed. Many very small refineries function in various parts of Latin America, either to process oil from small producing fields or as a token of progress in less developed areas. As in western Europe (e.g. southern Italy, Spain, Northern Ireland), the establishment of an oil refinery is increasingly coming to be thought of as a convenient starting point or development pole for industrialization, especially in an area deficient in energy, even if the oil is imported, hence the establishment of small refineries in the Central

TABLE 8.11[18]

	Number of plants		Crude capacity			Number of plants		Crude capacity	
	1963	1966	1963	1966		1963	1966	1963	1966
Mexico	6	7	407	530	Antigua	0	1	0	10
Guatemala	1	2	4	12	Trinidad	3	3	301	301
El Salvador	1	1	14	14	Neth. Antilles	2	2	650	650
Honduras	0	1	0	15	Venezuela	11	11	1,026	1,049
Nicaragua	1	1	5	5	Colombia	5	8	78	159
Costa Rica	0	1	0	5	Ecuador	2	2	16	16
Panama	1	1	55	55	Peru	4	5	54	67
Cuba	8	9	82	122	Brazil	9	11	300	440
Haiti	0	1	0	10	Paraguay	0	1	0	5
Dominican					Uruguay	1	1	46	46
Republic	0	1	0	10	Argentina	16	17	377	395
Jamaica	0	1	0	28	Chile	3	4	47	83
Puerto Rico	2	2	90	110					
					Latin America: 76 94 2,635 2,928				

American countries, in Haiti, the Amazon region (Manaus, Iquitos). The development of oil refining has also perhaps contributed more than anything else to the growth of a chemicals industry in several Latin American countries, and this branch is therefore considered in the next section. In view of the growing importance of oil refineries it is useful to list again in more detail the actual refining capacity (in thousands of barrels daily) of each country in 1963 and the proposed capacity in 1966. It will be noted that by 1966 *all* the 22 independent countries will have at least one refinery.

8.5. CHEMICALS

Latin America has numerous raw materials for the manufacture of chemicals but this branch of manufacturing lagged behind most others until recently. So far the manufacture of fertilizers has made most progress, but other branches are now expanding as well. Raw materials available include oil and natural gas and by-products obtained from the refining of oil in most countries, nitrates in Chile, guano in Peru, sulphur in Mexico, phosphates in several countries, as well as by-products from the processing of metallic ores.

Chilean nitrates were for a time a major world source of fertilizers. Natural nitrate in the mineral *caliche* is found widely in the desert area of

North Chile, and after extraction and purification by simple processes has been shipped to industrial countries. When nitrogen was obtained by other processes the industry declined in Chile, but $1\frac{1}{2}$ m. tons, with a nitrate equivalent of about 200–250,000 tons are still produced each year. Until the late 1950s, Latin America imported most of its needs of nitrogenous fertilizers, but thanks to the establishment recently of plants in several countries, based mainly on the use of waste gases from the oil industry, the capacity for producing synthetic nitrogen is expected to increase as follows:

1960	85,000 tons of N content
late 1961	290,000 tons of N content
1963	512,000 tons of N content
1965	710,000 tons of N content

Most of this will be from plant in or near existing oil refineries: Cubatão (Brazil), Minatitlán, Salamanca (Mexico), Morón (Venezuela), Cartagena (Colombia). Smaller quantities are produced in association with the iron and steel industry, while new factories are planned in backward agricultural areas, including Cusco (Peru), near Salvador (Northeast Brazil), as well as in Trinidad (to 235,000 tons per year of ammonia) for world markets. By the mid-1960s, nitrogenous fertilizers will be under production in varying quantities in about 20 localities, and some may soon be available for export outside Latin America.

Other types of fertilizer are not produced in such large quantities. Phosphate rock is extracted in Brazil (650,000 tons in 1962) and Peru (200,000 tons), and superphosphates have been produced in Brazil since 1954 (220,000 tons in 1961) and in Mexico (about 110,000 tons). Potash is not produced in Latin America at all except in very small quantities in Chile, and potassium fertilizers are imported if used at all.

Native sulphur is produced in large quantities only in Mexico, while very little is produced from pyrites. The Mexican output has increased impressively from very little in 1953 to $\frac{1}{2}$ m. tons in 1955 and around 1,300,000 per year in 1958–61, almost 20 per cent of the world total. Mexico is the largest producer of sulphuric acid in Latin America (300,000 tons in 1961) but even this is far less in *per caput* terms than the output of leading industrial countries; Brazil and Argentina produce smaller amounts. Sulphuric acid is an ingredient in many branches of chemicals and as it is not easily transported it must be made on the spot by any country aspiring to develop its chemicals industry. Around 1960 the output of other acids and of caustic soda was also very limited in Latin America. Salt (sodium chloride) is however produced in some quantity in virtually every country, often as a state monopoly. Even so, the total production for Latin America (about 2,750,000 tons in 1960) is only about one tenth that of North America and much is used directly for domestic purposes and food preserving. Production per country is roughly related to size of population and there is little trade in the commodity, but the Bahamas have a large surplus, while Bolivia, Paraguay and Uruguay apparently produce very little.

More sophisticated branches of the chemicals industry, such as the manufacture of paints and dyes, of synthetic fibres, rubber and so on are only beginning to develop in Latin America. These products often require costly equipment and considerable technical experience. Ironically, Brazil, the home of natural rubber, is manufacturing synthetic rubber, while plastics are made or planned in several countries. Leading centres of the chemicals industry are the São Paulo–Rio area, Morón in Venezuela, and

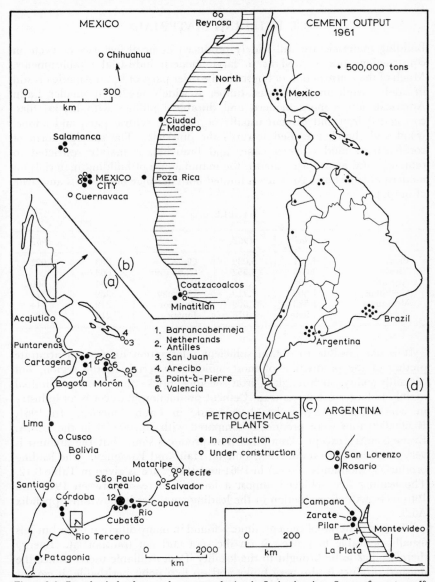

Figure 8.4. Petrochemicals plants and cement production in Latin America. Sources for maps a-c[19]

Mexico City and other centres in Mexico, while there are developments also near Rosario (San Lorenzo) in Argentina.

Figure 8.4 shows the distribution of petrochemicals works in Latin America[18], both existing and proposed; no indication is given of size of works or of the range of products. There is clearly a close relationship to the distribution of oil refineries, but places not on oilfields (e.g. Salamanca, San Lorenzo) and even without their own oil refineries (Bogotá, Recife) can receive crude oil or refined products by pipeline or sea.

8.6. BUILDING MATERIALS

Building materials are still widely produced in small factories or even on construction sites as well as in large modern industrial establishments. Much of the construction of houses in the drier parts of Latin America is still in adobe, while in the forests, timber is widely used. In smaller Latin American towns more modern and durable buildings with bricks, tiles, corrugated iron and cement usually occupy the central part, and adobe, wood and thatch are used towards the outskirts. The simplest form of construction, mud covered canes and branches, is mainly restricted to remoter rural areas. In general, the manufacture of building materials on modern lines in Latin America is limited both in range of products and scale of output.

TABLE 8.12

	1961	1962		1961	1962
Brazil	4,711	5,039	Chile	883	1,022
Mexico	3,035	3,352	Cuba (59)	663	
Argentina	2,906	2,945	Peru	594	660
Colombia	1,569	1,719	Uruguay	389	374
Venezuela	1,513	1,509	Ecuador	219	214
Puerto Rico	966	1,078	Jamaica	216	200

It is not possible to obtain sufficient information to give an accurate picture of the production of most building materials in the region, but certainly many, such as glass, iron sheeting, bricks and so on are limited mainly to larger urban centres. Cement production however is an industry in which great progress has been made in Latin America. In 1961, 18,600,000 tons were produced, compared with 56,700,000 in the U.S.A. Every country except Costa Rica now produces some, but the amount is very small in Central America, Bolivia, Haiti and Paraguay. The leading producers (thousands of tons) in 1961 and 1962[20] are as given in Table 8.12. The leading five achieved almost a fourfold increase between 1948 and 1961. Growth of production in the leading countries is shown in Appendix A5.3.

The raw material of cement, lime, is found in many different rocks but it is usually desirable to process it on the spot and not transport it. Energy therefore has to be brought to the locality if not available there. Since the finished product is also very bulky and up to a point perishable, it cannot conveniently be transported far except by sea in Latin America. Most of the larger cement works are therefore in or near large towns or in mining areas. Since the demand for cement in urban areas is growing rapidly, rural markets, usually difficult to reach anyway, fare very badly or pay very highly for the product. For special purposes cement may even be flown to remote areas, but to do this is absurd; the answer is either to put up a large number of small and presumably inefficient cement works, or to improve communications.

The sequence of cement works in Peru illustrates the expansion of the industry. Until 1956 the only cement produced at home came from a works in the capital, Lima. A second works was opened at Pacasmayo in the north in 1956 to serve the sizable and growing centres of north Peru. A third works is under construction to supply the south. Thus there has been not only an increase in total output (280,000 in 1948, 654,000 in 1961) but decentralization of manufacture. In Uruguay, in contrast, there is still only one works, Montevideo. Brazil and Mexico on the other hand have had regional works for some time but some of the smallest countries (Honduras, Haiti, Paraguay) did not manufacture cement at all before the 1950s.

8.7. NON-FERROUS METALS*

The production of metals has probably been the field of production in which Latin America has made most impact on the economy of the world in the last four centuries. The export of silver and to a lesser extent gold in the sixteenth century is considered to have influenced the economies of west European countries profoundly. Later, Brazilian minerals were important, while in the nineteenth century Chile (1857–1880) was the leading producer of copper in the world. At present, Latin America produces over half of the bauxite of the world and Mexico is the leading producer of silver and a major producer of zinc. Up to a point, too, the occurrence of metallic minerals guided the direction of colonial settlement in the sixteenth century.

In the mid-twentieth century the names of several Latin American countries still bring to mind certain metals, even though in several cases mining has declined in relative importance as a source of exports (e.g. in Mexico from 90 per cent in 1837 to 15 per cent now), and the oil industry has eclipsed other branches of mining in a number of countries. Nor does the extraction of metallic minerals and their processing and shipment employ a large labour force. Mining encampments are isolated, remain small, and can be a liability because they sometimes have to be supplied with food, water and energy from distant sources.

The relative contribution of major Latin American producers of metals was shown in Section 8.2. Here output is listed in 1961[21]:

	Thousand tons of metal content				Tons	
	Copper	Lead	Zinc	Tin	Silver	Gold
Mexico	48	176	52		1,255	8,4
Peru	182	77	32		1,044	4,2
Bolivia				21	121	0,9
Chile	502				54	1,6
Argentina		28	15		44	
Colombia						11,8
Brazil						3,8

* See *Figure 8.5.*

187

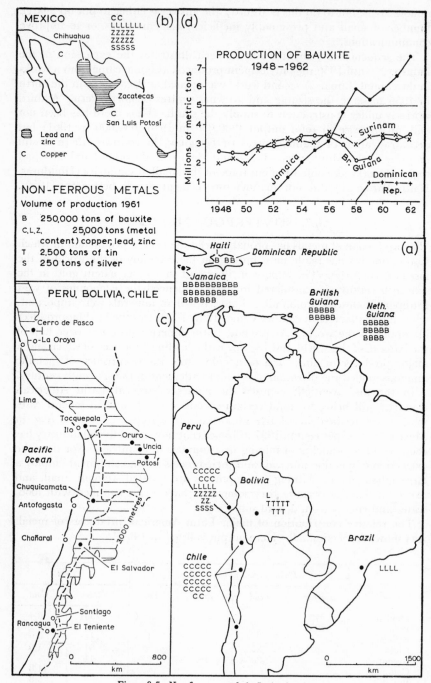

Figure 8.5. Non-ferrous metals in Latin America

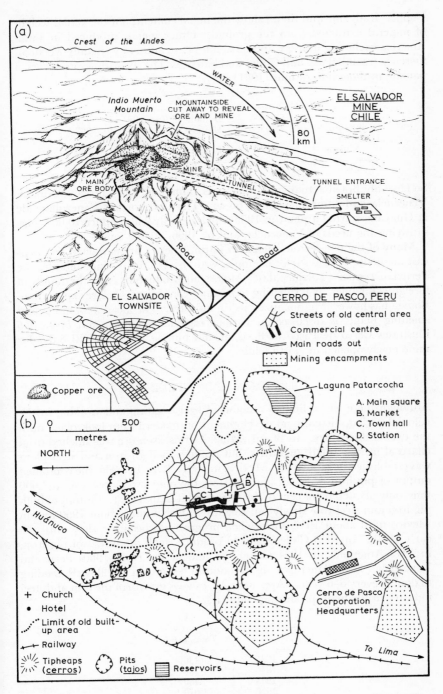

Figure 8.6. (a) El Salvador copper mine of the Anaconda Company, Chile. (b) Cerro de Pasco, Peru

189

Copper, lead, zinc and tin all show the metal content, not the actual weight of mineral extracted from the ground. Other metals produced in Latin America excluding iron ore and ferro-alloys are antimony (mainly Mexico), mercury (mainly Peru and Chile) and bauxite. The six leading producers of bauxite in thousands of tons (1961) are:

Jamaica	6,615	Dominican Republic	734
Surinam	3,405	Haiti	267
British Guiana	2,412	Brazil	98

So far, only Brazil actually manufactures aluminium but Mexico, Surinam, Venezuela and Jamaica plan to do so. The Corporación Venezolana de la Guayana started a plant in 1963 which initially will produce 10,000 tons, satisfying the needs of Venezuela, and by 1966, 20,000 tons.

Many of the non-ferrous metals in Latin America are extracted by open-cast methods. This is so, for example, with most of the bauxite and also the Peruvian copper (Tocquepala). Almost all production is in the hands of foreign companies, as is smelting to produce concentrates before exportation. Bolivia has however nationalized its tin industry. The location of mines and smelting plants is discussed in various regional chapters, and *Figure 8.6* illustrates Cerro de Pasco in Peru, an old mining town, and El Salvador mine newly opened in North Chile.

8.8. IRON AND STEEL

Although there was a limited amount of iron smelting and working in the colonial period, virtually no development on modern lines took place until the twentieth century. In Brazil (Minas Gerais) iron ore was smelted from charcoal in very small quantities, but the first modern iron and steel plant was established in Monterrey, Mexico, in 1897. Even by 1935, the combined output of pig iron of Brazil and Mexico, the only producers, was 130,000 tons, only about 0·6 per cent of the U.S. output in that year. Output of both pig iron and steel rose slowly but steadily in Brazil until about 1950 and in Mexico until about 1957, since when progress has been less slow until the early 1960s. In 1940 Chile began to produce small quantities of pig iron, in 1947 Argentina, in 1954 Colombia, and in the early 1960s Peru and Venezuela. Latin American pig iron output has grown as follows[23], tending to double every 5–6 years. Appendix A5.4 shows growth of the iron and steel industry in the main producing countries

	Thous. tons
1935	130
1940	280
1945	480
1950	1,070
1955	1,800
1960	3,055

Obviously it cannot do this indefinitely, but may continue to do so in the next 10–15 years.

While it is possible to establish a steel industry on scrap metal or on imported pig iron, this has not been done to any great extent in Latin America, while individual countries, although with iron ore deposits, have been slow to develop integrated works. In the mid-1930s Latin America was only producing about ½ m. tons of iron ore per year, a small part in Mexico for home consumption, the rest in Chile for export (Cruz Grande). A peak of about 2 m. tons iron content per year was reached in the middle of the Second World War, as ore was exported to the U.S.A., but the rapid increase that has made Latin America one of the leading iron ore producers of the world began only in the early 1950s. Compare 3,6 m. tons iron content in 1950 with 26,5 m. in 1960, nearly half produced by Venezuela. The following figures show iron content in millions of tons[24]:

	1955	1961	1962		1955	1962	1963
Venezuela	5,4	9,3	8,5	Peru	1,1	3,1	3,2
Brazil	2,3	6,7	n.a.	Mexico	0,4	0,7	1,1
Chile	0,9	4,4	5,2	Colombia	0,1	0,3	0,3

Most of the iron ore produced in Latin America is of very high grade and the actual ore extracted amounts to only about 50–60 per cent more in weight than the iron content figures given above. About 90 per cent of the total production is exported, so far mainly without being concentrated. Production is almost entirely in the hands of large foreign companies but ore may be sold by these to producing countries at advantageous prices. Most of the exports go to the U.S.A., which now derives from foreign sources about one third of the iron content of all the iron ore it consumes.

Figure 8.7 shows the main iron ore producing countries in Latin America. Almost all the ore produced so far has come from four main areas, Minas Gerais in Brazil, north-central Chile, eastern Venezuela and southern Peru, in all but the first place, from deposits close to the coast. The ore produced in Mexico and Colombia is mainly for home consumption. Some of the principal reserves are listed below:

Mexico: proved, about 230 m. tons mainly at Cerro del Mercado in Durango, Las Truchas in Michoacán

Venezuela: about 1,420 m. tons in the Imataca iron belt, of which 1,200 m. in the so-called Cuadrilátero Ferrífero Bolívar

Peru: mainly at Marcona, with 410 m. tons (planned to produce 7 m. tons in 1965 and 10 m. in 1970)

Chile: proved, about 200 m., plus perhaps 3,000 m. (see Chapter 18.2)

Brazil: 35,000 m. tons in Minas Gerais alone.

Bolivia: Mutun (near Puerto Suárez, eastern Bolivia) 40–50,000 m.

Argentina: Sierra Grande (Rio Negro) 50 m.

The only large producers and consumers of iron and steel in 1961 were as follows (thousands of tons):

TABLE 8.13[26]

	Pig iron 1962	Steel 1961	Steel 1962	Steel consumption	Steel consumption, kilograms per caput
Brazil	1,821	2,400	2,800	2,701	37
Mexico	912	1,728	1,851	1,840	51
Argentina	396	441	644	2,379	113
Chile	383	363	495	506	65
Colombia	149	176	137	405	28
Peru				246	24
Venezuela				448	59
Cuba				277	40
Uruguay				86	30

All the producing countries except Argentina also produced metallurgical coke, while Brazil is a major producer of manganese ore. Other ferro-alloys produced formerly in Latin America but not now are chrome ore (Cuba) and vanadium (Peru).

One drawback in Latin America, lack of coking coal, has now largely been overcome. One way has been to use charcoal for smelting, derived mainly from eucalypts, especially in Minas Gerais (Monlevade, Coronel Fabriciano), but this is wasteful. Much more important has been the use of electricity (e.g. Venezuela), while gas is being considered for a proposed works in Salvador, Brazil. What is more, U.S. coking coal can be transported to some works very cheaply in ore carriers otherwise returning empty.

Figure 8.7 shows the distribution of most of the centres of the iron and steel industry in the mid-1950s[25a], but is by no means complete. Several major new works have come into production since the publication of *Iron and Steel Works of the World*[25a], a number of others have been started, and many more have been proposed. In view of the importance of the industry to the future industrialization of Latin America and the lack of recent information on the subject, Table 8.14 summarizes the main features of existing works and shows proposed features of ones that are under construction or are seriously being considered; unfortunately it is not complete. More details are mentioned in later chapters under the countries concerned.

The iron and steel works in Latin America are so varied in size and type of location that they defy simple classification. *Figure 8.7* therefore merely shows the relationship of each of the main works to the iron ore it uses, the main source of energy, and the market it serves. Only Paz del Rio, Colombia has all three main ingredients in one locality. San Nicolás in Argentina has none on the spot, but is very well placed to serve the national market. The same is largely true also of Volta Redonda, which does however have hydroelectric power in the vicinity. Several fairly small new works such as Recife and Barranquilla are planned to serve regional markets. Others, such as Huachipato and Chimbote are basically designed to serve national needs, though Huachipato has had a surplus of steel for export at times. A number of new works, on the other hand, have clearly been planned with international markets, or at least the LAFTA market, in mind, particularly the eastern Venezuela and Vitória (Brazil) works. Venezuela has actually already exported small amounts of steel to the U.S.A., Japan and West Europe, as well as to Colombia, Panama and Argentina. By 1975 Brazil hopes to be exporting 2 m. tons per year to LAFTA countries.

TABLE 8.14

Summary

Country	Locality (No. of works) Coastal italicized	Type of energy	Output 1960–62	Projected output	Products
Mexico	Monclova	C	300		
	Monterrey (2)	C	600		
	Mexico (several)	E	100		
	Las Truchas (Mich.)			Very large	
Venezuela	Puerto Ordaz	E, C	400 (63)	−700–1·2 m.	Ingot steel,
	Caracas (small)				seamless steel, tubes, wire
Colombia	Paz del Rio	C	70	220 (68)	
	Barranquilla				
Ecuador	with Chilean			25 (1965)	
	financial help				
Peru	Chimbote	E, C			
Chile	Huachipato	C	440 (pig)		
			520 (steel)	600 (by 64/5)	
Argentina	Zapla	Ch			
	Prov. of Rio Negro				
	San Nicolás	C			
	Villa Constitución				
	Campana				
	Buenos Aires		100		
	La Plata			1,400	Steel ingots
Brazil	Santa Cruz (Rio)				
	Volta Redonda	C	1,200	3,600	
	Belo Horizonte				
	(Mannesmann)	Ch	120	350	
	Usminas	C	500 (63)	1 m. (65)	
				2 m. (70)	
	Monlevade	Ch	130	380 (67)	Medium and fine steels
	Vitória	C		2 m.	
	São Paulo (Cosipa)	E	400		Ingot steel
	Santa Catarina state	C		100	
	Salvador (Usiba)	Gas		130	Finished steel
	Porto Alegre				
	Recife				

C—coal, E—electricity, Ch—charcoal
Plants have also been proposed for Central America, Cuba and Ecuador.

Almost all the larger works make pig iron as well as steel, but some smaller works, both in existing industrial concentrations such as Mexico City and São Paulo, and in smaller centres, produce only steel, using scrap or pig iron from elsewhere. A wide range of products is now being turned out by the major works, including not only relatively simple items such as rods for ferro-concrete construction, girders, rails and so on, but also equipment for the oil industry, including seamless steel tubes (Venezuela). In addition, metal working is becoming fairly widespread, especially in

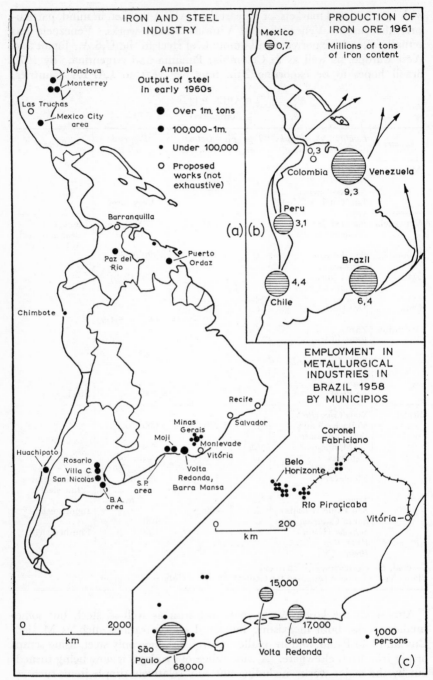

Figure 8.7. Iron and steel industry in Latin America (a)[25a], (c)[25b]

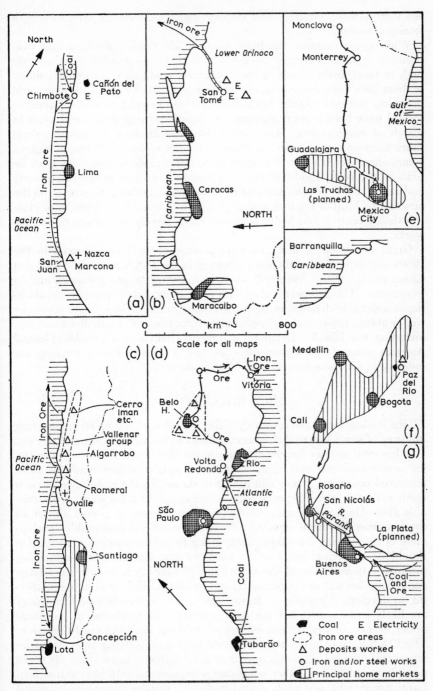

Figure 8.8. The main centres of iron and steel manufacturing in Latin America. To facilitate comparison, the maps are all on the same scale. (a) Peru. (b) Venezuela. (c) Chile. (d) Brazil. (e) Mexico. (f) Colombia. (g) Argentina

195

the three largest countries, and engineering, also, is closely associated with steel production.

While great progress has been made in developing the iron and steel industry in Latin America since the mid-1950s, production costs are still high in most works owing to their relatively small size. Moreover, many of them have been slow to start producing (e.g. San Nicolás, Chimbote) and provision has not usually been adequate for housing workers. Even so several have been a great attraction to people moving from rural areas in search of employment. The population of Chimbote increased several times even before any steel was produced there, and the area in eastern Venezuela in which the new town of San Tomé de la Guayana is to be built for the heavy industrial complex based on the new steelworks, already had about 50,000 people, many of them squatters, before work started on the new town. Most of the iron and steel mills of Latin America are in or close to existing centres, but Volta Redonda exists largely as a result of its steel works.

Great expansion of iron and steel production may be expected in the 1960s—an expansion of the kind achieved in the U.S.S.R. in the 1930s and China in the 1950s. Most will come in the three largest countries and in Venezuela. The prospect is that with economies of scale possible thanks to the considerable demand in their own home markets these larger countries will be able to produce cheaply enough to serve many of the smaller countries, including the Islands, Uruguay, Paraguay, Bolivia and possibly Central America none of which may therefore find it worth while to develop the industry at all, though each would like to do so.

8.9. ENGINEERING

All the leading industrial countries of the world have built up an engineering industry of some sort and this seems almost to be a prerequisite of success. It is less vital to later developers than to the first countries to industrialize, for newer countries can equip themselves with machines made in more advanced countries, if they can afford to do so. In the end, however, it is costly to do this, and if dependence on other countries is not wanted, undesirable also. Until now, Latin American countries have imported almost all the machines they have required. Recently, however, considerable development of engineering has taken place, and a decade or two hence the region should be satisfying many of its needs of less sophisticated engineering products. Indeed, one of the main aims of LAFTA is to provide a large enough market and sufficient capital and training facilities to enable engineering to develop. Virtually no major innovations in engineering technology are likely to be made, nor are they necessary, for products can be made under licence, or designs can be copied, without slow and costly research. The U.S.S.R. and Japan both depended largely on copying other countries for several decades, although now they are capable of innovating. It is not possible therefore to predict what stages engineering will pass through in Latin America for if it could afford to do so, virtually any underdeveloped country could buy complicated machinery, pay foreign technicians, and make very advanced products without having gone through the stages of making simpler items such as textile machinery and steam locomotives. In fact, the larger Latin American countries have tended to go from simpler stages to more complex ones and it may be assumed that the stages listed below would be passed through in turn, but the list is only suggested tentatively.

Iron or now usually steel can be made immediately into girders, rails, pipes and so on and be used without being made into machines, or can be worked into simple products such as horseshoes, nails and ploughshares without great skill or capital investment. A proper engineering industry arises from the assembly of various parts to make machines. Even such relatively simple pieces of equipment as clocks, carpenters' tools, agricultural implements and so on are not widely made in Latin America, and outside a factory equipped from Europe or North America, the manufacture of a cycle would still be far too exacting a task.

Suggested stages of complication in engineering	Stage reached by selected countries
Simple textile machinery	
Steam engines	
Locomotives and rolling stock	
Ships (small)	
Motor vehicle assembly	
Simple electrical goods	Chile
Motor vehicle parts	Venezuela
Complete motor vehicle manufacture	Argentina, Mexico
Machine tools	
Power station equipment	Brazil, China
Precision engineering	Italy
Electronics	W. Germany, Japan
Supersonic aircraft	
Nuclear power	U.K., France
Space rockets and satellites	U.S.A., U.S.S.R.

1958 figures[27] show that metal working and engineering in that year was much more confined to certain countries than were most other branches of industry. The distribution by country (in percentages of the Latin American total) of basic metal and of metal working and engineering, was as follows:

	Metallurgical	Metal working and engineering
Brazil	21·5	30·6
Argentina	15·7	29·0
Mexico	41·6	21·7
Venezuela	0·5	4·0
Colombia	1·5	3·3
Chile	17·4	3·2
Uruguay	0·4	3·1

With only 60 per cent of the population, Brazil, Mexico and Argentina together had over 80 per cent of engineering. Most of the remainder was in the next four countries. Venezuela is likely to increase its share, but there are few signs of great progress in any other countries, and the major powers seem likely to dominate the industry even more, unless smaller countries are allocated certain branches in which to specialize for LAFTA. Small size of home market and lack of internal capital are against them, however, and by the time they reach a stage when they can manufacture say steam locomotives, these will be obsolete anyway.

Just as oil has come to play a dominant role in the economy of nearly every Latin America country, however, it seems probable that one branch of engineering, the manufacture of motor vehicles, may find expression widely, and come to be the leading branch, and its development therefore deserves special attention. The procedure has usually been first for the importation of motor vehicles to be organized through sales centres in the major towns, then for these to stock parts and to service and repair vehicles. Later, some parts begin to be made in the importing countries, and finally vehicles are imported in knocked down condition and assembled locally rather than transported in finished condition from the factory. All this is usually done by the motor vehicle firms themselves, but eventually there is enough skilled labour for the manufacture of complete vehicles to be contemplated and the establishment of subsidiary factories to be worth while. This is a gradual procedure, and has usually been achieved by raising the proportion of parts that must be made in the host country. In Venezuela, for example, the situation is that 13 per cent by weight of the parts will have to be home produced in 1963, 30 per cent in 1964 and 60 per cent in 1970. By 1963 Brazil was already making about 80 per cent of the parts used in its motor vehicle industry and some types were almost entirely Brazilian made; the proportion in Argentina was 60 per cent. In the end it has become more advantageous for large U.S. and West European firms to have complete factories in Latin America than for them to continue exporting vehicles. As in Australia, so now in Brazil, complete motor vehicles are being made on the spot. This stage is near in Argentina, Mexico, Venezuela and Chile as well, while assembly is carried out in at least five other countries, Colombia, Uruguay, Peru, Ecuador and El Salvador. For example, General Motors has six overseas units in Latin America importing, distributing and assembling: in Argentina, Brazil, Mexico, Peru, Uruguay and Venezuela, and most of the world's large motor vehicle manufacturing firms are represented somewhere in the region.

Actual figures for motor vehicle manufacture give only a rough picture of the degree of development and of capacity of the industry since a clear distinction cannot be made between the varying stages ranging from simple assembly to complete manufacture, and types of vehicle cannot be sorted out easily. Brazil is the most advanced, however, while Argentina, Mexico, Chile and Venezuela follow. The main centres of the industry are the São Paulo area, Greater Buenos Aires, Mexico City, Arica in Chile, and Caracas in Venezuela.

In reality no single domestic market in Latin America has been large enough to need several motor vehicle firms, yet 23 plants have been set up in Argentina alone since 1959 to produce for a market needing only about 100,000 per year. By 1963 there were 14 in Chile and 6 in Venezuela. To overcome this, a number of the companies operating in more than one LAFTA country have made plans to integrate their efforts, concentrating manufacture in a single country to achieve economies of scale. Thus in 1963 for example one firm was contemplating establishing its works in Central

Chile to serve Brazil, Argentina and Mexico as well as Chile, and using parts from these countries. This is the first serious attempt to break down the nationalistic tradition and to make use of the possibilities offered by LAFTA. In general terms the idea is to avoid duplication in the manufacture of models and to standardize parts. Other interesting developments are the exportation of Brazilian made vehicles to other Latin American countries (e.g. to Chile, Ecuador) and the plan to set up a plant in Ecuador to *assemble* vehicles manufactured in Argentina.

The development of the motor vehicles industry will be interesting to watch in the next few years. Circumstances in Latin America are so different from those in West Europe and the U.S.A. that many factors affecting the location of the industry there are absent. Perhaps the most striking but not surprising feature has been the way the industry has remained in or near the largest concentrations of population, precisely the places through which imported vehicles were and still are distributed. But whereas the mere assembly of vehicles does not benefit much from economies of scale, this is essential for a complete cycle of manufacturing.

The development of other branches of engineering must also be mentioned. Several countries now make sizable metal ships (Brazil, Peru, Chile and Colombia) but much of the machinery in these is of course imported. Brazil is making advances in marine engineering and the following example illustrates the way in which an industry can be forced by legislation into becoming entirely home based. Three firms in Brazil make marine diesel engines; these are obliged quite arbitrarily to incorporate an increasing percentage of Brazilian made parts in the following way:

	Percentage		
	1963/64	*1965/6*	*1967*
Larger engines	40	50	75
Smaller engines	50	60	80

Brazil is also making rapid strides in the manufacture of machine tools; output rose by 260 per cent between 1956 and 1961, and by the latter year some 40 per cent of the national needs were being produced in Brazil (90 per cent in the São Paulo area); by 1971 Brazil could be producing 85 per cent of its needs. In 1963 it was being planned to build helicopters in Brazil in collaboration with the French firm Sud Aviation, the first step towards establishing the manufacture of aircraft in Latin America. Latin America also has the beginnings of a nuclear energy industry, while the establishment of a LAFTA Institute for the Electric and Electronic Industry shows interest in this important field. It goes without saying, of course, that many of the more complicated machines will not be produced in Latin America for a long time to come and expansion of engineering in Latin America will mean more, rather than fewer, imports of many types of capital engineering goods from outside the region.

8.10. TEXTILES AND OTHER INDUSTRIES

As already stressed in the previous chapter, Latin America is a leading world producer of both cotton and wool, though its share of the latter has declined

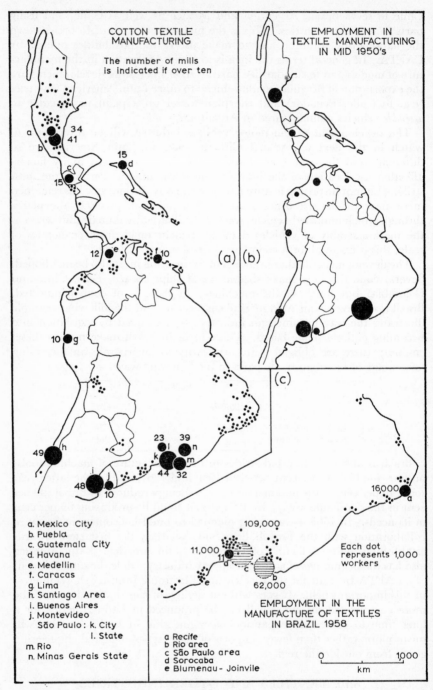

Figure 8.9. Textile manufacturing in Latin America. (a) The distribution of cotton manufacturing establishments[30]. (b) Employment in textile manufacturing by countries. (c) Employment in textile manufacturing in Brazil in 1958[31]

in recent decades. Cotton is produced in almost every country and forms the basis of textile manufacturing in most. Sheep (and llamas) are raised mainly outside the tropics or at high altitudes. Spinning, weaving, and the manufacture of clothing were widely practised in the colonial period though rarely at more than domestic level. In the nineteenth century, however, textile machinery was bought in Europe, and, as in Russia, Italy, Spain, India and other parts of the world, modern manufacturing industry in Latin America commenced in most parts of Latin America with cotton manufacturing. None of the factors so often quoted as essential in determining the location of cotton manufacturing in Lancashire seem to have contributed. The first consideration was of course sufficient capital to establish an industry, the second, protection to give it a chance to consolidate itself against foreign competition. Quite independently, groups of industrialists set up mills in Puebla and Orizaba, Mexico, in Medellin, Colombia, and in Juiz de Fora, Brazil; not one is a national capital. Subsequently the industry has tended to grow up more in capitals than anywhere else, with the exception of São Paulo and towns in its vicinity.

The general distribution of textile manufacturing can be gained from figures of employment[28] (in thousands) for the mid-1950s

Brazil	338	Peru	25
Argentina	175	Uruguay	24
Mexico	138	Venezuela	8
Chile	37	Ecuador	7
Colombia	25	Central America	12

There would probably be about 50–60,000 more in the remaining areas, bringing the total to 850,000. Although this branch of manufacturing has not increased so fast as others, quite possibly 1 m. people are now employed in modern textile manufacturing, not counting perhaps as many again spinning or weaving part time in poorer agricultural areas (the Andes, southern Mexico). It is possible to obtain a breakdown for Brazil in 1958[29]. The total number employed in textile manufacturing was 335,000, of which only 47,000 were in the Northeast, 109,000 in the São Paulo area and 62,000 in the Rio area (see *Figure 8.9c*). After São Paulo and Rio, Recife was a secondary concentration and Blumenau–Joinvile an additional district. A very rough guide to the manufacture of cotton alone, based on mills listed[30] suggests that there are seven main concentrations of important mills:

Mexico City	Santiago	Rio
Puebla	Buenos Aires	São Paulo
Medellín		

and secondary centres of importance are Havana, Caracas, Lima, Montevideo, Juiz de Fora and Recife. Few of the cotton textile mills in Latin America are very large but some, including those of Colombia, are very well equipped.

The manufacture of woollen textiles in modern mills is limited to a few countries only[30]. Buenos Aires and Montevideo are wool merchanting centres and have most of the mills in their respective countries. Peru,

Chile and southern Brazil also produce and manufacture some wool. Lima and Santiago are the main but not the only centres of the industry, while São Paulo appears to dominate manufacturing in Brazil. Other branches of textile manufacturing in Latin America are of limited and localized importance: silk and linen have not flourished anywhere, but artificial and synthetic fibres are both produced and woven on a limited scale and the jute industry is being established by some countries.

In general, Latin American countries satisfy their needs in textiles, though the higher quality goods, especially woollens and worsteds, have to be imported from Europe. The industry has developed within the tariff protection of each individual country to serve national markets and little inter-Latin American trade in textiles therefore exists at present or is contemplated under LAFTA conditions. Nor is the industry likely to expand appreciably compared with other branches. In most countries it has tended to grow up and remain confined in one centre (Medellín, Montevideo) or a small number (Puebla-Orizaba-Mexico City-Guadalajara), but in Brazil it is to be found in many centres away from the Rio-São Paulo area and is one of the branches being expanded in the Northeast to help this region.

Although food, textiles, metal-smelting and engineering, and chemicals are the leading branches of industry, many other branches are also represented in Latin America and several deserve mention. The larger Latin American countries satisfy many of their needs of light industrial products. The following figures, for want of complete sets for a more recent year, at least give an idea of the relative importance of various branches, showing persons employed in 1953 in thousands:

TABLE 8.15

	Mexico	Venez.	Col.	Peru	Chile	Arg.	Brazil
Clothing	51	14	29	9	23	123	77
Leather	8	1	4	2	4	19	21
Rubber	6	1	3	1	2	10	11
Wood	44	9	10	4	11	125	107
Paper	10	1	2	2	3	22	25
Printing	16	4	8	4	7	42	49

Of these branches, only the manufacture of paper tends to take place in large sized establishments. The other branches are often carried out in small workshops or by self-employed individuals (tailors, cobblers, furniture makers and so on). Many of the above figures must have become larger by the early 1960s, while some, particularly clothing, certainly do not include all persons engaged, since many are employed part time only. Clothing and footwear are made throughout Latin America on a small scale, and factory made clothing is only a recent feature, though it is likely to reduce the role of small scale manufacturers drastically, as has happened in so many more advanced countries. Several smaller countries, notably Uruguay, Cuba, Puerto Rico, Ecuador and El Salvador are not shown in the table but have made considerable progress in light manufacturing.

8.11. CONCLUSIONS

With regard to the general distribution of industry in Latin America, as already shown in Chapter 7.10, agricultural processing is widespread; although associated above all with areas of commercial agriculture, the preparation of foods and beverages is carried on throughout the region. If sugar, cotton and coffee are usually processed in large or moderate sized establishments, manioc, maize, potatoes and other such subsistence crops are prepared for consumption throughout the agricultural areas of the continent. Along the Pacific coast of South America the expansion of fishmeal production has led to the establishment of many new factories. Mining products are also processed where possible where they are mined in order to reduce their weight and bulk. This is essential for non-ferrous metals and requires a large consumption of energy. More steps are now also being taken to concentrate iron ore before shipping it, particularly in Chile and Peru (Marcona). The refining of oil was initially the privilege of countries importing this product from Latin America but in the last 20 years producing countries have tried to ensure that as much refining as possible is done before the oil is exported. Oil refineries in Latin America are located therefore both in and near oilfields (e.g. Venezuela) and near large importing centres (e.g. Rio, La Plata).

The remaining industries of Latin America, which have mostly been protected at some stage or other in their development, still cater largely for the consumer market, and generally it has been advantageous to have a location in or near a large city, usually the capital, with an appreciable market on the doorstep. Indeed, this has been the procedure in countries of all sizes, although some other centres already mentioned (e.g. Monterrey, São Paulo), which are not national capitals, are also important industrially. Presumably earlier, if not now, capital has been much more readily available in the larger cities than elsewhere. A further type of location is beginning to become prominent in certain circumstances. In certain industries, bulky raw materials from different areas can most conveniently be assembled at some place not necessarily near where they are produced nor near a large city. This is the case in the iron and steel works of Volta Redonda in Brazil.

Some of the drawbacks and advantages of industry in Latin America may now be suggested. Industrialization in Latin America has been hindered by the very small size of most national markets. For example, the purchasing power in Guatemala or Ecuador is only as great as that in an English county the size of say Norfolk or Devon. That in Brazil is roughly equal to the purchasing power of Belgium spread (unevenly) over an area the size of Europe. The total gross domestic product of Brazil in 1963 was very roughly equal in value to the total sales of the single U.S. firm of General Motors in that year. Lack of capital and of a class of entrepreneurs has further delayed the progress of industrialization, while foreign capital has been mainly though not entirely directed towards obtaining raw materials for export. The resulting lack of skilled labour and of an interest in technology are added disadvantages. Lack of good reserves of coal is a further debatable disadvantage. In the century 1840–1940 industry throughout the world depended heavily on energy from this source, but now gas, oil and hydroelectric energy

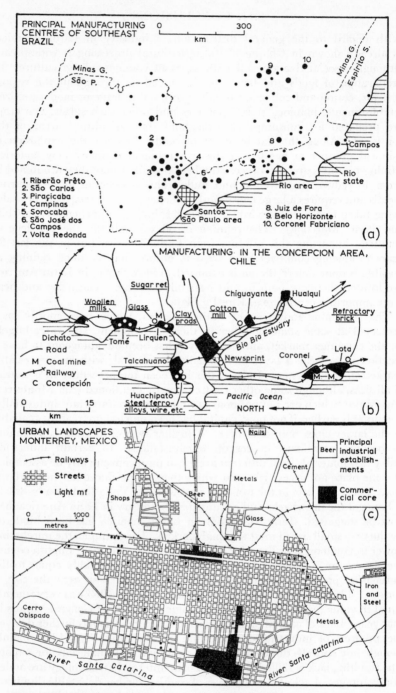

Figure 8.10. Examples of manufacturing areas in Latin America. (a) Southeast Brazil[33]. (b) Concepción area, Chile[34]. (c) Monterrey[35] by kind permission of the authoress

can replace coal in almost every branch of industry and only a few million tons is imported by Latin America, mainly to serve the iron and steel industry and mining activities. The fact that there were so few coalfields in Latin America does not necessarily mean that this held up industrial development; China has very large reserves of coal but these were hardly used until the 1930s, were exploited on a large scale only in the 1950s, and have only recently become the basis of modern industry. Scandinavia and Italy began to industrialize at a fairly early stage *without* home produced coal.

Among the advantages of Latin America as a whole are its large quantity and variety of raw materials and of sources of energy other than coal, and the fact that the old industrial countries whether they like it or not are passing on their discoveries and techniques to the new industrial countries. Very few innovations in technology have been made in Latin America, yet many complicated industrial items are produced, initially often under licence. A further stimulus to the development of those branches of industry requiring a reasonably large home market before economies of large scale are achieved are the interest in, and the moves towards economic union among the leading industrial countries.

Some more detailed features of industrial areas will be discussed and illustrated in regional chapters to follow. *Figure 8.10* shows the industries of three areas, a large area in Southeast Brazil[33], a small area in Chile, and the town of Monterrey in Mexico.

REFERENCES

[1] *Towards a Dynamic Development Policy for Latin America*, p. 71; United Nations
[2] Crossley, J. C. 'The Growth of Manufacturing Industry in Latin America', *J. Inst. Bankers* Oct. 1963
[3] *UNSY, 1962*, Table 164
[4] *Patterns of Industrial Growth 1938–1958*, Part II, Data for Industrial Countries, 1960, New York; United Nations
[5] *UNSY, 1961*, Tables 10 and 11
[6] *UNSY, 1962*, Table 11
[7] *UNSY, 1962*, Table 122 and 1963, Table 129
[8] *UNSY, 1962*
[9] *UNSY, 1962* Table 10
[10] *UNSY, 1962* Table 11
[11] *UNSY, 1962*, Table 122
[12] *UNSY, 1963*, Table 45
[13] *UNSY, 1962*, Table 43; Petroleum Press Service, January 1964
[14] *UNSY, 1963*, Table 47
[15] *UNSY, 1962*, Table 125
[16] *UNSY, 1955*, Table 102
[17] *Petroleum Information Bureau*
[18] *Annual Refinery Review*, 1963
[19] *World Petroleum*, 'The World's Petrochemical Plants', July 15, 1963
[20] *UNSY, 1963*, Table 113
[21] *UNSY, 1962*, Various tables
[22] *Andes Copper Mining Company*, Anaconda
[23] *UNSY, 1955, 1962*
[24] *UNSY, 1963*, Table 50
[25] (a) Cordero, H. G. (Ed.) *Iron and Steel Works of the World*; (b) Producão industrial brasileira, 1958, IBGE, Serie Regional 1958
[26] *UNSY, 1962* and 1963
[27] *UNSY, 1962*, Table 11

[28] *UNPIG, 1938–1958*, Part 2
[29] *Produção Industrial Brasileira, 1958*, p. 81; *serie regional* pp. 199–392
[30] *Skinners Wool Trade Directory of the World*
[31] *Produção industrial brasileira, 1958*
[32] *UNPIG, 1938–1958*, Part 2
[33] *Boletim Geográfico, IBGE XXI*, Implantação Industrial no Brasil Sudeste', Jan–Feb. 1963, No. 172, pp. 50–62
[34] Butler, J. H. *Manufacturing in the Concepción Area of Chile*, 1960, National Academy of Sciences, Washington D.C.
[35] Megee, M. C. *Monterrey*, Mexico: Internal Patterns and External Relations, 1958, Chicago

CHAPTER 9

INTRODUCTION TO THE REGIONS OF LATIN AMERICA

9.1. REGIONAL DIVISIONS OF LATIN AMERICA

The aim of this book so far has been to stress the unity of Latin America. Now it is necessary to divide the region into appropriate parts in order to investigate the particular problems of smaller areas. Latin America has been divided satisfactorily on several bases. In Chapter 3.5 a number of physical environments were suggested and the distribution of population in relation to these distinct habitats was calculated. But the same kind of physical environment occurs in areas that are far apart and have little or no contact economically speaking. It would also be possible to divide the region mechanically into a number of parts of more or less equal size, but this would violate both physical environments and national boundaries. Platt* saw the population of Latin America as being distributed in a number of clusters, like islands separated by sea, or by large stretches of virtually uninhabited forest or desert. All other things being equal, the inhabitants of these clusters of population might be expected to be more closely related economically and socially with one another than with people in other clusters. Such a situation can only be expected to occur in an area in which population is very unevenly distributed.

Platt's view of Latin America can to some extent be reconciled with the division of the region into political units (sovereign states), for many of these have a single cluster of population, although this may not be always central†. *Figure 9.1* illustrates this in selected countries. In Mexico for example the main concentration of population, indicated very roughly by areas with a density of population exceeding the national mean, is distant from the boundaries of both the United States and Central America. In Uruguay the main concentration of population is peripheral but against the coast and not against an international boundary. In Venezuela also it is peripheral but the area of high density in the northwest continues across the boundary into Colombia. In El Salvador areas of relatively high and low density are indiscriminately distributed in relation to the national area and on the evidence of the limited number of major civil divisions cannot be called central or peripheral.

The idea behind this is that in the Latin American context it is desirable to have one state per cluster of population. This obviously occurs in all the Islands except Hispaniola. On the mainland, however, several clusters

* Platt[1], p. 158, 'The South American Countries are like islands in the same way as those of Central America, separated by boundary zones that might as well be water from certain points of view'.

† James[2] uses a country by country basis in his book on Latin America and has been followed by Butland[3] and largely by Robinson[4].

207

are shared by two countries (e.g. Guatemala–El Salvador, Venezuela–Colombia), while other countries have two or more clusters within the one national area (Brazil, Argentina). In the case of Bolivia there is no cluster at all large enough to form a nucleus for such an inflated national area. The advantages of using sovereign States as a basis for the study of regions of

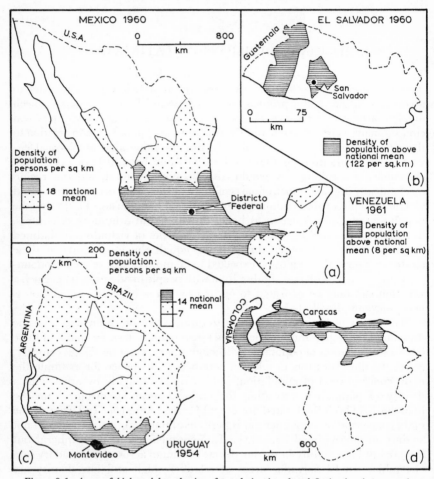

Figure 9.1. Areas of high and low density of population in selected Latin American countries

Latin America include the usefulness of having a ready-made boundary (although a few areas are still disputed), the fact that each State has tended to organize itself as an economic as well as an administrative unit, and the availability of statistical data on a country by country basis. Most important of all, perhaps, is the idea of attaining some degree of self-sufficiency within each country and of integrating each by means of a suitable system of transportation. In this book, in the following chapters, the more important countries are dealt with individually, but for certain purposes, two or more have been grouped together.

9.2. ECONOMIC DEVELOPMENT AND INTEGRATION*
IN LATIN AMERICAN COUNTRIES

Before embarking on a study of individual regions in Latin America it will be useful to consider some of the processes that are taking place over time as each moves towards a more complex and sophisticated economy. As already stressed, the 22 Latin American countries are at widely different stages of economic development, ranging from very poor, simple economies to relatively complicated ones, though none is so advanced as North America or Western Europe. Within countries the extremes are between the most primitive economies in the world, and big cities, which if resting on a shaky economic and social basis, still have many of the features of their North American counterparts. In fact, in a world context many Latin American countries might be considered to have reached an intermediate stage of development. This development involves a number of closely connected processes, some of which, as they take place over time, result in profound changes in the human geography of the countries. These processes may be summed up as follows:

(a) From agricultural to non-agricultural activities (reflected in changing employment structure).
(b) Subsistence economy to commercial economy (local self-sufficiency to regional specialization).
(c) Isolation to integration (improvement of transport facilities).
(d) Rural settlement to urban settlement (increasing concentration of population in limited areas).
(e) Illiteracy to literacy.

Agriculture diminishes in relative importance as mining, manufacturing, and various services increase, a feature reflected both in changing employment structure and in changing contribution of different economic activities to total gross domestic product, aspects already discussed in Chapter 5.2. It has involved the massive movement of population to urban areas, particularly existing ones, and to particular parts of countries favoured by the presence of minerals or by their particularly advantageous position. Each part of a country tends to specialize more and more in what it is best able to produce and farms tend to sell more of their produce elsewhere instead of consuming it locally. All this requires greatly improved communications to make the flow of goods between regions reasonably cheap. The process starts with a single rural community and theoretically ends with complete integration of the whole world. In Latin America at the moment it has largely revolved round the integration of each existing sovereign State. The establishment of LAFTA, however, implies that such integration is now envisaged on a continental level.

As railways, roads, air services, and sometimes shipping routes and inland waterways, are improved, and integration begins to take place, some areas in a country are for a time placed at an advantage over others. This is

* Integration has a distinct meaning in several different disciplines. In this book, unless otherwise indicated, it implies the provision of a reasonably complete system of communications in a given area, making possible interregional movement of both people and goods.

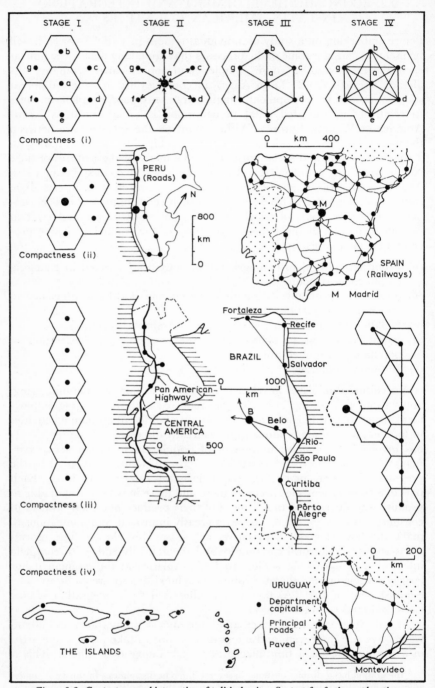

Figure 9.2. Compactness and integration of political units. See text for further explanation

because obviously complete integration cannot take place immediately and at early stages certain places and certain routes are better served with modern transportation services than others. In addition it may be assumed that the more compact a national area is, the more easily it can be integrated. If the shapes of areas may very roughly be classed as compact, fairly compact,

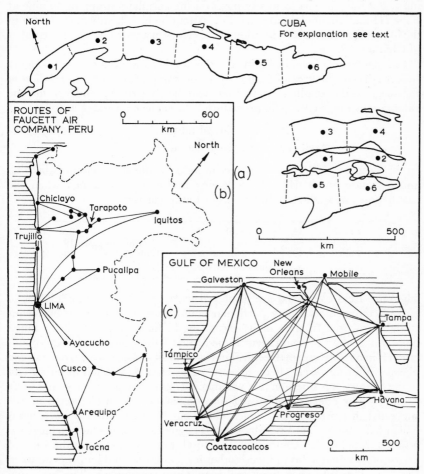

Figure 9.3. Compactness and integration. See text for further explanation

elongated and fragmented (here transhipment is usually necessary), then the viability diminishes appreciably from one end of the scale to the other.

Figure 9.2 is a rough summary of possible situations arising firstly from increasing degrees of integration (stages I—IV along the top)[5] and secondly from increasing degrees of uncompactness (down the side). Complete integration (imagine stage V), implying the possibility of a direct journey from any one of an infinite number of points to any other in an area can, of course, only be achieved on land under conditions such as those in a playground or a football pitch, but, as illustrated in *Figure 9.3c*, theoretically almost exists in a sea area such as the Gulf of Mexico. Looking at the various

211

stages of integration, it will be seen that at stage II a set of journeys from the central point (a) to the six others (b–g) is only six units of distance, while one from any of the peripheral points to the six others is eleven units. The advantageous position of the centre remains in the next two stages (III and IV) but diminishes somewhat, the six journeys from the centre still being six units, but the journeys from any point on the periphery dropping to nine at stage III and about eight at stage IV. Attention has already been drawn to the inherent advantageous position of the centre of an area over the periphery in Chapter 6.7.

Compactness of areas in Latin America has been worked out very roughly by considering the area of each country or group of countries in relation to the area of the smallest circle that contains it (see Appendix 7 for the calculations involved). The procedure is to achieve an index as follows:

$$\frac{\text{Area of political unit}}{\text{Area of smallest circle containing it}} \times 100$$

In this system a circle, of course, has an index of 100, a hexagon of about 83 and a square about 64. The following indices were obtained when the calculation was applied to nine areas in Latin America:

Brazil	54	Colombia	40	Mexico	22
Venezuela	45	Peru	36	Central America	19
Bolivia	43	Argentina	27	Chile	5

Mean for the nine areas 34

The nine areas concerned are displayed in *Figure 9.4*. The implications of lack of compactness in any particular country are, of course, by no means straightforward. In spite of its great length, for example, Chile is much more viable than it would seem to be at first sight, since most of the population is in a relatively small central part and most journeys are made between places within this area. If there were a cluster of population at either end of the country it is questionable whether it could have survived at all as one country. The effect of increasing the compactness of an elongated unit is suggested in *Figure 9.3a*, in which Cuba has been split into three sections which have been placed side by side. The greater compactness achieved is assessed roughly by comparing the total journeys between the central points of six equal areas in the island as it is, with the total journeys between the same six points when the island is split and rearranged. The new total is reduced to 40 per cent of the actual total. On the other hand, Brazil, with its compact though large territory, has in reality operated as an elongated unit, since almost all the population has been strung out in a long narrow belt fairly close to the coast and just as long from end to end as Chile itself.

These considerations of compactness and integration must be thought of more as a guide to understanding the problems of Latin American countries than as models for studying each particular country with great precision. They do, however, draw attention to, and throw light on certain problems that affect the distribution of economic activity in Latin American countries as they advance economically.

One of the most outstanding features and problems of Latin America has been the rapid growth of population in the last few decades. In Chapter 19.2 it will be shown that much of this has taken place in a relatively limited number of individual urban centres, or clusters of urban centres, and along

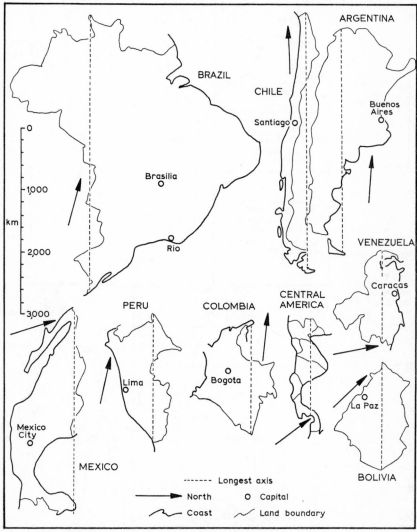

Figure 9.4. Compactness of larger Latin American countries. See text and Appendix 7 for further explanation

bands or axes between these. The attraction of large centres is obvious, at least until they become so inconvenient that congestion occurs. The attraction of transport axes can also be seen in a number of instances in the world and several are quoted and discussed by Chisholm*. The railways of Asiatic U.S.S.R. have attracted industry and settlement as they

* Chisholm[6]. See especially Chapter 5.

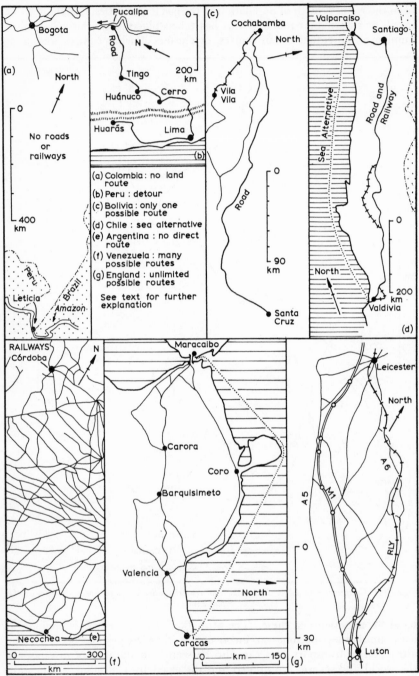

Figure 9.5. Availability of transport routes between selected pairs of towns in Latin America (a–f).
Maps are on different scales

have become established in new areas. Such axes are usually more difficult to define and to make convincing assertions about than single large centres but in certain circumstances they can easily be seen. *Figure 9.5* is an attempt to summarize the various situations in which an axis of attraction may or may not be expected to occur. The most favourable situation would seem to be the existence of a single road and/or railway between two large centres not very far apart. This occurs between Cochabamba and Santa Cruz in Bolivia, between Rio and São Paulo and between Buenos Aires and Rosario. The more alternative routes there are between two centres or clusters (e.g. between Caracas and Maracaibo in Venezuela, between Toledo and Chicago in the U.S.A., or between London and Birmingham in England) the wider becomes the zone of attraction and the more dispersed the places to which population might move. A stretch of road, railway or waterway can, of course, be attractive even if there is not a large centre at either end.

The implications of these various ideas on a continental or LAFTA level are that Latin America is very uncompact, and that the population is very broadly peripheral rather than central. Indeed, at the moment the region might be considered fragmented because in addition to the Islands of the Caribbean there are several distinct parts that are not linked by land communication and can therefore only be connected by sea-links. It goes without saying, also, that integration of the Latin American region has as yet not proceeded far.

9.3. THE REGIONAL DISTRIBUTION OF ECONOMIC ACTIVITIES

This section is intended to show in the broadest outlines the uneven distribution among five major regions in Latin America of selected economic activities, thus both summarizing the findings of the two preceding chapters and preparing the way for a more detailed survey of individual countries.

Section A of Table 9.1 shows the absolute amount involved with the explanation and source of each set of figures given below. Section B shows the amount in each region in per *mil* of the Latin American total. If everything were shared out among the five regions in the same proportions as population is, then each would have the same proportion as of population. This does not of course happen in reality, nor is there any reason to expect it to happen, but by further adapting the figures it is possible quickly to see in Section C the disparity between the actual amount and the amount a region would have if everything *was* shared out according to population.

An example will illustrate the procedure. Column XIII deals with cattle. Section A shows roughly how many (in million) each region had in 1960/61; Brazil, for example, had 74 m. This absolute number was 370 per thousand of the Latin American total of 200 m., and is shown for Brazil in Section B. Brazil has a somewhat bigger share of cattle than of population (370 per thousand compared with 337 per thousand). The index in Section C is calculated by:

$$\frac{\text{per thousand of cattle}}{\text{per thousand of population}} \times 100, \text{ or } \frac{370}{337} \times 100 = 110$$

TABLE 9.1

	I Area	II Pop'n	III GNP	IV Crop land	V Energy cons.	VI Mining	VII Manuf.	VIII Elec.	IX Oil	X Coffee	XI Sugar	XII Cotton lint	XIII Cattle	XIV Cement	XV Oil refining	XVI Steel
	absolute figures															
A																
Mexico—C. America	2,507	47,0	12,240	24	37	n.a.	n.a.	13	15,3	457	1,8	601	27	3,4	15	1,7
Andean	4,669	39,3	12,580	11	34			10	166,6	609	1,5	217	33	4,0	53	0,2
Islands—Guianas	738	20,6	6,730	4	16			8	6,5	142	10,3	negl.	7	2,3	58	0
Brazil	8,514	70,8	11,750	19	25			24	4,5	2,085	3,4	603	74	4,7	10	1,8
South	4,114	32,3	12,240	37	38			18	13,3	0	0,8	151	59	4,2	15	0,8
Latin America	20,542	210,0	55,540	95	150			73	206,2	3,293	17,9	1,572	200	18,6	151	4,5
B *Per mil*																
Mexico—C. America	122	224	220	252	246	111	230	178	74	139	101	382	135	183	99	378
Andean	227	187	227	116	227	702	151	137	808	185	89	138	165	215	351	44
Islands—Guianas	36	98	121	42	107	76	92	110	31	43	575	0	35	124	385	0
Brazil	415	337	212	200	167	18	236	329	22	633	190	384	370	252	66	400
South	200	154	220	390	253	93	291	246	65	0	45	96	295	226	99	178
Latin America	1,000	1,000	1,000	1,000	1,000	1,000	1,000	1,000	1,000	1,000	1,000	1,000	1,000	1,000	1,000	1,000
C *Index of dispersal*																
Mexico—C. America	55	100	98	113	110	50	103	79	33	62	45	171	60	82	44	169
Andean	121	100	121	62	121	378	81	73	432	99	48	74	88	115	188	236
Islands—Guianas	37	100	124	43	109	76	92	112	32	44	586	0	36	127	393	0
Brazil	123	100	63	59	50	5	70	98	7	188	56	114	110	75	20	119
South	130	100	143	254	164	60	188	160	42	0	29	62	192	147	64	116

For explanation see text.   n.a. = not available.

KEY:
I Area in thousands of square kilometres.
II Population in 1961 in millions.
III Total gross national product in millions of U.S. dollars in 1958.
IV Area of cropland in millions of hectares[7].
V Consumption of energy in millions of tons of coal equivalent in 1961[8]
VI Distribution of value of mining production in 1958[9].
VII Distribution of value added in manufacturing in 1958[9].
VIII Electricity generated in 1961[10] in thousands of millions of kWh.
IX Output of oil in millions of tons in 1961[11].
X Production of coffee in thousands of metric tons in 1961[12]
XI Output of sugar (refined) in millions of tons in 1960/61[13].
XII Production of cotton lint in thousands of metric tons in 1961[14].
XIII Cattle in millions in 1960/61[15].
XIV Output of cement in millions of tons in 1961[16]
XV Production of oil refineries in millions of tons in 1961[17].
XVI Output of steel in millions of tons in 1961[18].

In section C, therefore, if a region has an index above 100 for a particular item it has more of its share of that item than it has of population, while the converse is true if its index is below 100. In column XI, for sugar, contrast for example, 586 for the Islands—Guianas, with only 29 for the South.

The table therefore brings out the activities in which each region is strong or weak. Thus the South is shown to be well developed both in manufacturing and in agriculture apart from tropical crops. For the Islands, sugar and oil refining are the obvious specialities. Further study of the table will bring out a number of interesting facts of great general importance in appreciating Latin America that are easily overlooked unless such fundamental figures as these are clearly presented.

REFERENCES

[1] Platt, R. S. *Latin America: Countrysides and United Regions*, 1942, New York; McGraw-Hill

[2] James, P. E. *Latin America*, 1942, London; Cassell

[3] Butland, G. J. The Human Geography of Southern Chile, The Institute of British Geographies, Publication No. 24, 1957; London.

[4] Robinson, H. *Latin America* 1961, London; MacDonald and Evans

[5] Snyder, D. E. 'Commercial Passenger Linkages and the Metropolitan Modality of Montevideo' *Economic Geography* 38 (1962) 95–112

[6] Chisholm, M. *Rural Settlement and Land Use*. 1962; London

[7] *FAOPY*, 1962, Table 1

[8] *UNSY*, 1962, Table 122

[9] *UNSY*, 1962, Table 11

[10] *UNSY*, 1962, Table 125

[11] *UNSY*, 1962, Table 43

[12] *UNSY*, 1962, Table 28

[13] *UNSY*, 1962, Table 75

[14] *UNSY*, 1962, Table 31

[15] *UNSY*, 1962, Table 32

[16] *UNSY*, 1962, Table 107

[17] *UNSY*, 1962, Table 105

[18] *UNSY*, 1962, Table 109

CHAPTER 10

CENTRAL AMERICA

10.1. GENERAL

Central America consists for the purposes of this section of six republics and British Honduras*; Panama does not strictly belong and the future of British Honduras is uncertain. It is a long narrow land, almost 2,000 km from end to end, but only half as long as Mexico and about one quarter the area, being about as large as France. Like Mexico, Central America has had very strong links with the U.S.A. dating particularly from the 1900s. The U.S.A. has intervened on many occasions in the affairs of individual countries, having had marines in Nicaragua almost continuously from 1912–1933 and for frequent short periods in Guatemala and Honduras. The Central American republics in general and Guatemala in particular are also somewhat apprehensive of Mexico, which is much more advanced industrially. In addition, Guatemala claims British Honduras, and Honduras, and Nicaragua have an unsettled frontier dispute. The region is in some ways a miniature version of Latin America and is appropriate to begin this part of the book.

Central America has two coasts, and high mountain regions in the interior with much of the population. It lies well within the tropics (8–18°N) and most was originally densely forested, dry conditions prevailing only in a few limited areas. It consists of six sovereign States, each with a seat in the United Nations, plus British Honduras and the Panama Canal Zone, still dependent. There is a heavy dependence on agriculture, virtually no important mineral production, and hardly any large scale industry. The make up of population varies greatly from country to country however, for Guatemala is largely Indian or mestizo (ladino), but the middle republics are more mestizo, while Costa Rica is mainly European (Spanish), and the negro element, introduced in the nineteenth and twentieth centuries, is strong along the Caribbean coast and in much of Panama. There have been few immigrants since independence in the 1820s except to Costa Rica.

Central America has for the most part an undistinguished history. Home of the Maya civilizations in the north, most was thinly inhabited by Indians, who were eliminated by or mixed with the Spaniards as they penetrated the region in the sixteenth century from Mexico and Panama and settled in small numbers. There were few minerals to attract the Europeans, and during the colonial period and nineteenth century the region remained largely agricultural, with several clusters of population that now form the cores of the present republics. Under the Viceroyalty of New Mexico, the captaincy of Guatemala controlled the region, which for a time remained intact after Spanish control was removed, but soon broke down

* British Honduras[1] is covered very thoroughly and will not be discussed.

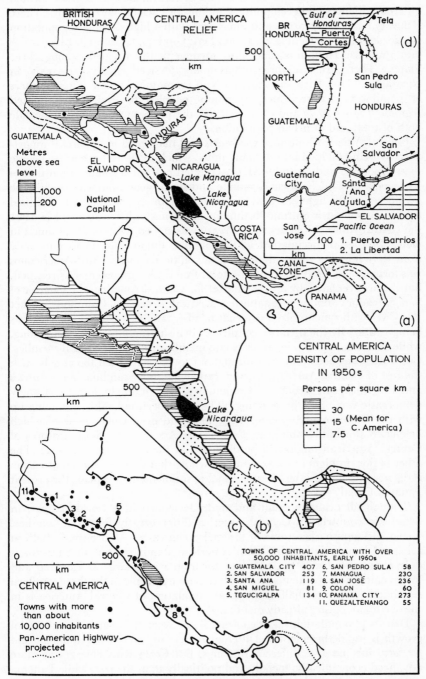

Figure 10.1. Central America. (a) Relief. (b) Density of population. (c) Towns with more than 10,000 inhabitants. (d) Communications in Guatemala and El Salvador

into a number of separate units, which in the nineteenth century formed different alliances and even political unions for various short periods. There is now one relatively large continuous area with a high density of population (see *Figure 10.1b*) stretching across southern Guatemala, through El Salvador into southern Honduras, and thus inconveniently divided among three States. There are also three other moderate sized clusters, one each in Nicaragua, Costa Rica and Panama, and many minor ones. These clusters of population are separated by thinly peopled or even uninhabited regions. *Figures 10.1b* and *c* show clearly the preference for the Pacific side both of total and of urban population.

Central America is at once weakened and magnified in apparent import-ance by being divided into so many units, which together have fewer people than Colombia and a combined gross domestic product smaller than that of Venezuela or Chile. Their economic and social geography can usefully be considered in the light of recent moves to form an economic union. Political union was sought from time to time in the nineteenth century and in 1921 the central American Federation Treaty was signed, with political union in view. Serious preoccupation with economic union appears to date only from 1951 however, when the Organización de Estados Centro-Americanos was formed. In 1958–59 a multi-lateral free trade agreement was reached, but this was replaced by a new Charter for Central America, the Charter of San Salvador, aiming to establish a Central American Common Market (CACM) with synchronized external tariffs[2]. In 1963–64 this Charter was being ratified by the member countries. British Honduras does not belong, while Panama hopes to be an associate member rather than a full member. Costa Rica has been reluctant throughout to associate itself too closely with the rest of Central America, fearing, rather like the Scandinavian countries and the European Economic Community, that it might lose its strongly democratic way of life by so doing. There has been talk, also, of linking up with the Dominican Republic, Venezuela and even Cuba, none of which belong to the Latin American Free Trade Association. Some features of Central American union will be discussed at the end of this chapter. The other major problem of the region as a whole that deserves special attention is the need for a new inter-oceanic canal to supplement or replace the present Panama Canal.

Though all dismally small and underdeveloped in a world context, in detail the countries of Central America differ greatly from one another. Table 10.1 summarizes some of the major contrasts. All are small, both in area and in population, by Latin American standards, but El Salvador is only about the size of Wales, while Nicaragua is as large as England and Wales combined. Guatemala alone has as many people as the three southern republics, while over half of the total population of Central America is in the one major cluster already mentioned.

Density of population varies enormously between the countries, but rate of growth is rapid throughout. Different indices of level of development and *per caput* income give different rankings, but Costa Rica emerges as more advanced economically, socially and politically than the rest, while Panama has an artificially high index due to the Canal. El Salvador and Costa Rica are somewhat more advanced industrially than the rest, but all are heavily dependent on agriculture for employment and for the provision of export commodities; emphasis differs among coffee, cotton and bananas.

TABLE 10.1[3,4]

	Population				Per caput		
	Area thous. km²	1961–1962		Persons per km²	Av. annl. growth 1958–61 (per cent)	Consumption of energy 1961 (kg)	GNP (1962) U.S. $	Exports 1962 U.S. $
Br. Honduras	23	93	96	4	2·4	216	n.a.	n.a.
Guatemala	109	3,886	4,017	36	3·1	174	174	29
El Salvador	21	2,709	2,627	127	3·6	121	220	51
Honduras	112	1,893	1,950	17	3·0	186	210	39
Nicaragua	148	1,526	1,578	10	3·5	177	220	53
Costa Rica	51	1,225	1,274	24	4·4	223	356	67
Panama	74	1,109	1,146	15	2·7	520	434	26

	Land use (percentages)			% of active popn. in agric.	Indl. origin of GDP, % agricultural
	Arable etc.	Pasture	Forest		
Br. Honduras	24		47	40	n.a.
Guatemala	14	5	44	68	32
El Salvador	26	33	13	63	36
Honduras	9	25	43	66	44
Nicaragua	13	n.a.	47	68	n.a.
Costa Rica	6	14	13*	55	37
Panama	7	11	70	50	24

* Only part of total.

10.2. PHYSICAL BACKGROUND AND AGRICULTURE

Central America consists of two main mountain regions, separated by a low depression across Nicaragua. Neither mountain region is continuous or clearcut structurally, but each for most of its length presents a formidable barrier to movement between the two coasts, while at the same time containing numerous valleys and basins at around 500–2,000 m, which contain much of the total population except in Nicaragua and Panama with their lowland populations. The northern mountain region is on the whole higher, with impressive volcanic peaks in Guatemala, but only very small areas exceed 3,000 m. The mountains leave only relatively narrow, discontinuous lowlands along most of the Pacific side; in places rugged peninsulas project into the ocean. The interoceanic watershed is close to the Pacific most of the way and rivers are short on this side. On the Caribbean side, much of the land to the east and north of the main ranges is still very broken, but Nicaragua and Honduras have fairly broad plains along their coasts.

The presence of high mountain regions and two seas complicates climatic conditions in Central America, as in Mexico. Temperature is reduced by altitude to give *tierra templada* conditions in a few places but except in Guatemala even the highest settlements have a sub-tropical rather than a temperate appearance. Mean annual precipitation almost everywhere exceeds 1,000 mm and along the Caribbean coast and also on the Pacific side in the south, exceeds 2,000 mm in places. It falls mainly during the

221

summer and autumn (May–November) but the dry season is so limited on the Caribbean side that tropical rain forest occurs here almost throughout. On the drier Pacific side, tropical semi-evergreen and deciduous forest prevail, while the higher parts combine tropical montane forest with coniferous species. There is virtually no thorn forest or scrub, and even the so-called savannas of parts of the region seem dubious and probably due to human interference. Central America still has a much larger proportion of its surface under forest than Mexico, and commercially useful hardwood and softwood species both occur, including mahogany and pine. There is no immediate need for irrigation, but on the Pacific side there are projects, such as the Rivas scheme (10,000 hectares) in Nicaragua and the Zacapa project in Guatemala to supplement rainfall with irrigation water. The general impression is that the forest soils are not fertile, but that volcanic and alluvial soils are widespread and that these form the basis of agriculture in most areas.

Between half and two thirds of the population is still engaged in agriculture in different parts of Central America but, as elsewhere in Latin America, this activity makes a smaller contribution to total gross domestic product than its employment suggests. Land tenure varies greatly from region to region, with extreme concentration in a few hands in parts of Guatemala; the 1950 agrarian census showed that 70 per cent of the cultivated land was possessed by 2 per cent of the owners. In El Salvador there are many medium sized farms, while in central Costa Rica, family farms are widespread. Most of the banana plantations are controlled by two large U.S. Companies, United Fruit and Standard Fruit. Except in El Salvador, only a small part of each country is actually cultivated, and in spite of rugged conditions and relatively poor soils, there would appear to be considerable scope for extending cultivation and grazing.

Very broadly, Central American agriculture falls into three types: the cultivation of basic food crops such as maize, rice, beans, millet, roots, tubers and even sugar, for local or regional consumption; the cultivation of special crops, notably coffee, cotton and bananas, largely for export; and the raising of cattle. These three branches are not mutually exclusive but do tend to be concentrated in certain parts of the region. The following figures summarize the country by country distribution of production of major agricultural items in 1961/62[5]:

	Thousands of tons					Cattle '000 head
	Maize	Coffee	Cotton seed	lint	Bananas	
Guatemala	500	98	45	26	197	1,130
El Salvador	150	106	110	61	negl.	800
Honduras	285	22	7	4	893	1,120
Nicaragua	100	23	99	57	negl.	1,500
Costa Rica	80	68	negl.		434	1,100
Panama	80	5	negl.		452	770

The special crops tend to occupy the best land and receive most attention and they must be near roads or railways giving access to ports. The coffee, mild in quality and high in value, occupies land mainly between about 600 and 1,800 m in Guatemala, El Salvador and Costa Rica. Altogether there are about 400 million trees, about two-thirds as many as in Colombia, in which physical conditions are comparable. Coffee cultivation was introduced before 1800 in Costa Rica around 1850 in El Salvador, and about the same time in Guatemala by German settlers, who successfully cultivated it until the Second World War. In all three countries the coffee harvest accounts for 40–50 per cent of the total value of farm production. It is cultivated mainly in medium sized estates but also on small farms. In contrast, bananas have been grown for export only in the last few decades. They were grown initially almost entirely in the Caribbean lowlands, as close as possible to the U.S.A., but as plantations became afflicted by diseases here, cultivation has shifted to the Pacific side as well, while recently Ecuador has become a serious rival. Some of the abandoned banana plantations on the Caribbean side now grow cacao, abaca and basic food crops, and the total production of Central America has declined since the 1920s.

The great dependence of Central America on coffee and bananas has been reduced since the Second World War by the expansion of cultivation of other crops, both for export, particularly cotton (for seed and lint) on the drier Pacific lowlands, especially of El Salvador and Nicaragua, and for home consumption, particularly sugar cane, rice and tobacco. But many areas, especially in Guatemala and Honduras, remain essentially backward, with a near subsistence economy while agriculture in Panama lacks integration, and the Canal settlements import large quantities of food. The third element, the cattle, are poor in quality, with little attention given to breeding and fodder, and although Honduras and Nicaragua each export livestock, Central America as a whole is deficient in meat.

10.3. INDUSTRY, TOWNS AND TRANSPORT

Much of the employment in industry is concerned with agricultural products. Coffee *beneficios* are usually small and are scattered throughout the areas of coffee cultivation, but there is now a large plant in San Salvador making instant soluble coffee for the U.S. market. Bananas are shipped as quickly as possible after cutting, but cotton, henequen, tobacco and other crops are also processed.

Significant figures for employment in industry in Central America are difficult to obtain but certainly considerable numbers of people are involved in small-scale processing and manufacturing, whereas even medium sized factories with modern equipment are few, and there are no very large establishments at all. The absence of a single large home market and of any spectacular mineral deposit may partly explain the lack of large-scale industry but this may be due also to the backwater nature of the region and its failure to escape from an agricultural economy. Lack of local sources of energy, of capital and of a technological background have left Central America at the level of the poorer Islands and the smaller South American countries. The following figures suggest different degrees of industrialization, and stress the heavy dependence on agricultural processing.

223

Although gold has been one of the principal exports of Nicaragua, coal and iron ore are both known to exist in Honduras and oil is now being sought in Guatemala (El Peten province) and elsewhere, there has been virtually no mining in most of Central America. A considerable hydro-electric potential exists, too, but until the 1950s this was neglected. The first moderate sized plant has been the 75,000 kW '5 de Novembre' on the R. Lempa in El Salvador. Energy has therefore been terribly short, and consumption is still far lower than in Mexico. The establishment of small oil refineries to process imported oil, mainly from Venezuela, has been regarded as a partial solution. Each Central American country has sought to have its own refinery and if the possibility of placing one or two reasonably large refineries to serve the Central American market was ever seriously

TABLE 10.2[6]

		Total value of industrial production in millions of U.S. $	Per caput value U.S. $ per inhabitant	Value of food and drink	Food and drink as % of total
Costa Rica	(1957)	111	90	76	69
El Salvador	(1956)	192	71	160	83
Panama	(1957)	59	53	39	66
Honduras	(1960)	58	30	31	53
Guatemala	(1958)	99	25	42	42
Nicaragua	(1953)	38	25	22	58

considered by the countries themselves, as it was by the oil companies concerned, then it was abandoned[7] in the interests of nationalism. At least four new refineries have been opened recently (see *Figure 8.3*) (tons per annum).

1962 Panama, Las Minas Bay, 2,600,000
1962 Guatemala, Matias de Gálvez, 200,000
1963 El Salvador, Acajutla, 700,000
1964 Nicaragua, Managua, 250,000

Apart from the Panama refinery, these are all small, but it is doubtful if the economies of large scale, achieved by building one large central refinery, would have been offset by the much greater average length of land hauls to its customers, given the elongated shape of Central America.

These new refineries may emerge as foci of attraction for new industries, replacing the larger towns, which at present have most of what manufacturing there is. It would be superfluous to repeat several times more or less the same list of manufacturing products turned out by each country at present, but the following typical list for El Salvador is worth quoting: cement, furniture, henequen bags (San Miguel), cotton textiles, knitwear, footwear, soap, cigarettes, matches, beer, soft drinks. Metal working and engineering is largely confined to the making of spare parts for and the maintenance of imported machinery. Any machines to equip factories are of course imported. The industries listed can flourish with little capital, and limited skilled labour, in small establishments. With the progress of economic union, however, and the assurance of a much larger though still modest home market of 12 million people, industrialists in Central America are planning for a new stage in industrialization, the idea being that each country should specialize in a particular branch of manufacturing, for which it is best equipped. In the late 1950s, for example, it was agreed that Honduras should establish a large paper mill, Guatemala should make motor tyres, El Salvador insecticides and so on. The host country would provide at least 30 per cent of the capital, each of the others at least 10 per cent. This would avoid duplication, at the same time leading quickly to inter-dependence. As yet there has been no serious talk of a large integrated iron and steel works for Central America; this would have to be in one plant to be economic. El Salvador, however, plans to expand steel production (at Villa Delgado) and Guatemala, Honduras and Nicaragua all have under construction or plan to have small works; El Salvador is also developing light engineering: bicycles and motor cycles, spare parts for aircraft, coach-work and motor vehicles, agricultural equipment (Santa Ana) and electric light bulbs. Other countries also have plans; for example Managua is to make galvanized steel tubing and refrigerators for the Central American market, Guatemala to have a large new textile mill at Quezaltenango. The central position of San Salvador in the major cluster of population in Central America makes it an attractive location for serving the whole market. Panama and even Costa Rica are very peripheral in this sense, while Honduras lacks even a reasonable sized cluster of population to serve as a local market.

Central America is not so highly urbanized as most of Latin America but urban growth has been rapid in the last decade. In the mid-nineteenth century, when the region had few connections with the outside world, towns were small and were mostly in the highlands. Many of these com-mercial and administrative centres have stagnated, but some, particularly the national capitals, have grown rapidly in recent decades and have attracted industries; the population of Managua for example doubled between 1950 and 1963, to 230,000. As in Latin America as a whole, capitals tend to be multi-functional centres. Secondly, a large number of ports, all small except Colón and Panama, which are special anyway, have grown up along the coasts, often at points conveniently near to interior centres but with nothing more than roadsteads. Until the 1950s the orientation of major routes and traffic flows was from interior to coast. Thirdly, a limited number of new centres have grown up or been extended by the large fruit companies to house their workers. It is premature to do more than suggest the possibility that the new oil refineries may turn some of the ports into proper industrial centres, which none is at present, and to antici-pate the establishment of a new capital for the region, perhaps in a federal district in El Salvador.

Great distances between clusters of population, and poor, devious routes, ensured the isolation of different parts of Central America until the 1930s, for the limited railway system built by then consisted of many individual lines linking interior centres with ports or serving banana plantations, and failing to provide a backbone along the isthmus, and it was more easy to travel from a Central American country to the U.S.A. than to reach a neighbouring one. Air transport increased contacts in the interwar period, but for the serious movement of goods and of large numbers of people over considerable distances, roads were necessary. During and since the Second

World War the main preoccupation has been to provide an international highway to link the six countries. Existing stretches with suitable alignments were linked, and through the 1950s it became more and more practicable to travel along Central America as well as across it. It is now possible to travel by bus from the Mexican border to San José in Costa Rica; the Inter-American highway is paved nearly all the way. The system of communications has thus been transferred into a major longitudinal axis, well over towards the Pacific, with many offshoots to hitherto remote interior localities as well as to coasts. Air services are still vital for maintaining rapid transport between capitals and for reaching more remote localities.

10.4. INDIVIDUAL COUNTRIES

The individual features and problems of the various Central American partners have not been stressed, but some of these must now briefly be noted. Guatemala[8] is characterized by a concentration of population in the higher southern part, with many poor Indian and metizo communities growing food crops above the more prosperous coffee zone, and a rapidly growing capital with now about 10 per cent of the total population, but few industries. Large tracts of forest in the north remain virtually untouched, but it is planned to resettle 100,000 families in this area in the next 15 years. The main outlet, Puerto Barrios, lies in a relatively remote and unimportant area; a modern road now links it with the south.

El Salvador differs from the rest of Central America in being virtually full, agriculturally speaking. There is little new land to take into farms, and pressure of population on existing land is considerable, while food products are now being imported; several hundred thousand people have emigrated, many into neighbouring Honduras. Here, certainly, is a reason for industrializing, and the central position in Central America (in relation to population, if not area) is an advantage. Possibly sufficient capital from coffee cultivation (*cf.* Brazil, Colombia) together with U.S. aid, may ensure considerable advances in manufacturing here, and efforts are currently being made also to improve higher educational facilities.

The problems of Honduras are like those of Latin America on a very small scale. Much of the population is in one part in the south, the capital is somewhat separate and until recently inaccessible, and the main source of exports, the banana plantations, are at the other side of the country, but there are also many agricultural clusters of several tens of thousands of inhabitants, linked only by air or by very poor roads and tracks in the west and centre. Resources are considerable: forests, grazing lands and minerals, but population, over 80 per cent of which is still rural, is so thinly spread that it is difficult to know where to start making improvements. Unfortunately the Inter-American highway only passes through the extreme south. *Figure 10.2d* gives an impression of the problems facing Honduras.

Nicaragua has a more compact population than Honduras, mainly lowland, close to its two large lakes. It grows relatively little coffee and has not had large banana plantations, but grows good cotton. The Caribbean side has so far been neglected and the interior contributes only limited quantities of forest and grazing products.

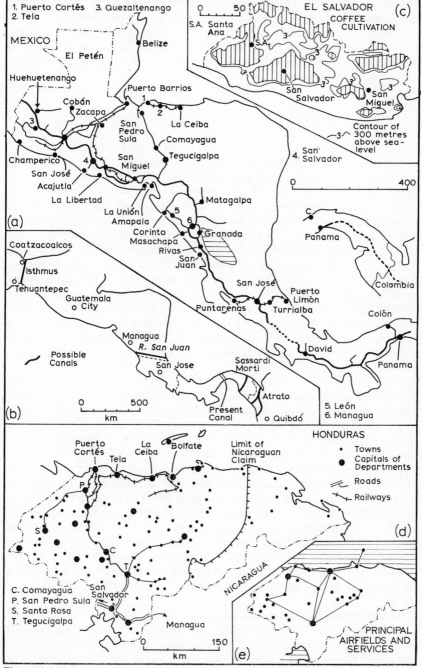

Figure 10.2. Central America. (a) Communications. (b) Possible sites for new inter-oceanic canal. (c) Coffee cultivation in El Salvador. (d), (e) Towns and routes in Honduras

227

Costa Rica and Panama differ from the rest of Central America for their population make up, though coffee and bananas are their major exports. European farmers have spread out in Costa Rica from the central valley around San José and the country is reasonably well integrated and organized. Panama[9], on the other hand, consists of a main cluster of agricultural population on the Pacific side in the west and a service population based on the Canal in the centre.

10.5. ECONOMIC INTEGRATION AND FOREIGN TRADE

It is not easy to assess at any given time the precise state of Central American union, but by the mid-1960s considerable progress had been made, and it was proposed to eliminate all internal tariffs by 1966. At the risk of confusing what has been achieved with what has been proposed, some features deserve mention, since here is probably the smallest and simplest of economic unions in the world. Financial difficulties are to be eased by the establishment of uniform currency, a Central American Bank and a Clearing House. Integration is to be improved by the completion of the intercontinental highway and the formation of a Central American Aviation Company (initial investment U.S. $ 5 m., one fifth from each country). A single electricity grid is proposed eventually. Some duplication of administrative services may be avoided, and a new capital has been proposed. Most important of all, manufacturing is to be put on a rational basis by the introduction of regional specialization in bigger, more efficient plants than is possible at present. Some advantage may be expected, also, from greater power to bargain over exports.

The success of Central American Union is not automatic. In its favour are a common language, Spanish, a reasonably integrated system of communications since the late 1950s, and a definite consciousness of belonging to the same part of the world (many motor vehicles in the region bear the initials C.A. for Centro America as well as their own national registration numbers). The countries were long united in the Spanish Empire and some have been united at times since. Against rapid integration are the considerable distances involved between clusters of population and the fact that they all produce roughly the same commodities and at present trade between them is slight. But other countries in the world with about the same number of inhabitants as Central America are equally unwieldy in shape yet succeed. Lack of trade between them, however, undermines the very raison d'etre of a common market. In the late 1950s only a few per cent of the trade of each country was with the rest of the area, but intraregional trade has been increasing in the last few years and between 1960 and 1962 alone increased six times.

Central America still depends heavily on the U.S.A. as a trading partner, but less in the early 1960s than in the Second World War. 1961 figures were as shown at top of facing page. German and Japanese trade with the region has grown recently and is now considerable. There is very little trade with the rest of Latin America apart from oil imported from Venezuela.

Dependence on coffee and/or bananas has diminished recently but is still

	Percentage of	
	Imports from U.S.A.	Exports to U.S.A.
Guatemala	48	53
El Salvador	43	35
Honduras	52	66
Nicaragua	49	45
Costa Rica	45	59
Panama	50	91

greater than is thought desirable. The percentage of exports in 1961 (and 1957 in brackets) was made up as follows:

	Coffee	Bananas	Cotton
Guatemala	63 (75)	10	10
El Salvador	59 (80)	18	—
Honduras	17 (15)	50 (60)	—
Nicaragua	25 (45)	—	31 (30)
Costa Rica	54 (50)	23 (40)	—
Panama	— —	62 (70)	—

Other exports of the region include cacao, sugar, live cattle, meat and gold.

To some extent the fortunes of the whole of Central America are related to the interoceanic canal, since the reluctance of Panama to join the union has been due to its special position and problems, while Nicaragua offers a possible route for another canal. Moreover, the opening of a canal has given the Pacific coast of Central America more easy contact with eastern U.S.A. and with Europe. The Panama Canal and its trade have been discussed in Chapter 6.3. At different stages in the last four centuries several countries, including Spain, England and France, contemplated the possibility of a canal across Panama, but the U.S.A. finally built the canal in about ten years at the beginning of this century in the newly created republic, formerly a department of Colombia. There had been a road, the Camino Real, when Panama was a colony of Spain, and in 1855 the first transcontinental railway in the Americas was completed to take settlers from eastern U.S.A. to California. The French began to construct a canal in the 1880s but disease decimated the labour force and the project was abandoned. The U.S.A. started the Canal in 1904 and completed it in 1914, but the official opening was only in 1920. The original railway was submerged, but is now super-seded by a new one and by a modern highway. The Canal runs through a 10 mile wide zone leased to the U.S.A. in perpetuity for the yearly payment of a modest sum; the U.S.A. virtually has sovereignty over the zone. Much of the course of the Canal is through the artificially created Gatun Lake at about 85 ft. above sea level, but there is a cut through hills, and three pairs of locks* carry the canal up to the 85 ft. level from each ocean. Small engines (mules) tow the larger vessels through the locks.

Cristóbal and Balboa are ports at each end, within the Canal Zone, while the adjoining towns of Colón and Panama are the largest towns in the Republic.

* Dimensions 1,000 ft. × 110 ft. × 70 ft. now exclude many large U.S. warships and also large liners and tankers.

Approximately 15,000 persons are engaged in operating the Canal, most of them Panamanians, while the existence of Colón and Panama is due largely to commercial activities, services and the purchases of transit passengers connected with the Canal. Panama is the national capital and also a great focus of intercontinental and international air routes (Tocumen airport). The Canal cuts the republic of Panama in two, but a fine new high steel arch bridge (U.S. $ 20 m. completed in 1962) now crosses it near Panama, replacing unsatisfactory lifting bridges. Colón now has a free zone for goods in transhipment, and sites for industry, and there is an oil refinery nearby. At first sight the place would seem to be favourable for industrialization, since a great variety of raw materials could easily be assembled and manufactured products easily distributed over much of Latin America by frequent services. But a market on the spot is virtually non-existent. Comparable places in the world such as Port Said, Malta and Aden have not become industrialized, but Singapore and Hong Kong have.

A few of the many courses proposed for a new Canal are shown in *Figure 10.2b*. The present Canal could be improved to prolong its life for a considerable time but ultimately a new one, preferably at sea level will be needed[10]. It is possible that Central America may miss the new Canal altogether, for in April, 1964 a U.S.-Colombian agreement was signed to survey the sea level route via the Atrato River in Colombia.

REFERENCES

[1] *Land in British Honduras*, Colonial Research Publication No. 24, 1959, London; H.M.S.O.
[2] *BOLSA (QR)* Central America, Regional Integration, Jan. 1964, pp. 36–46
[3] *UNSY, 1962*
[4] *FAOPY, 1962*, Pick's Currency Yearbook 1963, pp. 27, 29
[5] *FAOPY, 1962*
[6] *BOLSA (FR)* 13 July 1963, p. 627
[7] Odell, P. R. *An Economic Geography of Oil*, 1963 pp. 133–9, 167–9, London
[8] Whetten, N. L. *Guatemala, The Land and the People*, 1961; New Haven
[9] Bennett, C. F. 'The Bayano Cuna Indians, Panama: An Ecological Study of Livelihood and Diet', *A.A.A.G.* March 1962 pp. 32–50
[10] Fox, D. J. 'Prospects for the Panama Canal', *Tijdschr. econ. Geogr.* April, 1964

CHAPTER 11

MEXICO*

11.1. INTRODUCTION

Though Mexico is typically Latin American in many ways, several features make it distinct from the South American countries. Firstly, it adjoins the United States, with which it shares a long common boundary; a rewarding study would be a comparison of the ways in which Mexico and Canada are linked with and depend on their great neighbour. For example, in 1963 about two thirds of the foreign trade of Mexico was with the U.S.A., and 10 years ago it was appreciably more, while in 1959, some 700,000 U.S. tourists visited the country. Secondly, Mexico was organized by Spain during the colonial period as a separate entity from South America, and there was little direct contact between the viceroyalties of Mexico and Peru; more indeed with East Asia than with South America. Distance and lack of communications until the air age have tended to perpetuate this situation. Thirdly, the Indian, still the basic component of the population, though largely now in mestizo form, has for some decades held a respectable, almost exalted position in the life of Mexico, certainly superior in status to that of the Andean Indians, even if still little more prosperous economically. To some extent Mexico is a larger version of Central America, having two coasts, interior mountains and scattered clusters of population, but it is larger, more varied physically and diversified economically, yet more fully integrated.

Mexico is about one quarter the size of the U.S.A. (without Alaska), nearly four times the size of France, had a population in 1963 of about 38 m., which during 1958–61 was growing at a rate of about 3 per cent per year. Much longer from end to end than it appears at first sight on atlas maps, the longest axis across Mexico is as long as the whole width of the United States (Jacksonville, Florida to Los Angeles, California), some 3,500 km. Mexico is not a compact unit, and movement between the extremities involves very great distances. In addition, Mexico is extremely rugged, a feature of the natural environment that affects the life of the country adversely in many ways, and greatly hinders movement over most interregional routes. Unlike Central America, Mexico has virtually no negroes and few nearly pure Europeans. Of the total population, some 10 per cent are white, 60 per cent mestizo and 30 per cent Indian, but this is only a very rough classification and by now is based on cultural features such as retention of Indian language, rather than on physiological characteristics; many communities of Indians, such as the Tarascan of Michoacán and the Zamora of Quiroga, are very little changed so far. Fifty one per cent of the population was classed as urban in 1960 compared with only 43 per cent in 1950, and urbanization continues. Employment in agriculture as a percentage of total employment has declined as follows: 85 per cent in 1910, 70 per cent in 1930, 58 per cent

* See Ref. 1 for a study of Mexico in a North American context.

231

in 1950, and 49 per cent in 1963. Some states are still deeply rural and agricultural (in 1950 Guerrero had 80 per cent in agriculture, Chiapas 79 per cent, Oaxaca 78 per cent) while others depend heavily on non-agricultural activities. In the early 1960s about 2 m. persons were engaged in manufacturing, which accounted for about 25 per cent of the total gross domestic product. The early 1960s find Mexico a country of great regional contrasts in level of development, with a rapidly increasing population, a changing employment structure, concern over the use of new resources and, after several decades of irregular progress, apparently steady economic growth.

Much of the area of present day Mexico had been the home of relatively advanced civilization before the Spaniards arrived early in the sixteenth century, at which time the south central area was dominated by the Aztecs. The Spaniards quickly took over the densely peopled high basins of this area, organized mining especially to the north, and spread their influence over most of the country during the following decades. Later in the colonial period the Mexico viceroyalty also had loose control over much of what is now western U.S.A. Even by the early nineteenth century the population was still basically Indian, and since then few settlers have come to Mexico from Europe*. Independence from Spain came around 1820, but in the mid-nineteenth century the expanding U.S.A. acquired by various means the large but thinly peopled lands north of the Rio Bravo (Rio Grande). For over a century now Mexico has had approximately its present form, with a fairly centralized government after the breakdown of several experiments in federation. Modern industry and railways penetrated the country slowly until the last part of the nineteenth century, but after many setbacks Mexico at last appears to have reached a stage of sustained economic growth, and since the Revolution around 1910 and especially since the mid-1950s (particularly 1934–40) the government has taken an increasing share in the economic organization of the country, promoting profound land reform changes, including the breaking up of large estates, financing large irrigation projects, and acquiring control of the oil industry and most railways.

11.2. PHYSICAL BACKGROUND AND RESOURCES

Mexican geographers divide the country into a widely accepted scheme of physical divisions, with variations in detail. One version is reproduced in *Figure 11.1b*. This already complex picture is a summary of extremely varied relief features on a very complicated structure, a continuation of the features of the western United States, at least to the Balsas Depression, south and east of which, however, there is a new orientation of major features. To the north of the volcanic range (1 on map), the northern part of the country has three main ranges, only one of which, the Sierra Madre Occidental, is very high and continuous. The two Sierra Madres are separated by two extensive plateau areas, the larger, lower northern one consisting mainly of bolsons (interior drainage areas) and the higher southern one of a number of basins encircled by high mountains. The west-east volcanic area has three

* A small but influential group has been some 12,000 Spanish republican refugees received by Mexico during the Spanish Civil War (1936–39).

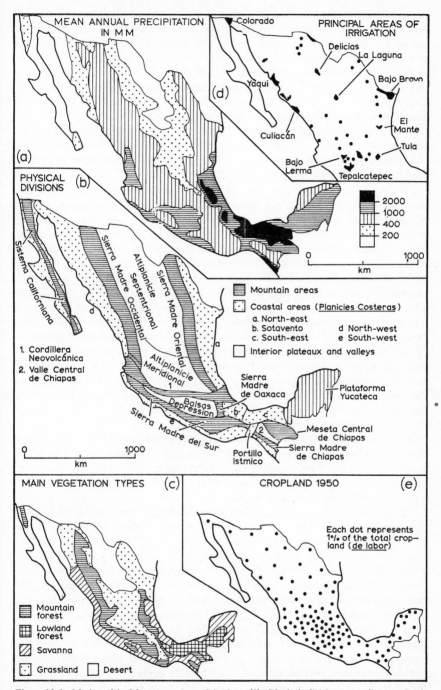

Figure 11.1. Mexico. (a) Mean annual precipitation. (b) Physical divisions according to J. A. Vivó[16], (c) Main vegetation types. (d) Principal areas of irrigation. (e) Distribution of cropland in 1950

peaks of over 5,000 m: Pico de Orizaba (5,747 m), Popocatépetl (5,450 m) and Ixaccíhuatl (5,288 m). Much of the southern plateau is drained westwards by the Lerma. To the south, the Balsas Depression and the discontinuous Sierra Madre del Sur have an east-west orientation but terminate in the east at the narrow Isthmus of Tehuantepec, beyond which the ranges of Chiapas state have an orientation and appearance more comparable with Central America. Similarly structurally the low limestone plateau of Yucatan is not unlike parts of Cuba and Florida. Coastal lowlands are non-existent to the south of the Sierra Madre del Sur and are discontinuous by the Gulf of California, the western side of the Sierra Madre Occidental being characterized by ranges and basins. The Gulf coast lowlands are generally wider and less interrupted by upland areas.

Mexico is situated astride the Tropic of Cancer (about 15° to 32°N), roughly in the latitude of the Sudan and Egypt. But the climate is complicated by the great variety of relief features and the presence of two seas with somewhat different temperature conditions at the same latitudes. Mean annual precipitation varies from less than 200 mm in large areas of the north and northwest to over 2,000 mm along the southern shores of the Gulf of Mexico (see *Figure 11.1a*). Most of Mexico is distinguished by a very marked dry season in the first part of the year and heavy rain in the summer and autumn; but there are many local variations, while much of the south has no true dry season. Precipitation is generally very unreliable. One pessimistic version of the usefulness of precipitation assesses Mexico as 52 per cent arid, 41 per cent semi-arid and only 7 per cent humid. Unfortunately, even the limited parts that receive a heavy and reasonably reliable rainfall happen to be mainly the more rugged parts of the country such as the Sierra Madre Occidental and the southern mountain slopes. It has been calculated that some 50 per cent of the water resources of the country occur in only 15 per cent of the national area.

Temperatures of course decrease regularly with altitudes and bring temperate climatic conditions into the high central basins, as well as frosts much of the year. The southern part of the country is completely frost free, however, as are the Pacific coast north to the middle of the Gulf of California and the Gulf coast to near Támpico.

Figure 11.1c shows the main types of vegetation. The types distinguished differ from those in Chapter 3.4 and the main questionable feature is the savanna, which is more correctly thorn forest in the drier parts or tropical evergreen and semi-deciduous forest along the more humid parts of the Gulf coast. At its simplest, Mexico consists of a complicated mixture of arid lowlands and low plateaux, semi-arid or reasonably well watered rugged mountain regions and high plateaux, and forested lowland and upland. None of these environments offers good conditions for farming over more than scattered areas of limited extent, and there is no continuous area of good farmland comparable with the Middle West in the U.S.A. or even the pampa of Argentina. A commentary on this is the fact that throughout the last few centuries and in spite of considerable economic changes, most of the population has lived above about 1,500 m, in only a small part of the national area. Lowland areas have mostly been either too dry or too heavily forested to support large agricultural populations. The presence of Mexico

City at a height of some 2,240 m contribute appreciably to the high altitude of population. According to a study* of 1950 census data, there were 4 m. rural dwellers above 2,000 m (on about 10 per cent of the total area), 5 m. between 1,000 and 2,000 m and only 5 m. below 1,000 m. Of the 32 capitals of major civil divisions (see *Figure 11.3c*) seven, including Mexico City, with more people than the rest put together, were above 2,000 m, and nine were between 1,500 and 2,000 m (see table in footnote) †.

11.3. AGRICULTURE

In 1950 roughly 10 per cent of the total area of Mexico was under field or tree crops or fallow (see *Figure 11.1e*), nearly 40 per cent was classified as pasture, yet much of it poor in quality, and about 20 per cent was forested, though much is forest of little commercial use. Most of the total value of farm production comes from the cropland, the extent of which has been appreciably increased since 1950 by new irrigation projects, which bring the irrigated land to about 15 per cent of the total cropland area. More could still be done to use the water of the rivers of the northern part of the country before they reach the sea, but even the higher parts from which these rivers flow do not have a heavy rainfall. Some progress has been made in regulating the waterways of the even more rugged central region of the country but costly reservoirs are necessary, even if hydroelectric power is an important by-product. There are few long rivers and often no suitable gently sloping areas with good soils that could be irrigated once water is regulated. Yucatán is characterized by the virtual absence of surface drainage and limited irrigation from wells is all that is possible. Since the 1920s Mexico has been preoccupied with water supply, and most of the present major projects have been completed or extended since then. Interest is now shifting to whole valleys such as the Papaloapan in Oaxaca-Puebla-Veracruz, the Tepalcatepec in Michoacán, the Fuerte in Sinaloa and the Grijalva in Chiapas‡: (see *Figure 11.3e* for their location). The north still

* By the Universidad Nacional Autónoma de México[2].

†	Capitals of major civil divisions of Mexico more than 500 m above sea level (in metres)[3]				
over 2,000		1,500–2,000		1,000–1,500	
Toluca	2640	Durango	1889		
Zacatecas	2442	Morelia	1886		
Pachuca	2426	San Luis Potosí	1877	Jalapa	
Tlaxcala	2252	Aguascalientes	1869	Chihuahua	
Mexico City	2240	Querétaro	1821	Chilpancingo	
Puebla	2162	Saltillo	1589	500–1000	
Guanajuato	2008	Oaxaca	1546	Tuxtla Gutiérrez	
		Cuernavaca	1542	Tepic	
		Guadalajara	1540	Monterrey	

‡ The Grijalva and Usumacinta basins in the extreme southeast of Mexico have over 25 per cent of all the run-off in Mexico, the Papaloapan, Coatzacoalcos and Tonala about 20 per cent. These five together occupy only 10 per cent of the area of Mexico[4].

has most of the irrigated land however, the lower Colorado, lower Rio Grande (Bajo Bravo) and the Yaqui each having about 200,000 hectares or 10 per cent of the national total. According to one estimate, about 8 m. hectares could eventually be irrigated compared with about 2 m. hectares at present.

As yet little of the land in the high, densely populated basins of central Mexico is irrigated, but precipitation is adequate (750–1,000 mm), evaporation restricted by lower temperatures and cloudiness, and soils sufficiently fertile for crop farming with sub-tropical or temperate crops according to altitude. Since frosts are frequent, tropical cultivation is impossible and even the traditional widespread cultivation of maize seems unsound. Southern Mexico is characterized by more rugged agricultural conditions, with cultivation on excessively steep slopes poor soils and serious soil erosion aggravated by heavy downpours; Yucatán has its own distinct problems.

Agricultural land, then, is dispersed in many small areas, whether oases in the north hemmed in by desert, basins and valleys enclosed by mountain sides in the centre, valleys floors and steep hillsides on the south, or patches of more fertile soil on the limestone of Yucatán. Undoubtedly new patches could be brought into cultivation, but to do this, much investment would be needed to provide access roads, regulate water supply, clear vegetation, and move (often over great distances) and equip settlers from existing overpopulated farmlands. The most promising new areas are the irrigated lands in the north and the forested lowlands of the south. Agricultural production could also be greatly increased by achieving higher yields in existing areas of cultivation through the more widespread use of fertilizer, the introduction of better seed, more suitable plants and so on.

The relative importance of different crops to the Mexican economy can best be summarized by the value of their production[5].

	Millions of pesos				
	1960	*1962*		*1960*	*1962*
Maize	3,900	4,510	Sugar cane	860	1,100
Cotton (lint)	2,760	3,420	Beans (frijol)	760	920
Wheat	1,060	1,290	Oranges	380	540
Coffee	1,020	1,070	Alfalfa	370	450

Tomatoes, henequen, rice, and tobacco were between 200 and 350 m. in 1960. Since value of production per unit of area varies greatly, proportion of area occupied by each crop does not correspond to its share of value. There is a lack of precise data about the actual area under crops, but the 1950 census revealed that of a total area of 19,900,000 hectares classified as cropland (*de labor*), only 8,600,000 yielded harvests and 1,188,000 hectares were irrigated. In 1961–1962, 1,900,000 hectares were irrigated*.

* The water was obtained as follows: for 1,180,000 hectares from reservoirs, 360,000 direct from waterways, 70,000 pumped from waterways, and 270,000 pumped from deep wells[6]. New dams under construction in the early 1960s include:

Benito Juarez, Oaxaca State
El Tunal, Durango
El Humaya, Sinaloa
Tehuantepec River, Oaxaca

The area harvested in 1960 was about 11 m. hectares. This was divided among the main crops as follows (thousands of hectares):

	1960	1961		1960	1961		1960	1961
Maize	5,550	5,700	Sugar cane	317	320	Henequen	169	170
Beans	1,305	1,300	Coffee	290	290	Chickpeas	146	150
Cotton (lint)	885	820	Barley	245	245	Rice	131	135
Wheat	840	846	Rapeseed	190	205			

Under 100,000: groundnut, chiles, potatoes, bananas, tomatoes, lemons, tobacco, alfalfa, oranges, cacao.

Cattle numbered 21,6 m. in 1960, pigs 9 m., horses, mules and asses 10 m. and sheep and goats 16 m. (1961, 24 m., 10 m., 6 m. and 15 m).

Maize, which still occupies roughly half of the cropland of Mexico, is grown throughout the country but is of particular importance in the economic life of the high central basins and humid Gulf coast (Veracruz). Wheat and barley are cultivated mainly in the north; Sonora accounts for nearly one third of the wheat. Rice is grown mainly in Veracruz.

Beans, chickpeas, potatoes, bananas, tobacco, sugar cane and fruits are also widely grown, but mainly for local or regional consumption. Little fodder is grown for livestock and the quality of this is consequently poor. Alfalfa cultivation represents a modest attempt to improve cattle raising. Cotton, coffee and henequen are the principal agricultural exports. Cotton is grown almost entirely on irrigated land in the north, with Tamaulipas (30 per cent), Baja California and Sonora (20 per cent each) and Sinaloa and Coahuila accounting for nearly all the national total. Coffee, in contrast, is grown on sloping land of moderate altitude in the uplands of Veracruz (over 30 per cent), Chiapas (nearly 30 per cent) and Oaxaca, while nearly 90 per cent of the henequen comes from Yucatán. Thus the main export crops are grown in distinct parts of the country, but the central farmland and the states to the south (Guerrero, Michoacán) contribute little to the export total. Live cattle are a considerable item of export to the U.S.A. and since the war, over 20 meat packing plants have been opened in the northern states.

As a result of the attempt to raise the poor and unprivileged level of the mass of rural population in Mexico at the beginning of this century, agrarian reform programmes have transformed the agricultural life of the country. Reforms have taken place at irregular intervals, but for some time substantial increases in production could not be detected even though socially much of the agricultural population emerged more satisfied. Since the Second World War, however, agricultural output has risen in a spectacular fashion, but to what extent agrarian reform has been responsible and to what extent modernization of techniques in the broadest sense, it is difficult to say. Around 1910, almost all the agricultural land was in the hands of about 5 per cent of the population, and some 300 owners each had over 10,000 hectares. As elsewhere in Latin America the Spanish conquerors had shared out the land in large units and their descendants, together with the Church, had squeezed the peasants out. Since little of the total area was farmed and owners were satisfied with limited incomes from low yields, these large units were uneconomic, and were reduced, the land being shared out among individual farmers or more often ejidos (collective farms), or co-operatives. The state was involved in compensating owners and financing the peasants to put them on their feet. Between 1915 and 1950, 30 m. hectares were redistributed but most of this was land of little use, and included forest, scrub, poor pasture, and even waste, while little was irrigated and much lay away from routes. In the late 1950s, further redistribution of land began, and had exceeded 10 m. hectares by 1963.

A landless aristocracy was one by-product of the reforms, while many owners who remained with land felt insecure and were reluctant to make improvements. At the other extreme, the peasants with limited education, no experience at organizing farms and no capital could make little progress. Some resemblance to the land reforms in the U.S.S.R. may be noted. Collectivization was carried out much more abruptly in the U.S.S.R. (most during 1928–32) but production dropped, and only recovered in the 1950s.

In 1959 agriculture in Mexico still employed 6,230,000 persons, 55 per cent of the employed population, industry, including mining, only 1,700,000 or under 17 per cent. Agriculture only accounted for 25 per cent of the national income, however, while manufacturing made up 23 per cent and mining over 6 per cent. The relative importance of industry is increasing rapidly, and industrial output rose by over 60 per cent between 1954 and 1959 alone.

11.4. MINING AND MANUFACTURING

Although Mexico has been predominantly an agricultural country at least until the Second World War, it has had industries based both on local crafts and on the processing of mining products since the sixteenth century. Several districts rose to prominence at different periods for their mines (see *Figure 4.4*), among them San Luis Potosí, Zacatecas, Guanajuato and Pachuca to the north of Mexico City and Taxco to the south. Textiles, leather, wood, and in a limited way, iron, were manufactured. Modern industry in Mexico developed out of the modernization of mining, with non-ferrous metals and later oil, developing alongside gold and silver, and out of the importation from as early as 1830–40 on of textile machinery by enterprising capitalists in certain centres such as Puebla and Orizaba. The first steel to be made in Latin America was produced around 1900, but engineering dates only from the 1950s, with, for example, the beginning of the manufacture of railway wagons in 1954, textile machinery in 1955 and sewing machines in 1958; during the same period a motor vehicles industry has been formed, based initially on assembly. The chemicals industry on any but a modest scale dates from the 1940s. The ingredients of modern industry in Mexico are based on home produced oil, gas and hydro-electricity, on other minerals, both metallic and nonmetallic, including non-ferrous metals, iron ore and sulphur, and on agricultural products such as cotton and henequen, plus imported machinery and both home and foreign capital.

Although Mexico has several small coalfields and produces about 1½ million tons of coal per year (1.8 m. tons in 1961), its total reserves, most of which are in the Salinas basin, are only put at 1,690 m. tons, equal to about eight times the yearly U.K. output. Oil and gas are the principal sources of energy. For a time after the First World War Mexico was the leading exporter of oil in the world but the industry was nationalized in 1938 and there followed a period of stagnation. Recently great progress has been made by Petróleos Mexicanos (Pemex) in increasing both oil and gas output. Crude oil production rose from $5\frac{1}{2}$ m. tons in 1938 to 14 m. in 1959 and 16 m. in 1962; most is refined in the country. Gas increased from 1,762 m. cubic metres in 1950 to 9,328 in 1959 and 10,510 m. in 1962. In 1959, over 75 per cent of the oil came from the general area of Támpico, most from Tuxpan and Nueva Faja de Oro, 20 per cent from the southern Gulf coast, and a small amount from near the U.S. boundary (Frontera), but about half of the gas came from this northern area (Reynosa), the remainder coming about equally from the other two main areas. The pipeline system has been extended rapidly in recent years both to distribute refined products from the coastal refineries and to take crude oil to new refineries in the interior (see *Figure 11.3a*). Oil and gas pipelines now extend also to Torreón and Chihuahua and a gas pipeline from Minatitlán to Mexico city. The other source of energy is hydroelectricity. Roughly half of the electricity in the country comes from this source, the rest being generated from oil or gas. In 1962 there was a total installed generating capacity of 3,476,000 kW, of which 1,590,000 was hydroelectric. The leading states for hydroelectricity were Puebla (400,000 kW), Mexico (380,000), Michoacán (230,000), Oaxaca (160,000) and Jalisco (100,000)*.

The relative importance of other minerals in Mexico can be seen from the following figures of percentage of value of total production in 1959 and 1961

	1959	1961		1959	1961
Zinc	24	25	Sulphur	11	10
Lead	18	16	Iron ore	4	5
Silver	14	13	Gold	4	3
Copper	12	11	Coal	3	4

The more important mining centres are widely scattered over the northern part of the country with concentrations to the south of Chihuahua, north of Zacatecas, and in northern Coahuila (see *Figure 11.3a*). There are many mining encampments of moderate size such as Real del Monte near Pachuca, still producing silver, and Santa Eulalia and Parral, near Chihuahua. Smelters are usually located in or near the mining centres. The main reserve of iron ore is at Cerro del Mercado in Durango. Large deposits of asbestos have recently been confirmed in the Novillo Canyon, in southern Tamaulipas. These various mineral deposits are almost all in the mountains and plateaux of the interior; only the sulphur is mined in the south (Jaltipan).

* The following power stations were under construction or planned in the early 1960s[7].

Hydroelectric: Mazatepec, Puebla state
Cupatitzio, Michoacán (95,000 kW)
El Infiernillo, Guerrero (600,000 kW)
Apulco (208,000), El Novillo (90,000), Santa Rosa (90,000)
Thermal: Fresnillo, Zacatecas state

239

Various widely differing estimates of the number of persons engaged in manufacturing in Mexico occur in different sources, but the number appears to be about 2 m. One source[8] puts the number of persons employed in manufacturing (industrias de transformación) in 1955 at 2,171,000, of which 1,322,000 were in the Distrito Federal and 95,000 in Nuevo Leon state: 45 per cent of all investment in manufacturing was in the Distrito Federal and 55 per cent of industrial output came from it. Certainly a large share of manufacturing production comes from the capital, but this estimate of employment seems excessively large.

Although most branches of industry are represented in the capital, which has about one third of the purchasing power of the country, other centres tend to specialize in one or a limited number of branches. The iron and steel industry has hitherto been confined largely to the northeast, with coking coal and iron ore being assembled and iron made at Monclova and Monterrey. But with the use of electricity and gas in steel-making it has been possible to establish the industry on the outskirts of Mexico City and in Veracruz (steel tubes). Mexico is now constructing a very large modern integrated iron and steel works at Las Truchas in Michoacán. Total steel production (tons) has risen as follows:

1950	39,000	1960	1,500,000
1955	725,000	1961	1,725,000
1957	1,049,000	1962	1,850,000

If expansion continues at this rate for another decade, Mexico will soon be able to count on a suitable base for really large scale industrialization; the target for 1965 is 3,875,000 tons.

The distribution of oil refineries is shown in *Figure 8.3*. These are either oilfields or market orientated and are becoming centres of chemicals manufacturing. Cement is also an expanding industry in Mexico. Textile manufacturing, mainly cotton, is the speciality of Puebla and Orizaba, while León

TABLE 11.1

Towns in Mexico With Over 50,000 Inhabitants
in 1960 (Census) in Alphabetical Order

1	Aguascalientes	127	22	Nuevo Laredo	93
2	Celaya	59	23	Oaxaca	72
3	Chihuahua	150	24	Orizaba	70
4	Ciudad Juárez	262	25	Pachuca	65
5	Ciudad Madero	54	26	Puebla	289
6	Ciudad Obregón	68	27	Querétaro	68
7	Ciudad Victoria	51	28	Reynosa	74
8	Culiacán	85	29	Saltillo	99
9	Distrito Federal	4,871	30	San Luis Potosí	160
10	Gómez Palacio	61	31	Támpico	123
11	Guadalajara	737	32	Tepic	54
12	Hermosillo	96	33	Tijuana	152
13	Irapuato	84	34	Toluca	77
14	Jalapa	66	35	Torreón	180
15	León	210	36	Veracruz	145
16	Matamoros	92	37	Victoria de Durango	97
17	Mazatlán	76	38	Villahermosa	52
18	Mérida	171			
19	Mexicali	175			
20	Monterrey	597			
21	Morelia	101			

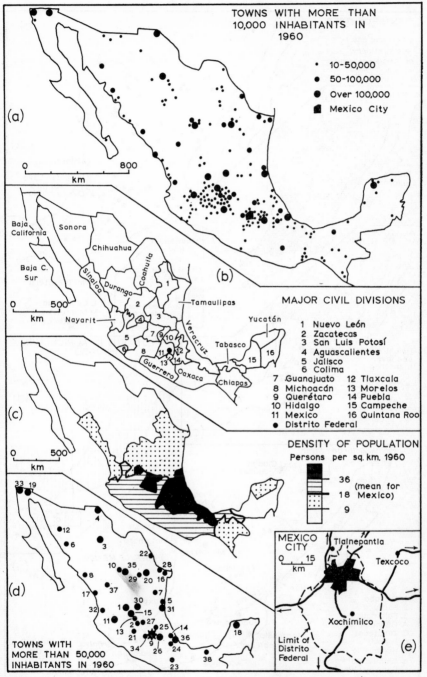

Figure 11.2. Mexico. (a) Towns with more than 10,000 inhabitants in 1960. (b) Major civil divisions. (c) Density of population. (d) Towns with more than 50,000 inhabitants. (e) Mexico City area

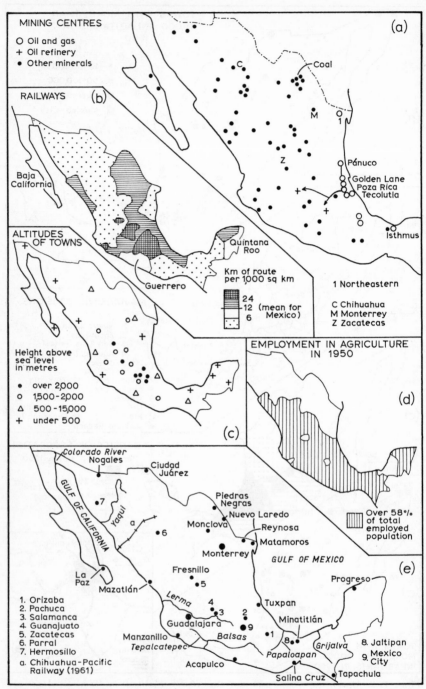

Figure 11.3. Mexico. (a) Mining centres. (b) Density of railway network. (c) Altitude of towns. (d) Employment in agriculture. (e) Miscellaneous places mentioned in text

makes shoes. Guadalajara, on the other hand, has industries based on traditional crafts and located in small establishments producing glassware, pottery, clothing and other consumer goods. Many medium sized towns of Mexico (e.g. Hermosillo, Torreón, Mérida, Oaxaca) have little industry at all other than the processing of agricultural products; they exist and are growing essentially as commercial and administrative towns. *Figure 11.2d* shows the distribution of towns with over 50,000 inhabitants and these are listed in Table 11.1.

11.5. TRANSPORT

Growing regional specialization in agriculture, the development of new manufacturing, the increasing need to move raw materials, and even the expanding tourist industry, have all contributed to make a system of inter-regional transport links necessary in Mexico. Although the Mexican system is more complete than that of most Latin American countries it is far from integrated yet. There were numerous trails served mainly by pack animals in the country in the colonial period, those running Veracruz-Mexico-Acapulco and Mexico-Zacatecas and beyond, and Mexico-Oaxaca and beyond, being particularly busy. However, most areas remained very isolated. The first railway was built in 1837, but the great period of railway construction, as in Argentina, was roughly 1870–1910. More lines are still being added (e.g. the Chihuahua-Pacific line was completed in 1961 but is only single track) and very few have been closed so far, but some are so little used they could better be replaced by roads. In addition to a fairly close network of lines in the high basins of Central Mexico, a number of radial lines were built between Mexico City and the extremities of the country: three to the north, and one to the south, branching at the Isthmus to serve the coasts of Chiapas and Yucatán. There are links with the U.S. system in the north and with Guatemala in the south. Even now it is much more easy to travel in directions radiating from Mexico City than at right angles to these. What is more, some areas, including the southwest, have no lines at all, while the Sierra Madre Occidental was only crossed in 1961.

Road improvement and construction has progressed rapidly, and the main arteries tend to follow the same general courses as the main railways (see *Figure 11.5c*). The following figures illustrate the rise of motor transport:

	Paved road	Motor vehicles registered	No. of which were commercial vehicles
1950	13,600 km	308,000	111,000
1960	27,000 km	827,000	293,000
1962	n.a.	902,000	354,000

The distribution of both good roads and vehicles in circulation is of course very irregular. Again the states of the southwest are the worst provided, and there is a general deterioration southwards, understandable since the roads north of Mexico have to carry most of the tourist traffic and much of the interregional and international trade of Mexico. In 1960, Mexico already had about 30,000 km of paved road, about twice as much as Brazil.

Veracruz is the principal seaport of the country, and handles much of the European traffic, but many of the exports of Mexico go via land to the U.S.A. Now that the country is roughly self-sufficient in oil and its products, Támpico handles less foreign trade than previously. Coastal shipping is concerned mainly with the distribution of oil and Támpico, Minatitlán and Coatzacoalcos are the busiest on the Gulf side, while Salina Cruz distributes oil to Pacific coast ports. Most of the 3 m. tons of goods handled by coastwise shipping in 1959 was oil.

Like other Latin American countries, Mexico has been integrated as a political and social unit by air transport. In 1960 there were about 860 landing places, but many were only capable of receiving small aircraft. The main air routes radiate from the capital, but many cross routes provide direct links between regional centres separated by physical barriers and not linked by road or rail.

11.6. REGIONAL CONTRASTS

From what has been said so far it will be clear that Mexico is a land of great contrasts in both physical and human conditions. Regional differences can be assessed in different ways. Here they will be approached briefly from two angles, the study of data recording levels of economic and social development in the major civil divisions, and the study of transport axes and their accompanying belts of developing area.

There is a considerable amount of data for the 32 major civil divisions of Mexico* on value of sales per inhabitant, consumption of goods, motor vehicles in circulation, degree of illiteracy, illegitimacy and so on. Some of this is mapped in *Figure 11.4* and a visual impression of the different distributions is achieved. But in the view of the author, a more precise idea of the relationship of any pair of these distributions (or of others not mapped) may be achieved in the way shown in Table 11.2. Some preliminary findings of this exercise suggest that a high standard of living and of literacy are fairly closely associated with urbanization, that population is increasing fastest in the most prosperous areas, but that occurrence of illegitimacy is not related either to lack of education (low literacy) or to non-urban areas†.

Using partly the type of data outlined above, partly other regional differences discussed in this chapter, some broad socioeconomic regions may be suggested. The fringe bordering the United States consists of a number of oases with dense agricultural populations and a number of border towns, usually twins with a counterpart on the other side. These most northern parts of Mexico are the most prosperous, even though the basis of their prosperity is precarious. Secondly, the northern part of the country with its expanding oases, relatively efficiently run farms, mines and industries, and busy roads and railways across it, is more prosperous than the rest of the country; Yucatán might perhaps be included. Almost all the exports of the country apart from coffee actually come from the north. Thirdly, Mexico City stands out from the country around it as having a far higher *per caput* income, though a large part of the population is relatively poor. Its level of

* There are 29 states, two territories and the Federal District.

† Work has been done on regional differences in Mexico as illustrated by data for states by Megee[9]. See also Appendix 8.

244

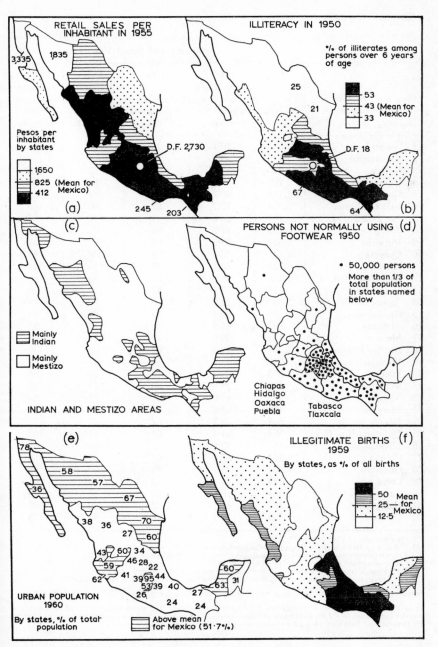

Figure 11.4. Mexico. (a) Sales per inhabitant in 1955. (b) Illiteracy in 1950. (c) Indian and mestizo areas. (d) Persons not normally using footwear. (e) Urban population in 1960. (f) Illegitimate births in 1959

TABLE 11.2

Economic and Social Variations in Mexico.

States and Territories (T) arranged according to distance from the U.S.A.	Ia Per caput sales	IIa Percentage of population urban	IIIa Percentage of population over 5 literate	IVa Legitimate births as percentage of all births	Va Percentage increase of population 1940–60
1 Nuevo León	1,505	70·4	79	95	100
2 Tamaulipas	1,172	59·8	74	77	124
3 Sonora	1,843	57·6	73	75	115
4 Chihuahua	793	57·2	73	86	97
5 Coahuila	1,111	66·7	75	91	65
6 Baja California	3,334	77·7	82	80	460
7 San Luis Potosí	461	33·6	49	86	54
8 Zacatecas	195	27·2	61	92	45
9 Durango	310	35·5	69	78	57
10 Querétaro	322	28·1	38	88	45
11 Sinaloa	751	38·2	58	53	71
12 Baja California (T)	1,156	36·3	78	65	60
13 Hidalgo	134	22·4	42	49	29
14 Aguascalientes	507	59·9	69	90	49
15 Guanajuato	292	46·4	46	84	66
16 Tlaxcala	97	43·9	56	77	55
17 Mexico	153	38·6	49	77	66
18 Distrito Federal	2,731	95·8	82	84	176
19 Yucatán	417	59·8	65	77	51
20 Puebla	375	39·2	46	66	53
21 Veracruz	492	39·6	50	45	69
22 Nayarit	387	42·6	63	55	80
23 Morelos	489	53·2	60	61	111
24 Jalisco	564	58·5	62	89	72
25 Quintana Roo (T)	507	31·4	62	74	168
26 Michoacán	248	40·6	47	85	57
27 Colima	482	61·8	64	71	108
28 Guerrero	207	25·7	33	80	62
29 Oaxaca	245	24·4	39	48	46
30 Tabasco	384	26·6	58	57	74
31 Campeche	394	63·2	62	79	87
32 Chiapas	203	24·4	36	45	78

I *Per caput* sales in 1955 in pesos[10].
II Urban population as a percentage of total population in 1960[11].
III Literate population as percentage of total population over age of five years in 1950[12].
IV Legitimate births as a percentage of all births in 1959[13].
V Percentage increase of population, 1940–1960. The mean for Mexico itself was 78 per cent[14].
    An approximate idea of the degree of correlation of the various distributions can be achieved by applying Spearman Rank Correlation Coefficient to any pair. The formula is $r = 1 - \dfrac{6\Sigma d^2}{n^3 - n}$ where d = the difference in ranking of each state and n (in this case 32) the number of states. The result ranges from $+1$ for a complete positive correlation to -1 for a complete negative correlation. See Appendix 8 for a correlation matrix (13 × 13) for 13 variables. Note that Vb is a consensus ranking giving equal consideration to I–IV.

I–Va, *per caput* data, I–Vb, ranked

Ib	IIb	I and II applying Spearman (see below)		IIIb	IVb		Sum of rankings I–IV	Re-ranked according to I–IV	Vb
Per caput sales	Per cent urban 1960	d	d²						
4	3	1	1	3	1		11	1	7
5	9	4	16	6	19		39	7	4
3	11	8	64	7	20		41	9	5
8	12	4	16	8	8		36	6	9
7	4	3	9	5	3		19	4	19
1	2	1	1	2	12		17	3	1
16	24	8	64	24	7		71	16	25
29	27	2	4	17	2		75	18	31
23	23	0	0	9	15		70	15	22
22	26	4	16	30	6		84	23	30
9	21	12	144	20	28		78	24	15
6	22	16	256	4	24		56	13	21
31	32	1	1	28	29		120	31	32
11	7	4	16	10	4		32	5	27
24	14	10	100	27	11		76	20	18
32	15	17	289	21	18		86	25	24
30	20	10	100	23	17		90	27	17
2	1	1	1	1	10		14	2	2
17	8	9	81	11	16		52	10	28
21	19	2	4	26	23		89	26	26
13	18	5	25	22	31		84	22	16
19	16	3	9	13	27		75	19	11
14	13	1	1	18	25		70	14	8
10	10	0	0	14	5		39	8	14
12	25	13	169	16	21		74	17	3
25	17	8	64	25	9		76	21	23
15	6	9	81	12	22		55	12	6
27	29	2	4	32	13		101	29	20
26	30	4	16	29	30		115	30	29
20	28	8	64	19	26		95	28	13
18	5	13	169	15	14		52	11	10
28	31	3	9	31	32		122	32	12

Comparing *per caput* sales (Ib) with degree of urbanization IIb the following is the procedure (see appropriate columns):
Σ (the sum of) all d^2 is 1,792. Thus:

$$r = 1 - \frac{6 \times 1,792}{32^3 - 32} = 1 - \frac{10,752}{32,736} = 1 - 0.33 = +0.67$$

The following results, suggesting a fairly close correlation, were obtained:

I and II (Sales and urbanization): +0·67
II and III (Urbanization and literacy): +0·73
I and V (Sales and increase of population): +0·64

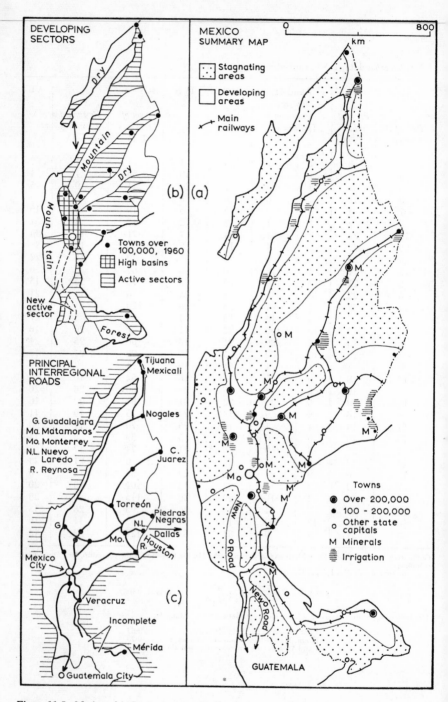

Figure 11.5. Mexico. (a) Summary map. (b) Developing sectors. (c) Principal interregional roads

development is due both to industries and services. Fourthly, the mountain basins around Mexico, especially the higher eastern ones, are particularly poor, but being at the centre of economic life of the country, have the prospect of being caught up in the industrial expansion and are reasonably well served by roads and railways. Fifthly, the south remains the poorest, least attractive and most difficult part of Mexico to develop, but a new road through Oaxaca to the Isthmus is likely to bring gradual improvements, and it is hoped eventually to resettle perhaps $2\frac{1}{2}$ m. people in this area[15].

The Mexican economy can be looked at in quite a different light, spatially speaking. If Central America is type (iii)/II in *Figure 9.2*, a number of clusters strung out on a line, Mexico, though very distorted in shape from a compact form, is nevertheless type (i)/II to III at a moderate stage of development, with radials from a centre strongly developed, but weak cross routes. It is along the radial roads and railways that much of the population is clustered, and between them that most of the backward, subsistence areas lie. *Figure 11.5a* is only suggestive of the developing and stagnating sectors. Physical conditions of course have something to do with the alignment of the routes, as does the focal role of the capital. From this view, Mexico may be regarded as a central core with the capital and a surrounding area of dense mainly agricultural population, and positive and negative sectors radiating from this core. Six developing sectors may be suggested.

(*a*) East from Mexico City, roads and railways descend to the principal port, Veracruz. Puebla and Orizaba are textile centres in this sector. The rail route continues southeast, to proceed into Yucatán and Chiapas.

(*b*) South from Mexico City a modern highway succeeds the old trails to the Pacific port of Acapulco; there is no railway here and not much development yet, but the places close to the road have been brought into the economic life of Mexico better than those away from it.

(*c*) Southeast from Mexico City, a new road has opened up Oaxaca and Chiapas states, following a more direct course to the Guatemala boundary than the main railway.

(*d*) To the northwest, the Pacific coast road and railway links the many oases of this area (with a surplus of cotton and food) and carries the traffic from California to the centre of Mexico. Lower California largely remains a stagnating sector. The Sierra Madre Occidental separates (*d*) from

(*e*) The axis linking the metal mining centres of the western part of the plateau and the cotton oases at the foot of the Sierra Madre Occidental with Mexico City.

(*f*) Finally a wider sector in the northeast contains the main oilfields, coalfields and iron and steel centres as well as important cattle grazing lands, and carries the roads and railways to Texas and eastern U.S.A.

It would seem reasonable to think that distance from the centre of the country means proportionately less integration in the economic life, but the picture is distorted by the proximity of the northern region to the U.S.A. and its dependence on the U.S.A. (tourists from its neighbour, labour and commodities to it). Inevitably, some of the prosperity of the U.S.A., whose *per caput* income is ten times as high as the mean for Mexico, has spilled into this northern part of the country. Tijuana is actually considerably closer (in a straight line) to Vancouver, Canada, than to Mexico City, while

Mérida in Yucatán is roughly the same distance from Havana and Miami as from Mexico City.

11.7. PROBLEMS OF MEXICO

Some of the outstanding problems of Mexico must now be outlined: the rapid process of urbanization and especially the growth of the capital, the need to increase agricultural production and to integrate the country even more.

By 1930 Mexico had a total population of 16,600,000, of which only about 5,600,000 were urban. By 1960, total population had more than doubled, while urban population had risen from 33 per cent to 51 per cent of total population, 17,700,000, or considerably more than three times. The impact of this increase in towns in little over a generation on food and water supply, housing, health services and so on is far more drastic than anything known in Britain for over a century. Of the absolute increase of urban dwellers, 12 m., about 30 per cent has occurred in the capital itself. The population of Mexico City grew gradually through the colonial period to reach about 140,000 in 1800 and by 1850 it was about 250,000. The following table shows how in the present century it has been steadily increasing its share of the national total (population in thousands)[16]:

	Distrito Federal	All Mexico	% in D.F.		Distrito Federal	All Mexico	% in D.F.
1895	476	12,600	4	1930	1,229	16,600	7
1900	541	13,600	4	1940	1,758	19,700	9
1910	721	15,200	5	1950	3,050	25,800	12
1921	906	14,300	6	1960	4,870	34,900	14

No less impressive has been the mushroom growth of the larger towns on or near the U.S. boundary. Together the six largest now have about 850,000 inhabitants, compared with only about 100,000 thirty years ago. The success of the capital seems due to its central position and the special place it has in relation to rail, air and road networks. The more advanced an economy becomes, the more certain areas seem to become attractive, as changing employment structure drives people from the land. At the present level of development of Mexico, and given the alignment of routes, the capital, with its relatively high standard of living, employment opportunities and superior amenities, exerts centripetal forces that seem irresistible. Greater Mexico City is growing at least by 200,000 people per year, and on the north side is spreading beyond the Distrito Federal*. But the presence of the capital has not greatly changed the rural areas of its own and nearby basins.

Mexico City occupies the site of a former lake area, lake Texcoco, which is gradually being drained. The central part of the town has suffered from serious subsidence. The original gridiron centre still serves partly as the central business district, but long avenues to the west carry tall new blocks of offices for several kilometres (see *Figure 11.6*). Most of the town has low

---

* See also Section 19.2 and *Figure 19.4*.

buildings, with widespread slum housing arranged along narrow alleys. Some 30 per cent of the population live in *colonias proletarias* on the outskirts; these originated as squatter settlements but are gradually being integrated in the urban life. Much of the industry is on the northwest side of the town. Water supply is rapidly becoming inadequate and electricity is short while traffic problems are grave.

So long as a large urban concentration does not choke itself out there seems nothing wrong in having industries and services concentrated in one locality. It is considered, however, that by 1980 the population could be

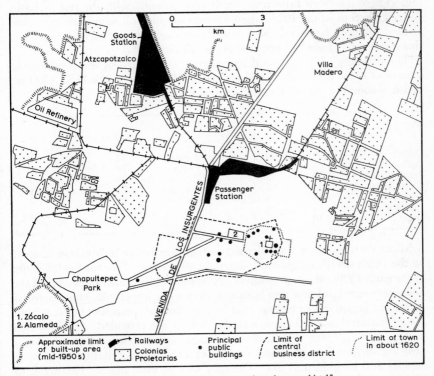

Figure 11.6. Mexico City centre and northern outskirts[17]

15 m. But the growth of the capital and other large regional centres depends on a sound agricultural basis and the establishment of a sound energy base. Much has to be done to increase agricultural production and to attract people discontented with the rural areas in which they dwell or unable to find employment there to new areas of development. At the same time, the network of communications has to be extended to improve interregional lines and divert some of the traffic that converges on and passes through the capital.

Finally, Mexico lies next to the U.S.A. and whether it likes it or not cannot cut itself off from its neighbour. Admittedly U.S. investments in Mexico are now regulated in various ways and much U.S. financial assistance is in enterprises more than half Mexican owned.

11.8. FOREIGN TRADE

For some decades, a large share of the foreign trade of Mexico has been with the U.S.A. In 1938, for example, 58 per cent of the imports came from the U.S.A. and 67 per cent of Mexican exports went there. The proportions were higher during and after the Second World War. In 1952, for example, the U.S.A. supplied 83 per cent of the imports and took 77 per cent of exports, but by the early 1960s the proportion each way was back to about two-thirds, while Mexico's trade with the EEC, especially West Germany, was expanding. There has been little trade until very recently with the rest of Latin America except in the 1920s when Mexico supplied oil to certain countries. Under LAFTA, however, there have been moves to encourage trade, but this is still only about 2–3 per cent of the Mexican total.

The diversity of Mexico and its economy is reflected in the considerable variety of items exported. Total exports in 1959 were worth U.S. $ 723 m. Items accounting for more than 2 per cent were:

	U.S. $ m.	%	% 1961		U.S. $ m.	%	% 1961
Cotton	199	28	15	Lead	34	5	4
Coffee	63	9	7	Copper	29	4	2
Shrimps	39	5	5	Zinc	25	4	3
Cattle, meat	38	5	5	Sulphur	24	3	4
Tomatoes	24	3	—	Fuel oil	21	3	3
Henequen	20	3	—				
Sugar	15	2	9	— small			

Minerals account for a smaller share than ever before in Mexican history. In the 1830s silver and gold accounted for 90 per cent of the total value while in the early 1920s oil was prominent. Now most of the minerals produced are being consumed at home and bauxite is even to be imported. Manufactured goods are beginning to be exported in very limited quantities but it is from the agricultural sector that most of the exports are provided. Here Mexico is striving to achieve a precarious balance—self-sufficiency in food plus a growing surplus from the land for export. Its own population is growing rapidly and its industries too. The only way to maintain the balance is to develop the production of fertilizers and to mechanize agriculture more. Mexico's balance of trade is very unfavourable. Imports were $ U.S. 1,100 m in 1959 compared with exports of only 723 m. At this stage in its development, without a sophisticated engineering industry, Mexico has to import so much machinery and equipment to keep its economy expanding that it must go on exporting. It looks to the U.S.A., Europe and Japan as outlets for food and mineral products but it has its eyes on the rest of Latin American as an outlet for manufactured goods in the future.

U.S. tourists spend as much money as half of the value of all Mexican exports, and this business seems likely to continue and expand; 220,000 visited Mexico in 1962 for periods over 3 days. Mexican labourers (*braceros*), as many as 450,000 a year, have gone seasonally to work in farms in California, Arizona and Texas, especially those in the irrigated lands of the southwest, which require much labour at certain times in the year. These Mexican workers are usually housed in special encampments and have little contact with ordinary life in the U.S.A., but as well as bringing back large sums of money to Mexico they are considered to have brought in new ideas and to have had some hand in urging social reform and possibly also in improving farming techniques in their own rural areas. The towns along the northern boundary of Mexico are however an embarrassment economically since understandably their citizens make heavy purchases in neighbouring parts of the U.S.A.

REFERENCES

1a Watson, W. *North America, its Countries and Regions*, 1963, Ch. 23, London, Longmans
1b Vivó, J. A. *Geografía de México*, 1950. Barcelona; Editorial Labor
2 Instituto de Geografía, 1962. *Distribución geográfica de la población en la República Mexicana*
3 *Anuario Estadístico* 1958–1959, p. 33
4 Winnie, W. W. 'The Papaloapan Project: An Experiment in Tropical Development' *Econ. Geogr.* 34 (1958) 227–48
5 *Compendio Estadístico*, 1960, p. 73 and 1962, pp. 97–8
6 *Compendio Estadístico*, 1962, p. 109
7 *Compendio Estadístico*, 1962, p. 118
8 *Anuario Estadístico* 1958–1959, p. 522
9 Megee, M. 'Social and Economic Factors in the Differential Growth of Mexican States' *Papers presented to the First Latin American Conference on Regional Science* held at Cendes, Caracas, Nov. 1962
10 Tamayo, J. L. *Geografía moderna de Mexico*. 1960, 353–4
11 *Compendio Estadístico*, 1960 p. 15
12 *Anuario Estadístico*, 1958–1959, pp. 48–50
13 *Anuario Estadístico*, 1958–1959, pp. 85–86
14 *Compendio Estadístico*, 1960, pp. 13–14
15 *The Times*, 4 Aug. 1964. 'Mexico Develops the South-East'
16 *Anuario Estadístico*, 1959, pp. 36–39
17 *Colonias Proletarias, Problemas y Soluciones*, INV, 1958, Mexico

CHAPTER 12

VENEZUELA

12.1. INTRODUCTION

Venezuela is distinct from the other Latin American countries on account of its great oil industry. Four decades ago it was among the poorer and less progressive countries of Latin America, with most of its population confined to a small part of the national area and very heavy dependence on agriculture. For more than two decades now it has been either the second or third oil producing country in the world and by the late 1950s its *per caput* gross national product was more than twice as high as that of any other country in Latin America except for some Islands, though the wealth is very unevenly spread among the population. As the oil industry has expanded, the contribution of agriculture to total gross domestic product has shrunk to a mere 6 per cent in the early 1960s; surplus rural population has moved to oilfield areas and to towns elsewhere and has spread from the original clusters; a magnificent system of roads serves the northern part of the country. Yet about 10 per cent of the population is unemployed, 30 per cent destitute and 50 per cent illiterate. In 1961 oil accounted for 21 per cent of the gross national product, 56 per cent of government revenue and 93 per cent of the value of exports. The following figures for oil production in selected years illustrate the expansion of the industry (millions of metric tons):

1925	2,5	1945	47,3	1961	155,9
1930	19,0	1950	80,0	1962	166,1
1935	21,7	1955	115,2	1963	171,1
1940	26,9	1960	152,4		

Venezuela is roughly $1\frac{1}{2}$ times the size of France, but its population in 1920 was only 2,400,000, concentrated very much in the Andean region. The figure for mid-1963 was 8,140,000, of which 4,200,000 were under 18

TABLE 12.1[2]

Andean Countries: Summary Table

	Venezuela	Colombia	Ecuador	Peru	Bolivia
Area (thousands of sq. km)	912	1,138	271	1,285	1,099
Population (thousands)	7,600	14,400	4,600	10,400	3,500
Population of capital (thousands)	1,265	1,329	362	1,978	340
Capital as % of total population	17	9	8	19	10
Employment in agric. % (thous.)	40	54	50	50	72
Agriculture as % of total GDP	6	34	37	25	n.a.
Per caput GDP (1958) (thous.U.S. $)	715	301	180	150	96
Per caput consumption of energy 1961, in kilograms of coal equivalent	2,764	549	184	354	145

years of age, indicating a rapidly growing population, about 3 per cent per year[1]. In fact the population roughly doubled in 20 years between 1941 and 1961, but immigration, particularly in the 1950s, made a considerable contribution to this growth. Italians, Spaniards and Colombians were the main immigrants, arriving at the rate of about 30,000 a year in the 1950s, the peak period being 1953–57 (40–50,000 per year). Currently emigration exceeds immigration. Growth of population has been accompanied by urbanization; the urban share of total population rose from about one third in 1936 to over half in 1961; Greater Caracas alone has nearly 20 per cent of the total.

The key to an understanding of Venezuela and its problems is the great discrepancy between the percentage of the contribution of different economic activities to total gross domestic product and to the percentage of employment. Different sets of figures vary considerably, but the same broad picture emerges: agriculture accounts for only about 6 per cent of total gross domestic product but still employs about 35 per cent of the working population. The oil industry accounts for about 20 per cent but employs only about 2 per cent. The productivity of an oil worker is 50–100 times as high as that of a worker in agriculture, though wages are not of course that many times higher. Employment in agriculture has risen gradually in the 1950s (1950, 704,000; 1959, 833,000) but has dropped from 41 per cent of total employment to 34 per cent. Employment in the oil industry has actually declined in spite of a great increase in output: 1948, 60,000; 1956, 50,000; 1962, 34,000; but it is hoped to stabilize it at around 40,000. Employment in manufacturing has in fact risen considerably since the early 1950s: about 170,000 in 1951 to 280,000 in 1962, accounting for rather more than 10 per cent of both employment and gross domestic product. Finally, some 50 per cent of the gross domestic product is accounted for by services. 1959 figures bring out the great discrepancy in productivity. The average value in $ U.S. of production per person employed during 1959 was: agriculture 590, oil 52,400, other mining 10,700, remaining activities 3,170.

12.2. PHYSICAL BACKGROUND AND AGRICULTURE

Physically, Venezuela may be divided into several fairly clearly distinctive regions, though climate and relief features are only roughly related. The most simple division is into the cordilleras, the lowlands and uplands of the northwest, the lowlands of the llanos, reaching to the Orinoco, and the uplands and highlands of the Venezuelan Guiana beyond. Within these, subdivisions such as the Orinoco delta may be distinguished.

The Cordillera de los Andes and their continuation eastwards in the Cordillera de la Costa are broken into three parts by the two depressions, one near Barquisimeto and the other the Unaré basin. They are high, exceeding 5,000 m in one place, but narrow. For much of the length there are two or more ranges enclosing high valleys and basins (e.g. Mérida, Lake Valencia). There is a considerable area with temperate (*templado*) conditions between about 1,000 and 2,000 m but the cold (*frío*) and *páramo* zones are much smaller than in other Andean countries. Permanent snow occurs above about 4,600 m. Mean annual precipitation varies greatly from one

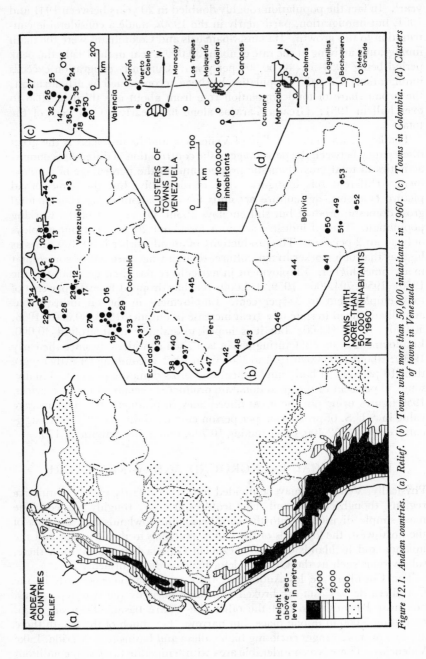

Figure 12.1. Andean countries. (a) Relief. (b) Towns with more than 50,000 inhabitants in 1960. (c) Towns in Colombia. (d) Clusters of towns in Venezuela

256

TABLE 12.2

Towns With Over 50,000 Inhabitants in the Andean Countries
Arranged Alphabetically by Country (See *Figure 12.1*)

Venezuela (1961 Census)				
1	Barquisimeto	197	28 Montería*	104
2	Cabimas	93	29 Neiva	70
3	Ciudad Bolívar	96	30 Palmira	120
4	Cumaná	72	31 Pasto*	124
5	Distrito Federal	1,265	32 Pereira	170
6	Lagunillas	68	33 Popoyán	60
7	Maracaibo	433	34 Santa Marta*	64
8	Maracay	134	35 Sevilla	60
9	Maturín	53	36 Tuluá	110
10	Puerto Cabello	51	*Ecuador* (1962 Census)	
11	Puerto La Cruz	55	37 Cuenca	75
12	San Cristóbal	96	38 Guayaquil	515
13	Valencia	161	39 Quito	362
Colombia (Late 1950s or			40 Riobamba	50
1962 estimate*)			*Peru* (1961 Census)	
14	Armenia	100	41 Arequipa	142
15	Barranquilla*	474	42 Chiclayo	87
16	Bogota*	1,329	43 Chimbote	64
17	Bucaramanga*	222	44 Cusco	60
18	Buenaventura*	60	45 Iquitos	56
19	Buga	50	46 Lima	1,978
20	Cali*	693	47 Piura	66
21	Ciénaga	80	48 Trujillo	100
22	Cartagena*	185	*Bolivia* (Late 1950s)	
23	Cucutá*	148	49 Cochabamba	90
24	Girardot	60	50 La Paz	340
25	Ibagué*	149	51 Oruro	50
26	Manizales*	176	52 Potosí	50
27	Medellín*	691	53 Santa Cruz	70

part of the cordillera to another, with semi-arid conditions prevailing in places; usually it is steepness of slope and poor quality of soil that limit agricultural possibilities.

On its northwest side, the high Cordillera of the Andes overlooks the lowlands of Maracaibo, partly filled by shallow sea, but almost encircled by mountains or uplands. This lowland is covered by dense tropical rain forest in the south but is remarkably dry towards the north. There is little agriculture at present but with drainage and control of the rivers in the south and irrigation further north cultivation could be extended.

Roughly between the Andes and the Orinoco lie the llanos. This is a lowland area with a gradual slope east or southeast, filled mainly with relatively new deposits from the cordilleras, well watered in the west and crossed by many large rivers here, but rather more broken, and generally drier in the east. A savanna vegetation is associated with the region, but much of the surface in the west, especially close to the Andes, and in the delta as well, is heavily forested, while the Unaré basin has thorn forest rather than savanna. Little of the region is cultivated, though much is used for grazing. Improvements for agriculture depend both on regulating the flow of rivers to prevent flooding and to improve drainage, and on arranging irrigation systems.

Beyond the Orinoco the land rises irregularly towards the southeast of the country, where much of the land is above 1,000 m, but there are also lowlands, as in the extreme south. Though mostly receiving more than

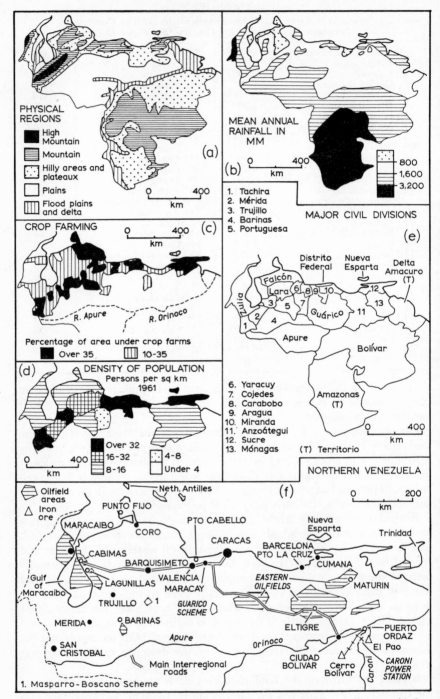

Figure 12.2. Venezuela. (a) Physical regions. (b) Mean annual rainfall in millimetres. (c) Crop farming. (d) Density of population. (e) Major civil divisions. (f) Northern Venezuela

about 3,000 mm of rain per year, the region is not entirely covered by tropical rain forest (selva), for patches of savanna interrupt this.

Venezuela lies well within the tropics (1°N–12°N) and the regional contrasts in its relief, amount of rain, and vegetation, are not matched by contrasts in temperature or seasonal occurrence of rain over most of the country. Over 90 per cent of Venezuela has a mean annual temperature of over 24°C. Moderate differences in altitude do of course make appreciable differences: contrast Caracas, 22°C, with its nearby port, La Guaira, 26°C. The subtle division of the country by some Venezuelan geographers into tropical land below 500 m and hot (caliente) between 500 and 1,000 m seems superfluous.

1956 figures for land use in Venezuela show that only a very small part of the country is seriously used for agricultural production. About 6 per cent of the total area was actually in crop farms, but only 20–25 per cent of this or less than 1·5 per cent of all Venezuela, actually grows field or tree crops, and about the same area has cultivated pastures. Another 20 per cent of Venezuela is classed as pasture land, while much of the remainder is forest, but this has not been accurately assessed. Most of the cropland is in the cordilleras or at their foot, grazing is practised in the llanos and in a more limited way in the Maracaibo lowlands, but the half of the country south of the Orinoco is farmed only by primitive shifting cultivators. In 1960, out of a total value of production from the land and from fisheries of about $ U.S. 550 m., 56·5 per cent came from crops, 37 per cent from livestock and only a few per cent each from the fisheries and forests.

In 1960, 1,437,000 hectares were under field and tree crops. Cereals occupied 31 per cent of the area, coffee and cacao 37 per cent, and tubers, roots, beans and other vegetables 19 per cent. The small remaining part of the total area grew more valuable crops per unit of area including sugar cane and cotton, bananas and other fruits, tobacco and oilseeds. Basic foods of the rural population are maize, yuca, beans and bananas, while coffee and cacao are the only agricultural products exported. Yields of all crops have generally tended to be low in Venezuela, even by Latin American standards, but improvements are at last being made; for example the number of tractors rose four times in the 1950s. Cattle number about 6 m., an impressive quantity considering the population, if the beasts were of good quality; most are not, being criollo breeds. Brahman are being introduced for breeding, especially to improve meat production. About half of the cattle are in the three states of Apuré, Guárico and Zulia. There are also about 1½ m. pigs and the same number of goats and sheep, but there is a drive to eliminate goats.

Agriculture in Venezuela is organized very broadly in three basic types of holding. Firstly commercial crop farms (fincas comercializadas), usually over about 20 hectares, use labour paid in regular wages, have some mechanization and use fertilizers and insecticides; products include sugar and cotton, often grown virtually as monocultures. Secondly there are family size farms (conucos), not usually owned by the operators, usually small, concentrating on food crops for consumption on the farm and on tree crops, mainly coffee, for sale in towns or abroad. Two crops are often harvested each year but techniques are inefficient and yields low. Both coffee and cacao trees are usually grown too close together. Thirdly, there are large pastoral farms

LA GUAIRA — CARACAS MOTORWAY

BLOCK OF LUXURY FLATS, CARACAS

BRIDGE ACROSS
THE ENTRANCE
OF THE GULF
OF MARACAIBO

260

VENEZUELA

LEFT:
SIMÓN BOLÍVAR CENTRE,
DOWNTOWN CARACAS

BELOW:
SHANTY TOWN (*RANCHO*)
" ON CARACAS HILLSIDE

(*fincas ganaderas*), often over 2,500 hectares in area. They use unenclosed land with very low quality pasture and gather in and trade their cattle at yearly meetings—*vaqueras* or *rodeos*. One feature of land improvements in the llanos, as at the Guárico dam (Calabozo), is the provision of fodder crops for fattening.

Actual land tenure is very complicated in Venezuela, as in other Latin American countries, but sweeping changes are now being made in the hope that the backwardness of rural areas will at least be reduced and agricultural output boosted. A study of farm sizes in 1950 showed that there were 235,000 units, but that a mere 445 of these, all over 10,000 hectares each, had 42·6 per cent of the total area, while the 196,000 under 20 hectares had only 4·2 per cent of the area. Some small farmers do actually own their land but usually it is too small to support a family and provide a surplus for sale off it. Most farm workers actually work as labourers on larger farm units, and the number of tenants and share croppers is limited. Though labour is now more or less free to move about the country, the system of land tenure still has the basic features of the encomienda system with large properties owned by the Europeans or their mestizo descendants and Indians included with the land. Until recently, 2 per cent of the owners had about 80 per cent of the land. Land reform programmes of the late 1950s and early 1960s envisage the reorganization of 350,000 farm families, roughly half of the agricultural population, at the enormous cost of $ U.S. 6,900 m., a sum that only Venezuela among Latin American countries could expect to find over a short period (taking into account its size).

Agriculture in Venezuela is in a state of rapid transition. In the 1950s the country awoke to the fact that it was importing much of its food while having, even from the most pessimistic point of view, large areas that could be brought into use. Much of the farm land is in areas with frequent steep slopes, cannot be mechanized, and suffers from soil erosion. Farm incomes are very low, diet poor, educational standards dismal, tradition strong. Facilities for collecting, transporting, storing and retailing farm products have been bad, and supplies in the vicinity of large towns inadequate. Production has been expanding irregularly—at about 5 per cent per year, but powdered milk, cheese, eggs, tinned meat, fruit, wheat and rice are being imported. In time the relative importance of the mountain areas will diminish as improvements are made in the lowlands. So far the Guárico scheme is the only very large one but the Masparro-Boscano irrigation scheme should bring into use 220,000 more hectares.

12.3. MINING AND MANUFACTURING

Some general aspects of oil production in Venezuela have been described in Sections 5.2 and 8.3. Its position in the life of Venezuela must now be discussed. Until the last few years the oil industry of Venezuela was entirely in the hands of a limited number of U.S. and European oil companies. Of the seven largest companies in the U.S.A. in terms of sales in 1962 (see *Fortune*, July 1963, p. 178) three were oil companies with a large interest in Venezuela (Standard Oil/N.J., Socony Mobil Oil and Texaco), two were motor vehicles concerns (General Motors and Ford) with plants there and one, U.S. Steel, has an interest in Venezuelan iron ore. In the same year, Royal Dutch Shell had larger sales than any other private company outside the U.S.A. If not dominated by large foreign companies, Venezuela is at least entirely dependent on them for its high level of development.

Only about 6 per cent* of the total area of Venezuela is actually in oil concessions and only a small part of this actually has oil beneath it. Concessions were granted to foreign companies usually for 40 years, and tax was paid to explore, and by those companies who were lucky enough to find oil, to exploit, the concessions, while profits on the sale of oil were also taxed. In the early 1950s taxation was arranged so that the government received in revenue roughly 50 per cent (e.g. 52 per cent in 1958) of the profits. The country as a whole also benefited by the wages paid to oilfield, refinery and transportation personnel. By the early 1960s revenue had risen to about 66 per cent of profits. Even so it is worth while continuing to produce, though there has been reluctance to explore further by several companies, and in the early 1960s only about 500 new wells were being drilled yearly compared with over 1,700 in 1957 after the Suez crisis. Initially Venezuela could not possibly have developed a large modern oil industry with its own capital, but the position is changing and the Venezuelan Company† had about 10 wells in production by 1964, a negligible production but a development setting the pattern for the future. The plan is to stop granting new concessions to foreign companies and to co-operate with these in new developments on the basis of contracts of association.

There are two main general areas of oil production at the moment, the Maracaibo area and the eastern fields, the latter being more dispersed but only accounting for about a third of the total production. Two other areas are of interest in oil prospecting but produce little at present, Barinas in the west and the continental shelf in the northeast. At first, almost all the oil produced in Venezuela left in crude form but now nearly a third is refined within the country, the two largest refineries being on the Paraguaná Peninsula. There is a very extensive network of pipelines in both main oilfield areas. The complexity of these is suggested in *Figure 8.2* which shows only those belonging to Shell in western Venezuela.

Although only about 40,000 persons are now directly employed by the oil companies, several times as many people appear to find employment serving the oil workers themselves. The population of Zulia state has grown from about 120,000 in 1920 to 910,000 in 1961 and that of the town of Maracaibo from 47,000 to 443,000. Growth has been on a somewhat smaller scale in the eastern fields, and more dispersed, but has probably involved an increase of about ½ m. people in the general area. Large new towns such as Cabimas, Lagunillas and El Tigre depend entirely on oil, and excellent roads serve the oilfield areas which, however, are mostly in areas with poor prospects for agriculture.

The development of iron ore mining in Venezuela is more recent than that of oil but has been no less spectacular. Large reserves of high grade iron ore exist in the so-called Imateca iron belt of Venezuela, extending

---

* Actual area of concessions in force at the end of 1962 was 3,780,000 hectares of which only 13 per cent had been effectively explored.

† Corporación Venezolana de Petróleo (CORVEPET).

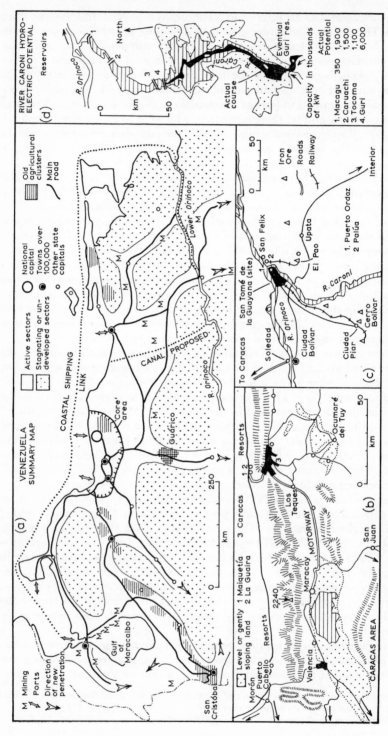

Figure 12.3. Venezuela. (a) Summary map. (b) Caracas area. (c) Lower Orinoco. (d) River Caroni hydroelectric potential[5]

from British Guiana west to Las Galeras del Cinaruco in Apuré state; 1,420 m. tons was the estimate in 1963, 80 per cent of it in the Ciudad Bolívar area (Cuadrilátero Ferrífero Bolívar), some with 70 per cent iron content. The principal mining districts (see *Figure 12.3*) are Cerro Bolívar and El Pao. The San Isidro deposits belong to the State and are to supply the new steel works, while Cerro Bolívar is worked by the Orinoco Mining Company (of U.S. Steel Corporation) and El Pao by the Bethlehem Steel Company. The ore is carried downhill by rail for shipment via the Orinoco. Exports rose during the 1950s but have dropped in the early 1960s. Venezuela apparently has other minerals as well, including large deposits of argil, a mineral with a 25 per cent aluminium content, also in the east, diamonds further south in the Guiana highlands (Salto El Venado) and in the extreme west, in Tachira state, phosphorite.

Until the Second World War Venezuela had very little modern manufacturing apart from plants concerned with processing agricultural products and oil, but in the last two decades, and especially since 1955, manufacturing has been transformed. The background is a considerable home market with a relatively high *per caput* purchasing power, abundant oil, natural gas and hydroelectricity, a good variety of raw materials, and considerable capital within the country, though much foreign capital is also invested in Venezuela. Oil is the principal source of energy. The amount of electricity generated increased ten times between 1948 and 1961, still coming mostly from oil-fired stations in the early 1960s. The Caroni power station is now producing in the east, however, and the Macagua station should also be completed in the early 1960s. Each has a capacity of 300–350,000 kW. The Caroni river is finally to have an installed capacity of about 6 m. kW.; the next stage, the Guri dam, was being considered in 1963 (see *Figure 12.3*).

Very broadly, the modern industries of Venezuela fall into three groups. First are the oil refineries and associated petrochemicals plants. There is now a State oil refinery at Morón, which is small and runs at a loss, but is to be greatly expanded and will feed chemical works producing fertilizers, explosives, plastics and eventually synthetic rubber. Secondly, much of the production of consumer goods takes place in the Valencia-Marcay-Caracas area with Barquisimeto also contributing. The usual list of goods is produced, including textiles, leather, paper, tyres, tobacco, light engineering products and motor vehicles (assembled), but the rapid expansion in the last few years is most striking. For example the production of cigarettes rose by 180 per cent between 1958 and 1962. Such changes are reminiscent of those in communist economies at certain stages of development. Surprisingly, even the manufacture of cotton textiles and of footwear is only relatively new in Venezuela and is also rapidly expanding. Thirdly, a new industrial complex on the lower Orinoco has appeared in the last few years. The whole enterprise is under the Corporación Venezolana de Guayana. The Guayana Corporation (CVG) is an autonomous institution. It was set up in 1960 by the Government to develop the Guayana area. Its interests include the State steel mill, an aluminium reduction plant, the Guri hydroelectric power scheme and the already completed Macagua plant (see the *Informe Anual* 1962 of CVG). It is based on the iron ore reserves already mentioned, coking coal brought in by ore carriers returning from foreign markets, aluminium minerals, oil from nearby parts of the eastern fields and hydro-electric power, with timber, cattle and diamonds as other products of the region. The major development has been the construction of a large integrated iron and steel works (Matanzas) near Puerto Ordaz at a cost for the first stage of U.S. $ 200 m. Output of steel reached 400,000 tons per year in 1963 and is planned to reach 1 m. tons by 1966. Venezuela cannot use it all yet but has found markets in the U.S.A., Europe, Latin America and Japan for small quantities of both steel ingots and simple products from the rolling mills. One of the principal items produced will be seamless steel tubes for use in the oilfields, and oil companies in the country are expected to buy these if they can, rather than import them. Aluminium and electro-chemicals plants are to be built in the area and the regional centre is to be the new town of San Tomé de la Guayana, initially to have 25,000 inhabitants and ultimately 250,000. Already in the early 1960s there were some 50,000 squatters in this area. Ciudad Bolívar is the administrative centre at present, while there are also several mining encampments and ports (see *Figure 12.3*). The total population of the area should soon reach $\frac{1}{4}$ m., repeating under different circumstances, the congregation of population in hitherto empty areas in which oil was discovered.

12.4. POPULATION AND TRANSPORT

Until a few decades ago, different clusters of population in Venezuela were separated by considerable distances, and even the few railways did not form strong links, as they did already by 1900 in Mexico, parts of Brazil and some other countries. The integration of Venezuela came in the interwar period with air transport and roads, and road transport seems the answer, given the difficulty of building railways in and across the cordilleras. At first the best roads were mostly in the oilfields, but now the whole of the northern quarter of the country is well served, and almost every state capital is linked to the system by a paved road. The actual length of paved roads rose from 5,500 km in 1958 to 12,000 in 1964. In addition to its ordinary roads, Venezuela has several exceptional engineering feats, including the motor-ways from La Guaira to Caracas and Caracas to Maracay, and the bridge across the entrance to the Gulf of Maracaibo, built high enough for large tankers entering the Gulf to pass under. Air transport is also vital for the economic life of Venezuela, and all self-respecting centres of reasonable size, apart from some in difficult localities in the high Andes, have an airfield. There are 150 small landing places in the southern part of the country and much of the meat produced here is flown to towns in the north.

There is a plan to make the Orinoco navigable far upstream and even to build a canal through from the Caribbean coast via the Unaré and Pao rivers to the Orinoco. But the main line of movement of goods carried by water extends between Ciudad Bolívar and Maracaibo, a distance of 2,000 km. The principal ports are shown in *Figure 12.3*.

The spatial arrangement of population and production in Venezuela has been profoundly altered over the last few decades. The essential features have been little change in the cordilleras, much of the llanos, or the southern half of the country, but a great increase in population in the mining areas and in the Caracas-Valencia area, as well as in some larger towns (e.g. San Cristóbal) elsewhere in the country. Roads have been built to link the main clusters of population, old and new, and to facilitate the spread of population into and the development of new areas. The result has been to replace a main axis of population along the Andes between San Cristóbal and Caracas by a longer axis from the Gulf of Maracaibo, through Valencia to the Lower Orinoco. Comparative distances along these axes are in a straight line 600 km and 1,100 km respectively and by road 1,060 km and 1,340 km. As in Mexico, developing and stagnating sectors of the national area may be suggested, if only very tentatively. In contrast to Mexico, however, only the northern third of the country is actually affected so far, while railways play virtually no role at all, but pipelines complicate the picture considerably.

There is a central core with some 2 m. people, most of the light industry and possibly half of the purchasing power of the national market. Radiating from this are major interregional roads to the east and west, as well as one to the south. Between these are less developed, generally thinly peopled areas that make little contribution to the national life. *Figure 12.3* shows in summary form the main features.

12.5. ECONOMIC GROWTH AND FOREIGN TRADE

The political and economic problem of Venezuela has been to spend its oil revenues as usefully as possible. At first, much went towards improving Caracas. Then there has been a period during which interest turned to improving the infrastructure of the country; building roads, improving conditions in rural areas and so on. More recently, the idea of establishing poles of development in limited areas, such as the steel works and the Morón oil refinery seems to have been predominant. Whatever the policy, if any at all, there has always been a fear that the oil revenues would not last, and the final and logical stage has been to initiate the gradual process of taking over the oil industry itself. Spatially the problem of Venezuela is to integrate a limited population spread unevenly but mostly very thinly over a large area, and either to curb or accommodate the growing megalopolis between Caracas and Puerto Cabello, expected to have 7–10 m. people by the end of the century or 40–50 per cent of the expected population of Venezuela. Socially the problem is to reduce the enormous gap between high and low income groups and rehabilitate the large part of the population still living in wooden or adobe houses with earth floors, poor roofs, and no glass in the windows, and living on an unsatisfactory diet of maize, beans or roots and tubers, whether they live in the shanty settlements around Caracas and other big centres, or in remote rural localities.

In 1963[4] Venezuela embarked on a revised Four-Year Plan (1963–66). The developments envisaged are of course far more ambitious than could be expected in other Latin American countries of comparable size, but the main projects are worth listing, even if they may not all be completed in the time stipulated.

1. Eight per cent growth of gross domestic product each year (but population increases by 3 per cent).

2. Iron ore production to reach 22 m. tons by 1966, of which 16 m. to be exported.
3. Total investments of U.S. $ 6,300 m., of which two thirds in private sector, one third in public.
4. Guri hydroelectric plant to have an installed capacity of 1,750,000 kW by 1968.
5. To increase oil output by 4 per cent per year, reducing however the contribution of oil from 22·6 per cent of total gross domestic product in 1963 to 18·6 per cent in 1966. Oil would still account for about 92 per cent of the value of exports.
6. By 1966, manufacturing should meet 77 per cent of the needs of the country.
7. 1,750 km of main roads and 2,000 km of access roads to be built.
8. 200,000 families to be resettled under agrarian reform by 1966, compared with only 57,000 up to the end of 1962.
9. 230,000 additional areas of land to be irrigated.

One aspect of the plan is that it will change the pattern of Venezuelan imports[5]. The following were the principal imports of the country in 1962, by percentage of value:

Food products and beverages	8	Machinery and accessories	21
Other consumer goods	23	Transport materials	12
Raw materials	31		

With the encouragement of national industry by protective tariffs and the drive to increase agricultural production, most consumer needs should soon be provided locally, and imports will include more capital and specialist goods. In 1962, exports were made up as follows:

Oil and derivatives	93 per cent
Iron ore	4·5
Coffee and cacao	1
Others	1·5

In the mid-1950s the U.S.A. was supplying about two thirds of Venezuelan imports, but by 1962 the proportion had dropped almost to half. Venezuela provided in 1962 almost half of all U.S. oil imports and was the principal supplier of oil to the importing countries of Latin America (the Islands, Central America, Brazil). Most of its iron ore exports go to the U.S.A. (78 per cent in 1962) but West European countries also import (West Germany, U.K., Italy almost all the rest).

REFERENCES

[1] Lopez, J. E. 'La expansión demográfica de Venezuela'. *Rev. geogr* (*Mérida*) Vol. III, No. 8, pp. 195–275
[2] *UNSY, 1962*
[3] *BOLSA* (*FR*) *1963*, 13 July, p. 622
[4] *BOLSA* (*FR*) *1963*, W.H.E.C. Mission to Venezuela, 15 June.
[5] *BOLSA* (*FR*) *1963*, 13 July. pp. 624–65

CHAPTER 13

COLOMBIA

13.1. INTRODUCTION AND PHYSICAL BACKGROUND

Colombia has a *per caput* national income only about one third that of Venezuela yet gives the impression of having a more balanced and complete economy. There has not been the spectacular growth of the oil industry as in Venezuela nor the great social upheavals of Mexico, yet during the present century considerable progress has been made in both commercial agriculture and in manufacturing. The country does not have the problem of one very large urban centre.

Colombia is roughly twice the size of France, but the southeastern half of the national area is virtually uninhabited and even many parts of the more developed half are hardly touched. The population in 1963 was 16,525,000, of which about 30 per cent are European, 40 per cent mestizo, a few per cent each Indian and negro, and about 20 per cent mulatto. It is distributed in about 15 main clusters and many smaller ones in the mountain region, and thinly over the northwest lowlands. The yearly increase around 1960 was little more than 2 per cent, less than in Venezuela. In 1960, agriculture accounted for 34 per cent of gross domestic product (contrast only 6 per cent in Venezuela), mining 4 per cent and manufacturing 17 per cent (rising from 15 per cent in 1950 to 18 per cent in 1961).

Colombia lies within the tropics, roughly between the equator and 12°N, but its tropical climate is modified by the Andes, which occupy only a small part of the total area, but contain most of the population. From the extreme southwest of the country the Andes, which are under 150 km wide, but high, with two parallel ranges separated by a high plateau, open out to form for much of the length of Colombia three main ranges, called very simply the Cordillera Occidental (western), Central, and Oriental (eastern). These are separated by two depressions, the Cauca and Magdalena valleys. The crests of the western and central Cordilleras run roughly parallel, only 70–80 km apart, with summits well over 3,000 m along most of the central one. They close at the northern extremity, only allowing the Cauca to drain through a narrow valley to the wide lowlands to the north. Northwards the crest of the eastern range increases in distance from the central range, leaving the Magdalena a widening valley that opens on the northern lowlands. The Cordillera widens north of Bogotá to contain a high plateau with parallel but discontinuous ranges. At the Venezuelan boundary it divides, the main branch becoming the high Andes of Venezuela, the other separating the Maracaibo lowlands, a small part of which is in Colombia, from the Magdalena lowlands. A fourth, lower, range close to the Pacific coast runs roughly parallel to the western Cordillera, but is much more modest in scale. Quite different and distinct from the Andes is the high Sierra Nevada de Santa Marta whose 5,800 m high snow clad peak exceeds the highest points

269

in the main ranges. East of the Andes almost all the land is below 500 m but contains upland areas as well as an isolated range south of Bogota.

The crest of the eastern range forms the main watershed between rivers draining to the Caribbean or Pacific and those draining to the Orinoco or Amazon. Only short rivers drain to the Pacific, except in the extreme southwest, where the western range is broken and the southern continuation of the Cauca valley drains westwards. Large areas in the Magdalena and Atrato lowlands are ill-drained.

Altogether, Colombia is one of the most well-watered countries of Latin America. Only the extreme northeast, the Guajira peninsula, is arid in character, but there is a low rainfall and dry vegetation along the Caribbean coast and on the floors of the more enclosed valleys between the high ranges of the Andes. The remaining lowlands are either covered with tropical rain forest or, in the Orinoco lowlands, llanos, with gallery forest. The Pacific coast is particularly wet, with as much as 6–7,000 mm of rain per year in places. The Amazon lowlands of the southeast receive less rain but are still heavily forested. The remaining variations in climate and vegetation are caused by altitude, with many of the lower slopes of the Andes clothed in mountain forest but the higher parts basically grassland. Lowland Colombia is of course hot throughout the year with a mean annual temperature around 25°C and a small annual range, but many areas of settlement lie either in the so-called temperate zone (1,000–2,000 m) or the cold zone (over 2,000 m), and above about 2,000 m frosts may occur (see *Figure 3.4*).

Physical conditions restricting agriculture include low temperatures, but only in the very limited areas above about 3,000 m, and inadequate rainfall along the northeast coast and in some valley floors. The main obstacles have been steep slopes in the Andes, dense forest, poor drainage and poor soils in the forested lowlands. In fact the agricultural possibilities of most of the surface of Colombia have not been seriously explored yet, and the lowland areas of the country, whether grassland or forest, have so far mostly been used only to support large herds of cattle or shifting cultivators. There is little need for irrigation except in certain localities, but some is practised to supplement rainfall. Physical conditions also profoundly affect the life of Colombia by making movement in certain directions extremely difficult.

13.2. AGRICULTURE[1]

Precise figures for agriculture are elusive and many data are inconsistent. About 5 m. hectares, or over 4 per cent of the total area, is in agricultural holdings, excluding extensive cattle farms, but only about half is actually under field or tree crops. Another 13 per cent of Colombia is classified as grazing land, and over 60 per cent forest, while the remainder consists of useless mountain areas, swamps and unused arid areas. Some 500,000 hectares were provided with irrigation of some sort. Agriculture still employs roughly half the total population of Colombia, but the proportion exceeded 70 per cent in the late 1930s and was about 55 per cent in the early 1950s.

Until recently, Colombian agricultural products could be divided into three main groups, coffee, produced essentially for export, other crops, grown for regional or local consumption, and cattle raising. Coffee occupies land between a few hundred and about 2,000 m. Other crops range from the potato, barley, wheat and temperate fodder crops grown in the cool zone, to maize, grown at every altitude except the very highest, and sugar, cotton, bananas, yuca and other tropical plants, at low altitudes.

The cultivation of coffee is found in long narrow belts along the sides of the three main ranges within the altitudes mentioned. It avoids both the valley floors and the higher parts (see *Figure 13.1e*). Around 1960 Colombia was producing about 460,000 tons of coffee a year, about one fifth as much as Brazil, but roughly as much as Mexico and Central America combined. In 1959, 370,000 tons were actually recorded as being purchased for processing. The total was distributed as follows by departments[2]:

	Thousands of tons	Percentage of total
Caldas	130	35
Valle del Cauca	72	19
Antioquía	63	17
Cundinamarca	42	11
Cauca	16	4
Tolima	15	4

Manizales is at the centre of the most heavily cultivated area. Coffee exports from farms in the northern part of Colombia are sent to the Caribbean ports, those from farms to the south are shipped via Buenaventura (*Figure 13.3c*). Coffee is relatively valuable in relation to its bulk and Colombia can compete better in world markets with this crop than it could with more bulky items. Around 1950, some 650,000 hectares were under coffee and the number of trees was about 600 m., yet this enormous number of trees, which have been contributing up to 80 per cent of the value of Colombia's exports, only covered about 1/200 of the total national area, a sobering thought leading one to question the visual impression given by maps showing a distribution such as this and to marvel at how special the small part of the national area growing coffee must be, or how under-used the rest of the land is.

Colombian coffee is a mild variety, obtaining a high price abroad, and its quality is carefully preserved. The land tenure situation is satisfactory, most of the coffee being grown in family farms with a few thousand trees each. The crop is gathered throughout the year, and this places a minimum strain on the difficult transport facilities of the country. Successful though Colombia has been in expanding its coffee production in the post-war period, this heavy dependence on one agricultural commodity is not considered desirable; some of the changes proposed will be noted at the end of this account of Colombia.

The main crops of Colombia in 1961/62 or nearest period were[3]:

	Thousands of hectares	Thousands of tons
Maize	710	760
Rice	240	410
Wheat	160	145
Cotton lint	160	80
Potatoes	100	550
Beans	100	50
Manioc	80	825
Bananas	40	500
Tobacco	15	30

271

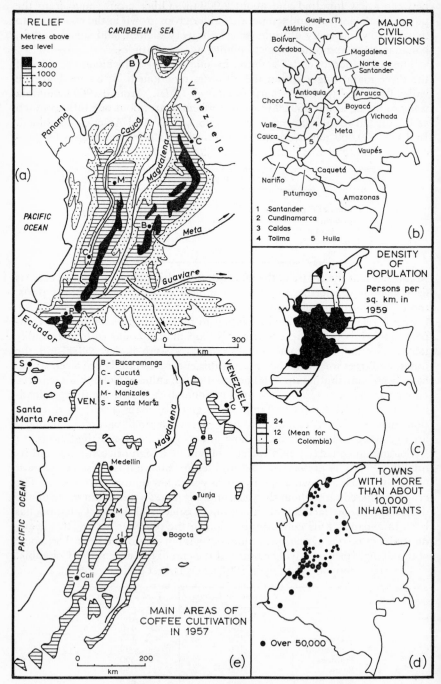

Figure 13.1. Colombia. (a) Relief. (b) Major civil divisions. (c) Density of population. (d) Towns with more than about 10,000 inhabitants. (e) Main areas of coffee cultivation in 1957

In contrast to coffee, the state of field crop farming in Colombia is very disappointing. Yields are low even by Latin American standards, productivity per worker very low. The basic foods listed above, together with other roots and tubers, satisfy most of the needs of the country, but are hardly totals worthy of 2½ m. farm workers. Much of the existing land under cultivation cannot usefully be mechanized, but Colombia plans to make much more intensive use of such areas as the Cauca and Magdalena valleys, where mechanized agriculture is possible.

The third main branch of agriculture in Colombia is cattle raising. 1960/61 livestock totals were as follows: cattle 15,400,000 or roughly one per inhabitant, pigs about 1½ m., sheep about 1 m. only. It is surprising to find that very few of the cattle in Colombia are in the southeastern lowland half of the country. 1950 figures show the bulk in a few of the northwestern departments: Córdoba 2,9 m., Antioquia 1,6 m., Magdalena 1,3 m. As in Venezuela, meat is flown to the major urban centres from the lowlands, but new roads and the Magdalena railway are making access to markets easier.

Colombia is less concerned with agrarian reform than most other Latin American countries, but there has been a programme in the early 1960s to redistribute 500,000 hectares over 18 months. In the long run, the movement of settlers to new areas, and the more intensive use of existing land with fertilizers and mechanization are the two ways in which agricultural production will have to be raised.

13.3. INDUSTRY

Colombia is often quoted as being one of the more advanced Latin American countries industrially. This is misleading, for it is not so advanced as Mexico, southeast Brazil, Argentina or Chile and it has not made the rapid recent progress of Venezuela. But it seems probable that the generally remote and inaccessible position from the coast of most of the population, and the difficulty of trading with other countries, at least until the opening of the Panama Canal in 1914 put the new outlet of Buenaventura on the Pacific coast within reasonable reach of North Atlantic ports, Colombians sought ways of decreasing dependence on imports. Modern industry began around 1900 with the establishment of textile manufacturing in Medellín, and light manufacturing developed gradually. In the early 1950s textiles employed about 40,000 persons, clothing and footwear 60,000. But even in 1960 only about 250,000 persons were employed in manufacturing altogether, 20 per cent of them still artisans (small craftsmen), and most in or around the few largest towns. In 1958, only 163 manufacturing establishments had over 200 persons each, almost all of them in or near Bogota, Medellín, Cali or Barranquilla. It is calculated, however, that the number of persons in manufacturing will almost double in the 1960s (to 490,000 in 1970). The industries employing most workers according to 1953 data were (in percentages of total industrial employment):

Food	39	Textiles	13
Drinks	11	Footwear and clothing	9

Non-metallic minerals and chemicals each accounted for a few per cent, but iron and steel production and engineering were virtually non-existent.

273

The basis for industrialization in Colombia has included an isolated market protected to some extent by distance from ports, capital derived from the coffee industry, and certain raw materials including cotton (about 30,000 tons are consumed in Colombia) and hides, and more recently oil, and other minerals. The country has considerable coal deposits but these are not easily accessible and have only been mined in limited quantities, while hydroelectric potential is large but so far there are few sizable power stations. Enough oil is produced both for home needs and some export but has not been easy to transport to markets until recent pipeline construction; natural gas deposits also exist. Even around 1960 however, Colombia only had an installed capacity of 900,000 kW, half of which was hydroelectricity, a weak basis for heavy industry. Though coal, iron ore and limestone occur close together near Paz del Rio, the integrated iron and steel works, which began production in the late 1950s, still has a very small output. Somehow the process of rapid industrialization expected and encountered in other Latin American countries has been restrained in Colombia, but the early 1960s may be the beginning of more rapid expansion.

Oil and gas production are the key to progress in the near future, since the large hydroelectric power stations projected at the moment will not be completed for some time. Oil production has grown as follows (millions of metric tons):

1948	3,3	1960	7,7	1963	9,0 (estimate)
1958	6,4	1961	7,3		
1959	7,4	1962	7,6		

About 3,5 m. tons were refined in 1961 the rest being exported in crude form. The principal centre of the industry is Barrancabermeja, headquarters of the Empresa Colombiana de Petróleo (formerly de Mares) and almost half of the refining capacity is here. The other main area of production up to the present has been in the Barco field, but several new oil and gas deposits have been found lately. An increasing share of the national production is being directed towards the home market and the growing system of pipelines is shown in *Figure 13.3c*. The contribution of hydroelectric power stations was still small by 1960, their capacity being roughly 500,000 kW but this should be increased several times in the next decade. The Bogota area alone, for example, is expected to raise generating capacity in all kinds of power stations from 250,000 kW in 1963 to 1,250,000 kW in 1970. In addition to energy minerals, Colombia produces a number of other minerals, including gold, platinum and precious stones largely for export, and salt; the very large deposits of salt at Zipaquirá north of Bogota are to form the basis of a new chemicals industry.

Apart from oil refining and the processing of agricultural products, large scale industry is mostly confined to four main concentrations, each with distinctive features. The Bogota-Paz del Rio area, with coal, iron and steel, salt and cement is becoming the principal heavy industrial area, but Bogota has some light industry as well. The Medellín area continues to lead in textile manufacturing, while Cali has recently attracted a wide range of light manufactures. The Caribbean ports are better placed than the three interior centres to receive imported raw materials and are at the pipeline terminals, but they are more remote from the centre of the national market. Petrochemicals at Cartagena and Mamonal and a steelworks projected for Barranquilla to cost U.S. $ 50 m., to use imported ore and scrap, and to make tin-plate, suggest that this may become a second area of heavy industry.

The key to greater industrialization seems to lie in the expansion of steel production and the development of engineering. Small amounts of steel are made near Medellín and a steel forging plant is planned at Bucaramanga but it seems desirable to concentrate effort in one main works. Paz del Rio is being expanded, and part of the new equipment is being made in Chile. The fact that motor vehicle assembly only began in 1962 is evidence, however, that in engineering Colombia lags behind the larger countries of Latin America.

13.4. TOWNS AND REGIONAL INTEGRATION

Colombia differs considerably from most Latin American countries, especially those of medium size, in lacking a single urban centre that dominates the life of the country in many ways. In Venezuela, Peru and Chile, provincial centres are very second-rate places compared with the capitals, but this is not so in Colombia, where regional consciousness is strong, while not apparently interfering with national cohesion. This may be because although centres have been isolated from one another and have developed in their own ways, they are still closer to each other than to the outside world.

A brief survey of the eleven largest towns in Colombia in 1962 (see Table 13.1) shows a number of features that are unusual in Latin America. Bogota, the national capital, has only as many inhabitants as the next two in size. One of these, Cali, like some smaller centres, is growing more rapidly, in relative, though not absolute terms, than the capital. Although the capital has a somewhat higher index per inhabitant for retail sales, financial transactions and other such activities, the difference is much less than is usual in Latin America. Some smaller places have a greater movement of air passengers (per thousand inhabitants) than the capital. In other words, Bogota dominates the country only in certain respects: firstly, as the national capital, secondly, to a lesser extent, as the financial and cultural centre. It is not the industrial capital, nor is it situated in that part of the country from which most of the exports are derived.

Whether the influence of Bogota increases or diminishes in the future depends on the particular direction of future developments in Colombia. The development of heavy industry in places immediately to the north and the opening up of the eastern regions of the country could both strengthen its position. The proposed development of the Cauca valley and improvements to Buenaventura mean on the other hand that the further rapid growth of Cali seems likely. Medellín is in something of a backwater position at the moment, but could receive further impetus from the opening of the road north to Cartagena and in the long run from the completion of the Pan-American Highway between Panama and Colombia. The three main Caribbean ports, with Barranquilla as the principal regional centre, also have the possibility of developing with the further exploration of oil and gas and the encouragement of trade with LAFTA countries.

TABLE 13.1

Features of Major Urban Centres in Colombia

	Population[4] 1962	Population[5] 1912	Times increased 1912–1962	Retail sales[6]		Cheques cashed[6]		Air passengers leaving[6]	
				In millions of pesos 1959	Per caput, thousands of pesos	In millions of pesos 1959	Value per caput in pesos	In thousands 1959	Per thousand population
Bogota	1,329	121	11	1,765	1,310	23,184	17,400	365	274
Cali	693	26	26	735	1,060	5,340	7,700	132	191
Medellín	691	71	10	607	880	8,632	12,500	197	286
Barranquilla	474	49	10	503	1,060	3,138	6,400	163	344
Bucaramanga	222	20	11	142	640	1,238	5,600	73	329
Cartagena	185	35	5	219	1,080	1,065	5,700	45	244
Pereira	184	n.a.	n.a.	186	1,010	1,033	5,600	36	196
Manizales	176	35	5	160	910	1,142	6,500	11	62
Ibagué	149	n.a.	n.a.	144	970	563	4,400	negligible	
Cúcuta	148	20	7	154	1,040	801	5,400	50	338
Pasto	124	n.a.	n.a.	71	570	208	1,700	8	64

* n.a. not available.

276

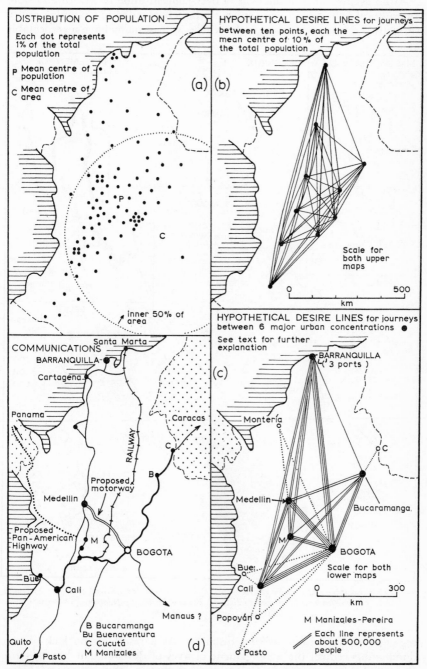

Figure 13.2. Colombia. (a) Distribution of population. (b) Hypothetical desire lines for journeys. (c) Hypothetical desire lines for journeys. (d) Communications

Note: in (b) and (c) no account is taken of diminishing frequency of journeys (according to the gravity model) with increase in distance

277

At all events, some of the evils of over-concentration of wealth and non-agricultural activities in one centre are largely avoided in Columbia and if rural areas remain very poor on the whole, at least many have a respectable

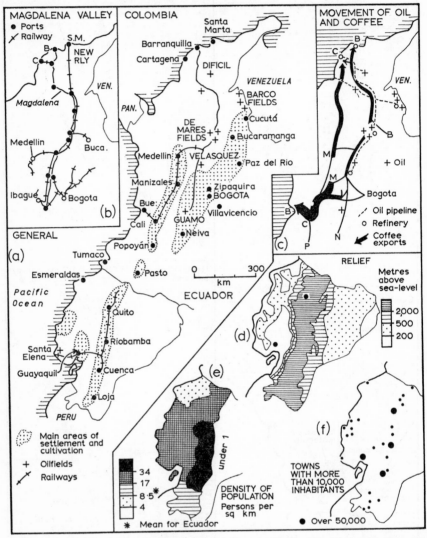

Figure 13.3. Colombia and Ecuador general map. (a) General. (b) Magdalena Valley. (c) Movement of oil and coffee in Colombia. (d) Ecuador relief. (e) Ecuador density of population. (f) Ecuador towns with more than 10,000 inhabitants.

regional capital within striking distance. As a result of the lack of one dominating centre, the arrangement of axes of development has taken a somewhat different form in Colombia from that in other countries. *Figure 13.2* suggests three main points of growth at the corners of a roughly equilateral triangle and outlets to the coast or lines of penetration towards the interior branching from these. The most attractive sector would appear to be the triangle itself, for any place within this triangle is reasonably close to the three largest centres. Somewhat less attractive would be a position on one of the routes leading away from the triangle. The areas off routes altogether are obviously likely to stagnate or decline, and it is departments such as Córdoba, Choco and Nariño (see *Figure 13.1*) that have the lowest indices of development. Contrasts in living standards between regions are not however as marked as in Mexico (see Chapter 11.6). Even so there are sufficient data in the *Anuario General de Estadística** of Colombia to show for example that per 1,000 people, the distribution of such features as leprosy, venereal diseases and illegitimate births is very irregular and that health services are very much concentrated in certain areas. Two thirds of the doctors, for example, are in the departmental capitals. Financial contrasts are also marked.

A major problem in Colombia, therefore, is lack of integration and failure especially to bring certain of the remoter rural areas into contact with the economic life of the country. A serious study of the impact of difficult physical conditions on the organization of transportation and the location of economic activities would be very rewarding in Colombia. The effects of rugged conditions on transportation have been discussed in Chapters 3.8 and 6.7 and generalizations made there apply of course in Colombia.

The transport problems of Colombia can best be considered firstly under access to the coast and secondly under movement between centres of population in the interior. The Magdalena has been the main outlet to the Caribbean until the opening of a railway in 1961, and roads or railways link it fairly directly to most of the major interior centres of Colombia; but it is inconvenient to navigate as water is low during November–April and the river journey is slow; 500 ton steamers can reach La Dorada and Puerto Salgar. The other principal outlet is a road and railway to Buenaventura, which can now be reached by road or rail from most parts of the country.

The internal movement of passengers and goods has always been difficult until air services were established. Colombia claims to have the oldest airway system in Latin America and more perhaps than in any other country, has benefited from the advantages of air transport. There are over 650 airfields. Now, however, road improvements are reducing times between many centres and the special role of air transport in providing cohesion has diminished. For the movement of goods between regions, roads seem much better suited to Colombian conditions than railways. In recent years long stretches have been paved; for example from Cúcuta in the north via Bogotá to beyond Cali. A motorway (U.S. $ 35 m.) is proposed between Medellín and Bogota while a new road from Medellín to Cartagena (via Planeta Rica and Montería) is beginning to open up the western part of the Caribbean lowlands.

Colombia's interest in coastwise shipping is very limited and the four main ports (see *Figure 13.2d*) handle mainly international cargoes. Apart from the

---

* e.g. 1959 edition[6], illegitimate births, p. 31, venereal diseases, p. 136, leprosy, p. 169, savings, p. 484, public spending, p. 536, motor vehicles in circulation, p. 648. See also *Estudio sobre las condiciones del desarollo de Colombia.*

export of several million tons of oil each year, the volume of goods handled is small, about $1\frac{1}{2}$ m. tons in 1960, expected to reach $2\frac{1}{2}$ m. by 1970. All four are being improved, however, with most effort being put into improving Buenaventura.

13.5. PROBLEMS, PROJECTS AND FOREIGN TRADE

A number of current problems and projects of Colombia may now be put in perspective. Population is very unevenly spread over the national area but apart from a few roads down from the eastern range of the Andes to draw on food supplies from the empty southeastern half of the country, as from Villavicencio below Bogotá, virtually no important development project is planned here and no serious move has been made to settle new areas*. In other words, Colombia is concentrating its energy on improving the part that has already been developed, and as tentatively suggested in *Figure 13.2b* and *c*, the effectively used part of the country is only a small part of the total national area. Admittedly the difficulty of access to the lowlands beyond the Andes makes this policy of integration for the already settled and developed part reasonable.

One of the various programmes for development in Colombia is to reduce the uneven distribution of the wealth of the country. Other aims are firstly to achieve greater integration territorially, secondly to achieve greater self-sufficiency in industry (the development of iron and steel, oil and hydro-electricity has been mentioned), and thirdly to reduce dependence on coffee.

Colombia has a ten year transport programme for the period 1961–70, in which U.S. $ 275 m. is to be spent, two thirds on roads, only 15 per cent on railways. Industrial development during the 1961–70 period is seen as a massive programme of import substitution. Industrial growth of 8·6 per cent per year is planned compared with 6·8 per cent in the 1950s, and Paz del Rio is to produce 220,000 tons of steel by 1968, 400,000 by 1970 (satisfying home demand) and 600,000 by 1975. Even this however, will only be as much steel as Chile is expecting to produce in 1965. Diversification of exports involves firstly expansion of oil production to achieve a greater surplus for export, and secondly, the expansion of cultivation of tropical products such as sugar, cotton, the African oil palm (in the Buenaventura area to 100,000 hectares) and bananas. An increase in the area and output of sugar cane is envisaged, and 450,000 hectares could be mechanized in the Cauca valley and 3·2 m. tons of refined sugar, worth about U.S. $ 700 m. per year, twice the current value of coffee exports, could be exported.

Colombian exports still consist largely of coffee (70 per cent in the early 1960s by value) but the share of coffee has declined from around 80 per cent not long ago (77 per cent in 1958) thanks to an increase in the contribution of crude oil and of cotton. Unlike Venezuela, Colombia hardly imports any agricultural products, and about half of the value of imports is made up of machinery and other metal goods. Its *per caput* trade is lower than that of the other medium sized countries, a reflection more perhaps of an economy cut off from easy access to world trade than of a more complete range of goods produced at home. About two thirds of Colombian exports go to the U.S.A.

* For a study of one new settlement area in the east, see Stoddart and Trubshaw[7].

and most of the remainder to Western Europe. There is little trade with other LAFTA countries, but increased trade with Mexico is currently proposed, while a small but promising trade in coffee is developing with East Europe.

REFERENCES

[1] Parsons, J. J. 'The Settlement of the Sinu Valley of Colombia, *Geogr. Rev.* Vol. XLII (1952) pp. 67–86
[2] *Anuario General de Estadística* 1959, Colombia, 1960, p. 647
[3] *FAOPY,* 1962
[4] *BOLSA (FR)* 16 July 1963, p. 622
[5] *Statesman's Yearbook* of 1913
[6] *Anuario General de Estadística* 1959, Colombia 1960, pp. 470, 645, 658
[7] Stoddart, D. R. and Trubshaw, J. D. 'Colonization in Action in Eastern Colombia' *Geography,* Jan. 1962, pp. 47–53

CHAPTER 14

ECUADOR, PERU AND BOLIVIA

14.1. INTRODUCTION

Three basic types of physical environment, desert, mountain and forested lowland can clearly be distinguished in western South America. The Andes consist for most of their length of two roughly parallel ranges separated by a high plateau. But between southern Ecuador and central Peru is a relatively low pass (Cuello de Porculla, about 2,000 m) and to the south of this for some distance there are three ranges separating two depressions. The proximity of the main Pacific-Atlantic watershed to the Pacific coast has already been noted; it follows the western range most of the distance. The coastal region between the Andes and the Pacific includes few extensive lowlands; much of it is hill country, while in southern Peru mountainous conditions reach very close to the coast. The coastal region is drained by a large number of small rivers and only in a few places, notably in northern Ecuador and in the Santa valley of Peru, do they run parallel to the Andes for an appreciable distance. East of the Andes the forested lowlands of the three countries consist of wide flood plains, undulating country between these, and a number of low ranges, the precise features of which have not in some cases been mapped yet.

The coastal region of Ecuador is characterized by a great variety of climatic and vegetation conditions but in the southern part dry conditions prevail and the coastal belt is arid for the whole length of Peru and in northern Chile. The cold current, which extends north almost to the Equator along this coast, has a profound influence on climate. The Andes of Ecuador and Peru receive considerable rainfall but the dry conditions of the coastal desert extend progressively higher into the Andes as one passes into southern Peru, and in southern Bolivia the plateau itself is arid. Rainfall in the Andes of Peru and Bolivia falls mainly during the period December to May and except in the extreme south of Peru is sufficient to provide some water for irrigation in the coastal desert, though most drains towards the Atlantic. The eastern lowlands are characterized by high rainfall, in most places 2,000–3,000 mm, and a short dry season, except in the south where it is longer. There is a dense cover of tropical rain forest, which however thins out in southern Bolivia, where thorn forest prevails. The forest extends up the eastern slopes of the Andes to about 2,000 m but the Andes themselves are largely treeless except for eucalyptus plantations.

Ecuador and Peru each have part of the three main environments mentioned already but Bolivia lacks a Pacific coast, having lost this to Chile in 1883 after the War of the Pacific (1879–83). All three countries are characterized by a large Indian element in the Andean region and by the limited number of Spanish settlers arriving in the Colonial period and the virtual absence of immigration in the modern period by other Europeans.

The coastal region has the most mixed population, with a strong negro element in Ecuador and northern Peru. In recent decades there has been a shift of population from the Andes into the coastal regions of Peru and Ecuador, while in Bolivia movement into the eastern lowlands is now beginning. The interior lowlands are very sparsely populated and so far make little contribution to the economic life of their respective countries.

14.2. ECONOMIC ACTIVITIES

Only a little more than 1 per cent of the total area of these three countries is under crops (see Table 12.1 for data) but considerable areas in the Andes are used for grazing. Agriculture in the Andes is concerned mainly with growing food crops for local consumption, for sale in the mining and service centres, or in Peru, to some extent for sale also in the coastal lowlands. Altitude and climatic conditions determine the emphasis on particular crops in different areas with potatoes and other tubers forming the basis of cultivation in the highest parts, and being particularly vital in southern Peru and northern Bolivia. Wheat and barley are grown at somewhat lower altitudes, but maize appears to be preferred where temperatures are high enough and rainfall adequate. Livestock farming depends traditionally on llamas and sheep, and cattle raising has not made great progress so far. Cultivation is carried out in the Andean region in a very large number of small favourable areas separated by large tracts of poor pasture or useless land. Irrigation is practised in places to supplement rainfall.

Agriculture in the coastal lowlands is completely different. In Ecuador the forested areas have been cleared for the cultivation of cacao, and more recently bananas for export, while sugar, cotton and rice are cultivated for consumption within the country. Irrigation is desirable in the southern part of the coastal lowlands. In coastal Peru* crop farming depends entirely on the availability of water for irrigation; here again crops are grown both for export and for home consumption, this time sugar and cotton being the main export crop, while rice, maize and fodder crops are for home consumption. In Bolivia there is a deficiency of food in the Andean region and food products have long been imported, but attempts are being made to achieve a large surplus in the eastern lowland region, particularly of sugar and rice.

Forestry and fishing have played little part in the economic life of the three countries until very recently, while the vast forest resources of Amazonia cannot easily be transported even into the Andean region, let alone to the coast. The planting of eucalypts in the last hundred years in the Andes provides a useful but limited source of timber in that region. Coastal Ecuador has its own local sources of timber, but coastal Peru is completely deficient. Through lack of organization, the fishing resources of the Pacific were hardly touched until the mid-1950s, but since then Peru has risen to second place among the fishing countries of the world. Almost all of its catch consists of anchovies (see Chapter 7.9).

The mineral resources of the three countries are varied, and several promising new deposits have been found recently. All three countries produce

* For examples of agricultural activities in areas of irrigation in Peru see Smith[1].

oil, but the small fields of coastal Ecuador and northern Peru have only limited reserves and most of the oil appears to be in the interior beyond the Andes. Oil and gas have both been discovered in the central part of the interior lowlands of Peru, and along the foot of the Andes in southern Bolivia (see *Figure 3.12*). Metallic minerals occur widely in the Andes, the main products being non-ferrous metals from Cerro de Pasco and tin from central Bolivia. Recently iron ore has been exploited in coastal Peru (Marcona) and in 1964, $4\frac{1}{2}$ m. tons were produced here, while 10 m. tons are projected for 1970. Bolivia is reputed to have the world's largest iron ore deposit at Mutun, a total of some 50,000 m. tons (about twice the amount claimed for Minas Gerais in Brazil) in an area covering 60 km² with the ore 200 m thick, but this is too inaccessible to be exported at the moment. In addition, manganese ore has recently been discovered beyond the Andes in central Peru, while for some years now a large copper deposit has been worked at Tocquepala in the coastal region of southern Peru. Of non-metallic minerals the most spectacular find has been a large deposit of phosphate rock in northern Peru. No important mineral deposits have yet been found in Ecuador. What is more, none of the three countries is sufficiently developed industrially to make use itself of the minerals produced apart from oil, which is the main source of energy in all three, coal production being negligible. Nor are the deposits in the Andes and the lowlands beyond conveniently located to serve world markets.

Consumption of energy per inhabitant is lower than in most other parts of Latin America and in Peru and Bolivia a considerable part of the consumption is used in mining and processing activities. The total generating capacity of electricity in the three countries was only about 1 m. kW in 1960, about half of it hydroelectric. Coal has been imported in small quantities for special purposes such as smelting, and for the railways; timber is used as a source of fuel but is not abundant where most needed, while Ecuador and Peru, unlike Colombia, have reached a stage when they consume virtually all the oil they produce, even if reserves exist in the Amazon lowlands. It is not surprising that interest has turned to hydroelectricity. All three countries have a large potential, but the sites with the greatest capacity are in difficult localities, often far from the nearest roads. Several moderate sized power stations already serve regional needs in Peru but a much more ambitious project is to generate electricity on the Mantaro river in the central Andes of Peru. The potential of this site ($2\frac{1}{2}$ m. kW) is about five times the total capacity of all existing hydroelectric power stations in the three countries.

Industrial development has also been limited in the three countries. Most of the capacity is in the processing of minerals or agricultural products and the manufacture of textiles, clothing and other consumer goods. Only Peru has the beginnings of an iron and steel industry, while developments in chemicals and in engineering have been very limited so far. Before they can be exported the metallic minerals produced in the Andes have to be processed, while it is convenient to reduce iron ore in weight, and in Marcona a new plant for enriching the ore before export has been established. Again, most of the oil is refined locally. The manufacture of textiles and clothing is only partly on a factory basis. Both spinning and weaving are carried out in rural areas in the Andes, while in Ecuador, for example, 30,000 domestic craftsmen depend for a living largely on the manufacture of leather footwear, and to keep them in employment, the manufacture of plastic shoes has been prohibited. The assembly of motor vehicles is beginning in Peru and Ecuador but the home markets of these countries seem too small for a complete motor vehicles industry to be worth while. In Ecuador, Guayaquil is the outstanding industrial centre, but many new industries are moving into towns such as Cuenca and Riobamba on various routes between the port and the capital*. In Peru almost all the light manufacturing is concentrated in Lima. In Bolivia there is very little manufacturing at all, and what few factories there are in La Paz have declined in recent years. Some new industries are being established in Cochabamba (tyre factory) and in the Santa Cruz area.

14.3. ECUADOR

Ecuador only seriously uses two of its three main regions. So far only short roads run beyond the Andes into the Amazon region and there has been little settlement there, although ironically the existence of a large area of potential agricultural land in the east (Oriente) has been held as an excuse for delaying land reform in the Andean region. Formerly the Andes was the most important region economically but in recent decades most of the development has been in the coastal Pacific lowlands. For example, population changes between 1910 and 1960 show an increase of population of between 8 and 9 times in the four entirely lowland provinces compared with only a twofold growth in four provinces in the southern part of the Andes. During this period the total population of Ecuador increased three times. The more rapid growth of the coastal area is also reflected in the great expansion of Guayaquil compared with the slow growth of Quito. During this period of course there was little change at all in the eastern region.

One of the major development projects in Ecuador recently has been the construction of a new port (U.S. $ 20 m.) near Guayaquil (see *Figure 14.1*). Guayaquil handles at least 90 per cent of the imports and 65 per cent of the exports of the country, is becoming the base of Ecuador's fishing industry, and with the improvements of roads both over the lowland area and into the Andes, is now able to reach its hinterland more easily than before.

In spite of the developments in Ecuador, the country is still very isolated, having little contact with its neighbours and until recently a low foreign trade per inhabitant. Even now, the bulk of the population in the Andean region makes no contribution to the exports of the country and remains what might be called a regional subsistence economy. Bananas, which come entirely from the coastal lowlands, now account for 60 per cent of the value of exports, having risen from around 40 per cent in the early 1950s, and Ecuador now supplies about one quarter of the world's exports. This is a remarkable achievement, considering the great distance of Ecuador from its markets and is partly due to the satisfactory land tenure system, partly to

* The following, for example, were under construction or projected in the early 1960s: Cuenca, batteries and transistors, sewing machines, a tyre factory; Latacunga, electrical equipment and lime; Azogues, cement.

† The banana industry of Ecuador is thoroughly covered in a paper by Preston[3]. Material has also been obtained from *El Universo*[4]. See also Parsons[5] and Burt[6].

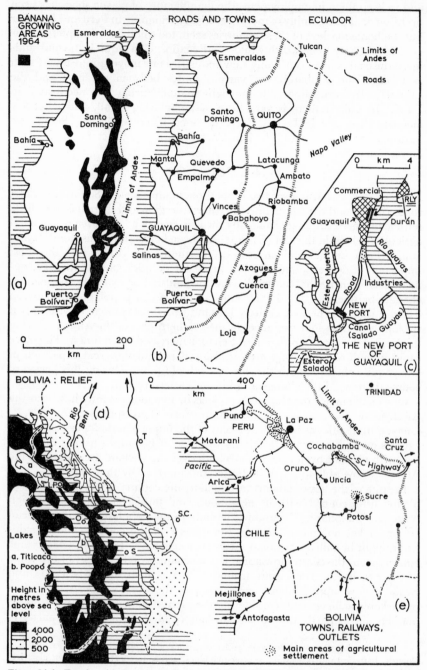

Figure 14.1. Ecuador. (a) Banana growing areas 1964[3,4]. (b) Roads and towns. (c) The new port of Guayaquil. (d) Boliva relief. (e) Boliva towns, railways outlets

preoccupation with the elimination of diseases and the improvement of marketing facilities. Cacao and coffee account for most of the remainder of the exports and these also come from the lowlands or more accessible Andean slopes.

Ecuador has a ten-year development project (1961–70) during which a growth of the economy of almost 5 per cent per year is planned. It is hoped to attract foreign capital and priority is being given to the establishment of industries using Ecuadorean products (e.g. fruit canning, the extraction of castor oil) and to the chemicals industry (sulphuric acid, caustic soda, fertilizers, detergents and plastics).

14.4. BOLIVIA[7,8]

The progress recently achieved in Ecuador contrasts with the stagnation or even decline of many branches of the economy in Bolivia. Bolivia has had a long record of instability, including some 60 revolutions in the first 100 years of its existence. It is unfortunate therefore that having achieved reasonable political stability since the revolution of 1952 it has been saved from complete economic collapse only by large amounts of U.S. aid, some U.S. $ 300 m. Indeed, on paper there have been improvements, for *per caput* national income increased from $60 to $100 during 1952–62. Tin production has declined however, for reasons of both organization and the exhaustion of more accessible deposits, and is being rehabilitated with U.S. and West German help in the so-called Triangular Operation. Even less encouraging has been the decline in oil production since a peak in the late 1950s. More perhaps than any other single Latin American country, Bolivia suffers from having a small population dispersed over a large area, even though this effectively occupied area is itself only a limited part of the total country. Apart from its metals and its limited agricultural land, the high plateau of Bolivia has little to offer, and it is in the lowlands east of the Andes that most of the resources for future development appear to be located. The two regions are separated by extremely difficult country along the eastern range of the Andes and although tracks, roads and railways penetrated this region it was virtually impossible to carry goods across it until the completion of the Cochabamba–Santa Cruz highway in 1954. The problem of cohesion was to some extent solved as Bolivia developed its airlines (Lloyd Aereo Boliviano) established in 1925, the second oldest in South America, but only with the road has it been possible to contemplate the resettlement of large numbers of Indians from the Andes; some 130,000 people have already been moved. At the same time, to distribute oil products over the national market it has been necessary to establish an extensive and hardly economical system of small diameter oil pipelines (see *Figure 3.12*).

It is in the eastern region of Bolivia that the largest areas of potential agricultural land are to be found. Santa Cruz is the centre of the main area of colonization. Its population has grown between 1955 and 1960 from 15,000 to 60,000, while the smaller centre of Mantaro for example has grown over the same period from 1,500 to 14,000. Sugar and rice are the principal products of this area and are sent now by road into the Andean region. In spite of large investments in oil prospecting by several foreign companies, as well as by the Bolivian oil company, YPBF, the oil output is very small and has not changed much in recent years. Until the discovery of the Caranda field near Santa Cruz (see *Figure 14.1*) proved deposits were not large, but this discovery has changed the situation, since oil and gas reserves are large enough to make it worth while considering piping gas to São Paulo in Brazil; such a pipeline would cost about U.S. $ 250 m. The Caranda field is already linked to the Bolivian pipeline system and a new refinery is under construction at Santa Cruz. One other activity of the eastern lowland area is to be developed, the gathering of rubber in the provinces of Beni and Pando; this is expected to give employment to some 40,000 workers, in gathering, washing and laminating the material, which will then be sent to the Cochabamba tyre factory.

Not only is Bolivia hampered by great difficulties and physical obstacles within the country itself; it is a landlocked state. It has at least six possible outlets (see *Figure 14.1*) across the territories of four of its five neighbours and there are various concessions allowing Bolivia free access to places on the Pacific coast, but not one of the routes is an easy one. The railways to Arica and Antofagasta are said to have the highest freight charges in the world, while to reach Matarani in Peru, goods have to be ferried across Lake Titicaca. Bolivia is agitating for a piece of sovereign territory on the coast of Chile at Mejillones, its case being that Chile interferes with its traffic to overseas countries; this might be granted to Bolivia in exchange for concessions to Chile regarding the use of water in five rivers originating in Bolivia. Bolivian foreign trade has long depended heavily on tin, which in 1962 accounted for over three quarters of the value of all exports; silver, gold and other metals made up most of the remainder.

14.5. THE THREE REGIONS OF PERU

The geography of Peru is profoundly affected by the existence of three completely distinct physical regions. These are separated, of course, by narrow areas of transition which, however, are abrupt because of the great change in altitude over short horizontal distances. The three regions are the Costa, Sierra and Selva (often referred to as the Montaña). Of the total population of the country, about 40 per cent is in the coastal region, almost 60 per cent in the Andes and only a few per cent in the Selva. The Selva region, however, covers nearly two thirds of the total area, leaving one quarter in the Andes and only one tenth in the coastal region. The capital, Greater Lima, now has nearly 20 per cent of the total population. The Andean region is still inhabited largely by the Indian descendants of the Inca empire while the Selva region is inhabited by about 100 tribes of savages (*chunchos*). The population of the coastal region is more varied, having both European and negro elements as well as Indian.

The economy of the country still depends heavily on agriculture, which in 1959 employed 50 per cent of the total employed population, yet only about 1·5 per cent of the total area is under crops. Mining employs only a small number of people but minerals account for about 40 per cent of the total value of exports. Manufacturing is increasing, but is not so advanced as in the larger countries of Latin America. Most impressive of all has been the recent rise of the fishing industry. Indeed the coastal waters of Peru might almost count as a fourth major region, and the value of what they produce is now greater than that of the whole of the Selva region.

The coastal region of Peru is a desert with negligible rainfall over most of its length (e.g. about 35 mm/year in Lima) and cultivation depends entirely on water brought by some fifty rivers of varying size flowing from the western range of the Andes to the Pacific, much of it coming during the early months of the year. Much of this water is already used for irrigation in some valleys and in a few the rivers never reach the sea, but a great deal is wasted, and theoretically with the use of reservoirs all the water could ultimately be retained for use in agriculture and none need reach the sea. In addition, by tapping the headwaters of rivers flowing to the Amazon it is possible to divert water through tunnels beneath the main watershed to the coastal oases. This has been done on a small scale already in three places. The main drawback is that works of construction become progressively more costly as reservoirs and tunnels have to be built. Although below the average for lowland areas at this latitude on account of the cold currents, temperatures are high enough for the cultivation of tropical crops. At present some 500,000 hectares are cultivated, but this area could be doubled.

Sugar, grown in large plantations organized mainly by foreign companies, and cotton, grown on smaller farms, both mainly for export, cover about half of the total area under crops, but a wide range of other crops is grown for the national market. The yields are high and the land well farmed, and guano fertilizer from the coastal islands is easily transported to the oases. One obvious advantage of the coastal region over the Andes is the ease with which agricultural products can be exported, another is lack of steeply sloping cultivated land and little danger of soil erosion.

In the Sierra, about 1 m. hectares are cultivated, but yields are much lower than in the coastal region. The cultivated area lies mainly between 2,500 and 4,000 m. Rain here is generally adequate for cultivation and falls mainly during January–April. There are many small agricultural communities dispersed through the Andean region, and a few larger valley floors with concentrations of population up to several hundred thousand; for example, around Huarás, Huancayo, Sicuani and Puno. It seems doubtful if the cultivated area could be greatly extended, but changes in land tenure should make it possible to bring new land into use in some areas. A small surplus of agricultural products such as wool, meat, cheese and vegetables is sent from the Andean region to the coastal towns, but only from districts served by rail or motor transport. It is difficult to see how the very low standard of living among agricultural workers in the Andes can be raised, except by a slow process of small-scale improvements. Such improvements seem likely to spread from a few centres such as Cusco, Ayacucho (a new University has recently been established here with courses in Indian languages) and Huancayo, as fertilizer factories are built and power stations completed in the vicinity of such centres. Much could be done to increase yields, and fish meal fertilizer is abundant in the coastal regions, but it is very costly to move this into the Andes. Changes could be made in crop rotations, terraces reconstructed in the more rugged areas, irrigation works improved and trees planted.

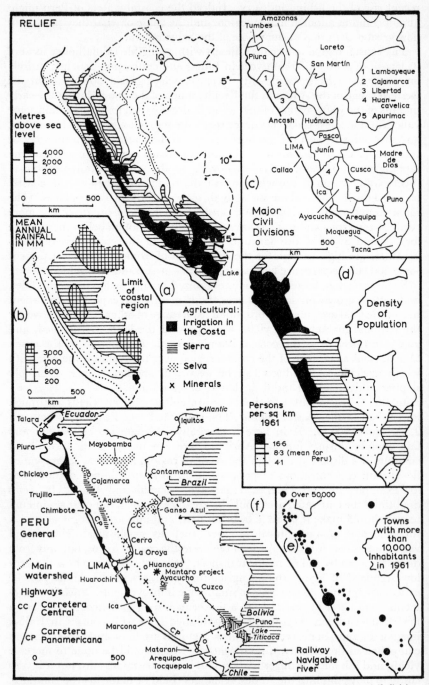

Figure 14.2. Peru. (a) Relief. (b) Mean annual rainfall in millimetres. (c) Major civil divisions. (d) Density of population. (e) Towns with more than 10,000 inhabitants in 1961. (f) Agricultural irrigation in the Costa

The Selva region at present makes very little contribution to the agricultural production of Peru[9]. The difficulties of the tropical rain forest environment have already been stressed. In Peru a lack of adequate knowledge about physical conditions, the danger of soil erosion when the forest is cleared, and other obstacles to the development of the forests are accompanied by additional considerations resulting from inaccessibility. There is only one road at present to markets and ports in coastal Peru and a large amount of capital is needed to link any part of the Selva with the rest of the country. Colonization cannot take place without careful preparation and large numbers of settlers must be placed in any one area to make road construction worth while. Field crops such as maize, cotton, sugar and rice can be grown, but the prospects seem better for tree crops including tea, coffee and cacao on the lower slopes of the Andes, rubber trees, bananas and other tree crops in the lowlands. Possibly the most satisfactory combination will be cattle raising combined with the cultivation of tree crops. Unless areas of cultivation in the Selva are able to keep on a commercial basis by selling most of their products off the farm, they very easily revert to an unsatisfactory kind of subsistence farming, based on bananas and fishing. *Figure 14.2* shows the two main areas of settlement beyond the Andes, the more active one being that along the central highway.

The prospect for Peru at the moment is either to satisfy its own needs in agricultural products from the three regions, as it could do under present conditions, or to use its best land for export crops, notably cotton and sugar, and to import food from abroad at considerable cost and move it to the deficient areas as it does at the moment. But in all three regions agricultural production could be increased greatly. Unfortunately there has never been sufficient capital to make large enough improvements at any one time to transform the picture completely. The lack of a chemicals industry has held back the manufacture of fertilizers, the lack of an iron and steel industry has delayed the development of engineering, and all machinery still has to be imported. Equipment to build roads quickly is lacking, and much manual labour is still used. Improvements in education, water supply and housing are all needed in agricultural areas.

The foreign trade of Peru is characterized by the diversity of the products it exports (as Mexico) but it does not export large quantities of any one product. Its exports contain a roughly equal proportion of mineral products and of agricultural and fishing products. From the late 1950s two new items have appeared, copper and fish meal, to challenge the traditional exports, cotton, sugar and other non-ferrous metals. The proportions in 1961 were copper 21 per cent, cotton 16 per cent, fish 14·5 per cent, sugar 13 per cent, iron ore 7·5 per cent. Unfortunately these five leading exports all come almost entirely from the coastal region, which supplies about 80 per cent of all exports; the other main items, coffee, lead, zinc and silver come from the Andean region, while the Selva region provides almost nothing. At present the U.S.A. takes about one third of the exports, considerably less than a decade ago, but it provides about half of the imports; there appears to be a time lag between the postwar reorientation of exports and of imports from North America towards western Europe.

One reason why the coastal region makes such a large contribution to the foreign trade of the country is the accessibility of its various resources to ports. For some time now Peruvian leaders have contemplated ways of integrating the various regions of the country. The two main railways were built to link certain parts of the Andes with the coast but the road system and the internal airways system have had the effect of linking all parts of the country with the capital (see *Figure 9.3b*), which now has an extremely advantageous location in relation to routes compared with that of any other single place. Evidence of this appears from the calculations shown in Chapter 6.7. It seems that the country could either continue to be organized on this basis, in which case the rapid growth of the capital would probably continue, or it could be divided into a number of more self-sufficient regions, each with a section of the Costa, Sierra and Selva, and good routes at right-angles to the coast as well as along it.

14.6. THE VALLEY OF HUAROCHIRÍ, PERU[10,11]

The problems of the valley of Huarochirí are like those of innumerable other small isolated agricultural communities in Latin America. The valley is located in the western Andes of Peru on the Pacific side of the main water-shed in the headwaters of the River Mala, which have cut a great hollow in the high plateau with its surface at about 4,000 m above sea level. The Mala leaves this valley through an impassable gorge starting about 2,000 m above sea level. The Huarochirí area has about 10,000 people in a cluster of population of about 25 × 10 km set in a virtually uninhabited area of poor pasture. Population is mainly found at a number of nucleated settlements between about 2,000 and 4,000 m. The only resource of this small region is its cultivated and pasture land, for there is very little timber, no economic minerals are produced other than building materials, and no hydroelectricity is generated. Until 1946 the region could only be reached from the outside world along tracks suitable for pack animals. Integration into the national economy has been very gradual and has still not proceeded far.

The valley was annexed by the Inca empire during its expansion in the fifteenth century and a main road passed through it at this time, but it must have been almost entirely self-sufficient, depending on the cultivation of tubers, maize and beans, the land being cultivated by hoes; the llama was the only form of livestock. Metals were virtually unknown and the wheel was not used for transportation. In the sixteenth century the area began to feel the influence of Spanish conquest. For military and administrative purposes population was grouped into nucleated settlements. The population was theoretically converted to Christianity, but many old beliefs and customs last to this day. Spanish began to be used and gradually came to replace quechua, but many quechua words are still used and the two languages occur side by side, as for example in the place name Santiago de Anchucaya. New plants and livestock were introduced, and Old World cereals, cattle and sheep have come to supplement the range of New World items, but new methods of cultivation made little impact. Some new techniques were adopted, such as weaving with a more complicated form of loom.

For almost four centuries the valley remained very much on the fringe of

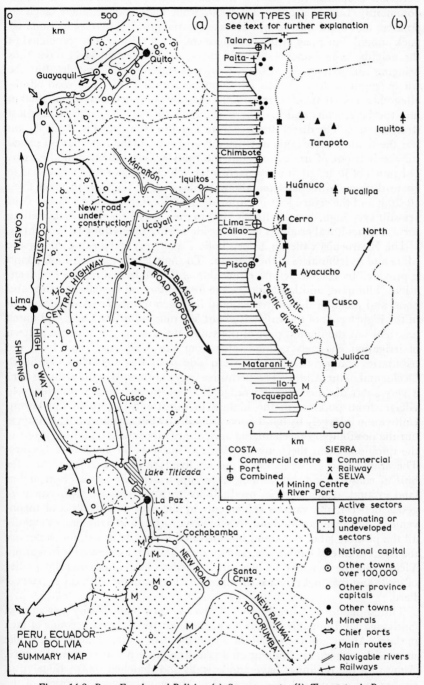

Figure 14.3. Peru, Ecuador and Bolivia. (a) Summary map. (b) Town types in Peru

Peruvian economic life, with a mestizo culture superimposed on a predominantly Indian people. By 1900, wool and food products, such as potatoes and dried meat could be taken to the growing market in Lima by pack animal, but early in the twentieth century a railway was completed in the neighbouring Rimac valley and this could be reached in $1\frac{1}{2}$ days, thus bringing Lima closer. In 1920 a road was started to Huarochirí, but the whole length of the road was not completed until 1946. The road climbs altogether more than 4,000 m from the coast before it descends about 1000 m into the Huarochirí valley. There are some 40 hair-pin bends in this last stretch alone. The direct distance from Lima to Huarochirí is about 80 km but the road distance is about twice this amount. As the road has no paved surface it is out of use throughout the rainy season, about half the year. For much of its length it is too narrow for vehicles to pass and traffic has to go in different directions on alternate days. The journey up takes from 10–20 h and the return journey from about 8–16. Obviously transport costs are still very high, but this link is vital to the valley because only by selling surplus agricultural products to the outside world can anything be brought in.

The Huarochirí valley is a deep hollow with very steep sides, cut by the Mala and its tributaries in the plateau. The only level or gently sloping land is provided by terraces left on either side of the Mala as a result of rejuvenation. Slumping and landslides occur frequently, soil is generally thin and poor, and much of the cultivated land has been terraced. Annual rainfall in the higher part of the valley is about 500 mm but at the lower end much less. All but the highest part of the valley depends on an intricate pattern of irrigation channels taking water from the Mala itself and from the tributaries coming in on the eastern side from the snow-clad Cordillera Occidental of the Andes. Temperatures vary enormously with altitude over a very short distance and the range of crops grown varies from village to village, from potatoes in the highest to sub-tropical crops in the lowest. Cultivation is largely by hand or occasionally by ploughs drawn by livestock, but the possibility of mechanizing agriculture on conventional lines is out of the question, when there are in places as many as 50 'fields' per hectare. The arable land grows fodder crops for livestock as well as food crops for human consumption, but fodder crops supplement the pastures on higher land around, which vary in productivity with the seasons. Movement of goods between the various settlements in the area is difficult and inconvenient, for the motor road only reaches Huarochirí and Santiago. Virtually all the possible land that could be cultivated is already in use, for slopes are too steep to extend cultivation, and no more water is available for irrigation. Yields could be increased by bringing in fertilizers and improving the quality of seeds and livestock; hence the need for closer contact with other parts of Peru.

The population of nearly 10,000 gives a very high density per unit of cultivated land but this cannot be worked out precisely on account of lack of data. About half the population is in the two largest villages which, like most of the others, are laid out on a grid-iron pattern with a central square. Almost all the buildings have adobe walls and thatched roofs. Eucalyptus timber and corrugated iron are used by the more affluent members of the community. Furniture is usually very poor, the kitchens outside the main building are traditionally too low to stand up in, and cooking is done on open fires. Water supply is provided in the villages from a few communal taps. Fuel is too scarce for heating and there is no gas and no electricity. Again, sanitation is unknown. Considering the size of the villages, they all have a surprisingly large number of shops, but the turnover is minute and most shopkeepers have other occupations as well. Each village has a church, but in the 1950s there was only one priest, an American. The valley has no doctor and no hospital facilities. There are primary schools in most of the villages and education is available for most of the children up to the age of about eleven, but facilities for secondary education had to be found outside the region until a small start was made in the 1950s to provide this locally.

Not surprisingly the inhabitants of the valley, many of whom have travelled to the capital, or have relatives who have settled there, are conscious of the need to improve conditions in their own area. To do this they have to bring in an enormous number of ingredients: fertilizers, better implements, seed and stock for agriculture, fuel (mainly kerosene), building materials such as corrugated iron and glass, and all the machinery and consumer goods beyond the limited range of clothing produced locally, as well as the services of teachers, doctors and so on. These can be obtained only through the sales of agricultural products which, in fact, are marketed now in a reasonably well-organized way in the wholesale markets of Lima. If variety in diet is desired then items such as sugar, rice and tinned foods also have to be brought into the valley.

The valley of Huarochirí is isolated and is relatively though not desperately poor. Many other areas in the Andes of Peru are both more isolated and poorer. Population appears to be growing fairly fast and only part of it finds an outlet in Lima and other places along the coast. Agricultural production is difficult to increase on account of the many reasons already suggested but it is unthinkable at the moment to try to diversify the economy by introducing non-agricultural activities. Improvements are coming, but they can only be gradual. For a region such as this which in miniature has many of the problems of the under-developed world, there seem to be three possible lines of approach. Firstly, the region could be left to itself, in which case nothing very much would change. Secondly, a massive attempt could be made to improve it; in the case of Huarochirí for example a first class road could be built right into the valley, eliminating its isolation, but the cost of building such a road could not possibly be offset by the limited advantages to the economy of the country as a whole of integrating such a region. Or, thirdly, it could be deliberately abandoned, retaining only a caretaker population to keep agriculture going and having the rest of its population resettled in some more promising agricultural area or in an urban centre.

14.7. LIMA AND OTHER URBAN CENTRES OF PERU[12,13]

By way of contrast it is interesting to compare Lima, only 80 km away, with Huarochirí. The story of Greater Lima is matched by that of about at least a dozen other large cities in Latin America. Lima occupies about 1/5,000 of the total area of Peru but has about one fifth of the total population, half the motor vehicles in circulation, and about three quarters of the manufacturing. Between about 1940 and 1960 the population increased from about 650,000 to nearly 2 m. The town has a fairly central position on the Pacific coast of both Peru and Latin America. The next towns of comparable size are Bogotá to the north and Santiago to the south. Lima is in a desert region, but the area in which it is situated is supplied with water by three rivers, the central one being the Rimac, on which Lima is located. These three rivers irrigate the rich alluvial soils of the area, but the local farms have long ceased to satisfy the food requirements of the capital.

Lima was founded in 1535 by the Spaniards who after some indecision, chose a site for the future capital of their new empire in South America near the coast and not in the Andes. They chose an area in which there was already an agricultural population and therefore a local food supply, as well as water. An almost level site was used so that the town could spread indefinitely, and the streets were laid out in the usual grid-iron fashion (*Figure 14.4a*). It was not long before Lima began to have at least six clearly defined functions. It was a military base for the continuation of the Conquest, an administrative centre, becoming the capital of a viceroyalty soon after its foundation, a religious centre, an educational centre (a University from about 1550), the main commercial centre handling the trade with Spain, and in a limited way a manufacturing centre. Between 1550 and 1850 the population of Lima grew only gradually, rising from about 40,000 in 1700 to about 100,000 in 1850, by which time it was the capital of Peru, its original sphere of administration, which for a time around 1600 spread over the whole of South America, having been progressively reduced through the Colonial period. The building of walls in the seventeenth century and a very serious earthquake in 1743, which attracted attention in Europe at that time, were outstanding events in an otherwise undistinguished history.

Technological changes spreading to Latin America from Europe and North America began to transform the economy of Peru from about 1840. Shipping services along the coast grew more efficient and frequent and first guano and then cotton, metals and sugar were exported to Europe. From this time on Lima began to grow both in population and in area, at first slowly and then more rapidly; its links with the rest of the country were strengthened, first along the coast by shipping services, then with the central Andes by rail, and especially since the Second World War with the rest of the country by road. Population grew from about 100,000 in 1850 to about 250,000 in 1910 and 500,000 in 1935. Since then, the quantity of people arriving from the provinces each year has increased steadily, to add to the high natural rate of growth of the population of the town itself. A journey that took several weeks by land from the southern Andes can now be accomplished in a day by bus, and the hazardous journey from Iquitos, which lasted about a month, now takes only 2 h by air. The prerequisite for this accumulation of population in one locality has, in other words, depended on improved transportation and integration.

The built-up area of Lima has spread in three successive phases. Until the latter part of the nineteenth century most of the population was still within the limits of the walls, which were demolished late in the nineteenth century, but railways were built in the 1860s and tramways around 1900 in three directions towards the nearby coast to Callao, Magdalena and Miraflores (see *Figure 14.4c*), and development began to spread along these transport axes. By the 1930s these had been supplemented by good roads, and by the early 1950s a Greater Lima region was recognized by planners to fill the triangle Lima-Callao-Chorrillos, though some agricultural land remained within this triangle. By the early 1950s it was also possible to recognize several distinct land-use zones, including a central business district, the remains of the old town around this, by now largely consisting of slum dwellings, areas of better-class suburbs, especially in Miraflores, an industrial zone* extending most of the length of one of the avenues between Lima and its port, the port area itself, and finally the shanty towns. These already housed about 100,000 people by 1950 and occupied land of no use for agriculture or other developments including hillsides close to or even within the built-up area, the gravel covered bed of the Rimac, places in the desert outside the town and even blocks awaiting development within Lima.

But a third phase of development is now in progress, the emergence, partly planned, partly unplanned, of a Greater Greater Lima (see *Figure 14.4d*), a discontinuous urban area extending some 80 km along the coast and some 40 km from San Lorenzo island, inland up the Rimac valley. This includes a considerable number of new shanty towns†, the total population of which was estimated to be around 350,000 in the early 1960s, and at least three new satellite towns, one of which, Ventanilla, was completed in the early 1960s to house 100,000 people. Many new resorts serving as outer suburbs of Greater Lima have also grown up along the coast, thanks to the excellent conditions for motor transport. The construction of new fish meal factories, a large new airport (see *Figure 14.5*) and an oil refinery outside the established triangle of Greater Lima, and the plan to link the island of San Lorenzo to Callao by a causeway, all add to the reality of the concept of a Greater Greater Lima.

To this day Lima depends mainly on six functions noted at the beginning of this section, but its commercial and manufacturing functions are far more serious now than in the colonial period. Some idea of the importance of Lima can be judged by the disproportionate share it has of many material and cultural amenities of the country. Some features of land use are illustrated in *Figure 14.5a*.

With nearly 20 per cent of the total population of Peru and about half of the truly urban population Lima completely dominates the country. It is the administrative, commercial, financial and industrial capital; its port handles most of the imports of Peru. Culturally it is also much better provided than the rest of the country, having about 40 per cent of the places in secondary schools and 80 per cent of students in higher education, while about 60 per cent of the periodicals and reviews are circulated there. In Peru as a whole there are about 5,000 doctors, roughly 1 per 2,000 inhabitants, but about half are in the capital, many of the others in province capitals and few at all in remote rural areas. About 75 per cent of the money

---

* A surprising variety of industries are found strung out along one main avenue, with branches adjacent to one another that in older and more complex industrial countries are associated with quite distinct regions.

† See Ref.[14] for a fascinating detailed study of a *barriada* (shanty town) in Lima.

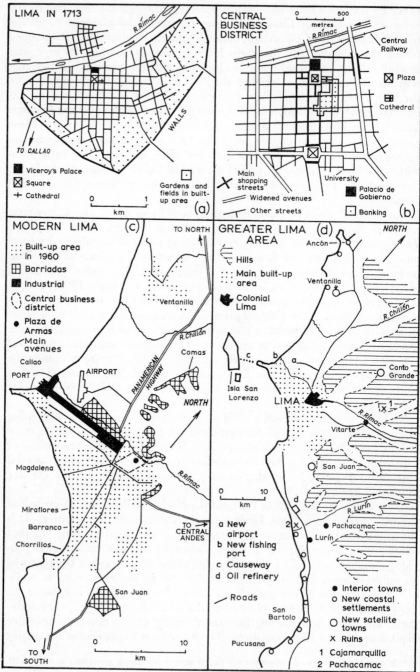

Figure 14.4. Peru. (a) Lima in 1713. (b) Central business district. (c) Modern Lima. (d) Greater Lima area

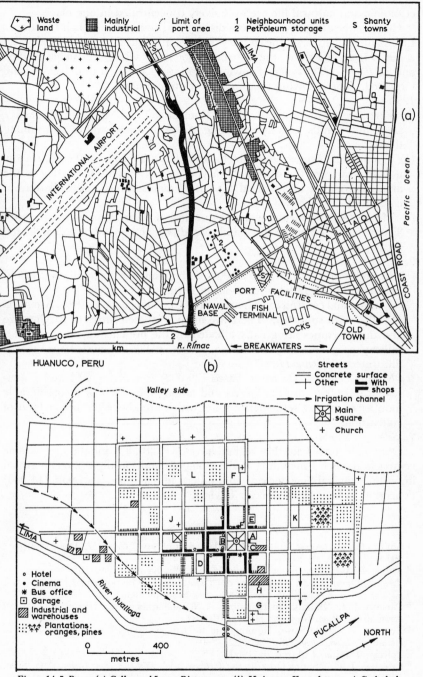

Figure 14.5. Peru. (a) Callao and Lower Rimac area. (b) Huánuco. Key to letters: A Cathedral, B Town Hall, C Tourist Hotel, D Main market, E Post Office, F Secondary School, G Hospital, H Motor vehicle dealers, J Convent, K Prison, L New market

deposited in banks is in Lima. These are only some of the ways in which the economic and cultural life are excessively concentrated in one place.

How are the other towns of Peru distributed, and what are their functions? Like so many features of the country they are influenced by the main physical zones. *Figure 14.2* shows the distribution of towns with over 10,000 in 1961 and in *Figure 14.3b* types of town according to function and location are indicated. The following types may be distinguished:

1. *Coast*
(*a*) Ports, e.g. Paita (33,000). Apart from Callao and Matarani, these have small hinterlands, usually consisting of one or a few valleys or a mining district[15].

(*b*) Commercial centres, e.g. Chiclayo (87,000), Trujillo (100,000), usually a little way from the coast and varying in size roughly according to the area of irrigated agricultural land they serve. Lima and Callao are a combination of the two types.

(*c*) Mining encampments, e.g. El Alto near Talara, Marcona (iron ore), Tocquepala. These are small and specialized, and are all outside irrigated areas.

2. *Sierra*[16]
(*a*) Route centres. La Oroya (20,000) with its smelter, and Juliaca (21,000) are the only two railway junctions in Peru.

(*b*) Commercial centres, e.g. Huarás (21,000), Huancayo (46,000), Arequipa (157,000 with suburbs). There are many of these centres of varying size and their fortunes are greatly affected by the presence or otherwise of a railway or good road. Huánuco (about 20,000), founded in 1545, is illustrated in *Figure 14.5*.

(*c*) Mining centres. Cerro de Pasco (20,000) (see *Figure 8.6*) and Huancavelica (12,000) are the largest and among the oldest of a considerable number of mining settlements, some which are above the upper limit of cultivation.

3. *Selva*
Only four towns in this region have over 10,000 inhabitants. Some centres in the Selva including Iquitos (56,000) and Pucallpa (26,000) are on important navigable waterways, but others, for example, Tarapoto (14,000) depend at present largely on air services.

REFERENCES

[1] Smith, C. T. 'Agriculture and Settlement in Peru,' *Geogr. J.* Dec. 1960, pp. 397–412

[2] Miller, E. V. 'Agricultural Ecuador' *Geogr. Rev.* XLIX (1959) 183–207

[3] Preston, D. A. *I.B.G. Transactions and Publications* (To be published)

[4] *El Universo* (Guayaquil) 4 April 1964 (special supplement)

[5] Parsons, J. J. 'Bananas in Ecuador: A New Chapter in the History of Tropical Agriculture' *Econ. Geogr.* 33 (1957) 201–216

[6] Burt, A. L. *et al.* Santo Domingo de los Colorados—A New Pioneer Zone in Ecuador', *Econ. Geogr.* 36 (1960) 221–230

[7] Bolivia, *The Statist* March 26, 1960

[8] Crossley, J. C. 'Santa Cruz at the Cross-roads' *Tijdschr. econ. Geogr.* Aug./Sept. 1961

[9] Eidt, R. C. 'Pioneer Settlement in Eastern Peru', *A.A.A.G.* Sept. 1962, pp. 255–78

[10] *Las actuales comunidades de indígenas Huarochirí en 1955*, Instituto de Etnología, San Marcos University, Lima, 1958

[11] Cole, J. P. Huarochirí, une petite région des Andes du Pérou, *Rev. Géogr. alp.* June 1956, pp. 445–62

[12] Cole, J. P. 'Some Town Planning Problems of Greater Lima', *Town Plann. Rev.* Vol. XXVI, No. 4, Jan. 1956

[13] Cole, J. P. 'La Grande Lima: note di geografia urbana', *Riv. geogr. ital.* LXIII June 1956, pp. 120–43

[14] *Archit. Design* Aug. 1963

[15] Cole, J. P. 'Ports and Hinterlands in Peru' *Tijdschr. econ. Geogr.* June/July 1956

[16] Ortolani, M. and Cole, J. P. 'Tipi di sedi sulle Ande Centrali' *Riv. geogr. ital.* LXX, Dec. 1963

CHAPTER 15

THE ISLANDS AND GUIANAS

15.1. GENERAL FEATURES OF THE ISLANDS

Although the Islands of the Caribbean differ from one another in size, physical conditions and level of economic development, they have certain features in common which justify their being considered together. The fact of being insular and having every part of the national area close to the coast, given their relatively small size, is an obvious attribute. On the other hand, collectively they are like other parts of Latin America in that they consist of a number of clusters of dense population separated by empty areas, in their case the sea, of course, and not thinly populated land. Movements by sea between the various clusters of population may indeed be easier and cheaper than by land between concentrations of population on the mainland. There is some resemblance in this respect between the Islands and Central America, but Central America has roughly twice the area with only half the population.

The Islands have many important features in common. First of all their proximity to Europe and to North America must partly be responsible for the way in which greater influence has been exerted by various European powers and much more recently by the U.S.A., than in most other parts of Latin America. The Islands remained colonial longer than any other part of Latin America and have been more involved in world affairs and in the strategy of the Second World War than the rest of Latin America. Physically they have much in common, having equable temperatures, a high rainfall except in limited areas, and a population living mainly below a few hundred metres, although high mountain sides are cultivated. They suffer from an unreliable rainfall and frequent hurricanes. With regard to relief, however, there is a basic contrast between most of Cuba except parts of the southeast and a few small Islands on the one hand, and the rest of the region on the other, Cuba being essentially flat or gently undulating, the rest of the larger islands, except Trinidad, being rugged, with only limited areas of level or gently sloping land.

In comparison with the rest of Latin America the Islands are small and densely populated. Even Cuba, with only about a third of the total population on half the area, is many times more densely populated than the other countries of medium size (size meaning population) in Latin America (Venezuela, Chile, Peru). There may be limited areas into which cultivation could be extended but the Islands are virtually full, agriculturally speaking. Another feature shared by the Islands is a large negro element compared with that in the areas so far studied. The proportion varies, however, from about 10 per cent in Cuba to almost 100 per cent in Haiti. There has of course been a great deal of mixing of population. In sheer numbers the quantity of negroes brought to the Caribbean is rivalled only by that taken to Northeast Brazil.

Economically, the Islands almost all depend heavily on the cultivation of sugar and therefore have in common various problems associated with this crop, such as seasonal variations in labour requirements. Table 15.3 summarizes production over the last 3 decades. Bananas too are very widely grown, but less on a commercial basis than in Ecuador or Central America, the frequent occurrence of hurricanes making them a risky investment*. The Islands account for about 10 per cent of the Latin American total, the chief producers being (1961–2): the Dominican Republic 500,000 tons, Guadeloupe and Martinique 330,000, Jamaica 260,000, Puerto Rico 115,000.

Industrially the Islands are not so far advanced as most of Latin America and much of the industrial capacity is in agricultural processing and the refining of minerals, especially oil. The Islands themselves suffer from an almost complete lack of energy resources apart from the oil and gas fields of Trinidad. There is no coal, and the limited hydroelectric potential makes only a small contribution. Most of the Islands aspire to having a tourist industry, another feature they have in common†.

There are of course great contrasts between the different Islands, some illustrated in Table 15.1. Contrasts are due partly to differences in physical conditions; for example, with exactly the same historical background Cuba could not have failed to produce a more prosperous community than Haiti, since conditions for agriculture are so much more favourable. On the other hand, the great difference between Haiti and the neighbouring Dominican Republic can only partly be explained in physical terms since difficult conditions extend throughout the island they share; it is due more to differences in their history over the last few hundred years. The Indian element in the Islands almost completely disappeared in the 16th century but through the colonial period intensity of economic exploitation varied from place to place. On account of the lack of precious metals the region was of little interest to the Spaniards except as a series of stepping stones on the routes between Spain and the mainland of Latin America. Those areas held by Spain, notably Cuba, the Dominican Republic and Puerto Rico were not so intensively developed as Haiti and smaller islands held during much of the colonial period by the English and French. The Islands have therefore developed in different directions, and continue to do so. They will be considered in this chapter on this basis.

Cuba is a relatively large island and was neglected by the Spaniards throughout the colonial period which in its case lasted until 1898. It attracted considerable numbers of settlers from Spain but few negroes were brought in and sugar cultivation was only of limited importance, much of the island being devoted to cattle raising. In the twentieth century it changed direction abruptly as sugar cultivation spread across the island and it

* Hurricane Flora (1963), for example, destroyed 80 per cent of the banana plants in Dominica, 75 per cent in Granada and 60 per cent in St. Lucia.

† The following are the number of visitors, most of them from the U.S.A., to the various islands in 1961 or nearest year[1]: Bahamas 370,000, Puerto Rico 300,000, Bermuda 110,000, Haiti 90,000, Jamaica and Trinidad 75,000 each, Barbados 40,000. The greatest development has been in the Bahamas (only 35,000 in 1948). Cuba has declined sharply.

TABLE 15.1

Summary of Population and Economic Features in Late 1950s or Early 1960s

	I	II	III	IV	V	VI	VII	VIII	IX	X
	Area	*Population*	*Density*	*Yearly population increase 1958–61*	*Per cent employment in agriculture*	*Cropland*	*Cropland as % of total area*	*Area under sugar*	*Sugar as % of cropland*	*Per caput energy cons.*
Cuba	114,5	6,933	61	2·1	42	19,7	17	14,3	70–75	866
Haiti	27,8	4,249	153	2·2	83	3,7	13	0,1	3	36
Dominican Rep.	48,7	3,098	64	3·4	56	6,8	14	1,5	22	148
Puerto Rico	8,9	2,409	271	1·6	24	3,1	35	1,5	ca 50	1,448
Jamaica	11,4	1,631	143	1·6	49	2,3	20	0,8	ca 35	602
Trinidad	5,1	859	168	2·9	25	1,7	33	0,3	18	2,390
Barbados	0,4	236	548	n.a.	29	0,3	75	0,2	65	350
French West Indies	2,9	560	193	2·4	n.a.	1,0	35	0,45	45	300
Netherlands Antilles	1,0	194	202	1·3	n.a.	n.	n.a.	n.	n.	very high
British Guiana	215,0	582	3	3·0	46	0,5	∨1	0,3	60	576
Netherlands Guiana	143,0	283	2	4·5	n.a.	0,3	∨1	n.	n.	750
French Guiana	91,0	32	n.	1·7	n.a.	n.	∨1	n.	n.	350

n. = negligible.   n.a. = not available

I Area in thousands of square kilometres.
II Population in 1961 or nearest year in thousands.
III Persons per square kilometre.
IV Average annual increase of population 1958–61.
V Employment in agriculture as a percentage of total employed population.

VI Area under crops in thousands of square kilometres.
VII Area under crops as a percentage of total land area.
VIII Area under sugar cane in thousands of square kilometres.
IX Sugar cane as a percentage of all land under crops (very approximate).
X Per caput consumption of energy (all sources) in kilograms of coal equivalent in 1961.

became the chief source of sugar for the United States. From the late 1950s it has again changed very abruptly and has been developing on lines very different from those followed by the rest of the Islands in the last few years. The Dominican Republic has a somewhat similar history to that of Cuba up to the early nineteenth century but then became independent from Spain, only to be for a time part of Haiti. It has stagnated up to the 1920s but commercial agriculture has advanced and some industrialization has taken place since then. Haiti on the other hand reached its peak of relative importance in the Caribbean in the eighteenth century since when it has reverted from a commercial agricultural economy to a regional subsistence economy accompanied by a great increase in population; its economy might be called retrogressive. Puerto Rico became more densely populated than the other Spanish colonies in the Caribbean, but when the United States gained control of it around 1900 it had little to export and pressure of population on land was very great. Under the United States it was converted to a sugar exporting colony but improvements were limited until about 1940 when the United States began to reconsider its policy towards the island, and from 1950 improvements have been very rapid indeed. Jamaica and Trinidad have a similar history of development under the British, their main purpose being to export tropical crops. Large numbers of negroes were brought into both islands and also Asians into Trinidad in the nineteenth century. These islands, together with the smaller British islands in the Caribbean, have to some extent benefited from an assured market in Britain, but by the 1930s they were beginning to feel the effects of over-population. With its asphalt and oil, Trinidad, has been able to diversify its economy during and since the inter-war period, while the exploitation of bauxite in Jamaica during and since the Second World War has given it also an alternative resource to agriculture. Since the Second World War therefore these two islands have been able to break away from their dependence on tropical crops and to industrialize, and together with Puerto Rico they have recorded the highest increase in national income per inhabitant of any part of Latin America in the last two decades, apart from Venezuela. Some of the smaller islands have been less fortunate and remain basically agricultural but fortunately only limited numbers of people are involved. It is interesting to compare the way in which some of the smaller islands have found a function of international importance while others struggle to export tropical crops. The Bahamas for example have a great tourist industry, the Netherlands Antilles two of the world's largest oil refineries, while the French colonies Martinique and Guadeloupe specialize for the French market.

15.2. PRODUCTION AND OTHER FIGURES

This section contains a number of sets of figures intended to illustrate the main features of economic development in the Islands and Guianas and to bring out important contrasts. Table 15.1 is a summary of the main features. Table 15.2 lists all towns with more than about 50,000 inhabitants in the early 1960s. Table 15.3 shows sugar production in the main areas of cultivation, Table 15.4 deals with the electrification and Table 15.5 oil refineries.

TABLE 15.2

Towns with Over 50,000 Inhabitants in the Islands and Guianas Around 1960. (See *Figure 15.1c* for location)

1.	La Habana (Havana)	1,220	12.	Santiago	60
2.	Matanzas	70	13.	Santo Domingo	370
3.	Cárdenas	50	14.	Mayagüez	70
4.	Cienfuegos	70	15.	Ponce	150
5.	Santa Clara	90	16.	San Juan	590
6.	Camaguëy	110	17.	Willemstad	70
7.	Holguín	70	18.	Fort-de-France	70
8.	Santiago de Cuba	160	19.	Bridgetown	80
9.	Guantánamo	70	20.	Port-of-Spain	94
10.	Kingston	380		Georgetown	100
11.	Port-au-Prince	250		Paramaribo	150

TABLE 15.3

Raw Sugar Production in Selected Years in Thousands of Metric Tons[2]

	1935	1940	1945	1950	1955	1960	1962
Cuba	2,606	2,472	4,060	5,759	4,528	5,862	4,815
Puerto Rico	840	845	825	1,123	1,057	933	913
Dominican Rep.	457	400	459	532	637	1,112	902
Jamaica	92	157	181	272	403	431	441
Trinidad	153	132	111	143	196	221	204
Guadeloupe					122	159	177
Barbados	131	102	136	191	174	162	161
Martinique					86	83	88
Haiti	37	32	40	58	56	73	69

TABLE 15.4

Electricity Output in the Post-war Period[3]

	Output of electricity millions of kWh		Increase 1948–1960 (times)
	1948	1960 or 1961	
Cuba	1,000*	3,000*	3
Haiti	10*	60	6
Dominican Rep.	60	350	6
Puerto Rico	480	2,440	5
Jamaica	100	600	6
Trinidad	50	500	10
Martinique-Guadeloupe	12	45	4
Barbados	10	43	4
British Guiana	30*	125	4
Surinam	5	90	18

* very approximate figure.

TABLE 15.5

Oil Refineries[4]

	Number of refineries		Crude capacity (1,000 barrels per day)		Investment in millions of U.S. $
	1963	1965	1963	1965	
Cuba	6	7	87	127	30
Haiti	0	1	0	10	8
Dominican Rep.	0	1	0	10	10
Puerto Rico	2	2	105	105	
Jamaica	0	1	0	28	15
Antigua	0	1	0	10	16
Trinidad	2	2	305	305	
Neth. Antilles	2	2	650	605	

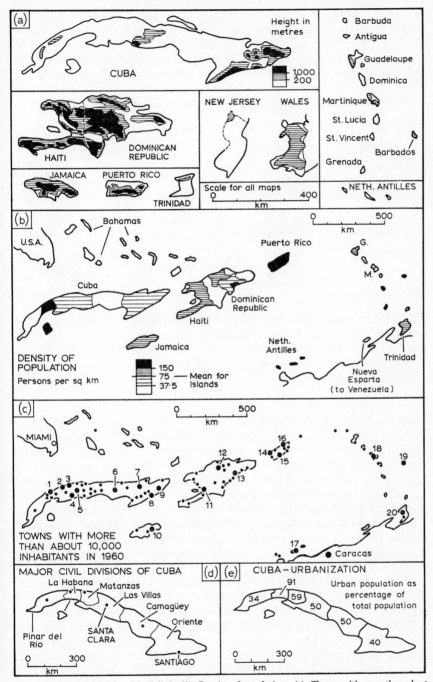

Figure 15.1. The Islands. (a) Relief. (b) Density of population. (c) Towns with more than about 10,000 inhabitants in 1960. (d) Major civil divisions of Cuba. (e) Cuba urbanization

During 1963–65 it is not planned to extend the capacity of the very large refineries producing entirely or largely for export. Four refineries are projected for countries without any, however, while Cuba is expecting to increase its existing capacity. The sites of the new refineries are to be Port-au-Prince in Haiti, Kingston in Jamaica, and Santiago de Cuba. The plant in Antigua is St. Johns and that in the Dominican Republic was undecided in 1963.

The location of the existing refineries was as follows[5]:

Country	Plant	Company	Total refined 1963 (thousands of tons)
Neth. Antilles	Aruba	Lago	22,000
	Caracas	Shell	14,750
Trinidad	Point-à-Pierre	Texaco	11,750
	Point Fortin	Shell	3,050
	La Brea	Brighton	250
Puerto Rico	Guayamilla	C.O.R.	4,500
	Bayamon	Carib. Ref.	1,500
Cuba	Belot		1,750
	Havana	Nationalized	1,350
	Santiago		1,000
	Cabaignan		105

The Netherland Antilles exports virtually all the oil it refines. Trinidad consumes only 3–4 per cent of its production, while 15 per cent goes on bunker sales in the island. There is already a large petrochemicals plant at Point-à-Pierre and plants are also being constructed in the Netherlands Antilles.

15.3. HAITI*

Haiti has attracted considerable attention as one of the poorest countries in the world. Its yearly national income per inhabitant (70$) is roughly one fortieth that of the United States, and one quarter that of the mean for Latin America. Its agriculture has declined in efficiency since the eighteenth century. It has a growing population, and dwindling resources, for the need to cultivate on progressively steeper slopes has caused soil erosion. Its mineral and hydroelectric resources are small considering the population. Haiti is one of the most densely peopled, impoverished and thoroughly rural nations in the western hemisphere. Two centuries ago its foreign trade surpassed in value that of all Spanish America and it was the world's leading exporter of coffee and sugar†.

Haiti is about 28,000 km² in area, somewhat larger than Wales but smaller than Switzerland. The density of population is 2½ times as high as in the adjoining Dominican Republic. The island consists of four mountain areas with a roughly east-west alignment, separated by lowlands or low plateaux, and ending in most places abruptly at the coast without any coastal plain. A north-south journey across Haiti involves crossing the four mountain areas, varying from 1,000 to 3,000 m (see *Figure 3.13*). About 80 per cent

* See Bibliography, p. 461.
† Street[6], p. 9.

of the country is rugged, and the level or reasonably gently sloping land occupies only about 10 per cent. Soils vary greatly from region to region, and some are very fertile, including the alluvial soils in the depressions and some soils derived from the widespread limestone of the island. Temperatures are uniformly high, with occasional frosts occurring only in the highest parts, but rainfall varies from 3,000 mm in the exposed areas, especially in the northern part of the island, to less than 500 mm in sheltered depressions in the interior (see *Figure 3.3c*). Haiti is particularly afflicted by hurricanes. One (Hazel) in 1954 destroyed many of the coffee trees; it was followed by a very serious drought in part of the island. In 1963 Hurricane Flora is calculated to have left 4,000 dead and 100,000 homeless. In August 1964, Hurricane Cleo again took a heavy toll of life and property including 122 deaths, and the destruction of half the buildings in Les Cayes. Most of the original vegetation has been cleared for cultivation or otherwise modified in some way but some high forest is presumably original.

As elsewhere in the Caribbean, the American Indian population almost entirely disappeared after colonization, and a few Spaniards settled in the island in the sixteenth and seventeenth centuries. Already in the seventeenth century France began to take an interest in Hispaniola and its sovereignty over the western end was recognized by Spain in 1697. Both European and negro labour was brought in to develop Haiti as the principal colony of France in the tropics. Initially Africans and Europeans were to be in similar proportions, but by the end of the eighteenth century there were roughly $\frac{1}{2}$ million negroes compared with only 40,000 whites; most of the negroes were still slaves, but some had been freed. There had been some mixing, and mulattoes were fairly numerous, but French had become the official language of the country and a dialect of French remains the language of the whole population. In 1794 the negro and mulatto population fought for and achieved independence from France and the whites left the island or were eliminated. From then on the country has been largely run by the mulattoes, who have lacked technicians and any experience in organizing an independent country as an economic unit. The plantation system of the eighteenth century broke down almost completely in the nineteenth century and almost all the sugar still grown has been consumed within the country itself. Haiti was recognized by France in 1838, but its independence dates from before that, and for a time from 1814 to 1844 it controlled the whole of the island of Hispaniola. Until the twentieth century Haiti had little to do with the outside world, but from 1915 to 1934 it was occupied by the United States, its finances were reorganized, and its foreign trade began to grow; it had favourable tariffs for its trade with the U.S.A. Even so, progress has been modest in the twentieth century whereas the population, which had risen to about $1\frac{1}{4}$ m. in 1900, exceeded 3 m. in 1950 and was estimated to be $4\frac{1}{4}$ m. in the early 1960s. Only about one tenth of this population is urban, a good indication of the lack of non-agricultural activities.

In the sixteenth and seventeenth centuries the economy of the island was based on the cultivation of maize, manioc and sweet potatoes, and the Spaniards brought in cattle, but crops that could be exported to Europe, such as tobacco and plants producing dyes, were hardly grown. Towards the end of the seventeenth century sugar, cacao, coffee and cotton were all introduced, and in the eighteenth century France invested much money in the establishment of plantations, building sugar refineries and, as cultivation shifted to drier parts of the island, providing irrigation works. As in Northeast Brazil in the seventeenth century, large numbers of slaves were brought in throughout the eighteenth century to work in the plantations. Food crops were grown but these were not sufficient to feed the whole population of the island and both food and timber, as well as manufactured goods, were imported. Haiti was the world's leading producer of sugar. After the decline of plantation agriculture much of the equipment and many of the irrigation works were abandoned. Only in the twentieth century has there been an attempt to find markets abroad for sugar, cultivated in the wetter lowland areas, for sisal grown in the drier lowlands, and for coffee cultivated on slopes at appropriate altitudes; the coffee and certain other export crops such as cotton tend, in fact, to be grown widely as a cash crop in farms concerned essentially with growing crops for their own needs. There are a few cattle in the island now but pigs, goats and poultry of low quality are kept widely to supplement and diversify the many food crops grown. With a density of population of about 5 people per hectare of cultivated land, Haiti has greater pressure on agricultural land than almost any country in the world except Japan and Egypt, but its yields per unit of area are much lower than in those two countries. There is virtually no mechanization and almost all agricultural work is done by hand using hoes and machetes, rather than with the help of livestock. Hardly any mineral fertilizers are produced on the island or imported. The view is held by some that to maintain such a high density of population in such difficult conditions of slope, heavy downpours and often soils of poor or only moderate quality, it has been necessary to develop a variety of land use that simulates the natural vegetation. Not only is there very little monoculture, but on farms themselves several tree and field crops are often grown together and are often not arranged in an orderly fashion at all; the appearance is of disorderly gardens rather than farms.

The state of agriculture in Haiti is not helped by land tenure conditions. Large estates are rare and in theory most of the agricultural land is owned by individual farmers, but there are few records of land and its ownership, and few titles to land, and over much of the island there is great scope for disputes over ownership, and lack of interest by individuals in particular pieces of land. Collective cultivation of fields with a large number of owners, known as *coumbite*, is carried out widely but does not amount to specialization, and is of dubious use economically: 'The quality and volume of work contributed in a coumbite are almost entirely a matter of individual determination and the loss in efficiency caused by concentrating so many individuals on a given task that they get in each others way, is taken to be compensated for by the gains in social satisfaction'[7].

Haiti is one of the most rural countries in the world and although there are several towns in the island, the capital, which now has about 200,000 inhabitants, is the only place that is urban in appearance, though even it lacks many of the amenities that would elsewhere be considered essential in a town of its size. Since inter-regional trade is limited in volume if not in variety of goods exchanged, regional commercial centres do not appear to have been necessary. Much trade is carried out in rural localities, the scene of markets and fairs held at certain occasions during the year. Nor is there a need to process most agricultural products anywhere but in the farms themselves. Activities other than agriculture include fishing, which involves only a few thousand persons and is run very inefficiently, and charcoal and lime burning. There is one modern cotton mill in the capital and a few sugar refineries in the lowlands. Inter-regional movement of goods is very difficult, there being only about 100 km of paved road and very few bridges; many of the roads are therefore closed during the rainy season. There are only a few thousand motor vehicles in the whole country and many of these are in the towns.

Socially the island is also by far the most backward region in Latin America. Less than 4 per cent of the population is literate and it was calculated that in the 1950s only one seventh of the children attended school at all, and even those that did could not usually stay long. Housing is very poor and medical facilities almost non-existent outside the towns. Most families live in a single room: 'the typical home is a long single room, usually less than 10 m², with a bare dirt floor, a wood-frame construction, woven grass and clay in-filling, and thatched roof. The houses have no sanitary facilities or running water. The cooking is done on the ground outside, over a metal brazier and charcoal fire ... Rarely has a peasant family more than one bed, if any, and several people share it; the less fortunate sleep on mats on the bare ground'[8].

Haiti offers an extreme example of regional inequality in social services. There are only a few hundred physicians in the whole of the island, of which half are in the capital, and most of the remainder in the province capitals; in 1948 there were said to be only 26 in the rest of the island to cater for $2\frac{1}{2}$ million people. With water rarely clean, lack of hygiene, and many parts of the country isolated even from emergency medical services, it is not surprising that diseases such as malaria, tuberculosis, hook-worm and yaws, go untreated. Malnutrition is also widespread. Inadequate health facilities and diet appear to be the main reason why the growth of population in Haiti is currently much slower than in most other parts of Latin America.

Although little has been done yet to change conditions in Haiti, much work has now been done on assessing its problems and making recommendations. Changes in agriculture depend both on sorting out land tenure problems and on increasing yields. There are few new areas to be brought into cultivation and if anything it would be best to retreat from some of the steeper slopes. Throughout the country, forest conservation and the control of torrential streams is essential. In many parts, terraces need improving, and in some lowland areas irrigation works are needed. While it would seem unwise to interfere with the characteristically varied type of farm already described, productivity could be greatly increased with plant selection, pest control, and the improvement of pastures and livestock. But even if agricultural productivity was increased two or three times, Haiti would still be one of the poorest countries in the world, and it is obvious that dependence on agriculture must be reduced. At present, industry is confined almost entirely to domestic activities and small workshops, and only about 50,000 people are employed. The consumption of energy in the country is very small and the total generating capacity of all electric power stations, about 10,000 kW, is only equal to about one fiftieth of the capacity of a single large modern power station in an industrial country. An oil refinery is to be completed in 1965 and although this will be small, it is the nearest that the island can hope to get towards establishing its own fuel base, since the hydroelectric potential is dispersed in many small rivers and is not great in total quantity. But Haiti has no mineral resources that can at present be used in the island although some bauxite is exported, while there are few agricultural products apart from cotton and sisal that could be processed or manufactured.

The prospect is altogether bleak for there is little chance that other parts of Latin America will accept settlers from Haiti; indeed both the Dominican Republic and Cuba do all they can to keep them out. But there is a prospect that if improvements are made, and a somewhat higher standard of living is achieved, then the rate of increase of population will become higher and a greater population in two or three decades time will have to face the same problems all over again.

15.4. CUBA

Physically Cuba consists mainly of undulating lowland but there are limited mountain areas in the extreme west and especially in the southeast where the Sierra Maestra exceeds 1,800 m. Rainfall is high over most of the island, which originally was largely forested, but where a lower rainfall and particular soil conditions combine, especially in the central part of the island, drier types of vegetation prevail.

Compared with the other islands of the Caribbean, Cuba was little developed in the Colonial period and a figure of 170,000 for its population in 1774 (contrast $\frac{1}{2}$ m. in Haiti at that time) is small; but the figure for 1877 is $1\frac{1}{2}$ m. and for 1900, 2 m., while in the early 1960s the total probably passed 7 m. Even now, however, density of population is much lower than in most of the other islands and bears no comparison with that of Java, which is only slightly larger in area but has almost ten times as many people. The make-up of the population in Cuba (1953) shows clearly that the negro element has been more limited than elsewhere: white 73 per cent, black 12 per cent and mixed 15 per cent.

Although less densely populated than the other islands, no large part of Cuba is thinly populated, but locally, some coastal marshes, especially in the south, and the mountain areas, support only a small population. The country is highly urbanized by Latin American standards; in the late 1950s the figure was 57 per cent, with Greater Havana containing about one quarter of the total population or 1·7 m. The degree of urbanization varies among the provinces. The following figures show percentage urban and percentage illiterate (24 per cent for Cuba as a whole) in the six provinces:

	Percentage				Percentage	
	Urban	Illiterate			Urban	Illiterate
Havana	91	9	Las Villas		50	25
Matanzas	59	19	Oriente		40	25
Camagüey	50	27	Pinar		34	29

In addition to being highly urbanized, Cuba has a good system of roads and railways. There are 14,500 km of railway, of which 8,000 are main lines, and a trunk road running the whole length of the island.

In the nineteenth century the economy of Cuba was based almost entirely on agriculture but like many less developed parts of the Spanish Empire it had been used for cattle raising rather than plantation agriculture. Still a colony of Spain in the nineteenth century it tended to be neglected and with the abolition of slavery, a growing competition from beet sugar in Europe, and the small population of the island, sugar cane was cultivated only on a very limited scale. This changed entirely after 1898 as the island came more and more under U.S. influence. The cultivation of sugar cane spread into the large 'capitalist' estates and on a smaller scale the cultivation of tobacco increased in the western part of the island. As the cultivation of these two crops for export grew, and population increased, Cuba had to begin to import food products. *Figure 15.2* shows the growth of sugar production during the twentieth century[9]. Year to year fluctuations due to climatic influence do not hide the rapid expansion in the first three decades:

1900	300,000	1919	4 m.
1903	1 m.	1925	over 5 m.
1913	2 m.	1952	over 7 m.
1916	3 m.	1963	only 3·8 m.

Before 1959, 20–25 per cent of the area of Cuba, excluding the extreme west, was occupied by sugar companies, some 27,000 km^2, not all of which was cultivated. In Camagüey Province, six U.S. sugar companies had 7,500 km^2, over 20 per cent of the area of the province. Even so, this was not as large as the 40,000 km^2 in large 'capitalist' estates. The sugar industry employed about $\frac{1}{2}$ m. people and sugar was grown on more than half of the arable land, mainly the better land, but even so, yields in Cuba have tended to be lower than in the other Islands. Before 1959 Cuba was estimated to have $\frac{1}{2}$ m. persons permanently unemployed (about 20 per cent of its potential labour force), 650,000 agricultural workers out of work for half the year, and 90,000 sugar mill workers similarly affected.

Cuba has some minerals including chrome, nickel and iron ore and small oil deposits, but its hydroelectric potential is very limited. It has not made much use of these minerals and for its energy supply has permanently depended on imports.

The revolution of 1959 and subsequent developments have transformed the economic life of the country. In the first place United States interests were completely taken over, assets worth about U.S. $ 1,000 m. being expropriated. The importation of goods diminished rapidly as the U.S.A. cut and then prohibited sugar imports from Cuba*; these had entered at a

* The following figures illustrate the decline[10]:

Millions of U.S. $:		1957	58	59	60	61	62	63
	U.S. exports to Cuba	619	547	439	224	14	13	37
	U.S. imports from Cuba	482	528	475	357	35	7	negl.

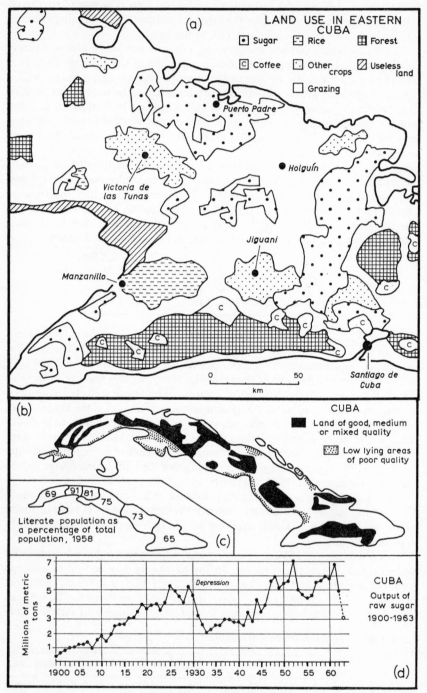

Figure 15.2. Cuba. (a) Land use in Eastern Cuba. (b) Cuba quality of farm land. (c) Literate population as a percentage of total population. (d) Cuba output of raw sugar 1900–1963

preferential rate. Tourists from the United States, an important source of income, ceased to arrive. Cuba turned to the Communist countries as trading partners and a source of aid. During 1960–62 Soviet aid, half of it in raw materials, and excluding military equipment, amounted to U.S. $ 850 m. Machinery and equipment, transportation material and food were also provided by the U.S.S.R. and its East European partners in COMECON. In return these were forced to import large quantities of sugar and tobacco, in spite of the fact that the U.S.S.R. has gone to great lengths to become self-sufficient in beet sugar; presumably, if Cuba could be relied on as a source of sugar, some of the best land in the Ukraine could be released for other crops.

The internal policy has been for the state to take over many economic activities, both agricultural and non-agricultural (e.g. oil refining). Agrarian reform has brought profound changes in land tenure. At first a maximum size of 400 hectares was established, and then 50 hectares. Before the revolution about 2 per cent of the population owned half of the land. Now it is mostly run in collective or state farms with a preference on the part of farm workers for state farms, in which a regular wage is paid. Attempts have been made to reduce unemployment, to inspire the rural population to improve housing conditions and to eliminate illiteracy. Initially there was a move to reduce dependence on sugar and to increase the production of basic foods and cattle raising. More recently (1963) the aim has been to concentrate on what Cuba is best suited to produce, obviously sugar, and moves have been made to establish industries using the residue of the plant after the sugar has been removed, for the manufacture of paper and other items. Equipment for this kind of industry can only be obtained from North America or Western Europe.

15.5. DOMINICAN REPUBLIC[11]

Physically, the Dominican Republic is a continuation of Haiti, with several ranges running roughly east to west, and varying from 1–3,000 m in altitude. As in Haiti, too, precipitation varies greatly over short distances, from extremes of about 600 to 2,500 mm. Altogether, however, conditions are more favourable for agriculture, and given a larger size and smaller population, there is about three times as much cultivated land per inhabitant[12]. Although independent from Spain since the 1820s the Dominican Republic was controlled by Haiti for much of the first half of the nineteenth century and although the Spanish tradition was maintained, in contrast to Cuba few European settlers arrived. The island was for a time occupied by the United States (1916–24) but few developments took place until the 1930s, when transport and marketing facilities were improved, land reforms introduced, new areas opened up and large sugar farms established. In Cuba, sugar cultivation supplanted food and livestock farming, while in Haiti subsistence agriculture replaced sugar cultivation. In contrast, the Dominican Republic has managed to maintain a balance between the two, achieving a surplus of sugar, cacao and coffee for export, self-sufficiency in food crops such as rice and bananas, and even a small surplus of meat. Until recently the country was very agricultural but in the last three decades the share of employment in farming has dropped from 75 per cent to 55 per cent, while in the 1950s employment in industry doubled from 50,000 to 100,000, and electricity production increased four times. New developments have been the introduction of light industries (e.g. footwear, textiles) and of cement production. The extraction of bauxite, starting from nothing in the late 1950s, reached 1·3 m. tons in 1960. In the 1950s coffee production doubled and more cotton and sisal were grown, while since the Cuban revolution sugar exports to the United States have gone up and now account for more than half of all exports, most of the remainder consisting of coffee, cacao fruits and bauxite.

The country is small and reasonably easy to integrate but routes tend to focus on the capital, Santo Domingo, which has more than 10 per cent of the total population. Like most of the other islands the Republic lacks energy resources, but it is to have an oil refinery. *Per caput* national income is considerably lower than in Puerto Rico, Jamaica and Trinidad, but progress of the kind achieved by these three islands in the 1950s is hoped for in the Dominican Republic in the 1960s.

15.6. PUERTO RICO[13]

Since the Second World War Puerto Rico has become something of a show-piece among the underdeveloped countries of the western world. Its *per caput* national income has risen at a rate only comparable with that of Venezuela. Taken over from Spain by the United States around 1900, it was run more or less on colonial lines until 1940, being developed particularly by four large U.S. sugar estates; it suffered heavily in the depression in the early 1930s. The turning point in its career was the granting of self-government in 1940, the introduction of agrarian reforms and the establishment of a Government Industrial Development Corporation. It was later given the status of a commonwealth with many of the advantages of a U.S. state but without the financial commitments. Throughout the twentieth century almost all its trade has been with the United States, around 90 per cent most of the time and reaching a peak of 95 per cent in 1941–42. One reason for the interest of the United States in the island was its strategic position in relation to the Caribbean area. With changing emphasis in world strategy its military significance has diminished, and as yet attempts to exploit this position in an economic sense by attracting industries to process products brought by sea to this convenient stopping place have not been successful; an international free-trade zone in Mayagüez has made little progress so far.

Puerto Rico is smaller and more rugged than Cuba and even Hispaniola, with land rising to 1,300 m a short distance from the coast, some 25 per cent of the surface with slopes exceeding 45 per cent, and only 25 per cent reasonably level. In spite of these difficulties about one third of the island is under crops, but even this gives a density of 8 persons per hectare, far too little land to support the population without non-agricultural activities. Indeed, soils are generally poor anyway, but fishing, forests and mineral resources are even more meagre.

The population of Puerto Rico has increased fast in the first half of this century but the birth-rate as well as the death-rate has been declining since the late 1940s, and in addition there has been large-scale emigration to the United States, and between 1950 and 1960 the population increased only by 6 per cent, while many parts of the island, including the town of Mayagüez actually lost population. The number of Puerto Ricans in New York City rose from 63,000 in 1940 to 750,000 in the early 1960s, but by 1962 more Puerto Ricans were leaving the U.S.A. than arriving there. Demographic trends in Puerto Rico and particularly the slowing down of the increase of population are of great interest to other Latin American countries. It appears that as *per caput* income rose (doubling in the 1950s) and material conditions improved, the size of families began to diminish. Urban and rural attitudes to large families differ. At what level of income per inhabitant did the change begin to take place? Certainly it was at least several hundred dollars per head, a figure considerably higher than is found or could be expected in the near future in most parts of Latin America. Puerto Rico has achieved considerable material progress since 1940, partly through improvements in agriculture and partly through the development of industry and to a lesser extent tourism. Even now, however, most of its industries are concerned with the processing of raw materials, but the kind of industry wanted is branches that employ a large labour force such as light engineering, for the exceptionally high unemployment rate of 16 per cent in the early 1950s had only diminished to about 10 per cent in the 1960s. Moreover, much of the industry is concentrated in the capital San Juan, where there are oil refineries, and in smaller places nearby. In addition, Puerto Rico has only a small home market and although it is compact, on busy sea routes, and associated with the United States, it lacks the resources of more extensive countries on the Latin American mainland which are roughly comparable in population (e.g. Nicaragua, Paraguay). For various reasons, therefore, Puerto Rico may not be a good model on which to base development plans for other countries.

15.7. JAMAICA[14]

Like Puerto Rico, Jamaica has been closely associated with a large industrial country in the present century and its problems of development have been similar in some ways. In the 1950s population was increasing more rapidly than in Puerto Rico with a natural increase of about 3 per cent per year, but this has been offset by emigration to the United Kingdom, which during the period 1954–63 totalled about 180,000 (reaching a peak of 39,000 in 1961 but dropping to only 7,000 in 1963 following restrictions on immigration) and involving more than 10 per cent of the total population, which in 1963 had reached 1·7 m. Since the early 1950s however, conditions have improved in the island and in 1963, 4,000 emigrants returned. Employment in agriculture has diminished sharply, dropping from about 260,000 in 1954 to 165,000 in 1961 (with farm population diminishing from 900,000 to 740,000), and agriculture now only accounts for about 13 per cent of the gross domestic product. Improvements have been due to the growth of bauxite mining and the establishment of two plants to process this into alumina, but in 1963 fewer than 6,000 people altogether were employed by the mining companies,

317

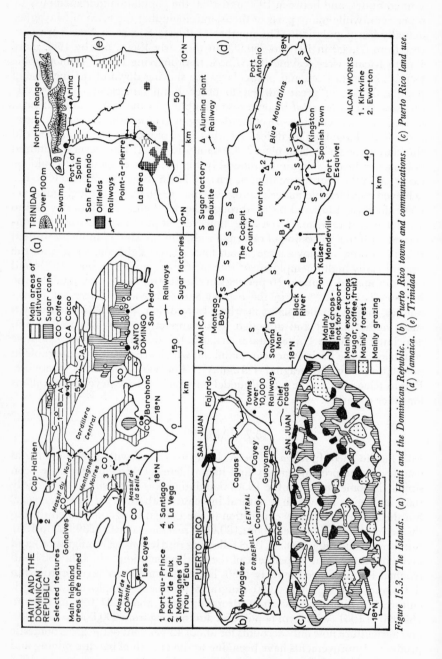

Figure 15.3. The Islands. (a) Haiti and the Dominican Republic. (b) Puerto Rico towns and communications. (c) Puerto Rico land use. (d) Jamaica. (e) Trinidad

318

although they received wages averaging some U.S. $ 2,000 per head, which is very much higher than the wage of an agricultural worker.

The economy of Jamaica is much more diversified than in the interwar period but attempts are being made to raise agricultural production, which still provides about half of the value of exports. The island grows nearly 80 per cent of the food it requires and the value of agricultural products exported is twice as great as the value of food imports. Land tenure in Jamaica is characterized by very large estates and very small farms; over 70 per cent of the farms are less than 2 hectares in area; under a land reform programme in the early 1960s, several thousand four-hectare family farms were being created. Altogether the sugar industry employs 80–90,000 persons, over a third of these working on 18 large estates; small cane farmers still produce about half of the harvest however. Output of raw sugar has risen from 375,000 tons in 1959 to 478,000 in 1963 and it is hoped to reach 600,000 by 1966; some 80 per cent of the crop is exported, and the U.K. and North America are the principal importers. Other crops contributing to exports include bananas (about 12 m. stems per year) almost all of which go to the U.K., citrus fruits, coffee, and cocoa beans.

During the Second World War the bauxite reserves of Jamaica were seriously assessed and large surface deposits with 50 per cent aluminium content were discovered. Reserves are estimated at 500–600 m. tons and production in the late 1950s reached 5–6 m. tons while the 1963 figure was 7 m. Several large North American Companies operate in Jamaica, including Alcan, which started in 1942, completed Port Esquivel in 1954, and now has two alumina plants, Kirkvine (capacity $\frac{1}{2}$ m. tons per year) and Ewarton ($\frac{1}{4}$ m.). The other companies, which include the Kaiser Bauxite Co. and Alcoa Minerals, which began in 1963, ship the bauxite directly overseas. Gypsum, the output of which is declining, is the only other commercial mineral of note.

Since the early 1950s, Jamaica has made great efforts to attract manufacturing industry. In addition to sugar refining and bauxite processing it produces textiles, clothing, soap, porcelain and cement, and even exports clothing. Esso West Indies Oil Refinery near Kingston was opened in 1964 and the capacity of this will be large enough to provide a surplus of products either for export or to be the basis of a petrochemicals plant. One drawback is the small size of the home market.

With the expansion, then, of sugar production, bauxite exports and tourism in the 1950s and large scale emigration to the U.K., prospects at that time seemed bright. Now, however, there is new apprehension about population pressure as people return from the U.K., tourism stagnates, and rival producers (Dominican Republic, West African countries) threaten Jamaica's large share of world bauxite exports. Exports in 1963 according to percentage of value were:

Bauxite and alumina	42
Sugar and products	33·5
Bananas	7
Other tropical crops	8

Fortunately, traditional connections with the U.K. and Canada are strong, although since independence in 1962, the share of the U.K. in Jamaican trade has diminished.

15.8. TRINIDAD AND OTHER ISLANDS

These interesting and varied small island regions will only be discussed briefly here in view of their small size. Trinidad[15], with a population of about 875,000, is the largest in size and population. It is extremely cosmopolitan, with about 40 per cent each of negroes and South Asians (brought in from the 1830s to 1917) and small numbers of Chinese, Syrians, Spaniards, French and British. As in Jamaica, sugar is the principal agricultural export but the quantity produced is much smaller and Trinidad depends much more than Jamaica on minerals, of which asphalt, extracted from La Brea lake, is world famous. The oil industry, which employs some 18,000 people altogether and accounts for up to 85 per cent of the exports and 30 per cent of gross domestic product, is the chief reason for the relative prosperity of the island. Almost 7 m. tons were produced in 1963 and in addition almost as much again is imported, mainly from Venezuela, to be refined in the Texaco refinery at Point-à-Pierre and in two smaller refineries. Exploration for oil in Trinidad continues and new developments are taking place offshore (e.g. Soldado oilfield). Like Jamaica, Trinidad has an Industrial Development Corporation that has attempted to attract light manufacturing; there are industrial estates at Port of Spain, Arima and Point-à-Pierre, where, also, is one of the largest petrochemicals plants in Latin America.

The small islands of the British West Indies[16], with a total population of several hundred thousand and in some cases an extremely high density of population, differ greatly among themselves in relief features. The negro element is much greater than in Trinidad, one reason why Trinidad was reluctant to support the larger Federation of the British West Indian possessions. The islands depend mainly on the export of sugar and bananas, have little to exchange among themselves and virtually no resources to enable them to diversify their economies. If they fail to do so, however, very serious pressure of population is expected in the 1980s or 1990s.

The two principal French possessions in the West Indies, Guadeloupe[17] and Martinique have similar problems. Both have volcanic peaks exceeding 1,400 m, but part of Guadeloupe is low lying. The population is mainly negro and the economy has been geared to sugar cultivation, particularly in Guadeloupe, while Martinique has recently diversified its agriculture, turning to bananas and pineapples. The total population exceeds 500,000, and food has to be imported to compensate for the exports of agricultural products. Much of the trade is with France.

The tiny Netherlands Antilles are of little use agriculturally but thanks to their position have achieved economic distinction far greater than their size merits by having two of the largest oil refineries in the world (see Table 15.5), established by Lago (Esso subsidiary) on Aruba and Royal Dutch Shell on Curaçao, processing crude oil from Venezuela. The greatest single problem is lack of fresh water and now altogether 12 m. gallons (about 60,000 tons) are distilled each day from sea water.

15.9. THE GUIANAS[18]

The present form of the three colonial territories comprising the Guianas was agreed on after the Napoleonic Wars, but Holland, England and France all had interests in the area by the early seventeenth century. In spite of their relatively close proximity to Europe (see *Figure 4.4*), their difficult conditions, lack of obvious resources and small Indian population made them less attractive to the Spaniards and Portuguese than other parts of Latin America. What is more they lay in a no-mans-land between the Orinoco

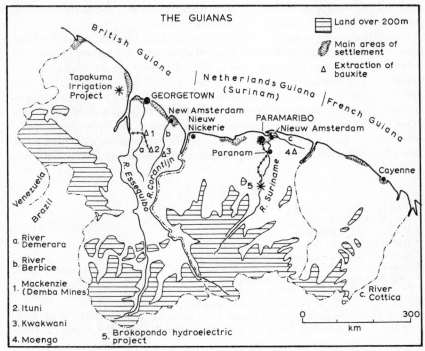

Figure 15.4. The Guianas

basin, controlled, if only loosely, by the Spaniards, and the Amazon, penetrated by the Portuguese.

Most of the area consists of the crystalline massif of the Guianas, with features similar to those in Southeast Brazil, but if anything more rugged conditions still. A cover of tropical rain forest on steep slopes in an area with a very heavy rainfall is perhaps the most difficult environment of all to develop in the tropics. Nevertheless, the Guianas have large timber reserves, a considerable hydroelectric potential and, in addition to bauxite, iron ore, gold and diamonds already located, may, like adjoining parts of Venezuela and Brazil, have various other metals. A narrow coastal plain extending almost the whole length of the coast is the only place where cultivation is seriously practised, but even here conditions are marshy and drainage has been necessary. Rice is the principal cereal crop cultivated, while in British

Guiana, sugar is grown for export. In the British and Netherlands Guianas less than 1 per cent of the land is cultivated, while in French Guiana, the proportion is a mere 1/3,000.

Bauxite has been exported from both British and Netherlands Guiana since the First World War, with a great increase during and since the Second (see *Figure 8.5*). As in Jamaica, the Canadian company Alcan operates in British Guiana, the main area of extraction being near Mackenzie on the Demerara river. The whole bauxite industry only employs some 3,000 persons, however, or about 2 per cent of the labour force in the colony. Trade is mainly with Canada (bauxite) or the U.K. (sugar). In Surinam the main mining company is the U.S. firm Alcoa, but a new Netherlands Company is now also operating on the Suriname River.

Population is very much concentrated in the three capitals, which together have about one third of the total population. A very varied population makes racial troubles a danger, and in 1964 there was great unrest in British Guiana. Independence is now seriously considered, especially for the British colony, but even as a union the three Guianas are too small in population and too narrowly specialized economically to form a viable sovereign State. Yet their size and resources make them potentially more useful economically than the tiny West Indian islands and some see their future role as a place for resettlement of surplus population from the Caribbean area.

REFERENCES

[1] *UNSY*, 1962, Table 146
[2] *UNSY*, 1955 and 1963
[3] *UNSY*, 1962, Table 125
[4] *World Petroleum*, April 1963, pp. 40–43
[5] *Petroleum Information Bureau*, 1964
[6] Street, J. M. *Historical and Economic Geography of the Southwest Peninsula of Haiti*, 1960 Berkeley; Univ. of California
[7] *U.N. Mission to Haiti*, p. 102, 1949; New York
[8] *U.N. Mission to Haiti*, pp. 38, 60, 1949; New York
[9] Dyer, D. R. 'Sugar Regions of Cuba', *Econ. Geogr.* 32 (1956) 177–84; Crist, R. E. 'Some Notes on Recent Trends in Rice Production in Cuba' *Econ. Geogr.* 32 (1956) 126–131
[10] *BOLSA (QR)*, April 1964, pp. 82–3
[11] Augelli, J. P, 'The Dominican Republic' *Focus*, Vol. X, No. 6, Feb. 1960
[12] Dyer, D. 'Distribution of Population in Hispaniola', *Econ. Geogr.* 30 (1954) 337–346; Augelli, J. P. 'Agricultural Colonization in the Dominican Republic, *Econ. Geogr.* 38 (1962) 15–27
[13] Augelli, J. P. 'Sugar Cane and Tobacco: A Comparison of Agricultural Types in the Highlands of Eastern Puerto Rico; *Econ. Geogr.* 29 (1953) 63–73
[14] *Economic Survey Jamaica*, 1963, Government of Jamaica, 1964
[15] Dyson, A. 'Land Use in the Maracas—St. Joseph Basin, Trinidad in Geographers,' and the Tropics: Liverpool Essays (Eds. Steel and Prothero) 1964; London. Augelli, J. P. and Taylor, H. W. 'Pace and Population Patterns in Trinidad'. *A.A.A.G.* June 1960, pp. 123–138
[16] Augelli, J. P. 'Patterns and Problems of Land Tenure in the Lesser Antilles: Antigua, B.W.I., *Econ. Geogr.* 29 (1953) 362–367
[17] Hoy, D. R. 'Changing Agricultural Land Use on Guadeloupe, French West Indies,' *A.A.A.G.* Dec. 1962, pp. 441–454
[18] Lowenthal, D. 'Population Contrasts in the Guianas', *Geogr. Rev.* Vol. L (1960) 41–58

CHAPTER 16

BRAZIL

16.1 INTRODUCTION

Physically, Brazil consists of a particular combination of several of the ingredients commonly found in Latin American countries, but it differs basically in at least two main respects: it is much larger than any other, being roughly comparable in size with China, Canada, the U.S.A. and Australia but about three times as large as Argentina; and it was colonized by the Portuguese, not the Spaniards. Like the Islands but unlike almost all the other mainland countries of Latin America it has a large concentration of negroes. Like Argentina, however, the European element is also large, while the Indians, who numbered about 3 m. before the colonial period, are now mixed with the other elements or survive intact only in small numbers in the Amazon region.

Almost all of the population of Brazil lives in a continuous belt of country about 4,000 km long and a few hundred kilometres wide extending from the northeast to the extreme south; density of population in this belt tends to diminish away from the coast. Throughout colonial and modern Brazilian history there has been a tendency for population to spread towards the interior, and the movement continues, receiving the encouragement of the Brazilian government. This shift towards the interior is not the only direction of movement of population, but has long been the main one, and contrasts with the tendency noted in Mexico and in Central American and Andean countries, for population to tend to move from high altitudes to lowland areas, often away from the interior towards the coast (e.g. in parts of Mexico, in Ecuador, Peru). Indeed, although substantial areas of Brazil may be defined as highland, especially near the southeast coast, few people live above about 1,000 m and movement of population between appreciably different altitudes therefore involves very small numbers. Nor does Brazil have any large, extremely dry areas; the Northeast suffers at irregular intervals from dry years, but the area so affected is only a few per cent of the total area of Brazil. Droughts do also occur widely from time to time elsewhere.

Brazil is often referred to as a land of enormous potential resources. Perhaps it is too soon to say whether this is true or not, but at least some reservations should be made. In spite of having climatic conditions that appear to favour agriculture, fertile soils are of limited occurrence and in general soils lose their fertility easily. Nor is the present mineral production of Brazil as large as is often suggested. Certainly the country has very large reserves of iron ore, but coal reserves are small and inaccessible and there are greatly differing views about the possibility of finding oil and gas, proved reserves of which are very limited at present. At all events, all other things

323

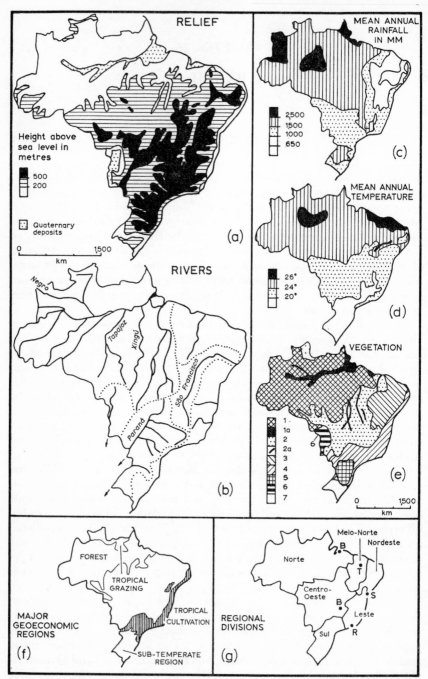

Figure 16.1. Brazil. (a) Relief. (b) Rivers. (c) Mean annual rainfall in millimetres. (d) Mean annual temperature. (e) Vegetation. (f) Major geoeconomic regions. (g) Regional divisions. Vegetation types in (e) are 1, 1a Tropical rain forest (1a in flood plain) 2, 2a Savanna (2a gallery forest), 3 Caatingas (thorn forest), 4 Tropical rain forest of east coast, 5 Sub-tropical forest with pines, 6 Pantanal complex, 7 Grassland

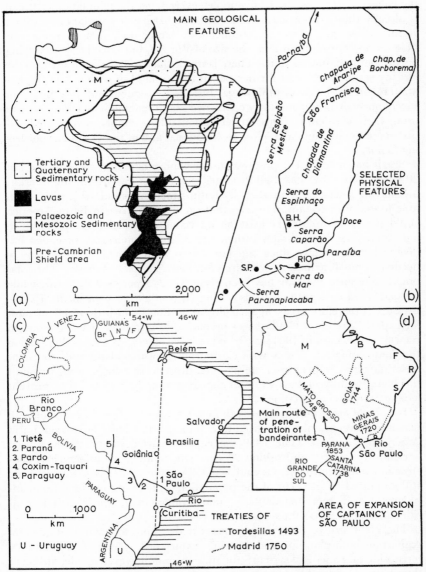

Figure 16.2. Brazil. (a) Main geological features. (b) Selected physical features. (c) Colonial period treaties. (d) Expansion of São Paulo Captaincy

being equal, the larger a country, the larger its resources may be expected to be, and there seems some justification in assuming that because of its sheer size Brazil can anticipate further resources somewhere in the empty interior. To develop the interior and integrate it into the economic life of the country, great distances have to be covered, yet the population of Brazil is already thinly dispersed over a vast area. It has a population of about 70 m. with a gross domestic product little larger than that of Sweden or Belgium in control of an area the size of Europe, but effectively occupying only about one quarter of it. There is much slack to be taken up within the already settled area, and further penetration inland of such a small population might not be wise at this stage. But the Portuguese and their Brazilian successors have been constantly concerned about making it look as if they are using their vast land. This anxiety about filling empty spaces is also a preoccupation of Australia, close to Indonesia, and of the U.S.S.R., bordering China.

Brazil has made great progress in developing manufacturing in the last 20 years, a fact that has itself attracted population away from the interior, and having such a large market (by Latin American standards), it has been able to establish certain industries that smaller countries in Latin America could not contemplate, at least on an economic basis. But progress in agriculture has been disappointing, the relative importance of coffee has declined dramatically since the late 1950s, and something is obviously needed to put Brazilian agriculture on a more satisfactory basis. The total population since the war has been rising by 2–3 per cent per year, while *per caput* food consumption is also rising (it rose 20 per cent in the 1950s). Pressure is therefore great on agricultural products and little is left of most for export. President Goulart was preparing to introduce massive agrarian reforms in 1963 but in 1964 was forced to leave office. As well as threatening the landowning aristocracy with expropriation of their land and (to them) unsatisfactory compensation, he planned drastic tax reforms aimed against the more wealthy classes, while at the same time he had failed to prevent a dangerous level of inflation.

In spite of great industrial growth in the Southeast, Brazil as a whole still depends more heavily on agriculture than do the most advanced Latin American countries. The 1959 makeup of gross domestic product was: agriculture, forestry and fishing 27 per cent, mining, manufacturing, construction and electricity, gas and water 25 per cent. In 1950 agriculture still employed 58 per cent of the population. There is considerable unemployment and, more particularly, underemployment, and Brazil is considered to need 800,000 new jobs each year.

The great size of the country makes it desirable to have a number of regions for both planning and descriptive purposes. There are 24 states or territories, and a federal system; the states cannot however secede, although they have considerable autonomy, and the state governors are influential persons. *Figure 16.1g* shows one set of six major regions commonly used in certain Brazilian publications*. For the purposes of description in this book and this chapter in particular, the regions shown in *Figure 16.10c* are used. Thus unless otherwise indicated, the Northeast refers to all states from

* For further material on regions in Brazil see Serebrenick and Rizzini[1].

326

Maranhão round to Bahia; the Southeast to those from Minais Gerais to Paraná; the South, the two most southerly; and the Interior to Goiás and Mato Grosso. Southern Brazil refers more loosely to all Brazil south of about Belo Horizonte. *Figure 16.1f* represents in very simple terms the major economic regions of Brazil and is a useful introduction. Special regions have also been devised for planning and other purposes; for example the dry poligon (*polígono das sêcas*) and São Francisco valleys in the Northeast, the Amazon region and the Paraná-Uruguay basin.

16.2. POPULATION

The total area of Brazil is about 8,512,000 km^2, and its population in the early 1960s already exceeded 70 m. The actual figure for the 1960 census was 70,799,000, but since there was an increase of only 10 m. between 1940 and 1950 and 19 m. between 1950 and 1960 it would seem that the 1960 census has been more complete than its predecessors and that to have a true picture earlier census figures should be increased by a progressively larger amount the farther back they were collected. Nor should it be overlooked that the 1960 census might not be complete. A mid-year estimate for 1964 was 79 m.

The main features of the present distribution of population of Brazil are shown in *Figure 16.4*. Almost 50 per cent of the total population is in the Southeast, in an area covering little over 10 per cent of the national area (Minas Gerais–Espirito Santo–Rio de Janeiro–Guanabara–São Paulo–Paraná). About another 25 per cent is in part of the Northeast, in less than 10 per cent of the total area (Ceará–Rio Grande do Norte–Paraíba–Pernambuco–Alagoas–Sergipe–part of Bahia). Other features of distribution will be evident from the maps and will be referred to elsewhere in the chapter.

Even in Latin America, with its rapidly growing population, the growth of the population of Brazil has been spectacular. The unreliability of figures make the following only an approximate picture of growth, but the implications are terrifying[2]:

		Population passed	Period over which 10 m. increase took place
Actual	1872	10 m.	
	1905	20 m.	33 years
	1925	30 m.	20
	1939	40 m.	14
	1950	50 m.	11
	1956	60 m.	6
	1960	70 m.	4
Expected	1965	80 m.	5
	1969	90 m.	4
	1973	100 m.	4
	1976	110 m.	3
	1979	120 m.	3

As in the U.S.A., modern immigration has made a considerable contribution to population growth, but the numbers involved in the last hundred years are only about 5 m. in Brazil compared with about 35 m.

TROPICAL RAIN FOREST IN THE BRAZILIAN AMAZON REGION

TROPICAL RAIN FOREST BEING CLEARED FOR CULTIVATION

DRY FOREST (*CAATINGA*), NORTHEAST BRAZIL

CARNAÚBA PALM,
NORTHEAST BRAZIL

ARAUCÁRIA PINE, SOUTHERN BRAZIL

in the U.S.A.[3]. Nevertheless, the economic and cultural life of southern Brazil has been transformed by the modern immigrants. A small number of Swiss settled in Brazil as early as 1818 (Nova Friburgo near Rio) and some Germans in 1824 (Rio Grande do Sul) but the main reason for the great influx was the demand for labour in the rapidly expanding coffee plantations from about 1870 and the decline of the slave trade (officially after 1850). Between 1884 and 1941 the following numbers were involved (in thousands):

Italians	1,413	Japanese	189
Portuguese	1,222	Various	
		Slavs	180
Spaniards	582	Germans	172

Small numbers of Turks and Syrians also came. In some years there were as many as 150,000 arrivals. The Portuguese have had freest access but any Europeans have been encouraged. Since the Second World War only limited immigration has occurred and in 1960, for example, there were 41,000 arrivals, half from Iberia; 65 per cent went to São Paulo state and 27 per cent to Rio.

The makeup of population in Brazil has therefore changed profoundly in the last hundred years. Around 1860 the three main elements were the Indians, the Portuguese, and the Africans, of which it has been estimated that between 4 m. and 12 m. were introduced as slaves between about 1550 and 1850; slavery itself, as opposed to the slave trade, was actually abolished in Brazil only in 1888. Slaves were derived mainly from two great African cultural groups, the Sudanese (not restricted to the present Sudan) and the Bantus; the former were moved particularly to Bahia, the latter to Pernambuco and Rio.

Currently the population of Brazil consists officially of some 60 per cent white (*branco*), 30 per cent mixed (mestiço—mainly African and European), a few per cent negro (*prêto*) and a few per cent Indian. *Caboclo* is a term loosely used for peasants mainly of mixed Portuguese and Indian origin. The whole classification is largely fictitious; the aim appears eventually to have an 'all-white' population. Although pure Europeans exist in Southern Brazil, virually pure Africans in parts of the north, particularly Maranhão, and pure Indians over large areas of the Amazon, most Brazilians are mixed, and incredibly complicated schemes for classifying different combinations exist locally*. 'Assimilation' is the final aim, but for differing reasons the Germans, Japanese, Africans and Indians have been integrated only gradually in recent decades, and the negroes, in particular, tend to remain a class apart in most regions, but reach all levels of society in some parts, particularly Bahia. In addition to terms related to 'racial' features, many interesting regional types exist in the Brazilian mind; for example, the cowboys of different regions—the *vaqueiros* of the Northeast, with a strong Indian element, the *boiadeiros* of the centre, and the *gauchos* of the extreme south.

Urbanization has been rapid in Brazil in recent decades, but as a whole the country is somewhat less highly urbanized than most of Latin America.

* See, for example, Hutchinson[4], especially Chapter 6, Class and Race.

About 40 per cent of the total population is urban, and about half of this is contained in the six largest urban concentrations alone (see Table 16.5). Towns continue to attract population as industry and services expand and as the superior cultural and material standards of the larger ones become appreciated among the rural population. Since the largest towns are almost all on or near the coast (see *Figure 16.4*), urbanization in total means in reality a general tendency for population to move away from the interior towards the coast. At the same time the old pull of the interior still exerts its influence and in places there is a still thinly populated but rapidly filling fringe. The treaty of Tordesillas in 1493–94 gave Brazil an area of approximately 2,600,000 km^2, less than one third of its present area (see *Figure 16.2c*), but Portuguese penetration beyond this line, associated with the search for Indian labour and minerals (*bandeirismo*), the spread of livestock farming and the activity of missions, forced Spain in the eighteenth century to recognize the Portuguese occupation of a much greater area. The principal line of penetration was along the valleys of the following rivers: Tietê–Paraná–Pardo–Coxim–Taquari–Paraguay (see *Figure 16.2c* and *d*). Since then the main areas of attraction have not been far from the coast; the mines of Minas Gerais, the coffee lands of the Southeast, the forests and grasslands of the extreme South and finally the modern industrial centres. Only the rubber boom of 1870–1910 drew many people into the remoter parts, but the twentieth century has seen the pushing forward of the fringe of settlement in Mato Grosso and Goiás, the establishment of special territories to encourage settlers to the political frontiers, and the movement of the national capital from Rio de Janeiro to Brasilia in 1960.

16.3. PHYSICAL BACKGROUND*

Brazil occupies the crystalline shield of eastern South America but this is buried along the valley of the Amazon by thick Tertiary and Quaternary sedimentary rocks, leaving to the north the Guiana highlands and to the south the Brazilian massif, with its covering in many places of older sedimentaries, not, however, of marine origin. *Figure 16.2a* shows the main geological features and *Figure 16.2b* names some major relief features. The highlands and uplands of the Brazilian shield are referred to very broadly as the Planalto Brasileiro, which is mainly between 300 and 1,000 m and rarely exceeds 1,000 m. Relief is to some extent related to solid geology, as where in places the basalt plateau of the south ends abruptly, or where some particularly resistant part of the shield remains as a scarp or isolated mountain. In spite of the widespread use of the term *serra* (= range), the 'ranges' of Brazil are not the result of folding, uplift and subsequent erosion, but are the relics of pediplanation and are often markedly asymmetrical. Such are many of the chapadas of the Northeast and the serras of the Southeast. Perhaps the most striking feature of the relief of Brazil is the so-called escarpment which lies close behind the coast over great distances in southern Brazil. It is irregular both in altitude and in distance from the coast but is responsible for bringing the watershed between the rivers of the Paraná

* See also Chapter 3.1.

basin and those draining direct to the Atlantic very near indeed to the sea.

Very rugged conditions are of limited extent in Brazil and much of the countryside consists rather of plateaux at various levels, separated by abrupt slopes. In some areas, isolated mountain massifs stand above extensive low plateaux. Only about 10 per cent of the country could be considered lowland, but even the largest area of this, in Amazonia, is mostly a very low plateau, in which the present flood plain of the Amazon is cut. Penetration from the coast towards the interior is nowhere so difficult as it is along the Pacific side of South America. The Amazon offers easy access to the interior and there are reasonably straightforward ways in from the Northeast. The most difficult conditions are behind Rio, while at São Paulo a climb of nearly 1,000 m has to be negotiated before the plateau is reached (see *Figure 3.13*).

By far the largest drainage basin is that of the Amazon (Amazonas). This basin occupies 56 per cent of the total area of Brazil or 4,750,000 km², but it extends outside Brazil to cover 6,500,000 km² altogether. The main stream is already only 80 m above sea level when still about 3,000 km from its mouth. The Paraná basin occupies about 10 per cent of the total area in the south of the country, the São Francisco only 7 per cent or 670,000 km². The Amazon has a complicated regime since it drains areas lying on both sides of the Equator and also derives much of its water from the Andes. South of the Amazon, January to March is the season in which most of the rivers are at their full flow.

Figure 16.1c and *d* show mean annual precipitation and temperature. The northwest of Brazil is defined as super-humid, having heavy annual rainfall, with over 1,900 mm, and rain at all seasons. The eastern part of the Amazon basin is similarly wet but has a marked dry season. A rainfall over 1,900 mm occurs locally also in places in southern Brazil, as along the coast of the Paraná and Santa Catarina, and behind Rio. A large part of Brazil receives between about 1,900 mm and 1,300 mm, and is classed as humid rather than super-humid. Almost throughout there is a marked dry season. The general area of the Northeast is considered to be semi-humid and receives under 1,300 mm. Within this area, the *sertão nordestino* and the middle São Francisco receive only 250–600 mm. The map of temperatures is self-explanatory, but it should be appreciated that in spite of high mean annual temperatures throughout the country, cold conditions occur in the southern part. Snow sometimes falls in the mountains of the south, while frosts have on several occasions devastated large areas of coffee plantation in Paraná and São Paulo states.

Figure 16.1e shows the main types of vegetation in Brazil according to *Atlas do Brasil*. The so-called floresta equatorial or Hileia (1, 1a in *Figure 16.1e*) occupies about 40 per cent of the total area of Brazil. Its main features have been noted in Chapter 3.4. Trees are 40–50 m high and lianes and epiphytes are widespread. In Brazil a distinction is drawn between forest on land above the flood plains (terra firme) and that subject to periodical flooding (*várzea*) or permanently submerged (*igapó*). The Amazon forests at present make little contribution to the economic life of the country, and the whole area is sometimes referred to as the *inferno verde*.

Second in extent is the *cerrado*, the savanna vegetation[5]. In Brazil the trees are generally no more than 3–6 m high while the herbaceous plants reach about 50 cm. There are considerable variations in the closeness of the tree cover and the nature of the grassland, and local conditions of soil and slope appear to have considerable influence. Along the main river valleys the tongues of forest stretch south from the Amazon forest lands. At present the cerrado lands of Brazil are devoted largely to extensive cattle raising.

The *caatingas* (also catingas) (3) consist of small trees and shrubs in a very hot environment with a moderate but very irregular rainfall. Many species are equipped to store water, while leaves are small and wax covered. Once rain has fallen, many plants are able to come to life quickly after long dry periods. Much of the caatingas is today poor grazing land and only limited areas have been brought into cultivation.

The *floresta tropical* (4) consists of a more humid coastal belt about 50–100 km wide with mainly evergreen species, like the Amazon forest, and behind this, mixed evergreen and deciduous forest, more open than along the coast. Most of the cultivated land in tropical Brazil has been cleared in this forest. South of the tropic is the so-called floresta subtropical of the uplands of the southern states. The widespread occurrence of the pine *Araucaria angustofolia*, has given this area the name of *pinheirais* (pine forests), the main source of timber in Brazil at present.

The *campos limpos* (7) (limpo = clear) of the extreme south are a grassland vegetation occurring on undulating lands and widely used now for both grazing and crop farming. The *Pantanal* (6) is characterized by its flat character and periodic inundations. It contains both forest and grassland and at present is used mainly for grazing. Finally, the coastal region has its own special types of vegetation associated with swamps, dunes, coral reefs and lagoons.

More than other parts of Latin America, Brazil has a number of plant species that occur wild or semi-wild (their spread sometimes being facilitated by deliberate clearance of vegetation in suitable areas) but yield products of particular interest and use. One of the earliest to be exploited was the *pau-brasil*—the Brazil wood (*Caesalpinia echinata*) occurring in the eastern forests and providing a dye. In recent decades the following have been widely exploited:

In the Amazon forests:	Hevea brasiliensis, natural rubber; Bertholletia excelsa, Brazil nut
In transitional and dry forests:	Orbigny speciosa, the babacu oil palm (*cocais de babaçu*) Copernicia cerifera, the carnaúba wax palm
In the southern forests:	Erva-maté, a kind of tea.

16.4. ECONOMIC DEVELOPMENT

The economic history of Brazil has been interpreted in terms of a number of cycles during each of which a particular product was exploited and formed the main item of export, after which it was largely abandoned (see *Figure 4.4d*). The exploitation of each product gave rise to a particular economic and social system. This is only part of the truth, for the cycles are not mutually exclusive but overlap and in certain cases have occurred roughly contemporaneously; nor have the more important ones died out completely. At the same time, the production of food crops and the raising of cattle have continued in the background throughout the fluctuations of the critical branches of the economy. The following cycles have been distinguished[6]. Firstly, the *pau brasil* tree was exploited in the sixteenth century. Secondly, sugar production for export to Europe began seriously around 1550, reached its climax in the seventeenth century and by 1700 had been eclipsed by the Caribbean area. Sugar has however been grown in the same areas ever since and appreciable quantities have been exported. Sugar cultivation in Pernambuco and Bahia was associated with a powerful rural aristocracy (the *senhor de engenho*, the mill proprietor) based on African slaves. The eighteenth century saw interest and political power shift from the Northeast to Minas Gerais as gold and precious stones were discovered here. The period of Mineração resulted in the rise of many new centres on the plateau of Minas Gerais, and minerals were sought much further west, far beyond the Tordesillas line. Again, there is some continuity in mining and metal working between the eighteenth and twentieth centuries, even if nearly 200 years separate the major discoveries of minerals from the finding of very large high grade iron ore deposits as well as other minerals in Minas Gerais. The nineteenth century saw the rapid expansion not only of coffee cultivation but also of cacao cultivation and the gathering of wild rubber. All have suffered their setbacks: cacao diseases and African competition, coffee frosts and overproduction, and wild rubber competition from Asian plantation rubber, but only the rubber cycle terminated abruptly and almost completely without trace. Some Brazilians have interpreted the great expansion of modern manufacturing as the beginning of a new cycle[7]. Certainly emphasis is at present on the development of heavy industry, the production of electricity, the search for oil and the improvement of transportation, rather than on improving agriculture.

In agriculture itself, according to one writer[8], Brazil has been going through a painful process of adaptation to a new outlook and way of organization. This transformation is the result of new technology and affects not only Brazil but many other Latin American countries. There are two philosophies: 'the old tradition that the land is a divine gift and on it man works to redeem himself of original sin; and the present view that wealth is derived from human effort converted into utilities (goods). It is evident that these two philosophies have different meanings for agriculture. In other words, there is a shift from intensive agriculture to extensive, because what is sought is the least human effort for the quantity of things produced rather than the largest quantity possible from each unit of land worked.' It is possible that industrialization, by creating new demands from the land and a new set of labour relations, and by feeding fertilizers and equipment back into agriculture, will facilitate this necessary change of attitude.

Although the deposition of President Goulart in 1964 will no doubt be followed by changes in planning policy, the main features of the 1963–65 development plan, devised in answer to the offers of the Alliance for Progress, may usefully be outlined here. 18 per cent of gross national product was to be reinvested, and national income raised by 7 per cent per year (but *per caput* national income only by about 4 per cent per year because of rapidly growing population). Two thirds of the funds were to come from private sources. The following proportions were to be invested in particular sectors (in per cent): transport 25, industry 16, electricity 13, oil 7, agriculture (only) 7. Among the principal projects to be completed were large iron and steel works in Minas Gerais (USIMINAS) and São Paulo (COSIPA) states, a very large new iron ore port at Vitória, the Furnas hydroelectric station, to supply São Paulo, and an extension of the Paulo Alfonso station in the Northeast.

An appreciation of the relatively backward state of Brazil at present is helped by a comparison with the U.S.A., which is roughly similar in size but now has three times as many people. Up to the end of the eighteenth century, Brazil sent a greater value of exports to Europe than did the English North American colonies, and in 1800 the two areas still had roughly the same number of people. Both areas had at this time plantations depending on slaves, and in a remote way the Northeast bears the same relationship to Brazil as the deep south does to the U.S.A. What has held Brazil back? The explanation seems to lie both in a less favourable endowment of resources (including agricultural land), and in a less favourable population make-up, with social and cultural conditions less conducive to economic advance on account of the much more limited influx of European settlers in the nineteenth century and early twentieth century. On the resource side Brazil has lacked coal, oil and natural gas as well as many metals used in the U.S.A. at some stage, even if imported there now, while it has not had any large area with uniformly good farm conditions like the Middle West. Brazilians are very optimistic about their future, however, and the title of one book, *Brasil, La Gran Potencia del Siglo XXI* (the great power of the twenty-first century)[9] suggests that there is no limit to prospects. G. Freyre[10] (see pp. 145–7) points out that the Europeans have failed to produce techniques needed to practise agriculture successfully in the tropics. He sees Brazil, to him the most advanced large country in the tropics, as the leader of a future tropical civilization '. . . some modern students of these (agricultural) and other problems concerned with the expansion of civilization think that a new science has to be developed to deal with these complex problems from a tropical point of view or angle complementary to, if not in place of, the European or boreal one, so far overdominant in science and technology.'

16.5. AGRICULTURE AND FISHING[11]

A recent figure for Brazil (1960) puts the total extent of arable land at about 26,200,000 hectares, or 3 per cent of the total national area, while about 13 per cent of the country is classed as permanent pasture and 61 per cent as forest. Several reasons may be suggested why no more land is actually cultivated. The population is small compared with the total area; often cultivation has exhausted the soil of an area and this has reverted to grazing; physical conditions are less favourable than might be expected, though many promising areas may lie beyond the present fringe of settlement. Although climatic conditions are generally favourable and slopes less of an obstacle than in most Latin American countries, soils are generally unsuitable for the continued arable cultivation of field crops. Soils on the ancient crystalline

335

rocks are low in fertility except locally, as for example where the gneisses in the Northeast give a soil known as *massape*, excellent for sugar growing. The older sedimentary rocks are generally poor, while the more recent ones of Amazonia consist widely of sandy soils from which the removal of the thin layer of humus after cultivation has locally in many places left the land virtually useless. Regionally the volcanic areas of southern Brazil give fertile soils known as *terra roxa* in São Paulo and are widely used for coffee cultivation. Locally, alluvial soils support rice cultivation and pastures. In the drier parts of the Northeast, improvements in farming depend on water supply, and many small reservoirs (*açudes*) are being constructed, especially in Ceará and Paraíba.

The following table summarizes the main crops grown in Brazil in 1960.

TABLE 16.1[12]

	Value (thousand million cruzerios)	Area (millions of hectares)	% of area
Coffee	77	4,4	17
Rice	52	3,0	11
Maize	49	7,0	27
Cotton lint	43	3,0	11
Beans (feijão)	40	2,5	10
Sugar cane	30	1,3	5
Manioc	24	1,3	5
Wheat	12	1,0	4
Bananas	11	n.a.	
Potatoes	10	n.a.	
Cacao	8	0,5	2
Citrus fruits	7	n.a.	
Tobacco	7	0,2	1

n.a. = not available.
Others (value): 4 sweet potatoes; 3 sisal, grapes, coconut, *babaçu*; 2 soybeans, *rubber*, *carnaúba*, *brazil nut*; 1 *erva-mate*, jute.

The five main wild or semi-natural plants (italics in Table 16.1) together were only equal on value to about 12 per cent of the coffee crop. Jute, soybeans, groundnuts (about 100,000 tons in 1961) and a number of other crops are relative newcomers. Wheat, potatoes and grapes are largely restricted to the sub-tropical southern area of Brazil. Sisal (agave) and cacao are localized in the dry Northeast and in the coastal tropical forest of Bahia respectively. The remaining major crops are widely grown within the general farming area of Brazil but each tends to prefer certain areas.

The volume of cereals produced in 1961/62 was[13]:

	Thousands of metric tons	
Maize	9,036	(1960/61)
Rice	5,300	
Wheat	545	

In 1962–63 only 300,000 tons of wheat were produced in Brazil, roughly 11 per cent of home consumption; 90 per cent came from Rio Grande do Sul. Rice is mostly grown in the southern half of Brazil; in the early 1960s, São Paulo contributed 25 per cent of the production, while most of the rest came from other parts of the Southeast, South or Interior. Even maize is not grown much in the Northeast whereas Minas Gerais and São Paulo each account for about 20 per cent. Manioc and bananas on the other hand are grown throughout the tropical agricultural lands. Cereal yields are low by world and even Latin American standards. For example, the 1963 maize crop of Brazil, 10,200,000 tons, gave only 1,350 kg per hectare compared with 4,000 kg in the U.S.A.

The cultivation of cane sugar was largely a monopoly of Northeast Brazil in the colonial period thanks to the proximity of this part of the country to Africa (for slaves) and Europe (for markets), but in the last hundred years sugar cultivation has spread to southern Brazil and in the early 1960s São Paulo state alone was producing 40 per cent of the national total, more than the whole of the Northeast, which only grew a third. Brazil now consumes nearly all its sugar production (1963–64 production 58 m. bags of which 52 m. were consumed at home) but it is hoped to raise output to 100 m. by 1970–71 thus increasing or at least maintaining exports. Cotton has also long been grown in Brazil but output has increased especially in the last few decades with the development of cotton textile manufacturing, while the precarious position of coffee exports, especially around 1930, led farmers to widen their range of interests, and many turned to cotton, which is now widely grown in the western part of São Paulo state, often on less fertile soils in the valleys below the coffee lands. In 1961–62, about two thirds (370,000 tons) of the cotton was grown in southern Brazil, only one third (180,000) in the Northeast, and São Paulo state accounts for about one third of the national total. The 1963 crop in southern Brazil (310,000 tons) suffered through unfavourable climatic conditions, but the crop in the Northeast was 200,000 tons. The annual plant *Gossypium herbaceum* is grown in the Southeast but the tree variety *Gossypium vitifolium* is grown in parts of the Northeast, and the quality of the lint in the dry Northeast is generally superior to that in southern Brazil.

The revolution in coffee growing in Brazil has been referred to in Chapter 7.6. In the early 1960s Brazil was still providing some 40 per cent of the world's coffee and was allowed that proportion of export quotas. By July 1963, about 350,000 hectares of coffee plantations, nearly 10 per cent of the national total, had been replaced by pasture, food crops and cotton. In the winter of 1963, widespread frost destroyed most of the coffee trees in Paraná and in 1964 Brazilian coffee stocks stood at a very low level.

Coffee came to Brazil from the Caribbean via French Guiana, was first grown in the Northeast, and reached Rio in 1774 where for a time it was a garden crop. The importance of coffee to the economy of Brazil can be gauged by its growing share of the value of exports in the nineteenth century: 1821, 16 per cent, 1852, 50 per cent, 1889, 67 per cent. The main area of production was at first the Paraíba valley, but subsequently cultivation has spread into and across São Paulo state almost to the River Paraná (see *Figure 7.4*), leaving the earlier areas mostly without traces of coffee trees, much of the land becoming poor pasture. The latest areas of development have been in the northern part of Paraná state and in southeast Minas Gerais. In the early 1960s, São Paulo was accounting for about 50 per cent of Brazilian coffee, Paraná 30 per cent, and Minas Gerais most of the rest.

337

In the search for fertile soils such as the terra roxa of the volcanic plateau, planters have moved into areas with unfavourable climatic conditions. As early as June 1918, some 400 m. trees were destroyed by frost. But such setbacks have not prevented Brazil from over-producing at certain periods in the last few decades, and in the 1930s, altogether 4 m. tons were burned.

In spite of its devastating influence on the land and its precarious position on world trade, coffee has had a far greater impact on the Brazilian economy than any other single product in the last hundred years. During this time it has accounted for most of the exports of Brazil, has helped to attract millions of key settlers from Europe, has necessitated the construction of a close rail network in the coffee lands, has allowed the accumulation of capital, and of urban population, which has virtually been forced to turn to manufacturing to maintain its existence*. The work of clearing, planting, tending and harvesting 3,000 m. trees and of processing the products has required a very large labour force, and as coffee declines, mechanization in farming increases and crops requiring less labour are replacing coffee, a further influx of population into São Paulo city and other urban centres may be expected.

Livestock farming in Brazil has tended to be relegated to more remote, less fertile areas away from the sugar and coffee plantations and other arable lands. The caatinga and cerrado lands of the Northeast and São Francisco valley provided leather and dried meat for the colonial plantations. Much of Minas Gerais and Rio Grande do Sul became grazing lands in the eighteenth century, and since then, Mato Grosso and Goiás have come to provide pastures for large herds. At the same time, the cultivation of fodder crops in areas of arable farming and the development of dairying near large towns have brought cattle more than previously into the coastal region. Altogether, then, cattle raising is found throughout the settled parts of Brazil and is one of the main means of colonizing new areas such as the west of Mato Grosso and the territory of Rio Branco. In 1960 the cattle population of Brazil was 74 m., larger than the human population, but almost all are still of inferior quality and some are still used for draught purposes. They were distributed as follows[15]:

The Northeast except Bahia	8 m.	Rio Grande do Sul	10 m.
Bahia	6 m.	Mato Grosso	10 m.
Minas Gerais	16 m.	Goiás	6 m.
São Paulo	10 m.		

Pigs and pountry are kept widely in association with arable farming, but sheep are largely confined to Rio Grande do Sul, which has over half the national total and produces nearly all the wool.

Fishing in Brazil is one of the least efficient of all branches of the economy. In 1961 a mere 280,000 tons were caught, but this gave employment, some of it presumably part time, to 234,000 workers, an output of little over 1 ton per person compared now with about 100 tons per person in Peru. Fish are one of the principal sources of protein in Amazonia and along the coasts of the Northeast, however, and for want of anything better, seem difficult to

* P. Mombieg concludes his work[14] with the view that in spite of its devastating effect on the land, coffee has given São Paulo state enormous economic strength for the future.

replace, yet the industry could not easily be made more efficient. In 1964, however, plans were announced to raise the catch to about 1 m. tons per year by 1970.

16.6. MINERALS AND ENERGY

The extraction of minerals makes only a very small contribution to the total value of production in Brazil. Very broadly it consists of two main types, that organized by large companies, national or foreign, to extract oil, manganese ore and iron ore, and that run by small enterprises or individuals who still search for gold and precious stones on the surface, a practice called *garimpagem*. The contrast in efficiency and value of output per worker is great. Figures for the relative importance (by value) of some Brazilian minerals are available[16] for 1960 (value in millions of cruzeiros)

Coal	2,765
Iron ore	1,444
Salt (marine)	900
Lead	600

There seems little likelihood that appreciable coal reserves will be discovered in Brazil. In the early 1960s about 2–3 m. tons was being mined each year, about 1 per cent of the U.K. production. The coal comes from small inefficient mines in Santa Catarina (Rio Tubarão) and Rio Grande do Sul (Arroio dos Ratos) and to some extent caters for the needs of the growing Brazilian iron and steel industry.

Oil and natural gas production have risen rapidly since the mid-1950s but opinions differ as to the probability of finding large reserves (see *Figure 8.2*). In the early 1960s U.S. experts were not hopeful, but Soviet geologists predicted large reserves in Amazonia, pointing out the resemblances of this area to Siberia[17], and they forecast self-sufficiency in oil by 1968. Oil has been discovered in Bahia (Recôncavo), Alagoas, the Parnaíba valley, the Tocantins valley, and at Nova Olinda (near Manaus), and exploration is starting at Lagôa dos Patos in Rio Grande do Sul. Most of the oil at present comes from the Recôncavo are of Bahia (AEB[18] gives for 1960; 60 per cent from Agua Grande, 15 per cent from Candeias and 12 per cent from Taquipe). Reserves here are put at between 3,000 m. and 12,000 m. barrels. Brazilian oil production was as follows in the early 1960s :

1961	4,549,000 tons
1962	4,324,000 tons
1963	5,000,000 tons

The State enterprise, Petrobras, has a monopoly on the extractive side and the government has also been contemplating the control of imports, refining and retail distribution.

A considerable number of metallic minerals are mined in commercial quantities in Brazil but until recently have made a negligible contribution to the economy of the country through being exported. Gold is still widely extracted, though in limited quantities; for example the Morro Velho near Nova Lima in the heart of Minas Gerais, established in 1831, continues to produce, and has one shaft reaching to a depth of over 2,500 m. Much more

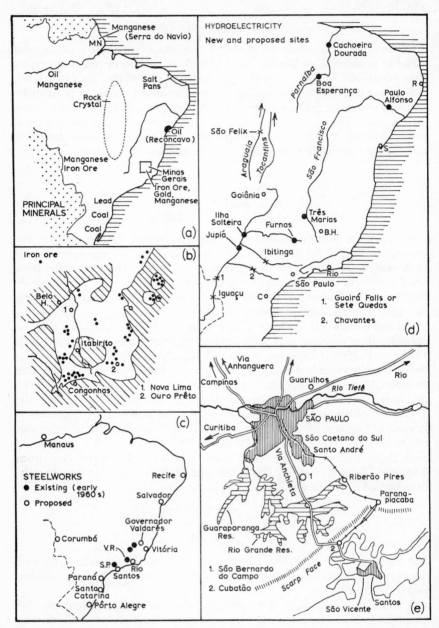

Figure 16.3. Brazil. (a) *Principal minerals.* (b) *Iron ore.* (c) *Steelworks.* (d) *Hydroelectricity* (e) *São Paulo area*

recently Brazil has become one of the world's leading producers of high grade iron ore (haematite), with 60–65 per cent iron content. Deposits are put in two different sources at 16,000 m. and at 35,000 m. tons in the Quadrilátero Central of Minas Gerais, southeast of Belo Horizonte (see *Figure 16.3b*). Total production has been as follows around 1960:

Year	Ore	Iron content
1958	5,200	3,526
1959	8,900	6,057
1960	9,300	6,355
1961	9,300	6,351

Most is produced for export and production has therefore been geared largely to foreign demand, while the improvement of facilities for moving the ore to the coast and for loading it has been necessary. A growing proportion of the ore is now being used in Brazil, and the lack of coking coal in the country is to some extent compensated for by the very high grade of the ore. Manganese ore is also mined in Minas Gerais and much is used in the iron and steel industry of this part of Brazil. The Companhia Vale do Rio Doce with its subsidiaries handles much of the export of ore, using the port of Vitória. In 1961 it exported 4,900,000 tons, in 1962, 6,040,000. The company is planning to establish the largest iron ore loading facilities in the world at Ponto do Tubarão (not to be confused with Tubarão in the south) near Vitória. Rio de Janeiro is also to export up to 10 m. tons of iron ore a year. Both iron ore and manganese ore have been found elsewhere in Brazil (see *Figure 16.3a*) and most of the growing exports of manganese ore are shipped from Macapá in Amapá territory, the ore coming from the Serra do Navio mines. Iron ore and manganese ore deposits exist also in Piauí and Ceará and in southern Mato Grosso, near Corumbá. Nickel reserves are found in Goiás (Niquelândia) and it is planned to use local hydroelectric power to smelt these. Lead is mined in limited quantities in the south, and in Bahia state, the latter producing two thirds of the total of 14,000 tons in 1963, and bauxite is available in Minas Gerais for the new aluminium industry. Most of the salt consumed in Brazil is produced in the saltpans of the dry northeast coast (Ceará and Rio Grande do Norte).

Short of both coal and oil, the Brazilian economy has suffered from the lack of home produced energy, but some consolation may be derived from the presence of a large hydroelectric potential, much of it conveniently situated in the southern part of the country. The energy balance of Brazil is made up at present roughly as follows in coal equivalent, using the following conversion of hydroelectric energy:

$$1000 \text{ m. kWh} = 0 \cdot 6 \text{ tons of coal}$$

Home produced $\begin{cases} \text{Coal} & 2\frac{1}{2} \text{ m.} \\ \text{Oil} & 7 \text{ m.} \\ \text{HEP} & 12 \text{ m.} \end{cases}$

Imported oil, coal   15 m.

Wood is also used as a fuel for heating, smelting and traction purposes.

341

At the end of 1962, out of a total installed generating capacity of 5,728,000 kW, 4,125,000 (72 per cent) was in hydroelectric power stations. Capacity was increasing impressively, as follows, in the early 1960s:

1961   5,2 m. kW

1962   5,7 m. kW

1963   6,5 m. kW

and it is planned to reach 20·4 m. by 1970. Output of electricity from thermal and hydro sources combined was in 1961, 24,000 m. kWh, and in 1962, 26,900 m. Public capacity has been gaining on private capacity.

Given the poor scope of coal reserves, the doubtful potential of oil reserves and the undesirability of importing large amounts of fuel, it is not surprising that Brazil has a very ambitious programme for developing its hydroelectric potential. The first sizable hydroelectric power station in South America was built near Juiz de Fora. In the 1930s some impressive works were completed near São Paulo; most ingenious was the damming of headwaters of of the River Tietê on the edge of the plateau south of São Paulo and the diversion of water from these over the plateau edge to the Cubatão and other power stations some 700 m below (see *Figure 16.3e*). Although work is only now beginning on several large stations and others are only projected it is important to note the main projects of the late 1950s and 1960s. The potential is shared out roughly as follows[19] by basins (in per cent)

Amazon   33   Eastern rivers   18

Paraná   32   São Francisco   10

Northeast only   1·5

TABLE 16.2

Major Power Stations

River	Locality	kW capacity	Completion
Rio Grande	Furnas (Minas G.)	150,000 eventually 1 m.	1963 1964
Rio Grande	Urubupunga	3 m.	1969
Tietê	Ibitinga	140,000	
Paranapanema	Chavantes	400,000	1966
Paraná	Ilha Solteira	3 m.	
Paraná	Jupia (Tres Lagoas)	1,2 m.	under construction 1963
Paraná	Sete Quedas Iguaçu	10 m.	
São Francisco	Tres Marias		start 1964
São Francisco	Paulo Alfonso	Enlarging	1963
Parnaíba	Cariri (Ceará) Boa Esperança Cachoeira Dourada		
Araguaia	San Félix		
Thermal at Santa Cruz, Guanabara		150,000	

The main plants being constructed or expanded in the early 1960s are already at considerable distances from the large industrial centres of the

Southeast. From the Furnas plant to São Paulo, for example, the transmission distance is 316 km; the line is to pass via Poços de Caldas (Minas Gerais) to serve the new aluminium works there, which will require a 100,000 kW capacity. The Tres Marias station will serve the mining and industrial areas of Minas Gerais. The sites with the greatest potential of all in southern Brazil are further away still, on the Paraná itself. Among these is the Sete Quedas site, the potential capacity of which is some 10 m. kW, about twice the total generating capacity of *all* power stations in Brazil in 1960, and four times the capacity of the giant power stations at Kuybyshev and Volgograd in the U.S.S.R. It would involve Paraguay and would generate roughly as much as 20–25 m. tons of coal, but would cost U.S. $ 1,000 m. In spite of its limited potential, the Northeast is to have some moderate sized hydroelectric power stations in addition to the Paulo Alfonso plant already completed. The Parnaíba, which separates the states of Maranhão and Piauí, is the most promising river in the area and a station with a capacity of 210,000 kW is to be completed by 1966.

Although still working largely on imported oil, the oil refineries of Brazil might be considered the second main source of energy in the country. Their combined output in 1963 was 15,053,000 tons and the following were the main plants:

Place	State	Output 1963 in thousands of tons
Cubatão	São Paulo	5,500
Rio de Janeiro		4,500
Mataripe	Bahia	2,340
Capuava		1,450
Rio Grande	Rio Grande do Sul	460
Manguinhos	Rio	450
Manaus	Amazonas	250

It appears to be the ambition of several other states to have at least one oil refinery, and as new ones are being completed, the oil refining capacity of Brazil is becoming very dispersed. Medium refineries (45,000 barrels per day—roughly 15 m. barrels per year) are due for completion soon in Pôrto Alegre and Belo Horizonte, the latter served by a pipeline from Rio de Janeiro.

16.7. MANUFACTURING

The relative importance of the various main branches of industry in Brazil can be gauged roughly by the value of production in each in 1958[20]. (*See Table 16.3.*) It would be wrong to draw very precise conclusions from these figures and in particular from the apparent low output of textile workers. All branches contain a large number of persons employed in small, inefficient establishments, while the servicing of machinery inflates the engineering industry. The *Brazilian News*[21], puts the number employed in manufacturing in Brazil at 3 m., in 150,000 factories.

The overwhelming importance of the Southeast of Brazil in manufacturing may be judged from the fact that about one half of all persons employed are in the urban areas of São Paulo and Rio (Guanabara). Modest concentrations of manufacturing population occur in and around Recife, Belo Horizonte and Pôrto Alegre, but much of the remainder is in the general area of eastern São Paulo state and in Rio de Janeiro state (see *Figure 8.9a* and *Figure 16.5b*).

TABLE 16.3

Selected Main Branches of Industry

	Value (thousand million cruzerios)	% of value	Total number of persons employed in thousands	% of employment
Food, drink and tobacco	186	26	238	15
Textiles	99	14	335	21
Chemical and pharmaceutical	94	13	107	7
Engineering etc.	94	13	179	11
Metallurgical	77	11	164	10
TOTAL	724		1,581	

The iron and steel industry is rapidly becoming the basis of modern industralization in Brazil and its distribution will be considered first[21]. The principal ingredients are the iron ore and manganese of Minas Gerais, coal from the South and from abroad, and electricity, and the main market is Southeast Brazil. Steel production (thousands of tons) has risen in recent years as shown below, but in 1962, 600,000 tons still had to be imported.

1958, 1,360   1961, 2,400
1959, 1,603   1962, 2,800
1960, 1,843   1963, 3,800

In 1960 Brazilian iron and steel output was distributed as follows[23]:

	Pig iron	%	Steel	%
Rio and Espírito Santo	887	51	1,081	59
Minas Gerais	747	43	587	32
São Paulo	100	6	175	9·5
Brazil	1,750	100	1,843	100

Clearly the industry has up to now been completely dominated by the triangle Rio–São Paulo–Belo Horizonte, but as the industry expands, new areas in Brazil are entering the picture. Until recently, about half has been produced by the works at Volta Redonda: 1,120,000 tons in 1961 and 1,150,000 in 1962, but by 1963 its contribution was only one third. A very large expansion programme (U.S. $ 150 m.) is underway here to extend the capacity at Volta Redonda to about 3,6 m. tons within the next few years. At this stage it is difficult to give a complete account of the rest of the industry but in view of its importance not only to Brazil but to the whole of LAFTA, the main works and projects may usefully be noted [24].

	Place	Approx. capacity early 1960s and proposed increase
1. Southeast, already producing		
Cia Siderurgica Nacional	Volta Redonda	1 m. tons (3½ m.)
Belgo-Mineira	Monlevade, Sabara	150,000
Mannesmann		120,000 (350,000)
2. Southeast, proposed		
Usiminas	Governador Valdares	1 m. (1965), 2 m. (1970)
Cosipa (opened 1963)	Piçagueira near Santos, São Paulo State	(400,000) (800,000)
Cosigua	Santa Cruz (Rio)	(500,000)
Ferro e Aço de Vitória	Vitória	130,000 (1963), 2 m. (1970)
3. Rest of Brazil, proposed		
Siderama	Manaus Amazonas	
	Recife Pernambuco	
	Salvador Bahia	
Usipar	Paraná	
Sidesc	Santa Catarina	100,000
Cia Piratini	Rio Grande do Sul	700,000
	Corumbá Mato Grosso	

By about 1930, Brazil was producing some 60,000 tons of steel, a very modest part of its requirements. Most came from Minas Gerais, and smelting was with charcoal. By an agreement with the U.S.A. in 1940 the Brazilian government established the Companhia Siderúrgica Nacional at Volta Redonda, and expansion here has been considerable but erratic up to about 1960. German, Belgian, Luxembourg, French and Japanese investors have all taken an interest in the Brazilian iron and steel industry, especially in Minas Gerais. In and around São Paulo there are also many small steel works (e.g. Barão de Cocais, Caete), while Rio itself is also soon to have a plant using ore from Minas. Fuel for smelting has been a problem in the industry and wood and electricity are both used, while the new works near Salvador (at Cambaçari or Aratu) is to use local gas and is expected to produce very cheap steel.

The engineering industry is even more recent than the steel industry, but this branch of manufacturing is now growing impressively and may soon become the leading single branch. The way in which engineering has been taking root in various Latin American countries was discussed in Chapter 8.9. Brazil has certain advantages not shared by most of the others: a well established iron and steel industry, some tradition in metal working, and a relatively large market, making reasonably large-scale production feasible even without dependence on exports. Industries that have grown up mainly in the last ten years include shipbuilding, the making of motor vehicles, tractors (beginning around 1960 and expected to produce 12,000 units in 1964), machine tools (some are exported), factory equipment (e.g. for cement works), ball bearings (e.g. SKF the Swedish firm, at Guarulhos, São Paulo), sewing machines (Singer at Campinas). Brazil is now building vessels up to 18,000 dwt and has a building programme of 16 vessels over 3½ years, including five cargo vessels for Mexico*. The early stages of the

* One of 10,500 tons, two of 7,250 each and two of 4,500.

motor vehicle industry illustrate the rapidity with which engineering has expanded. Vehicles produced to nearest thousand[25]:

Firm	1957	1958	1959	1960
Fábrica Nacional de Motores	3	4	2	3
Ford	6	11	17	19
General Motors	5	9	17	18
International			1	1
Mercedes-Benz	6	11	9	10
Simca			1	4
Vemag (and Scania-Vabis)	1	5	7	10
Volkswagen		6	17	28
Willys	9	16	24	39
TOTAL	31	61	96	133

No indication is given here of the types of vehicle (many were commercial) nor of the actual percentage of Brazilian parts, but this has been increasing. 1956 was the year in which production began (6,000 vehicles). More recent figures[26] have been: 1961, 73,000 passenger cars and 73,000 commercial vehicles manufactured or assembled, and 1962, 97,000 and 94,000. In 1963 the manufacture of motor vehicles was employing some 140,000 persons in 11 main factories and 1,300 small establishments making parts. The engineering industry of Brazil is concentrated almost entirely in and near São Paulo, but in 1964 it was planned to build a new assembly plant for Willys-Overland do Brasil in Recife.

Industries that have not expanded so rapidly in the post-war period are textiles and clothing, food processing, the manufacture of wood and leather and other branches more directly connected with products of the land and with the consumer market. Some of these also tend to be very much concentrated in the Southeast. The manufacture of textiles, for example, is largely confined to this part of the country but there are secondary areas such as the towns of the Northeast (Recife in particular), and of the South (Blumenau, Joinvile, Pôrto Alegre). Cement, too, is a fairly old industry, but has recently started to expand more quickly (thousands of tons):

$$
\begin{array}{ll}
1960 \ 4,420 & 1962 \ 5,040 \\
1961 \ 4,709 & 1963 \ 6,000
\end{array}
$$

São Paulo (29 per cent) and Minas (27 per cent) dominated production in 1962 but many other states had some production*.

One industry that has expanded in the post-war period has been chemicals and associated branches. The oil refineries have provided a new raw material, and associated branches. The oil refineries have provided a new raw material, and fertilizers, synthetic fibres, synthetic rubber and plastic materials are being made for the first time. Two places, Duque de Caixas (Rio), and Recife are to make synthetic rubber (capacity 50,000 tons and 25,000 tons per year respectively). Tyres and tubes are also nearly all home produced now, São Paulo having the main plant. Again, the production of

* See Ref.[27] for regional production.

artificial fibres is increasing, with output of cellulose rising from 105,000 tons in 1956 to 310,000 tons in 1962. Brazilian timber, including the southern pine and eucalypts, is used. The factories are distributed unevenly, as usual, with six of the thirteen in São Paulo, two in each of the three most southern states and one in Manaus.

From this brief survey of modern industry in Brazil the dominant position of the Southeast will have become clear. 1958 figures showed 55 per cent of the total value of production in São Paulo state, which only has 18 per cent of the population of Brazil, and 24 per cent in Guanabara, Rio state and Minas Gerais (which, however, also have 24 per cent of the population). If anything, the concentration in the Southeast would appear to have increased slightly since 1958, but the effects of decentralization may be felt soon as new industrial 'poles', based on oil refineries, hydroelectricity and regional steel works, are encouraged to develop. While it is obviously unsound to break up the São Paulo–Rio–Belo Horizonte complex, there seems no way of raising the level of the poorer parts of Brazil unless they can capture some of the new expansion. What is more, the Southeast is already subject to water and power shortages and its ports easily become congested. New electric potential is at a considerable distance, and transmission costs will rise; there is even talk of piping natural gas from the Santa Cruz area in Bolivia to São Paulo, a direct distance of about 1,800 km.

16.8. TRANSPORT

The cohesion of Brazil since the Portuguese first colonized the country has depended largely on water transport, with the main centres of the country served by shipping along the east facing coast, which continues almost in a straight line, the great circle line from Lisbon to Pernambuco, and the rivers serving either to penetrate the interior (Amazon particularly) or to supplement contact between the Northeast and Southern Brazil (São Francisco). The São Francisco, though now largely replaced by rail, road and air routes, is still thought of in Brazil as the 'river of national unity'. Shipping services link the coastal ports and penetrate far up the Amazon, but distances are enormous, the quantity of goods carried coastwise is limited, vessels are mostly small and antiquated, and the facilities of many ports inadequate. Under these conditions, water transport is neither particularly cheap nor quick.

The principal ports of Brazil are mapped in *Figure 6.1*. The total tonnage of goods handled in Brazilian ports (both coastal and foreign trade) has been rising (in millions of tons):

1958 41 m.   1960 44 m.   1962 48 m.
1959 42 m.   1961 47 m.

1960 figures for individual ports[28] were as follows (arranged in order of value of exports*).

* It is interesting to contrast the relative importance of Brazilian ports nearly a century ago with the situation now[29]: Of the total value of imports in 1869, Rio handled 54 per cent, Recife 16 per cent, Salvador 14 per cent, Belém 5 per cent, Santos little over 1 per cent.

Value in thousands of millions of cruzerios, volume in millions of tons.

TABLE 16.4

Foreign Trade of Brazilian Ports

	Value		Volume		Total volume of goods handled including coastal trade
	Exports	Imports	Exports	Imports	
Santos	46	110	1,3	7,3	12,4
Rio-Niteroi	19	58	1,3	4,6	11,0
Vitória	12	2	4,3	0,1	4,7
Salvador	11	3	0,8	0,2	1,0
Paranaguá	9	2	0,2	0,3	0,7
Recife	7	5	0,5	0,7	2,1
Angra dos Reis	5	0,3	0,1	negl.	0,5
Ilhéus	5	negl.	0,1	negl.	0,2
Fortaleza	5	1	0,1	0,2	n.a.
Macapá	5	0,5	0,7	negl.	n.a.
Cabedelo	3	0,3	0,1	0,1	0,3
Belém	3	1,5	0,4	0,2	0,9
All ports	147	201	10,6	15,6	n.a.

Rio de Janeiro (with Niterói), Angra dos Reis and Santos together account for about half of the value of Brazilian exports, but receive about 85 per cent of the value of imports. The principal ports are shown in *Figure 16.5f* and the products of their hinterlands indicated. Coastal trade is considerable in bulk but low in value and consists of salt, refined oil products, coal and various raw materials, all of which tend to converge on the Southeast. Pôrto Alegre and Rio Grande have little foreign trade but a large coastal trade.

International shipping lines are tending to use fewer and fewer ports, and those of the Northeast are often by-passed now. This is partly through inadequate facilities (e.g. Ilhéus) partly because there are few products for exports, and also a result of Brazilian policy to carry goods coastwise in its own ships. Even so, port improvements are planned not only at Santos (São Sebastião could be used as an alternative and is being developed as an oil terminal) and Vitória, but also at Paranaguá to the south, the principal outlet of Paraná state, and a possible outlet for Paraguay, at Ilhéus, Fortaleza (Mucuripe) and São Luis. The main oil terminals of Petrobras will be at Madre de Deus (Bahia), Guanabara, São Sebastião, Ilhéus and Tramandaí (Rio Grande do Sul).

The first railway in Brazil was started in 1845 between Mauá (Rio) and a point near Petrópolis*, but serious construction dates from the 1870s. The length of route in use given in years was as follows:

1880	3,400 km	1920	28,600
1890	10,000	1930	32,500
1900	15,300	1950	36,700
1910	21,500	1960	38,000

Considering the size of the country this length is small. In addition, much of the route is narrow gauge and single track. The underused nature of most

* Viscount Mauá was one of the people interested in improving communications at this time.

Brazilian railways has been criticized[30], and although few lines have been closed yet it seems only a matter of time before roads make many of the lines unnecessary. Behind Rio and São Paulo there is apparently a close network of lines, but it is not always possible to run through trains over considerable distances except towards ports. The incompleteness of the network in the Northeast is clear from *Figure 16.7*. Recently Brazil has however concentrated on improving certain lines, particularly those from the iron ore fields of Minas Gerais to Vitória via the Doce valley, to Rio and to Volta Redonda, and rail links are considered vital between Rio and Brasilia, and São Paulo and Brasilia (via Pires do Rio). By 1960, 2,500 km were electrified. The line south from São Paulo to Pelotas is also being improved, and the stretches Rio Negro–Ponte Alta–Lajes have been completed. A considerable amount of useful material is available on the railways of Brazil[31].

An early interregional road in Brazil linked Minas Gerais and Rio in the eighteenth century, and in 1861 a road (União e Industria) was constructed from Rio to Petrópolis and Juiz de Fora. Until after the Second World War, however, road transport played only a limited part in the Brazilian economy, thanks to the development of railways and coastal shipping. In 1960 there were 477,000 km of road used for traffic, of which 34,000 were federal roads, 83,000 state roads and the rest municipal. But of the federal roads, only 9,000 km were paved, and of the state roads, only 4,000. Obviously in view of climatic conditions, many of the roads are usually in a very poor state. The length of paved federal road was 11,000 km in 1962 and is to reach 20,000 in 1965. Early roads of the motor vehicle era in Brazil were the Via Anchieta linking São Paula and Santos, with a dual carriageway most of the distance, five tunnels and 31 viaducts, and the Via Anhanguera between São Paulo and Campinas.

Some of the principal interregional arteries of the late 1950s and early 1960s are mapped in *Figure 16.10*.

They include

BR2 from Rio to Pelotas, almost all paved now
BR3 Rio–Belo Horizonte
BR4 Rio–Salvador, 1,657 km in length, all paved by 1963*
BR5 Rio–Vitória, paved
BR7 Belo Horizonte–Brasilia
São Paulo–Brasilia

Important roads also run inland from the coastal region of São Paulo and Paraná to the coffee lands behind. Two new improvements are on BR87 from São Paulo to Maringa and from Paranaguá to Apucarana (Estrada do Café).

Since the late 1950s Brasilia has consciously been prepared as the new centre of the road system, and ambitious projects include the road to Belém, which is 2,200 km long, already had some 50 settlements on it in 1964, and carried about 160 vehicles per day, to Santarem, probably via Cuiabá, and to Lima (Peru) via Port Velho (BR29, Trans-Brasiliana). BR30 is

* Most of this road was paved in 1962–63 with a labour force of 10,000 men. It is now used by about 1,500 vehicles per day, 90 per cent of them commercial.

TABLE 16.5

Towns With Over 50,000 Inhabitants in Brazil
in 1960 (Census) Arranged Alphabetically

1	Anápolis	51	23	Ilhéus	57	45	Recife*	974
2	Aracajú	113	24	Itabuna	68	46	Riberão Preto	119
3	Araçatuba	54	25	Jequil	51	47	Rio de Janeiro*	4,370
4	Araraquara	61	26	João Pessoa	138	48	Rio Grande	88
5	Bagé	50	27	Joinvile	56	49	Salvador	639
6	Barra Mansa	52	28	Juazeiro do	54	50	Santa Maria	84
7	Bauru	86		Norte	54	51	Santos*	359
8	Belém	381	29	Juiz de Fora	128	52	São Carlos	51
9	Belo Horizonte*	684	30	Jundiaí	84	53	São José do C.	57
10	Brasilia†	90	31	Londrina	77	54	São José do	
11	Campina Grande	126	32	Maceió	162		R. Preto	139
12	Campinas	185	33	Manaus	154	55	São Luis	139
13	Campo Grande	65	34	Marília	54	56	São Paulo*	3,872
14	Campos	132	35	Moji	71	57	Sorocoba	119
15	Caruaru	65	36	Natal	156	58	Taubaté	66
16	Caxias do Sul	69	37	Nova Friburgo	56	59	Teresina	100
17	Curitiba	351	38	Passo Fundo	51	60	Uberaba	72
18	Feira de Santana	70	39	Pelotas	130	61	Uberlândia	72
19	Florianópolis	78	40	Petrópolis	120	62	Uruguaiana	51
20	Fortaleza	471	41	Piracicaba	82	63	Vitória*	139
21	Goiânia	133	42	Ponta Grossa	79	64	Vitória da C.	53
22	Governador		43	Pôrto Alegre*	722	65	Volta Redonda	84
	Valdares	76	44	Presidente				
				Prudente	55			

* Adjoining urbanized municipio or municipios added.
† By 1964 Brasilia had more than 300,000 inhabitants.

planned to run from Brasilia to La Paz (Bolivia), and there is already a good link with Montevideo. Finally a trans-Amazon road is projected, via Manaus to Caracarai with branches into Colombia and Venezuela.

Air transport in Brazil has been of enormous importance in bringing together the various regions, and exploring and consolidating the remote frontier areas, but it is still too costly to allow the movement of goods except of very high value or in special circumstances. Nor have the interregional movements of population been caused or appreciably increased by air traffic. The first regular air service was introduced in 1927. Today Brazil is one of the most air-minded countries in the world and the aircraft, fuel and various equipment are one of the main items of import. Very frequent services link the three corners of the triangle Rio–São Paulo–Brasilia, and since Brasilia became the capital, people have been commuting regularly each week by air between Brasilia and Rio and there are even stories of this being done daily in exceptional circumstances; the distance is roughly 1,000 km. The busiest airports in Brazil are São Paulo (Viracopos), Rio (Galeão) and Brasilia, with Belo Horizonte fourth.

Other forms of transport used in Brazil include oil pipelines and electricity transmission lines. As yet these play only a small part in the economic life of the country, but an electricity grid seems essential for the Southeast if the various hydroelectric stations are to be put to the best use.

16.9. URBAN DEVELOPMENT

Although less highly urbanized than the most advanced countries of Latin America, Brazil now has about 40 per cent of its population living in urban

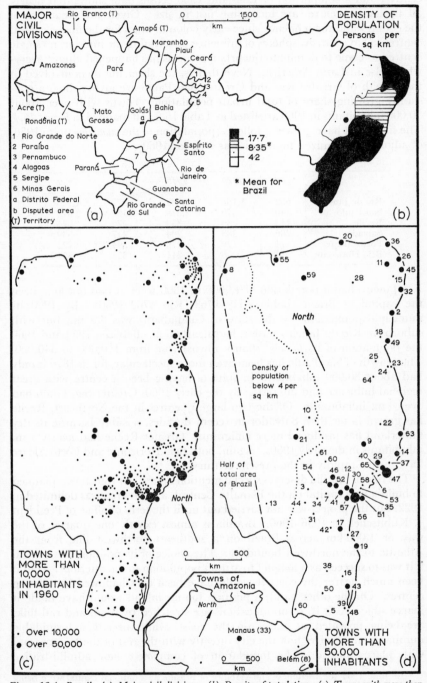

Figure 16.4. Brazil. (a) Major civil divisions. (b) Density of population. (c) Towns with more than 10,000 inhabitants in 1960. (d) Towns with more than 50,000 inhabitants (see Table 16.5)

351

centres, and a comparison of 1950 and 1960 census data shows that nearly all the larger centres are increasing fast in size. Given the great size of the country and the tendency since early colonial times for the major coastal centres to have narrow spheres of influence penetrating the interior, no single centre has come to dominate the urban scene as has happened almost everywhere else in Latin America. Nevertheless, the sheer numbers involved in the growth of Greater Rio and Greater São Paulo are giving these a constantly growing share of total urban population. Towns with over about 50,000 inhabitants in 1960 are listed in Table 16.5 and mapped in *Figure 16.4*. The six largest have grown as follows (population of the *municipio* up to 1950, of adjoining urbanized municipios as well for 1960).

	1900	1920	1940	1950	1960
Rio de Janeiro	692	1,158	1,782	2,377	4,370
São Paulo	240	579	1,319	2,198	3,872
Recife	113	239	353	525	974
Salvador	206	283	294	417	639
Pôrto Alegre	74	179	276	394	722
Belo Horizonte	13	56	211	353	684

Rio Janeiro had a population of 43,000 in 1800 when it had not long been the capital of Brazil (Bahia 1549–1763, Rio 1763–1960). By 1960 its municipio population (= the state of Guanabara) was 3,3 m., but with suburbs in Rio de Janeiro state it had nearly 5 m. Between 1950 and 1960 the population of its *favelas* (shanty towns) rose from 170,000 to 340,000. The growth of São Paulo has been even more spectacular, for in 1870 it only had about 30,000 inhabitants in spite of having been a centre with great regional influence and interests. By the early 1960s Greater São Paulo had over 4 m. inhabitants. Of the two largest centres in the Northeast, Recife has grown faster than Salvador in recent decades, possibly because its dry hinterland has produced more emigrants. Greater Recife had nearly 1 m. inhabitants in the early 1960s. Again, both Belo Horizonte and Pôrto Alegre have grown rapidly in the present century.

The role of Brasilia deserves special mention here[32]. In 1891 it was planned to build a new capital on the Planalto Central, and an area was delimited in 1922, but the project was not carried out until the term of office of President J. Kubitschek in 1956–1960. Brasilia is almost exactly one quarter of the way or 1,000 km across Brazil on a southeast–northwest line from the Atlantic to the northwest boundary. The choice of its position was critical if it was to succeed as a magnet to attract population to the interior*. Had it been much nearer the coast it would have been overshadowed by existing centres. On the other hand, a position too far inland would have made it inaccessible. As it is, communications are stretched by road, and rail links are being provided to places on the coast, while already a formidable number of air services link the city directly with the rest of the country and with places abroad. The foundation of completely new administrative

---

* In June 1964 the usefulness and viability of Brasilia as a national capital were being reviewed by the new government. Some Brazilians consider it a matter of time only before the place is abandoned as a capital.

centres is not new in Brazil. Teresina was founded in 1852, Belo Horizonte was started in 1894 and completed in 1897, and Goiânia replaced Goiás as state capital in 1937, each replacing unsatisfactory existing capitals. Brasilia lies in a very thinly populated grazing region with a small amount of crop farming, and the promise of mineral and forest resources. It is intended to be both a regional service centre and a manufacturing centre as well as the national capital, but water, food and power supplies will have to be built up before serious progress can be expected and at present Brasilia could not by any stretch of the imagination be considered well placed for the location of industrial establishments hoping to serve the whole national market.

16.10. FOREIGN TRADE

Throughout the post-colonial period Brazil has been one of the world's principal sources of tropical products. The export of minerals such as iron ore and manganese is a recent feature, and the export of manufactured goods has hardly started, but currently the nature of both imports and exports is changing fundamentally. During the Second World War Brazil was able to sell many products normally of secondary importance, and although in the post-war period coffee returned to dominate the exports, it has been possible to diversify these in the last few years. At the same time, Brazil is now sufficiently advanced industrially not to have to import many kinds of manufactured product any longer. As the industrial countries of Europe and elsewhere have found, the importation of consumer goods is now very limited. Indeed, about 20 per cent of the imports of Brazil are fuels, and 10–15 per cent food, but the principal need still is capital goods.

In 1961 the exports of Brazil were as follows[33]:

	Value U.S. $ m.	% of total value
Coffee	710	50·6
Cotton	110	7·8
Sugar	66	4·7
Iron ore	60	4·3
Pinewood	48	3·4
Cocoa beans	46	3·3
Manganese ore	32	2·3

Other items exported were sisal, tobacco, castorseed oil, crude petroleum, Brazil nuts, carnauba wax, cacao butter and tinned meat. By far the largest share of the tonnage of exports was accounted for by iron ore (12 m. tons in 1963, 20 m. expected in 1964). Japan alone has agreed to import 10 m. tons per year for ten years.

The direction of Brazilian foreign trade in 1961[34] in U.S. $ millions was as shown at top of next page. Growing population, the general failure to improve agriculture, and bad harvests, have prevented Brazil from reducing its dependence on foreign food supplies. By 1964 it had to resort to obtaining surplus wheat from the U.S.A., since Argentina, its traditional source, no longer had sufficient to export. At the same time Brazil imports certain minerals that could be produced at home. Over the next few years it is hoped to expand the export of manufactured goods, especially to LAFTA countries;

	Exports value	%		Imports value	%
U.S.A.	563	40·1	U.S.A.	515	35·3
W. Germany	114	8·1	W. Germany	141	9·7
Netherlands	71	5·1	Venezuela	99	6·8
Argentina	67	4·8	Japan	79	5·4
U.K.	62	4·4	Neth. Antilles	54	3·7
France	51	3·6	U.K.	47	3·2
Italy	48	3·4	Italy	44	3·0
Sweden	44	3·1	France	43	2·9
Japan	43	3·1			

machine tools, ships, synthetic rubber and steel, rather than consumer goods, are the kind of products envisaged, but in 1964 small quantities of woollen textiles were even being exported to the U.S.A. It is planned to export 2 m. tons of steel by 1975.

In the immediate post-war years Brazilian trade was directed mainly towards the U.S.A., but in the 1950s, trade with traditional partners in Western Europe was restored. Recently it has grown with Japan and with East Europe, as well as with LAFTA countries. During 1960–62, there was considerable trade with East Europe—about U.S. $ 235 m. for the three years each way; the main partners were the U.S.S.R. (70 m.), Poland and Czechoslovakia (50 m. each). Coffee accounted for 40 per cent of the exports to this area, iron ore, cotton, cacao and sisal 10 per cent each. But Brazil is still far from being a world trading nation and the trade with Africa, almost all of Asia and Australia is negligible.

16.11. ECONOMIC AND SOCIAL PROBLEMS

Although the major regions of Brazil are still very distinct and conscious entities, in many respects the country has always had greater cohesion than the Spanish possessions in the Americas, and today Brazil must be considered as a single economic unit. As such it is faced with a number of problems related to its great size and the uneven distribution of both population and resources. As a result of the tendency for some of the agricultural activities practised so far to exhaust the land after a time, large areas once intensively used have been left with a relatively thin population. In such areas the railway and roads needed to serve what is characteristically a dispersed rural population tend to be greatly under-used. As population spreads inland this problem is increased. But new resources do exist in the interior and rightly or wrongly it is the policy of Brazil to encourage movement into areas so far little touched by modern development. The result of these trends is to reshape the effectively occupied area of the country, adding to the series of clusters arranged in a line along the coast new clusters in the interior orientated to one particular part of the coast, at the same time stretching distances (see *Figure 9.2*). In addition, rehabilitation of agricultural land in the coastal clusters is desirable, and diversification of the economy with the introduction of industry into new areas is essential in the long run.

Altogether it seems unlikely that the more remote agricultural areas can satisfactorily be integrated in the economic life of Brazil at this stage, and commercial agriculture is likely to flourish along the major axes of communication, especially the new interregional roads, rather than away from these. As employment structure changes and manufacturing develops, larger urban centres are claiming a growing share of total population. Under these conditions, great interregional movements of population are taking place. These are further encouraged to some extent by the very uneven regional spread of wealth in Brazil. The general tendency therefore is for people to move either towards new areas of development in the interior, particularly in Mato Grosso or Goiás, or for them to move to towns on or near the coast, whether or not the immediate prospects of employment in manufacturing are hopeful. In addition there is a limited movement from the Northeast to the Southeast, but as the distance is so great, and usually the poorer members of the community are likely to move farthest from their home area in search of employment, not many have left up to now. The great influx of population into Rio has come mainly from areas to the north, within a radius of a few hundred kilometres (Minas Gerais, southern Bahia), while São Paulo has been populated largely by people from overseas and from its own state. In very general terms there must be an intermediate area of decline or below average increase between the coastal belt with its fast growing towns and the fringe of new settlement spreading towards the interior. More than a suspicion of this trend is conveyed in *Figure 19.3*, showing population changes in São Paulo state, 1950–60. A careful study of appropriate municipio data would be necessary to show whether or not it is a widespread feature.

Once a complete paved system of interregional roads is completed, movement of population over great distances will undoubtedly increase. Brazil has gone to great lengths to create an impression of integration, and the possibility of going by road across the country was celebrated in 1960 by a convoy of some 50 Brazilian made vehicles of all kinds, pompously termed the Caravana de Integraçao Nacional, which made the journey from Belem to Bagé via Brasilia. As integration proceeds, greater regional specialization should be possible, at least if the economy develops on the lines of that of the U.S.A. But there are signs that regional self-sufficiency is also being aimed at, at least in certain respects. This is partly due to the federal system and the strong influence of states on the location of economic activities (*cf.* Australia). Thus all the more influential states appear to be anxious to have a steel works and an oil refinery. In the immediate future this may help to raise the level of the more backward areas, but in the long run it will leave Brazil with many small or medium scale and presumably inefficient industrial establishments. Much could be learned from the experience of the U.S.S.R. in this respect.

At all events the contrast between different regions of the country has reached such a magnitude that something must be done. It revolves largely round the fact that the Southeast has had a virtual monopoly of Brazilian exports for about a century now, also has the best agricultural land, hydro-electric potential and proved reserves of iron ore, and has received almost all the immigrants from Europe in the modern period. The result is that as

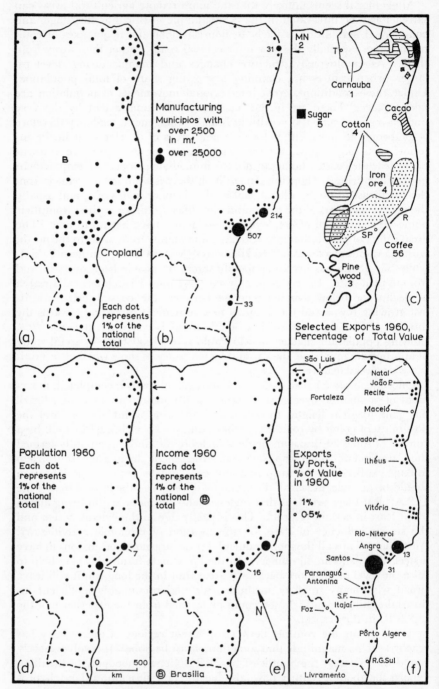

Figure 16.5. Brazil. (a) Cropland. (b) Manufacturing. (c) Selected exports percentage of total value. (d) Population 1960. (e) Income 1960. (f) Exports by ports, percentage of value in 1960

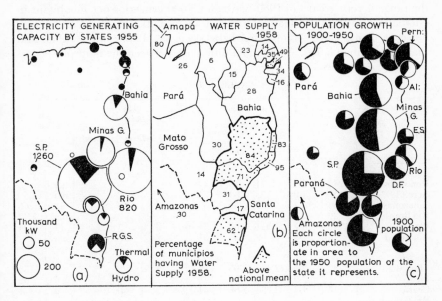

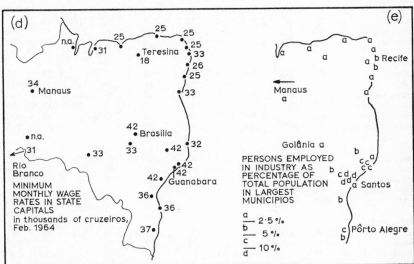

Figure 16.6. Brazil. (a) *Electricity generating capacity by states 1955.* (b) *Percentage of municipios having water supply 1958.* (c) *Population growth 1900–1950.* (d) *Minimum monthly wage rates in state capitals.* (e) *Persons employed in industry as percentage of total population in largest municipios. Maps* (a) *and* (c) *are based on Atlas do Brasil*

well as having a generally more prosperous agricultural population, the Southeast has almost all of the large scale industry, and dominates the country financially. *Per caput* income figures are available for states and the range is very great: in 1960 between 65,000 cruzerios per inhabitant in Guanabara and 6,000 in Piauí. Guanabara is exceptional for several reasons, however, and a fairer comparison is between São Paulo state, 37,000 and Piauí–Maranhão 6,500. The sixfold difference between the most prosperous

TABLE 16.6[35]

State or Territory (*T*)	I Area		II Population			III Industry			IV Finance	
						Mfg. and extr.		cement		
	a	b	a	b	c	a	b	c	a	b
Norte										
Rondônia (T)	243	2·9	71	0·3	44				n.a.	
Acre (T)	153	1·8	153	1·1	21				n.a.	
Amazonas	1,564	18·4	721	0·5	33	2			14	266
Rio Branco (T)	230	2·7	29	0·1	43				n.a.	
Pará	1,248	14·7	1,551	1·3	41	3			11	224
Amapá (T)	140	1·6	69	0·5	51	2			n.a.	
Nordeste										
Maranhão	329	3·9	2,492	13·5	18	2			7	35
Piauí	251	2·9	1,263	5·0	24				6	62
Ceará	148	1·7	3,338	22·6	34	5	1		9	71
Rio Grande do Norte	53	0·6	1,157	21·8	38	3			11	117
Paraíba	56	0·7	2,018	35·8	35	4	1	108	10	87
Pernambuco	98	1·2	4,137	42·1	45	20	3	259	13	104
Alagoas	28	0·3	1,271	46·0	34	4	1		10	94
Leste										
Sergipe	22	0·3	760	34·6	39	2			12	95
Bahia	561	6·6	5,991	10·7	35	11	2	135	11	221
Minas Gerais	583	6·9	9,799	18.8	40	40	6	800	16	290
Espírito Santo	39	0·5	1,189	30.2	32	2		36	14	350
Rio de Janeiro	43	0·5	3,403	80·8	61	48	7	797	20	303
Guanabara	1	negl.	3,223	very high	97	82	11		65	795
Sul										
São Paulo	248	2·9	12,975	52·3	63	398	55	1,230	37	1,000
Paraná	200	2·3	4,110	not completed		22	3	154	23	340
Santa Catarina	96	1·1	2,147	22.5	32	15	2	47	18	238
Rio Grande do Sul	282	3·3	5,449	20·4	45	56	8	179	24	470
Centro-Oeste										
Mato Grosso	1,232	14·5	910	0·7	40	2		63	15	214
Goiás	642	7·6	1,955	5·0	31	2			12	167
Distrito Federal	6	0·1	142	24·4	63				n.a.	n.a.
Brazil*	8,512	100	70,800	8·3	35	724	100		21	396

* Note: small disputed areas are not listed with states and territories.

I a Area in thousands of square kilometres.
 b As percentage of total.
II a Population in thousands, 1960.
 b Persons per square kilometre.
 c Percentage urban.
III a Value of manufacturing and extractive activities in 1958 in thousands of millions of cruzeiros.
 b Percentage of total.
 c Output of cement in thousands of tons in 1960.
IV a *Per caput* income in thousands of cruzeiros in 1960.
 b Expenditure *per caput* on education in cruzeiros in 1960[36].

and the poorest areas is much greater than in the U.S.A. in which the most prosperous state is only three times as high as the poorest (Mississippi). In Italy however, which like Brazil, but on a much smaller area, has most of the industry *and* the best agricultural land in one part of the country, the difference is 5–6 times as great (see also Chapter 19.1). Table 16.6 shows the kind of data available for studying economic and social contrasts between Brazilian states, and Table 16.7 shows some of the ways in which the disproportionate share of the Southeast can be gauged. Column II in Table 16.7 shows the proportion in each state or group of states of the total population. If the wealth of the country were shared out evenly according to

TABLE 16.7[37]

Percentages of Total Wealth in States or Groups of States

	I	II	III	IV	V	VI
	Area	population	Value of mining and mfg in 1958	Deposits in banks in 1960	Commercial turnover in 1960	Internal income in 1959
São Paulo	2·9	18·3	55	38	48	32
Guanabara-Rio-E.S.	1·0	11·2	18	19	18	20
Minas Gerais	6·9	13·8	6	22	7	10
Paraná	2·3	5·8	3	2	5	6
Santa Catarina	1·1	3·0	2	1	2	3
Rio Grande do Sul	3·3	7·7	8	7	8	9
Bahia-Sergipe	6·9	9·5	2	4	2·5	5
Alagoas-Pernambuco Paraíba-R.G.N.	2·8	12·1	4	3	4·5	7
Ceará	1·7	4·7	1	1	1	2
Maranhão-Piauí	6·7	5·3	<0·5		0·5	2
Goias-Mato Grosso-D.F.	22·1	4·3	0·5	2	2	2
Pará-Amapá	16·3	2·3	0·5	1	1	1
Amazonas-Rondônia-Acre-Rio Branco	25·7	1·4	<0·5		0·5	1

Column *III.* see p. 91, value of production[37]
IV. see p. 190 (*movimento bancário*)[37]
V. see p. 263 (*giro comercial*)[37]
VI. see p. 269 (*renda interna*)[37]

population, each subsequent column would have the same proportion. In reality very great discrepancies can be detected. For example, the Greater Northeast has almost one third of total population but only about 7 per cent of the value of mining and manufacturing. Rio Grande do Sul, in spite of not being highly industrialized, has indices close to the national mean, thanks to its more favourable farming conditions. The interior states and Amazonia have indices below the national mean but not so low as the poorest parts of the Northeast.

The particularly strong position of São Paulo state may be appreciated from the following figures: it has about 3 per cent of the national area, 18 per cent of the population, but accounts for 35 per cent of the cotton and 50 per cent of the coffee grown in Brazil, 55 per cent of the industrial production, and almost all the engineering, a key industry in Brazilian manufacturing. Most of the financial life of Brazil is based on São Paulo, and around 1960 the state had 75 per cent of the foreign investments. Obviously this position cannot be expected to last, for it is absurd that such a small part of the national area should make such a large contribution to the national income, but such situations occur in other parts of the world (e.g. Australia, Canada, Argentina) and it is not easy to break down such a monopoly nor necessarily desirable to attempt to do so too quickly.

16.12. THE NORTHEAST

O Nordeste is a characteristic region of Brazil with its own particular history, landscapes and ways of life. Already highly developed in its own way in the seventeenth century with the use of the fertile east facing coastal area for sugar cultivation and the interior for cattle raising, like Haiti, though in a less complete way, it has seen its economy slip back from one based on exports to one based largely on production for regional needs. Agriculture has however been diversified somewhat (cotton, cacao, tobacco) especially away from the two main concentrations of sugar cultivation around Recife and Salvador, and irrigation has been extended in the drier parts. There are now several times as many people in the region as during the colonial period, and it has remained essentially agricultural. Land tenure has not changed much, and inefficiently run large units are widespread in the interior. For the purposes of this section the greater Northeast consists of the nine states from Maranhão to Bahia and contains somewhat more than 30 per cent of the population of Brazil but has only 16 per cent of the national income and 7 per cent of manufacturing. The Northeast often refers only to the five states from Ceará to the lower São Francisco.

Only locally in the region are relief conditions particularly rugged. Land over 1,000 m is rare but narrow steep sided *chapadas*, the result of pediplanation, twist about the area, tending to isolate the various river basins. Most of the surface consists of low plateaux (*tabuleiros*) with steep edges and with scattered inselbergs. There is little evidence of a coastal scarp. It is climate, rather than relief that presents a major problem in much of the region. Low and unreliable rainfall (see *Figure 3.3d*) which occurs in a short wet season, and very high temperatures, result in a very dry environment (*caatingas*) with thorn forest and cactus. The mean annual rainfall for one place, Cabeceiras, is only 278 mm. This dry belt extends from the middle São Francisco to the coast of Ceará. The southeast facing coast, however, has a heavier and more reliable rainfall and is an area of tropical rain forest. Westwards, with increasing humidity, the tropical rain forest reappears (in Piauí, Maranhão), while southwards in Bahia the *cerrado* vegetation is predominant.

The total population of the Northeast has grown about five times in the last hundred years without cultivated land being extended to the same degree. Catastrophic droughts have periodically driven people out of the dry area either east into the already overcrowded coastlands of Recife and Bahia or west into Amazonia. It has been estimated[39] that in the drought of 1877, half of the population of Ceará, about 500,000 people, perished through sheer starvation, thirst, or diseases such as smallpox. Many people died of food poisoning through eating unsuitable vegetation or even soil. Others migrated into Amazonia to participate in the gathering of wild rubber, often to disappear without trace. Such dry periods have been repeated several times since, even as recently as 1958, but with less devastating results. But in years favoured with adequate rain the *região do sertão*, as the dry interior is called, can provide an abundance of agricultural products and after each setback the population has increased again. Future prospects seem reasonably bright as new reservoirs are built to store water and artesian wells drilled (e.g. 200 in 1963) but apart from the São Francisco, not much surface water is available.

The problem of the eastern coastal strip (the *terras úmidas*) is different. This area is largely populated by descendants of the slaves, brought in particularly between 1550 and 1700. Great emphasis is still placed on the cultivation of sugar cane and little land is available either for food crops or for livestock. Manioc, maize, beans, rice and vegetables are grown, but not in sufficient quantities to ensure either an adequate or a balanced diet. With basically a carbohydrate diet, malnutrition is common. Fishing along the coast by primitive means (*jangadas* that use local winds to take them far out to sea) in an area in which prospects of a good catch are limited, supplements the diet to a small extent.

The third region, the Meio-Norte (Maranhão-Piauí) as it is now called, is the most backward part of Brazil altogether. Agriculture is practised locally, forest products are gathered and livestock raised but there are no minerals and no manufacturing, transport facilities are poor and amenities inadequate. Virtually no contribution is made to the economy of the rest of Brazil.

The description of the Greater Northeast so far has been dismal, but recently the Brazilian government initiated a very ambitious programme to try to raise it to the level of southern Brazil. In essence, the region must make much fuller use of its own resources, since resettlement in the interior is difficult, given that it means moving into either the forests of the Amazon or the *cerrado* lands to the south of this. Some emigration to Southeast Brazil and to Brasilia is taking place, but with the rapid growth of population, the answer must be found in the Northeast itself, and only funds and technical assistance can be added to what is there.

Brazil now has a development plan for the Northeast (Sudene). The main aim of this is to ensure that much more money is invested in the region than previously. For example, in 1960 only 3 per cent of all domestic private investment was placed there; the aim is 17 per cent. Outside aid is also being directed here, and funds from the Alliance for Progress are now being used. It is planned, surely unrealistically, to catch up with the rest of Brazil in a few years. In agriculture attempts are being made to introduce new crops (e.g. ramie, the vine), to plant useful trees (e.g. mesquit trees to protect soil) and to improve rural water supply. But the success of the plan depends largely on creating employment in manufacturing for about 500,000 people in a matter of 3–4 years, particularly in a few favourable places. There are three major hydroelectric schemes: Paulo Alfonso enlargement, Cariri and Cachoeira Dorada. The Bahia oilfield is another centre for development and a steel works is planned here. The manufacture of petro-chemicals is to be established at Cabo near Recife (COPERBO making synthetic rubber), a steelworks is planned, and a large new textile factory,

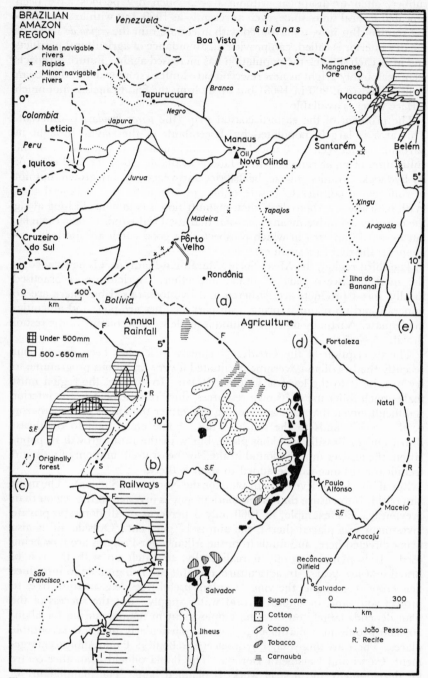

Figure 16.7. Brazil. (a) Brazilian Amazon region. (b)-(e) Northeast Brazil. (b) Annual rainfall. (c) Railways. (d) Agriculture. (e) Towns

sponsored by capital from São Paulo, is being established in Natal. Irrigation projects in the interior include improvement in the Acaraú area west of Fortaleza (50,000 hectares) and Jaguaribe area in eastern Ceará (145,000 hectares). It is hoped to find oil or natural gas in the younger sedimentary rocks of Piauí and Maranhão and small oil reserves have recently been found in Alagoas. The asphalting of the main road from Salvador south to Minas Gerais and Rio in 1963 has made it more easy to reach places away from the coast in the Southeast.

In the second general plan of Sudene (1963–5) electricity alone is taking 35 per cent of the investment; this is going towards the construction of a main transmission line from Paulo Alfonso to Fortaleza, to smaller lines to bring electricity to smaller settlements, and on the Cariri power station. Some 15 per cent is for the improvement of roads and 15 per cent for water supply.

16.13. SOUTHEAST

Southeast Brazil is unfortunately usually divided by Brazilian geographers and planners, and Rio, with Minas Gerais, is included in the Leste, together with Bahia, while São Paulo goes with the South. Given the very close links between the hinterlands of Rio and São Paulo (exchange of energy, minerals, agricultural products and so on) it is unrealistic to separate these. For this reason the Southeast in this chapter is taken to include the states of Minas Gerais, São Paulo, Espirito Santo, Rio and Guanabara, while northern Paraná, part of which is orientated towards São Paulo rather than Curitiba anyway, could realistically belong as well.

There are considerable physical differences in the region, with a humid, once densely forested coastal lowland northeast of Rio (still largely forested north of the Doce) and southwest of Santos, the most rugged mountains in Brazil close to the coast between these two centres[41], and the trough of the Paraíba valley making movement into the interior doubly difficult. The road and railway between São Paulo and Rio follow this valley, while the Serra da Mantiqueira is avoided by the main lines of penetration, and by settlement from Rio north through Belo Horizonte to the central plateau and upper São Francisco, and from São Paulo northwest down the tributaries of the Paraná. The coastal mountains receive a very heavy rainfall, have also been heavily forested, and offer many opportunities for hydroelectric power stations. Northwards across Minas Gerais, savanna conditions appear, but westwards the land was forested as far as the Paraná, which now forms a marked break in settlement and land use.

Most of the agriculture in the coastal lowlands and Paraíba valley is directed towards producing food for regional needs: sugar cane, bananas and pastures for dairying. On the higher land behind are the main coffee plantations (see *Figure 7.4*). In a belt extending from the Rio Doce valley to northern Paraná, narrowing almost to nothing behind the Serra da Mantiqueira, is the coffee growing region of Brazil. In the eastern part, in Minas and northeastern São Paulo a more mixed kind of agriculture prevails, with cereal cultivation and cattle raising alongside coffee. In the western part coffee growing has been more of a monoculture, occupying the favoured fertile sloping land, with cotton, sugar, cereals and pastures on the lower

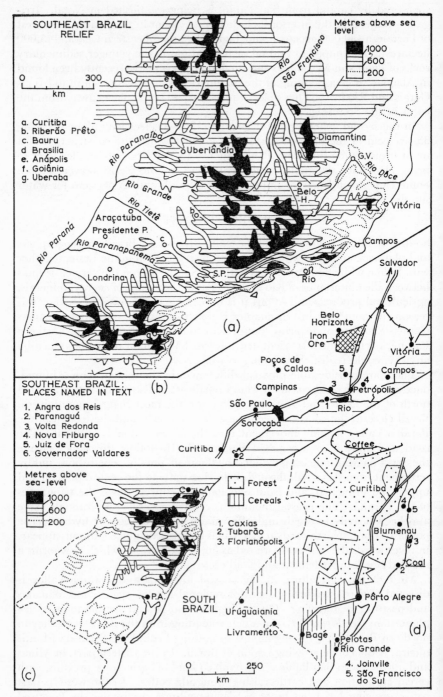

Figure 16.8. Southeast Brazil. (a) Relief. (b) Places named in text. (c)–(d) South Brazil, (c) Relief. (d) Land use and towns

land. The coffee belt ends abruptly against the mountains of southern Paraná and here forestry and grazing intervene between the tropical cultivation of Paraná[42] and the subtropical cultivation of Rio Grande do Sul (see *Figure 16.8*). The extreme western part of Paraná state is still largely forested and offers opportunities for colonization, but could not be expected to produce coffee.

The great contribution of the Southeast to Brazilian agriculture and especially exports has been emphasized already. The mineral deposits have been noted and the present and projected major hydroelectric stations mapped (see *Figure 16.3*). Although almost all of the area has now been occupied and much of the surface is used for crop farming, forestry or grazing, population is very unevenly distributed and is tending to become more concentrated in Rio and São Paulo and along axes radiating from these centres. Roughly one third of the population of the region is in or near these two towns, while there are many towns with 50–150,000 inhabitants north-west and west to São Paulo, north of Rio and along the Paraíba valley. Several of these are highly industrialized by Latin American standards: Campinas, Sorocaba, Jundiaí near São Paulo, Volta Redonda, Petrópolis and Juiz de Fora near Rio and several smaller centres in Minas Gerais. Metal-working is the principal branch of manufacturing in southern Minas Gerais and the Paraíba valley, but textile manufacturing is also wide-spread.

Rio de Janeiro occupies a difficult site in a beautiful setting. The continuity of the built-up area is broken by mountains several hundred metres high, and as the town has spread westwards, several tunnels have been built to serve new quarters and maintain cohesion. The bay of Rio, with its islands, offers a great length of coastline for port development and many of the industries lie along its western side. About half a million people live east of the entrance to the bay, in Niteroi and São Gonçalo, and it is planned to supplement the ferries by a tunnel or bridge. When Brasilia became the capital in 1960 the Federal District was made into the city state of Guanabara, which then had a population of 3,3 m. About 1½ m. more people live in the adjoining state of Rio de Janeiro but within Greater Rio. Rio is less highly industrialized than São Paulo and at the same time is slowly losing one of its main functions, that of national capital. The transition has fortunately been slow, but the artificially high standard of living seems to be threatened. Rio has attracted large numbers of people from nearby parts of Brazil in recent decades, and while parts of the town are luxuriously constructed, the *favelas* on the lower slopes of many of the hillsides are growing in size to house the poorer immigrants, mainly negro or with some negro element, from rural areas to the north.

Although roughly the same size as Rio, São Paulo differs fundamentally from its rival*. Very difficult access to the coast only 50 km away in a direct line but about 700 m below is compensated for by much easier access to the hinterland than Rio has. The modern growth of São Paulo has been more rapid than that of Rio. It has been more closely associated with coffee, with foreign trade and with financial matters than Rio, and within about

* See Ref.[43] for a great deal of material on São Paulo, past and present.

the last 30 years has taken the lead industrially, thanks partly to the availability of hydroelectric power in the immediate vicinity. Like Rio, São Paulo is a sophisticated modern city, but its central area, clearly defined banking district, large number of skyscrapers, and absence of the equivalent of favelas at least in more conspicuous parts of the town give it a different character, and nowhere in Latin America are more industries concentrated in one district than in its southern suburbs, particularly along the Via Anchieta and the railway leading to Santos.

16.14. SOUTH BRAZIL, THE INTERIOR AND AMAZONIA[44]

South of the coffee lands of northeast Paraná is an extensive rugged area with a considerable proportion of its surface over 1,000 m. Covered mainly with mixed forest, in which the Araucaria pine predominates, this area has been developed only relatively recently, mainly by settlers who have arrived in the last hundred years. The coastal regions between Curitiba and southern Santa Catarina depend largely on the cultivation of food crops, but the products of the interior are timber and livestock. The region is poorer than the regions to the north and south, bleak in the winter and isolated except near the main roads. Mining and manufacturing are of limited importance in spite of the presence of Brazil's main coal mines. Curitiba is a rapidly growing centre but has few industries so far.

Rio Grande do Sul is an area of older settlement. Much of the area was occupied by the eighteenth century and cattle and sheep raising have been the dominant activities. The state now grows almost all of Brazil's wheat as well as rice, tobacco, sub-tropical fruits, and fodder for livestock, and the processing of agricultural products is widespread. The principal concentration of population is in and around Pôrto Alegre, and a fairly dense rural population spreads across the lowlands to the northwest, but density is low in the southern part of the state, towards Uruguay.

Although a wave of immigration is still filling up the western parts of São Paulo, Paraná and Santa Catarina states (see 1950–60 population data), the area west to the Paraná river is virtually integrated. West, beyond the Paraná, in Mato Grosso, and northwest, beyond the settled southeastern part of Goiás state (see *Figure 16.9*) lie the lands that are likely next to be developed. Given the vast size of the area involved and the limited number of people moving into the area it seems probable that development will take place along certain axes such as the railway to Corumbá and the roads to Acre and Belém. Apart from the establishment of Brasilia and the construction and improvement of roads little is currently being invested in the area beyond the Paraná.

Taken as the two states and four territories of the north, Amazonia or the Norte region, has 40 per cent of the area of Brazil but less than 4 per cent of its total population. The region has been called 'a world apart' and much of the population lives its own life, selling a small surplus of forest products to traders, for sale either in the rest of Brazil or in foreign countries. Other parts of Brazil are reached either by sea or by air, but the recent completion of the road Brasilia–Belém may begin to break down its isolation. As far as Brazil is concerned at present, Amazonia might not exist. Its only serious

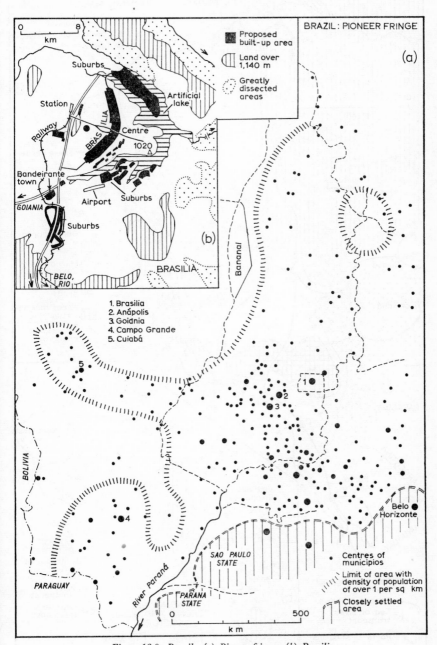

Figure 16.9. Brazil. (a) Pioneer fringe. (b) Brasilia

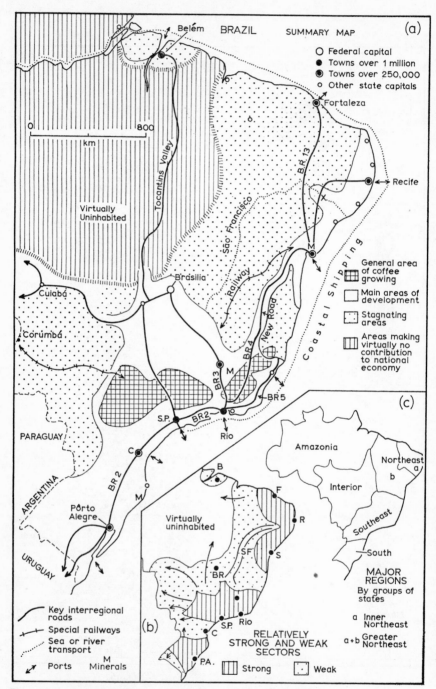

Figure 16.10. Brazil. (a) Summary map. (b) Relatively strong and weak sectors. (c) Major regions by groups of states

contribution to the economic life of the country has been the wild rubber boom of 1870–1910, during which the only two towns of size grew fast:

Belém   1851,   18,000   Manaus   1879,   5,000
         1900,   100,000   1910,   50,000
         1920,   236,000

Present interest in Amazonia lies mainly in the prospects of finding minerals, and manganese ore in Amapá and oil and manganese ore near Manaus are the chief new finds.

REFERENCES

1 Serebrenick, S. 'Planejamentos Regionais no Brazil' *Bol. geogr.* IBGE, XX, Nov.–Dec. 1962, No. 171, pp. 664–68; Rizzini, C. T. 'Nota previa sobre a divisão fitogeográfica do Brazil', *Rev. bras. Geogr.* IBGE, XXV Jan.–Mar. 1963, No. 1. pp. 3–63

2 *Anuario Estatístico do Brasil* 1961 IBGE, p. 29–1960; *UNSBLA*, Vol. 1, No. 1, p. 17–1979

3 Carneiro, J. F. *Imigração e Colonização no Brazil*, Universidade do Brasil, Rio de Janeiro, 1950; Augelli, J. P. *The Latvians of Varpa: A Foreign Colony on the Brazilian Pioneer Fringe*, Vol. XLVIII, 1958, pp. 365–387; Augelli, J. P. *Cultural and Economic Changes of Bastos, a Japanese Colony on Brazil's Paulista Frontier*, A.A.A.G., March 1958, pp. 3–19

4 Hutchinson, H. W. *Village and Plantation Life in Northeastern Brazil*, Seattle, 1957

5 Cole, M. M. Cerrado, Caatinga and Pantanal, Distribution and Origin of the Savanna Vegetation of Brazil, *Georgr. J.* June 1960, pp. 168–79

6 Prado, Caio, Jnr. *Historia Económica do Brasil*, Editora Brasiliense, 1961 (6th edn)

7 Castro, Josué de, *Geografia da fôme*, São Paulo, 1961

8 Ferreira, Jurandyr Pires. *Atlas do Brasil*, IBGE (Preface), 1960, p. XVI

9 Pardo, A. M. *Brasil, La Gran Potencia del Siglo XXI*, Santiago de Compostela (Spain), 1955

10 Freyre, G. *New World in the Tropics*, The Culture of Modern Brazil, 1959, London; Knopf

11 O'Reilly, H. 'Agriculture and Industry in Brazil', *Geogr. J.* CXXI, Dec. 1955. pp. 488–502; James, P. E. 'Trends in Brazilian Agricultural Development', *Geogr. Rev.* Vol. XLIII, 1953, pp. 301–328; Webb, K. E. 'Origins and Development of a Food Economy in Central Minas Gerais', *A.A.A.G.*, Dec. 1959, pp. 409–419; and Stevens, R. L. and Brandão, P. R. 'Diversification of the Economy of the Cacao Coast of Bahia, Brazil,' *Econ. geogr.* 37, 1961, pp. 231–253

12 *Anuario Estatístico do Brasil*, 1961, pp. 76–82

13 *FAOPY*, 1962, Tables 11, 16, 18

14 Mombieg, P. *Pionniers et Planteurs de São Paulo*, Paris, 1952, pp. 361–64

15 *Anuario Estatístico do Brasil*, 1961, IBGE, p. 83

16 *Anuario Estatístico do Brasil*, 1961, p. 59

17 *BOLSA (FR)* 2 Nov. 1963, p. 926

18 *Anuario Estatística do Brasil* 1961, p. 62

19 *Anuario Estatística do Brasil* 1961, p. 13

20 *Anuario Estatística do Brasil* 1961, pp. 89–90

21 *Brazilian News*, No. 24, April 1964

22 Strauch, Ney. *Zona Metalúrgica de Minas Gerais e Vale do Rio Doce*, Conselho Nacional de Geographia, Rio de Janeiro, 1958

23 *Anuario Estatístico do Brasil*, 1961, p. 97

24 *BOLSA (FR)*, 28 Dec. 1963; *Brazilian News* No. 26, June 1964

25 *Anuario Estatístico do Brasil*, 1961, p. 101

26 *UNSY*, 1963, Table 124

27 *Anuario Estatístico do Brasil* 1961 p. 95

28 *Anuario Estatístico do Brasil* 1961, p. 160 and p. 220–221

29 *The Statesman's Yearbook*, 1872, p. 501

[30] Sodré, N. W. O Problema Ferroviário, *Boletim Geográfico*, IBGE, XXI, Jan.–Feb. 1963, No. 172 pp. 39–43

[31] *Anuario Estatístico do Brasil*, 1961, pp. 147–52

[32] James, P. E. and Faissol, S. 'Problems of Brazil's Capital City' *Geogr. Rev.* Vol. XLVI (1956) 301–317

[33] *BOLSA (FR)*, 9 March 1963, p. 243

[34] *BOLSA (FR)*, 23 March 1963

[35] *Anuario Estatístico do Brasil*, 1961, various tables

[36] *Anuario Estatístico do Brasil*, 1961, p. 383

[37] *Anuario Estatístico do Brasil*, 1961, pp. 91, 190, 263, 269

[38] Lacerdo de Melo, M. 'Bases Geográficos dos Problemas do Nordeste' *Rev. bras. Geogr.* XXIV Oct–Dec. 1962, No. 4, pp. 503–41; Castro, J. de, Operación Nordeste El Correo (Courier), UNESCO, May 1963; James, P. E. 'Patterns of Land Use in Northeast Brazil', A.A.A.G., XLIII, June 1953

[39] Castro J. de, *Geografia do fôme*, São Paulo, 1961

[40] AB'Saber, Aziz Nacib and Bernardes, Nilo, 'Vale do Paraíba' *Serra da Mantiqueira e Arredores de São Paulo*, Conselho Nacional de Geografia, Rio de Janiero, 1958; Muller, N. L. *Sitios e Sitantes no Estado de São Paulo*, São Paulo, 1951

[41] Haggett, P. 'Land Use and Sediment Yield in an Old Plantation Tract of the Serra do Mar, Brazil, *Geogr. J.* Mar. 1961, pp. 50–62

[42] Dozier, C. L. 'Northern Paraná', Brazil: An Example of Organized Regional Developments' *Georg. Rev.* Vol. XLVI, 1956, pp. 318–333

[43] *A cidade de São Paulo, Estudos de geografia urbana*, (Ed. A. de Azevedo) in 4 vols., São Paulo, 1958

[44] Bernardes, H. 'Bases Geográficas do Povoamento no Estado do Rio Grande do Sul,' *Bol. geogr.* IBGE, XX, Nov.–Dec. 1962, No. 171, pp. 587–620 and XXI, Jan. Feb. 1963, No. 172, pp. 3–29

CHAPTER 17

PARAGUAY, URUGUAY AND ARGENTINA

17.1. INTRODUCTION

This chapter deals with Paraguay, Uruguay and Argentina but for convenience some features of southern South America have been mapped together in *Figures 17.1–17.3*. *Figure 17.1* shows certain physical features; the vegetation of Argentina is included in *Figure 3.7*. In *Figure 17.2*, the density of population is shown for the whole area, using data for major civil divisions in the three smaller countries and for minor civil divisions (departments) in Argentina. *Figure 17.3a* and Table 17.1 gives the recent population for all towns with over about 50,000 inhabitants.

17.2. PARAGUAY

In many respects Paraguay is similar to Mato Grosso state in Brazil and to the Chaco and Misiones provinces of Argentina. It is mainly flat or gently undulating, is situated on the Tropic of Capricorn, has very hot summers and a high though seasonal rainfall, and forest, scrub and savanna vegetation. Moreover, like these interior parts of Brazil and Argentina it has small areas that are densely settled and large areas that remain virtually untouched, and is far from the coast and from any large urban-industrial complex. The fact that it is a sovereign state has helped to ensure its isolation, for it is less susceptible to pressure from such centres as São Paulo and Buenos Aires, the impact of which is naturally felt in adjoining parts of Brazil and Argentina. Policy in the nineteenth century was for a time, indeed, to exclude all contacts with the outside world.

Although about four fifths the size of Spain and several times as large as Cuba, Paraguay had only 1,800,000 inhabitants in 1961 (an increase of 35 per cent over 1949). About 450,000 are in and around Asunción, the capital, but other towns are small. Over half of the population is still agricultural, but in 1961 agriculture only accounted for 38 per cent of the total gross domestic product (having dropped from 45 per cent in 1950). Of the total area of Paraguay, little over 1 per cent is actually under field or tree crops and less than 25 per cent is classed as permanent pastures and meadows, although rough grazing extends over a much larger area than this. Somewhat more than 50 per cent is forested, while the rest of the land includes a small potential area of farmland and much waste. Agriculture is based on the cultivation of maize, sugar, oilseeds and cotton of high quality as well as various basic food crops, and on cattle raising. The country has 4–5 m. cattle, more than twice as many as its human population. Paraguay does not however satisfy its food requirements, and food products, including wheat (15 per cent of all imports), are imported, while exports, which are very

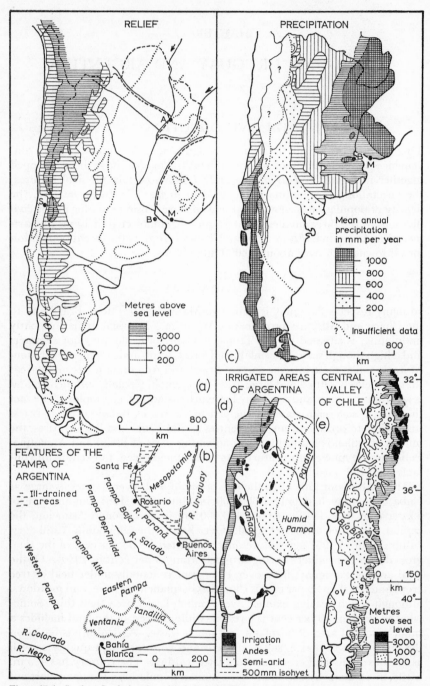

Figure 17.1. Southern South America. (a) Relief. (b) Features of the pampa of Argentina. (c) Precipitation. (d) Irrigated areas of Argentina. (e) Central valley of Chile

diverse, include meat and hides (about 35 per cent), wood and quebracho (about 30 per cent) and several arable products including oilseeds and cotton.

Concessions have been granted to oil companies for exploration but nothing useful has yet been discovered and Paraguay has to import its fuel

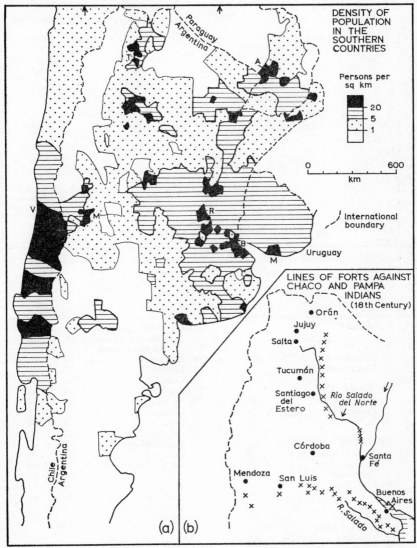

Figure 17.2. (a) Density of population in the southern countries. (b) Lines of forts against Chaco and Pampa Indians (eighteenth century)

needs (oil is 10 per cent of the value of imports). There appear to be virtually no other minerals either. Consumption of energy per inhabitant is very low and the electricity generating capacity of some 50,000 kW is almost as small as that of Haiti. An oil refinery with an initial capacity of 10,000 barrels per

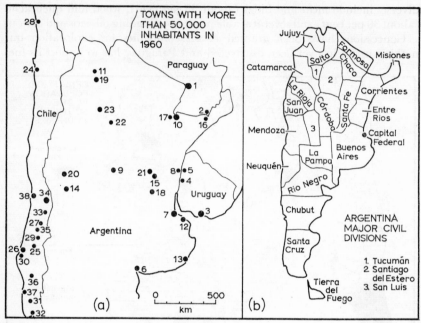

Figure 17.3. Southern South America. (a) *Towns with more than 50,000 inhabitants in 1960.* (b) *Argentina major civil divisions*

TABLE 17.1

PARAGUAY		CHILE (1960 figures obtained after the drawing of the map are given in the r.h. column)		
1. Asunción	310	24. Antofagasta	91	88
2. Encarnación	50	25. Chillán	83	59
		26. Concepción	286	232
URUGUAY		27. Curico	83	33
3. Montevideo	1,173	28. Iquique	54	51
4. Paysandú	60	29. Linares	51	28
5. Salto	60	30. Lota	52	49
		31. Osorno	55	55
ARGENTINA (1960)		32. Puerto Montt	50	42
6. Bahia Blanca	150	33. Rancagua	62	53
7. Buenos Aires	6,763	34. Santiago (Greater)	2,114	1,989
8. Concordia	80	35. Talca	80	68
9. Córdoba	590	36. Témuco	117	72
10. Corrientes	110	37. Valdivia	85	61
11. Jujuy	60	38. Valparaiso-Viña		
12. La Plata	330	del Mar	385	368
13. Mar del Plata	230			
14. Mendoza	380			
15. Paraná	130	* Includes Talcahuano.		
16. Posadas	50			
17. Resistencia	90			
18. Rosario	670			
19. Salta	120			
20. San Juan	110			
21. Santa Fé	260			
22. Santiago del Estero	90			
23. Tucumán	290			

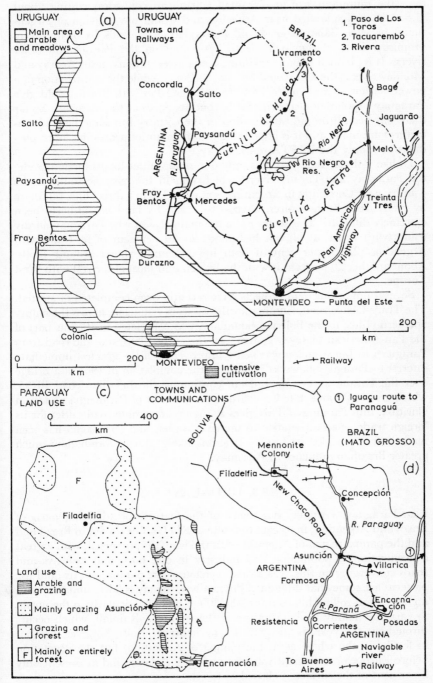

Figure 17.4. (a)–(b) Uruguay. (a) Main area of arable land and meadows. (b) Towns and railways. (c)–(d) Paraguay. (c) Land use. (d) Towns and communications

day (the minimum size in the small Caribbean countries) costing about U.S. $ 10 m. is planned near Asunción and would use Bolivian or Argentinian or even Saharan crude oil unless Paraguay finds its own. More promising is the large hydroelectric potential on the Paraná and other rivers. It is planned to build medium sized power stations on the Acaray and Monday rivers (the cost would be U.S. $ 22 m.), while the construction of a power station at the Guaira Falls, in collaboration with Brazil, could give Paraguay supplies of electricity far beyond its needs at the moment. So far there has been little industrialization in the country but some light manufactures are made and it is hoped to establish factories processing forest products to supply the LAFTA market.

Unlike Bolivia, Paraguay has only one main outlet for its foreign trade, the Paraguay and Paraná rivers, which join in the extreme south of the country near Corrientes in Argentina, some 800 km in a direct line, but more by river, from Buenos Aires. Access to Brazil by land has hitherto been extremely difficult. This seems to be the main reason why Paraguay hardly trades with Brazil at all but has about 25–30 per cent of its trade with Argentina (27–28 per cent of both imports and exports around 1960). About another 20 per cent is with the U.S.A. and most of the rest with West Europe.

Several important road projects have recently been completed or started. The Trans-Chaco road, running northwest from Asunción, across the empty northern lands, to the Bolivian boundary, was completed in 1963 as part of the Pan-American highway system. In the early 1960s, too, the road from Paraguari to Encarnación was being improved. Of the greatest immediate interest to Paraguay however is perhaps the completion in 1961 of a bridge over the Paraná at Foz de Iguaçu, continuing the Brazilian road BR35, which crosses Paraná state westwards from the port of Paranaguá and from Curitiba, into Paraguay. This gives Paraguay a possible road outlet for its foreign trade as an alternative to the river outlet, and Paranaguá has been made a free port for its trade. It seems likely also to foreshadow much greater Brazilian influence in Paraguay.

17.3. URUGUAY[1]

Like Paraguay, Uruguay has many of the features of adjoining parts of Brazil and Argentina, in its case the state of Rio Grande do Sul in Brazil and and the pampa region of Argentina. In the way it is organized, with a great concentration of population and industry in one port, and railways and roads converging on this, it is a small version of the pampa, but its land use patterns are somewhat different. Physically Uruguay is fairly uniform, with no more than rolling hill country 200–300 m high, particularly in the north, to vary the mainly lowland nature of the country. Rainfall, which occurs throughout the year, is adequate for agriculture. Soils, however, are not so fertile on the whole as in the pampa of Argentina, but the vegetation before European settlement was also mainly grassland, and at present only 2 per cent of the surface is classed as forest.

Uruguay is not only more prosperous than Paraguay but much more highly urbanized. Of the total population of 2,560,000 (1963), 1,173,000 were in the district of Montevideo, and less than 20 per cent of the total population was classed as agricultural. Agriculture is still the basis of the economy, supplying all the exports, but Uruguay seems to have drifted into a more sophisticated stage of economic development without having been compelled to do so through pressure on the land. Only 13·5 per cent is classed as arable or under permanent crops and the actual area under field crops is considerably less than 10 per cent of the whole country. Permanent pastures of varying quality occupy about two thirds of the surface, and some 10 per cent of the remainder is considered to be potential farm land. There is a great amount of slack to be taken up therefore, both by bringing more permanent pasture under the plough and by increasing yields by the application of fertilizers. The principal crops grown are wheat (400–500,000 hectares in the early 1960s) and maize (about 275,000 hectares) but yields of these and of barley and oats are low compared with those in Argentina, and from time to time wheat even has been imported. Other crops include linseed and the sunflower. Little is done to improve the natural fodder supply for the 8 m. cattle and 20 m. sheep, which together provide almost all the exports of Uruguay. In the early 1960s, exports were made up roughly as follows (in per cent):

Raw wool	35	Meat	25
Wool tops	15	Hides	10

Uruguay has not so far discovered economic minerals of importance and has only a limited hydroelectric potential except on the Uruguay river, which forms the boundary with Argentina. The relatively high consumption of energy is provided for either by imports of oil (mainly from Venezuela), much of it crude, to be processed in the Montevideo refinery, or by the Rio Negro power station. About 75 per cent of the electricity is in fact provided from hydroelectric sources, but this is insufficient, and in the immediate future the emphasis is on increasing the thermal electric capacity in Montevideo. Imported oil, together with natural gas, to be piped from Argentina, probably across the Plate estuary from Buenos Aires to Colonia, and even peat from reserves near the Atlantic coast, are sources for power station and other needs. It seems probable, however, that the Salto Grande rapids, on the Uruguay River some 20 km above Salto, may be used to generate very large quantities of electricity. Construction works would, however, cost some U.S. $ 400 m.

Lack of data for the departments of Uruguay makes it difficult to study the distribution of economic activities and of other features of the human geography. Only very broad aspects can be noted here. The density of population tends to diminish away from the southern coast and from the Uruguay River towards the more remote interior and the Atlantic coast region. No sizable areas remain unoccupied however and there is no longer a fringe of settlement facing completely empty lands, as around much of Amazonia.

Like the pampa of Argentina, the arrangement of population and of economic activities can be thought of in terms of a series of zones of increasing distance from Montevideo. With 46 per cent of the total population of Uruguay, the Montevideo area probably dominates the economic life of its country more than any other Latin American capital does. It handles almost all the international trade, consumes about 75 per cent of the electricity and has most of the industries. Secondly, there is a zone about 600 km long, curving round from Punta del Este (a resort) in the east, through Colonia del Sacramento (the ferry port for Buenos Aires) up the Uruguay valley to Salto. This contains most of the other towns of Uruguay and much of the arable land. The rest of the country, mostly grazing land, has only about 20 per cent of the total population on about two thirds of the area, but contributes a large part of the exports.

Like Argentina, most of the foreign trade of Uruguay is with West Europe since apart from wool it has little that is needed in North America. Trade was shared out among the main partners roughly as follows in 1960:

	Exports to per cent	Imports from per cent
U.S.A.	15	25
U.K.	25	8
EEC	35	15
Venezuela	negligible	15

Brazil and Argentina each account for about 5 per cent of the total trade.

17.4. ARGENTINA—INTRODUCTION AND HISTORY

Argentina is second in area but third in population among Latin American countries. Unlike the other large and medium countries, its population of 20 m. is almost entirely European, since the Indians were virtually exterminated by the end of the nineteenth century except in the extreme north. It is also more highly urbanized than any other, having as early as 1914 some 53 per cent of its population in places with over 2,000 inhabitants, and in the early 1960s, about two thirds. Population growth is somewhat slower than in most of Latin America. Economically, Argentina differs greatly from the rest of Latin America since in the first place agriculture employed only 30 per cent of the total active population in 1947[*] and 25 per cent in the early 1960s, and accounts for only about 20 per cent of gross domestic product (manufacturing 20 per cent, mining only 1 per cent) yet provides virtually all the exports. Moreover, the exports are almost entirely warm temperate products, although tropical and subtropical crops are grown for home consumption.

The *per caput* gross domestic product is much higher than in Brazil or Mexico and other indices of a reasonably high standard of living are the large food consumption and high percentage of literate population. This can only be explained by its possession of a magnificent farming region, the pampa, with fertile soils, adequate rainfall and a level or gently undulating surface, covering an area about the size of Spain. In some respects, Argentina resembles Australia or even Canada rather than the rest of Latin America, but if it were organized as efficiently as these, its standard of living would be much higher than it is.

[*] 1,534,000 out of 5,163,000[2].

Argentina is a puzzle to economists because its economy is stagnating, yet it has the features of a developed country and the conditions for growth: 'The case of Argentina has intrigued many present observers because its social and economic structure is more like that of dynamic and developed countries than of underdeveloped and stagnating ones'[3]. In Latin America, only Haiti, Paraguay and Bolivia have failed to advance appreciably in the last two decades.

In Argentina, the sown area has remained roughly the same for three decades, and yields of most agricultural products have hardly changed. Exports in the late 1950s were roughly only two thirds what they were 30 years previously, and on account of population growth, only half as much *per caput*. Indices for gross domestic product have changed little since the mid-1950s.

1950 = 100		1960	117
1958	119	1961	124
1959	113	1962	119

In contrast to Mexico and Brazil, industrial production has not grown since the mid-1950s, and in the early 1960s, much capacity was idle, while the actual value of manufacturing diminished in 1963, being 20 per cent less than in 1962. Nor is a comparison with 1952 flattering:

1952 = 100	
1961	120
1962	108

Various reasons have been put forward to explain the situation. In the first place, the system of land tenure in the pampa region has failed to provide incentives to increase yields. Much of the land is in the hands of a limited number of owners and is worked by labourers or tenant farmers; the owners were disliked by Perón anyway, and on the whole did not collaborate with his regime. Secondly, energy consumption has risen fast, but home production of energy, never adequate, has lagged behind, and imports have been crippling. Thirdly, the traditional importers of Argentinian foodstuffs, notably the industrial countries of Western Europe, have been increasing the productivity of their own agriculture. Moreover, industry was expanded during the Perón period without an adequate justification either in terms of ingredients or size of market.

Until the nineteenth century Argentina was one of the less developed parts of Latin America. Thanks to its peripheral and extra tropical position and its lack of precious metals it exported little to Spain at all and the population of the parts actually controlled by Spain practised subsistence agriculture or sent pastoral products such as hides, as well as mules, to the Andean mining communities. The main area of settlement lay in the triangle between Mendoza, the Plate estuary and Tucumán (see *Figure 17.2b*). Missions operated to the northeast of this area, but untamed Indians prevented effective occupation of lands south of Buenos Aires–Mendoza. The most active part of the country was the northwest, closest to Bolivia and Peru, and for much of the colonial period Buenos Aires itself was not permitted to trade directly with Spain.

The Argentinian economist Aldo Ferrer in a recent economic history of Argentina[3] recognizes a number of stages in Argentinian development. A period of regional subsistence economies lasted until about 1800. This was followed by a period of transition from 1800–1860, during which the dominance of Buenos Aires was established, as it became the main outlet for the country, and livestock farming expanded, but the interior stagnated. 1860 to 1930 was the great period of development based on the export of primary products; during this period the Indians were cleared from the lands south of Buenos Aires, land was enclosed and arable farming spread over the pampa, most of the railways were built,* most of the immigration took place (reinforcing the dominance of the coast) and refrigeration made the export of fresh meat to Europe possible. According to Ferrer, Argentina entered a period of non-integrated industrial economy around 1930; industrial because manufacturing had become by then the key to the economic life of Argentina, but non-integrated because manufacturing depended on the importation of most of its equipment and of fuel and many raw materials. It was developed *at the expense* of agriculture, which was therefore unable to maintain a level of exports sufficient to keep manufacturing expanding. At the end of 1962 it was stated that 'while the industrial and State sectors of the economy had been capitalized by 17 and 42 per cent, respectively, between 1940 and 1955, agriculture and livestock had been decapitalized by 20 per cent and public services by 30 per cent'.[4]

Figures to illustrate the growth of employment in manufacturing in Argentina are only very approximate and the definition clearly varies at different periods. By 1895 there were some 170,000 persons employed in 23,000 establishments. Most of these were very small places, making furniture, clothing and other light manufactures, or processing food. Many of the new immigrants were employed in them, and were even responsible for establishing some. In 1914 the number employed had risen to 410,000 in 49,000 establishments, and a textile industry had by then been developed, but the number included many service activities. The First World War encouraged development, while in the 1930s, large importing companies began to make or assemble some of their goods in Argentina. The Second World War and national policy continued to encourage the expansion of employment in manufacturing, which rose from 420,000 in 1935 to 920,000 in 1948.

Throughout the modern period, Argentina, like Australia, has been a highly urbanized country, since much of the development of new areas has

	Population in thousands		Percentage	
	urban	rural	urban	rural
1869	493	1,244	28	72
1895	1,488	1,466	37	63
1914	4,152	3,728	53	47
1947	9,932	5,917	62	38
1960	13,000	7,000	65	35

* By 1930, 38,000 km, to which only about another 6,000 had been added by 1960.

been on a commercial rather than subsistence level with relatively high productivity per worker and a considerable population engaged in processing and service activities. Thus in 1870, almost before any railways had been built, nearly 30 per cent of the population was urban, the proportion for Brazil in 1950. There has been a fairly steady increase since[5].

17.5. ARGENTINA—PHYSICAL BACKGROUND AND AGRICULTURE

Although Argentina is fortunate in having the only large, relatively densely, populated lowland area in Latin America, much of the country is high and rugged. The roughly north-south Argentina–Chile boundary follows the Andes almost the whole of its length, keeping along or close to the main watershed except in the southern third. The Andes are higher and wider north of Mendoza, and a small part of the Altiplano of Bolivia extends into the northwest; much of the way the crest exceeds 5,000 m and passes are high and difficult. South of Mendoza the crest is lower and there are many easy passes across the range. The northern part of the Andes is flanked by lower, parallel, ranges, while the mountains of Córdoba stand some 500 km to the east. This is an area with basin and ranges features, and with extensive salinas. The eastern part of Argentina consists of lowlands rarely exceeding 500 m, mostly gently undulating, but in places flat and ill-drained, especially between the rivers Paraná and Uruguay. Roughly to the south of the Río Negro is the plateau of Patagonia, with only limited coastal lowlands, but wide deep valleys.

Mean annual precipitation in Argentina diminishes westwards from over 1,000 mm in the extreme east (Misiones) to under 200 mm in many valleys in the west and over most of Patagonia. The northern Andes are on the whole dry, and, as in Chile, serve only as a modest source of water for the irrigated areas to the east, but precipitation is higher on the Andes in the south. Many of the rivers flowing east from the northern Andes drain into interior basins, and almost all the water entering the Plate estuary comes from the Paraná and Uruguay rivers.

The principal types of vegetation according to Rampa[6] are mapped in *Figure 3.7b*. They are divided into sub-tropical and temperate. There are two limited areas of dense sub-tropical forest, that in Misiones being the extremity of the forests of South Brazil, and a belt of forest extending along the eastern foot of the Andes to Tucumán. Between these, the Chaco area consists of a mixture of forest and of savanna, while the Mesopotamian region, lying between the Rivers Paraná and Uruguay, is partly forested, partly open grassland.

The temperate zone consists of the pampa, a grassland with virtually no trees originally, and a dry summer period. The northern limit of the pampa is considered to be its junction with the forests and savanna lands, but on the west and southwest, diminishing precipitation is the usual criterion, and 500–600 mm is considered to mark the margin. Beyond lies the semi-arid *monte* region with a xerophytic vegetation of small trees and shrubs. Patagonia is also semi-arid, but vegetation varies considerably with relief conditions. The valleys have grassland suitable for pasture, but much of the intervening mass is dry and windswept, with a thin cover of shrubs. Only in the Andes in the west is there a forest cover. The northern Andes is distinguished as a separate vegetation region on account of its low temperatures, arid conditions and shrub vegetation. A considerable part of the drier margin of the pampa has already been adversely affected as a result of cultivation, and one geographer[5] puts the area already ruined by soil erosion as $\frac{1}{2}$ m. hectares, 7 m. as in danger and 34 m. as susceptible.

Of the total area of Argentina (2,750,000 km²), 300,000 km² or over 10 per cent is arable, and another 1,113,000 permanent meadows and pastures, while 994,000 is classed as forest, but much of this is only partially tree covered; 353,000 is useless. These figures are old but still reasonably true of the situation now. There were in 1957 some 15,000 km² of irrigated land. The outstanding feature of the geography of Argentinian agriculture is the contrast between the pampa region and the rest of the country. Almost all of the pampa region consists either of arable land or of pasture that could be improved, though towards the margins the intensity of use diminishes. In the early 1960s, 53 per cent consisted of unimproved pastures, only 17 per cent was cultivated for fodder, and most of the rest was cultivated for other crops. Throughout the rest of the country, arable land is the exception, and the few sizable concentrations are set in areas of forest, poor grazing or virtually semi-desert. In western Argentina irrigation is necessary for crop farming but in the northeast rainfall is sufficient.

In very broad terms, the pampa covers 15 per cent of the total area but has nearly 88 per cent of the cultivated land and most of the cattle raised for beef. But the contribution to the total value of Argentinian agricultural production made by the pampa has diminished considerably in the last 30 years; in the late 1920s it accounted for nearly 80 per cent, in the late 1950s, less than 70 per cent. While the pampa has stagnated agriculturally, considerable progress has been made in clearing new land in the north and extending irrigation in the west. This continues, for example, in the construction of dams, as in Chubut, 140 km west of Trelew (the Florentino Ameghino dam to irrigate 30,000 hectares), and in Río Negro province (Instituto de Desarrollo del Valle Inferior, 75,000 hectares). As a result, the rest of the country accounts now for nearly half of the value of field and tree crops, but the pampa, with its production of fodder crops and its improved pastures, still accounts for 75 per cent of pastoral products.

The contrast between the pampa and the rest of the country is also brought out in the range of products. Agriculture in the pampa is now based on the cultivation of cereals, both for human consumption and for livestock, of other crops for livestock and of oilseeds, and on permanent pastures that could be improved, and the raising of cattle. These crops are only grown in limited quantities elsewhere in Argentina, but cattle raising is spreading northwards into Chaco and Corrientes–Misiones. Commercial agriculture outside the pampa is based on cotton in the north, sugar in the northwest, vines and deciduous fruits in the west and sheep raising in the south.

Within the pampa there are regional differences in emphasis, with maize, for example, especially important in the area of highest rainfall, wheat on the southern margins and so on. Local differences, on the other hand, depend not so much on physical features, which change only gradually over great distances, but on the choice of particular farmers. Platt[7] illustrates excellently how two adjacent large units of land tenure, once similar in function, now have very different uses of land in virtually identical physical conditions.

Table 17.2 shows the main products of Argentinian arable farming.

TABLE 17.2*

Argentina: Main Crops Around 1960 (1961/62 average)
Yields in Hundreds of kg/per hectare

	Area (thous. of hectares)	Production (thous. of tons)	1948/49–1952/53	1961/62
Maize	2,757	5,220	14·8	18·9
Maize U.S.A.	23,653	92,092	24·9	38·9
Wheat	4,198	5,100	11·5	12·1
Wheat France	3,997	9,574	18·3	23·9
Rye	694	510	7·3	7·3
Barley	742	800	12·1	10·8
Oats	597	700	11·7	11·7
Millet	159	215	8·1	13·5
Sorghum	893	1,642	n.a.	18·4
Rice	53	182	30·5	34·4
Groundnuts	280	433	10·1	15·5
Cotton seed	540	204	4·5	3·8
Linseed	1,172	818	6·4	6·9
Sunflower seed	1,185	834	7·4	7·0
Cotton lint	540	110	2·4	2·0
Sugar cane	253	8,805	229	223
Vines	244	2,247		

* More recent data: Maize 1961/62 5,900, 1962/63 4,350
Wheat 1962/63 4,900, 1963/64 6,250
Sugar 1963/64 10,650
Sunflower seed 1962/63 550.

With the inclusion of the remaining crops not listed in Table 17.2, little more than half of the 30 m. officially recorded as arable land, or some 16 m. hectares, is actually used for crops other than those grown for fodder; these occupy 9 m. more hectares (alfalfa over 7 m.). The difference appears to consist largely of pastures that have not recently been improved. The remainder of the pampa is used for grazing and the natural pastures here only carry 0·8 cattle per hectare.

The five provinces that contain the pampa region account for almost all the wheat, oats, rye, barley, linseed and sunflower grown in Argentina, and most of the maize, but the proportions of each crop contributed by the different provinces varies. In 1960/61, roughly half of the volume of cereals grown in the pampa region came from Buenos Aires province alone.

Of the other main crops grown in Argentina, Chaco had nearly 90 per cent of the cotton area, Tucumán nearly 80 per cent of the sugar, and Mendoza and San Juan 87 per cent of the vineyards and most of the olives. The western oases also grow fodder crops to supplement the poor natural pastures around them. This high degree of regional specialization, more typical of North America and Australia than of Latin America, reflects both the great variety of physical conditions in Argentina and the advanced

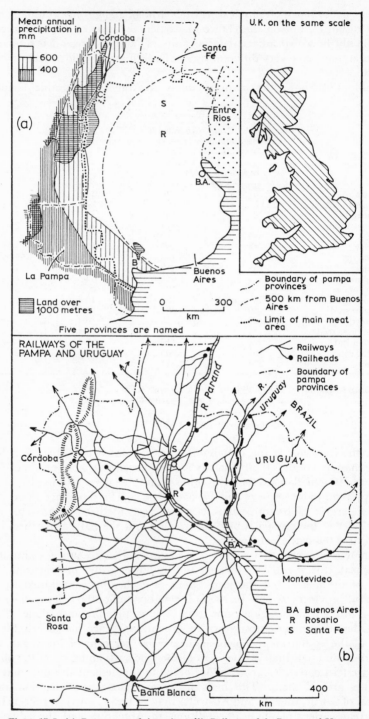

Figure 17.5. (a) *Pampa area of Argentina.* (b) *Railways of the Pampa and Uruguay*

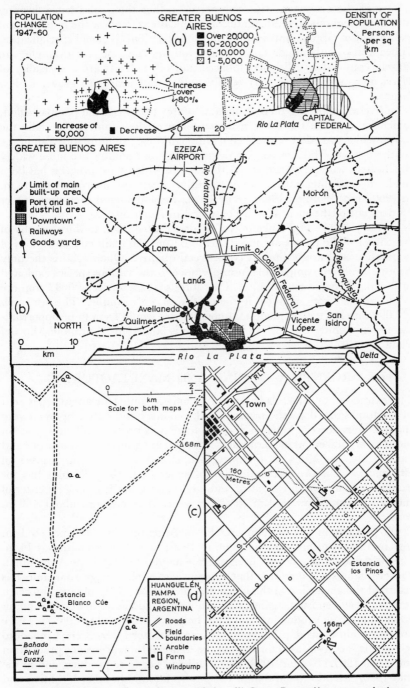

Figure 17.6. (a) Greater Buenos Aires; population. (b) Greater Buenos Aires; communications. (c) and (d) Farming areas in Argentina. (c) in Corrientes. (d) in Buenos Aires State (Huanguelen)

385

nature of the economy, with commercial rather than subsistence farming almost throughout, and adequate communications to allow the interregional movement of large quantities of farm products. This regional specialization appears also with minor crops[9]: tung oil and manioc, for example, are largely confined to Misiones, tobacco and citrus fruits are a speciality of Corrientes, and a large part of the apples and pears are grown in Río Negro.

In livestock farming there is again a contrast between the pampa region, which has most of the cattle[10], and the rest of the country, especially the south, which has most of the sheep, although these are numerous also in the southern part of Buenos Aires province. Pigs and poultry are more widely distributed, while the northeast is the area in which most progress has been made in extending cattle raising recently. Cattle numbered about 45 m. in 1960, only 43 m. on 1963; some 11 m. are slaughtered each year. Over 75 per cent of the meat is now consumed in Argentina.

Forestry and fishing make only a modest contribution to the economy of Argentina. The forests are mostly remote from the main concentrations of population and are of limited commercial quality. Quebracho is the only semi-natural tree comparable in importance to the various species exploited in Brazil. A major contribution of the forests is as a source of fuel; iron ore is still smelted from charcoal in the northwest, for example. The fish catch (77,000 tons in 1959) is modest, although there would seem to be opportunities for expanding this. Most of the catch is landed at Altura and Mar del Plata.

17.6. ARGENTINA—MINING AND MANUFACTURING

The extraction of minerals in Argentina only accounts for about 1 per cent of the total gross domestic product of the country and only employs a very small labour force. Most of the production consists of oil and gas, an industry organized on modern lines; the remaining minerals, numerous and varied, but negligible in quantity, are mined with varying degrees of efficiency. Coal production in the extreme south (Río Turbio) has for example recently been expanded and modernized, but it is only a matter of increasing from $\frac{1}{4}$ m. to 1 m. tons per year. Reserves are about 450 m. tons.

Oil production began commercially in Argentina in 1907, passed 1 m. tons in 1926, 2 m. in 1930 and 5 m. in 1956; the 1963 estimate was 14 m. tons. Production has largely been in State hands* or by private Argentinian concerns, and some maintain that reluctance to admit foreign companies has retarded the expansion of the industry. In 1959, the help of several foreign companies was enlisted, against national policy and almost in desperation, in order to increase production, but their help was discarded in 1963†. There are four main areas of production in Argentina (see *Figure 8.2*): Comodoro Rivadavia has accounted for most of the national total ever since production started in 1907. Around 1920, Plaza Huincul began to produce, and in the mid-1920s, Mendoza and Salta. Oil has been found in other localities, and

* Yacimientos Petrolíferos Fiscales.
† Compensation was being considered in 1964.

considerable areas are promising. The oilfields are all distant from the main consuming area of the Lower Plate and their development has to some extent depended on the provision of transport facilities, once demand in their local areas has been satisfied. In contrast to agriculture and manufacturing, mineral production has expanded rapidly in Argentina on account of the recent growth of oil production: 1952 = 100, 1961 = 302, 1962 = 346, and in a matter of a few years, oil imports have been cut almost to nothing thanks to roughly a threefold increase in output. Imports dropped from U.S. $ 317 m. in 1957 to U.S. $ 60 m. in 1963, a gratifying achievement considering that in the mid-1950s oil made up 20–25 per cent of the value of imports.

About three quarters of the energy consumed in Argentina in 1958 was oil. The following figures show the main sources consumed in percentages (after conversion to oil equivalent):

Oil	75
Natural gas	4
Coal	5
Wood	15
Hydroelectric	1

In that year nearly two thirds of the oil and much of the coal were imported. Since 1958 there has been little change in the relative importance of different sources, only in their origin (home produced or imported), but natural gas and hydroelectricity are likely to gain relatively. The energy was consumed as follows in 1958 (in per cent):

Industry	36	Domestic	12
Transport	28	Mines	5
Thermal electricity	15	Rural	2

Very little of the hydroelectric potential has yet been developed and over 90 per cent of the electricity generated comes from thermal stations burning oil or other fuel. The Greater Buenos Aires area both produced and consumed roughly 70 per cent of all the thermal electricity, Rosario (10 per cent), Santa Fé, Córdoba and Mendoza (each about 5 per cent) most of the rest. So far there has been no serious attempt to establish an electricity grid, but with the completion of large hydroelectric stations in the Andes this will be desirable. Oil and natural gas on the other hand are now moved great distances by pipeline. The hydroelectric potential is distributed roughly as follows: Patagonia has 40 per cent, the Andes 20 per cent, and the Paraná and Uruguay systems most of the rest. Work is in progress on a large multipurpose project in the south on the Limay River, and power stations with a total capacity of about 1 m. kW are planned, costing about U.S. $ 300 m. There is also a project near Mendoza (Puente del Inca) on the Tunuyan River.

Although the industrial growth of Southeast Brazil has received great publicity lately, the Plate area in Argentina has an older complex with some

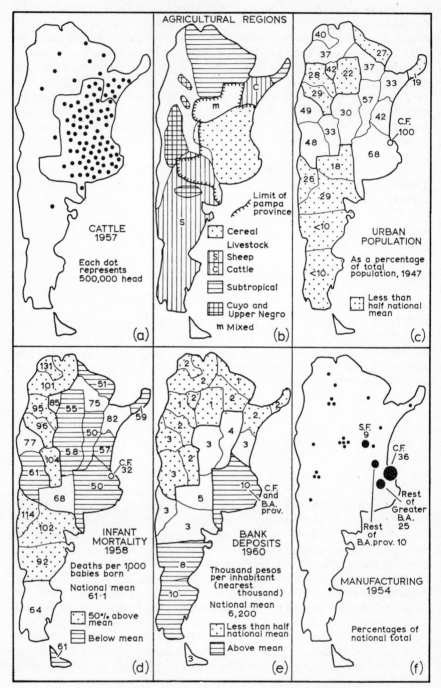

Figure 17.7. Argentina. (a) Cattle 1957. (b) Agricultural regions. (c) Urban population. (d) Infant mortality 1958. (e) Bank deposits 1960. (f) Manufacturing 1954

very large factories*, with a comparable number of people employed, and perhaps still a wider range of branches represented. Of the industries of Argentina, food and drinks account for about 20 per cent of the value, textiles 13 per cent, metals 10 per cent and vehicles 11 per cent. In spite of slow progress since about 1950, industry is becoming more sophisticated and near self-sufficiency has been achieved in cellulose and paper, some chemicals, rubber, and many metal goods. For example, the value of motor vehicle imports declined from U.S. $ 166 m. in 1961 to about U.S. $ 40 m.

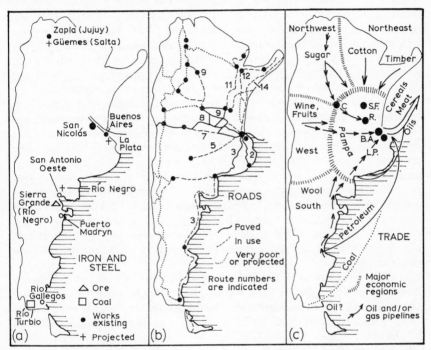

Figure 1.7.8 Argentina. (a) Iron and Steel. (b) Roads. (c) Trade

in 1964. However, the iron and steel industry has only been slightly developed and the manufacture of chemicals, excluding oil refining, has been very modest until recently. The weakness of Argentinian industry lies therefore in the lack of a heavy industrial base and the need to import many semi-finished products.

In the mid-1950s Greater Buenos Aires alone accounted for about 60 per cent of the value of manufacturing, while about 20 per cent more came from the La Plata–Santa Fé belt. Córdoba, which has certain attractions, including good electricity supplies, is the only concentration of any size outside the main area mentioned and one of the largest hydroelectric stations, La Vina, with a capacity of 300,000 kW is here. Mendoza and Tucumán are large towns, but their industry is mainly concerned with processing local agricultural products.

* For example, Alpargatas footwear factory in Buenos Aires is by far the largest in Latin America and produces 60 m. pairs a year.

There are, however, signs of some decentralization. The following are examples of new industries being established outside the main concentration in the early 1960s: Córdoba area, pulp and cardboard (Almafuerte), cement (Malagueño); cement in San Juan; petrochemicals in Puerto Madryn (Chubut), in Cinco Saltos (near Neuquén); cellulose from bagasse in Ledesma, Jujuy. Few of the small towns of the pampa away from the lower Plate seem to be attracting industry at the moment but a large new pulpboard factory is being built at Tornaquist. One disadvantage of a location in the interior of the pampa region is that the railway system, although dense, has evolved mainly to cater for the movement of goods towards or away from Buenos Aires (see *Figure 17.5*). In the Buenos Aires area itself there has been considerable decentralization of industry away from the districts near the port, such as Avellaneda. La Plata is becoming attractive with its large oil refining capacity, while places such as Pilar and Campana (chemicals) to the northwest of Buenos Aires are expanding.

The future success of industry in Argentina is considered to depend on the growth of a successful iron and steel industry. Although Argentina has iron ore reserves it has never used these in large quantities, and although it has many small coal deposits, these are not usually suitable for coking. The steel that has been produced up to now has been made largely from imported pig iron, from scrap, or from iron smelted locally with charcoal, mainly at the State controlled Zapla works in Jujuy. Many small steelworks function in the vicinity of Buenos Aires, but in no year before 1960 did the Argentinian total exceed 250,000 tons a year, while the pig iron produced was usually a mere 20–40,000 tons. This situation is now changing and steel production rose to 440,000 tons in 1961 and about 1 m. tons in 1963, but demand has risen sharply too.

At the moment most of the efforts to establish an iron and steel industry have been concentrated on the complex at San Nicolás near Rosario. On a large site here (about 350 hectares) by the navigable Paraná, which takes vessels with a draught up to 28 ft., work has been in progress since 1952 on the General Savio plant. The cost of construction has been about U.S. \$ 300 m., and has been financed from several sources. Within a radius of about 250 km is 85 per cent of the home market for steel. The first steel was produced in 1961, but the plant has not been working to full capacity, for in 1963 it only produced ¾ m. tons out of a capacity of 1·2 m. Eventually it is planned to have a capacity of 1·8 m. tons. In addition to the iron and steel works itself there are a coking plant, a thermal electric power station (300,000 kW) and rolling mills. In 1961 the following ingredients were used:

> 420,000 tons of coal imported or from Río Turbio*
> 415,000 tons of iron ore, mostly imported
> 160,000 tons of limestone from inland.

In 1963 the plant was employing 2,000–2,500 workers in the production of steel, 4,000–4,500 in the construction of new plant.

---

* The national coal is not satisfactory itself for metallurgical coke, but can be mixed, forming 15–25 per cent of the total; this would consume about 300,000 tons a year.

The plant at San Nicolás cannot satisfy the entire needs of Argentina and the establishment of other works is being considered. One plan is for a U.S. $ 200 m. iron and steel works at La Plata (Propulsora Siderúrgica) financed by European interests and with a capacity of 1·4 m. tons of ingot steel and 1·1 m. of semi-finished products. Another is to increase the capacity of the already mentioned Zapla works from about 40,000 to 150,000 tons and to have a steel and rolling plant at Güemes. An iron and steel works is also proposed for the province of Río Negro, near the Sierra Grande iron ore deposits; it would use electricity from the new hydroelectric station on the Limay.

The motor vehicle industry in Argentina has grown up independently from steel. Several major plants are now functioning; those listed below are not all but give an idea of the location and scale of the new industry:

Buenos Aires area

(a) Ford Motor Co. at Pacheco near Buenos Aires.

(b) Fevre y Basset, with Chrysler, at San Justo.

(c) IAFA making Peugeot models under licence and financed partly by French and Swiss interests. The plant in Buenos Aires was started in 1961, is to produce 30,000 vehicles a year, and to employ 7,000 persons, housed in a special settlement.

Córdoba

(a) IKA (Kaiser) with main works at Córdoba supplying 40 per cent of the Argentinian market. The firm employs some 50,000 persons altogether in various activities.

(b) Fiat, main works, plus plant at Caseros in Buenos Aires province.

17.7. ARGENTINA—TRANSPORT AND REGIONAL PROBLEMS

In comparison with most Latin American countries, conditions in the more densely peopled parts of Argentina are very easy for rail and road construction, but the great size of the country should not be forgotten (see *Figure 17.5*). Between the Andes in the west and the coast in the east, only the Sierras de Córdoba and the Paraná river form serious obstacles to movement. While serving as a very important route to the interior of South America, the presence of the Paraná has tended to isolate and retard development in the Mesopotamian area, although there are several ferries, and a road tunnel has now been built between Santa Fé and Paraná. Otherwise the railway system is continuous as far south as Río Negro province, while poor quality roads reach to the southern extremity of Argentina. But in practice the south depends on shipping and air services and a pipeline to link it with the rest of the country.

Like Brazil, Argentina has a long coastline, with a navigable waterway, continuing into the interior in the north. But unlike Brazil, Argentina is at the end of international shipping routes, not on them, and most in fact terminate at the Plate estuary; few coastal links are therefore provided by international vessels. A rough guide to the relative importance of different ports for foreign trade can be obtained from the figures for the tonnage of non-coastal shipping using them (in 1959). The total was roughly 12 m. tons:

	Thousands of tons	Percentage
Buenos Aires	8,867	74
La Plata	605	5
Campana	782	6·5
Rosario	541	4·5
Bahía Blanca	545	4·5
Quequen (Necochea)	205	1·5
Others	390	

The four ports on the Paraná-Plate Estuary have about 90 per cent of the traffic. The actual value of goods handled is very much concentrated in Buenos Aires, which receives 90 per cent of the imports, but handles only 35 per cent of the exports. Numerous other ports handle the products of extensive but thinly peopled hinterlands in the south: for example, Rawson, Comodoro Rivadavia, Rio Gallegos. The latter, together with San Nicolás on the Paraná, and a port in Río Negro or Chubut to serve the Sierra Grande iron ore deposits, are being improved or constructed to cater for the new iron and steel industry.

The internal movement of goods in Argentina has depended almost entirely upon the railways until the Second World War, with local hauls to the nearest railway siding by animal drawn vehicles. Until after the Second World War motor vehicles were largely confined to the main towns and to this day the route length of paved roads outside these is only about one third that of the railways. The construction of railways began in Argentina before 1860, but not until the 1870s did rapid construction begin. 1900–10 was the decade in which the largest amount was built, and since 1950 little has been added, while it was planned to close in the early 1960s nearly 4,000 km and to cut down the staff on the railways from 210,000 to 135,000:

The following amount was added in successive decades (kilometres)[11].

	Additional	Total		Additional	Total
Pre 1880	2,500	2,500	1910–20	5,900	33,900
1880–90	6,900	9,400	1920–30	5,300	38,100
1890–1900	7,100	16,600	1930–40	3,100	41,300
1900–1910	11,400	28,000	1940–50	2,400	43,700

Very broadly the system consists firstly of a relatively close network covering most of the pampa, secondly of several important interregional lines extending from this region, and reaching out to the boundaries of Chile (near Mendoza), Bolivia (Jujuy province) and Paraguay, and thirdly of a system in Mesopotamia, and individual lines in the South, not linked to the main system. The map of railways in Argentina gives a false impression of completeness, however, for in the first place up to the 1940s the now nationalized system had largely been developed by several separate companies, each with its own running practices, and involving at least three gauges. Secondly, the main concern was to link the interior with the ports, and although there are transverse lines, as from Bahía Blanca to Rosario, journeys at right angles to the radial lines usually involve many detours, even if they are possible at all. Little has been done to modernize the system since nationalization in 1949 except to introduce diesel traction on some lines, and journeys are usually slow.

Since the Second World War, increasing attention has been given to road improvement and construction, and since the late 1950s, with the increase in the manufacture of motor vehicles in Argentina, the great expansion in oil production and the neglect of the railways since the 1930s (rehabilitation will cost U.S. $ 300 m.), particularly of rolling stock, road transport has become more attractive and several major interregional roads have been paved (see *Figure 17.8*), but most still duplicate the railways, and nothing so impressive has been done as in Brazil to bring remote areas into the main sphere of economic life. In 1960 only about one third of the 60,000 km of major roads were paved, but another 20,000 are to be paved by 1970 in a programme costing some U.S. $ 900 m. As in other Latin American countries, air transport is highly developed in Argentina, but except in the south is less vital to the cohesion of the country than in most others.

The stagnation of the Argentinian economy in the last three decades has been stressed and illustrated throughout this chapter. Obviously this has been due partly to organization obstacles connected with land tenure, personal ambitions and the creation of industries lacking a sound basis. It has undoubtedly been due also to the tendency to neglect the rest of the country and concentrate most of the manufacturing and the purchasing power of the country in and near the national capital. As long as a large urban concentration does not actually choke itself out of existence through congestion of movement there seems no objection to having a large part of the population of a country or of a large major civil division in one place. California has almost the highest standard of living in the world yet most of its population is in two small areas. Australia has over half of its population in five major centres and is three times as large as Argentina. There would be nothing wrong with Greater Buenos Aires if other parts of the country were given more attention.

One can perhaps most usefully think of regional problems in Argentina in terms of concentric zones around Buenos Aires. The administrative, commercial and financial life of Argentina, as well as many of the higher educational institutions, are concentrated in the *Capital Federal*. This is set in Greater Buenos Aires, whose share of the population of Argentina has grown steadily in the last few decades from the already surprisingly high figure of 26 per cent in 1914 to 30 per cent in 1947 and 34 per cent in 1960, passing 7 m. probably in 1962. Greater Buenos Aires handles most of the foreign trade, produces nearly two thirds of Argentinian manufactures, and consumes about this proportion of the electricity.

The attractions of Greater Buenos Aires to industries include an infrastructure superior to that in any other part of the country, its large share of the home market, its access to imported fuel, raw materials and equipment, its skilled labour. It has absorbed both immigrants from Europe and from rural Argentina, mainly the pampa region, which with mechanization and stagnation of production has had a surplus recently. The pressure of population in the Greater Buenos Aires area is reflected in the housing shortage and the failure to provide low rent housing. It has been calculated that some 300,000 people, or about 4 per cent of the total population, live in shanty towns, *villas miserias*, of which there are about 55. The industrial district of Avellaneda has 90,000 such people in its total population of some 400,000. Certainly the problem of shanty towns is not so great as elsewhere in Latin America; nor is it confined to Buenos Aires in Argentina*. What is more, about 90 per cent of the shanty town population is employed, and on the whole lives reasonably well thanks to its not having to pay rents. As a whole, however, and particularly in the five largest towns, Argentina has an enormous housing problem, and it is considered desirable to rehouse in about ten years some $1\frac{1}{2}$ m. families or nearly one third of the total population; the cost would be U.S. $ 7,500 m.

Extending northwest and southeast of Greater Buenos Aires is a belt of country along the lower Paraná and Plate estuary between Santa Fé and La Plata, a distance of nearly 500 km, containing roughly another 3 m. people, or, with Greater Buenos Aires, roughly half the total Argentinian population. This is in no sense a conurbation but, given the particular configuration of the coast and lower Paraná (a convex face looking to the interior), forms a narrow band of particular attraction, with a coast or navigable waterway, busy land routes parallel to this and a reasonably central position in the national market. The high proportion of almost all branches of manufacturing has already been referred to.

Beyond this belt lie the fertile lands of the pampas. Well served by railways, but little affected by industrialization, possessing no minerals and lacking urban centres of more than moderate size, the region remains the best and most prosperous predominantly rural region in Latin America, but many districts are actually losing population (see *Figure 19.4a*). It is roughly twice as large as the whole of the United Kingdom. Here, given the incentive, there is great scope for increasing agricultural production; the incentive could come from growing population and pressure on food supplies in other LAFTA countries.

At a distance of at least several hundred kilometres from Buenos Aires, on or beyond the fringes of the pampa region, lie a number of regional centres, in secondary clusters of population. Closest of these to Buenos Aires and formerly central in the main triangle of colonial settlement (see *Figure 17.2*) is Córdoba, which has recently attracted many industries. Another centre of influence is Tucumán, in the northwest, centre of the sugar growing region and roughly half way between Buenos Aires and La Paz. In the west, Mendoza occupies a comparable position on the route to Chile but is much closer to Santiago than to Buenos Aires. A number of other smaller clusters and centres occur in the northern half of Argentina, such as around Corrientes and Resistencia, the oases of Catamarca and of San Juan, but to the southwest and south of the pampa total population is very small. Thus, a further region may be suggested, the fringe of the country, with a low density of population and no large towns, but with resources

---

* Comodoro Rivadavia, for example, has nearly half of its 60,000 inhabitants in *villas miserias*.

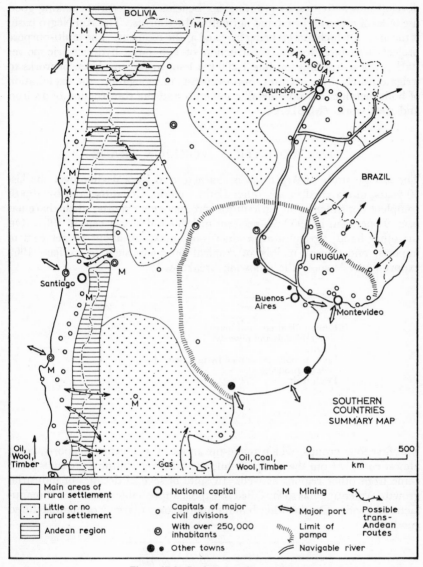

Figure 17.9. Southern countries, summary map

valuable enough still to attract settlers in spite of the pull of the capital: particularly, the sub-tropical lands of Misiones and Formosa, the minerals of Patagonia, and places in and near the Andes, especially south of Mendoza, in which hydroelectric power and irrigation are being developed.

While it cannot be hoped to alter fundamentally the present distribution of non-agricultural activities in the country, either by dispersing industry too much in various regional centres or by creating a new major industrial area, a chance has been given both to Patagonia and to the Northwest to

395

develop new activities, by granting tax benefits to enterprises making good use of local mineral, forest and agricultural resources. The Río Negro basin is the area in which most is being invested at the moment. The multi-purpose project here includes the construction of two large hydroelectric power stations, of a transmission line 1,200 km long to Buenos Aires, of works to irrigate nearly 1 m. hectares, improvements to navigation, the exploitation of both metallic and non-metallic minerals and the construction of an iron and steel works (MISIPA).

17.8. ARGENTINA—FOREIGN TRADE

The foreign trade of Argentina is characterized by a decline over the last 30 years, unmatched in any other Latin American country, and by almost complete dependence on agricultural products for exports; their share has been 94 per cent in 1959, 95 per cent in 1960 and 97 per cent in 1961. On the other hand, agricultural products only make up about 10 per cent of imports, and consist mainly of tropical products such as coffee. 1962 export figures[12] show the following breakdown:

Items	Percentage
Cereals, flour etc. and linseed	30·6
Vegetable oils and oilseeds	13·8
Meat	18·7
Live animals and animal by-products, dairy products	6·1
Fresh fruit	2·3
Wool	11·9
Hides	7·5
Other products	9·1

The first four groups, which make up about 70 per cent of exports, come almost entirely from the pampa, while the other agricultural products listed come from other regions as well. In spite of several decades of industrial growth, Argentina has so far failed to export appreciable quantities of manufactured goods. On the other hand, imports consist largely of manufactured goods:

	1962 per cent
Machinery	54
Iron and steel and manufactures	10
Fuels and lubricants	7

Even since the late 1950s there has been a substantial drop in the relative importance of iron and steel and of fuels, and in this has enabled the country to spend more on machinery of various kinds.

The direction of the trade of Argentina differs fundamentally from that of most other Latin American countries, as the following percentages show (1962):

	Exports to	Imports from
North America	8	31
West Europe	78	45·5
EEC	*45*	*30·5*
UK	*17*	*9*
Soviet area	6	2
Latin America	13	11
Brazil	*5·6*	*5*
Chile	2·6	Small

Since the U.S.A. and Canada both export or at least have surpluses of cereals and meat, there is little chance for Argentina to sell such items to them, yet much of the machinery requirements of Argentina come from North America. It has been suggested, however, that more linseed, sugar and wines might be tried on the U.S. market. Trade is currently very one-sided in this direction.

West Europe and, increasingly, East Europe and the U.S.S.R. as well, require the agricultural products of Argentina, but agricultural policies and increased productivity in West Europe have tended to diminish dependence on Argentinian meat and cereals, while wool production has been eclipsed by that of Australia and New Zealand. Japan and communist China would seem to be possible future markets for Argentinian products. Ironically, precisely since Argentina has joined LAFTA its imports of oil (from Venezuela and the Netherland Antilles) and steel (which could be supplied by Chile) are diminishing. On the other hand, greater trade with Brazil seems likely.

REFERENCES

[1] Fitzgibbon, R. H. 'Uruguay's Agricultural Problems'. *Econ. Geogr.* 29 (1953) 251–262
[2] *FAOPY*, 1962, p. 23
[3] Ferrar A. *La Economía Argentina*, Buenos Aires, 1963, p. 239
[4] *BOLSA (FR)* 12 Jan 1963, p. 6
[5] Isacovich, M. *Argentina económica y social*, Buenos Aires 1961, p. 21
[6] Rampa, A. C. *Geografica física de la República Argentina*, Buenos Aires 1961, pp. 190–203
[7] Platt, R. Latin America, *Countrysides and United Regions*, 1942, pp. 355–361, New York; McGraw-Hill
[8] *FAOPY*, 1962, various tables
[9] Stewart, N. R. 'Tea—A New Argicultural Industry for Argentina'. *Econ geogr.* 36 (1960) 267–76
[10] *BOLSA (QR)* July 1964, pp. 119–32, Argentina—Cattle Farming and Beef Trade
[11] Defelippe, B. A. *Geografía económica Argentina* Buenos Aires 1959, p. 257
[12] *BOLSA (FR)* 6 April 1963

CHAPTER 18

CHILE

18.1. INTRODUCTION AND REGIONS

Although approximately the same area as Venezuela or Bolivia, Chile is distinguished by its great length, over 4,000 km from north to south, while it averages only 200 km in width. Such great distortion of shape increases interregional distances, but since the population of Chile is mostly concentrated in a limited central area, the average distance of many journeys is not great. If the population were evenly spread, the problem would be much greater, while if there were a concentration at either end, there would probably be two States, not one.* In practice the narrowness of Chile has not been a disadavantage in its modern history in every respect because all its resources are arranged within a short distance of the coast, and given well-organized shipping services it has not been difficult to move goods between the various parts of the country or to ship them to foreign markets.

The population of Chile in 1959 was approximately 7,500,000 and it probably passed 8 m. in 1963. It is increasing at about 2·5 per cent per annum and at the same time the proportion of urban dwellers is increasing and is currently about 60 per cent of the total. The population of Chile is mainly mestizo, since the pure Indian communities that persisted in places well into the nineteenth century are gradually being absorbed, while the number of European immigrants arriving in the modern period has not been large.

The economy of Chile depends very heavily on minerals, for although mining only accounts for 5–6 per cent of total gross domestic product and roughly the same proportion of employment, minerals contribute up to 85–90 per cent of the value of exports. As in most Latin American countries the relative importance of agriculture has been diminishing since the Second World War (18 per cent of gross domestic product in 1950, 14 per cent in 1960) while manufacturing has been gaining (14 per cent in 1950, 20 per cent in 1960). Agriculture still employs about 30 per cent of the total population but has dropped from 40 per cent in the mid-1930s. Over 60 per cent of the gross domestic product is now accounted for by non-productive activities, a high proportion in a country at the level of development of Chile.

Although at the same latitude as Argentina, Chile has a very different agriculture from that of its larger neighbour and from the rest of Latin America, since although it also grows temperate crops it lacks the large area of good agricultural land in Argentina, and consequently has failed to develop either cereal or meat production on a comparable scale.

Under no circumstances could conditions of relief be called favourable in Chile. There is little level or gently sloping land and a large part of the

* See Section 9.2 for a discussion of further aspects of compactness.

country is rugged mountain. For convenience of description Chile can be divided into three very narrow north to south regions, the Andes in the east, a central depression, and a western coast range. All three features diminish progressively in altitude southwards, and in the south the Andes range is not only lower but discontinuous, the central depression largely submerged, and the coast range a number of islands. In addition, the southern part has been heavily glaciated. In the north the continuity of the central depression is in reality interrupted in several areas by ridges linking the Andes and the coastal range. Nevertheless both the railway and the road follow the depression the whole length from Arica to Puerto Montt. Although distances from the coast to places in the interior are not great, access to the interior from places on the coast suitable for ports is made difficult by the coastal range.

Precipitation increases from north to south from virtually nothing in the northern part of the country to a few hundred millimetres in the centre and 2–3,000 mm or even more in the south. It occurs mainly in the winter in central Chile but throughout the year in the south. As far south as Santiago it is inadequate for most kinds of agriculture unless supplemented by irrigation, but since the rivers draining northern Chile are small and originate in the Andes, which themselves are dry, little is available north of Coquimbo. Desert conditions prevail here, and there is only thin vegetation as far south as Santiago. South of here, first in the Andes, and then in the valleys and along the coast south of the Bío Bío river, forests appear, and except in the extreme south (Patagonian Chile and Tierra del Fuego) cover most of the surface.

Thanks to its shape, Chile can be divided into five reasonably clear-cut regions from north to south, each containing part of the three elements, the coastal range, the central valley and the Andes. The oldest area of colonization by the Spaniards lies roughly in the centre between Santiago and the Bío Bío valley. This now contains nearly two thirds of the population of the country and includes much of Chile's agricultural land, but progress in agriculture has been held back by unsatisfactory land tenure, and contrasts with advances in industrialization. To the north, between Santiago and Copiapó, agriculture depends almost entirely on irrigation, and the cultivated area is very limited. Here, on the other hand, are most of the iron ore deposits worked at present. To the north again there is virtually no agriculture, but the presence of both nitrates and copper have brought considerable activity to the region, and the development of fishing promises to revive stagnating ports in the extreme north. To the south of the Bío Bío valley agriculture based on settlement since about 1870, together with forests and a considerable hydroelectric potential, have formed the basis for the opening up of this region in the last hundred years. To the south again, the rugged mountains and inaccessible forests of most of southern Chile at present make virtually no contribution to the economic life of the country, but the extreme south has Chile's only oilfield and some useful grazing land.[1]

The fortunes of these five regions have changed greatly in the history of Chile. Initially, Spanish influence was largely confined to the central part of the country which, however, had little to export to Spain during the colonial period. Since about the middle of the nineteenth century population has spread both north and south; thinly northwards into the desert in

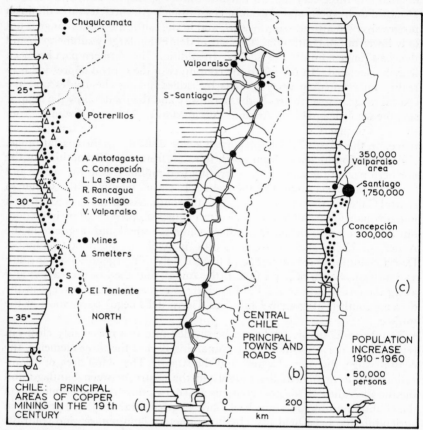

Figure 18.1. Chile. (*a*) *Principal areas of copper mining in the nineteenth century**. (*b*) *Central Chile: principal towns and roads.* (*c*) *Population increase 1910–1960*

* Some modern mines are also shown.

TABLE 18.1

Groups of provinces (as numbered in Figure 18.2b)	Population 1910	% of national total	Population 1960	% of national total	Absolute gain	Increase (1910 = 100)
Northern (1–3)	300	8·8	480	6·2	180	160
North-Central (4, 5)	312	9·1	535	6·9	223	172
Santiago-Valparaiso (6, 7)	846	24·8	2,932	38·0	2,086	346
Central (8–15)	1,117	32·7	1,963	25·4	846	166
South Central (16–22)	682	20·0	1,601	20·8	919	235
Southern (23–25)	116	3·4	209	2·7	93	180
Chile	3,373	100	7,720	100	4,347	229

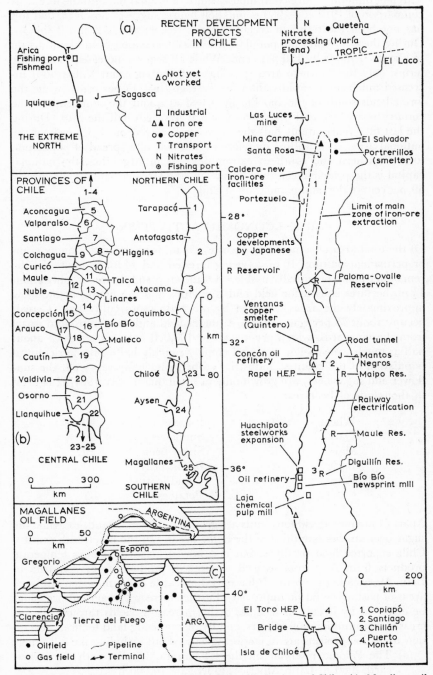

Figure 18.2. (a) Recent development projects in Chile. (b) Provinces of Chile. (c) Magallanes oil field

search of minerals, more continuously south of the Bío Bío into the forest. A comparison of 1910 and 1960 population figures suggests, however, that this has not been the trend in recent decades (see *Figure 18.2* and Table 8). During these 50 years the population of Chile increased from about 3.4 m. to about 7·7 m. or by 130 per cent. While all regions increased in absolute terms, only the Santiago area (provinces of Santiago and Valparaiso) increased much more rapidly than the average (by 245 per cent), while the forest lands south of the Bío Bío increased at about the same rate as the country as a whole and the rest of Chile at less than half the rate. During the last fifty years, about half the increases occurred on 3 per cent of the national area. It is absurd therefore to talk now of a spread of population to the northern and southern extremities. As in Argentina, the national capital is the principal centre of attraction, and Greater Santiago has nearly 30 per cent of the total population of Chile.

18.2. ECONOMIC ACTIVITIES

Of the total area of some 73 m. hectares, $5\frac{1}{2}$ m. is recorded as having crops or permanent pasture, 16 m. as being forested and 44 m. as unusable, the remainder being potentially usable.[2] Of the cropland, however, only about $1\frac{1}{2}$ m. hectares is used for field and tree crops and the figures below show approximately the areas occupied by the main crops cultivated. Cereals occupy about 75 per cent of the area under field and tree crops, and apart from the vineyards, which occupy about 100,000 hectares, produce about half as much wine as Portugal and employ roughly half of the agricultural population of the country, industrial crops (principally rapeseed, the sunflower and sugar beet) are grown only in small quantities: 1961/62 figures[2] in thousands of hectares:

Wheat	850	Rapeseed	40
Oats	110	Sunflower	30
Maize	75	Sugar beet	20
Barley	65	Beans, peas	
Rice	30	and lentils	145
		Potatoes	85

Apart from vines, deciduous fruits are grown in modest quantities, while the sugar beet satisfies one third of the home needs. In the nineteenth century Chile exported food products, but it is now deficient and buys temperate products from Argentina as well as tropical products from countries in Latin America to the north. It has only 3 m. cattle and 6 m. sheep but large areas of pasture could be improved. Further increases in agriculture could be achieved by irrigation schemes or by increasing yields through the increased consumption of fertilizers, and by reorganizing land tenure. Several new irrigation projects are in fact being carried out including the following:
- (a) The Paloma reservoir on the R. Lamira, Ovalle, with the largest earth dam in Latin America, to irrigate 70,000 has.
- (b) The Yeso reservoir on the R. Maipo near Santiago (120,000 hectares).
- (c) The Diguillín reservoir, Ñuble, 50,000 hectares.

But major improvements in agriculture seem to await political changes, and agriculture is being by-passed by continuing industrial expansion, a great revival of mining, and projects to use much more fully the forest and fishing resources of the country.

There are plans to increase the felling of pinewood timber in south central Chile and to continue reafforestations. The Monterey pine, introduced from the U.S.A. early in the twentieth century, matures in 20 years, while the thinnings serve for the new pulp mills. In the north, Chile is following the example of Peru and expanding its fishing on modern lines. The fish catch rose by 50 per cent in 1961–62 alone, but most of the catch is anchovies, destined for the fishmeal factories. There is a drive to increase consumption of other types of fish such as tuna and bonito, and it is planned to catch 1·2 m. tons of fish in 1965 and 1·5 m. in 1966 and to obtain 10 per cent of the value of exports from fishmeal.

Chile produces a wider range of minerals than almost any other Latin American country, some types almost exclusively for export, others almost entirely for home consumption. It is the leading producer of copper and nitrates in Latin America and one of the leading producers of iron ore, while its coal and oil makes it almost self-sufficient in sources of energy. The mining industry hardly existed in the colonial period, and dates almost entirely from the nineteenth century. Foreign capital has entered the country, mainly to exploit minerals, while many of the ports in the northern part of the country exist solely to ship minerals abroad. In the nineteenth century both nitrates and copper were extracted in a very large number of small mines, and Chile was actually the world's leading producer of copper for a time (1857–1880); *Figure 18.2a* shows the distribution of copper mines in the last century. Although both copper and iron ore are produced in numerous small establishments the bulk of the production now comes from a few large mines while the large companies buy the limited output of the small producers. Deposits of nitrates occur widely in the extremely dry northern part of Chile but this source no longer has the monopoly of the last century. The industry has been contracting steadily for the last 50 years, but an effort is now being made to modernize the processing of nitrates and a large-scale plant has been completed at María Elena by the Anglo-Lautaro Company and this will account for two thirds of Chilean production. For some time now almost all the copper mined has come from three places, the relative importance of which can be judged from the figures below.

	Foundation	
Chuquicamata	about half	1915
El Teniente	about 40 per cent	1912
Potrerillos	about 10 per cent	1926

The Potrerillos mine was closed in 1959 but has been replaced by the new El Salvador mine nearby (see *Figure 8.6*). A very large amount of ore is involved (the Chuquicamata mine handles up to 100,000 tons per day), and processing is of course desirable before export. Various new deposits have been found and a more favourable position in world markets for Chilean copper in the 1960s appears to be the reason for plans both to develop new deposits and to increase the refining capacity in Chile itself. Both copper and nitrates remain largely in the hands of foreign companies, but this is not so with iron ore, which now exceeds nitrates in value exported. Until the 1950s most of the iron in Chile came from El Tofo mine of the Bethlehem Chile Iron Company, but this was closed in 1957 after producing about 50 m. tons, and the company now works El Romeral mine nearby, but its output is now exceeded by that of the Chilean Santa Fé Company, established in 1952. Chile has at least 200 m. tons of proved high grade iron ore, together with much larger probable reserves occurring both in sands in central Chile and in the very large El Laco magnetite deposit in the north, estimated to have between 1,000 and 3,000 m. tons. To make the exploitation of this latter deposit worth while the Santa Fé Company would have to be assured of a yearly output of 7–10 m. tons. The main area of iron mining is shown in *Figure 18.2a*. Total output of ore, averaging about 63 per cent iron content, rose from about 5 m. tons in 1960 to nearly 6 m. in 1961 and over 7 m. in 1962.

In the Concepción (Lota and Coronel) area Chile has one of Latin America's principal coalfields. Modest though the output is, this has undoubtedly contributed to the industrial development of the country, most of the coal being used either for metal smelting or the generation of electricity. Mining conditions are difficult and efficiency low but the mines are being modernized. Of more importance now are the oil and gas deposits first exploited in 1945, in the extreme south of the country (see *Figure 18.2c*). These are worked by ENAP*, the State oil company, and since the mid-1950s output has been increased so quickly that by 1963, 75 per cent of Chile's needs were being satisfied. The search for oil and gas has now also begun in South central Chile, particularly between Chillán and Puerto Montt. Much of the oil from the extreme south is transported by sea to the Concón Refinery (44,000 barrels per day) near Valparaiso and products are piped to Santiago, while a new refinery is being constructed at Concepción. These sources of energy are supplemented by hydroelectricity, and several medium-sized power stations are under construction at the moment, including one at Rapel (350,000 kW) near Santiago and one near Puerto Montt (El Toro 280,000 kW for 1969). Chile has a higher consumption of sources of energy per inhabitant than almost any other Latin American country, but much of course is used to refine copper for export.

Chile is also one of the most highly industrialized countries in Latin America and while all main branches have expanded greatly in the last 30 years the most impressive progress has been made in developing the iron and steel industry and in engineering, while the production of paper and newsprint is also a feature of recent years. Even so, as in Argentina industrial progress has not been entirely satisfactory and in 1961 a survey showed that only about 80 per cent of the total capacity was actually in use. This is attributed basically to the fact that the market is small and industrial establishments are mostly too small to be economical. Demand in the home market is limited and irregular, heavy protection is needed and many raw materials cannot easily be imported. The future of Chilean industry seems

* Empresa Nacional de Petróleo.

to lie in the assurance of a much larger Latin American market and the establishment of much larger plant. A development on these lines has been the establishment of a large newsprint mill on the Bío Bío near Concepción and a chemical pulp mill at Laja, each costing about U.S. $ 20 m. The mills are to use the pine thinnings of the nearby forests and to export most of their output.

The Huachipato iron and steel works, run by CAP (Compañía de Acero del Pacífico) though small as an integrated iron and steel works by world standards, has nevertheless been a success. The project was started in 1946, the initial plant completed in 1950 and in 1951 about 170,000 tons of steel were produced, while output had risen irregularly to 430,000 tons in 1961 and capacity is being raised to 600,000 for the middle 1960s. Most of the coal consumed comes from the nearby coalfields, but about one third is imported. The iron ore comes from El Romeral. Most of the output of steel is consumed in Chile, and an engineering industry is growing up in Concepción (see *Figure 8.10*) and other towns in central Chile*, but in some years a surplus has been available for export, and although Argentina has been the principal customer, even the United states has imported small quantities. With several Latin American countries expanding their iron and steel production at the moment, the prospects of a large share of the Latin American market for Chilean steel outside Chile itself seem very poor.

18.3. TRANSPORT AND TRADE

Given the great length of Chile and the proximity of every part of the country to the coast, coastal shipping services have probably been more important in maintaining cohesion than in any other Latin American country. There are some 50 ports in use but many do not have proper berthing facilities and from some access to the interior is difficult. Valparaiso and Concepción handle general cargoes but most of the ports of the northern coast have been established to serve particular mineral deposits. Iron ore accounts now for much of the volume transported and several ports are specially equipped to handle this. Arica and Iquique are the principal centres of the new fishing industry, while Arica (in 1953) and Punta Arenas (in 1957) have been designated free ports to stimulate the economic life of the extremities of the country; one result has been the establishment of several motor vehicles assembly plants in Arica; Arica is also to have special facilities for handling Peruvian cargoes (under a 1928 agreement). Several ports are undergoing improvement at the moment.

Chile also has a good network of railways and roads by Latin American standards, except in the southern third of the country. Major rail improvements have lately been limited largely to the electrification of the line Santiago–Chillán and the lines from Valparaiso to Santiago and to the Andean pass on the Mendoza line. Roads are receiving more attention than railways, and a major project, completed in 1964, has been the paving of the 3,200 km Camino Longitudinal running from Arica to Puerto Montt.

* Recent examples are a plant for producing steel balls for crushing ores, and shipbuilding yards (for 1966) to build vessels up to 8,000 tons.

Chilean exports have been based on minerals throughout the modern period, and for some decades now copper has been the most valuable, accounting for two thirds of exports, and nitrates and iron ore each for a few per cent more. But Chile appears to be about to diversify its exports appreciably by adding such items as paper and pulp products (aimed at LAFTA partners), fishmeal and liquefied gas. Much of its trade is with the U.S.A., which in 1961 took about one third of the exports, but here again, other markets are being sought, and both the U.S.S.R. and China have taken part of the copper exports in recent years.

Chile has one of the highest standards of living in Latin America and one of the most literate and politically stable populations, but unless population growth slows down or great improvements are made in agriculture it will become excessively dependent on imports of food, without having sufficient raw materials or manufactured goods to export. There is no question of exhaustion of its principal minerals, while prospects for fishing, forest products and hydroelectricity seem excellent, but even though ocean transport is normally cheap, a remote location at the end of world shipping routes is a basic disadvantage which has no complete remedy. One partial solution is for Chile to trade more with Argentina and Peru, both of which are to some extent complementary with Chile in their products.

REFERENCES

[1] Holdgate, M. W. 'Man and Environment in the South Chilean Islands', *Geogr. J.* Dec. 1961 pp. 401–16
[2] *FAOPY* 1962

CHAPTER 19

REGIONAL INCOME DIFFERENCES AND POPULATION CHANGES

19.1. THE UNEVEN DISTRIBUTION OF ECONOMIC WEALTH IN LATIN AMERICA

National income* expresses in a very rough way the production of goods and services in a country†, and its distribution within the country is a reflection of the distribution of economic activity in that country. National income is distributed very unevenly in Latin America, both by countries and within them, firstly among different social classes‡, and secondly, expressed in *per caput* terms, among different clusters of population. One important reason why *per caput* national income varies from one part of Latin America to another is that agriculture in Latin American countries invariably employs a larger share of total population than it provides of gross national produce, and predominantly agricultural areas therefore usually have a much lower *per caput* index than predominantly non-agricultural areas in the same country. This feature was discussed in Chapter 5.2. The following situation is roughly what occurs in the less developed countries: agriculture engages say 50 per cent of the labour force but contributes only 25 per cent of gross domestic product. The other sectors of the economy, therefore, employ 50 per cent of the labour force but provide 75 per cent of the gross national product, productivity being three times greater. Examples of this situation will be recalled; at one extreme, in Venezuela, the productivity of an oil worker, for example, could be 50 to 100 times higher than that of a person employed in agriculture, while at the other, in Argentina the difference between the efficiency of workers in agriculture and in other activities is not great. Differences in *per caput* income between different parts of individual countries are largely related to degree of dependence on agriculture, and up to a point this is true also of differences between countries, which must however also to some extent be related to differing population/resource balance (contrast, for example, Haiti and Uruguay), and differences due to organizational ability of different groups of population. The regions with a predominance of Europeans tend to be the most prosperous but this can be related to their choice of the areas favoured with the best resources as well as to an ability, brought from a more

---

* Figures may in practice be available for gross domestic product, gross national product or some other comparable measure of total economic activity.

† For example Pounds[1] suggests that gross national product is the most useful measure of the strength of a country.

‡ 'The social contrast is striking indeed. While 50 per cent of the population accounts for approximately two-tenths of total personal consumption, at the other end of the scale of distribution 5 per cent of the inhabitants enjoy nearly three tenths of that total.....'[2]

407

advanced region, to organize an economy and introduce technology better on the whole than non-European groups.

Table 19.1 is an attempt to summarize, unfortunately in a very generalized and approximate way, regional differences in *per caput* income and in living standards in Latin America, and the areas used are shown in *Figure 19.1*. The influence of international boundaries has been taken into account, but where areas with similar conditions lie on either side of one (e.g. Andean Ecuador,

TABLE 19.1
Income in U.S. $ *Per Caput* Per Year

	A *VERY POOR* *Below about 150*	*Pop'n*	*B* *MEDIUM* *150–450*	*Pop'n*	*C* *RELATIVELY* *PROSPEROUS* *Above about 450*	*Pop'n*	*Total*

I
Thin
rural
	(i) S. Mexico and
	   C. America
	(ii) Ven.-Col.-
	   Ecu.-Peru-Bol.
	(iii) Brazil Amazon
	   and west
	(iv) Paraguay
		1,0
		
		1,0
		
		5,5
		n.
			(i) N. Mexico 4,5
			
			(ii) Guianas 1,0
			
			(iii) N. and S. Arg. 0,5
			
			(iv) N. and S. Chile 0,5				

		7,5		6,5			14

II
Rural
and
medium
town
	(i) C. ans S. Mexico 11,5
	(ii) Ecu.-Peru-Bol. 12
	(iii) Haiti 3,5
	(iv) N.E. Brazil 21,0
	(v) Paraguay 2,0
			(i) N.C. Mexico 12
			(ii) C. America 10,5
			(iii) Venezuela 6
			(iv) Colombia 11
			(v) Coastal Ecu.
			   and Peru 3,5
			(vi) Islands except
			   Haiti 15,5
			(vii) S. Brazil 32,5
			(viii) Uruguay 2,5
			(ix) Argentina 11,5
			(x) Chile 5,0				

		50		110			160
III Towns over 500,000			12 towns (see map)	10,5	10 towns (see map)	26,5	37
TOTALS		57,5		127	·	26,5	211

Peru and Bolivia) they have been grouped together. Regions are divided firstly (A–C) according to *per caput* national income*, distinguishing areas that are clearly very poor (*A*, under about U.S. $ 150 *per caput*), and those which by Latin American standards are very prosperous (*C*, over about U.S. $ 450 *per caput*), leaving a middle level (*B*) around the mean for Latin America (U.S. $ 300 *per caput*), between about 150 and 450. Regions are obviously only classed according to the predominant level within them (e.g. in Central Chile, classed as *B*, there are some very poor people and some very prosperous ones). Regions are divided secondly (I-III) according to the

* The basis has been the data for various whole countries, discussed in Section 1.4 and data for major civil divisions within individual countries where this is available.

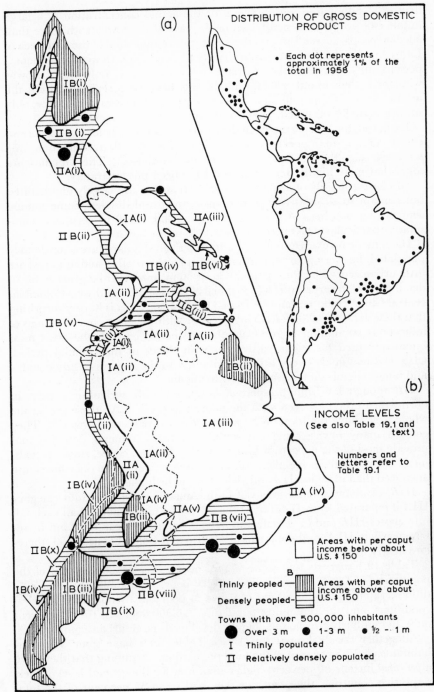

Figure 19.1. Latin America. (*a*) *Income levels.* (*b*) *Distribution of gross domestic product*

Outline of coast based on a map in the Oxford Atlas published by the
Oxford University Press

density of population within them, or the actual concentration of a large number of people in a small area in the case of the towns with more than 500,000 people. Area I in practice represents roughly half of the total area of Latin America having the lowest density of population (fewer than about 3 persons/km²). At the other extreme, for convenience, only the 22 towns with more than about 500,000 inhabitants have been separated from the urban sector of the population. Of the nine possible classes in the table, only six are actually occupied. Each deserves a brief comment:

I*A* is roughly the virtually undeveloped tropical rain forest; it does of course contain small pockets of dense population and relatively high income *per caput* (e.g. the banana plantations of Honduras). The Guianas are somewhat more highly developed and have been put separately.

I*B* consists mainly of arid or semi-arid areas that are largely uninhabited but contain small relatively prosperous agricultural districts, some mining centres (e.g. southern Argentina, northern Chile) and in certain circumstances, particularly favoured towns (e.g. in north Mexico).

II*A* is made up of areas that by Latin American standards are often densely populated, but very poor agriculturally, yet have few other activities and are little urbanized. The total population of 50 m. may well be greater, for in detail parts of the areas in II*B* (e.g. much of Guatemala, southwest Colombia, central Chile) could perhaps be moved into this class. It is hardly surprising that these areas coincide fairly closely either with the great concentrations of indigenous population in pre-Columbian America or with the areas most intensively used for sugar cultivation with slaves in the colonial period. Class II*A* now makes very little contribution to the exports of any country and often remains on the fringe of economic life.

II*B* though far from prosperous compared with agricultural areas in northwest Europe, or even with the poorest in the U.S.A., these are on the whole well above the level of the most backward parts of the world. They contain many towns, some industries, and many mineral deposits, and provide most of the exports of Latin America (cotton, coffee, sugar, cereals, meat, oil, non-ferrous metals). Agricultural practices are on the whole more advanced than in region II*A* and yields tend to be higher.

III*B*, *C*. Some smaller towns of Latin America would fall into category III*A* if separated from II*A*, but of the 22 largest towns, about half each fall into classes III*B* and *C*. Recife and Salvador must be near 150 (and therefore nearly in III*A*) and the towns of Mexico and Colombia near 450 (therefore nearly in III*C*).

Table 19.1 suggests that some 57½ m. people, say 25–30 per cent of the population of Latin America, live in very poor, predominantly rural conditions, 126 m. or about 60 per cent live in poor but by no means hopeless conditions, and the remaining population, 26,500,000, say 10–15 per cent only, live in fairly prosperous, highly developed, large urban communities. Altogether the 22 largest towns (see Table 19.2) have some 37 m. inhabitants, or 17·5 per cent of the total population. Assuming that they have a *per caput* income 50 per cent higher than that for the general level of their respective countries, then together they had some 25 per cent of the total national income of Latin America. The 25 capitals (of 22 sovereign states and 3 dependent areas, Table 19.2) which include 10 of the 22 towns in the previous list, have 14 per cent of the total population of Latin America, and again, probably 25 per cent of the wealth of Latin America. Almost everywhere in Latin America, a move from a rural community to an urban one in the same general area means a move to an area with superior economic prospects.

Given the great differences in level of development in different parts of Latin America it would be a very fruitful exercise to map more precisely the distribution of national income and then relate this to other distributions. Even from the small amount of material presented in this book it is clear that there are marked differences over quite limited distances. Locally there is often a sharp difference between a town and its adjoining rural area. On a regional level there are gradual changes from one part of a country to another (e.g. from northwest to south Mexico). In theory, also, there should be sudden changes in level along national boundaries (e.g. between Venezuela and Colombia, Haiti and the Dominican republic, Argentina and Paraguay). Certainly there is between the U.S.A. and Mexico. The magnitude of differences in *per caput* income between countries or between regions within countries can be summarized by expressing the indices of different units as percentages of the index of the highest. Thus for example, among the states of the U.S.A. the highest income *per caput* in 1960 was in Delaware (U.S. $ 2,996 *per caput*), the lowest in Mississippi (1,169), while the U.S. mean was U.S. $ 2,215*. If Delaware = 100 then Mississippi is 39. Some decades ago the gap was wider, with New York (then the highest) about four times as high as the poorest (still Mississippi). If this procedure is applied to different countries or groups of countries, the following results are obtained (the figures are based on various criteria, all however roughly comparable with national income):

U.S.A.[3]	Delaware	100	Mississippi	39
Spain†	Vizcaya	100	Granada	38·5
U.K.[5]	Hertfordshire	100	County Down	28·5
France[5]	Seine(Paris)	100	Corsica	26
Italy‡	Milano	100	Potenza	18
Brazil§	Guanabara	100	Piauí	9
	São Paulo State	100	Piauí	16
Latin America	Venezuela	100	Haiti	12
World	U.S.A.	100	Ethiopia	1·7

At first sight it would seem that the larger the area involved, the greater would be the regional differences expected. On the other hand, it may be

* The highest in the U.S.A. were Delaware, Connecticut, New York, Nevada, Alaska and California, the lowest were mostly in the Southeast. The poorest area, as in Latin American countries, is also the most heavily dependent on agriculture and the least highly urbanized[3].

† In per caput terms, income was highest in the north and east and lowest in much of the south and west. Compare 26,000 in Tarragona and Vizcaya with 10,000 in Granada and Orense[4].

‡ Much work has been done on this subject by Italian economists, especially G. Tagliacarne. For a brief study see reference[6].

§ 1959 figures in cruzeiros *per caput:* Guanabara 64,966, São Paulo 36,787, Maranhão 7,187, Piauí 5,960[7].

assumed that if a country is very poor, even if it is large (e.g. India, China, Indonesia), there cannot be very great regional differences, unless some area is particularly favoured and stands out above the rest. On the whole, too, it is the policy in planned economics, as in the U.S.S.R. and presumably in China, to reduce regional differences as far as possible. Finally, it may be assumed that once a country becomes very prosperous (Sweden, Australia), either through government planning, or spontaneously, the wealth will spread out into less fortunate areas and reduce regional differences (the policy in France, Italy, the U.K., the U.S.A. in the 1960s).

The countries in which the greatest regional differences may be expected appear, therefore, to be those in between the very poor and the very prosperous countries, in which rapid economic development has taken place only in certain parts of the national area (e.g. Venezuela, Brazil, Mexico) whether in areas rich in minerals, particularly favoured agriculturally, or attractive (particularly large cities) to manufacturing. This situation has occurred particularly in the U.S.S.R. (where it is recognized but is not publicized), Italy and Japan in recent decades, and is now found widely in Latin America, as already made clear.

From *Figure 19.1* and Table 19.1 it is reasonably clear which are the poorer and more prosperous regions of Latin America. It will also be appreciated, though not enough data has been assembled in this book to allow it to be mapped precisely, that there are some places in which there is a very abrupt 'gradient' between low and high income areas, as between Mexico City and adjoining states to the south and east, between Lima and the central Andes of Peru, even between Buenos Aires and the adjoining pampa. Elsewhere, there may be fairly uniform conditions and little change over a great distance, as throughout the length of northern Chile as far south as the capital, or across Amazonia say from Belém to Iquitos.

Is it possible that migration of population is related to spatial variations in *per caput* income? And if so, does population move more rapidly and in greater quantities the steeper the gradient between low and high *per caput* income? This perhaps suggests an analogy with atmospheric pressure that is not justified, and it must be stressed that only a possible tendency is being considered, not an inevitable law. The basis for the tendency is the very reasonable assumption that if people are going to move from one area to another, they will move, as individuals or families anyway, from areas with unemployment, under-employment or generally low incomes to areas with assured or at least prospective employment and/or with a higher income. Presumably people only move to areas with less favourable material prospects either if they are forced to do so (African slaves to the Americas in the colonial period, Koreans from Japan back to Korea after the Second World War) or if for religious or other reasons they prefer to do so. More favourable employment can be expected either in non-agricultural activities, mainly found of course in towns, or in agricultural settlements in which new development is being well organized. Such a movement of population to more favoured areas has happened frequently in the modern period of world history alone. Now, for example, Italian and Spanish workers move to the Benelux and France, Irish, West Indians and Pakistani workers to England, and so on.

412

Besides, you just re-locate problem

If this is what happens, then at first sight there seems an easy answer to the problem of the very poor quarter or third of the population of Latin America: to move it to areas with a higher income. This is certainly happening gradually, as will be suggested in the next section, but it obviously is absurd to imagine it could happen overnight or that the poor areas could be cleared completely*. In the end the level of these will have to be raised with help from more prosperous areas as for example is already beginning to happen in Northeast Brazil, and, under special circumstances, has already happened in Puerto Rico. *Not typical*

19.2. POPULATION CHANGES IN LATIN AMERICA

During the twentieth century and particularly since the 1920s, the population of Latin America has both increased rapidly, probably doubling between 1930 and the early 1960s, and has changed in distribution. It is widely assumed that as it has increased in recent decades it has tended to become more dispersed, or at least that if it has not, it should have done so. The reasonable assumption is that population tends spontaneously to move from areas with a high density to areas with a low density, though a perfectly even spread could not possibly be expected. An investigation of population changes in major civil divisions of Latin American countries between 1935 and 1960 suggests that in reality the reverse is true: population has become more concentrated, and probably more people are now living on a smaller part of the total area than ever before in the history of the region. Before discussing the possible influence of differences in *per caput* income level on migration of population suggested in the previous section, some basic facts about recent population changes in Latin America must be presented.

It is not easy to summarize in a few sentences the way in which the distribution of population has been changing in such a varied and unwieldy region as Latin America. *Figure 19.2* merely indicates very inadequately the main features of change during 1935–1960. A comparison of this map with *Figures 2.1* and *2.2* indicates that very broadly the bulk of the increase of some 90 m. people has occurred in the area that already in 1935 had most of the population and was most densely populated. Very little occurred in the interior or extreme south of South America. The attraction of certain very large towns is also evident. What has in fact happened is that although the relative increase may have been greater in some of the thinly peopled areas than in areas with a high density already, the absolute numbers involved have been much smaller. This situation may be illustrated by comparing the following fictitous units:

	Unit A	Unit B
Area in square kilometres	100,000	100,000
Population 1935	200,000	1,000,000
Population 1960	500,000	2,000,000
Density of popn. 1935	2	10
Density of popn. 1960	5	20
Percentage increase 1935–1960	150	100
Absolute volume of increase	300,000	1,000,000

* Some aspects of this problem are covered by Brown[8].

413

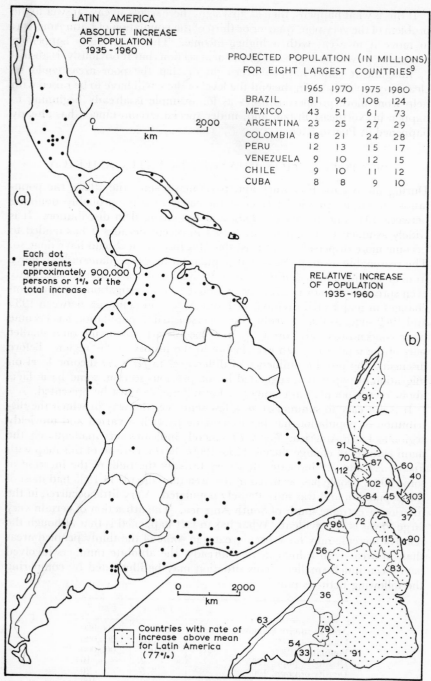

Figure 19.2. Latin America. (a) *Absolute increase of population 1935–1960.* (b) *Relative increase of population 1935–1960*

Outline of coast based on a map in the Oxford Altas published by the Oxford University Press

Population increased more rapidly in unit A than in unit B but in absolute terms the volume of increase was less than a third as great. The contrast in density increased from 2:10 persons/km² to 5:20.

Population in Latin America has become more concentrated than it was in 1935. This may be illustrated in a very general way by reconsidering data used in Chapter 2.2 to show features of concentration and dispersal. Two sets of major civil divisions were involved, those having the highest density of population in 1960 and containing in that year some 25 per cent of the total population of Latin America on 2·5 per cent of the total area, and those having the lowest density of population in 1960 and containing in that year about 5 per cent of the population on 50 per cent of the area. During 1935–60 the total population of Latin America increased from 118 m. to 210 m., or by 78 per cent. During the same period, that of the first group of major civil divisions rose from 30 m. to 54 m. or by about 80 per cent, while that of the second group rose from 6,8 m. to 10,2 m. or by 50 per cent. The astounding implications of this are that 24 m. more people appeared on a mere 2·5 per cent of the total area while only about 3¼ m. more appeared on half of the total area. In the light of these figures it is utterly absurd to say that population is becoming more evenly spread in Latin America.

A study of the growth of the largest towns of Latin America and of national capitals (Rio, not Brasilia for Brazil) during 1930–60 further emphasizes the tendency towards concentration. Table 19.2 contains all towns that are national capitals and/or had more than 500,000 inhabitants in 1960.

During 1930–1960 the total population of Latin America roughly doubled (105 m.–210 m.). During that period the population of the 22 largest towns in 1960 increased from about 10 m. to 37 m., more than 3¼ times, while that of the 25 capitals increased from about 8 m. to 28½ m., about 3½ times. A study of the population of the 20 main capitals between 1880 and 1960 shows that without exception these now contain a larger share of the total population of their respective countries than they did in 1880. In 1960, the share of the 25 in Table 19.2 was 14 per cent of the total population of Latin America. It may be noted in passing that there is no significant correlation* between the number of inhabitants of a country and the proportion of total population in the capital. A study of population trends in other towns of Latin America having more than 100,000 inhabitants in 1960 suggests that the rate of growth of capital cities in total has only been slightly faster than that in other medium and large towns.

Much of the growing concentration of population on a small part of the total area is clearly closely related to urbanization. Has there also been a movement of population in recent decades from overcrowded rural areas to more promising, pioneer, agricultural lands? Looking back over the period of European influence in Latin America, great waves of population have swept into the region, lapping round and spreading over the fairly stable areas of Indian population. Newcomers moved into all kinds of environment to extract minerals, grow tropical crops and raise cattle. In

* Spearman Rank Correlation Coefficient, comparing rank by number of inhabitants and by percentage of population in capital in 1960 gives $r = +0.06$. See Chapter 11.6 for an explanation of the technique. See also Berry[10].

the post-colonial period they colonized new lands in extra-tropical South America. But there has been little of this kind of movement since 1930: some movement into northeast Argentina, and up to and across the Paraná in Brazil, into the oilfields in Venezuela, into specially prepared areas of

TABLE 19.2

	National capital		Over 500,000 in 1960	
	1930	1960	1930	1960
Mexico City	900	4,871	900	4,871
Guadalajara			150	737
Monterrey			100	597
Guatemala City	120	407		
San Salvador	110	253		
Tegucigalpa	30	134		
Managua	35	230		
San José	60	236		
Panama City	70	273		
Caracas	200	1,265	200	1,265
Bogotá	170	1,329	170	1,329
Medellín			100	691
Cali			80	693
Quito	120	362		
Guayaquil			110	515
Lima	250	1,978	250	1,978
La Paz	130	340		
Havana	600	1,220	600	1,220
Port au Prince	120	250		
Santo Domingo	35	370		
San Juan	80	590	80	590
Kingston	120	380		
Port of Spain	65	94		
Georgetown	60	100		
Paramaribo	45	150		
Recife			350	974
Salvador			350	639
Belo Horizonte			50	684
Rio	1,500	4,370	1,500	4,370
São Paulo			1,000	3,872
Porto Alegre			200	722
Asunción	110	310		
Montevideo	450	1,173	450	1,173
Buenos Aires	2,000	6,763	2,000	6,763
Córdoba			200	590
Rosario			400	670
Santiago	600	1,989	600	1,989
	7,980	29,337	9,840	36,932

agricultural colonization such as new irrigated lands in Mexico, resettlement areas in Bolivia. But the number of people involved here has been small compared with the number of people moving into towns. Indeed the establishment of a large new urban centre, Brasilia, and the promise of another, San Tomé in Venezuela, have actually been used as magnets to attract population into relatively remote areas. Whether to developing rural areas or to towns, however, the movement of population has almost all been *within* the limits of national boundaries, and in Brazil even interregional movement between northeast and southern Brazil has so far been small.

A brief study of population trends in the recent past in Brazil, Mexico and Argentina (see *Figures 19.3* and *19.4*) is all that space allows here to illustrate features of population change in more detail. In *Figure 19.3* population changes during 1950–60 in three separate states of Brazil are mapped (see

TABLE 19.3

Population of the Capital City as a Percentage of Total Population
in Selected Years

Rank according to number of inhabitants of country in 1960	*Capital*	*1880*	*1905*	*1930*	*1960*
1 Brazil	Rio	3	4	4	7
2 Mexico	Mexico	3	3	5	15
3 Argentina	Buenos Aires	12	20	20	32
4 Colombia	Bogota	1	2	2	8
5 Peru	Lima	3	3	5	19
6 Chile	Santiago	6	10	13	22
7 Cuba	Havana	13	15	15	18
8 Venezuela	Caracas	3	4	7	20
9 Ecuador	Quito	7	5	5	7
10 Guatemala	Guatemala City	4	5	5	10
11 Haiti	Port-au-Prince	1	4	4	3
12 Bolivia	La Paz	3	4	5	10
13 Dominican Rep.	Santo Domingo	1	2	3	12
14 Uruguay	Montevideo	12	30	28	31
15 El Salvador	San Salvador	4	5	8	9
16 Honduras	Tegucigalpa	3	4	4	5
17 Paraguay	Asunción	3	12	14	18
18 Nicaragua	Managua	3	6	5	13
19 Panama	Panama City	(7)	14	16	25
20 Costa Rica	San José	15	10	12	22

Figure 16.4 for their location). During 1950–60 the three states in question increased in population (in thousands) as follows[10]:

	1950	*1960*	*Percentage increase*
São Paulo	9,134	12,975	42
Alagoas	1,093	1,270	16
Santa Catarina	1,561	2,147	38

In the state of São Paulo, changes by *zonas* (groups of municipios) were very uneven; one actually lost population. Of the absolute increase of 3,841,000, the *zona* of São Paulo, stretching in fact into rural areas beyond the limit of the conurbation, accounted for 2,363,000 or over 60 per cent of the total. Several *zonas*, both near the coast and in the interior had only small increases, but all those at the western extremity of the state, along the River Paraná, increased fast and presumably represented the last stage of pioneer development in the state.

In the state of Alagoas in Northeast Brazil the rate of increase for the state as a whole was less than in São Paulo. There are too few *zonas* to draw

417

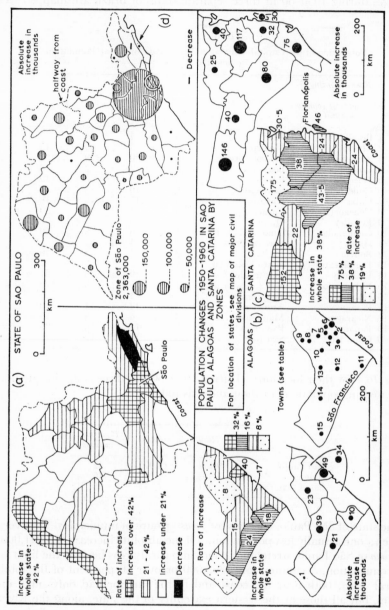

Figure 19.3. Population changes 1950–1960 in São Paulo, Alagoas and Santa Catarina States of Brazil by zones

useful conclusions about the distribution of different rates of increase but a study of the municipios themselves suggests greater increases along the coast and the lower São Francisco than in the interior. Very striking, on the other hand, is the rapid growth of most of the urban centres. Of the 15 with over 5,000 in 1960, all but two increased in population faster than the state as a whole. Maceió, the capital, had about 30 per cent of the total state increase. As a result, the 15 towns increased their share of total population from 18 per cent to 23 per cent, which is impressive over 10 years in a pre-dominantly agricultural area.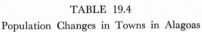

TABLE 19.4

Population Changes in Towns in Alagoas

	Population in thousands		Increase	
	1950	*1960*	*Percentage**	*Absolute*
1 Maceió	99	153	55	54
2 Marechal Deodoro	5	5	5	—
3 São Miguel	5	7	38	2
4 Pilar	7	7	5	—
5 Rio Largo	14	17	24	3
6 Fernão Velho	4	6	54	2
7 Murici	4	6	65	2
8 União dos Palmares	7	10	50	3
9 São José	4	6	37	2
10 Viçosa	6	7	21	1
11 Penedo	14	17	21	3
12 Arapiraca	9	20	124	11
13 Palmeira dos Indios	9	16	69	7
14 Santana do Ipanema	3	8	154	5
15 Delmiro Gouveia	5	6	21	1
Total	195	291	49	96
Rest of state	898	980	9	82
Whole state	1,093	1,271	16	178

* Calculated from actual, not rounded, figure.

In the state of Santa Catarina, the capital, Florianópolis, possibly for its somewhat inaccessible situation, has not increased much faster than the state as a whole, and much of the increase has actually taken place in the extreme west, an area in which colonization has recently been taking place.

Figure 19.4 shows changes of population in the states of Mexico between 1940 and 1960. During this period the total population of the country increased from 19,654,000 to 34,923,000 or by 78 per cent. The rate of increase varied greatly, however, from one major civil division to another. This could have been due partly, but certainly not entirely, to differing rates of natural increase, due to superior health and to other conditions in certain areas, but much was due to interregional movement. The percentage increase ranged from 460 per cent in Baja California and 176 per cent in the Distrito Federal to less than 50 per cent in several central states. *Figure 19.4* shows the increase both according to the absolute gain and to the relative increase. It would be possible to comment on and attempt to explain the change recorded in each individual unit, and such influences as the construction of irrigation works in the drier north, the expansion of manufacturing

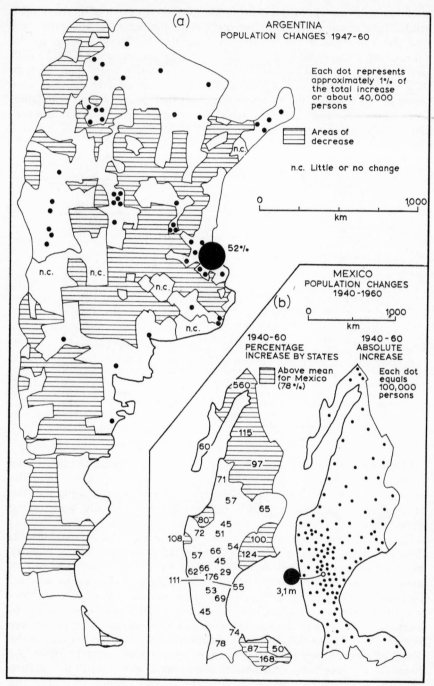

Figure 19.4. (a) *Argentina, population changes 1947–60.* (b) *Mexico, population changes 1940–60*

in certain places and the attraction of the capital city would emerge*. But by considering the relationship of rate of population growth to *per caput* sales (see Chapter 11.6) for all 32 states and territories simultaneously, it is possible to test in a very rough way if there is a correlation between these two variables. The result, a correlation of $+0.64$ is significant and shows a fairly close though far from complete correlation (the data appear in Table 11.2), suggesting that the more prosperous areas have tended to attract population from the less prosperous areas. It would seem that the arrangement of data into the 32 major civil divisions, while being the only basis readily available, tends to reduce the strength of the correlation that exists in reality by giving excessive emphasis to several small (in population) units such as the two territories, which influence the calculations more than their populations merit and have big discrepancies in ranking. The greatest movement of all appears to have been from the very poor agricultural regions in central Mexico, especially those to the east and south, into the capital. Unfortunately the number of people moving between each pair of states is not known, but by analogy with Brazil, in which interstate migration is known, most movement would be expected to take place over fairly short distances. Certainly there is a very steep 'gradient' in incomes between the capital and nearby agricultural areas.

Figure 19.4 shows population changes in Argentina between the censuses of 1947 and 1960[13]. During this period, the total population of Argentina increased from 15,897,000 to 20,009,000, an absolute increase of 4,112,000. Of this, 2,040,000 or almost half, was in Greater Buenos Aires. In contrast to Brazil and Mexico, in which few areas appear actually to have fewer people now than a decade or two ago, about half of the total area of Argentina actually had a decrease between 1947 and 1960. Most of the pampa region diminished in population, though the decrease was usually slight. Only a small percentage of all departments increased in population by more than 26 per cent, the figure for the country as a whole. In addition to Greater Buenos Aires and the pampa region within a radius of about 100 km of it, Córdoba, Rosario, Tucumán and Mendoza all had big increases. The only large rural area in which a substantial increase took place was Misiones in the extreme northeast and to a lesser extent the Chaco. In Argentina, the pull of the largest city is probably stronger than in almost any other Latin American country but thanks to a more gradual natural rate of increase and less sharp differences between attractiveness of the agricultural and industrial sides of the economy, there is less of an atmosphere of a revolution in the re-distribution of population than in Brazil or Mexico.

* Snyder[12], in his paper concludes: 'Differential growth (in the last 50 years) relative to area, a consequence of inter-regional migrations, tended toward a general equilibrium in which sparsely peripheral areas gained at the expense of densely inhabited, traditional areas of settlement in the southern and central plateau areas. The powerful vector of rural to urban migration both aided and abated the equalizing trend. Most notable of the former was phenomenal growth of urban places in the northern frontier states. Population growth substantially above the national average within the Federal district posed the most significant element of the minority counter trend. Decelerating growth in Federal District relative to second order urban places (Guadalajara and Monterrey) and third order relative to lower order places is indicative of a spatial and structural maturing of the urbanizing process in which the regulating mechanism of the threshold concept is seemingly operative.'

Much other evidence of movement of population from low income to high income areas has been given in this book, whether into larger towns with manufacturing and services, or into new mining or agricultural areas*. The movement into manufacturing and service centres has been dealt with, but it may be useful to recall also movement into new mining areas such as the oilfield areas of western and eastern Venezuela, the Orinoco iron ore area, new mining centres in Peru and Chile, and also movement into agricultural lands in which new developments are taking place: new irrigated areas in Mexico, Peru, Chile, Venezuela, new commercial agriculture in coastal Ecuador, eastern Bolivia, Goiás and Mato Grosso in Brazil.

There appears to be little evidence of any movement in the opposite direction. There is not sufficient data, of course, to say that movement invariably takes place in a situation in which low and high income areas are close together. In reality this may be difficult anyway, on account of lack of transport facilities, or even on account of the presence of an international boundary or the existence of regulations. On the whole, however, within individual Latin American countries there have rarely been serious regulations to prevent movement in the twentieth century; nor has there been much compulsion.

In contrast there has so far been little migration from one country to another in the way that people move among states in the U.S.A. or regions in the U.S.S.R. Exceptions are worth noting: the movement of Puerto Ricans to the U.S.A. and of West Indians to the U.K., the tendency for Colombians to migrate officially or even to infiltrate into Western Venezuela, Haitians into the Dominican Republic, citizens of El Salvador into Honduras and of Chile into Argentina. Caracas has become an attraction to professional people from all over South America. In each case except the last, the movement is clearly from a relatively poor country to one associated politically or adjoining territorially, either with better jobs to be obtained or with land to spare. Finally, it may be noted that even migration into Latin America from Europe in recent decades, especially since the Second World War, has tended to be very selective. Almost all the people arriving in Brazil since the war have for example settled in Rio and São Paulo, the only places that now offer attractive enough prospects to people from Portugal, Spain and Italy, all of which have become more affluent recently. Similarly, in Venezuela, Caracas has been the main centre of attraction to foreigners.

Even a brief study of changes of distribution of population in Latin America in the last three or four decades leads one to the inescapable conclusion that people are becoming more and more concentrated in smaller and smaller areas, that this is a result of changing employment structure, and that the direction of movement is largely determined by spatial differences in per caput income. Population is becoming concentrated in certain centres and along certain axes, a trend that seems likely to remain the dominant one in Latin America for some decades to come. The fact that population is not moving as fast as many governments would like into parts of Latin America that are empty, remote from major concentrations of population and often embarrassingly conspicuous in the vicinity of international boundaries, is

* e.g. in Venezuela, urban population *doubled* between 1950 and 1961.

one reason for the creation of many major civil divisions (usually designated territories) with special conditions to attract people. But there appears to be a contradiction between what is actually happening, greater concentration, a reflection of economic development, and what is desired, greater dispersal, a political aim.

In the view of the author the best prospect for Latin America for some time to come is to encourage the rapid growth of the economy in a limited number of large concentrations and to establish new poles of attraction, growth centres, such as oil refineries and steel works, but in a few key places, rather than indiscriminately in any backward area. It seems inevitable that there will for some time at least be a great disparity between *per caput* income in poorer and more prosperous parts of countries. It would hinder development that would ultimately be to the benefit of the whole country if too much were spent at this stage in raising standards as evenly as possible throughout.

The idea that population should be as evenly spread as possible is an attractive one but more suitable for a community with an agricultural outlook. Strategic considerations, now out of date, have something to do with it—the fear that a small area with the bulk of the population or all the key industries could be captured or put out of action in a modern war more easily than a dispersed population*. In addition, many Latin American countries are large in relation to their population, which is often concentrated in a small part only. The fear that neighbouring powers might move in or that more densely peopled countries might argue that there was space for their own populations has not only worried Brazil and its neighbours with which it shares a frontier in Amazonia, but even such countries as Australia (the north) and the U.S.S.R. (the Soviet Far East).

In conclusion, then, it appears that an understanding of the distribution of economic activities and of population in Latin America requires a sympathetic consideration of the possibility that greater concentration is desirable at least at the present stage of development of many countries, so long as it does not lead to congestion. This problem, of course, occurs in miniature (in terms of area involved) in the U.K. at present. Moreover, if this redeployment of economic activity and population is to take place, either spontaneously or in a planned fashion, it must not be restricted by the existence of over 20 virtually self-contained compartments, the present sovereign states. In addition to *Figure 19.5* which suggests tentatively the centres and axes that are attractive to population, *Figure 20.3* has been constructed to show in a highly schematic fashion the kind of way in which the main urban centres are related in Latin America and in North America, and the new links that are being sought in Latin America as LAFTA develops.

It would be dangerous to try to predict precisely what changes will take place in the distribution of population in Latin America, but if the population doubles in the next 35 years, a conservative forecast by demographers, and if 60 per cent is urban by then instead of 40 per cent now, then Latin

* e.g. industrial northeast France in the First World War, the Donbass in the Second. Latin American Revolutions (e.g. the capture of Havana by Castro, Cuba 1959) and Wars (e.g. occupation of Lima and Arequipa by the Chileans in the Pacific War).

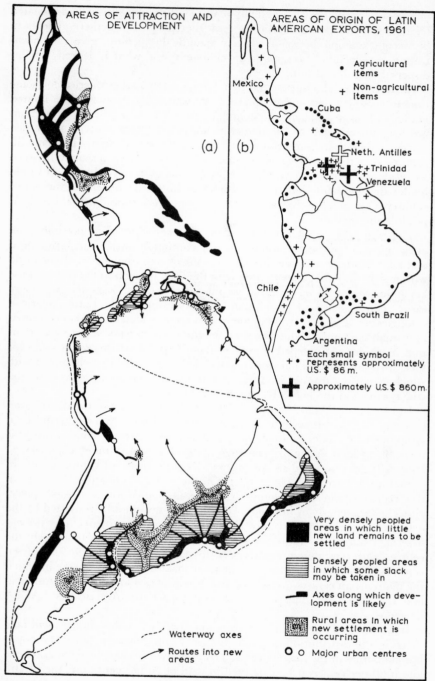

Figure 19.5. Latin America. (a) Areas of attraction and development. (b) Areas of origin of Latin American exports, 1960

Outline of coast based on a map in the Oxford Atlas published by the Oxford University Press

America should have some 240 m. urban dwellers, and by analogy with regions such as North America and the U.S.S.R., in the 1990s the following kinds of population figures may be expected unless there is some fundamental change in trend such as a sudden drop in birthrate or deliberate policy to keep people out of these places:

Mexico City	15 m.	Caracas-Valencia	
Buenos Aires	12 m.	conurbation	5 m.
São Paulo area	12 m.	Lima	4 m.
Rio area	8 m.	Santiago	4 m.

REFERENCES

1 Pounds, N. *Political Geography*. p. 164, 1963, New York; McGraw-Hill
2 *Towards a Dynamic Development Policy for Latin America*, p. 5, 1963; United Nations
3 *Statistical Abstract of the United States, 1963*
4 *España, Anuario Estadístico, 1963*, Instituto Nacional Estadística, p. 594 National Income by Provinces
5 *The European Markets, The Chase Manhattan Bank*, January 1964, data from purchasing power survey
6 Cole, J. P. *Italy*, Ch. 14, Section 2, 1964, London; Chatto and Windus
7 *Anuario Estatístico do Brasil, IBGE, 1961*, p. 269.
8 Brown, A. J. *Introduction to the World Economy*, 1959, London; Allen and Unwin
9 *United Nations Statistical Bulletin for Latin America*, Vol. 1, No. 1, Table 4, 1964, New York
10 Berry, B. J. City Size Distributions and Economic Development, *Economic Development and Cultural Change*, Vol. ix, No. 4, Pt. 1, July 1961
11 *IBGE Serviço Nacional de Recenseamento Sinopse Preliminar do Censo Demográfico*, appropriate volumes.
12 Snyder, D. E. 'Urbanization and Population Growth in Mexico', *20th. Int. Geographical Congr.* London, July 1964
13 *Censo Nacional de 1960, Población, Resultados Provisionales*, Buenos Aires, 1961

CHAPTER 20

FOREIGN TRADE AND ECONOMIC UNION

20.1. FOREIGN TRADE*

As has become clear already, the foreign trade of Latin America as a whole has been and still is largely characterized by the export of primary products to and the import of manufactured goods from North America and Western Europe. It has also become clear that the economy and material development of almost every Latin American country revolves round one or a limited number of export items. The importance of foreign trade to the region as a whole can be judged by the fact that the export coefficient for the late 1950s was 16† per cent, compared with 18·5 per cent in West Europe, only 4–5 per cent in the U.S.A. and about 2 per cent in the U.S.S.R. The figure is arrived at by expressing total value of imports as a percentage of total gross national product. Although the total value of Latin American imports and exports is much less than that of West Europe, so also is total gross national product, and it can be seen that foreign trade is almost as important to Latin American countries as to West Europe. In fact it has tended to decline somewhat since the immediate post-war period, for the value of trade in Latin America has not risen as fast as gross national product, or as fast as total world trade; of this, Latin America's share (excluding Cuba) has dropped from 9·4 per cent in 1950–54 to just under 7 per cent in the early 1960s. This may partly be a reflection of increasing self-sufficiency in manufactured products.

The actual amount of foreign trade carried on by individual Latin American countries varies greatly, firstly, of course, because of great differences in population, and secondly on account of varying levels of development. In Table 20.1 the figures in column I–II show the absolute amount involved. In spite of its much smaller population, Venezuela precedes the three largest countries, accounting for about 20 per cent of the value of all Latin American trade, while having less than 4 per cent of total population. Per caput figures in column III show very great differences, but are a less meaningful guide to the importance of trade to the economy of each country than import coefficient figures in column IV (how these are derived is shown above). It is, of course, possible also to express value of exports, or value of imports and exports combined, as a percentage of total gross national product.

The total value of Latin American foreign trade in 1961 was U.S. $17,210 m., with exports in that year worth slightly more than imports. This

* Important material on Latin American foreign trade is published in *BOLSA (FR)* at frequent intervals. *UNSY*[1] puts Latin America in its world context. *BOLSA (QR)*[2] has a useful article: Latin American Trade, Difficulties and Trends.

† It is hoped to reduce this to 8 per cent by 1975. If political union of Latin American countries has taken place by then, inter-Latin American trade, which is being encouraged, will presumably no longer technically count as foreign.

TABLE 20.1

	I	II a	II b	II c	III a	III b	IV a	IV b	V a	V b	VI	VII (principal exports, %)					
1 Brazil	1,214	1,403	1,460	2,863	16	20	11,750	12	35	486	86	coffee	56	cacao	8	veg. fibres	6
2 Mexico	937	826	1,139	1,965	25	31	9,900	12	73	797		cotton	21	coffee	9	sugar	7
3 Argentina	1,210	964	1,460	2,424	56	62	8,300	18	26	424	97	meats	31	cereals	29	wool	26
4 Colombia	464	434	557	991	31	36	3,100	18	57	252	81	coffee	72	crude oil	17	bananas	3
5 Peru	538	494	468	962	49	49	1,500	31	44	173	c. 50	copper	22	cotton	17	fish etc.	12
6 Chile	532	508	585	1,093	66	65	2,820	21	48	227	c. 5	copper†	70	iron ore	6	nitrates	5
7 Venezuela	2,585	2,413	1,051	3,464	331	152	6,800	15	57	510	1·4	oil	91	iron ore	7	coffee	1
8 Cuba*	617(60)	763	808	1,571	115	134	2,500	35	negl.	14		sugar	76	tobacco	10		
9 Ecuador	140	127	101	228	30	24	780	13	43	49	94	bananas	62	coffee	15	cacao	14
10 Guatemala	109	115	134	249	29	34	530	13	49	60		coffee	66	bananas	17		
11 El Salvador	136	119	112	231	51	47	410	26	43	35	92	coffee	69	cotton	14	wood	10
12 Honduras	77	73	72	145	39	40	310	27	53	37	87	bananas	46	coffee	19	gold	12
13 Nicaragua	80	61	74	135	53	66	310	23	53	32	83	coffee	34	cotton	26	cacao	7
14 Costa Rica	85	84	107	191	67	89	420	24	47	42	96	coffee	49	bananas	28	cacao	3
15 Panama	46	30	124	154	26	134	360	25	53	125	93	bananas	73	coffee	12	sugar	11
16 Haiti	42	32	35	65	10	10	250	34	65	26		coffee	56	sisal	13	cacao	8
17 Dominican Rep.	173	143	69	212	54	44	680	14		29		sugar	50	coffee	21	machinery etc.	11
18 Puerto Rico	810	711	1,022	1,733			1,460	10				textiles etc.	25	sugar	24	bananas	9
19 Jamaica		178	211	389			575	37	{44	252	43	bauxite†	49	sugar	8	chemicals	2
20 Trinidad		346	336	682			615	55			13	oil†	84	chemicals	1		
21 Neth. Antilles		709	717	1,426	3,619	3,660					negl.	oil prods.	98				
22 Guianas	58	128	140	268	16	20	400	35		29	c. 45	bauxite†	44	sugar	30	rice	·10
23 Bolivia	56	56	73	129	18	22	400	18		26	negl.	tin	65	lead	7	silver	7
24 Paraguay	34	31	35	66			235	15		12	almost 100	meats	26	quebracho	11		
25 Uruguay	153	175	208	383	51	76	885	23		48	almost 100	wool	35	meat	24	hides	6
26 LATIN AMERICA		8,650	8,560	17,210						3,686		oil†	28	coffee	17	sugar	8

* Cuba mainly for 1958.
† includes refined products, concentrates, etc., as appropriate.
I Value of exports in 1962 in millions of U.S. $[3]
II Value in millions of U.S. $ of exports (a), imports (b) and total trade (c) in 1961[4].
III Per caput value in U.S. $ at official rate of exports (a) and imports (b) in 1962[5].
IV (a) Value in millions of U.S. $ of gross national produce in 1961[6].
(b) Value of imports as percentage value of total gross national products $\frac{IIb}{IVa} \times 100$

V (a) Percentage of total imports provided by U.S.A. (see also Figure 1.3)
(b) Value in millions of U.S. $ of U.S. exports to Latin America in 1961[7].
VI Agricultural products as a percentage of value of all exports in 1961[8].
VII Principal exports as percentages of total value of exports 1960 or near year[9].

was approximately 7 per cent of the total value of world trade. Latin American exports rose gradually in value from some U.S. $7,000 m. in 1952 to U.S. $8,650 m. in 1956 but hardly changed up to 1962 (U.S. $8,660 m. in 1961). There were of course fluctuations during the 1957–61 period with stagnation in individual countries, but in 1962–63 there were signs of an overall increase. During the same period, the balance of payments has tended to be unfavourable in most countries, with imports tending to exceed exports in value, and services also to be paid for. Some countries have put drastic restrictions on imports. Venezuela alone has an exceptionally favourable balance of payments.

During the last decade or so there have been great changes in the contribution of individual commodities. For example oil, contributed almost entirely by Venezuela, rose from 25 per cent to 28 per cent of the total value of Latin American exports during 1956–62, while coffee, hit by a 40 per cent drop in prices, dropped from 23 per cent to 16 per cent in the same period; the annual value of Colombian and Brazilian coffee exports declined by U.S. $500 m. during this period, coffee becoming one of the less attractive items to grow for export. Sugar prices also declined by 14 per cent during 1956–62 but the Cuban output dropped to about half in 1963, which was also marked by a poor beet harvest in Europe; prices of sugar then rose three times, thus encouraging many countries to consider growing more. Such drastic changes in the prices of primary commodities are a constant worry for Latin American economies and greatly affect patterns of trade and also influence what is grown at least on the more commercial farms of the region.

Latin American foreign trade is also affected by the existence of tariffs of varying severity protecting both Latin American countries themselves and partners with which Latin American countries trade. It should not be overlooked that tariffs on imports of foreign goods serve several purposes in Latin America: to protect home industries from outside competition, to discourage the import of luxury items, and as an important source of revenue, particularly since income tax and other forms of tax are generally inefficiently organized and contribute little. The U.S.A. manipulates much of its trade with primary producing countries by allowing quotas on its imports from these. The quota of fuel oil from Venezuela was increased in 1963, for example, while the elimination of imports of sugar from Cuba has led to a drastic reorganization of sugar import quotas from other suppliers of this commodity to the U.S.A. since the Cuban revolution. European tariffs tend to be low on raw materials such as copper, cotton and wool, but in recent years in Argentina and Uruguay have had difficulty in selling temperate food products to some countries, especially in EEC, while there is growing concern among tropical Latin American countries over the favoured position of many African countries for the export of coffee, cacao, and other tropical products to West Europe.

Turning to the exports of Latin American countries, it will be seen from column VII in Table 20.1 that most depend heavily on the export of agricultural products: for about 15 of the 25 areas listed, these are over 80 per cent of the total value of exports. Moreover, from the list of items exported it is clear that many countries depend heavily on a single item. Again, some

are equally dependent on one or a few mineral exports. Many of the agricultural and mineral exports are in some way processed before export, but
actual manufactures as yet hardly figure among the exports of any country.
There is a small export of textiles, clothing and chemical products, while
Brazil in particular is beginning to export engineering products, but altogether manufactures account for only a few per cent of total exports.

Imports, in contrast, consist largely of manufactured goods of various
kinds. Until two or three decades ago consumer goods formed a large proportion of these, but with the expansion of manufacturing capacity and the
policy of import substitution, many countries have been able to cut down on
imports of this kind and to spend more on capital goods: equipment for
factories, road building and so on. Such trends are well illustrated by the
changing imports of Colombia[10].

	Percentage of imports		
	1953–56	*1957–59*	*1960–61*
Raw materials	44·4	57·6	40·0
Consumer goods	17·1	11·0	9·2
Capital goods	38·5	31·4	50·8

Brazil has even reached a stage when the import substitution policy is being
extended to capital goods.

In addition to importing manufactured goods, many countries have to
import considerable quantities of fuel or food or occasionally both. The
paradox of countries both exporting and importing agricultural products is
explained by the advantage gained in using much of the best land to produce
tropical crops that can be exported to industrial countries while cutting
down the area on which food crops can be grown; in some cases, improvements could be made in the cultivation of food crops and imports virtually
eliminated. The importation of fuel, now almost entirely oil, crude or
refined, is another burden for many countries, and again efforts have been
made in most fuel deficient countries to discover oil and gas.

Many countries are concerned, naturally, over their dependence on one
particular crop or mineral and from time to time have attempted to diversify
their exports. In the last few years, alone, considerable changes have been
made. Thus several countries depending heavily on the export of coffee have
turned to other possible items: Brazil to food crops, cotton and manufactures,
Colombia to cotton and sugar, Central America to cotton and cotton seed
and so on. Similarly, the policy in Cuba after the revolution was for a time
to turn from excessive specialization in sugar cultivation towards food crops
and livestock. In Venezuela and Chile, iron ore has become an important
second export, following oil and copper respectively. Up to a point, these
changes cancel one another out, and leave the total pattern of trade little
changed, for while some are turning from coffee to other crops, other
countries are increasing their coffee plantations, and similarly while some
are reducing their dependence on sugar, others have great hopes of this in the
future. On the whole, however, there appears to be a general move towards
diversification of exports within countries, with the introduction of crops

429

such as the oil palm, and jute, little grown in Latin America before, and the expansion of manufacturing.

The direction of Latin American trade is summarized in Table 20.2. The proportions are based on exports only but in most cases differ little from those for imports. Considering Latin America as a whole it can be seen that in the early 1950s almost half of the total trade was with North America, compared with roughly a third in the interwar period*. In contrast, West Europe, which had half of Latin American foreign trade before the war, accounted for as little as a quarter in 1952, but has recovered somewhat since. Inter-Latin American trade has been somewhat higher in the 1950s

TABLE 20.2

Destination of Exports of Latin America[11]
(percentages of total value)

Year	Latin America	North America	West Europe	Rest
1938	6	31	47	16
1948	9	39	35	17
1952	9	52	25	14
1953	9	49	27	15
1954	9	45	29	17
1955	10	46	29	15
1956	8	47	31	14
1957	9	46	27	18
1958	9	46	32	13
1959	9	46	30	15
1960	8	43	32	17
1961	7	40	31	22
1962	7	39	33	21

than in 1938 but was diminishing relatively by the early 1960s. Increased inter-LAFTA trade is now reversing this trend (see next section). The principal remaining trading partners of Latin America have been Japan, East Europe and the U.S.S.R. (COMECON) and recently communist China. Attempts are also being made to increase or establish trading connections with such different countries as Australia and New Zealand, Israel and Nigeria.

As already shown in Chapter 1.2, the share of total trade in each country carried on with the U.S.A. tends to diminish with distance away from the U.S.A. Thus with the exception of Cuba and certain other Islands closely associated with Europe, Mexico, Central America, the Caribbean and northern South America have strong trading links with the U.S.A. Those least dependent on the U.S.A. are Argentina and Uruguay; as already stressed, distance is only one factor, for these more distant areas do not export many commodities needed by the U.S. economy anyway.

In conclusion, it seems that Latin American trade will continue to expand, as combined gross national product grows. Even if greater self-sufficiency is achieved in the simpler kinds of manufactured goods, more sophisticated kinds will be needed in much greater quantities. But there is a deliberate movement to reduce dependence on the U.S.A., and in their own ways,

* Enough data to build up a general picture of this can be collected from appropriate numbers of *The Statesman's Yearbook*.

Mexico and Cuba, the two countries closest to the U.S.A., have perhaps gone furthest to demonstrate this, Mexico by backing LAFTA and Cuba by cutting itself off altogether. In some countries, too, it has been regretted that traditional ties with West Europe from earlier in this century have been weakened, particularly as the U.K. has favoured trade with the British Commonwealth and France with its partners in Africa. This has to some extent been offset by growing Soviet interest in trade with Latin America, especially since Stalin's death in 1953. Japan, too, has revived its interest in the region, investing in the extraction of iron ore and the manufacture of steel; token quantities of Japanese settlers are being admitted to Brazil and Argentina. Other examples of entry into partnership with countries in other parts of the world include visits by Israeli missions to several countries in 1963, the establishment of an Uruguayan-Nigerian Chamber of Commerce in Montevideo, the export to mainland China of copper from Chile and meat from Argentina, and the opening in 1963 of a monthly freight service from Australia to the Pacific coast of South America.

Of more immediate interest to Latin American foreign trade, however, is the possibility of establishing more favourable terms of trade; that is, of ensuring greater payment from the same amount of exports. In other words, more remunerative prices are being sought for primary products, while at the same time obstacles to their free movement by developed countries importing them should be removed. The contention is that in the last decade or so primary commodity prices have stagnated or risen slowly, while the price of manufactured goods has been rising constantly. More favourable terms of trade would be more beneficial financially and less embarassing politically than more aid. In the meantime Latin American countries have been compelled to look for non-traditional goods to export, and have in some cases contemplated becoming exporters of manufactured goods.

In the near future, perhaps, the prospect of expanding Latin American exports is not bright, but the encouragement of inter-LAFTA trade may bring some improvement, while lack of stability in Africa and southern Asia may revive interest in Latin American tropical products. In the long run, as more and more parts of the world pass from being predominantly agricultural to predominantly industrial, there will surely be scope again for selling any primary products that Latin America, itself much more advanced industrially by then, still has available for export.

20.2. THE LATIN AMERICAN FREE TRADE ASSOCIATION*

The formal inauguration of the Latin American Free Trade Association (LAFTA) took place on Jan. 2nd 1962, with tariff rebates coming into force on that day. The idea of a trade association had been considered in the 1950s and was seriously proposed in 1958 by the United Nations Commission for Latin America (ECLA), and in 1959 a number of countries signed the Montevideo Treaty, which they ratified in 1961†, the year in which the

---

* There is much material on this topic. A useful recent article is 'Integration in Latin America'[12]. The name in Spanish of LAFTA is Asociación Latinoamericana de Libre Comercio (ALALC).

† A bewildering number of different dates are given for drawing up, signing, ratification and putting into operation. It is hoped that those given here are correct.

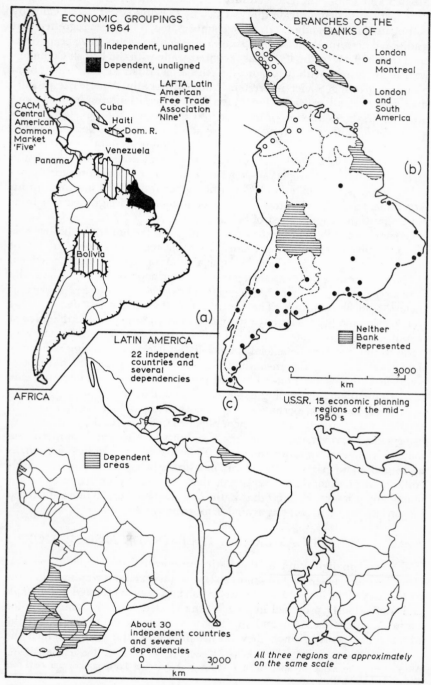

Figure 20.1. Latin America. (a) Economic groupings 1964. (b) Branches of the Banks of London and Montreal and of London and South America. (c) Latin America compared with Africa and U.S.S.R.

Punta del Este Conference was held. The seven founder members were Argentina, Brazil, Chile, Mexico, Paraguay, Peru and Uruguay; Colombia joined soon after and Ecuador later in 1962. Meetings between the member countries are held regularly (six in 1963 alone for example) and on some occasions Bolivia and Venezuela have sent observers. At the third Annual Conference late in 1963, for example, the question of shipping links between Member countries was discussed. Various subsidiary associations have been formed such as the Latin American Copper Association, the aim of which is to ensure that eventually Member countries supply all copper requirements of LAFTA.

At the moment, the countries of LAFTA are divided into three groups. There are special measures for Ecuador and Paraguay, which for eight years will have a special status as underdeveloped countries, and concessions on exports from them. Colombia, Chile, Peru and Uruguay form a separate group as countries with moderate development. Brazil, Mexico and Argentina form the third group. The remaining countries of Latin America, with the exception of Cuba (on account of its regime) may join the Association, but by 1964 had not chosen to do so. The six countries of Central America appear to be too concerned with their own union (see Chapter 10) which will however only bring their total population to the average size of a single Latin American country. Apart from Cuba, which at one stage was anxious to join, each of the Islands has its individual problems, most have special links with some other part of the world, and some possibly are not even wanted in LAFTA. Bolivia has been undecided about joining and one reason given for not doing so was that it prefers to obtain its manufactured goods from the U.S.A. and West Europe rather than be forced to buy goods of inferior quality from LAFTA. Venezuela perhaps is closest to joining LAFTA, but in recent years there have been no signs of its trade increasing with members and, moreover, the special nature of its foreign trade, including its reciprocal trade treaty with the U.S.A., together with its heavily protected new industries, high wages and system of collective labour contracts, make it difficult for Venezuela to enter*.

Although few major changes have yet come about as a result of the formation of LAFTA, the Association came into being without great difficulty and appears to have come permanently. There are several reasons why it came into existence so easily. The countries have at one time all been colonies of Spain or Portugal, although from the first they were operated in at least three distinct compartments, Brazil and the Viceroyalties of Mexico and Peru. They are located in the same part of the world, up to a point have similar economic problems and especially a similar trading pattern, and they have a common interest also in preserving the region from the excessive influence of the United States. In addition, apart from Brazil, they have the same language and, for what it is worth, the same religion; language conditions make contact and the spreading of ideas easy.

The general aims of LAFTA are not unlike those of the other large economic unions of the world. Basically there are supposed advantages in

---

* The president of Venezuela forecast the entry of his country into LAFTA by the end of 1964[13].

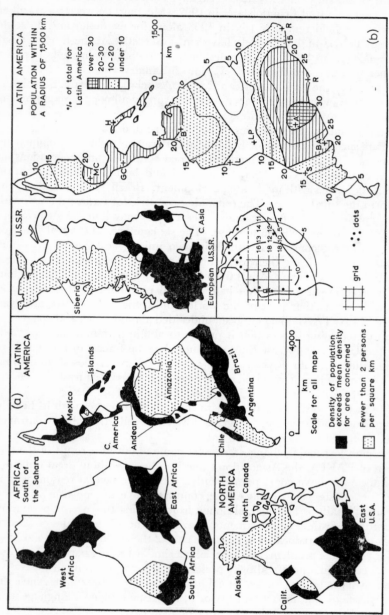

Figure 20.2. Latin America compared with Africa, North America and U.S.S.R.

scale in a large economic unit. These, without doubt, benefit certain industries (for example steel but not textiles), and they also allow resources to be pooled for research and administration. The collective aims of LAFTA include the following. Firstly, simply to encourage trade between the partners, thereby, among other things, decreasing dependence on the United States; trade is to be free by 1972 or 1973 and a reduction on tariffs of at least 8 per cent per year is aimed at on goods passing between the countries. Secondly, the enlarged 'home market' is expected to make greater regional specialization possible, with each country, presumably, producing what it is best suited to specialize in, if of course it has anything at all. This presupposes that the additional transport costs resulting from greater regional specialization do not make total costs greater than they would be if each region was self-sufficient and transport costs were limited. In particular a large market and co-ordination between member countries is needed if the engineering industry is to expand twenty-five times between 1958 and 1975. It is hoped that from a growth in the inter-LAFTA exchange of manufactured goods there may arise the exportation of manufactures to Europe and North America. Thirdly, by associating, the countries hope to be in a better position to bargain with the rest of the world in the sale of their export crops. Fourthly, some advantage should be gained by using the great size and diversity of the region to soften the fluctuations in yield of crops from year to year in different parts by compensating these from high yields elsewhere. Similarly, in the U.S.S.R., bad grain harvests in the Ukraine have usually been offset by good ones in Kazakhstan and vice versa. Finally it is planned that the Free Trade Association shall become a Customs union, with uniform external tariffs and possibly in the end a political union, which could considerably strengthen the position of Latin America in world affairs.

Each country no doubt also expects to derive some particular benefit from its membership. Mexico, for example has virtually no trade at all as yet with the rest of the countries but sees a way of resisting United States influence. Brazil is undoubtedly looking forward for assured markets for the products of its growing industries, while Paraguay is hoping for financial help from Argentina and Brazil.

What trade is there at the moment between LAFTA countries? The following table summarizes the main features of trade[14] (in millions of U.S. $ to nearest million in 1962).

From \ To	Mexico	Colombia	Ecuador	Peru	Chile	Argentina	Paraguay	Uruguay	Brazil
Mexico	—	2	1	2	2	2	n.a.	1	8
Colombia	n.	—	2	4	1	1	n.a.	n.	0
Ecuador	n.a.	3	—	n.	2	n.	n.a.	n.	n.a.
Peru	2	1	2	—	24	8	0	2	11
Chile	1	1	1	3	—	15	0	1	15
Argentina	1	2	n.	26	32	—	6	7	69
Paraguay	0	n.a.	n.a.	0	0	10	—	1	0
Uruguay	0	2	0	0	1	2	n.	—	3
Brazil	n.	n.	0	1	9	49	2	14	—

n.a. = not available.
n. = negligible.

435

It is ironical that the largest single item of inter-Latin American trade is Venezuelan oil, exported crude or refined from Venezuela or refined from the Netherlands Antilles and even Trinidad. The oil trade is affected by the policy of the Governments of the countries involved and of the large non-Latin American oil companies. Except when it exported limited quantities of oil to other parts of Latin America early in this century, Mexico has never had more than negligible trade with South America. Colombia has very little trade with the rest of the LAFTA countries and Ecuador not much. The remaining six countries trade regularly among themselves. The following figures show the LAFTA trade of each country as a percentage of its total foreign trade in 1962:

Paraguay	32	Chile	7	Ecuador	5
Argentina	12	Brazil	6	Mexico	1·8
Peru	9	Uruguay	5	Colombia	1·6

There are some convenient exchanges of commodities between LAFTA countries such as the exchange of Argentinian wheat for Brazilian coffee, of Chilean temperate fruits for Peruvian sugar, and so on. Such traditional trade was likely to continue anyway, without the help of trade liberalization. Much of the trade is in fact bilateral, which saves countries from using dollars, but this 'barter' arrangement is not very flexible, and to improve the organizational side of inter-LAFTA trade a compensation centre and eventually a true payments union will be necessary. It will be needful to unify or at least harmonize monetary, fiscal, exchange and other policies[15]. If further trade is to be fostered, reasonable shipping services between member countries must also be provided.

What are the present trends? Firstly, there is scope for encouraging certain regions to improve food production, others to concentrate on steel production and engineering and others still on chemicals. Argentina and Uruguay specially could increase wheat and meat supplies, items imported by most other parts of LAFTA. Brazil and Mexico seem the best equipped to specialize in heavy industry, while Chile and Peru have many useful raw materials. Already plans are being made in various countries to produce items for the new LAFTA market; for example, newspaper and print in Chile, plywood in Paraguay. Secondly, there have already been moves to improve the shipping services between the member countries, and early in 1964 it was proposed eventually to have all traffic carried by Latin American shipping. Apparently there are some 700 vessels of various kinds but these only take about 20 per cent of the mutual trade. One example of an attempt to improve services was the establishment in 1963 by Loide Brasileiro of a regular interval (20-day) shipping service between Salvador, Rio, other Brazilian ports, Montevideo and Buenos Aires[16]. Thirdly, by 1963 there were indications of an increase in mutual trade. It is too soon to see any serious trends, but in 1962 alone, trade between LAFTA countries rose by 36 per cent to U.S. $251 m.; Mexican trade rose by 112 per cent, that of Peru by 64 per cent.

There are already signs of closer economic co-operation among Latin American countries. In the first place there have been some achievements in Central America, which is more than can be said of the Islands, in which the Federation of the British West Indian colonies broke up and in which old centrifugal tendencies remain. Among LAFTA countries co-operation so far has largely been between pairs of countries. For example, a gas pipeline is to be built from Argentina into Uruguay, while Argentina and Uruguay (Salto Grande) and Brazil and Paraguay (Guaira) plan to build large hydroelectric power stations together, and Argentina and Chile are electrifying the railway between Mendoza and Santiago. Bridges are being built between Brazil and Paraguay over the Paraná River and between Argentina and Paraguay over the Paraguay River. In some cases collaboration is between more than two countries as for example between Chile, Brazil and

TABLE 20.3

Approximate Distance in Hundreds of Kilometres by Shortest Sea Distance (using Panama Canal where relevant) Between Representative Latin American Ports

	Veracruz	*Buenaventura*	*Callao*	*Valparaiso*	*Buenos Aires*	*Rio de Janeiro*	*Recife*	*La Guaira*	*San Juan*
Veracruz	—	34	56	81	120	99	79	35	34
Buenaventura	34	—	22	44	93	87	68	22	27
Callao	56	22	—	24	76	91	88	43	46
Valparaiso	81	44	24	—	51	68	87	68	70
Buenos Aires	120	93	76	51	—	22	42	87	90
Rio de Janeiro	99	87	91	68	22	—	20	64	67
Recife	79	68	88	87	42	20	—	44	47
La Guaira	35	22	43	68	87	64	44	—	10
San Juan	34	27	46	70	90	67	47	10	—

Argentina to avoid duplication in the motor vehicles industry. Most improbable of all is the construction by a Mexican firm of a bridge over the river Guayas at Guayaquil in Ecuador*.

LAFTA is a fact but its future success depends on its viability as an economic region. The unwieldy shape of Latin America and the great distances in journeys between one part of the continent and another have already been stressed several times. Conditions might be somewhat more easy if much of the population was concentrated in the hollow interior of South America. As it is, railways and roads are so bad, and distances so great, that the transportation of goods by land between most partners of LAFTA is out of the question, and almost all trade has to be by sea or air; the latter, of course, being out of the question at present except for special cargoes. One implication of this is that coastal areas will provide the most attractive sites for any industries hoping to sell products over LAFTA as a whole, as opposed to their own national markets†. The great distances involved between LAFTA countries appear often to be overlooked by economists. Table 20.3 shows distances between representative ports of each member country, and *Figure 20.3* compares distances in LAFTA with those in North America and West Europe.

* The cost would be U.S. $12 m.[17]
† An idea put forward by P. R. Odell in a paper at the annual meeting of the Geographical Association, London, December 1962.

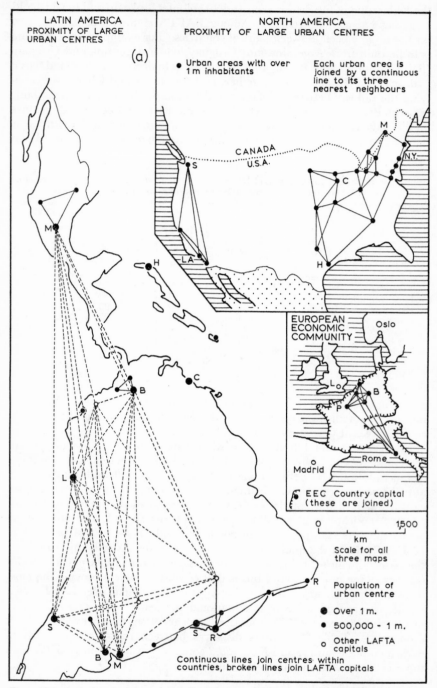

Figure 20.3. Latin America compared with North America and with the European Economic Community

Outline of coast based on a map in the Oxford Atlas published by
Oxford University Press

Given the present lack of trade between Mexico and Colombia on the one hand and the rest of South America on the other it would seem more realistic initially to develop LAFTA, together with any other countries that join it in the future, as two separate economic units (see *Figure 20.4*), and not to expect much trade between these two units for some time. This division of Latin America into two regions is nicely reflected in the spheres of influence of the Bank of London and South America and the Bank of London and Montreal (see *Figure 20.1b*). It is also suggested in *Figure 20.2* which shows the approximate number of people within a particular radius (1,500 km) of all points in Latin America. By this method* a more generalized picture of the distribution of population is shown than by dots (as in *Figure 2.1*). The result changes according to the radius taken, however, and the only justification for choosing 1,500 km is that it seems a reasonable distance over which goods could be sent to a regional market.

Whether Latin America develops as one or as two economic units, some aspects of the problems involved are summarized in *Figures 20.4a* and *20.4b*. The southern area with about 100 m. people and a combined gross national product two to three times that of Australia, although very long from end to end, seems large enough and varied enough to be usefully welded together as a fairly self-sufficient unit. The most central and accessible part would seem to lie between Buenos Aires and Rio, while Chile, Bolivia and Northeast Brazil would occupy peripheral positions, Chile at a dead end but Northeast Brazil passed by shipping services to the North Atlantic and Caribbean areas. The northern area, on the other hand, appears at first sight to be more fragmented than the southern area, though this might not be a drawback if suitable shipping services were introduced. A more serious drawback of the northern area, however, is the presence of the United States in such close proximity. The United States is the chief trading partner of almost every country in the area and it would be impossible to exclude it from any projects aimed at improving transport facilities or developing the economies of the various countries.

Finally, a comparison of LAFTA with certain other large areas that form economic units, or plan to do so in the future, throws further light on the problems of LAFTA. *Figure 20.2*, shows North America, the U.S.S.R. (not COMECON), and Africa south of the Sahara. The four regions are at present roughly equal in area and in population. The outstanding contrast between Latin America on the one hand, and North America and the U.S.S.R. on the other hand, is that Latin America has its population dispersed in a number of clusters of varying size, and an empty interior, whereas the other two have most of their population in a fairly small part of the total area and large empty areas to one side; that is not to say that the integration

* The procedure is to apply a 'running' mean to a spatial (areal) distribution, preferably represented by a convenient number of dots. For *Figure 20.2b*, the population of Latin America was represented by 100 dots, each equal to 1 per cent of the total. A grid with squares of appropriate size (see adjoining map to *Figure 20.2b*) was placed over the whole region. A circle with a radius equivalent to 1,500 km was then placed with its centre at each intersection on the grid in turn, where such an intersection fell on land. The number of dots contained in the circle was then counted and recorded on the map at the centre of the circle (e.g. first at *a*, then *b* and so on). The values recorded then formed the basis for an ordinary isopleth map.

439

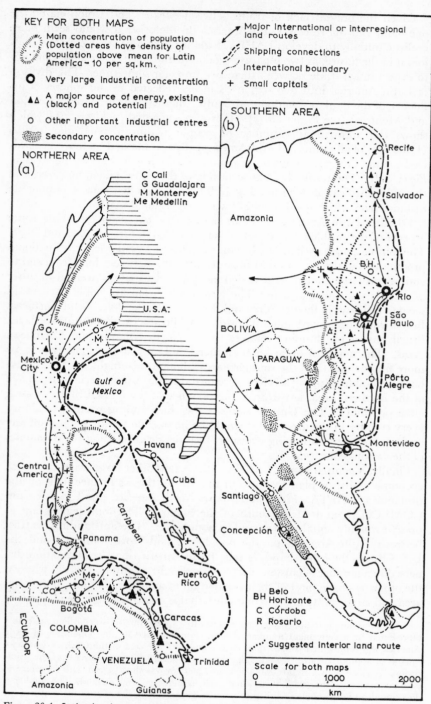

KEY FOR BOTH MAPS

Main concentration of population
(Dotted areas have density of
population above mean for Latin
America - 10 per sq. km.

O   Very large industrial concentration

▲Δ A major source of energy, existing
    (black) and potential

o   Other important industrial centres

    Secondary concentration

NORTHERN AREA
(a)

C Cali
G Guadalajara
M Monterrey
Me Medellin

Major International or interregional
land routes

Shipping connections

International boundary

+   Small capitals

SOUTHERN AREA
(b)

Amazonia

U.S.A.

Mexico
City

Gulf of
Mexico

Havana

Cuba

Caribbean

Central
America

Panama

Puerto
Rico

Me

Bogotá

Caracas

Trinidad

COLOMBIA

ECUADOR

VENEZUELA

Amazonia

Guianas

Recife

Salvador

BOLIVIA

PARAGUAY

B.H.

Rio

São
Paulo

Pôrto
Alegre

R

Montevideo

C

Santiago

Concepción

BH Belo
    Horizonte
C   Córdoba
R   Rosario

Suggested interior land route

Scale for both maps
0   1,000   2,000
              km

Figure 20.4. Latin America: recommended economic developments for Northern and Southern areas.
The two main industrial belts in South America are shown thus ≈

440

of northern Canada and of Siberia into the economic life of their respective regions is not without its problems, particularly those concerned with stretching communications. But these involve only a small part of the total population of the two regions. A brief comparison with Africa, south of the Sahara suggests that, here at least, there is some consolation for Latin America. If the Republic of South Africa is excluded, then the rest of the region has a combined gross national product no bigger than that of Brazil alone, spread among some thirty independent states. Here, as in Latin America, population is concentrated in a number of separate clusters and land travel between these is extremely difficult and costly even where possible at all.

In a study of the geography of Latin America one cannot help ending inconclusively. This book has been written during a period in Latin American history of particularly abrupt changes. If anything has emerged from what has been written it is the inadequacy of our traditional ways of studying the regional geography of a continent the size of Latin America in such a state of change. In the view of the author there are now sufficient quantitative data to allow a far fuller assessment of the economic, urban and social geography than has been carried out so far. And in the last resort, a comparison with other regions of the world of a continental scale could be fruitful, once satisfactory methods have been developed to do this. In conclusion, Latin America deserves special attention on account of its position as the most developed of the great underdeveloped regions of the world.

REFERENCES

[1] *UNSY*, 1962 Tables 152–156
[2] *BOLSA (QR)*, April 1964, Vol. IV, No. 2, pp. 75–91
[3] *UNSY*, 1963, Table 158
[4] *UNSY*, 1962, Table 152
[5] *Pick's Currency Yearbook*, 1963, p. 29
[6] *UNSY*, 1962
[7] *Statistical Abstract of the United States*, 1962, pp. 884–85
[8] *FAOTY* 1962, Table 1
[9] Centre of Latin American Studies, Univ. of California, *Statistical Abstract of Latin America*, 1962, pp. 98–99
[10] *BOLSA (FR)* 9 Feb. 1963, p. 116
[11] *UNSY*, 1962, Table 153; 1963, Table 159
[12] *BOLSA (QR)* Jan 1964, Vol. IV, No. 1. pp. 1–15
[13] *Peruvian Times*, 26 Jun 1964 p. 2
[14] *BOLSA (QR)* Jan 1964, table on p. 15
[15] *BOLSA (QR)* Jan 1964, p. 5
[16] *BOLSA (FR)* 30 Nov. 1963, p. 1017
[17] *BOLSA*, Oct. 1963, p. 900

APPENDIX 1

SELECTED PLACE NAMES OF LATIN AMERICA

Brazil assorted

Itacoatiara
São Domingos do
           Maranhão
Mombaça
Dona Inês
Delmiro Gouveia
Cotegipe
Barão de Cocais
Itanhandu
Rio Prêto
Magé
Elias Fausto
Palmital
Timburi
Teixeira Soares
Ibirubá
Aruana
Xambioá

Brazil long

Pindamonhangaba
Itaquaquecetuba
Jaboticabal
Guaratingüetá
Pirassununga

Brazil synthetic

Cafelândia
Brasilia
Nilópolis
Londrina
Uberlândia
Cosmópolis
Cristalândia

Mexico assorted

Asientos
Ensenada
San Antonio
Campeche
Nava
Villa de Alvárez
Ostuacán
Guadalupe Bravos
Hidalgo
San Luis de la Paz
Tlalchapa
Lolotla
Santa María de los Angeles
Temascalingo
Venustiano Carranza
Coatlán
Rosamorada

Mexico Indian

Ixtlahuaca
Coyotepec
Tepemaxalco
Ixmiquilpan

Mexico Spanish

Piedras Negras
Ascención
Saltillo
Buenavista
Compostela

Mexico Indian-Spanish

Santa Ana Ateixtlahuaca
Acatlan de Pérez Figueroa
Santiago Miahuatlan

San Martín Zacatepec
Tlacotepec Plumas

Peru Indian

Chuquibamba
Muquiyauyo
Paucartambo
Huarmicocha
Sumbilca
Corpacancha

Haiti assorted

Port-de-Paix
Maribaroux
Verrettes
Mirebalais
Croix-des-Bouquets
Changieux

Jamaica assorted

Hopewell
Adelphi
Clark's Town
Ocho Rios
Highgate
Santa Cruz
Mandeville

Miscellaneous

Kralendijk (Neth. Ant.)
Wageningen (Surinam)
Meerzorg (Surinam)
Filadelfia (Paraguay)
Rawson (Argentina)
Blumenau Brazil)
O'Higgins (Chile)

APPENDIX 2

TABLE A2

U.S. Exports and Aid to and Trade with Latin America[1]

	Population in millions in 1961	I U.S. exports 1962			II U.S. investments in 1961		III Major U.S. Govt. foreign assistance 1945–62	
		a	b	c	a	b	a	b
1 Cuba	6,9	13	2	negl.		negl.	40	6
2 Mexico	36,1	790	22	73	822	23	438	12
3 Haiti	4,2	24	6	65			86	20
4 Dominican Rep.	3,1	71	23	65			21	7
5 Guatemala	3,9	61	16	49			128	33
6 El Salvador	2,7	41	15	43			24	9
7 Venezuela	7,6	468	62	57	3,017	397	108	14
8 Colombia	14,4	227	16	57	425	30	272	19
9 Ecuador	4,5	45	10	43			73	16
10 Peru	10,4	184	18	44	437	42	200	19
11 Bolivia	3,5	32	9	44			244	70
12 Brazil	73,1	425	6	35	1,000	14	1,165	16
13 Chile	7,8	171	22	48	725	93	425	54
14 Argentina	21,1	375	18	26	635	30	371	13
15 Uruguay	2,9	44	15	25	49	17	49	17

I a Value in millions of U.S. $.
 b Per caput value in U.S. $.
 c U.S. exports as percentage of total exports to receiving country in 1961.
II a Value in millions of U.S. $.
 b Per caput value in U.S. $.
III a Value in millions of U.S. $.
 b Per caput value in U.S. $.

APPENDIX 3

TABLE A3

Population in Millions in Major World Regions, 1920–1961, and
as Percentages (in italics) of 1920 Figure. See *Figure 1.4*.

	1920	*1930*	*1940*	*1950*	*1961*
World	1,811	2,015	2,249	2,509	3,069
	100	*111*	*124*	*139*	*170*
Africa	141	157	176	207	261
	100	*112*	*125*	*147*	*186*
North America	117	135	146	167	204
	100	*115*	*125*	*143*	*174*
Latin America	91	109	131	162	218
	100	*120*	*144*	*178*	*240*
Asia	966	1,072	1,212	1,384	1,721
	100	*111*	*125*	*143*	*178*
U.S.S.R.	158	176	192	181	218
	100	*111*	*121*	*115*	*138*
Europe	329	356	381	395	430
	100	*108*	*116*	*120*	*131*

Projections of population (mid-year) for Latin America *excluding* all
dependent areas prior to 1962, are as follows:

1960	206 m.	1975	315 m.
1965	237 m.	1980	364 m.
1970	273 m.		

APPENDIX 4

FINANCIAL AND OTHER INTERNATIONAL BODIES

Capital now reaches Latin America from a great number of different sources. Below are listed some of the bodies that organize this finance. In addition to the essentially non-communist sources shown, Comecon countries are beginning to take an interest in the region. For example (BOLSA(FR), 6 April 1963) East Germany was planning to invest U.S. $50 m. in Northeast Brazil in industrial plants.

Financial Organizations

World Bank makes loans particularly to less developed countries either to their governments or, with their guarantee, to private enterprises. Much has gone to electricity and transport development.

IBRD International Bank for Reconstruction and Development (Washington). The institution through which loans are made by the World Bank.

IDA International Development Association (Washington). An affiliate of the World Bank, established in 1960, IDA makes credits available for developments in less developed countries without straining exchange reserves.

IFC International Finance Corporation (Washington). An affiliate of the World Bank, investing in private enterprises (first investment made in 1957).

IMF International Monetary Fund (Washington). One of the main functions of IMF is to act as a reserve on which countries having an unfavourable balance of payments can draw.

IADB Inter American Development Bank. This does not include Canada or the British West Indies. Capital is contributed by the U.S.A. (43 per cent), Brazil and Argentina (13 per cent each), Mexico (8 per cent), Venezuela (7 per cent) and other Latin American countries.

Export–Import Bank of Washington helps countries wishing to purchase U.S. goods.

AID U.S. agency for International Development. For further details see United Nations publication *Adventure in Development*, New York, 1962.

Economic and/or Political Associations

OAS Organization of American States. Canada and Cuba do not belong and Bolivia has not lately participated.

Alliance for Progress (Punta del Este). The target, not met up to 1963 (BOLSA(FR), 24 Aug. 1963) was to achieve an annual flow of U.S. $2,000 m. per year into Latin America.

446

ICAP   Inter-American Committee for the Alliance for Progress.
ADELA   Atlantic Community Group for Latin America is formed by
            private interests in the more advanced industrial countries of
            OECD (Organization for Economic Co-operation and De-
            velopment). It was set up in 1962 and is a multi-national
            private investment company.
ECLA   Economic Commission for Latin America.
BCIE   Banco Centroamericano de Integración Económica
BNDE   Banco Nacional do Desenvolvimento Econômico, Brazil.
CORFO   Corporación de Fomento de la Producción, Chile.
SUDENE   Superintendência do Desenvolvimento do Nordeste, Brazil.

As an example of the amount of aid given to a Latin American country in
recent years, the following is quoted from *BOLSA(FR)*, 21 Sept. 1963 (aid
to Colombia since Punta del Este): Total U.S. $566 m.; IBRD 160 m.;
IDA 19 m.; IFC 6 m; IMF 84 m.; IADB 59 m.; Export–Import Bank
24 m.; plus donations from the U.N. Special Fund and the U.S.A.

APPENDIX 5

GROWTH OF PRODUCTION OF KEY MINING AND MANUFACTURING ITEMS SINCE THE 1930s

TABLE A5.1

Electric Energy Generated in Thousands of Millions of kWh[4-6]

	Brazil	Mexico	Argentina	Colombia	Venezuela	Chile
1929	0,5	negl.	1,4			0,9
1937	3,0	2,5	2,2	0,2	0,1	1,6
1949	7,6	4,3	4,1	0,6	0,4	2,8
1950	8,2	4,4	4,4	0,7	0,5	2,9
1951	8,8	4,9	4,7	0,7	0,6	3,1
1952	10,0	5,3	4,7	0,8	0,7	3,3
1953	10,3	5,7	4,9	1,7*	1,0	3,3
1954	11,9	6,3	5,4	2,0	1,1	3,6
1955	13,7	7,0	n.a.	2,3	1,3	3,8
1956	15,4	7,8	n.a.	2,4	1,5	4,0
1957	17,0	8,5	n.a.	2,9	1,9	4,2
1958	19,8	9,1	9,4	3,0	2,3	4,2
1959	21,1	9,8	9,5	3,4	2,7	4,6
1960	22,9	10,7	10,4	3,8	3,0	4,4
1961	24,4	11,7	11,6	n.a.	3,4	4,8
1962	26,9	12,5	n.a.	n.a.	3,5	5,2

* Production for Colombia until 1953 was only for three principal enterprises.

APPENDIX 5

TABLE A5.2

Crude Oil Production in Millions of Metric Tons[7-9]

	Mexico	Trinidad	Venezuela	Colombia	Peru	Argentina
1935	5,8	1,7	21,7	2,4	2,3	2,0
1940	6,3	3,2	26,9	3,5	1,6	2,9
1941	6,2	3,0	33,2	3,4	1,6	3,1
1942	5,0	3,2	21,7	1,5	1,8	3,4
1943	5,0	3,1	26,2	1,9	1,9	3,6
1944	5,5	3,1	37,6	3,1	1,9	3,5
1945	6,2	3,1	47,3	3,2	1,8	3,3
1946	7,0	2,9	56,8	3,1	1,6	3,0
1947	8,1	3,0	63,6	3,5	1,7	3,1
1948	8,4	2,9	71,7	3,3	1,9	3,3
1949	7,8	3,0	70,5	4,1	2,0	3,2
1950	10,4	3,0	80,0	4,7	2,1	3,4
1951	11,1	3,1	91,0	5,3	2,1	3,5
1952	11,1	3,1	96,6	5,4	2,2	3,6
1953	10,4	3,2	94,2	5,5	2,1	4,1
1954	12,0	3,4	101,2	5,5	2,3	4,2
1955	12,8	3,6	115,2	5,5	2,3	4,4
1956	13,0	4,1	131,5	6,1	2,5	4,4
1957	12,6	4,9	148,4	6,3	2,6	4,9
1958	13,4	5,5	139,1	6,4	2,5	5,1
1959	14,0	5,8	147,9	7,4	2,4	6,4
1960	14,2	6,0	152,4	7,7	2,5	9,1
1961	15,3	6,5	155,9	7,3	2,6	12,1
1962	16,0	6,9	167,4	7,1	2,4	14,0

Other producers: Bolivia passed 100,000 tons in 1948 and 500,000 in 1957, since then, around 400,000.
Ecuador passed 300,000 tons in 1938, since then, around 350,000.
Brazil started in 1940, passed 100,000 in 1952 and reached 4,5 m. in 1961.
Chile started in 1949, passed 500,000 in 1956 and 1 m. in 1961.
Cuba produced for two short periods with maximum in 1950.

TABLE A5.3

Cement Production in Thousands of Metric Tons[10-11]

	Brazil	Mexico	Argentina	Colombia	Venezuela
1935	366	252	722	77	22
1941	768	537	1,164	211	115
1942	753	588	1,122	208	122
1943	747	589	997	253	112
1944	810	608	1,106	281	120
1945	774	741	1,100	303	116
1946	826	738	1,154	332	128
1947	914	708	1,371	346	146
1948	1,112	833	1,265	364	215
1949	1,281	1,228	1,457	476	300
1950	1,386	1,479	1,569	580	501
1951	1,456	1,615	1,563	648	621
1952	1,619	1,757	1,545	700	840
1953	2,030	1,753	1,655	873	982
1954	2,406	1,783	1,683	962	1,213
1955	2,771	2,057	1,844	1,046	1,282
1956	3,275	2,296	2,063	1,220	1,451
1957	3,393	2,560	2,363	1,356	1,747
1958	3,790	2,539	2,471	1,248	1,616
1959	3,841	2,709	2,368	1,348	1,872
1960	4,474	3,089	2,641	1,385	1,487
1961	4,709	3,035	2,906	1,567	1,513
1962	5,039	3,352	2,945	1,719	1,509

TABLE A5.4

Production of Pig Iron and Steel in Thousands of Metric Tons[14-15]

	Mexico		Brazil		Chile		Argentina		Colombia	
	Pig iron	Steel	Pig iron	Steel	Pig iron	Steel	Pig iron	Steel	Pig iron	Steel
1935	63	111	64	64						
1940	92	147	186	141						
1945	210	230	260	206						
1946	240	258	371	343		21				
1947	236	290	481	387		31				
1948	176	292	552	483		30	17	122		
1949	206	373	512	615		32	n.a.	n.a.		
1950	227	390	729	789	110	56	n.a.	n.a.		
1951	254	467	776	843	240	178	n.a.	n.a.		
1952	304	537	812	893	270	243	n.a.	n.a.		
1953	242	462	880	1,016	286	313	36	174		
1954	237	454	1,109	1,172	305	321	40	186	88	
1955	312	510	1,087	1,162	256	290	35	218	99	77
1956	409	591	1,170	1,375	368	381	29	202	128	90
1957	414	687	1,270	1,299	382	388	34	221	142	114
1958	478	988*	1,373	1,360	304	348	29	244	149	121
1959	556	1,213	1,560	1,603	290	415	32	214	125	109
1960	683	1,527	1,750	1,843	266	422	180	277	176	157
1961	851	1,728	1,821	1,995	285	363	399	441	190	176
1962	912	1,851	n.a.	2,800	383	495	396	644	149	137

* New method of calculating.

TABLE A5.5

Production of Metals by Major Producers—Copper (smelter) Production in Thousands of Tons. Iron Ore (iron content) Production in Millions of Tons; Bauxite Production in Thousands of Tons[14,15]

	Copper			Iron ore				Bauxite		
	Chile	Peru	Mexico	Brazil	Chile	Peru	Venezuela	Jamaica	Netherland Guiana	British Guiana
1935	259	29	41	0,03	0,5				113	140
1940*	456	28	41	0,4	1,1				614	614(sic)
1945	462	25	53	0,4	0,2				747	680
1946	359	20	52	0,4	0,7				1,020	1,134
1947	408	18	58	0,4	1,1				1,742	1,381
1948	425	13	49	1,1	1,7				1,983	1,996
1949	351	21	49	1,3	1,7				2,162	1,827
1950	345	20	48	1,4	1,8		0,1		2,045	1,679
1951	360	23	59	1,6	2,0		0,8		2,700	2,107
1952	383	21	51	2,1	1,4		1,3	420	3,168	2,426
1953	361	35	60	2,5	1,7	0,6	1,5	1,240	3,273	2,311
1954	364	38	55	2,1	1,3	1,2	3,5	2,098	3,362	2,347
1955	433	43	55	2,3	0,9	1,1	5,4	2,709	3,123	2,474
1956	490	46	55	2,8	1,6	1,6	7,1	3,256	3,485	2,521
1957	486	57	61	3,4	1,7	2,1	9,0	4,708	3,377	2,237
1958	467	54	65	3,5	2,3	1,5	9,1	5,874	2,988	1,611
1959	546	50	57	6,1	2,9	2,1	10,1	5,264	3,430	1,701
1960	536	182	60	6,4	3,8	3,1	12,5	5,872	3,455	2,511
1961	543	197	49	6,7	4,4	3,1	9,3	6,615	3,405	2,412
1962	557	150	46	n.a.	5,2	3,2	8,5	7,640	3,297	3,592

* 1941 for copper.

APPENDIX 6

TABLE A6

The Distribution of Major Branches of Mining and Manufacturing among Countries or Groups of Countries.
Percentages of Latin American Total[16]

	All mining and mfg.	All mining	Metals	Oil and gas	All mfg.	Light	Heavy	Food	Textiles	Chemicals, etc.	Basic metals	Metal working and engineering
Central America	2·0	0·4	1·3	—	2·4	3·8	0·7	4·9	0·9	0·6	—	0·9
Mexico	18·7	10·7	29·6	2·2	20·6	16·7	25·6	17·4	16·6	23·0	41·6	21·7
Venezuela	16·2	56·7	10·0	80·1	6·3	7·2	5·1	6·1	3·7	7·5	0·5	4·0
Colombia	5·1	4·6	2·1	5·1	5·2	6·6	3·5	6·7	8·1	4·2	1·5	3·3
Ecuador	0·6	0·3	—	0·1	1·0	1·5	0·3	1·3	0·9	0·5	—	0·3
Peru	3·0	6·3	17·9	2·6	2·3	2·9	1·5	3·0	3·6	2·3	1·0	0·9
Bolivia	0·5	2·3	7·6	0·6	0·3	0·3	0·2	0·2	0·4	0·4	0·1	—
Islands	8·5	6·6	11·7	5·2	9·0	9·8	7·9	15·7	1·6	17·3	0·3	2·8
Guianas	0·6	1·0	4·7	—	0·2	0·2	0·1	0·3	—	—	—	0·2
Brazil	19·3	1·8	2·8	0·4	23·6	22·1	25·5	18·5	29·7	21·3	21·5	30·6
Uruguay	2·3	0·1	—	—	2·7	3·2	2·2	2·6	4·2	2·1	0·4	3·1
Paraguay	0·2	—	—	—	0·1	0·1	—	0·3	0·2	0·1	—	—
Argentina	18·1	3·7	2·1	1·8	21·6	21·5	21·8	19·4	25·9	17·7	15·7	29·0
Chile	4·9	5·5	10·2	1·9	4·7	4·1	5·6	3·6	4·2	3·0	17·4	3·2
LAFTA	67	30·4	70·2	9·5	75·9	70·9	82·4	65·0	84·8	69·9	97·7	88·5

— none or negligible.

APPENDIX 7

The compactness of an irregularly shaped portion of the earth's surface can doubtless be assessed in various ways. For the purposes of a very approximate comparison of the compactness of countries the following procedure has been adopted: to compare the area (in square kilometres) of each country with the area of the smallest circle that encloses it. An index is derived as follows:

$$\text{Index} = \frac{\text{Area of country}}{\text{Area of smallest circle that encloses it}} \times 100. \quad \text{The exercise}$$

has been set out in full below:

	Radius in kilometres	Area in square kilometres	Radius squared	πr^2	Index $\frac{Area}{\pi r^2} \times 100$
1 Brazil	2,300	8,514,000	5,300,000	15,700,000	54
2 Argentina	1,800	2,778,000	3,240,000	10,200,000	27
3 Mexico	1,700	1,967,000	2,890,000	9,050,000	22
4 Peru	1,050	1,249,000	1,100,000	3,450,000	36
5 Colombia	950	1,138,000	900,000	2,820,000	40
6 Bolivia	900	1,099,000	810,000	2,540,000	43
7 Venezuela	800	912,000	640,000	2,010,000	45
8 Chile	2,100	742,000	4,410,000	13,830,000	5
9 C. America	950	540,000	900,000	2,820,000	19

APPENDIX 8

In Chapter 11, Section 11.6 several sets of figures were given for the 32 major civil divisions of Mexico, and coefficients expressing in an approximate way the correlation between selected pairs of distributions (variables) were

TABLE A8.1

Rankings for 13 Variables in Mexico

1 Altitude, low to high.
2 Mean annual precipitation increasing.
3 Percentage of land used for crop farming, diminishing.
4 Density of population, high to low.
5 Rate of increase of population, 1940–60, fastest to slowest.
6 Percentage of population of state born outside state, high to low.
7 Percentage of non-agricultural population as a percentage of all employed population, high to low.
8 Urban population as a percentage of total population, high to low.
9 Literate population as a percentage of total population over 5 years, high to low.
10 Legitimate births per 1,000 births, most to least.
11 Per caput purchasing power, high to low.
12 Distance from Mexico city, small to large.
13 Distance from the U.S.A., small to large.

	1	2	3	4	5	6	7	8	9	10	11	12	13
Nuevo León	15	11	24	18	7	7	2	3	3	1	4	20	1
Tamaulipas	8	12	25	23	4	4	7	9	6	19	5	17	2
Sonora	12	3	28	29	5	8	9	11	7	20	3	31	3
Chihuahua	23	4	31	28	9	11	6	12	8	8	8	29	4
Coahuila	17	5	30	27	19	10	4	4	5	3	7	25	5
Baja California	10	1	29	25	1	1	3	2	2	12	1	32	6
San Luis Potosí	21	7	23	17	25	20	23	24	24	7	16	14	7
Zacatecas	27	6	17	24	31	26	30	27	17	2	29	18	8
Durango	25	8	27	26	22	16	24	23	9	15	23	23	9
Querétaro	28	10	9	12	30	25	21	26	30	6	22	7	10
Sinaloa	7	15	20	20	15	18	18	21	20	28	9	26	11
Baja Calif. (T)	5	2	32	32	21	13	12	22	4	24	6	30	12
Hidalgo	22	29	7	7	32	21	26	32	28	29	31	5	13
Aguascalientes	29	9	10	8	27	9	5	7	10	4	11	15	14
Guanajuato	26	13	2	6	18	23	17	14	27	11	24	9	15
Tlaxcala	32	20	1	2	24	22	22	15	21	18	32	4	16
Mexico	30	17	5	3	17	14	15	20	23	17	30	2	17
Distrito Federal	31	19	4	1	2	3	1	1	1	10	2	1	18
Yucatán	4	18	6	21	28	32	13	8	11	16	17	27	19
Puebla	24	30	8	5	26	24	19	19	26	23	21	6	20
Veracruz	6	32	14	9	16	17	16	18	22	31	13	11	21
Nayarit	9	25	18	22	11	12	25	16	13	27	19	19	22
Morelos	20	23	3	4	8	6	14	13	18	25	14	3	23
Jalisco	18	16	15	11	14	19	8	10	14	5	10	16	24
Quintana Roo	3	27	26	31	3	2	20	25	16	21	12	28	25
Michoacán	19	21	13	10	23	27	28	17	25	9	25	10	26
Colima	11	14	12	13	6	5	10	6	12	22	15	12	27
Guerrero	13	22	11	15	20	30	31	29	32	13	27	8	28
Oaxaca	16	24	19	16	29	31	32	30	29	30	26	13	29
Tabasco	2	28	16	14	13	29	27	28	19	26	20	21	30
Campeche	1	26	21	30	10	15	11	5	15	14	18	24	31
Chiapas	14	31	22	19	12	28	29	31	31	32	28	22	32

TABLE A8.2

Matrix with Correlation Coefficients(r)

	1	2	3	4	5	6	7	8	9	10	11	12	13	1–13 as listed in table
1	1·000	−0·209	−0·467	**−0·588**	0·390	0·076	−0·026	−0·026	0·181	−0·433	0·339	**−0·617**	−0·270	Altitude, low to high
2	−0·209	1·000	−0·460	−0·412	0·049	0·357	0·473	0·365	**0·571**	**0·611**	0·471	−0·421	**0·774**	Precipitation, low to high
3	−0·467	−0·460	1·000	**0·881**	−0·332	−0·334	−0·197	−0·048	−0·475	−0·063	−0·511	**0·831**	−0·381	% of land used for agriculture
4	−0·588	−0·412	0·881	1·000	−0·246	−0·214	−0·105	−0·031	−0·439	−0·053	−0·381	**0·904**	−0·273	Density of population, high to low
5	0·390	0·049	−0·332	−0·246	1·000	0·730	0·544	**0·519**	**0·535**	−0·088	**0·641**	−0·305	0·013	Rate of inc. of popn. 40–60, high to low
6	0·076	0·357	−0·334	−0·214	**0·730**	1·000	**0·743**	**0·628**	**0·731**	0·130	**0·725**	−0·213	0·393	Popn. born elsewhere as % of popn. of state
7	−0·026	0·473	−0·197	−0·105	0·544	**0·743**	1·000	0·883	0·788	0·390	0·820	−0·242	0·458	% in non-agric. as % of all empl. popn.
8	−0·026	0·365	−0·048	−0·031	0·519	0·628	0·883	1·000	0·741	0·436	0·671	−0·158	0·289	% urban 1960, high to low
9	0·181	0·571	−0·475	−0·439	0·535	0·731	0·788	0·741	1·000	0·324	**0·799**	−0·518	0·500	% literate 1950, high to low
10	−0·433	**0·611**	−0·063	−0·053	−0·088	0·130	0·390	0·436	0·324	1,000	0·212	−0·025	0·457	Legitimate as % of all births, high to low
11	0·339	0·471	−0·511	−0·381	**0·641**	**0·725**	**0·820**	0·671	**0·799**	0·212	1·000	**−0·501**	0·446	Per caput purchasing power high to low
12	−0·617	−0·421	**0·831**	**0·904**	−0·305	−0·213	−0·242	−0·158	−0·518	−0·025	−0·501	1·000	−0·272	Distance from Mexico city, small to great
13	−0·270	**0·774**	−0·381	−0·273	0·013	0·393	0·458	0·289	0·500	0·457	0·446	−0·272	1·000	Distance from U.S.A., small to great

N.B. The matrix is square (13 × 13) and symmetric (the 'southwest' half is a repetition of the 'northeast' half) and the principal axis has a correlation of 1·000 in each cell, since each variable correlates completely (and positively) with itself.

given. The procedure has also been put in the form of a computer programme and for a negligible expense, calculations that would have taken
several days to work out manually were produced, comparing 13 variables.
These are shown in Table A8.1, with the 32 states ranked ready for the
application of Spearman Rank Correlation Coefficient (explained in Chapter
11) and the results set out in the matrix (Table A8.2). With 32 units
(the states) the 95 per cent confidence levels are approximately ± 0.3.
This means that an index outside -0.3 and $+0.3$ could have been obtained
by chance at most only once in 20 times. The 99 per cent confidence levels
are approximately ± 0.42. Any value above about $+0.5$ or below about
-0.5 suggests a true correlation and one outside ± 0.7 a strong one. The
matrix has been included more for general interest than to show what can
be done by this 'blanket' correlation. There are several ways in which the
data could be further refined and interpreted. It should be stressed, however,
that a high correlation between two variables does not imply a direct causal
relationship, either mutual (as urban and non-agricultural) or one way (as
lack of precipitation and low percentage of land used for agriculture). On
the other hand it is difficult to escape from the conclusion that some con-
nection, perhaps indirect, does exist. The results are also useful for pointing
out where apparent correlations, arising from preconceived ideas and backed
up by false interpretation of data on maps (e.g. high rate of illegitimacy and
low income) are not confirmed by the test.

REFERENCES

[1] *Statistical Abstract of the United States*, 1963, pp. 878–89, 856, 863
[2] *UNSY*, 1962, Table 2
[3] *Statistical Bulletin for Latin America*, Vol. 1, No. 1, p. 18, 1964, New York; United Nations
[4] *UNSY*, 1955, Table 120
[5] *UNSY*, 1962, Table 125
[6] *UNSY*, 1963, Table 132
[7] *UNSY*, 1955, Table 42
[8] *UNSY*, 1962, Table 43
[9] *UNSY*, 1963, Table 48
[10] *UNSY*, 1955, Table 104
[11] *UNSY*, 1963, Table 113
[12] *UNSY*, 1955, Tables 107–8
[13] *UNSY*, 1963, Tables 114–115
[14] *UNSY*, 1955, Copper—Table 109, Iron ore—Table 44, Bauxite—Table 49
[15] *UNSY*, 1963, Copper—Table 116, Iron ore—Table 50, Bauxite—Table 55
[16] *UNSY*, 1962, Table 11 (from which the figures have been extracted and rearranged)

BIBLIOGRAPHY

The references in this section are confined almost entirely to books. Articles from learned journals and other periodicals are referred to in appropriate places in the text. Publications are arranged under the following headings:
1. Statistical material.
2. Works of reference.
3. Series and periodicals.
4. Illustrative sources.
5. General works on Latin America.
6. Regional works.

1. STATISTICAL MATERIAL

(a) *General Statistical*
United Nations (published in New York)
   Statistical Yearbook especially the years 1955 and 1960–63
   Demographic Yearbook especially the years 1955 and 1960–62
   Patterns of Industrial Growth, 1960
   Statistical Bulletin for Latin America, Vol. 1, No. 1, 1964
   Economic Bulletin for Latin America, twice yearly, since 1955
Food and Agriculture Organization of the United Nations (published in Rome)
   Production Yearbook, especially Vol. 16, 1962
   Trade Yearbook, especially Vol. 16, 1962
   The State of Food and Agriculture, 1963
Committee on Latin American Studies, University of California, Los Angeles,
   Statistical Abstract for Latin America, 1957 and certain more recent years.
(b) *Country by Country Statistical*
   (i) *Costa Rica*
      Universidad de Costa Rica,
         El Desarrollo Económico de Costa Rica, 1958
         Estudio del Sector Industrial, 1959
   (ii) *Mexico*
      Dirección General de Estadística:
         Anuario Estadístico de los Estados Unidos Mexicanos 1958–1959, 1960, Mexico
         Compendio Estadístico 1960 and 1962
         VIII Censo General de Población, 1960 (Preliminary figures for places with over 5,000 inhabitants)
   (iii) *Venezuela*
      Dirección General de Estadística y Censos Nacionales
         IX Censo Nacional de Población, Resultados preliminares, 1962, Caracas
         Boletín Mensual de Estadística, Caracas
   (iv) *Colombia*
      Anuario General de Estadística, 1959, Departmento Administrativo Nacional de Estadística. 1960, Colombia
   (v) *Peru*
      Boletín de Estadística Peruana, Dirección Nacional de Estadística y Censos 1960, Lima

(vi) *Brazil*
   Conselho Nacional de Estatística:
   Anuario Estatístico do Brasil, 1960 and 1961
   Produção Industrial Brasileira, 1958
(vii) *Argentina*
   Dirección Nacional de Estadística y Censos
   Censo Nacional de 1960, Población, Resultados Preliminares, 1961, Buenos Aires
   Boletín de Estadística, monthly and three-monthly
(viii) *Chile*
   Dirección de Estadística y Censos
   Demografía Año 1960
   Estadística Chilena

2. WORKS OF REFERENCE

The South American Handbook, a yearly publication going back some decades, published by Trade and Travel Publications Ltd., London
Ibero-Amerika, ein Handbuch, 1960, Hamburg
The A B C World Airways Guide (Monthly), London
World Railways, yearly (Ed. Henry Sampson), London
Statesman's Yearbook, yearly, London. Macmillan
Martin, R. M. and G. H. Lovett, *An Encyclopedia of Latin America History*, 1956, London; Abelard Schuman Ltd.

3. SERIES AND PERIODICALS

(a) *Series*
   (i) The Royal Institute of International Affairs, London, has a series of books covering various aspects of the more important countries (e.g. *Ecuador, Country of Contrasts*, by L. Linke, 1954, London). O.U.P.
   (ii) Pan-American Union (Unión Panamericana), Washington, D.C., U.S.A., has various series of publications especially on economic and social aspects of Latin America.
   Instituto Panamericano de Geografía e Historia: Los Estudios sobre Recursos Naturales en las Americas
   Vol. 1. Central America
      2. Colombia, Venezuela
      3. Islands
      4. Mexico
      5. Summary of above
      7. Brazil
   Published 1953–54
   (iii) American Geographical Society of New York, Special Publications on Latin America (e.g. No. 12, McBride, G., *Land Systems of Mexixo*; No. 16, Jefferson, M., *Peopling of the Argentine Pampa*)
   (iv) University of Chicago, Department of Geography, Research Papers (e.g. Carmin, R. N., *Anápolis, Brazil*)
(b) *Periodicals*
   Bank of London and South America (BOLSA) London, *Fortnightly Review* and *Quarterly Review*
   Ibero-Americana, University of California Press, Berkeley and Los Angeles
   Americas, a monthly publication of general interest published by the Pan-American Union, Washington
   Anuario de Geografía, Universidad Nacional Autónoma de México, yearly from 1961
   Revista Venezolana de Geografía, first number, June 1961
   Revista Geográfica (Venezuela), twice yearly, published in Mérida

Venezuela Up-to-Date, a three monthly publication
Peruvian Times, weekly publication, Lima
Revista Brasileira de Geografia, quarterly by Instituto Brasileiro de Geografia e
Estatística, Rio de Janeiro
Boletim Geográfico (Brazil), Instituto Brasileiro de Geografia e Estatística
Brazilian News, monthly, issued by the Brazilian Embassy in the U.K.
The Review of the River Plate, weekly publication, Buenos Aires

4. ILLUSTRATIVE SOURCES (TRAVEL, PHOTOGRAPHS, ETC)

The Geographical Magazine (London)
  1964: July—Belem road, Brazil; March—Brasilia; Feb.—Cattle in British
     Guiana
  1963: June—Haiti; May—Martinique; Mar.—Venezuela; Feb.—Colombia
  1962: Dec.—Amazon; October—Tierra del Fuego, Ecuador; Sept.—Honduras;
     August—Rio de Janeiro; July—Mexico; March—Curaçao
  1961: October—Patagonia; Sept.—British West Indies; May—Amazon, Cusco
     (Peru); Feb.—El Salvador
National Geographic Magazine (Washington)
  1964: May—Amazon Indians; Feb.—Peru
  1963: March—Venezuela
  1962: Dec.—Puerto Rico; Sept.—Brazil
  1961: October—Mexico; March—Panama; February—Haiti
  1960: February—Chile

5. GENERAL WORKS ON LATIN AMERICA

(a) *General*
  Géographie Universelle
    Tome XIV *Méxique, Amérique Centrale,* 1928, Paris; Max Sorre
    Tome XV *Amérique du Sud.,* 1927, Paris; Denis, P.
  Carlson, Fred A. *Geography of Latin America,* 1937, New York; Prentice Hall
  Whitebeck, R. H. and Williams F. E. *Economic Geography of South America,* 1940,
    London; McGraw-Hill
  Jones, C. F. *South America,* 1930, London and New York; Allen and Unwin
  Platt, R. S. *Latin America: Countrysides and United Regions,* 1942, New York;
    McGraw-Hill
  James, P. E. *Latin America,* numerous editions since 1942, Cassell
  Wilgus, A. C. *Latin America in Maps,* 1951, New York; Barnes and Noble Inc.
  Atlas Général Larousse, pp. 216–233, 1959, Paris; Librarie Larousse
  Géographie Universelle Larousse, Director Pierre Deffontaines, 3rd volume,
    Paris (Libraire Larousse) 1960, pp. 212–354. Well illustrated and up to date
  Butland, G. A. *Latin America, a Regional Geography,* 1960, London; Longmans
  Robinson, H. *Latin America,* 1961, London; Macdonald and Evans
  El Correo (Courier), UNESCO, June 1961, América Latina, 150 años de inde-
    pendencia, July–Aug. 1962. La lucha contra el hambre
(b) *Physical*
  Rich, J. L. *The Face of South America, an Aerial Traverse,* 1942, New York; Ameri-
    can Geographical Society
  Roseveare, G. M. *The Grasslands of Latin America,* Bulletin 36 of Imp. Bureau of
    Pastures and Field Crops, 1948, Aberystwyth, G.B.
  King, Lester C. *The Morphology of the Earth, A Study and Synthesis of World Scenery,*
    1962, Edinburgh; Oliver and Boyd
(c) *Historical and Race*
  Von Hagen, V. W., in Mentor Books, New York, New American Library,
    Realm of the Incas (1957), *The Aztec: Man and Tribe* (1958), *World of the Maya*
    (1960)

Humphreys, R. A. *Evolution of Modern Latin America*, 1946, Oxford; O.U.P.
Vives, J. Vincens (Ed.), *Historia Social y Económica de España y América*, 1957, Barcelona, Editorial Teide, especially Vol. III
Steward, J. H. and Faron, L. C. *Native Peoples of South America*, 1959, New York; McGraw-Hill
Bailey, H. M. and Nasatir, A. P. *Latin America, The Development of its Civilization*, 1960, London; Constable
Herring, H. *A History of Latin America*, 1961, New York; Knopf
Halcro Ferguson, J. *Latin America, the Balance of Race Redressed*, 1961, Oxford U.P.
Pendle, G. *A History of Latin America*, 1963, Harmondsworth; Penguin
Wilgus, A. C., and R. d'Eca, *Latin American History*, 1963, New York; Barnes and Noble

(*d*) *General Economic*
Benham, F. and Holley, H. A. *A Short Introduction to the Economy of Latin America*, Royal Institute of International Affairs, 1960
Ellis, Howard S. (Ed.) and Wallich, Henry C. *Economic Development for Latin America*, 1961, London; Macmillan
UNESCO, *Social aspects of economic development in Latin America*, Vol. 1, 1963
Wythe, G. *Industry in Latin America*, 1945, New York; Columbia U.P.
Hughlett, L. J. (Ed.), *Industrialization of Latin America*, 1946, New York; McGraw-Hill
Vanzetti, C. *La terra e l'uomo nell' America Latina*, 1961, Milan; Societa Italiana di Sociologia Rurale
Agricultural Geography of Latin America, U.S. Govt. Printing Office
Rowe, J. W. F. *The World's Coffee*, 1963, HMSO
UN and FAO, *Coffee in Latin America*, Vol. 1. *Colombia and El Salvador*, 1958; 2. *Brazil, State of São Paulo*, 1960
United Nations, *Inter-Latin American Trade, Current Problems*, 1957
United Nations, *The Latin American Common Market*, 1959
Urquidi, V. L., *Free Trade and Economic Integration in Latin America*, 1962; University of California Press
Revista de Economía Latinoamericana, No. 6, April–June 1962 (Banco Central de Venezuela), a number devoted to papers on regional planning in Latin America given at the 1st Latin American Conference on Regional Planning held at Cendes, Caracas. An English version is also available.

(*e*) *Urban*
Violich, F. *Cities of Latin America*, 1944, New York; Reinhold
Wilhelmy, H. *Südamerika im Spiegel seiner Städte*, 1952, Hamburg; Cram. Gruyter & Co.
UNESCO, *Urbanization in Latin America* (Ed. P. M. Hauser), 1961

(*f*) *Social and Political*
Social Change in Latin America Today, Its Implications for U.S. Policy (Adams, R. N. *et al.*), 1960, New York; Harper, 1961, London; O.U.P
Alexander, R. J. *Today's Latin America*, Anchor Books, 1962; New York
Needler, M. C. *Latin American Politics in Perspective*, Van Nostrand, 1963; New York
Schmitt, Karl M. and Burks, David D. *Evolution and Chaos: Dynamics of Latin American Government and Politics*, Pall Mall, 1964; London

6. REGIONAL

(*a*) *Central America and Mexico*
United Nations (ECLA), *Los Recursos Humanos de Centroamérica, Panamá y México en 1950–1980*, published 1960
Colonial Office, *Land in British Honduras*, HMSO, 1959; London
Whetten, N. L. *Guatemala, the Land and the People*, Yale University Press, 1961, New Haven
Johannessen, Carl L. Savannas of Interior Honduras, 1963 (in *Ibero-Americana*)

Guzmann, L. E. *Farming and Farmlands in Panama*, University of Chicago, 1956

Vivó, J. A. *Geografía de México*, 4th edn. 1958, Mexico; Fondo de cultura económica

„ „ *La Conquista de Nuestro Suelo*, 1958, Mexico; Ediciones de la Cámara Nacional de la Industria de Transformacíon

Tamayo, J. L. *Geografía moderna de México*, 1960, Mexico; Editorial Patriad *Mexico 1960* and *Mexico 1963*, published by Banco Nacional de Comercio Exterior, S.A., Mexico, in both Spanish and English

Flores, E. *Tratado de Economica Agricola*, 1961, Mexico

Borah, W. and Cook, S. F. *The Population of Central Mexico in 1548*, 1960 (*Ibero-Americana*)

Distribución geográfica de la población en la Republica Mexicana, Universidad Nacional Autónoma de Mexico, 1962, Mexico

Megee, M. C. *Monterrey, Mexico: Internal Patterns and External Relations*, 1958, Chicago

Augelli, J. P. The Rimland-Mainland Concept of Culture Areas in Middle America, *A.A.A.G.*, June 1962, pp. 119–129

(b) *Andean*

Arraiz, A., and Egui, L. E. *Geografía económica de Venezuela*, 1957, Caracas

Uslar-Pietri, A. *Sumario de Economía Venezolana*, 1958, Caracas

Vila, P. *Geografía de Venezuela*, 1 El territorio nacional y su ambiante físico, Ministerio de Educación, 1960, Caracas

Atlas Agrícola de Venezuela, Ministerio de Agricultura y Cría, Dirección de Planificación Agropecuaria, Consejo de Bienestar Rural, 1960, Caracas

IBRD (International Bank for Reconstruction and Development), *The Economic Development of Venezuela*, 1961, Baltimore; Johns Hopkins Press

Romero, E. *Geografía del Pacífico Sudamericano*, 1947; Buenos Aires

Goez, R. C. *Geografía de Colombia*, 1947, Mexico

Cano, J. A. *Geografía física y económica de Colombia*, 1957, Bogota

Estudio sobre las condiciones de desarrollo de Colombia, Misión 'Economía y Humanismo', 1958, Bogota

Banco de la Republica, Departamento de Investigaciones Economicas, 1959, *Atlas de Economía Colombiana*, 3 volumes

Martz, John D. *Colombia—A Contemporary Political Survey*, Chapel Hill, 1962

Gordon, B. Le Roy. *Human Geography and Ecology in the Sinu Country of Colombia*, 1957 (*Ibero-Americana*, No. 39)

Paz Soldán, J. P. *Geografía del Peru*, 1950, Lima

Romero, E. *Historia económica del Perú*, 1949; Buenos Aires, and *Geografía económica del Perú*, 1961, Lima

Ford, T. R. *Man and Land in Peru*, 1955, Gainesville; University of Florida Press

Monge, C. *Acclimatization in the Andes*, 1948, Baltimore; Johns Hopkins Press

Plan regional para el desarrollo del Sur del Peru (various volumes and maps), 1959, Lima

Arze, W. G. *Plan inmediato de política económica del gobierno de la revolución nacional*, Memorandum, No. 2, Republica de Bolivia, 1955

(c) *Islands*

Jiménez, Antonio Núñez, *Geografía de Cuba*, 1960, La Habana; Editorial Lex

Huberman, L., and Sweezy, P. M. *Cuba, Anatomy of a Revolution*, MR Press, 1961; New York

United Nations, *Mission to Haiti*, 1949, New York

Rodman, Selden, *Haiti: The Black Republic*, 1954, New York; Devin Adair Co.

Street, John M. *Historical and Economic Geography of the Southwest Peninsula of Haiti*, 1960, Berkeley Univ. of California

Wood, H. A. *Northern Haiti: Land, Land Use and Settlement*, 1963, Toronto

Hanson, E. P. *Puerto Rico: Ally for Progress*, 1962, Princeton; Van Nostrand

Back, K. W. *Slums, Projects and People* (Puerto Rico), 1962, Durham, N.C. (Social Science Research Centre, College of Social Sciences, University of Puerto Rico)

461

Smith, M. G. *West Indian Family Structure*, American Ethnological Society, 1962, Seattle

Jamaica, Report for the year 1960, 1963, London; H.M.S.O.

(d) *Brazil*

Carta do Brasil ao Milionésimo, Instituto Brasileiro de Geografia e Estatística, 1960
IBGE, *Atlas do Brasil* (large and condensed versions), Conselho Nacional de Geografia, 1959, Rio de Janeiro
    ,, *Tipos e Aspectos do Brasil* 1956; Rio de Janeiro
de Azevedo, A. *Geografia do Brasil* (2 vols.) São Paulo, 1961
Waibel, L. *Capitulos de Geografia Tropical e do Brasil*, 1958, Rio de Janeiro
Prado Juniór, C. *Historia Económica do Brasil*, 1961, São Paulo
Boxer, C. R. *The Golden Age of Brazil 1695–1750*, Univ. of California Press, 1962, Los Angeles
Boxer, C. R. *Growing Pains of a Colonial Society*, 1962, Los Angeles, Univ. of California Press
Freyre, G. *The Masters and the Slaves*, A Study in the development of Brazilian civilization, 1956, New York
Freyre, G. *New World in the Tropics, The Culture of Modern Brazil*, 1959, New York
Schurz, Wm. Lythe *Brazil—the Infinite Country*, 1962, London
Wagley, C. *An Introduction to Brazil*, 1963, London
Wagley, C. (ed.) *Race and Class in Rural Brazil* (2nd ed) 1963, UNESCO
Harris, M. *Town and Country in Brazil*, 1956, New York; Columbia U.P.
Guerra, A. T., *Estudo Geográfico do Territorio do Acre*, IBGE, Conselho Nacional Geografia, 1955, Rio de Janeiro
IBGE, Conselho Nacional de Geografia, Vol. 1 Serie *A Grande Região Norte*, 1959, Vol. 2 Serie A *Grande Região Centro-Oeste*, 1960
de Castro, Josué, *Geografia da fôme*, 1961, São Paulo
Hutchinson, H. W. *Village and Plantation Life in Northeastern Brazil*, The American Ethnological Society, 1957, Seattle
Hunnicutt, B. H. *Brazil, World Frontier*, 1949, New York
Carmin, R. N. *Anápolis Brazil; Regional Capital of an Agricultural Frontier*, University of Chicago, Department of Geography Research Papers, No. 35
Mombieg, P. *Pionniers et Planteurs de São Paulo*, 1952, Paris
França, A. *A marcha do café e as frentes pioneiras*, 1960, Rio de Janeiro
Stein, S. J. *The Brazilian Cotton Manufacture, Textile Enterprise in an Underdeveloped Area, 1850–1950*, 1957, Cambridge (Mass)
Associação dos Geógrafos Brasileiros, Seção Regional de São Paulo, *A Cidade de São Paulo, Estudos de geografia urbana*, Companhia Editora Nacional São Paulo. 4 Vols, many maps
18th International Geographical Congress, Brazil, 1956, various Excursion Guide Books were published

(e) *South*

Service, Elman R., and Service, Helen S. *Tobati: Paraguayan Town*, 1954, Univ. of Chicago Press
Rampa, A. C. *Geografia física de la República Argentina*, 1961, Buenos Aires
Jefferson, Mark. *Peopling the Argentine Pampa*, American Geographical Society Research Series No. 16, 1926, New York
Defelippe, B. A. *Geografia económica argentina*, 1959, Buenos Aires
Isacovich, M. *Argentina económica y social*, 1961, Buenos Aires
Cortese, A. *Historia Económica Argentina y Americana*, 1961, Buenos Aires
Ferrer, A. *La economía argentina*, 1963, Buenos Aires
McBride, G. *Chile: Land and Society*, American Geographical Society, 1936
Butland, G. J. *The Human Geography of Southern Chile*, The Institute of British Geographers, Publication No. 24, 1957, London
Butler, J. H. *Manufacturing in the Concepcion Region of Chile*, National Academy of Sciences, 1960, Washington (D.C.)

INDEX

References to figures and diagrams are distinguished by italic type. References in bold type relate to important points.

466